COMPREHENSIVE MODEL OF THE

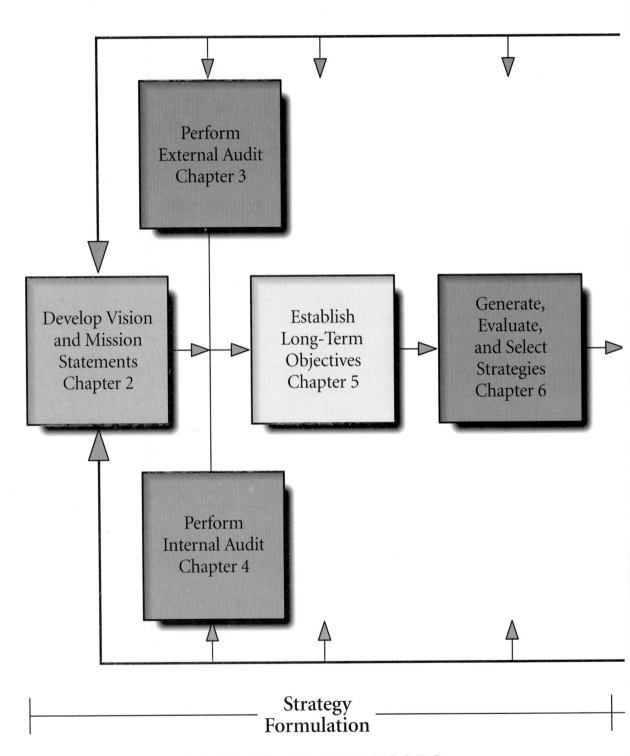

USED WIDELY AMONG BUSINESSES
AND ACADEMIA WORLDWIDE

STRATEGIC MANAGEMENT PROCESS

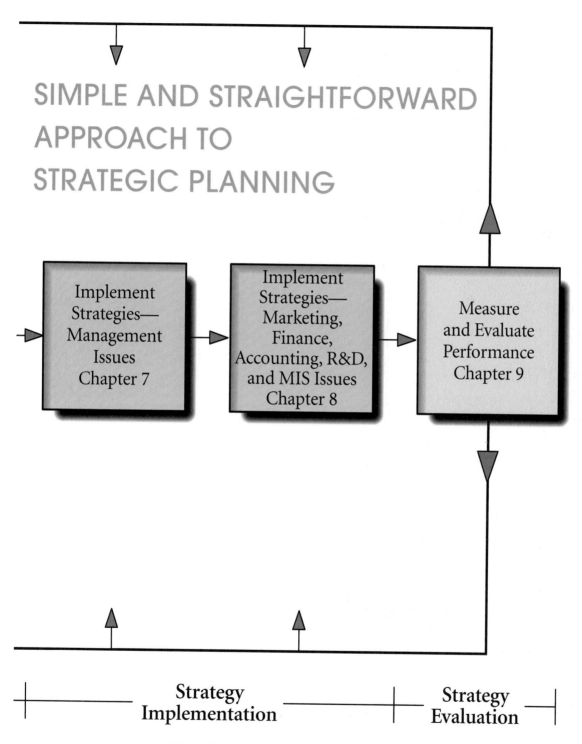

SIMPLE AND STRAIGHTFORWARD
APPROACH TO
STRATEGIC PLANNING

Implement Strategies—
Management Issues
Chapter 7

Implement Strategies—
Marketing, Finance, Accounting, R&D, and MIS Issues
Chapter 8

Measure and Evaluate Performance
Chapter 9

Strategy Implementation

Strategy Evaluation

USED TO INTEGRATE AND ORGANIZE
ALL CHAPTERS IN THIS TEXT

strategic management

concepts

strategic
management

concepts

Eleventh Edition

Fred R. David

Francis Marion University, Florence, South Carolina

Upper Saddle River, New Jersey 07458

Library of Congress Cataloging-in-Publication Data

David, Fred R.
   Strategic management: concepts / Fred R. David.— 11th ed.
     p.   cm.
   Includes bibliographical references and index.
   ISBN 0-13-186955-8
   1. Strategic planning—Case studies.   2. Strategic planning.   I. Title.

HD30.28.D3785 2007
658.4'012—dc22

2006001624

Senior Acquisitions Editor: Michael Ablassmeir
VP/Editorial Director: Jeff Shelstad
Product Development Manager: Ashley Santora
Project Manager: Melissa Pellerano
Editorial Assistant: Denise Vaughn
Media Product Development Manager: Nancy Welcher
Marketing Manager: Anne Howard
Associate Director, Production Editorial: Judy Leale
Managing Editor, Production: Renata Butera
Production Editor: Kelly Warsak
Permissions Coordinator: Charles Morris
Manufacturing Buyer: Diane Peirano
Design/Composition Manager: Christy Mahon
Composition Liaison: Suzanne Duda
Art Director: Kevin Kall

Interior Design: Karen Quigley
Cover Design: Michael Fruhbeis
Cover Photo: Getty Images
Illustration (Interior): Carlisle Publishing Services
Director, Image Resource Center: Melinda Reo
Manager, Rights and Permissions: Zina Arabia
Manager, Visual Research: Beth Brenzel
Image Permission Coordinator: Cathy Mazzucca
Photo Researcher: Melinda Alexander
Composition: Integra Software Services
Full-Service Project Management: Ann Imhof/Carlisle Publishing
   Services
Printer/Binder: Quebecor
Cover Printer: Lehigh
Typeface: 10.5 Minion-Regular

Credits and acknowledgments borrowed from other sources and reproduced, with permission, in this textbook appear on the appropriate page within text.

Photos on pages xviii and 2 courtesy of Google. Photos on pages 54, 80, 120, 166, 214, 260, 304, 334 courtesy of istock. Google logo courtesy of Google, Inc.

Pearson Education LTD.
Pearson Education Singapore, Pte. Ltd
Pearson Education, Canada, Ltd
Pearson Education—Japan

Pearson Education Australia PTY, Limited
Pearson Education North Asia Ltd
Pearson Educación de Mexico, S.A. de C.V.
Pearson Education Malaysia, Pte. Ltd.

10 9 8 7 6 5 4 3
ISBN: 0-13-186955-8

To Joy, Forest, Byron, and Meredith—my wife and children—
for their encouragement and love.

Brief Contents

Contents

Preface

The business world today is considerably different and more complex than it was just two years ago when the previous edition of this text was published. Today we experience rising consumer debt, rising oil prices, extensive outsourcing, a migration of work to developing countries, more attention to business ethics, ballooning federal budget deficits, continued globalization, consolidation within industries, a European Union in dispute over its constitution, a warming planet, and intense rivalry in almost all industries. E-commerce continues to alter the nature of business to its core.

Much has happened in recent years. Thousands of strategic alliances and partnerships, even among competitors, formed. Hundreds of companies have declared bankruptcy, and corporate scandals have highlighted the need for improved business ethics and corporate disclosure of financial transactions. Downsizing, rightsizing, reengineering, and countless divestitures, acquisitions, and liquidations have permanently altered the corporate landscape. Thousands of firms have begun global operations, and thousands more have merged. Thousands have prospered, and yet thousands more have failed. Many manufacturers have become e-commerce suppliers, and long-held competitive advantages have eroded as new ones have formed.

Both the challenges and opportunities facing organizations of all sizes today are greater than ever. China is rapidly becoming an economic powerhouse, and India is not far behind. The value of the euro has fallen dramatically, and the war on terrorism continues. Illegal immigration across the U.S.–Mexico border has reached emergency levels. Less room than ever for error exists today in the formulation and implementation of a strategic plan. This textbook provides a systematic effective approach for developing a clear strategic plan.

Changes made in this eleventh edition are aimed squarely at illustrating the effect of this new world order on strategic-management theory and practice. Due to the magnitude of the changes in strategic-management theory, research, and practice as well as changes in companies, cultures, and countries, this edition has been completely updated. The first edition of this text was published in 1986 and since that time has grown to be one of the most widely read strategic-management books in the world. This text is now published in nine languages other than English. Every sentence and paragraph has been scrutinized, modified, clarified, deleted, streamlined, updated, and improved to enhance the content and caliber of presentation. The structure of this edition parallels the last, with nine chapters and a Cohesion Case, but the improvements in readability and coverage are dramatic. Every chapter now features new strategic-management concepts and practices presented in a clear, focused, and relevant manner.

The skills-oriented, practitioner perspective that historically has been the foundation of this text is enhanced and strengthened in this edition. However, new and expanded coverage of strategic-management theories and research reflects companies' use of concepts such as value chain analysis (VCA), Balanced Scorecard, resource-based view (RBV), and outsourcing. To survive and prosper in the new millennium, organizations must build and sustain competitive advantage. This text is now trusted around the world to provide to future and present managers the latest skills and concepts needed to effectively formulate and efficiently implement a strategic plan—a game plan, if you will—that can lead to sustainable competitive advantage for any type of business.

In preparing the eleventh edition of *Strategic Management Concepts,* the mission was "to create the most current, well-written strategic management textbook on the market—a book that is exciting and valuable to both students and professors." To achieve this, every page has been revamped, updated, and improved. New strategic-management research and practice—such as the Industrial Organizational (I/O) Model, Market Commonality, Value Chain Analysis, Balanced Scorecard, and First Mover Advantages—are incorporated, and hundreds of new practical examples abound. The brand-new Cohesion Case focuses on Google (and replaces the tenth edition's Krispy Kreme Doughnuts case). Google is an exemplary company that is expanding aggressively around the world. Students will enjoy analyzing the Google case through exercises at the end of each chapter. This teaching tool is much improved in this edition, and it is highly recommended that it be used. Students will relate to it, especially because they probably do regular Internet searches using Google and may even have a Gmail account. New Experiential Exercises on Google are provided at the end of each chapter.

The reviewers and I believe you will find this eleventh edition to be the best strategic-management textbook available for communicating both the excitement and value of strategic management. Concise and exceptionally well organized, this text is now published in ten different languages—English, Chinese, Spanish, Thai, German, Japanese, Farsi, Indonesian, Hindi, and Arabic. A version in Russian is being negotiated. On five continents, this text is widely used in colleges and universities at both the graduate and undergraduate levels. In addition, thousands of companies, organizations, and governmental bodies use this text as a management guide.

This textbook meets all Association to Advance Collegiate Schools of Business (AACSB) guidelines for the business policy and strategic-management course at both the graduate and undergraduate levels, and previous editions have been used at more than 500 colleges and universities. This eleventh edition is fully updated to reflect the twenty-first century in terms of appearance, topical coverage, and today's business environment.

Prentice Hall maintains a separate Web site for this text at www.prenhall.com/david. The author maintains the Strategic Management Club Online at www.strategyclub.com, which offers many benefits for strategic-management and business policy students.

Chapter Themes

Three themes permeate all chapters in this edition and contribute significantly to making the text timely, informative, exciting, and valuable. Three types of boxed "Perspectives" in each chapter link concepts being presented to each theme. Most of the boxed inserts are new to this edition.

1. *Global Perspectives*

   Global factors affect virtually all strategic decisions, so the global theme is enhanced in this edition because doing business globally has become a necessity, rather than a luxury, in most industries. Today nearly all strategic decisions are affected by global issues and concerns. New global coverage in each chapter is consistent with the growing interdependence among countries and companies worldwide. The dynamics of political, economic, and cultural differences across countries directly affect strategic-management decisions. Doing business globally is more risky and complex than ever. The global theme illustrates how organizations can effectively do business today in an interdependent world community.

2. *E-Commerce Perspectives*

   E-commerce is a vital strategic-management tool, so the e-commerce theme is integrated throughout the chapters in response to immense e-commerce opportunities and threats facing organizations today. Almost all products can now be purchased on the Internet, with business-to-business e-commerce now being 10 times greater than business-to-consumer e-commerce. Accelerating use of the Internet to gather, analyze, send, and receive information has changed the way strategic decisions are made. Since the tenth edition of this text, thousands of companies have established World Wide Web sites and are conducting e-commerce internationally. A resurgence in the last two years of technology firms and wireless products is affecting all firms.

3. *Natural Environment Perspectives*

   Preserving the natural environment is a vital strategic issue, so this text's unique natural environment theme is strengthened in this edition to promote and encourage firms to conduct operations in an environmentally sound manner. This theme now includes social responsibility and business ethics issues. Countries worldwide have enacted laws to curtail the pollution of streams, rivers, air, land, and sea. Environmental concerns are a new point of contention in World Trade Organization (WTO) policies and practices. The strategic efforts of both companies and countries to preserve the natural environment are described herein, including coverage of ISO 14001 and the BELL Program. Respect for the natural environment has become an important concern for consumers, companies, society, and the AACSB.

Eleventh Edition Design Features

Some valuable design features have been added to this edition. The comprehensive strategic-management model is displayed at the front of the text. Near the start of each chapter, part of the comprehensive strategy model is highlighted and enlarged so students can easily see the focus of each chapter in the context of the model.

This edition of the book is especially appealing visually. Photographs throughout the text have changed and fit much better with the Google case and the Global, E-Commerce, and Natural Environment themes. The four-color printing used throughout the eleventh edition text is especially pleasing.

Time-Tested Features

This edition continues to offer many of the time-tested features and content that have made this text so successful for nearly 20 years. Trademarks of this text that have been strengthened in this edition include the following:

Chapters: Time-Tested Features

- This text meets AACSB guidelines that support a practitioner orientation rather than a theory/research approach. It offers a skills-oriented approach to developing a vision and mission statement; performing an external audit; conducting an internal assessment; and formulating, implementing, and evaluating strategies.
- The Global, Natural Environment, and E-Commerce themes permeate all chapters and examine strategic-management concepts in these important perspectives.
- The author's writing style is concise, conversational, interesting, logical, lively, and supported throughout by numerous current examples.
- A simple, integrative strategic-management model appears in all chapters and on the inside front cover of the text. This model is widely utilized for strategic planning among consultants and companies worldwide. One reviewer said, "One thing I have admired about David's text is that he follows the fundamental sequence of strategy formulation, implementation, and evaluation. There is a basic flow from mission/purposes to internal/external environmental scanning to strategy development, selection, implementation, and evaluation. This has been, and continues to be, a hallmark of the David text. Many other strategy texts are more disjointed in their presentation, and thus confusing to the student, especially at the undergraduate level."
- A new Cohesion Case (Google replaces Krispy Kreme Doughnuts) follows Chapter 1 and is revisited at the end of each chapter. This exciting new Cohesion Case allows students to apply strategic-management concepts and techniques to a real organization as chapter material is covered. This integrative (cohesive) approach readies students for case analysis.

- End-of-chapter Experiential Exercises effectively apply concepts and techniques in a challenging, meaningful, and enjoyable manner. Text material is applied to the Cohesion Case in 18 exercises; 10 more exercises apply textual material to a college or university; another 10 send students into the business world to explore important strategy topics. The exercises are relevant, interesting, and contemporary.
- Excellent pedagogy, including Notable Quotes and Objectives, open each chapter, and Key Terms, Current Readings, Discussion Questions, and Experiential Exercises close each chapter.
- Excellent coverage of strategy *formulation* issues includes such topics as business ethics, global versus domestic operations, vision/mission, matrix analysis, partnering, joint venturing, competitive analysis, governance, and guidelines for conducting an internal/external strategy assessment.
- Excellent coverage of strategy *implementation* issues includes such topics as corporate culture, organizational structure, outsourcing, marketing concepts, financial analysis, and business ethics.
- A systematic, analytical approach is presented in Chapter 6, including matrices such as SWOT, BCG, IE, GRAND, SPACE, and QSPM.
- Four-color printing is again used throughout the chapter material.
- Visit the Net (Internet) exercises are available online at www.prenhall.com/david, www.strategyclub.com, and in the margins of the text. This feature reveals the author's recommended Web sites for locating additional information on the concepts being presented, and it greatly enhances classroom presentation in an Internet environment since the recommended sites have been screened closely to ensure that each is well worth visiting in class. This feature also provides students with substantial additional material on chapter concepts.
- The Web site www.prenhall.com/david provides chapter and case updates and support materials.
- The nine chapters are organized in the same manner as the previous edition.
- A chapters-only paperback version of the text is available.
- SafariX, an Internet version of this text, is available at www.safarix.com.
- Custom-case publishing is available whereby an instructor can combine chapters from this text with cases from a variety of sources or select any number of cases you desire from the 38 cases in the full text.
- The outstanding ancillary package for the chapter material includes a comprehensive *Instructor's Manual* and a computerized test bank.

New Chapter Features/Changes/Content in This Edition

In addition to the special time-tested trademarks described, this eleventh edition includes some exciting new features, changes, and content designed to position this text as the clear leader and best choice for teaching business policy and strategic management.

First, the new Cohesion Case on Google, Inc. (GOOG) focuses on an exemplary company and replaces the previous Krispy Kreme Doughnuts Cohesion Case.

Cofounded by Larry Page and Sergey Brin in 1998, Google is a rapidly growing, global company headquartered in Mountain View, California. Many students use Google's e-mail services through Gmail, which offers a gigabyte of free storage for each user, along with e-mail search capabilities and relevant advertising. Most students are familar with Google, which offers advertising solutions and global Internet search solutions through its Web site and offers Intranet solutions via an enterprise search appliance. The company's products and services include Google.com, Google AdWords, Google AdSense, and Google Search Appliance. The AdWords and AdSense programs are used by advertisers to promote their products and services on the Web with targeted advertising. Google also provides means to search appliances to search corporate systems through the Google Search Appliance.

Experiential Exercises at the end of each chapter apply concepts to the new Google Cohesion Case to ready students for case analysis when they complete the chapter material. Over the past 20 years, the Cohesion Case for this text has changed from Ponderosa Steakhouse in the first and second editions, to Hershey Foods in the third through seventh editions, to AOL in the eighth edition, to American Airlines in the ninth edition, to Krispy Kreme Doughnuts in the tenth, and now to Google, which is a well-known company for students to focus upon throughout the semester.

In this edition, new features, changes, and content common to all nine chapters include the following:

- New Global, E-Commerce, and Natural Environment Perspectives (boxed inserts).
- New examples throughout.
- New Visit the Net (VTN) Web sites provided in the page margins.
- Improved coverage of global issues and concerns.
- Expanded coverage of business ethics.
- All new current readings at the end of each chapter that reveal fresh and relevant strategic-management research.
- More international flavor than ever. Textbooks for the U.S. market should include substantial coverage of how business functions vary among countries, so cultural and conceptual strategic-management differences among countries are covered in excellent new material.
- New research and theories of seminal thinkers in strategy development—such as Ansoff, Chandler, Porter, Hamel, Prahalad, Mintzberg, and Barney—are included. Such scholars have brought strategic management to its present place in modern business. Practical aspects of strategic management are still center stage and the trademark of this text.
- Excellent new Web sites that augment chapter concepts in the text margins throughout this edition. Many universities now teach in Internet-ready classrooms and utilize Web sites during lectures. These sites are also hot-linked at the www.prenhall.com/david and www.strategyclub.com Web sites.
- Substantial new material on business ethics throughout. Corporate fraud, scandals, and illegalities have become too numerous, so we in academia must be certain to emphasize that "Good ethics is good business." This notion is tied to the natural environment theme in this edition.

A few more new features/changes/content characterize this eleventh edition:

Chapter 1
- New Global Perspective boxed insert regarding the extent to which U.S. firms dominate industries, showing that many foreign firms lead the way in many industries.
- New Strategies in Action table featuring Walgreens, Outback Steakhouse, Nucor, and Autodesk.

Chapter 2
- New Global Perspective.
- New E-Commerce Perspective.

Chapter 3
- New coverage of the business conditions in Russia, Mexico, China, and Europe.
- New heading and discussion on Market Commonality and Resource Similarity.
- New E-Commerce Perspective.
- New information on Porter's Five Forces Model.
- New EFE matrix on Pilgrim's Pride Corporation.

Chapter 4
- New discussion of financial ratio analysis.
- New material on the use of dividends as a financial and investment tool.
- Two new diagrams and support material on Value Chain Analysis (VCA).
- New heading and information on Benchmarking.
- New IFE matrix on E*Trade Financial Corporation.

Chapter 5
- New discussion of objectives and the Balanced Scorecard.
- New headings and discussion for Related Diversification and Unrelated Diversification (replaces horizontal, concentric, and conglomerate diversification).
- New tables on divestitures and mergers.
- Substantially expanded new material on, and a new diagram of, Porter's Generic Strategies focusing now on five, not three, generic strategies.
- New coverage of joint ventures, cooperative arrangements, and partnerships, with good illustrations of the current trend toward mergers and acquisitions.
- New Figure 5-4: Meeting the Challenge of High-Velocity Change.
- New material on reasons why many mergers and acquisitions fail.
- New Global Perspective and E-Commerce Perspective.

Chapter 6
- New example of BCG Matrix and IE Matrix.
- New Global Perspective.
- New discussion of the limitations of SWOT analysis.
- New information on corporate governance.

Chapter 7

- New section: Some Do's and Don'ts in Developing Organizational Charts.
- Substantial new discussion of organizational structure.
- New diagram of a Matrix structure.
- New diagram showing typical titles for top managers of large firms so students can better devise organizational charts.
- New table: The Ten Best Firms for Women to Work for in 2005.
- Increased coverage of issues related to women and minority managers.

Chapter 8

- Expanded and improved coverage of financial statement analysis to match current new thinking in regard to ethical and legal handling of financial reporting.
- New EPS/EBIT and Value of the Company analyses, tables, and diagrams.
- New coverage of the Sarbanes-Oxley Act of 2002 concerning CEO and CFO responsibilities regarding financial statements.
- New Global, Natural Environment, and E-Commerce Perspectives (boxed inserts).

Chapter 9

- New Global, Natural Environment, and E-Commerce Perspectives (boxed inserts) are provided.
- New updates and examples throughout this chapter.

Ancillary Materials

- A new running update of the Google Cohesion Case is provided at www.prenhall.com/david. The Google Cohesion Case is kept fully updated online for both professors and students. Scores of excellent hot links for the Google case are provided at www.prenhall.com/david.
- The www.prenhall.com/david Web site is designed solely to support this textbook and has been dramatically improved. Content and information for both professors and students have been revised.
- The new PowerPoint Web site provided with this text offers professors easy-to-use lecture outlines for in-class presentations. Chapter headings and topics in this edition are highlighted on more than 80 PowerPoint slides per chapter.
- An *Instructor's Manual* provides lecture notes, teaching tips, answers to all end-of-chapter Experiential Exercises and Review Questions, additional Experiential Exercises that are not found in the text, a glossary with definitions of all end-of-chapter key terms and concepts, sample course syllabi, and a newly revamped test bank of nearly 1,500 mostly new questions with answers.
- A fully revised, printed, and Computerized Test Bank includes 425 true/false questions, 450 multiple-choice questions, 250 essay questions for the text chapters, and 250 discussion questions. Sample comprehensive tests for Chapters 1 through 5 and Chapters 6 through 9 are also provided, as are answers to all objective questions. The test questions in the *Instructor's Manual*

are also available on computerized test software to facilitate preparing and grading tests.

- Ancillary materials are provided to professors online at www.prenhall.com/david.

Special Note to Students

Whatever this class is called at your university—Business Policy or Strategic Management or something else—this is a challenging and exciting course that will teach you how to function as the owner or chief executive officer of different types of organizations. Your major task in this course will be to make strategic decisions and to justify those decisions through oral and written communication. Strategic decisions determine the future direction and competitive position of an enterprise for a long time. Decisions to expand geographically or to diversify are examples of strategic decisions.

Strategic decision making occurs in all types and sizes of organizations, from Exxon and IBM to a small hardware store or a small college. Many people's lives and jobs are affected by strategic decisions, so the stakes are very high. An organization's very survival is often at stake. The overall importance of strategic decisions makes this course especially exciting and challenging. You will be called upon in this course to demonstrate how your strategic decisions could be successfully implemented.

In this course, you can look forward to making strategic decisions both as an individual and as a member of a team. No matter how hard employees work, an organization is in real trouble if strategic decisions are not made effectively. Doing the right things (effectiveness) is more important than doing things right (efficiency). For example, companies such as Sears, Roebuck and AT&T were prosperous in the 1990s, but ineffective strategies led to revenue declines of 12 percent for each firm in 2004, along with profit declines of 114 percent and 446 percent, respectively. Even firms such as Kroger, Winn-Dixie, MCI, and Washington Mutual have pursued ineffective strategies of late. American icons General Motors and Ford are both struggling. You will have the opportunity in this course to make actual strategic decisions, perhaps for the first time in your academic career. Do not hesitate to take a stand and defend specific strategies that you determine to be the best based on tools and concepts in this textbook. The rationale for your strategic decisions will be more important than the actual decisions because no one knows for sure what the best strategy is for a particular organization at a given point in time. This fact accents the subjective, contingency nature of the strategic-management process.

Use the concepts and tools presented in this text, coupled with your own intuition, to recommend strategies that you can defend as being most appropriate for the organizations that you study. You also must integrate knowledge you acquired in previous business courses. For this reason, strategic management is often called a capstone course; thus, you may want to keep this book for your personal library.

This text is practitioner oriented and applications oriented. It presents techniques and content that will enable you to formulate, implement, and evaluate strategies in all kinds of profit and nonprofit organizations. The end-of-chapter Experiential Exercises allow you to apply what you've read in each chapter to the new Google Cohesion Case and to a case focused on your own university.

Definitely visit the Strategic Management Club Online at www.strategyclub. com. The templates and links there will save you time when performing analyses and will help make your work look professional. Work hard in policy this term and have fun. Good luck!

Acknowledgments

Many persons have contributed time, energy, ideas, and suggestions for improving this text over 11 editions. To all individuals involved in making this text so popular and successful, I am indebted and thankful. The strength of this text is largely attributed to the collective wisdom, work, and experiences of business policy professors, strategic-management researchers, students, and practitioners. Names of particular individuals whose published research is referenced in this edition are listed alphabetically in the Name Index.

Many reviewers contributed valuable material and suggestions for this edition. I would like to thank my colleagues and friends at Auburn University, Mississippi State University, East Carolina University, and Francis Marion University. These are universities where I have served on the management faculty. Scores of students and professors at these schools have helped to shape this text. Many thanks go to the following recent reviewers:

Dr. Kunal Banerji, Florida Atlantic University
Dr. Drew L. Harris, Longwood University
Dr. Jo Ann M. Duffy, Sam Houston State University
Dr. Dave Flynn, Hofstra University
Dr. Debbie Gilliard, Metropolitan State College
Dr. Robert C. Losik, Southern New Hampshire University
Dr. Leslie C. Mueller, Northwestern State University of Louisiana
Dr. Kenneth R. Tillery, Middle Tennessee State University
Dr. John Cote, Baker College
Dr. Rodley C. Pineda, Tennessee Technological University
Dr. Michael G. Goldsby, Ball State University College of Business
Dr. Warren S. Stone, University of Arkansas at Little Rock
Dr. Lindle Hatton, California State University, Sacramento

Individuals who develop cases for the North American Case Research Association Meeting, the Midwest Society for Case Research Meeting, the Eastern Case Writers Association Meeting, the European Case Research Association Meeting, and Harvard Case Services are vitally important for continued progress in the field of strategic management. From a research perspective, writing strategic-management cases represents a valuable scholarly activity among faculty. Extensive research is required to structure business policy cases in a way that exposes strategic issues, decisions, and behavior. Pedagogically, strategic-management cases are essential for students learning how to apply concepts, evaluate situations, formulate a plan, and resolve implementation problems. Without a continuous stream of updated business policy cases, the strategic-management course and discipline would lose much of its energy and excitement.

Professors who teach this course supplement lectures with simulations, guest speakers, experiential exercises, class projects, and/or outside readings. Case analysis, however, is typically the backbone of the learning process in most strategic-management courses across the country. Case analysis is almost always an integral part of this course.

Analyzing strategic-management cases gives students the opportunity to work in teams to evaluate the internal operations and external issues facing various organizations and to craft strategies that can lead these firms to success. Working in teams gives students practical experience solving problems as part of a group. In the business world, important decisions are generally made within groups; strategic-management students learn to deal with overly aggressive group members and also timid, noncontributing group members. This experience is valuable as strategic-management students near graduation and soon enter the working world on a full-time basis.

Students can improve their oral and written communication skills, as well as their analytical and interpersonal skills, by proposing and defending particular courses of action for the case companies. Analyzing cases allows students to view a company, its competitors, and its industry concurrently, thus simulating the complex business world. Through case analysis, students learn how to apply concepts, evaluate situations, formulate strategies, and resolve implementation problems. Instructors typically ask students to prepare a three-year strategic plan for the firm. Analyzing a strategic-management case entails students applying concepts learned across their entire business curriculum. Students gain experience dealing with a wide range of organizational problems that impact all the business functions.

In addition to the author of this text, the following individuals wrote cases that were selected for inclusion in this eleventh edition. These persons helped develop the most current compilation of cases ever assembled in a strategic-management text:

Dr. William L. Anderson, Frostburg State University
Dr. M. Jill Austin, Middle Tennessee State University
Dr. Alen Badal, The Union Institute
Dr. Mernoush Banton, Florida International University
Dr. Joe T. Baxter, Jr., Dalton State College
Dr. Henry H. Beam, Western Michigan University
Dr. Charles M. Byles, Virginia Commonwealth University
Dr. Scott K. Campbell, Francis Marion University
Dr. James A. Cunningham, National University of Ireland
Ms. Mary R. Dittman, Francis Marion University
Dr. William Golden, National University of Ireland
Dr. Fernán González, University of New Mexico
Dr. Richard J. Goossen, Trinity Western University
Dr. James Harbin, Texas A&M University–Texarkana
Dr. Marilyn M. Helms, Dalton State College
Dr. Michael P. Hughes, Francis Marion University
Dr. Van Johnston, University of Denver
Dr. Joe W. Leonard, Miami University
Dr. Michael Monahan, Frostburg State University
Dr. Vijaya Narapareddy, University of Denver
Dr. Evan H. Offstein, Frostburg State University
Dr. Nancy Sampson, University of Denver
Dr. Amit J. Shah, Frostburg State University
Dr. Claire Shultz, University of Denver
Dr. Doug E. Thomas, University of New Mexico

I especially appreciate the wonderful work completed by the eleventh edition ancillary authors as follows:

Case Instructor's Manual—Forest R. David, Francis Marion University
Instructor's Manual—Tracy Tuten Ryan, Virginia Commonwealth University
Test Item File and PowerPoints—Charles F. Seifert, Siena College
Internet Study Guide—Amit J. Shah, Frostburg State University

Scores of Pearson/Prentice Hall employees and salespersons have worked diligently behind the scenes to make this text a leader in the business policy market. I appreciate the continued hard work of all those persons.

I also want to thank you, the reader, for investing the time and effort to read and study this text. It will help you formulate, implement, and evaluate strategies for any organization with which you become associated. I hope you come to share my enthusiasm for the rich subject area of strategic management and for the systematic learning approach taken in this text.

Finally, I want to welcome and invite your suggestions, ideas, thoughts, comments, and questions regarding any part of this text or the ancillary materials. Please call me at 843-661-1431, fax me at 843-661-1432, e-mail me at Fdavid@Fmarion.edu, or write me at the School of Business, Francis Marion University, Florence, South Carolina 29501. I sincerely appreciate and need your input to continually improve this text in future editions. Drawing my attention to specific errors or deficiencies in coverage or exposition will especially be appreciated.

Thank you for using this text.

Fred R. David

Dr. Fred R. David is the sole author of three mainstream strategic-management textbooks: *Strategic Management: Concepts and Cases; Strategic Management Concepts;* and *Strategic Management Cases.* These texts have been on a two-year revision cycle since 1986, when the first edition was published. They are among the best-selling strategic-management textbooks in the world, if not *the* best-selling, and are used at more than 400 colleges and universities. Prestigious institutions that have used these textbooks include Harvard University, Duke University, Carnegie Mellon University, Johns Hopkins University, University of Maryland, University of North Carolina, University of Georgia, Florida State University, San Franciso State University, and Wake Forest University.

This strategic-management textbook has been translated and published in Chinese, Japanese, Farsi, Spanish, Indonesian, Hindi, Thai, and Arabic, and it is widely used across Asia and South America. It is the best-selling strategic-management textbook in Mexico, China, Peru, Chile, and Japan, and it is number two in the United States. Approximately 90,000 students read Dr. David's textbook annually, as do thousands of businesspersons. The book has led the field of strategic management for more than a decade in providing an applications/practitioner approach to the discipline.

A native of Whiteville, North Carolina, Fred R. David received a B.S. degree in Mathematics and an MBA from Wake Forest University before being employed as a bank manager with United Carolina Bank. He received a Ph.D. in Business Administration from the University of South Carolina, where he majored in Management. Currently the TranSouth Professor of Strategic Management at Francis Marion University (FMU) in Florence, South Carolina, Dr. David has also taught at Auburn University, Mississippi State University, East Carolina University, University of South Carolina, and University of North Carolina at Pembroke. He is the author of 150 referred publications, including 39 journal articles, 53 proceedings publications, and 58 business policy cases. Articles by Dr. David have been published in such journals as *Academy of Management Review, Academy of Management Executive, Journal of Applied Psychology, Long Range Planning,* and *Advanced Management Journal.* He serves on the editorial review board of the *Advanced Management Journal.*

Dr. David has received a Lifetime Honorary Professorship Award from the Universidad Ricardo Palma in Lima, Peru. He delivered the keynote speech at the twenty-first Annual Latin American Congress on Strategy hosted by the Centrum School of Business in Peru. Dr. David recently delivered an eight-hour Strategic Planning Workshop to the faculty at Pontificia Universidad Católica del Perú in Lima and an eight-hour Case Writing/Analyzing Workshop to the faculty at Utah Valley State College in Orem, Utah. He has received numerous awards, including FMU's Board of Trustees Research Scholar Award; the university's Award for Excellence in Research given annually to the best faculty researcher on campus; and the Phil Carroll Advancement of Management Award, given annually by the Society for the Advancement of Management (SAM) to a management scholar for outstanding contributions in management research.

Dr. David served for three years on the Southern Management Association's Board of Directors. Through his Web site, www.checkmateplan.com, he actively assists businesses around the world in doing strategic planning. He has developed and markets the CheckMATE Strategic Planning Software, which is an industry-leading business planning software package (www.checkmateplan.com).

strategic management

concepts

The Nature of Strategic Management

1

chapter objectives

After studying this chapter, you should be able to do the following:

1. Describe the strategic-management process.

2. Explain the need for integrating analysis and intuition in strategic management.

3. Define and give examples of key terms in strategic management.

4. Discuss the nature of strategy formulation, implementation, and evaluation activities.

5. Describe the benefits of good strategic management.

6. Explain why good ethics is good business in strategic management.

7. Explain the advantages and disadvantages of entering global markets.

8. Discuss the relevance of Sun Tzu's *The Art of War* to strategic management.

9. Discuss how a firm may achieve sustained competitive advantage.

10. Explain ISO 9000, 14000, and 14001.

AP Wide World Photos

experiential exercises

"notable quotes"

If we know where we are and something about how we got there, we might see where we are trending—and if the outcomes which lie naturally in our course are unacceptable, to make timely change.
Abraham Lincoln

Without a strategy, an organization is like a ship without a rudder, going around in circles. It's like a tramp; it has no place to go.
Joel Ross and Michael Kami

Plans are less important than planning.
Dale McConkey

The formulation of strategy can develop competitive advantage only to the extent that the process can give meaning to workers in the trenches.
David Hurst

Most of us fear change. Even when our minds say change is normal, our stomachs quiver at the prospect. But for strategists and managers today, there is no choice but to change.
Robert Waterman, Jr.

If business is not based on ethical grounds, it is of no benefit to society and will, like all other unethical combinations, pass into oblivion.
C. Max Killan

If a man takes no thought about what is distant, he will find sorrow near at hand. He who will not worry about what is far off will soon find something worse than worry.
Confucius

VISIT THE NET

Designed by the author, Fred David, especially for this textbook, this Web site provides strategic planning tools, templates, links, and information that will directly help strategic-management students analyze cases. Strategic Management Club Online. (www.strategyclub.com)

This chapter provides an overview of strategic management. It introduces a practical, integrative model of the strategic-management process; it defines basic activities and terms in strategic management; and it discusses the importance of business ethics.

This chapter initiates several themes that permeate all the chapters of this text. First, *global considerations impact virtually all strategic decisions*! The boundaries of countries no longer can define the limits of our imaginations. To see and appreciate the world from the perspective of others has become a matter of survival for businesses. The underpinnings of strategic management hinge upon managers' gaining an understanding of competitors, markets, prices, suppliers, distributors, governments, creditors, shareholders, and customers worldwide. The price and quality of a firm's products and services must be competitive on a worldwide basis, not just on a local basis. A "Global Perspective" box is provided in each chapter of this text to emphasize the importance of global factors in strategic management.

A second theme is that *electronic commerce (e-commerce) has become a vital strategic-management tool.* An increasing number of companies are gaining a competitive advantage by using the Internet for direct selling and for communication with suppliers, customers, creditors, partners, shareholders, clients, and competitors who may be dispersed globally. E-commerce allows firms to sell products, advertise, purchase supplies, bypass intermediaries, track inventory, eliminate paperwork, and share information. In total, e-commerce is minimizing the expense and cumbersomeness of time, distance, and space in doing business, thus yielding better customer service, greater efficiency, improved products, and higher profitability.

The Internet and personal computers are changing the way we organize our lives; inhabit our homes; and relate to and interact with family, friends, neighbors, and even ourselves. The Internet promotes endless comparison shopping, which thus enables consumers worldwide to band together to demand discounts. The Internet has transferred power from businesses to individuals. Buyers used to face big obstacles when attempting to get the best price and service, such as limited time and data to compare, but now consumers can quickly scan hundreds of vendor offerings. Or they can go to Web sites, such as CompareNet.com, that offer detailed information on more than 100,000 consumer products.

The Internet has changed the very nature and core of buying and selling in nearly all industries. It has fundamentally changed the economics of business in every single industry worldwide. Broadband, e-trade, e-commerce, e-business, and e-mail have become an integral part of everyday life worldwide. Business-to-business e-commerce is five times greater than consumer e-commerce. Fully 74 percent of Americans think the Internet will change society more than the telephone and television combined.[1] An "E-commerce Perspective" box is included in each chapter to illustrate how electronic commerce impacts the strategic-management process.

A third theme is that *the natural environment has become an important strategic issue.* Global warming, bioterrorism, and increased pollution suggest that perhaps there is now no greater threat to business and society than the continuous exploitation and decimation of our natural environment. Mark Starik at George Washington University says, "Halting and reversing worldwide ecological destruction and deterioration . . . is a strategic issue that needs immediate and substantive attention by all businesses and managers." According to the International Standards Organization (ISO), and in this textbook, the word *environment* refers to the natural environment and is defined as "surroundings in which an organization operates, including air, water, land, natural resources, flora, fauna, humans, and their interrelation." A "Natural Environment Perspective" box is provided in each chapter to illustrate how firms are addressing natural environment concerns.

What Is Strategic Management?

Once there were two company presidents who competed in the same industry. These two presidents decided to go on a camping trip to discuss a possible merger. They hiked deep into the woods. Suddenly, they came upon a grizzly bear that rose up on its hind legs and snarled. Instantly, the first president took off his knapsack and got out a pair of jogging shoes. The second president said, "Hey, you can't outrun that bear." The first president responded, "Maybe I can't outrun that bear, but I surely can outrun you!" This story captures the notion of strategic management, which is to achieve and maintain competitive advantage.

VISIT THE NET

Designed by the publisher, Prentice Hall, especially for this textbook, this Web site provides chapter quizzes to be used as a review tool. (www.prenhall.com/david)

Defining Strategic Management

Strategic management can be defined as the art and science of formulating, implementing, and evaluating cross-functional decisions that enable an organization to achieve its objectives. As this definition implies, strategic management focuses on integrating management, marketing, finance/accounting, production/operations, research and development, and computer information systems to achieve organizational success. The term *strategic management* in this text is used synonymously with the term *strategic planning*. The latter term is more often used in the business world, whereas the former is often used in academia. Sometimes the term *strategic management* is used to refer to strategy formulation, implementation, and evaluation, with *strategic planning* referring only to strategy formulation. The purpose of strategic management is to exploit and create new and different opportunities for tomorrow; *long-range planning*, in contrast, tries to optimize for tomorrow the trends of today.

The term *strategic planning* originated in the 1950s and was very popular between the mid-1960s and the mid-1970s. During these years, strategic planning was widely believed to be the answer for all problems. At the time, much of corporate America was "obsessed" with strategic planning. Following that "boom," however, strategic planning was cast aside during the 1980s as various planning models did not yield higher returns. The 1990s, however, brought the revival of strategic planning, and the process is widely practiced today in the business world.

A strategic plan is, in essence, a company's game plan. Just as a football team needs a good game plan to have a chance for success, a company must have a good strategic plan to compete successfully. Profit margins among firms in most industries have been so reduced that there is little room for error in the overall strategic plan. A strategic plan results from tough managerial choices among numerous good alternatives, and it signals commitment to specific markets, policies, procedures, and operations in lieu of other, "less desirable" courses of action.

The term *strategic management* is used at many colleges and universities as the subtitle for the capstone course in business administration—Business Policy—which integrates material from all business courses. The Strategic Management Club Online at www.strategyclub.com offers many benefits for business policy and strategic management students.

Stages of Strategic Management

The *strategic-management process* consists of three stages: strategy formulation, strategy implementation, and strategy evaluation. *Strategy formulation* includes developing a vision and mission, identifying an organization's external opportunities and threats, determining internal strengths and weaknesses, establishing long-term objectives, generating alternative strategies, and choosing particular strategies to pursue.

Strategy-formulation issues include deciding what new businesses to enter, what businesses to abandon, how to allocate resources, whether to expand operations or diversify, whether to enter international markets, whether to merge or form a joint venture, and how to avoid a hostile takeover.

Because no organization has unlimited resources, strategists must decide which alternative strategies will benefit the firm most. Strategy-formulation decisions commit an organization to specific products, markets, resources, and technologies over an extended period of time. Strategies determine long-term competitive advantages. For better or worse, strategic decisions have major multi-functional consequences and enduring effects on an organization. Top managers have the best perspective to understand fully the ramifications of strategy-formulation decisions; they have the authority to commit the resources necessary for implementation.

Strategy implementation requires a firm to establish annual objectives, devise policies, motivate employees, and allocate resources so that formulated strategies can be executed. Strategy implementation includes developing a strategy-supportive culture, creating an effective organizational structure, redirecting marketing efforts, preparing budgets, developing and utilizing information systems, and linking employee compensation to organizational performance.

Strategy implementation often is called the "action stage" of strategic management. Implementing strategy means mobilizing employees and managers to put formulated strategies into action. Often considered to be the most difficult stage in strategic management, strategy implementation requires personal discipline, commitment, and sacrifice. Successful strategy implementation hinges upon managers' ability to motivate employees, which is more an art than a science. Strategies formulated but not implemented serve no useful purpose.

Interpersonal skills are especially critical for successful strategy implementation. Strategy-implementation activities affect all employees and managers in an organization. Every division and department must decide on answers to questions, such as "What must we do to implement our part of the organization's strategy?" and "How best can we get the job done?" The challenge of implementation is to stimulate managers and employees throughout an organization to work with pride and enthusiasm toward achieving stated objectives.

Strategy evaluation is the final stage in strategic management. Managers desperately need to know when particular strategies are not working well; strategy evaluation is the primary means for obtaining this information. All strategies are subject to future modification because external and internal factors are constantly changing. Three fundamental strategy-evaluation activities are (1) reviewing external and internal factors that are the bases for current strategies, (2) measuring performance, and (3) taking corrective actions. Strategy evaluation is needed because success today is no guarantee of success tomorrow! Success always creates new and different problems; complacent organizations experience demise.

Strategy formulation, implementation, and evaluation activities occur at three hierarchical levels in a large organization: corporate, divisional or strategic business unit, and functional. By fostering communication and interaction among managers and employees across hierarchical levels, strategic management helps a firm function as a competitive team. Most small businesses and some large businesses do not have divisions or strategic business units; they have only the corporate and functional levels. Nevertheless, managers and employees at these two levels should be actively involved in strategic-management activities.

VISIT THE NET

Provides nice narrative regarding strategy formulation and implementation at Southern Polytechnic State University. (www.spsu.edu/planassess/strategic.htm)

Peter Drucker says the prime task of strategic management is thinking through the overall mission of a business:

> . . . that is, of asking the question, "What is our Business?" This leads to the setting of objectives, the development of strategies, and the making of today's decisions for tomorrow's results. This clearly must be done by a part of the organization that can see the entire business; that can balance objectives and the needs of today against the needs of tomorrow; and that can allocate resources of men and money to key results.[2]

Integrating Intuition and Analysis

The strategic-management process can be described as an objective, logical, systematic approach for making major decisions in an organization. It attempts to organize qualitative and quantitative information in a way that allows effective decisions to be made under conditions of uncertainty. Yet strategic management is not a pure science that lends itself to a nice, neat, one-two-three approach.

Based on past experiences, judgment, and feelings, most people recognize that *intuition* is essential to making good strategic decisions. Intuition is particularly useful for making decisions in situations of great uncertainty or little precedent. It is also helpful when highly interrelated variables exist or when it is necessary to choose from several plausible alternatives. Some managers and owners of businesses profess to have extraordinary abilities for using intuition alone in devising brilliant strategies. For example, Will Durant, who organized General Motors Corporation, was described by Alfred Sloan as "a man who would proceed on a course of action guided solely, as far as I could tell, by some intuitive flash of brilliance. He never felt obliged to make an engineering hunt for the facts. Yet at times, he was astoundingly correct in his judgment."[3] Albert Einstein acknowledged the importance of intuition when he said, "I believe in intuition and inspiration. At times I feel certain that I am right while not knowing the reason. Imagination is more important than knowledge, because knowledge is limited, whereas imagination embraces the entire world."[4]

Although some organizations today may survive and prosper because they have intuitive geniuses managing them, most are not so fortunate. Most organizations can benefit from strategic management, which is based upon integrating intuition and analysis in decision making. Choosing an intuitive or analytic approach to decision making is not an either–or proposition. Managers at all levels in an organization inject their intuition and judgment into strategic-management analyses. Analytical thinking and intuitive thinking complement each other.

Operating from the I've-already-made-up-my-mind-don't-bother-me-with-the-facts mode is not management by intuition; it is management by ignorance.[5] Drucker says, "I believe in intuition only if you discipline it. 'Hunch' artists, who make a diagnosis but don't check it out with the facts, are the ones in medicine who kill people, and in management kill businesses."[6] As Henderson notes:

> The accelerating rate of change today is producing a business world in which customary managerial habits in organizations are increasingly inadequate. Experience alone was an adequate guide when changes could be made in small increments. But intuitive and experience-based management philosophies are grossly inadequate when decisions are strategic and have major, irreversible consequences.[7]

VISIT THE NET

Reveals that strategies may need to be constantly changed.
(www.csuchico.edu/ mgmt/strategy/module1/ sld041.htm)

In a sense, the strategic-management process is an attempt both to duplicate what goes on in the mind of a brilliant, intuitive person who knows the business and to couple it with analysis.

Adapting to Change

The strategic-management process is based on the belief that organizations should continually monitor internal and external events and trends so that timely changes can be made as needed. The rate and magnitude of changes that affect organizations are increasing dramatically. Consider, for example, e-commerce, laser surgery, the war on terrorism, the aging population, the Enron scandal, and merger mania. To survive, all organizations must be capable of astutely identifying and adapting to change. The strategic-management process is aimed at allowing organizations to adapt effectively to change over the long run. As Waterman has noted:

> In today's business environment, more than in any preceding era, the only constant is change. Successful organizations effectively manage change, continuously adapting their bureaucracies, strategies, systems, products, and cultures to survive the shocks and prosper from the forces that decimate the competition.[8]

E-commerce and globalization are external changes that are transforming business and society today. On a political map, the boundaries between countries may be clear, but on a competitive map showing the real flow of financial and industrial activity, the boundaries have largely disappeared. The speedy flow of information has eaten away at national boundaries so that people worldwide readily see for themselves how other people live. People are traveling abroad more: 10 million Japanese annually travel abroad. People are emigrating more: Germans to England and Mexicans to the United States are examples. As the Global Perspective indicates, U.S. firms are challenged by competitors in many industries. We have become a borderless world with global citizens, global competitors, global customers, global suppliers, and global distributors!

The need to adapt to change leads organizations to key strategic-management questions, such as "What kind of business should we become?", "Are we in the right field(s)?", "Should we reshape our business?", "What new competitors are entering our industry?", "What strategies should we pursue?", "How are our customers changing?", "Are new technologies being developed that could put us out of business?"

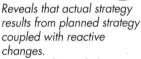

VISIT THE NET

Reveals that actual strategy results from planned strategy coupled with reactive changes.
(www.csuchico.edu/ mgmt/strategy/module1/ sld032.htm)

Key Terms in Strategic Management

Before we further discuss strategic management, we should define nine key terms: competitive advantage, strategists, vision and mission statements, external opportunities and threats, internal strengths and weaknesses, long-term objectives, strategies, annual objectives, and policies.

Competitive Advantage

Strategic management is all about gaining and maintaining *competitive advantage*. This term can be defined as "anything that a firm does especially well compared to rival firms." When a firm can do something that rival firms cannot do, or owns something that rival firms desire, that can represent a competitive advantage. Getting and keeping

GLOBAL PERSPECTIVE

The Largest Non-U.S. Companies in the World

Fortune maganize's annual ranking of the world's largest companies reveals that U.S. firms are being challenged in many industries. The world's largest twenty non-U.S. companies are listed here. Note how well the companies are competing in their respective industries. By way of comparison, the largest company in the world is Wal-Mart Stores with $287 billion in 2004 annual revenues and a revenue growth percentage of +09.

Company	Country	2004 Revenues (billions of $)	2004 vs. 2003 Revenue Growth (%)
BP	Britain	285	+22
Royal Dutch/Shell Group	Britain/Netherlands	268	+33
DaimlerChrysler	Germany	176	+13
Toyota Motor	Japan	172	+13
Total	France	152	+14
AXA	France	121	+09
Allianz	Germany	118	+04
Volkswagen	Germany	110	+12
ING Group	Netherlands	105	+10
Nippon Telegraph	Japan	100	+02
Siemens	Germany	91	+14
Carrefour	France	90	+13
Hitachi	Japan	84	+10
Assicurazioni Generali	Italy	83	+22
Matsushita Electric	Japan	81	+22
Honda Motor	Japan	80	+11
Nissan Motor	Japan	80	+21
Fortis	Belgium/Netherlands	76	+33
Sinopec	China	75	+36
ENI	Italy	74	+25

Source: Adapted from "Fortune Global 500, World's Largest Corporations," *Fortune* (July 25, 2005): 119.

competitive advantage is essential for long-term success in an organization. The Industrial/Organizational (I/O) and the Resource-Based View (RBV) theories of organization (as discussed in Chapters 3 and 4, respectively) present different perspectives on how best to capture and keep competitive advantage—that is, how best to manage strategically. Pursuit of competitive advantage leads to organizational success or failure. Strategic management researchers and practitioners alike desire to better understand the nature and role of competitive advantage in various industries.

Normally, a firm can sustain a competitive advantage for only a certain period due to rival firms imitating and undermining that advantage. Thus it is not adequate to simply obtain competitive advantage. A firm must strive to achieve *sustained*

TABLE 1-1   The Top Ten U.S. Newspapers (March 2005 data, compared to March 2004)

NEWSPAPER	WEEKLY CIRCULATION (IN THOUSANDS)	PERCENT CHANGE
USA Today	2,281	+0.05
Wall Street Journal	2,070	−0.80
New York Times	1,136	+0.24
Los Angeles Times	907	−6.47
Washington Post	751	−2.68
New York Daily News	735	−1.54
New York Post	678	+0.01
Chicago Tribune	573	−6.64
Houston Chronicle	527	−3.92
San Francisco Chronicle	468	−6.07

Source: Adapted from Joseph Hallinan, "Newspaper Circulation Declines 1.9%," *Wall Street Journal* (May 3, 2005):B4.

competitive advantage by (1) continually adapting to changes in external trends and events and internal capabilities, competencies, and resources; and by (2) effectively formulating, implementing, and evaluating strategies that capitalize upon those factors. For example, newspaper circulation in the United States is steadily declining. As indicated in Table 1-1, most national newspapers are rapidly losing market share to the Internet, cable, radio, television, magazines, and other media that consumers use to stay informed. Daily newspaper circulation in the United States totals about 55 million copies annually, which is about the same as it was in 1954. Strategists ponder whether the newspaper circulation slide can be halted in the digital age. The six broadcast networks—ABC, CBS, Fox, NBC, UPN, and WB—are being assaulted by cable channels, video games, broadband, wireless technologies, satellite radio, high-definition TV, and TiVo. The three original broadcast networks captured about 90 percent of the prime-time audience in 1978, but today their combined market share is less than 50 percent.[9]

Airbus has not been able to sustain its competitive advantage over Boeing, as indicated in the recent front page excerpt from the *Wall Street Journal*:

> Six months ago, Airbus's top salesman John Leahy looked unstoppable. The European jet maker had already surpassed Boeing Co. as the No. 1 builder of jetliners. In 2004, Airbus trounced Boeing in every key sales campaign. When Boeing replaced its chief salesman, Mr. Leahy took the opportunity to publicly mock his rival for "doing a good job of not selling airplanes." Since then, the U.S. giant has handed Mr. Leahy his hat. Underlining how quickly fortunes can swing in this storied business rivalry, Boeing is on track in 2005 to win more new orders than Airbus after four years in second place.[10]

Strategists

Strategists are the individuals who are most responsible for the success or failure of an organization. Strategists have various job titles, such as chief executive officer, president, owner, chair of the board, executive director, chancellor, dean, or entrepreneur. Jay Conger, professor of organizational behavior at the London Business School and author of *Building Leaders,* says, "All strategists have to be chief learning officers.

We are in an extended period of change. If our leaders aren't highly adaptive and great models during this period, then our companies won't adapt either, because ultimately leadership is about being a role model."

Strategists help an organization gather, analyze, and organize information. They track industry and competitive trends, develop forecasting models and scenario analyses, evaluate corporate and divisional performance, spot emerging market opportunities, identify business threats, and develop creative action plans. Strategic planners usually serve in a support or staff role. Usually found in higher levels of management, they typically have considerable authority for decision making in the firm. The CEO is the most visible and critical strategic manager. Any manager who has responsibility for a unit or division, responsibility for profit and loss outcomes, or direct authority over a major piece of the business is a strategic manager (strategist). In the last five years, the position of chief strategy officer (CSO) has emerged as a new addition to the top management ranks of many organizations, including Sun Microsystems, Network Associates, Clarus, Lante, Marimba, Sapient, Commerce One, BBDO, Cadbury Schweppes, General Motors, Ellie Mae, Cendant, Charles Schwab, Tyco, Campbell Soup, Morgan Stanley, and Reed-Elsevier. This new corporate officer title represents recognition of the growing importance of strategic planning in the business world.[11]

Strategists differ as much as organizations themselves, and these differences must be considered in the formulation, implementation, and evaluation of strategies. Some strategists will not consider some types of strategies because of their personal philosophies. Strategists differ in their attitudes, values, ethics, willingness to take risks, concern for social responsibility, concern for profitability, concern for short-run versus long-run aims, and management style. The founder of Hershey Foods, Milton Hershey, built the company to manage an orphanage. From corporate profits, Hershey Foods today cares for over one thousand boys and girls in its School for Orphans.

Vision and Mission Statements

Many organizations today develop a *vision statement* that answers the question "What do we want to become?" Developing a vision statement is often considered the first step in strategic planning, preceding even development of a mission statement. Many vision statements are a single sentence. For example, the vision statement of Stokes Eye Clinic in Florence, South Carolina, is "Our vision is to take care of your vision." The vision of the Institute of Management Accountants is "Global leadership in education, certification, and practice of management accounting and financial management."

Mission statements are "enduring statements of purpose that distinguish one business from other similar firms. A mission statement identifies the scope of a firm's operations in product and market terms."[12] It addresses the basic question that faces all strategists: "What is our business?" A clear mission statement describes the values and priorities of an organization. Developing a mission statement compels strategists to think about the nature and scope of present operations and to assess the potential attractiveness of future markets and activities. A mission statement broadly charts the future direction of an organization. An example of a mission statement is provided as follows for Microsoft.

> Microsoft's mission is to create software for the personal computer that empowers and enriches people in the workplace, at school and at home. Microsoft's early vision of a computer on every desk and in every home is coupled today with a strong commitment to Internet-related technologies

that expand the power and reach of the PC and its users. As the world's leading software provider, Microsoft strives to produce innovative products that meet our customers' evolving needs. At the same time, we understand that long-term success is about more than just making great products. Find out what we mean when we talk about Living Our Values (www.microsoft.com/mscorp).

External Opportunities and Threats

External opportunities and *external threats* refer to economic, social, cultural, demographic, environmental, political, legal, governmental, technological, and competitive trends and events that could significantly benefit or harm an organization in the future. Opportunities and threats are largely beyond the control of a single organization—thus the word *external.* The wireless revolution, biotechnology, population shifts, very high gas prices, changing work values and attitudes, illegal immigration issues, and increased competition from foreign companies are examples of opportunities or threats for companies. These types of changes are creating a different type of consumer and consequently a need for different types of products, services, and strategies. Many companies in many industries face the severe external threat of online sales capturing increasing market share in their industry.

Other opportunities and threats may include the passage of a law, the introduction of a new product by a competitor, a national catastrophe, or the declining value of the dollar. A competitor's strength could be a threat. Unrest in the Middle East, rising energy costs, or the war against terrorism could represent an opportunity or a threat.

A basic tenet of strategic management is that firms need to formulate strategies to take advantage of external opportunities and to avoid or reduce the impact of external threats. For this reason, identifying, monitoring, and evaluating external opportunities and threats are essential for success. This process of conducting research and gathering and assimilating external information is sometimes called *environmental scanning* or industry analysis. Lobbying is one activity that some organizations utilize to influence external opportunities and threats.

Internal Strengths and Weaknesses

Internal strengths and *internal weaknesses* are an organization's controllable activities that are performed especially well or poorly. They arise in the management, marketing, finance/accounting, production/operations, research and development, and management information systems activities of a business. Identifying and evaluating organizational strengths and weaknesses in the functional areas of a business is an essential strategic-management activity. Organizations strive to pursue strategies that capitalize on internal strengths and eliminate internal weaknesses.

Strengths and weaknesses are determined relative to competitors. *Relative* deficiency or superiority is important information. Also, strengths and weaknesses can be determined by elements of being rather than performance. For example, a strength may involve ownership of natural resources or a historic reputation for quality. Strengths and weaknesses may be determined relative to a firm's own objectives. For example, high levels of inventory turnover may not be a strength to a firm that seeks never to stock-out.

Internal factors can be determined in a number of ways, including computing ratios, measuring performance, and comparing to past periods and industry averages. Various types of surveys also can be developed and administered to examine internal factors such as employee morale, production efficiency, advertising effectiveness, and customer loyalty.

Long-Term Objectives

Objectives can be defined as specific results that an organization seeks to achieve in pursuing its basic mission. *Long-term* means more than one year. Objectives are essential for organizational success because they state direction; aid in evaluation; create synergy; reveal priorities; focus coordination; and provide a basis for effective planning, organizing, motivating, and controlling activities. Objectives should be challenging, measurable, consistent, reasonable, and clear. In a multidimensional firm, objectives should be established for the overall company and for each division.

Strategies

Strategies are the means by which long-term objectives will be achieved. Business strategies may include geographic expansion, diversification, acquisition, product development, market penetration, retrenchment, divestiture, liquidation, and joint ventures. Strategies currently being pursued by some companies are described in Table 1-2.

Strategies are potential actions that require top management decisions and large amounts of the firm's resources. In addition, strategies affect an organization's long-term prosperity, typically for at least five years, and thus are future-oriented. Strategies have multifunctional or multidivisional consequences and require consideration of both the external and internal factors facing the firm.

Annual Objectives

Annual objectives are short-term milestones that organizations must achieve to reach long-term objectives. Like long-term objectives, annual objectives should be measurable, quantitative, challenging, realistic, consistent, and prioritized. They should be established at the corporate, divisional, and functional levels in a large organization. Annual objectives should be stated in terms of management, marketing, finance/accounting, production/operations, research and development, and management information systems (MIS) accomplishments. A set of annual objectives is needed for each long-term objective. Annual objectives are especially important in strategy implementation, whereas long-term objectives are particularly important in strategy formulation. Annual objectives represent the basis for allocating resources.

Policies

Policies are the means by which annual objectives will be achieved. Policies include guidelines, rules, and procedures established to support efforts to achieve stated objectives. Policies are guides to decision making and address repetitive or recurring situations.

Policies are most often stated in terms of management, marketing, finance/accounting, production/operations, research and development, and computer information systems activities. Policies can be established at the corporate level and apply to an entire organization at the divisional level and apply to a single division, or at the functional level and apply to particular operational activities or departments. Policies, like annual objectives, are especially important in strategy implementation because they outline an organization's expectations of its employees and managers. Policies allow consistency and coordination within and between organizational departments.

Substantial research suggests that a healthier workforce can more effectively and efficiently implement strategies. The National Center for Health Promotion estimates that more than 80 percent of all U.S. corporations have no smoking policies. No smoking policies are usually derived from annual objectives that seek to reduce corporate medical costs associated with absenteeism and to provide a healthy workplace. Ireland recently banned smoking in all pubs and restaurants. Norway, Holland,

TABLE 1-2   Example Strategies in Action in 2005

WALGREENS

The large drugstore Walgreens now has 4,798 stores coast to coast serving over four million customers daily, but the firm faces intense competition on many fronts. Its biggest rival is CVS, which recently acquired 1,268 Eckerds stores to push its total store count to 5,415. Also, supermarkets and mass merchandisers such as Wal-Mart are rapidly moving into the pharmacy business. In addition, the rise in low-cost mail-order prescriptions, which represents a profound shift in the way Americans buy their medicines, threatens Walgreens. Drug purchases by mail grew 18 percent in 2004. So the Walgreens strategy is to open annually 450 new stores in "great" locations. CEO David Bernauer believes the United States has room for 12,000 Walgreens. The company also is a leader in driving down operating costs.

OUTBACK STEAKHOUSE, INC.

Outback Steakhouse, Inc., has pursued a strategy of diversification for more than a decade. Outback Steakhouse today owns Carrabba's Italian Grill (176 locations); Bonefish Grill, a seafood house specializing in wild-caught fish (72 locations); Fleming's Prime Steakhouse & Wine Bars, a white-tablecloth chain (32 locations); Roy's, a purveyor of Hawaiian fusion food (19 locations); Cheeseburger in Paradise, a tropical-theme outlet featuring nightly entertainment (14 locations); Paul Lee's Chinese Kitchens, a start-up business (3 locations); and Lee Roy Selmon's "Southern Comfort" (2 locations). Outback plans to open 163 new restaurants across these divisions in 2005 compared to 120 new openings in 2004.

NUCOR CORP.

Nucor Corp., based in Charlotte, Nucor Corp, has become the tenth-largest steel-producing company in the world by acquiring faltering steel plants. Nucor acquired ten steel plants from 2001 to 2005 as profits soared to $1.1 billion in 2004 on sales of over $11 billion. Nucor uses nonunion workers and state-of-the-art technology to outperform larger integrated steel companies. Previous CEO Ken Iverson led Nucor's pioneering mini-mill approach to steelmaking for decades before current CEO Daniel DiMicco led Nucor to become *Business Week*'s top performing company in materials/chemicals/forest products in 2004 based on both profit and revenue growth.

AUTODESK

Autodesk is among the best-performing stocks on the S&P 500, rising annually about 200 percent of late. Led by CEO Carol Bartz for the last thirteen years, Autodesk focuses on a strategy of product development and produces software for designing and manufacturing everything from skyscrapers to spoons. Since Carly Fiorina's exit from Hewlett-Packard, Carol Bartz of Autodesk is one of the most prominent women among U.S. technology firms (along with Meg Whitman, CEO of eBay). No CEO who is not a founder has served longer at any major tech company than Carol Bartz at Autodesk.

and Greece are passing similar laws. The Netherlands and Italy banned smoking in bars, cafes, and restaurants in January 2005. One European country that still allows smoking almost everywhere is Germany, where 34 percent of all people smoke compared to 22 percent in the United States. There is growing support in New Jersey and Colorado to require casinos to be nonsmoking. Currently the only nonsmoking casino in the nation is the Taos Mountain Casino in Taos, New Mexico. Casinos are fighting the nonsmoking initiative, contending that it would have a detrimental impact on revenues. When Delaware recently, enacted an indoor smoking ban at the state's racetracks revenues fell by 11 percent. An estimated one-third of casino customers are smokers but, of course, that means two-thirds are nonsmokers.

The Strategic-Management Model

The strategic-management process can best be studied and applied using a model. Every model represents some kind of process. The framework illustrated in Figure 1-1 is a widely accepted, comprehensive model of the strategic-management process.[13] This model does not guarantee success, but it does represent a clear and practical approach for formulating, implementing, and evaluating strategies. Relationships among major components of the strategic-management process are shown in the model, which appears in all subsequent chapters with appropriate areas shaped to show the particular focus of each chapter.

Identifying an organization's existing vision, mission, objectives, and strategies is the logical starting point for strategic management because a firm's present situation and condition may preclude certain strategies and may even dictate a particular course of action. Every organization has a vision, mission, objectives, and strategy, even if these elements are not consciously designed, written, or communicated. The answer to where an organization is going can be determined largely by where the organization has been!

FIGURE 1-1

A Comprehensive Strategic-Management Model

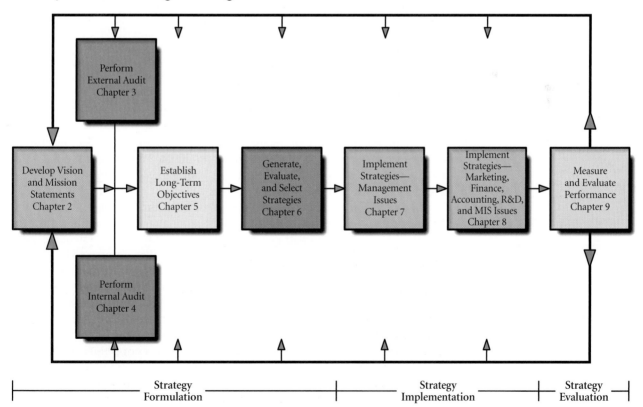

Source: Fred R. David, "How Companies Define Their Mission," *Long Range Planning* 22, no. 3 (June 1988): 40.

The strategic-management process is dynamic and continuous. A change in any one of the major components in the model can necessitate a change in any or all of the other components. For instance, a shift in the economy could represent a major opportunity and require a change in long-term objectives and strategies; a failure to accomplish annual objectives could require a change in policy; or a major competitor's change in strategy could require a change in the firm's mission. Therefore, strategy formulation, implementation, and evaluation activities should be performed on a continual basis, not just at the end of the year or semiannually. The strategic-management process never really ends.

The strategic-management process is not as cleanly divided and neatly performed in practice as the strategic-management model suggests. Strategists do not go through the process in lockstep fashion. Generally, there is give-and-take among hierarchical levels of an organization. Many organizations semiannually conduct formal meetings to discuss and update the firm's vision/mission, opportunities/threats, strengths/weaknesses, strategies, objectives, policies, and performance. These meetings are commonly held off-premises and are called *retreats*. The rationale for periodically conducting strategic-management meetings away from the work site is to encourage more creativity and candor from participants. Good communication and feedback are needed throughout the strategic-management process.

Application of the strategic-management process is typically more formal in larger and well-established organizations. Formality refers to the extent that participants, responsibilities, authority, duties, and approach are specified. Smaller businesses tend to be less formal. Firms that compete in complex, rapidly changing environments, such as technology companies, tend to be more formal in strategic planning. Firms that have many divisions, products, markets, and technologies also tend to be more formal in applying strategic-management concepts. Greater formality in applying the strategic-management process is usually positively associated with the cost, comprehensiveness, accuracy, and success of planning across all types and sizes of organizations.[14]

Benefits of Strategic Management

Strategic management allows an organization to be more proactive than reactive in shaping its own future; it allows an organization to initiate and influence (rather than just respond to) activities—and thus to exert control over its own destiny. Small business owners, chief executive officers, presidents, and managers of many for-profit and non-profit organizations have recognized and realized the benefits of strategic management.

VISIT THE NET

Explains in detail how to develop a strategic plan and compares this document to a business plan.
(www.planware.org/strategy.htm#1)

Historically, the principal benefit of strategic management has been to help organizations formulate better strategies through the use of a more systematic, logical, and rational approach to strategic choice. This certainly continues to be a major benefit of strategic management, but research studies now indicate that the process, rather than the decision or document, is the more important contribution of strategic management.[15] *Communication is a key to successful strategic management.* Through involvement in the process, managers and employees become committed to supporting the organization. Dialogue and participation are essential ingredients.

The manner in which strategic management is carried out is thus exceptionally important. A major aim of the process is to achieve the understanding of and commitment from all managers and employees. Understanding may be the most important benefit of strategic management, followed by commitment. When managers and employees understand what the organization is doing and why, they often feel that they are a part of the firm and become committed to assisting it. This is especially true when employees also understand linkages between their own compensation and organizational performance. Managers and employees become surprisingly creative and innovative when they understand and support the firm's mission, objectives, and strategies. A great benefit of strategic management, then, is the opportunity that the process provides to empower individuals. *Empowerment* is the act of strengthening employees' sense of effectiveness by encouraging them to participate in decision making and to exercise initiative and imagination, and rewarding them for doing so.

More and more organizations are decentralizing the strategic-management process, recognizing that planning must involve lower-level managers and employees. The notion of centralized staff planning is being replaced in organizations by decentralized line-manager planning. For example, Walt Disney Co., in 2005, dismantled its strategic-planning department and gave those responsibilities back to the Disney business divisions. Former CEO Michael Eisner had favored the centralized strategic-planning approach, but new CEO Robert Iger dissolved Disney's strategic-planning department within weeks of his taking over the top office at Disney. The process is a learning, helping, educating, and supporting activity, not merely a paper-shuffling activity among top executives. Strategic-management dialogue is more important than a nicely bound strategic-management document.[16] The worst thing strategists can do is develop strategic plans themselves and then present them to operating managers to execute. Through involvement in the process, line managers become "owners" of the strategy. Ownership of strategies by the people who have to execute them is a key to success!

Although making good strategic decisions is the major responsibility of an organization's owner or chief executive officer, both managers and employees must also be involved in strategy formulation, implementation, and evaluation activities. Participation is a key to gaining commitment for needed changes.

An increasing number of corporations and institutions are using strategic management to make effective decisions. But strategic management is not a guarantee for success; it can be dysfunctional if conducted haphazardly.

Financial Benefits

Research indicates that organizations using strategic-management concepts are more profitable and successful than those that do not.[17] Businesses using strategic-management concepts show significant improvement in sales, profitability, and productivity compared to firms without systematic planning activities. High-performing firms tend to do systematic planning to prepare for future fluctuations in their external and internal environments. Firms with planning systems more closely resembling strategic-management theory generally exhibit superior long-term financial performance relative to their industry.

High-performing firms seem to make more informed decisions with good anticipation of both short- and long-term consequences. On the other hand, firms that perform poorly often engage in activities that are shortsighted and do not reflect good forecasting of future conditions. Strategists of low-performing organizations are often preoccupied with solving internal problems and meeting paperwork deadlines. They typically underestimate their competitors' strengths and overestimate their own firm's strengths. They often attribute weak performance to uncontrollable factors such as a poor economy, technological change, or foreign competition.

Dun & Bradstreet reports that more than 100,000 businesses in the United States fail annually. Business failures include bankruptcies, foreclosures, liquidations, and court-mandated receiverships. Although many factors besides a lack of effective strategic management can lead to business failure, the planning concepts and tools described in this text can yield substantial financial benefits for any organization. An excellent Web site for businesses engaged in strategic planning is www.checkmateplan.com.

VISIT THE NET

Provides excellent narrative on the "Benefits of Strategic Planning," "Pitfalls of Strategic Planning," and the "Steps in Doing Strategic Planning."
(www.entarga.com/ stratplan/index.htm)

Nonfinancial Benefits

Besides helping firms avoid financial demise, strategic management offers other tangible benefits, such as an enhanced awareness of external threats, an improved understanding of competitors' strategies, increased employee productivity, reduced resistance to change, and a clearer understanding of performance–reward relationships. Strategic management enhances the problem-prevention capabilities of organizations because it promotes interaction among managers at all divisional and functional levels. Firms that have nurtured their managers and employees, shared organizational objectives with them, empowered them to help improve the product or service, and recognized their contributions can turn to them for help in a pinch because of this interaction.

In addition to empowering managers and employees, strategic management often brings order and discipline to an otherwise floundering firm. It can be the beginning of an efficient and effective managerial system. Strategic management may renew confidence in the current business strategy or point to the need for corrective actions. The strategic-management process provides a basis for identifying and rationalizing the need for change to all managers and employees of a firm; it helps them view change as an opportunity rather than as a threat.

Greenley stated that strategic management offers the following benefits:

1. It allows for identification, prioritization, and exploitation of opportunities.
2. It provides an objective view of management problems.
3. It represents a framework for improved coordination and control of activities.
4. It minimizes the effects of adverse conditions and changes.
5. It allows major decisions to better support established objectives.
6. It allows more effective allocation of time and resources to identified opportunities.
7. It allows fewer resources and less time to be devoted to correcting erroneous or ad hoc decisions.
8. It creates a framework for internal communication among personnel.
9. It helps integrate the behavior of individuals into a total effort.
10. It provides a basis for clarifying individual responsibilities.
11. It encourages forward thinking.
12. It provides a cooperative, integrated, and enthusiastic approach to tackling problems and opportunities.
13. It encourages a favorable attitude toward change.
14. It gives a degree of discipline and formality to the management of a business.[18]

Why Some Firms Do No Strategic Planning

VISIT THE NET

Gives reasons why some organizations avoid strategic planning.
(www.mindtools.com/ plfailpl.html)

Some firms do not engage in strategic planning, and some firms do strategic planning but receive no support from managers and employees. Some reasons for poor or no strategic planning are as follows:

- *Poor Reward Structures*—When an organization assumes success, it often fails to reward success. When failure occurs, then the firm may punish. In this situation, it is better for an individual to do nothing (and not draw attention) than to risk trying to achieve something, fail, and be punished.
- *Fire Fighting*—An organization can be so deeply embroiled in crisis management and fire fighting that it does not have time to plan.

- *Waste of Time*—Some firms see planning as a waste of time since no marketable product is produced. Time spent on planning is an investment.
- *Too Expensive*—Some organizations are culturally opposed to spending resources.
- *Laziness*—People may not want to put forth the effort needed to formulate a plan.
- *Content with Success*—Particularly if a firm is successful, individuals may feel there is no need to plan because things are fine as they stand. But success today does not guarantee success tomorrow.
- *Fear of Failure*—By not taking action, there is little risk of failure unless a problem is urgent and pressing. Whenever something worthwhile is attempted, there is some risk of failure.
- *Overconfidence*—As individuals amass experience, they may rely less on formalized planning. Rarely, however, is this appropriate. Being overconfident or overestimating experience can bring demise. Forethought is rarely wasted and is often the mark of professionalism.
- *Prior Bad Experience*—People may have had a previous bad experience with planning, that is, cases in which plans have been long, cumbersome, impractical, or inflexible. Planning, like anything else, can be done badly.
- *Self-Interest*—When someone has achieved status, privilege, or self-esteem through effectively using an old system, he or she often sees a new plan as a threat.
- *Fear of the Unknown*—People may be uncertain of their abilities to learn new skills, of their aptitude with new systems, or of their ability to take on new roles.
- *Honest Difference of Opinion*—People may sincerely believe the plan is wrong. They may view the situation from a different viewpoint, or they may have aspirations for themselves or the organization that are different from the plan. Different people in different jobs have different perceptions of a situation.
- *Suspicion*—Employees may not trust management.[19]

Pitfalls in Strategic Planning

Strategic planning is an involved, intricate, and complex process that takes an organization into uncharted territory. It does not provide a ready-to-use prescription for success; instead, it takes the organization through a journey and offers a framework for addressing questions and solving problems. Being aware of potential pitfalls and being prepared to address them is essential to success.

Some pitfalls to watch for and avoid in strategic planning are these:

- Using strategic planning to gain control over decisions and resources
- Doing strategic planning only to satisfy accreditation or regulatory requirements
- Too hastily moving from mission development to strategy formulation
- Failing to communicate the plan to employees, who continue working in the dark
- Top managers making many intuitive decisions that conflict with the formal plan
- Top managers not actively supporting the strategic-planning process
- Failing to use plans as a standard for measuring performance
- Delegating planning to a "planner" rather than involving all managers
- Failing to involve key employees in all phases of planning
- Failing to create a collaborative climate supportive of change

VISIT THE NET

Provides nice discussion of the limitations of strategic planning process within an organization. (www.des.calstate.edu/ limitations.html)

- Viewing planning as unnecessary or unimportant
- Becoming so engrossed in current problems that insufficient or no planning is done
- Being so formal in planning that flexibility and creativity are stifled.[20]

Guidelines for Effective Strategic Management

Failing to follow certain guidelines in conducting strategic management can foster criticisms of the process and create problems for the organization. An integral part of strategy evaluation must be to evaluate the quality of the strategic-management process. Issues such as "Is strategic management in our firm a people process or a paper process?" should be addressed.

> Even the most technically perfect strategic plan will serve little purpose if it is not implemented. Many organizations tend to spend an inordinate amount of time, money, and effort on developing the strategic plan, treating the means and circumstances under which it will be implemented as afterthoughts! Change comes through implementation and evaluation, not through the plan. A technically imperfect plan that is implemented well will achieve more than the perfect plan that never gets off the paper on which it is typed.[21]

Strategic management must not become a self-perpetuating bureaucratic mechanism. Rather, it must be a self-reflective learning process that familiarizes managers and employees in the organization with key strategic issues and feasible alternatives for resolving those issues. Strategic management must not become ritualistic, stilted, orchestrated, or too formal, predictable, and rigid. Words supported by numbers, rather than numbers supported by words, should represent the medium for explaining strategic issues and organizational responses. A key role of strategists is to facilitate continuous organizational learning and change.

R. T. Lenz offered some important guidelines for effective strategic management:

> Keep the strategic-management process as simple and nonroutine as possible. Eliminate jargon and arcane planning language. Remember, strategic management is a process for fostering learning and action, not merely a formal system for control. To avoid routinized behavior, vary assignments, team membership, meeting formats, and the planning calendar. The process should not be totally predictable, and settings must be changed to stimulate creativity. Emphasize word-oriented plans with numbers as back-up material. If managers cannot express their strategy in a paragraph or so, they either do not have one or do not understand it. Stimulate thinking and action that challenge the assumptions underlying current corporate strategy. Welcome bad news. If strategy is not working, managers desperately need to know it. Further, no pertinent information should be classified as inadmissible merely because it cannot be quantified. Build a corporate culture in which the role of strategic management and its essential purposes are understood. Do not permit "technicians" to co-opt the process. It is ultimately a process for learning and action. Speak of it in these terms. Attend to psychological, social, and political dimensions, as well as the information infrastructure and administrative procedures supporting it.[22]

An important guideline for effective strategic management is open-mindedness. A willingness and eagerness to consider new information, new viewpoints, new ideas, and new possibilities is essential; all organizational members must share a spirit of inquiry and learning. Strategists such as chief executive officers, presidents, owners of small businesses, and heads of government agencies must commit themselves to listen to and understand managers' positions well enough to be able to restate those positions to the managers' satisfaction. In addition, managers and employees throughout the firm should be able to describe the strategists' positions to the satisfaction of the strategists. This degree of discipline will promote understanding and learning.

No organization has unlimited resources. No firm can take on an unlimited amount of debt or issue an unlimited amount of stock to raise capital. Therefore, no organization can pursue all the strategies that potentially could benefit the firm. Strategic decisions thus always have to be made to eliminate some courses of action and to allocate organizational resources among others. Most organizations can afford to pursue only a few corporate-level strategies at any given time. It is a critical mistake for managers to pursue too many strategies at the same time, thereby spreading the firm's resources so thin that all strategies are jeopardized. Joseph Charyk, CEO of the Communication Satellite Corporation (Comsat), said, "We have to face the cold fact that Comsat may not be able to do all it wants. We must make hard choices on which ventures to keep and which to fold."

Strategic decisions require trade-offs such as long-range versus short-range considerations or maximizing profits versus increasing shareholders' wealth. There are ethics issues too. Strategy trade-offs require subjective judgments and preferences. In many cases, a lack of objectivity in formulating strategy results in a loss of competitive posture and profitability. Most organizations today recognize that strategic-management concepts and techniques can enhance the effectiveness of decisions. Subjective factors such as attitudes toward risk, concern for social responsibility, and organizational culture will always affect strategy-formulation decisions, but organizations need to be as objective as possible in considering qualitative factors.

Business Ethics and Strategic Management

Business ethics can be defined as principles of conduct within organizations that guide decision making and behavior. Good business ethics is a prerequisite for good strategic management; good ethics is just good business!

A rising tide of consciousness about the importance of business ethics is sweeping the United States and the rest of world. Strategists are the individuals primarily responsible for ensuring that high ethical principles are espoused and practiced in an organization. All strategy formulation, implementation, and evaluation decisions have ethical ramifications.

Newspapers and business magazines daily report legal and moral breaches of ethical conduct by both public and private organizations. For example, the Securities and Exchange Commission recently imposed on MCI (formerly WorldCom) a fine of $1.5 billion payable to shareholders for accounting fraud.

Managers and employees of firms must be careful not to become scapegoats blamed for company environmental wrongdoings. Harming the natural environment is unethical, illegal, and costly. When organizations today face criminal charges for polluting the environment, firms increasingly are turning on their managers and employees to win leniency for themselves. Employee firings and demotions are becoming common in pollution-related legal suits. Managers being fired at Darling International, Inc., and Niagara

VISIT THE NET

Describes "Why Have a Code of Ethics" and gives "Guidelines on Writing a Code of Ethics." (www.ethicsweb.ca/codes)

Mohawk Power Corporation for being indirectly responsible for their firms polluting water exemplifies this corporate trend. Therefore, managers and employees today must be careful not to ignore, conceal, or disregard a pollution problem, or they may find themselves personally liable. In this regard, more and more companies are becoming ISO 14001 certified, as indicated in the "Natural Environment Perspective" on pages 23–24.

A new wave of ethics issues related to product safety, employee health, sexual harassment, AIDS in the workplace, smoking, acid rain, affirmative action, waste disposal, foreign business practices, cover-ups, takeover tactics, conflicts of interest, employee privacy, inappropriate gifts, security of company records, and layoffs has accentuated the need for strategists to develop a clear code of business ethics. United Technologies Corporation has issued a twenty-one-page code of ethics and named a new vice president of business ethics. Baxter Travenol Laboratories, IBM, Caterpillar Tractor, Chemical Bank, ExxonMobil, Dow Corning, and Celanese are firms that have formal codes of business ethics. A *code of business ethics* can provide a basis on which policies can be devised to guide daily behavior and decisions at the work site.

The explosion of the Internet into the workplace has raised many new ethical questions in organizations today. The "E-Commerce Perspective on page 25" focuses on business ethics issues related to the Internet. Merely having a code of ethics, however, is not sufficient to ensure ethical business behavior. A code of ethics can be viewed as a public relations gimmick, a set of platitudes, or window dressing. To ensure that the code is read, understood, believed, and remembered, organizations need to conduct periodic ethics workshops to sensitize people to workplace circumstances in which ethics issues may arise.[23] If employees see examples of punishment for violating the code and rewards for upholding the code, this helps reinforce the importance of a firm's code of ethics.

An ethics "culture" needs to permeate organizations! To help create an ethics culture, Citicorp developed a business ethics board game that is played by forty thousand employees in forty-five countries. Called "The Word Ethic," this game asks players business ethics questions, such as how do you deal with a customer who offers you football tickets in exchange for a new, backdated IRA? Diana Robertson at the Wharton School of Business believes the game is effective because it is interactive. Many organizations, such as Prime Computer and Kmart, have developed a code-of-conduct manual outlining ethical expectations and giving examples of situations that commonly arise in their businesses. Harris Corporation's managers and employees are warned that failing to report an ethical violation by others could bring discharge.

One reason strategists' salaries are high compared to those of other individuals in an organization is that strategists must take the moral risks of the firm. Strategists are responsible for developing, communicating, and enforcing the code of business ethics for their organizations. Although primary responsibility for ensuring ethical behavior rests with a firm's strategists, an integral part of the responsibility of all managers is to provide ethics leadership by constant example and demonstration. Managers hold positions that enable them to influence and educate many people. This makes managers responsible for developing and implementing ethical decision making. Gellerman and Drucker, respectively, offer some good advice for managers:

> All managers risk giving too much because of what their companies demand from them. But the same superiors, who keep pressing you to do more, or to do it better, or faster, or less expensively, will turn on you should you cross that fuzzy line between right and wrong. They will blame you for exceeding instructions or for ignoring their warnings. The smartest managers already know that the best answer to the question "How far is too far?" is don't try to find out.[24]

VISIT THE NET

An excellent Web site to obtain additional information regarding business ethics is (www.ethicsweb.ca/codes); it describes "Why Have a Code of Ethics" and gives "Guidelines on Writing a Code of Ethics."

VISIT THE NET

Professor Hansen at Stetson University provides a strategic management slide show for this entire text. (www.stetson.edu/~rhansen/ strategy)

NATURAL ENVIRONMENT PERSPECTIVE

Using ISO 14000 Certification to Gain Strategic Advantage

Based in Geneva, Switzerland, the ISO (International Organization for Standardization) is a network of the national standards institutes of 147 countries, one member per country. ISO is the world's largest developer of standards. Widely accepted all over the world, ISO standards are voluntary since the organization has no legal authority to enforce their implementation. ISO itself does not regulate or legislate. Governmental agencies in various countries, such as the Environmental Protection Agency in the United States, have adopted ISO standards as part of their regulatory framework, and the standards are the basis of much legislation. Adoptions are sovereign decisions by the regulatory authorities, governments, and/or companies concerned.

Two widely adopted ISO standards are ISO 9000, which focuses on quality control, and ISO 14000, which focuses on operating in an environmentally friendly manner. More than a half million organizations in more than 60 countries are implementing ISO 9000, which provides a framework for quality management throughout the production and distribution of products and services. ISO 9000 has become an international reference for quality requirements in most industries. Companies that are not ISO 9000–certified often cannot get work.

Almost 37,000 companies have adopted the ISO 14001 standard for Environmental Management Systems since it was published in 1995. However, just 17 percent of the companies adopting the ISO 14001 standard are in developing countries. ISO 14000–certified Ford Motor Company, as of July 2, 2003, required all of its suppliers and all of its manufacturing sites to be ISO 14001 certified. General Motors requires all of its suppliers to be certified to the ISO 14001 standard. IBM Corporation strongly encourages its suppliers to be ISO 14001 certified. Skanska USA, Inc., was the first construction group in the United States to have all of its offices, job sites, and operations ISO 14001 certified. Washtenaw County, Michigan, is implementing an EMS based on 14001 for its sheriff's department.

What Are ISO 14000 and ISO 14001?

ISO 14000 refers to a series of voluntary standards in the environmental field. The ISO 14000 family of standards concerns the extent to which a firm minimizes harmful effects on the environment caused by its activities and continually monitors and improves its own environmental performance. Included in the ISO 14000 series are the ISO 14001 standards in fields such as environmental auditing, environmental performance evaluation, environmental labeling, and life-cycle assessment. ISO 14001 is a set of standards adopted by thousands of firms worldwide to certify to their constituencies that they are conducting business in an environmentally friendly manner. ISO 14001 standards offer a universal technical standard for environmental compliance that more and more firms are requiring not only of themselves but also of their suppliers and distributors.

Requirements for ISO 14001 Certification

The ISO 14001 standard requires that a community or organization put in place and implement a series of practices and procedures that, when taken together, result in an environmental management system. ISO 14001 is not a technical standard and as such does not in any way replace technical requirements embodied in statutes or regulations. It also does not set prescribed standards of performance for organizations. The major requirements of an EMS under ISO 14001 include the following:

- Establish an EMS that includes commitments to prevention of pollution, continual improvement in overall environmental performance, and compliance with all applicable statutory and regulatory requirements.

- Identification of all aspects of the organization's activities, products, and services that could have a significant impact on the environment, including those that are not regulated.

- Setting performance objectives and targets for the management system that link back to three policies: (1) prevention of pollution, (2) continual improvement, and (3) compliance.

- Implementing an EMS to meet environmental objectives that include training of employees, establishing work instructions and practices, and establishing the actual metrics by which the objectives and targets will be measured.
- Auditing the operation of the EMS.
- Taking corrective actions when deviations from the EMS occur.

Conclusion

ISO 14001 standards on air, water, and soil quality, and on emissions of gases and radiation, contribute to preserving the environment in which we all live and work. The U.S. Environmental Protection Agency (EPA) now offers a guide entitled "Environmental Management Systems (EMS): An Implementation Guide for Small and Medium Sized Organizations." The publication offers a plain-English, commonsense guide to becoming ISO 14001 certified. Not being ISO 14001 certified can be a strategic disadvantage for towns, counties, and companies as people today expect organizations to minimize or, even better, to eliminate environmental harm they cause.

Source: Adapted from the www.iso14000.com Web site and the www.epa.gov Web site.

A man (or woman) might know too little, perform poorly, lack judgment and ability, and yet not do too much damage as a manager. But if that person lacks character and integrity—no matter how knowledgeable, how brilliant, how successful—he destroys. He destroys people, the most valuable resource of the enterprise. He destroys spirit. And he destroys performance. This is particularly true of the people at the head of an enterprise. For the spirit of an organization is created from the top. If an organization is great in spirit, it is because the spirit of its top people is great. If it decays, it does so because the top rots. As the proverb has it, "Trees die from the top." No one should ever become a strategist unless he or she is willing to have his or her character serve as the model for subordinates.[25]

No society anywhere in the world can compete very long or successfully with people stealing from one another or not trusting one another, with every bit of information requiring notarized confirmation, with every disagreement ending up in litigation, or with government having to regulate businesses to keep them honest. Being unethical is a recipe for headaches, inefficiency, and waste. History has proven that the greater the trust and confidence of people in the ethics of an institution or society, the greater its economic strength. Business relationships are built mostly on mutual trust and reputation. Short-term decisions based on greed and questionable ethics will preclude the necessary self-respect to gain the trust of others. More and more firms believe that ethics training and an ethics culture create strategic advantage.

Some business actions considered to be unethical include misleading advertising or labeling, causing environmental harm, poor product or service safety, padding expense accounts, insider trading, dumping banned or flawed products in foreign markets, lack of equal opportunities for women and minorities, overpricing, hostile takeovers, moving jobs overseas, and using nonunion labor in a union shop.[26]

Internet fraud, including hacking into company computers and spreading viruses, has become a major unethical activity that plagues every sector of online commerce from banking to shopping sites. More than three hundred Web sites now show individuals how to hack into computers; this problem has become endemic nationwide and around the world.

E-COMMERCE PERSPECTIVE

Business Ethics and the Internet

May employees use the Internet at work to conduct day trading of personal stocks? May employees send e-mail to personal friends and relatives from the workplace? Is it ethical for employees to shop online while at work? May employees hunt for a new job while online at work? May employees play games online while at work? Before answering these questions consider the following facts:

- Employee productivity can suffer immensely when many workers surf the Web at work.

- Unlike phone calls, e-mail can often be retrieved months or years later and can be used against the company in litigation.

- When employees surf the Web at work, they drag the company's name along with them everywhere. This could be harmful to the company if employees visit certain sites such as racist chat rooms or pornographic material sites.

- Software packages are now available to companies that report Web site visits by individual employees. Companies such as Telemate Net Software, Inc. in Atlanta produce software that tells managers who went to what sites at what times and for how long.

- Some 27 percent of large U.S. firms have begun checking employee e-mail, up from 15 percent in 1997. BellSouth employees must regularly click "OK" to a message warning them against misuse of e-mail and the Internet and alerting them that their actions can be monitored.

- Many companies, such as Boeing, grant Internet usage to employees as a perk, but many of those firms are finding that this fringe benefit must be managed.

Lockheed Martin now directs its employees onto the Internet for extensive training sessions on topics that include business ethics, legal compliance, sexual harassment, and day trading. Lockheed even has an Internet ethics game, Ethics Challenge, which every single employee and manager must play once a year. During a recent six-month period, Lockheed discharged 25 employees for ethics violations, suspended 14 others, gave a written reprimand to 51 persons, and an oral reprimand to 146 employees.

Soon after installing the Telemate software, Wolverton & Associates learned that broadcast.com was the company's third most visited site; people download music from that site. And E*TRADE was the company's eighth most visited site; people day trade stocks at that site.

Recent research reveals that 38 percent of companies today choose to store and review employee e-mail messages; this represents a rise of 15 percent since 1997. In addition, 54 percent of companies also monitor employees' Internet connections, with 29 percent blocking access to unauthorized or inappropriate Web sites.

Source: Adapted from Michael McCarthy, "Virtual Morality. A New Workplace Quandary," *Wall Street Journal* (October 21, 1999): B1; Michael McCarthy, "Now the Boss Knows Where You're Clicking," *Wall Street Journal* (October 21, 1999); and Michael McCarthy, "How One Firm Tracks Ethics Electronically," *Wall Street Journal* (October 21, 1999): B1.

Ethics training programs should include messages from the CEO emphasizing ethical business practices, the development and discussion of codes of ethics, and procedures for discussing and reporting unethical behavior. Firms can align ethical and strategic decision making by incorporating ethical considerations into long-term planning, by integrating ethical decision making into the performance appraisal process, by encouraging whistle-blowing or the reporting of unethical practices, and by monitoring departmental and corporate performance regarding ethical issues.

In a final analysis, ethical standards come out of history and heritage. Our predecessors have left us with an ethical foundation to build upon. Even the legendary football coach Vince Lombardi knew that some things were worth more than winning, and he required his players to have three kinds of loyalty: to God, to their families, and to the Green Bay Packers, "in that order."

Comparing Business and Military Strategy

A strong military heritage underlies the study of strategic management. Terms such as *objectives*, *mission*, *strengths*, and *weaknesses* first were formulated to address problems on the battlefield. According to *Webster's New World Dictionary,* strategy is "the science of planning and directing large-scale military operations, of maneuvering forces into the most advantageous position prior to actual engagement with the enemy." The word *strategy* comes from the Greek *strategos,* which refers to a military general and combines *stratos* (the army) and *ago* (to lead). The history of strategic planning began in the military. A key aim of both business and military strategy is "to gain competitive advantage." In many respects, business strategy is like military strategy, and military strategists have learned much over the centuries that can benefit business strategists today. Both business and military organizations try to use their own strengths to exploit competitors' weaknesses. If an organization's overall strategy is wrong (ineffective), then all the efficiency in the world may not be enough to allow success. Business or military success is generally not the happy result of accidental strategies. Rather, success is the product of both continuous attention to changing external and internal conditions and the formulation and implementation of insightful adaptations to those conditions. The element of surprise provides great competitive advantages in both military and business strategy; information systems that provide data on opponents' or competitors' strategies and resources are also vitally important.

Of course, a fundamental difference between military and business strategy is that business strategy is formulated, implemented, and evaluated with an assumption of *competition,* whereas military strategy is based on an assumption of *conflict.* Nonetheless, military conflict and business competition are so similar that many strategic-management techniques apply equally to both. Business strategists have access to valuable insights that military thinkers have refined over time. Superior strategy formulation and implementation can overcome an opponent's superiority in numbers and resources.

Both business and military organizations must adapt to change and constantly improve to be successful. Too often, firms do not change their strategies when their environment and competitive conditions dictate the need to change. Gluck offered a classic military example of this:

VISIT THE NET

Provides a nice account of strategic planning, tracing history back to the military. (www.des.calstate.edu/ history.html)

When Napoleon won, it was because his opponents were committed to the strategy, tactics, and organization of earlier wars. When he lost—against Wellington, the Russians, and the Spaniards—it was because he, in turn, used tried-and-true strategies against enemies who thought afresh, who were developing the strategies not of the last war but of the next.[27]

Similarities can be construed from Sun Tzu's writings to the practice of formulating and implementing strategies among businesses today. Table 1-3 provides narrative excerpts from *The Art of War.* As you read through Table 1-3, consider which of the principles of war apply to business strategy as companies today compete aggressively to survive and grow.

T A B L E 1 - 3 Excerpts from Sun Tzu's *The Art of War* Writings

- War is a matter of vital importance to the state: a matter of life or death, the road either to survival or ruin. Hence, it is imperative that it be studied thoroughly.
- Warfare is based on deception. When near the enemy, make it seem that you are far away; when far away, make it seem that you are near. Hold out baits to lure the enemy. Strike the enemy when he is in disorder. Avoid the enemy when he is stronger. If your opponent is of choleric temper, try to irritate him. If he is arrogant, try to encourage his egotism. If enemy troops are well prepared after reorganization, try to wear them down. If they are united, try to sow dissension among them. Attack the enemy where he is unprepared, and appear where you are not expected. These are the keys to victory for a strategist. It is not possible to formulate them in detail beforehand.
- A speedy victory is the main object in war. If this is long in coming, weapons are blunted and morale depressed. When the army engages in protracted campaigns, the resources of the state will fall short. Thus, while we have heard of stupid haste in war, we have not yet seen a clever operation that was prolonged.
- Generally, in war the best policy is to take a state intact; to ruin it is inferior to this. To capture the enemy's entire army is better than to destroy it; to take intact a regiment, a company, or a squad is better than to destroy it. For to win one hundred victories in one hundred battles is not the acme of skill. To subdue the enemy without fighting is the supreme excellence. Those skilled in war subdue the enemy's army without battle.
- The art of using troops is this: When ten to the enemy's one, surround him. When five times his strength, attack him. If double his strength, divide him. If equally matched, you may engage him with some good plan. If weaker, be capable of withdrawing. And if in all respects unequal, be capable of eluding him.
- Know your enemy and know yourself, and in a hundred battles you will never be defeated. When you are ignorant of the enemy but know yourself, your chances of winning or losing are equal. If ignorant both of your enemy and of yourself, you are sure to be defeated in every battle.
- He who occupies the field of battle first and awaits his enemy is at ease, and he who comes later to the scene and rushes into the fight is weary. And therefore, those skilled in war bring the enemy to the field of battle and are not brought there by him. Thus, when the enemy is at ease, be able to tire him; when well fed, be able to starve him; when at rest, be able to make him move.
- Analyze the enemy's plans so that you will know his shortcomings as well as his strong points. Agitate him to ascertain the pattern of his movement. Lure him out to reveal his dispositions and to ascertain his position. Launch a probing attack to learn where his strength is abundant and where deficient. It is according to the situation that plans are laid for victory, but the multitude does not comprehend this.
- An army may be likened to water, for just as flowing water avoids the heights and hastens to the lowlands, so an army should avoid strength and strike weakness. And as water shapes its flow in accordance with the ground, so an army manages its victory in accordance with the situation of the enemy. And as water has no constant form, there are in warfare no constant conditions. Thus, one able to win the victory by modifying his tactics in accordance with the enemy situation may be said to be divine.
- If you decide to go into battle, do not anounce your intentions or plans. Project "business as usual."
- Unskilled leaders work out their conflicts in courtrooms and battlefields. Brilliant strategists rarely go to battle or to court; they generally achieve their objectives through tactical positioning well in advance of any confrontation.
- When you do decide to challenge another company (or army), much calculating, estimating, analyzing, and positioning bring triumph. Little computation brings defeat.
- Skillful leaders do not let a strategy inhibit creative counter-movement. Nor should commands from those at a distance interfere with spontaneous maneuvering in the immediate situation.
- When a decisive advantage is gained over a rival, skillful leaders do not press on. They hold their position and give their rivals the opportunity to surrender or merge. They do not allow their forces to be damaged by those who have nothing to lose.
- Brilliant strategists forge ahead with illusion, obscuring the area(s) of major confrontation, so that opponents divide their forces in an attempt to defend many areas. Create the appearance of confusion, fear, or vulnerability so the opponent is helplessly drawn toward this illusion of advantage.

(Note: Substitute the words *strategy* or *strategic planning* for *war* or *warfare*)
Source: Adapted from *The Art of War* and from the Web site www.ccs.neu.edu/home/thigpen/html/art_of_war.html

The Nature of Global Competition

For centuries before Columbus discovered America and surely for centuries to come, businesses have searched and will continue to search for new opportunities beyond their national boundaries. There has never been a more internationalized and economically competitive society than today's. Some U.S. industries, such as textiles, steel, and consumer electronics, are in complete disarray as a result of the international challenge.

Organizations that conduct business operations across national borders are called *international firms* or *multinational corporations.* The term *parent company* refers to a firm investing in international operations, while *host country* is the country where that business is conducted. The strategic-management process is conceptually the same for multinational firms as for purely domestic firms; however, the process is more complex for international firms because of the presence of more variables and relationships. The social, cultural, demographic, environmental, political, governmental, legal, technological, and competitive opportunities and threats that face a multinational corporation are almost limitless, and the number and complexity of these factors increase dramatically with the number of products produced and the number of geographic areas served.

More time and effort are required to identify and evaluate external trends and events in multinational corporations than in domestic corporations. Geographical distance, cultural and national differences, and variations in business practices often make communication between domestic headquarters and overseas operations difficult. Strategy implementation can be more difficult because different cultures have different norms, values, and work ethics.

The global war on terrorism and advancements in telecommunications are drawing countries, cultures, and organizations worldwide closer together. Foreign revenue as a percent of total company revenues already exceeds 50 percent in hundreds of U.S. firms, including ExxonMobil, Gillette, Dow Chemical, Citicorp, Colgate-Palmolive, and Texaco. Joint ventures and partnerships between domestic and foreign firms are becoming the rule rather than the exception!

Fully 95 percent of the world's population lives outside the United States, and this group is growing 70 percent faster than the U.S. population! The lineup of competitors in virtually all industries today is global. Global competition is more than a management fad. General Motors, Ford, and Chrysler compete with Toyota and Hyundai. General Electric and Westinghouse battle Siemens and Mitsubishi. Caterpillar and John Deere compete with Komatsu. Goodyear battles Michelin, Bridgestone/Firestone, and Pirelli. Boeing competes with Airbus. Only a few U.S. industries—such as furniture, printing, retailing, consumer packaged goods, and retail banking—are not yet greatly challenged by foreign competitors. But many products and components in these industries too are now manufactured in foreign countries.

International operations can be as simple as exporting a product to a single foreign country or as complex as operating manufacturing, distribution, and marketing facilities in many countries. U.S. firms are acquiring foreign companies and forming joint ventures with foreign firms, and foreign firms are acquiring U.S. companies and forming joint ventures with U.S. firms. This trend is accelerating dramatically. International expansion is no guarantee of success, however.

Advantages and Disadvantages of International Operations

Firms have numerous reasons for formulating and implementing strategies that initiate, continue, or expand involvement in business operations across national borders. Perhaps the greatest advantage is that firms can gain new customers for their products and services, thus increasing revenues. Growth in revenues and profits is a common organizational objective and often an expectation of shareholders because it is a measure of organizational success.

In addition to seeking growth, firms have the following potentially advantageous reasons to initiate, continue, and expand international operations:

1. Foreign operations can absorb excess capacity, reduce unit costs, and spread economic risks over a wider number of markets.
2. Foreign operations can allow firms to establish low-cost production facilities in locations close to raw materials and/or cheap labor.
3. Competitors in foreign markets may not exist, or competition may be less intense than in domestic markets.
4. Foreign operations may result in reduced tariffs, lower taxes, and favorable political treatment in other countries.
5. Joint ventures can enable firms to learn the technology, culture, and business practices of other people and to make contacts with potential customers, suppliers, creditors, and distributors in foreign countries.
6. Many foreign governments and countries offer varied incentives to encourage foreign investment in specific locations.
7. Economies of scale can be achieved from operation in global rather than solely domestic markets. Larger-scale production and better efficiencies allow higher sales volumes and lower-price offerings.

A firm's power and prestige in domestic markets may be significantly enhanced with various stakeholder groups if the firm competes globally. Enhanced prestige can translate into improved negotiating power among creditors, suppliers, distributors, and other important groups.

There are also numerous potential disadvantages of initiating, continuing, or expanding business across national borders. One risk is that foreign operations could be seized by nationalistic factions. Other disadvantages include the following:

1. Firms confront different and often little-understood social, cultural, demographic, environmental, political, governmental, legal, technological, economic, and competitive forces when internationally doing business. These forces can make communication difficult between the parent firm and subsidiaries.
2. Weaknesses of competitors in foreign lands are often overestimated, and strengths are often underestimated. Keeping informed about the number and nature of competitors is more difficult when internationally doing business.
3. Language, culture, and value systems differ among countries, and this can create barriers to communication and problems managing people.
4. Gaining an understanding of regional organizations such as the European Economic Community, the Latin American Free Trade Area, the International Bank for Reconstruction and Development, and the International Finance Corporation is difficult but is often required in internationally doing business.
5. Dealing with two or more monetary systems can complicate international business operations.
6. The availability, depth, and reliability of economic and marketing information in different countries vary extensively, as do industrial structures, business practices, and the number and nature of regional organizations.

CONCLUSION

All firms have a strategy, even if it is informal, unstructured, and sporadic. All organizations are heading somewhere, but unfortunately some organizations do not know where they are going. The old saying "If you do not know where you are going, then any road will lead you there!" accents the need for organizations to use strategic-management concepts and techniques. The strategic-management process is becoming more widely used by small firms, large companies, non-profit institutions, governmental organizations, and multinational conglomerates alike. The process of empowering managers and employees has almost limitless benefits.

Organizations should take a proactive rather than a reactive approach in their industry, and they should strive to influence, anticipate, and initiate rather than just respond to events. The strategic-management process embodies this approach to decision making. It represents a logical, systematic, and objective approach for determining an enterprise's future direction. The stakes are generally too high for strategists to use intuition alone in choosing among alternative courses of action. Successful strategists take the time to think about their businesses, where they are with their businesses, and what they want to be as organizations—and then they implement programs and policies to get from where they are to where they want to be in a reasonable period of time.

It is a known and accepted fact that people and organizations that plan ahead are much more likely to become what they want to become than those that do not plan at all. A good strategist plans and controls his or her plans, while a bad strategist never plans and then tries to control people! This textbook is devoted to providing you with the tools necessary to be a good strategist.

Success in business increasingly depends upon offering products and services that are competitive on a world basis, not just on a local basis. If the price and quality of a firm's products and services are not competitive with those available elsewhere in the world, the firm may soon face extinction. Global markets have become a reality in all but the most remote areas of the world. Certainly throughout the United States, even in small towns, firms feel the pressure of world competitors. Nearly half of all the automobiles sold in the United States, for example, are made in Japan and Germany.

We invite you to visit the David page on the Prentice Hall Companion Web site at www.prenhall.com/david for this chapter's review quiz.

KEY TERMS AND CONCEPTS

Annual Objectives (p. 13)	External Opportunities (p. 12)	Intuition (p. 7)
Business Ethics (p. 21)	External Threats (p. 12)	ISO 9000 (p. 23)
Code of Business Ethics (p. 22)	Host Country (p. 28)	ISO 14000 (p. 23)
Competitive Advantage (p. 8)	Internal Strengths (p. 12)	ISO 14001 (p. 23)
Empowerment (p. 17)	Internal Weaknesses (p. 12)	Long-Range Planning
Environmental Scanning (p. 12)	International Firms (p. 28)	(p. 5)

ISSUES FOR REVIEW AND DISCUSSION

1. Explain why the strategic management class is often called a "capstone course."
2. What aspect of strategy formulation do you think requires the most time? Why?
3. Why is strategy implementation often considered the most difficult stage in the strategic-management process?
4. Why is it so important to integrate intuition and analysis in strategic management?
5. Explain the importance of a vision and a mission statement.
6. Discuss relationships among objectives, strategies, and policies.
7. Why do you think some chief executive officers fail to use a strategic-management approach to decision making?
8. Discuss the importance of feedback in the strategic-management model.
9. How can strategists best ensure that strategies will be effectively implemented?
10. Give an example of a recent political development that changed the overall strategy of an organization.
11. Who are the major competitors of your college or university? What are their strengths and weaknesses? What are their strategies? How sucessful are these institutions compared to your college?
12. If you owned a small business, would you develop a code of business conduct? If yes, what variables would you include? If no, how would you ensure that ethical business standards were being followed by your employees?
13. Would strategic-management concepts and techniques benefit foreign businesses as much as domestic firms? Justify your answer.
14. What do you believe are some potential pitfalls or risks in using a strategic-management approach to decision making?
15. In your opinion, what is the single major benefit of using a strategic-management approach to decision making? Justify your answer.
16. Compare business strategy and military strategy.
17. What do you feel is the relationship between personal ethics and business ethics? Are they—or should they be—the same?
18. Why is it important for all business majors to study strategic management since most students will never become a chief executive officer nor even a top manager in a large company?
19. Explain why consumption patterns are becoming similar worldwide. What are the strategic implications of this trend?
20. What are the advantages and disadvantages of beginning export operations in a foreign country?
21. Describe the content available on the SMCO Web site at www.strategyclub.com.
22. List four financial and four nonfinancial benefits of a firm engaging in strategic planning.
23. Why is it that a firm can normally sustain a competitive advantage for only a limited period of time?
24. Why it is not adequate to simply obtain competitive advantage?
25. How can a firm best achieve sustained competitive advantage?
26. Compare and contrast ISO 9000, 14000, and 14001.

NOTES

1. Kevin Maney, "The Net Effect: Evolution or Revolution?" *USA Today* (August 9, 1999): B1.
2. Peter Drucker, *Management: Tasks, Responsibilities, and Practices* (New York: Harper & Row, 1974): 611.
3. Alfred Sloan, Jr., *Adventures of the White Collar Man* (New York: Doubleday, 1941): 104.
4. Quoted in Eugene Raudsepp, "Can You Trust Your Hunches?" *Management Review* 49, no. 4 (April 1960): 7.
5. Stephen Harper, "Intuition: What Separates Executives from Managers," *Business Horizons* 31, no. 5 (September–October 1988): 16.
6. Ron Nelson, "How to Be a Manager," *Success* (July–August 1985): 69.
7. Bruce Henderson, *Henderson on Corporate Strategy* (Boston: Abt Books, 1979): 6.
8. Robert Waterman, Jr., *The Renewal Factor: How the Best Get and Keep the Competitive Edge* (New York: Bantam, 1987). See also *BusinessWeek* (September 14, 1987): 100. Also, see *Academy of Management Executive* 3, no. 2 (May 1989): 115.
9. Ethan Smith, "How Old Media Can Survive in a New World," *Wall Street Journal* (May 23, 2005): R4.
10. Lynn Lunsford and Daniel Michaels, "After Four Years in the Rear, Boeing Is Set to Jet Past Airbus," *Wall Street Journal* (June 10, 2005): A1.
11. Daniel Delmar, "The Rise of the CSO," *Organization Design* (March–April 2003): 8–10.
12. John Pearce II and Fred David, "The Bottom Line on Corporate Mission Statements," *Academy of Management Executive* 1, no. 2 (May 1987): 109.
13. Fred R. David, "How Companies Define Their Mission," *Long Range Planning* 22, no. 1 (February 1989): 91.
14. Jack Pearce and Richard Robinson, *Strategic Management,* 7th ed. (New York: McGraw-Hill, 2000): p. 8.
15. Ann Langley, "The Roles of Formal Strategic Planning," *Long Range Planning* 21, no. 3 (June 1988): 40.
16. Bernard Reimann, "Getting Value from Strategic Planning," *Planning Review* 16, no. 3 (May–June 1988): 42.
17. G. L. Schwenk and K. Schrader, "Effects of Formal Strategic Planning in Financial Performance in Small Firms: A Meta-Analysis," *Entrepreneurship and Practice* 3, no. 17 (1993): 53–64. Also, C. C. Miller and L. B. Cardinal, "Strategic Planning and Firm Performance: A Synthesis of More than Two Decades of Research," *Academy of Management Journal* 6, no. 27 (1994): 1649–1665; Michael Peel and John Bridge, "How Planning and Capital Budgeting Improve SME Performance," *Long Range Planning* 31, no. 6 (October 1998): 848–856; Julia Smith, "Strategies for Start-Ups," *Long Range Planning* 31, no. 6 (October 1998): 857–872.
18. Gordon Greenley, "Does Strategic Planning Improve Company Performance?" *Long Range Planning* 19, no. 2 (April 1986): 106.
19. Adapted from: www.mindtools.com/plreschn.html.
20. Adapted from the Web sites: www.des.calstate.edu/limitations.html and www.entarga.com/stratplan/purposes.html.
21. Dale McConkey, "Planning in a Changing Environment," *Business Horizons* (September–October 1988): 66.
22. R. T. Lenz, "Managing the Evolution of the Strategic Planning Process," *Business Horizons* 30, no. 1 (January–February 1987): 39.
23. Joann Greco, "Privacy—Whose Right Is It Anyhow?" *Journal of Business Strategy* (January–February 2001): 32.
24. Saul Gellerman, "Why 'Good' Managers Make Bad Ethical Choices," *Harvard Business Review* 64, no. 4 (July–August 1986): 88.
25. Drucker, 462, 463.
26. Gene Laczniak, Marvin Berkowitz, Russell Brooker, and James Hale, "The Ethics of Business: Improving or Deteriorating?" *Business Horizons* 38, no. 1 (January–February 1995): 43.
27. Frederick Gluck, "Taking the Mystique Out of Planning," *Across the Board* (July–August 1985): 59.

CURRENT READINGS

Adner, Ron, and Daniel A. Levinthal. "What Is *Not* a Real Option: Considering Boundaries for the Application of Real Options to Business Strategy." *The Academy of Management Review* 29, no. 1 (January 2004): 74.

Alsop, Ronald J. "Anything but Superficial: The Deep but Fragile Nature of Corporate Reputation." *Journal of Business Strategy* 25, no. 6 (2004): 21.

Amis, John, Trevor Slack, and C. R. Hinings. "The Pace, Sequence, and Linearity of Radical Change." *The Academy of Management Journal* 47, no. 1 (February 2004): 15.

Anand, V., B. E. Ashforth, and M. Joshi. "Business as Usual: The Acceptance and Perpetuation of Corruption in Organizations." *The Academy of Management Executive* 18, no. 2 (July 2005): 39.

Argenti, P. A., R. A. Howell, and K. A. Beck. "The Strategic Communication Imperative." *MIT Sloan Management Review* 46, no. 3 (Spring 2005): 83.

Bansal, P. "Evolving Sustainable: A Longitudinal Study of Corporate Sustainable Development." *Strategic Management Journal* 26, no. 3 (March 2005): 197.

Boyd, B. K., S. Gove, and M. A. Hitt. "Construct Measurement in Strategic Management Research: Illusion or Reality?" *Strategic Management Journal* 26, no. 3 (March 2005): 239.

Branzei, O., T. J. Ursacki-Bryant, I. Vertinsky, and W. Zhang. "The Formation of Green Strategies in Chinese Firms: Matching Corporate Environmental Responses and Individual Principles." *Strategic Management Journal* 25, no. 11 (November 2004): 1075.

Brightman, Baird K. "Why Managers Fail, and How Organizations Can Rewrite the Script." *Journal of Business Strategy* 25, no. 2 (2004): 47.

Buckingham, M. "What Great Managers Do." *Harvard Business Review* (March 2005): 70.

Collier, Nardine, Francis Fishwick, and Steven W. Floyd. "Managerial Involvement and Perceptions of Strategy Process." *Long Range Planning* 37, no. 1 (February 2004): 67.

Cummings, S., and D. Angwin. "The Future Shape of Strategy: Lemmings or Chimeras?" *The Academy of Management Executive* 18, no. 2 (July 2004): 21.

Dalton, Catherine M. "The Changing Identity of Corporate America: Opportunity, Duty, Leadership." *Business Horizons* 48, no. 1 (January–February 2005): 1.

Gibbons, P. T., and T. O' Conner. "Influences on Strategic Planning Process Among Irish SMEs." *Journal of Small Business Management* 43, no. 2 (April 2005): 170.

Gupta, M., L. Boyd, and L. Sussman. "To Better Maps: A TOC Primer for Strategic Planning." *Business Horizons* 47, no. 2 (March 2004): 15.

"The HBR List: Breakthrough Ideas for 2005." *Harvard Business Review* (February 2005): 17.

Guttman, Howard M., and Richard S. Hawkes. "New Rules for Strategic Engagement." *Journal of Business Strategy* 25, no. 1 (2004): 34.

Hatch, N. W., and J. H. Dyer. "Human Capital and Learning as a Source of Sustainable Competitive Advantage." *Strategic Management Journal* 25, no. 12 (December 2004): 1155.

Jensen, M., and E. J. Zajac. "Corporate Elites and Corporate Strategy: How Demographic Preferences and Structural Position Shape the Scope of the Firm." *Strategic Management Journal* 25, no. 6 (June 2004): 507.

Mathews, John A. "Strategy and the Crystal Cycle." *California Management Review* 47, no. 2 (Winter 2005): 6.

Miller, C. Chet, and R. Duane Ireland. "Intuition in Strategic Decision Making: Friend or Foe in the Fast-Paced 21st Century." *The Academy of Management Executive* 19, no. 1 (February 2005): 7.

Resnick, Jeffrey T. "Managing Corporate Reputation— Applying Rigorous Measures to a Key Asset." *Journal of Business Strategy* 25, no. 6 (2004): 30.

Rindova, Violina P., Manuel Becerra, and Ianna Contardo. "Enacting Competitive Wars: Competitive Activity, Language Games, and Market Consequences." *The Academy of Management Review* 29, no. 4 (October 2004): 670.

Sadler-Smith, and E., E. Shefy. "The Intuitive Executive: Understanding and Applying 'Gut Feel' in Decision-Making." *The Academy of Management Executive* 18, no. 4 (November 2004): 76.

Schweitzer, Maurice E., Lisa Ordóñez, and Bambi Douma. "Goal Setting as a Motivator of Unethical Behavior." *The Academy of Management Journal* 47, no. 3 (June 2004): 422.

Spicer, A., T. W. Dunfee, and W. J. Bailey. "Does National Context Matter in Ethical Decision Making? An Empirical Test of Integrative Social Contracts Theory." *The Academy of Management Journal* 47, no. 4 (August 2004): 610.

Stevens, J. M., H. K. Steensma, D. A. Harrison, and P. L. Cochran. "Symbolic or Substantive Document? The Influence of Ethics Codes on Financial Executives' Decisions." *Strategic Management Journal* 26, no. 2 (February 2005): 181.

Tallman, Stephen, Mark Jenkins, Nick Henry, and Steven Pinch. "Knowledge, Clusters, and Competitive Advantage." *The Academy of Management Review* 29, no. 2 (April 2004): 258.

Thomas, T., J. R. Schermerhorn, Jr., and J. W. Dienhart. "Strategic Leadership of Ethical Behavior in Business." *The Academy of Management Executive* 18, no. 2 (July 2004): 56.

Trevino, L. K., and M. E. Brown. "Managing to Be Ethical: Debunking Five Business Ethics Myths." *The Academy of Management Executive* 18, no. 2 (July 2004): 69.

GOOGLE INC. — 2005

Ticker Symbol: GOOG
   www.google.com
Rick Goossen,
   Trinity Western University

The year is 2010. A professor is addressing his upper-year class of business students. They are talking about the former richest man in the world—Bill Gates—who was also regarded as one of the smartest men ever. Gates's company, Microsoft, used to dominate the software industry. Could Microsoft fall prey to Google by 2010? *Fortune* magazine's May 2, 2005, cover story was titled "Search and Destroy: Bill Gates Is on a Mission to Build a Google Killer." Google presents possibly the biggest challenge ever to Microsoft's position atop the high-tech mountain.

Microsoft has been the 800-pound gorilla that others in the high-tech jungle rankled at their considerable risk, but Google is now attracting the top techies, including a hundred "Microsofties" who are now "Googlers." The hot spot for the world's top grads is Google, which is first with technological innovations, even when being outspent by Microsoft. But will Microsoft prevail? Will Google simply be another of the foes vanquished by Microsoft, such as Netscape, WordPerfect, and Lotus 1-2-3? History may not repeat itself. There is one significant difference. Google doesn't need Microsoft's operating system—a user needs only Internet access to get into the Google orbit.

As a high-tech prima donna, Google has restored investors' faith, after the dot.com meltdown of March 2000, that high-tech companies can develop a profitable, indeed lucrative, business model. Google is earning gobs of cash through a compelling advertising model for its clients (clients pay only for the number of times their ad is actually viewed). Google has been profitable since the last quarter of 2001—and resisted the urge to go public too soon in the dot.com mania that ended in March 2000.

The founders of Google, Sergey Brin and Larry Page, met as graduate students in their early twentys at Stanford. They found a garage to start their small business, and word of mouth generated attention for their high-quality search engine, originally named "BackRub." Google went public on NASDAQ in August 2004 at $85 and in less than a year surpassed $300 a share. In the minds of many analysts, Google still looks reasonably priced in view of the huge potential of the company to create more extensions and to operate in more countries.

From its origins in 1995 to ten years later, Brin and Page have created a company with a market capitalization of over $80 billion, with each of the founders retaining about a 12 percent interest. Google has surpassed the market value of Time Warner Inc., owner of the venerable *Time* magazine, to become the most valuable media company in the world.

HISTORY

Sergey Brin and Larry Page clicked in spring 1995 at a gathering of Stanford University computer science candidates. Between January 1996 and December 1997, they created "BackRub," the precursor to the Google search engine. The objective was to better organize a mushrooming amount of data on the Internet. They created a new (less expensive and more effective) server environment that utilized networked low-end PCs. (It is now rumored that Google has 100,000 of these PC's networked). The company's name was eventually changed from

"BackRub" to "Google" to signify the immense amount of information on the Internet. Google is a play on the word *googol* (which refers to the numeral 1 followed by 100 zeros).

Brin and Page incorporated Google on September 7, 1998. They put their studies on hold and raised $1 million from family, friends, and investors. Andy Bechtolsheim, a founder of Sun Microsystems, chipped in $100,000. They also contacted Yahoo! founder David Filo, who "agreed that their technology was solid, but encouraged Larry and Sergey to grow the service themselves by starting a search engine company. 'When it's fully developed and scalable,' he told them, 'let's talk again.'"[1]

The quality of Google search technology attracted an ever-growing band of users. Corporate users are believers in the technology. AOL/Netscape selected Google as its Web search service (and that boosted traffic to more than 3 million searches per day), as did Italian portal Virgillo, Virgin Net (the United Kingdom's leading entertainment guide), and NetEase (China's leading portal).

The quality of Google's technology has been matched by its financial performance. The company was profitable by the fourth quarter of 2001. Growth continued, and an initial public offering was made in August 2004, with 19.6 million shares offered to the public at $85 per share and $1.7 billion raised. The offering was conducted as a "Dutch auction" where the market demand set the price, rather than the traditional pricing that is set by a syndicate of underwriters. A total of 271.2 million total shares were outstanding, and thus the initial market cap was $23.1 billion. A Google timeline of events is provided in Exhibit 1.

Google has continued to expand from being a Web search company to offering an increasing array of services and, as noted previously, is a possible competitor to Microsoft as a software company. In 2005 Google incorporated "Google Payment Corp." Google is working on a PayPal-like payment system and already has been testing it with some e-commerce players.[2] PayPal is well-established and has 72 million users. Eric Schmidt, CEO, stated during an interview with the Associated Press that "We do not intend to offer a person-to-person, stored-value payments system."[3] In other words, Google's product is not meant to be a direct competitor of Ebay's PayPal. Schmidt says, "The payment services we are working on are a natural evolution of Google's existing online products and advertising programs which today connect millions of consumers and advertisers." The mere *rumors* that Google might enter this space sent eBay's share price downward, as Google has a track record of launching new products that are superior to existing platforms.

Google is also rumored to be working on a Web-only video search that would allow people to watch a short clip of a video on the Web before shuttling visitors to the host's sight. Rumors have also been circulating of a Web browser to compete with Internet Explorer and even of a stand-alone operating system. (Check out the Web sites named in this footnote.[4])

INTERNAL ISSUES

Services

Google has more than 10 billion Web pages, 1 billion images, and 1 billion Usenet messages in search indexes. Google.com is one of the five most popular Web sites on the Internet.[5] A large part of Google's appeal is that many of its services are free to the general public. Seemingly everyone uses Google's Web search services first. This massive audience drives Google's advertising and revenue-generating model. This is afforded by Google's massive advertising system, which enables advertisers very specific target marketing. Google's key services are listed in Exhibit 2.

EXHIBIT 1 The Google Timeline

YEAR	MONTH	EVENT
1995	Mar.–Dec.	Sergey Brin and Larry Page meet at a Stanford University spring gathering of Ph.D. computer science candidates.
1996–7	Jan. '96–Dec. '97	Brin and Page create "Backrub," the precursor to the Google search engine.
1998	Aug.–Dec.	September 7, 1998, Google is incorporated; $1 million is raised from friends, family, and angel investors; four employees; Google answers 10,000 searches per day.
1999	Feb.–June	$25 million in equity funding from Sequoia Capital and Kleiner Perkins Caufield and Byers; eight employees; Google answers 500,000 searches per day.
	Aug.–Dec.	39 employees; Google answers 3 million searches per day.
2000	May–June	Google becomes the largest search engine on the Web, with 1 billion URLs; 18 million searches per day. Yahoo! selects Google as its default search results provider to complement Yahoo!'s Web directory and navigational guide.
2001	Mar.–Apr.	Eric Schmidt, Chairman & CEO of Novell, joins Google as Chairman of the Board of Directors.
	July–Aug.	Eric Schmidt is appointed CEO; Page becomes President, Products, and Brin becomes President, Technology.
	Sept.	Google announces that it has achieved profitability.
2002	Jan.–Feb.	Google announces the availability of "Google Search Appliance" (see products section). Google launches "Adwords Select" (the cost per click pricing model that makes search advertising cost-effective for any size of business).
	Mar.–Apr.	Google offers "Google Compute."
	Nov.–Dec.	Web index now includes 4 billion Web documents.
2003	Jan.–Feb.	Google acquires Pyra Labs, creator of Web self-publishing tool "Blogger."
	Mar.–Apr.	Google surpasses 100,000 active advertisers in its Google AdWords program.
	Nov.–Dec.	The Google Deskbar, a free software download that enables users to search Google without using a Web browser, is introduced on Google Labs.
2004	Mar.–Apr.	Gmail, a free Web-based e-mail service, is launched.
	July	Google acquires Picasa, Inc., a digital photo management company that helps users organize, manage, and share their digital photos.
	Aug. 19	Initial public offering of "GOOG" on NASDAQ at $85 per share, raising $1.7 billion.
	Nov.–Dec.	Google search index is now 8 billion pages.
2005	Mar.–Apr.	"Google Maps" is launched in Google Local, which enables users in the United States and Canada to find location information, navigate through maps, and easily and quickly get directions.
	July	GOOG share price passes $300 and becomes the world's largest media company by market value of approximate $85 billion

Source: Adapted from www.google.ca/intl/en/corporate/timeline.html

VALUATION

Less than one year after Google's initial public offering at $85 on August 17, 2004, its share price broke the $300 level. Google's market capitalization is approximately $83 billion. One analyst, Renaissance Capital, gushed about Google's fundamentals: "Incredibly strong cash flow, huge profit margins, compelling growth prospects and highly scalable

EXHIBIT 2 Google's Key Services

Google Web search—Advanced Search functionality; spell checker; Web page translation (French, German, Italian, Portuguese, Spanish, English); stock quotes; street maps; calculator; definitions; phone book; search by number (enables people to search by entering FedEx, UPS, USPS tracking numbers, vehicle ID numbers, product codes, area codes, patent numbers, and FAA airplane registration numbers); travel information (airline and weather info); cached links (allows users to view Web pages no longer available); movie information; weather; news and product information (when relevant); and book search.

Google Image Search—Access to more then 1.1 billion images by size, format, domain. . . .

Google News—News from 10,000 different sources tailored for twenty-two different international audiences.

Google Toolbar—making search technology constantly and easily available, (free), features include:

> Pop-up blocker.
> Page rank indicator (Google's rating of the Web site for specific key words).
> Autofill completes Web forms with information from previous fill-outs.
> Highlight highlights search terms where they appear on the Web page.
> Word Find finds any word on the Web site.
> Auto Link turns street addresses into links to online maps.
> Word Translator translates English words into other languages.
> Spellchecker checks spelling as you type into a form.

Froogle—free service to search the Web for products you wish to buy. Advertisements are separated from the objective search results.

Google Groups—expands upon 1 billion Usenet messages posted from 1981 and on. It is basically online discussion groups.

Google Mobile—search pages designed entirely for wireless devices that give access to results from Google's entire index.

Google Local—find relevant businesses near a city, postal code, or specific address. Google takes listings from the Yellow Pages, combines them with search results from the Web, and then plots their locations on interactive maps.

Google Print—Google allows a number of publishers to host their content in an online index. It also contains content from the AdSense Program.

Google Desktop Search—full text search of all contents on a user's computer. Free for individuals. There is also a commercial version. The commercial version allows for comprehensive network searches.

Google Alerts—e-mail updates on changes to the Google results of a Web/news search based upon the user's query or topic.

Google Labs—playground for engineers: basically prototypes.

Blogger—one of the most popular Web blog sites in the world.

Google Code—shares code for some upcoming Google projects for assistance from external developers.

Google Deskbar—enables Web search from the taskbar of a computer without launching a Web connection.

Picasa—software to help find, edit, and share all pictures on a computer (integrated with Gmail, Blogger, and Froogle). Acquired in July of 2004 (an amazing program and it is free). Every time you open Picasa, it automatically locates all of your pictures, even ones you had forgotten to add, and sorts them into visual albums with folder names and dates you recognize. Even password protects private pictures.

Google Earth (was Keyhole until June 2005, a satellite and aerial image provider for a fee)—free for consumers. Google Earth Plus ($20) is an optional upgrade that adds GPS support, the ability to import spreadsheets, drawing tools, and better printing. Google Earth Pro ($400 + subscription) is for professional and commercial users. It is the ultimate research, presentation, and collaboration tool for location information.

Gmail—a limited availability Web mail service that offers users 2 gigs and climbing storage space, 10-megabyte attachments, conversation organization, and service for finding messages.

business model."[6] Google key valuation benchmarks, such as price-to-earnings (P/E Ratio), P/E-to-growth (P/E/G), and enterprise value-to-cash-flow (EV/EBITDA), are attractive relative to its peer group, which includes companies such as Yahoo! and eBay. One cautionary note is that analysts at Renaissance Capital "remain cautious of Google's non-traditional governance style and are not fans of the insider selling, but management continues to execute well and maintains a large equity stake."[7]

Standard & Poor's "Stock Report" in July 2, 2005, stated that a $300 level share price is justified but questioned how much immediate upside exists for investors. On the one hand, Google will continue to leverage its leading position as a Web search company and to introduce new features and offerings, gain market share, and display strong pricing power. On the other hand, Microsoft and Yahoo! present stiff competition, and S&P analysts are uncomfortable with the corporate governance practices of Google.

GOVERNANCE

One issue that does not sit well with institutional investors and analysts is Google's "dual class stock ownership system." In its August 2004 prospectus, Google states, "We anticipate that our founders, executive officers, directors (and their affiliates) and employees will together own approximately 84.8 percent of our Class B common stock, representing approximately 83.6 percent of the voting power of our outstanding capital stock." Class A shares, listed on the NASDAQ under the symbol GOOG, entitle holders to one vote per share. Approximately 80 percent of the company is controlled by insiders (comprised mostly of management; see "Management" on page 40). Class B shares, which can be converted into Class A for liquidity purposes, have ten votes per share. Less than two-thirds of the company's directors are independent from management.

Institutional Shareholder Service recently gave Google a lower corporate governance rating than any stock in the S&P 500. Brin and Page have stated that they consider Warren Buffett's capital structure and corporate governance as a model to follow. Their present success blunts this weakness, but this may have to be addressed if the company's financial performance falters.

CODE OF BUSINESS ETHICS AND MISSION

Google's code of business ethics and mission statement are provided in Exhibit 3 and Exhibit 4 respectively. The company has no vision statement.

EXHIBIT 3   Google's Code of Business Ethics

Ten things Google has found to be true:

1. Focus on the user and all else will follow.
2. It's best to do one thing really, really well.
3. Fast is better than slow.
4. Democracy on the Web works.
5. You don't need to be at your desk to need an answer.
6. You can make money without doing evil.
7. There's always more information out there.
8. The need for information crosses all borders.
9. You can be serious without a suit.
10. Great just isn't good enough.

Source: www.google.com/corporate/tenthings.html

EXHIBIT 4   Google's Mission Statement

Our mission is to organize the world's information and make it universally accessible and useful. We believe that the most effective, and ultimately the most profitable, way to accomplish our mission is to put the needs of our users first. We have found that offering a high-quality user experience leads to increased traffic and strong word-of-mouth promotion. Our dedication to putting users first is reflected in three key commitments we have made to our users:

- We will do our best to provide the most relevant and useful search results possible, independent of financial incentives. Our search results will be objective and we will not accept payment for inclusion or ranking in them.
- We will do our best to provide the most relevant and useful advertising. If any element on a result page is influenced by payment to us, we will make it clear to our users. Advertisements should not be an annoying interruption.
- We will never stop working to improve our user experience, our search technology and other important areas of information organization.

We believe that our user focus is the foundation of our success to date. We also believe that this focus is critical for the creation of long-term value. We do not intend to compromise our user focus for short-term economic gain.

Source: www.sec.gov/Archives/edgar/data/1288776/000119312504143377/d424b4.htm (prospectus)

MARKETING

Google spent 7.4 percent of its revenues on sales and marketing in 2004. The vast majority of the expense was due to the increase in labor and facilities required for customer service in the sales departments. Google spent less than 3 percent of its revenue on advertising and promotional expenses. Google contends that a highly trusted and recognizable brand begins with high-quality products and services. Google's user base has grown almost entirely by word of mouth.

Google's early marketing efforts were focused on growing the word-of-mouth momentum of its users and utilizing public relations to assist its swell. Google does various test marketing through its Google Labs, where users are able to try out ideas devised by Google employees. Other products, such as Gmail, are selectively released as beta versions. Gmail is e-mail centered on the concept that you should never have to delete any e-mail. Simply archive it for when you need it. All the while, Google will provide you with advertising relevant to the key words in your e-mails on the right side of your screen. Google overcame a number of privacy concerns and successfully launched Gmail Beta.

Gmail and its 1,000 megabytes of storage space were released by invitation only, and during the summer of 2004 it became very chic. Both Yahoo! and Microsoft were forced to increase the amount of storage space in their customers' e-mail accounts, albeit their increases were only about one-fourth of the two gigabytes that Google was offering by mid-2005.

Google began as a technology company and has evolved into a software, technology, Internet, advertising, and media company. Building upon its philosophy and mission, Google maintains that it can put customers first by providing the world's best search service free of charge. Google's customers need only to click on the content-specific ads listed nonobtrusively on the right hand side of each Web page. Every click funnels advertising dollars to Google and, hopefully, assists customers with solutions to their queries. According to TNS Media Intelligence, Microsoft spent

$44 million marketing various MSN services in the first four months of 2005, while Yahoo! spent $14 million and Google spent just $2 million.

Google generates 99 percent of its revenue through its AdWords (50 percent) and AdSense (49 percent) advertising products. Google uses the cash generated to fund further expansion of its advertising scope. Yet most of Google's development efforts appear to be non-advertising. Google is largely a software/technology company striving for greater innovation and customer usability. It just happens to create revenue by offering the services for free and charging advertisers the benefit of access to its more than 82 million unique users worldwide.

Google's revenue-generating efforts are split into four segments: AdWords, AdSense, Search Appliance, and Wireless Service, as revealed in Exhibit 5.

PRODUCTION

At Google, employee time is expected to be divided "70–20–10"—70 percent of employee time is focused on the job description or on work regarding Web search and the advertising network; 20 percent is focused on adjacent areas that have some sort of overlap (i.e., Gmail and Google Desktop Search); and 10 percent is saved for anything else that employees' creative juices conjure. Google gives all its engineers one day a week to develop their own pet projects and the "free" days accumulate if "work" gets in the way for a few weeks.

The value of 70–20–10 is that incremental resources have diminishing returns over time in almost every undertaking. Google sees 70–20–10 as a necessity for all employees to add to innovation. Google employees are given significant ownership responsibilities—for example, engineers are responsible for the code that they write, and if a bug occurs, they are responsible for fixing it. Microsoft, by contrast, would pass the bugged code on to a system operations team to deal with it. At Google, the team that created the software and knows it best is responsible for fixing it.

MANAGEMENT

Google's upper management structure is composed of nine officers, including the founders, Sergey Brin and Larry Page. The founders, along with CEO Eric Schmidt, form the core of the management team and also are members of the nine-person board of directors. Exhibit 6 provides a graphic representation of the company's management structure.

EXTERNAL ISSUES

Despite its successes, Google faces numerous external challenges. The company must maintain vigilance to prevent click fraud, which could undercut confidence in one of its key revenue generators. In addition, Google has to monitor its associations through the Web. For example, a Kraft Foods ad appeared on a Web page of a self-described "White Nationalist" group. Kraft subsequently halted its Google advertising. Google is heavily reliant on certain key strategic relationships. For example, 12 percent of total revenue is received from the AdSense program with AOL (and Time Warner is looking to divest AOL).

There is likely to be ongoing and increasing demand for Internet products and services and an increasing number of online users and usage in the United States and worldwide. Google, Yahoo!, and Microsoft are fighting over a cut of the currently

EXHIBIT 5   Google's Revenue Reporting Segments

1. **AdWords**—purchase advertisements by purchasing rights to key words and paying per click on your advertisement.

   - Labeled as sponsored links
   - Campaign management tools to put budget on most profitable key words
   - Key word targeting through synonym generation and useful phrases
   - Traffic estimator (estimates cost of purchasing rights to key words/phrases)
   - Budget delivery (can set daily budgets and control timing of delivery of ads)
   - Performance reports continuous, timely reporting of ad's effectiveness
   - Multiple payment options, credit cards, debit cards, for selected advertisers invoicing and credit terms and payment in forty-eight currencies
   - AdWords discounter allows the freedom to increase maximum Cost per Click (CPC) as you never pay more then 1 cent above the next highest bidder
   - Conversion tracking measures the various conversions of an advertiser's campaign to give a better understanding of its return on investment

   Recent advertisers include Sony, Cisco, Alamo Car Rental, Ameritrade, Amazon.com, Canon, Disney, General Motors, L. L. Bean, Nordstrom, Sears, Smith & Hawken, Sprint, Volvo, and Xerox.

   For larger corporations:

   - Creative maximization (AdWord specialists help advertisers pick the most effective key words and focus on click-through and conversion rates)
   - Vertical market specialists (specialists in specific markets offer guidance for campaigns)
   - Bulk posting (assisting business with launching campaigns with 100s or 1000s of key words)
   - Dedicated client service representatives
   - AdWords API (the code)—for large advertisers and third parties Google's free API service lets developers engineer programs that interact directly with the AdWords system for more complete integration

2. **AdSense**—enables Web sites who join the Google network to offer targeted ads to browsers utilizing AdWords advertisements. Web sites can join the network online for terms that can be cancelled at any time. Google also actively pursues Web sites with high volume levels to join the network for specific durations. There are two products under this offering: "AdSense for search" and "AdSense for content."

   AdSense for search

   - Companies who do not have their own specific site or web search can offer Google's search services and provide searchers with AdSense results along the right side of the screen.
   - Google shares revenue with host Web site on a per click basis.

   AdSense for content

   - Automated technology analyzes the meaning of Web content and serves relevant advertising in a fraction of a second.
   - Google shares revenue with host Web site on a per click basis.
   - For Web sites with more then 20 million hits per month, customized services are made available.

   Recent customers include USATODAY.com, ABC.com, Forbes.com and 60 percent of the comScore Media Metrix top 100 sites, as well as thousands of other specialty content sites.

   Content features include:

   - competitive ad filters
   - sensitive content filters
   - choice of default ads in the event that Google is unable to serve targeted ads for the page
   - image ads available to add more visual incentives for consumers

3. **Search Appliance**—a complete software and hardware solution to enable companies to implement Google's search performance on internal and external information.

(Continued)

EXHIBIT 5   Continued

Four models:

- Google Mini—$4,995 for small business to provide search on public Web and intranets
- G-1001—$32,000 for midsize companies
- G-5005—$230,000 for dedicated high-priority search services
- G-8008—$525,000 for centralized deployments supporting global business units

Recent customers include PBS, The World Bank, Procter & Gamble, Cisco Systems, Boeing, Stanford University, Nextel, and Kaiser Permanente.

4. **Wireless Service**—Google search delivered via PDAs, mobile phones, and other wireless devices.

Recent customers include Sprint, Cingular, Qwest, Nextel, Bell Mobility (Canada), Vizzavi, Sprint PCS, Nextel, Palm, Handspring, and Omnisky.

Source: Adapted from www.google.com

$8 billion global search advertising business, which is expected to be worth $22 billion in five years. Thus, the overall outlook for the sector is extremely positive. In terms of company performance, since the dot.com shakeout of March 2000, many companies have focused on developing a profitable business model, improving operating procedures, and focusing on cash-generating activities. Companies such as Google and its competitors look for strategic acquisition to speed innovation and build economies of scale. The Internet companies that develop a significant brand name can further separate themselves from the pack through reduced competition for customers, revenues, employees, and investment capital.

EXHIBIT 6   Google's Management Structure

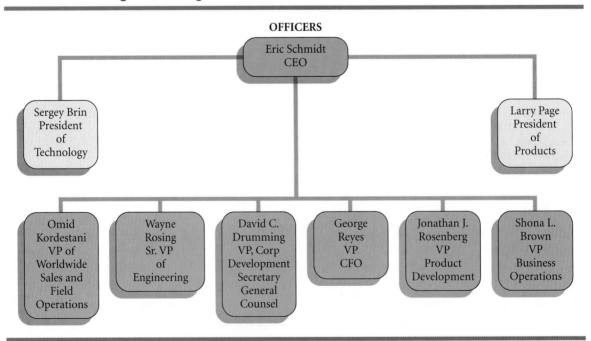

COMPETITION

How one defines the business of Google, then, determines the company's competition. Standard & Poor's classifies the sector as "Information Technology," the sub-industry as "Internet Software & Services," and the peer group as "Internet Content—General." If viewed traditionally as a Web search company, then Google's "peer group" (as classified by analysts) includes companies such as Ask Jeeves (ASKJ), CNET Networks (CNET), and Yahoo! (YHOO). But, as Google innovates, the competition changes. Thus, if Google launches a "Google Wallet," as rumored, it would be competing with eBay.com (EBAY) and its "PayPal." As noted earlier, if Google pursues grander aspirations, Yahoo! and Microsoft are its key competitors.

Microsoft

Microsoft (MSFT) develops computer software, mainly under the Windows name. Its businesses include operating systems for personal computers, servers, and personal information devices; productivity software (Microsoft Office); MSN web portal; the Xbox game console; video games; and enterprise software. Desktop software contributes around 60 percent of total revenue; server operating systems and applications represent more than 20 percent.

Microsoft is Google's number-one competitor, particularly as it relentlessly expands from its initial wedge of Web search. Microsoft has vanquished many competitors. In fact, Bill Gates may be more highly regarded as a cutthroat businessman than as a high-tech innovator. Microsoft's products are not typically regarded as the best, but Bill Gates outflanks the competition to make them the standard; thus Word replaced WordPerfect and Internet Explorer wiped out Netscape.

Microsoft is a formidable competitor that can throw $1 billion at a new venture without missing a step. Microsoft's revenue is more than ten times that of Google. Microsoft has more than $34 billion in cash and is generating $1 billion more each month. Microsoft is not perfect, however. It has experienced recent problems with release of its new operating system, Longhorn, which is one year behind schedule.

Exhibit 7 provides a comparison of Microsoft versus Google product names.

Yahoo!

Yahoo! is, of course, a well-known Web portal provider of search, shopping, information, and content to consumers and businesses around the world. Yahoo! derives about 87 percent of sales from advertising and search services and 13 percent from fee-based

EXHIBIT 7 Microsoft Versus Google Products

	GOOGLE	MICROSOFT
E-mail	Gmail	Hotmail
Blogs	Blogger	MSN Spaces
Photo Management	Picasa	Photo Story
Web Search	Google	MSN Search

Source: Adapted from *Fortune* (May 2, 2005) p. 76.

services/listings.[8] Yahoo! owns Inktomi and Overture, giving them software that enabled relevant search-based advertising with benefits and payoffs very similar to those of Google's AdSense and that included the search-engine technology that had run AltaVista. Yahoo! recently added photo tagging company Flickr and e-mail company Oddpost under its corporate banner.

Yahoo! is viewed as more corporate (professional and predictable) in the business world than Google, particularly in relation to some of Google's corporate governance practices (previously referred to). Yahoo! advertising sales teams focus on traditional partnerships and hand-holding with ad agencies. Yahoo! runs an internal telemarketing division to track down business with smaller ad agencies. Exhibit 8 provides some key statistics to compare Google, Microsoft, and Yahoo!.

Key Web search comparative data among Google and leading rival firms is given in Exhibit 9.

GLOBAL ISSUES

Google provides language interfaces in more then a hundred languages, results in thirty-five languages, and continuing translation efforts to enable Web sites to be viewed in one's native language. Currently Google translates between Chinese (sim-

EXHIBIT 8 2004 Key Competitors' Statistics

($ MILLIONS)	GOOGLE	MICROSOFT	YAHOO!
Revenue	3,189	36,835	3,574
R&D	225	7,779	369
Sales & Marketing	246	8,309	778
Net Income	399	8,168	840
Employees (worldwide)	3,021	57,000	7,600

Source: finance.yahoo.com

EXHIBIT 9 Web Search Comparison Data

SEARCH PROVIDER	SEARCHES (MILLIONS)	PERCENT OF EDIT LISTINGS	PERCENT OF PAID LISTINGS
Google	2,317	54	59
Yahoo!	908	21	34
MSN	592	14	0
Ask	232	5	0
Others	40	6	6
Total	**4,089**	**100**	**99**

Source: searchenginewatch.com/reports/article.php/2156451 US data. Numbers include searches done with Google technology through third parties, such as AOL.

plified), French, German, Italian, Korean, Japanese, Spanish, Portuguese, and English. Google has 3,021 employees worldwide. Google is the number-one search engine in the United Kingdom, Germany, France, Italy, the Netherlands, Spain, Switzerland, and Australia (Nielsen//NetRatings 6/04).

More than 50 percent of google.com traffic is from outside the United States. Google plans to be accessible in every language that creates issues related to international property right and copyright laws. Google was sued by Agence France Presse in the United States and France over the ability to give French Web searchers access to the press agency's headlines, pictures, and story leads on the French Google news Web site. An issue in China is freedom of speech and search. Google currently blocks search results to Web sites that China bars its citizens from viewing. Google's offices are globally illustrated in Exhibit 10.

EXHIBIT 10 Google's Offices Worldwide

Headquarters
Mountainview, California

U.S. Offices
New York
Atlanta
Boston
Chicago
Dallas
Denver
Detroit
Irvine
Santa Monica
Seattle

Global Offices
European Headquarters: Dublin, Ireland
Sydney, Australia
Toronto, Canada
Paris, France
Hamburg, Germany
Bangalore, India
Hyderabad, India
Milano, Italy
Shibuya-ku, Japan
Amsterdam, Netherlands
Madrid, Spain
Stockholm, Sweden
Zurich, Switzerland
London, England
Manchester, England

Source: www.google.com

EXHIBIT 11   Google's Income Statements

ALL AMOUNTS IN MILLIONS EXCEPT PER SHARE AMOUNTS	2004	2003	2002	2001
	12/31/2004	*12/31/2003*	*12/31/2002*	*12/31/2001*
Net Sales	3,189.2	1,465.9	439.5	86.4
Cost of Goods Sold	1,457.7	625.9	131.5	14.2
Gross Profit	**1,731.6**	**840.1**	**308.0**	**72.2**
SG & A Expenses	386.0	177.0	68.1	32.4
R & D Expenditures	225.6	91.2	31.7	16.5
Depreciation & Amortization	—	—	—	—
Income Before Depreciation & Amortization	1,119.9	571.8	208.1	23.3
Interest Expense	—	—	—	—
Investment Gains (Losses)	—	—	—	—
Total Operating Expenses	**611.6**	**268.3**	**99.9**	**48.9**
Non-Operating Income	−469.7	−225.2	−23.2	−13.3
Other Income	—	—	—	—
Income Before Tax	650.2	346.7	184.9	10.1
Provision for Income Taxes	251.1	241.0	85.3	3.1
Income After Tax	399.1	105.6	99.7	7.0
Minority Interest	—	—	—	—
Net Income Before Extra Items	399.1	105.6	99.7	7.0
Extra Items Discontinued Operations	—	—	—	—
Net Income	**399.1**	**105.6**	**99.7**	**7.0**

Source: finance.yahoo.com

CONCLUSION

Thus far, everything seems to be coming up roses for Google, as indicated in Exhibits 11 through 14. The founders are darlings of the media and the high-tech community. *Business Week* reported on July 18, 2005 (p. 45), that "Google's share of the U.S. searches hit 52 percent in June 2005, up from 45 percent a year ago, By contrast, Yahoo!'s and MSN's share slipped to 25 percent and 10 percent respectively."

Google has been able to maintain a stunning pace of innovation. To some extent, Google is viewed as a start-up that has had spectacular success. One challenge is to maintain its momentum. The company has done well in the public markets, but public perception and confidence can be fickle. Just as Google and its founders were unknown ten years ago, an upcoming generation is working on projects, technologies, and ideas that are born outside the incubators of well-heeled companies. Microsoft, with its billions, could not snuff out the emergence of a Google.

Google has had massive growth, and with that come the growing pains of managing that growth. Of course, this is a great problem to have, but all this growth is occurring under the microscope of the public markets, where any strategic miscalculation can erase billions from the market cap and cause a ripple throughout the organization.

EXHIBIT 12 Google's Balance Sheets

ALL AMOUNTS IN MILLIONS EXCEPT PER SHARE AMOUNTS	2004	2003	2002
	12/31/2004	*12/31/2003*	*12/31/2002*
Cash	426.9	149.0	57.8
Marketable Securities	1,705.4	185.7	88.6
Receivables	311.8	154.7	62.0
Inventories	—	—	—
Raw Materials	—	—	—
Work in Progress	—	—	—
Finished Goods	—	—	—
Notes Receivable	—	—	—
Other Current Assets	249.3	70.8	23.5
Total Current Assets	**2,693.5**	**560.2**	**231.8**
Property, Plant, and Equipment, Gross	378.9	188.3	53.9
Accumulated Depreciation	—	—	—
Property, Plant, and Equipment, Net	378.9	188.3	53.9
Intangibles	193.9	105.6	0.1
Investment Advances to Subsidiaries	—	—	—
Deferred Charges	47.1	17.4	1.1
Deposits and Other Assets	—	—	—
Other Non-Current Assets	—	—	—
Total Non-Current Assets	**619.9**	**311.2**	**55.1**
Total Assets	**3,313.4**	**871.5**	**286.9**
Notes Payable	—	—	—
Accounts Payable	32.7	46.2	9.4
Current Long-Term Debt	1.9	4.6	—
Current Portion Capital Leases	—	—	—
Accrued Expenses	269.3	148.6	25.3
Income Taxes	—	20.7	26.0
Other Current Liabilities	36.5	15.3	28.8
Total Current Liabilities	**340.4**	**235.5**	**89.5**
Mortgages	—	—	—
Deferred Charges to Income	—	18.5	2.5
Convertible Debt	—	—	—
Long-Term Debt	7.4	5.0	—
Non-Current Portion of Capital Leases	—	—	—
Minority Interest (Liabilities)	—	—	—
Other Long-Term Liabilities	36.5	9.8	21.0
Total Non-Current Liabilities	**43.9**	**33.4**	**23.4**
Total Liabilities	**384.3**	**268.8**	**112.9**
Preferred Stock	—	58.2	44.3
Common Stock, Net	0.3	0.2	0.1
Capital Surplus	2,582.4	725.2	83.4
Retained Earnings	590.5	191.4	85.7
Treasury Stock	—	—	—
Other Equity	−244.0	−372.3	−39.7
Total Shareholders' Equity	**2,929.1**	**602.6**	**174.0**
Total Liabilities Shareholders' Equity	**3,313.4**	**871.5**	**286.9**

Source: finance.yahoo.com

EXHIBIT 13 Google's Revenue by Geographic Area (year ended December 31)

(THOUSANDS)	2002		2003		2004	
United States	$341,570	78%	$1,038,409	71%	$2,119,043	66%
International	$97,938	22%	$427,525	29%	$1,070,180	34%
Total Revenue	**$439,508**		**$1,465,934**		**$3,119,223**	

Source: www.google.com

EXHIBIT 14 Google's Percent of Revenue by Segment (year ended December 31)

	2002	2003	2004
Google Web sites	70%	54%	50%
Google network	24	43	49%
Advertising	94%	97%	99%
Licensing & other	6%	3%	1%

Source: www.marketwatch.com

Apart from internal issues, Google competes in an industry that is constantly changing and in which innovation is a constant challenge. As the company has grown, it has attracted the attention of fierce competitors, notably Microsoft. Most companies would rather avoid the giant, rather than awaken its ire. Thus, the battle with Microsoft is highly significant. Microsoft has wiped out well-known brands in the past: Netscape was a high flyer, but today it is an historical footnote.

Ultimately, Google must keep delivering on its upside: ongoing innovation that is profitable. As the Google corporate Web site notes, "What's next from Google? Hard to say. We don't talk much about what lies ahead. . . . Our two chief competitive advantages are surprise, innovation and an almost fanatical devotion to our users." The founders of Google have done things in an unconventional style, from corporate governance to its "Dutch auction" IPO. But analysts and investors will view those idiosyncrasies as liabilities if the company can't deliver. Can Brin and Page maintain their run of success? The strategic moves of the main players will determine what our desktops will look like in the coming years.

CASE EXERCISE

Prepare a three-year strategic plan for Google's top management team. Google does not want Microsoft or Yahoo! to render them obsolete with their much larger bankrolls and experience in the high-tech business.

WEB SITES OF INTEREST

finance.yahoo.com
www.microsoft.com
www.yahoo.com
www.marketwatch.com
www.msn.money.com
www.edgar.com
www.wsj.com
news.google.com
www.googlefight.com
www.google-watch.org
googleguy.zorgloob.com

NOTES

1. www.google.com/corporate/history.html, para 6.
2. PiperJaffray. "Google Wallet May Be Launched by Q3." *Hot Comment* June 20, 2005.
3. www.marketwatch.com/tools/quotes/news article.asp?dist5&param5archive&siteid5mktw& guid=%7BD0F48E68%2DA223%2D4233%2D A83B%2D4F01A291B31C%7D
4. www.kottke.org/04/08/the-google-browser, blog.topix.net/archives/000016.html
5. www.google.com/corporate/facts.html
6. Renaissance Capital. Google (GOOG) Quarterly Update, May 10, 2005. www.IPOHome.com., p. 2.
7. Renaissance, 2.
8. Renaissance, 3.

experiential exercises

Experiential Exercise 1A	

Experiential Exercise 1A

Google (GOOG)

PURPOSE

The purpose of this exercise is to give you experience identifying an organization's opportunities, threats, strengths, and weaknesses. This information is vital to generating and selecting among alternative strategies.

INSTRUCTIONS

Step 1 Identify what you consider to be GOOG's major opportunities, threats, strengths, and weaknesses. On a separate sheet of paper, list these key factors under separate headings. Describe each factor in specific terms.

Step 2 Through class discussion, compare your lists of external and internal factors to those developed by other students. From the discussion, add to your lists of factors. Keep this information for use in later exercises.

Experiential Exercise 1B

Developing a Code of Business Ethics for Google (GOOG)

PURPOSE

This exercise can give you practice in developing a code of business ethics. Research was conducted to examine codes of business ethics from large manufacturing and service firms in the United States. The twenty-eight variables that follow were found to be included in a sample of more than eighty codes of business ethics. The variables are presented in order of how frequently they occurred. Thus, the first variable, "Conduct business in compliance with all laws," was most often included in the sample documents; "Firearms at work are prohibited" was least often included.

1. Conduct business in compliance with all laws.
2. Payments for unlawful purposes are prohibited.
3. Avoid outside activities that impair duties.
4. Comply with all antitrust and trade regulations.
5. Comply with accounting rules and controls.
6. Bribes are prohibited.
7. Maintain confidentiality of records.
8. Participate in community and political activities.
9. Provide products and services of the highest quality.
10. Exhibit standards of personal integrity and conduct.
11. Do not propagate false or misleading information.
12. Perform assigned duties to the best of your ability.
13. Conserve resources and protect the environment.
14. Comply with safety, health, and security regulations.
15. Racial, ethnic, religious, and sexual harassment at work is prohibited.
16. Report unethical and illegal activities to your manager.
17. Convey true claims in product advertisements.
18. Make decisions without regard for personal gain.
19. Do not use company property for personal benefit.
20. Demonstrate courtesy, respect, honesty, and fairness.
21. Illegal drugs and alcohol at work are prohibited.

22. Manage personal finances well.
23. Employees are personally accountable for company funds.
24. Exhibit good attendance and punctuality.
25. Follow directives of supervisors.
26. Do not use abusive language.
27. Dress in businesslike attire.
28. Firearms at work are prohibited.[1]

INSTRUCTIONS

Step 1 On a separate sheet of paper, write a code of business ethics for GOOG. Include as many variables listed above as you believe appropriate to GOOG's business. Limit your document to a hundred words or less.

Step 2 Read your code of ethics to the class. Comment on why you did or did not include certain variables.

Step 3 Explain why having a code of ethics is not sufficient for ensuring ethical behavior in an organization. What else does it take?

Notes
[1]Donald Robin, Michael Giallourakis, Fred R. David, and Thomas E. Moritz, "A Different Look at Codes of Ethics," *Business Horizons* 32, no. 1 (January–February 1989): 66–73.

Experiential Exercise 1C
The Ethics of Spying on Competitors

PURPOSE

This exercise gives you an opportunity to discuss in class ethical and legal issues related to methods being used by many companies to spy on competing firms. Gathering and using information about competitors is an area of strategic management that Japanese firms do more proficiently than American firms.

INSTRUCTIONS

On a separate sheet of paper, number from 1 to 18. For the eighteen spying activities listed as follows, indicate whether or not you believe the activity is ethical or unethical and legal or illegal. Place either an *E* for ethical or *U* for unethical, and either an *L* for legal or an *I* for illegal for each activity. Compare your answers to those of your classmates and discuss any differences.

1. Buying competitors' garbage.
2. Dissecting competitors' products.
3. Taking competitors' plant tours anonymously.
4. Counting tractor-trailer trucks leaving competitors' loading bays.
5. Studying aerial photographs of competitors' facilities.
6. Analyzing competitors' labor contracts.
7. Analyzing competitors' help-wanted ads.
8. Quizzing customers and buyers about the sales of competitors' products.
9. Infiltrating customers' and competitors' business operations.
10. Quizzing suppliers about competitors' level of manufacturing.

11. Using customers to buy out phony bids.
12. Encouraging key customers to reveal competitive information.
13. Quizzing competitors' former employees.
14. Interviewing consultants who may have worked with competitors.
15. Hiring key managers away from competitors.
16. Conducting phony job interviews to get competitors' employees to reveal information.
17. Sending engineers to trade meetings to quiz competitors' technical employees.
18. Quizzing potential employees who worked for or with competitors.

Experiential Exercise 1D

Strategic Planning for My University

PURPOSE

External and internal factors are the underlying bases of strategies formulated and implemented by organizations. Your college or university faces numerous external opportunities/threats and has many internal strengths/weaknesses. The purpose of this exercise is to illustrate the process of identifying critical external and internal factors.

External influences include trends in the following areas: economic, social, cultural, demographic, environmental, technological, political, legal, governmental, and competitive. External factors could include declining numbers of high school graduates; population shifts; community relations; increased competitiveness among colleges and universities; rising numbers of adults returning to college; decreased support from local, state, and federal agencies; increasing numbers of foreign students attending U.S. colleges; and a rising number of Internet courses.

Internal factors of a college or university include faculty, students, staff, alumni, athletic programs, physical plant, grounds and maintenance, student housing, administration, fund-raising, academic programs, food services, parking, placement, clubs, fraternities, sororities, and public relations.

INSTRUCTIONS

Step 1 On a separate sheet of paper, make four headings: External Opportunities, External Threats, Internal Strengths, and Internal Weaknesses.

Step 2 As related to your college or university, list five factors under each of the four headings.

Step 3 Discuss the factors as a class. Write the factors on the board.

Step 4 What new things did you learn about your university from the class discussion? How could this type of discussion benefit an organization?

Experiential Exercise 1E

Strategic Planning at a Local Company

PURPOSE

This activity is aimed at giving you practical knowledge about how organizations in your city or town are doing strategic planning. This exercise also will give you experience interacting on a professional basis with local business leaders.

INSTRUCTIONS

Step 1 Use the telephone to contact business owners or top managers. Find an organization that does strategic planning. Make an appointment to visit with the strategist (president, chief executive officer, or owner) of that business.

Step 2 Seek answers to the following questions during the interview:

a. How does your firm formally conduct strategic planning? Who is involved in the process?

b. Does your firm have a written mission statement? How was the statement developed? When was the statement last changed?

c. What are the benefits of engaging in strategic planning?

d. What are the major costs or problems in doing strategic planning in your business?

e. Do you anticipate making any changes in the strategic planning process at your company? If yes, please explain.

Step 3 Report your findings to the class.

Experiential Exercise 1F
Does My University Recruit in Foreign Countries?

PURPOSE

A competitive climate is emerging among colleges and universities around the world. Colleges and universities in Europe and Japan are increasingly recruiting U.S. students to offset declining enrollments. Foreign students already make up more than one-third of the student body at many U.S. universities. The purpose of this exercise is to identify particular colleges and universities in foreign countries that represent a competitive threat to U.S. institutions of higher learning.

INSTRUCTIONS

Step 1 Select a foreign country. Conduct research to determine the number and nature of colleges and universities in that country. What are the major educational institutions in that country? What programs are those institutions recognized for offering? What percentage of undergraduate and graduate students attending those institutions are U.S. citizens? Do these institutions actively recruit U.S. students?

Step 2 Prepare a report for the class that summarizes your research findings. Present your report to the class.

Experiential Exercise 1G
Getting Familiar with SMCO

PURPOSE

This exercise is designed to get you familiar with the Strategic Management Club Online (SMCO), which offers many benefits for the strategy student. The SMCO site also offers templates for doing case analyses in this course.

INSTRUCTIONS

Step 1 Go to the www.strategyclub.com Web site. Review the various sections of this site.

Step 2 Select a section of the SMCO site that you feel will be most useful to you in this class. Write a one-page summary of that section and describe why you feel it will benefit you most.

chapter objectives

After studying this chapter, you should be able to do the following:

1. Describe the nature and role of vision and mission statements in strategic management.

2. Discuss why the process of developing a mission statement is as important as the resulting document.

3. Identify the components of mission statements.

4. Discuss how clear vision and mission statements can benefit other strategic-management activities.

5. Evaluate mission statements of different organizations.

6. Write good vision and mission statements.

experiential exercises

"notable quotes"

A business is not defined by its name, statutes, or articles of incorporation. It is defined by the business mission. Only a clear definition of the mission and purpose of the organization makes possible clear and realistic business objectives.
Peter Drucker

A corporate vision can focus, direct, motivate, unify, and even excite a business into superior performance. The job of a strategist is to identify and project a clear vision.
John Keane

Where there is no vision, the people perish.
Proverbs 29:18

The last thing IBM needs right now is a vision. (July 1993)
What IBM needs most right now is a vision. (March 1996)
Louis V. Gerstner Jr., CEO, IBM Corporation

The best laid schemes of mice and men often go awry.
Robert Burns (paraphrased)

A strategist's job is to see the company not as it is . . . but as it can become.
John W. Teets, Chairman of Greyhound, Inc.

That business mission is so rarely given adequate thought is perhaps the most important single cause of business frustration.
Peter Drucker

The very essence of leadership is that you have to have vision. You can't blow an uncertain trumpet.
Theodore Hesburgh

This chapter focuses on the concepts and tools needed to evaluate and write business vision and mission statements. A practical framework for developing mission statements is provided. Actual mission statements from large and small organizations and for-profit and nonprofit enterprises are presented and critically examined. The process of creating a vision and mission statement is discussed.

We can perhaps best understand vision and mission by focusing on a business when it is first started. In the beginning, a new business is simply a collection of ideas. Starting a new business rests on a set of beliefs that the new organization can offer some product or service to some customers, in some geographic area, using some type of technology, at a profitable price. A new business owner typically believes that the management philosophy of the new enterprise will result in a favorable public image and that this concept of the business can be communicated to, and will be adopted by, important constituencies. When the set of beliefs about a business at its inception is put into writing, the resulting document mirrors the same basic ideas that underlie the vision and mission statements. As a business grows, owners or managers find it necessary to revise the founding set of beliefs, but those original ideas usually are reflected in the revised statements of vision and mission.

Vision and mission statements often can be found in the front of annual reports. They often are displayed throughout a firm's premises and are distributed with company information sent to constituencies. The statements are part of numerous internal reports, such as loan requests, supplier agreements, labor relations contracts, business plans, and customer service agreements. In a recent study, researchers concluded that 90 percent of all companies have used a mission statement sometime in the previous five years.[1]

What Do We Want to Become?

It is especially important for managers and executives in any organization to agree upon the basic vision that the firm strives to achieve in the long term. A vision statement should answer the basic question, "What do we want to become?" A clear vision provides the foundation for developing a comprehensive mission statement. Many organizations have both a vision and mission statement, but the vision statement should be established first and foremost. The vision statement should be short, preferably one sentence, and as many managers as possible should have input into developing the statement.

Several example vision statements are provided as follows and in Table 2-1.

VISIT THE NET

Gives an introduction to the vision concept.
(www.csuchico.edu/mgmt/strategy/module1/sld007.htm)

The Vision of the <u>National Pawnbrokers Association</u> is to have complete and vibrant membership that enjoys a positive public and political image and is the focal organization of all pawn associations.—National Pawnbrokers Association npa.ploygon.net

Our Vision as an independent community financial institution is to achieve superior long-term shareholder value, exercise exemplary corporate citizenship, and create an environment which promotes and rewards employee development and the consistent delivery of quality service to our customers.—<u>First Reliance Bank</u> of Florence, South Carolina

At <u>CIGNA</u>, we intend to be the best at helping our customers enhance and extend their lives and protect their financial security. Satisfying customers is the key to meeting employee needs and shareholder expectations, and will enable CIGNA to build on our reputation as a financially strong and highly respected company. www.cigna.com

TABLE 2-1 Vision and Mission Statement Examples

THE BELLEVUE HOSPITAL

Vision Statement

The Bellevue Hospital is the LEADER in providing resources necessary to realize the community's highest level of HEALTH throughout life.

Mission Statement

The Bellevue Hospital, with *respect, compassion, integrity,* and *courage,* honors the individuality and confidentiality of our patients, employees, and community, and is progressive in anticipating and providing future health care services.

U.S. POULTRY & EGG ASSOCIATION

Vision Statement

A national organization which represents its members in all aspects of poultry and eggs on both a national and an international level.

Mission Statement

1. We will partner with our affiliated state organizations to attack common problems.
2. We are committed to the advancement of all areas of research and education in poultry technology.
3. The International Poultry Exposition must continue to grow and be beneficial to both exhibitors and attendees.
4. We must always be responsive and effective to the changing needs of our industry.
5. Our imperatives must be such that we do not duplicate the efforts of our sister organizations.
6. We will strive to constantly improve the quality and safety of poultry products.

We will continue to increase the availability of poultry products.

JOHN DEERE, INC.

Vision Statement

John Deere is committed to providing Genuine Value to the company's stakeholders, including our customers, dealers, shareholders, employees, and communities. In support of that commitment, Deere aspires to:

- Grow and pursue leadership positions in each of our businesses.
- Extend our preeminent leadership position in the agricultural equipment market worldwide.
- Create new opportunities to leverage the John Deere brand globally.

Mission Statement

John Deere has grown and prospered through a long-standing partnership with the world's most productive farmers. Today, John Deere is a global company with several equipment operations and complementary service businesses. These businesses are closely interrelated, providing the company with significant growth opportunities and other synergistic benefits.

MANLEY BAPTIST CHURCH

The Vision of Manley Baptist Church is to be the people of God, on mission with God, motivated by a love for God, and a love for others.

The Mission of Manley Baptist Church is to help people in the Lakeway area become fully developed followers of Jesus Christ.

U.S. GEOLOGICAL SURVEY (USGS)

The Vision of USGS is to be a world leader in the natural sciences through our scientific excellence and responsiveness to society's needs.

The mission of USGS is to serve the Nation by providing reliable scientific information to

- describe and understand the Earth
- minimize loss of life and property from natural disasters
- manage water, biological, energy, and mineral resources; and enhance and protect our quality of life

(Continued)

TABLE 2-1 Continued

MASSACHUSETTS DIVISION OF BANKS

Vision Statement

To protect the public interest, ensure competition, accessibility and fairness within the relevant financial services industries, respond innovatively to a rapidly changing environment, and foster a positive impact on the Commonwealth's economy.

Mission Statement

To maintain a safe and sound competitive banking and financial services environment throughout the Commonwealth and ensure compliance with community reinvestment and consumer protection laws by chartering, licensing, and supervising state regulated financial institutions in a professional and innovative manner.

OHIO DIVISION OF HAZARDOUS WASTE MANAGEMENT

Vision Statement

Ohio's Division of Hazardous Waste Management is recognized as a leader among state hazardous waste management programs through our expertise, effectiveness, application of sound science, and delivery of quality service to our stakeholders.

Mission Statement

The Division of Hazardous Waste Management protects and improves the environment and therefore the health of Ohio's citizens by promoting pollution prevention and the proper management and cleanup of hazardous waste. We provide quality service to our stakeholders by assisting them in understanding and complying with the hazardous waste management regulations, and by implementing our program effectively.

ATLANTA WEB PRINTERS, INC.

Vision Statement

To be the first choice in the printed communications business. The first choice is the best choice, and *being the best* is what Atlanta Web *pledges* to work hard at being—*every day!*

Mission Statement

- to make our clients feel welcome, appreciated, and worthy of our best efforts in everything we do . . . each and every day
- to be recognized as an exceptional leader in our industry and community
- to conduct all our relationships with an emphasis on long-term mutual success and satisfaction, rather than short-term gain
- to earn the trust and respect of all we work with as being a Company of honesty, integrity, and responsibility
- to provide an environment of positive attitude and action to accomplish our vision, by increasing positive feedback and recognition at all levels of the Company
- to train and motivate our employees and to develop cooperation and communication at all levels
- to use our resources, knowledge, and experience to create win/win relationships for our clients, employees, suppliers, and shareholders in terms of growing compensation, service, and value

CALIFORNIA ENERGY COMMISSION

Vision Statement

It is the vision of the California Energy Commission for Californians to have energy choices that are affordable, reliable, diverse, safe, and environmentally acceptable.

Mission Statement

It is the California Energy Commission's mission to assess, advocate, and act through public/private partnerships to improve energy systems that promote a strong economy and a healthy environment.

What Is Our Business?

Current thought on mission statements is based largely on guidelines set forth in the mid-1970s by Peter Drucker, who is often called "the father of modern management" for his pioneering studies at General Motors Corporation and for his 22 books and hundreds of articles. *Harvard Business Review* has called Drucker "the preeminent management thinker of our time."

Drucker says that asking the question "What is our business?" is synonymous with asking the question "What is our mission?" An enduring statement of purpose that distinguishes one organization from other similar enterprises, the *mission statement* is a declaration of an organization's "reason for being." It answers the pivotal question "What is our business?" A clear mission statement is essential for effectively establishing objectives and formulating strategies.

Sometimes called a *creed statement,* a statement of purpose, a statement of philosophy, a statement of beliefs, a statement of business principles, or a statement "defining our business," a mission statement reveals what an organization wants to be and whom it wants to serve. All organizations have a reason for being, even if strategists have not consciously transformed this reason into writing. As illustrated in Figure 2-1, carefully prepared statements of vision and mission are

VISIT THE NET

Gives an introduction to the mission concept. (www.csuchico.edu/mgmt/ strategy/module1/sld008. htm)

Who we want to be whom we want to serve

FIGURE 2-1

A Comprehensive Strategic-Management Model

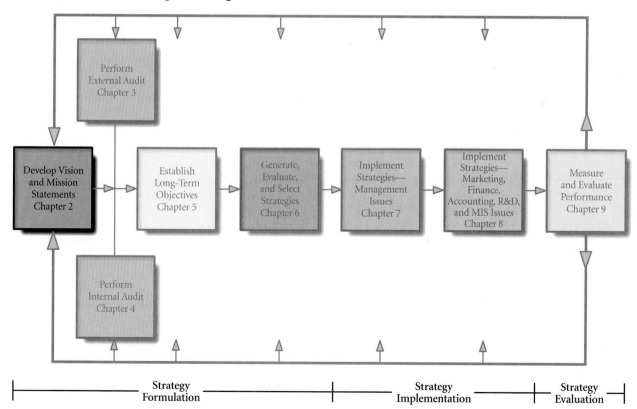

Source: Fred R. David, "How Companies Define Their Mission," *Long Range Planning* 22, no. 3 (June 1988): 40.

widely recognized by both practitioners and academicians as the first step in strategic management.

> A business mission is the foundation for priorities, strategies, plans, and work assignments. It is the starting point for the design of managerial jobs and, above all, for the design of managerial structures. Nothing may seem simpler or more obvious than to know what a company's business is. A steel mill makes steel, a railroad runs trains to carry freight and passengers, an insurance company underwrites fire risks, and a bank lends money. Actually, "What is our business?" is almost always a difficult question and the right answer is usually anything but obvious. The answer to this question is the first responsibility of strategists. Only strategists can make sure that this question receives the attention it deserves and that the answer makes sense and enables the business to plot its course and set its objectives.[2]

Some strategists spend almost every moment of every day on administrative and tactical concerns, and strategists who rush quickly to establish objectives and implement strategies often overlook the development of a vision and mission statement. This problem is widespread even among large organizations. Many corporations in America have not yet developed a formal vision or mission statement.[3] An increasing number of organizations are developing these statements.

Some companies develop mission statements simply because they feel it is fashionable, rather than out of any real commitment. However, as will be described in this chapter, firms that develop and systematically revisit their vision and mission statements, treat them as living documents, and consider them to be an integral part of the firm's culture realize great benefits. Johnson & Johnson (J&J) is an example firm. J&J managers meet regularly with employees to review, reword, and reaffirm the firm's vision and mission. The entire J&J workforce recognizes the value that top management places on this exercise, and these employees respond accordingly.

Vision Versus Mission

Many organizations develop both a mission statement and a vision statement. Whereas the mission statement answers the question "What is our business," the *vision statement* answers the question "What do we want to become?" Many organizations have both a mission and vision statement. Several examples are given in Table 2-1.

It can be argued that profit, not mission or vision, is the primary corporate motivator. But profit alone is not enough to motivate people.[4] Profit is perceived negatively by some employees in companies. Employees may see profit as something that they earn and management then uses and even gives away to shareholders. Although this perception is undesired and disturbing to management, it clearly indicates that both profit and vision are needed to effectively motivate a workforce.

When employees and managers together shape or fashion the vision and mission statements for a firm, the resultant documents can reflect the personal visions that managers and employees have in their hearts and minds about their own futures. Shared vision creates a commonality of interests that can lift workers out of the monotony of daily work and put them into a new world of opportunity and challenge.

VISIT THE NET

Gives questions that help form an effective vision and mission statement. (www.csuchico.edu/mgmt/strategy/module1/sld009.htm)

The Process of Developing a Mission Statement

As indicated in the strategic-management model, a clear mission statement is needed before alternative strategies can be formulated and implemented. It is important to involve as many managers as possible in the process of developing a mission statement, because through involvement, people become committed to an organization.

A widely used approach to developing a mission statement is first to select several articles about mission statements and ask all managers to read these as background information. Then ask managers themselves to prepare a mission statement for the organization. A facilitator, or committee of top managers, should then merge these statements into a single document and distribute this draft mission statement to all managers. A request for modifications, additions, and deletions is needed next, along with a meeting to revise the document. To the extent that all managers have input into and support the final mission statement document, organizations can more easily obtain managers' support for other strategy formulation, implementation, and evaluation activities. Thus, the process of developing a mission statement represents a great opportunity for strategists to obtain needed support from all managers in the firm.

During the process of developing a mission statement, some organizations use discussion groups of managers to develop and modify the mission statement. Some organizations hire an outside consultant or facilitator to manage the process and help draft the language. Sometimes an outside person with expertise in developing mission statements, who has unbiased views, can manage the process more effectively than an internal group or committee of managers. Decisions on how best to communicate the mission to all managers, employees, and external constituencies of an organization are needed when the document is in final form. Some organizations even develop a videotape to explain the mission statement and how it was developed.

An article by Campbell and Yeung emphasizes that the process of developing a mission statement should create an "emotional bond" and "sense of mission" between the organization and its employees.[5] Commitment to a company's strategy and intellectual agreement on the strategies to be pursued do not necessarily translate into an emotional bond; hence, strategies that have been formulated may not be implemented. These researchers stress that an emotional bond comes when an individual personally identifies with the underlying values and behavior of a firm, thus turning intellectual agreement and commitment to strategy into a sense of mission. Campbell and Yeung also differentiate between the terms *vision* and *mission,* saying that vision is "a possible and desirable future state of an organization" that includes specific goals, whereas mission is more associated with behavior and the present.

Importance of Vision and Mission Statements

The importance of vision and mission statements to effective strategic management is well documented in the literature, although research results are mixed. Rarick and Vitton found that firms with a formalized mission statement have twice the average return on shareholders' equity than those firms without a formalized mission statement have; Bart and Baetz found a positive relationship between mission statements and organizational performance; *BusinessWeek* reports that firms using mission statements have a 30 percent higher return on certain financial measures than those without such statements; however, some studies have found that having a mission statement does not directly contribute positively to financial performance.[6] The extent of manager and employee involvement in developing vision and mission statements can make a difference in business success. This chapter provides guidelines for developing these important documents. In actual practice, wide variations exist in the nature, composition, and use of both vision and mission statements. King and Cleland recommend that organizations carefully develop a written mission statement for the following reasons:

1. To ensure unanimity of purpose within the organization
2. To provide a basis, or standard, for allocating organizational resources
3. To establish a general tone or organizational climate
4. To serve as a focal point for individuals to identify with the organization's purpose and direction, and to deter those who cannot from participating further in the organization's activities
5. To facilitate the translation of objectives into a work structure involving the assignment of tasks to responsible elements within the organization
6. To specify organizational purposes and then to translate these purposes into objectives in such a way that cost, time, and performance parameters can be assessed and controlled.[7]

Reuben Mark, former CEO of Colgate, maintains that a clear mission increasingly must make sense internationally. Mark's thoughts on vision are as follows:

> When it comes to rallying everyone to the corporate banner, it's essential to push one vision globally rather than trying to drive home different messages in different cultures. The trick is to keep the vision simple but elevated: "We make the world's fastest computers" or "Telephone service for everyone." You're never going to get anyone to charge the machine guns only for financial objectives. It's got to be something that makes people feel better, feel a part of something.[8]

A Resolution of Divergent Views

Developing a comprehensive mission statement is important because divergent views among managers can be revealed and resolved through the process. The question "What is our business?" can create controversy. Raising the question often reveals differences among strategists in the organization. Individuals who have worked together for a long time and who think they know each other suddenly may realize that they are in fundamental disagreement. For example, in a college or university, divergent views regarding the relative importance of teaching, research, and service often are expressed during the mission statement development process. Negotiation, compromise, and eventual agreement on important issues are needed before people can focus on more specific strategy formulation activities.

> "What is our mission?" is a genuine decision; and a genuine decision must be based on divergent views to have a chance to be a right and effective decision. Developing a business mission is always a choice between alternatives, each of which rests on different assumptions regarding the reality of the business and its environment. It is always a high-risk decision. A change in mission always leads to changes in objectives, strategies,

organization, and behavior. The mission decision is far too important to be made by acclamation. Developing a business mission is a big step toward management effectiveness. Hidden or half-understood disagreements on the definition of a business mission underlie many of the personality problems, communication problems, and irritations that tend to divide a top-management group. Establishing a mission should never be made on plausibility alone, should never be made fast, and should never be made painlessly.[9]

Considerable disagreement among an organization's strategists over vision and mission statements can cause trouble if not resolved. For example, unresolved disagreement over the business mission was one of the reasons for W. T. Grant's bankruptcy and eventual liquidation. As one executive reported:

> There was a lot of dissension within the company whether we should go the Kmart route or go after the Montgomery Ward and JCPenney position. Ed Staley and Lou Lustenberger (two top executives) were at loggerheads over the issue, with the upshot being we took a position between the two and that consequently stood for nothing.[10]

Too often, strategists develop vision and business mission statements only when the organization is in trouble. Of course, it is needed then. Developing and communicating a clear mission during troubled times indeed may have spectacular results and even may reverse decline. However, to wait until an organization is in trouble to develop a vision and mission statement is a gamble that characterizes irresponsible management. According to Drucker, the most important time to ask seriously, "What do we want to become?" and "What is our business?" is when a company has been successful:

Don't wait until a crisis

> Success always obsoletes the very behavior that achieved it, always creates new realities, and always creates new and different problems. Only the fairy tale story ends, "They lived happily ever after." It is never popular to argue with success or to rock the boat. The ancient Greeks knew that the penalty of success can be severe. The management that does not ask "What is our mission?" when the company is successful is, in effect, smug, lazy, and arrogant. It will not be long before success will turn into failure. Sooner or later, even the most successful answer to the question "What is our business?" becomes obsolete.[11]

In multidivisional organizations, strategists should ensure that divisional units perform strategic-management tasks, including the development of a statement of vision and mission. Each division should involve its own managers and employees in developing a vision and mission statement that is consistent with and supportive of the corporate mission.

divisions should support the overall org.

An organization that fails to develop a vision statement as well as a comprehensive and inspiring mission statement loses the opportunity to present itself favorably to existing and potential stakeholders. All organizations need customers, employees, and managers, and most firms need creditors, suppliers, and distributors. The vision and mission statements are effective vehicles for communicating with important internal and external stakeholders. The principal value of these statements as tools of strategic management is derived from their specification of the ultimate aims of a firm:

> They provide managers with a unity of direction that transcends individual, parochial, and transitory needs. They promote a sense of shared expectations among all levels and generations of employees. They consolidate values over time and across individuals and interest groups. They project a sense of worth and intent that can be identified and assimilated by company outsiders. Finally, they affirm the company's commitment to responsible action, which is symbiotic with its need to preserve and protect the essential claims of insiders for sustained survival, growth, and profitability of the firm.[12]

Characteristics of a Mission Statement

A Declaration of Attitude

A mission statement is more than a statement of specific details; it is a declaration of attitude and outlook. It usually is broad in scope for at least two major reasons. First, a good mission statement allows for the generation and consideration of a range of feasible alternative objectives and strategies without unduly stifling management creativity. Excess specificity would limit the potential of creative growth for the organization. On the other hand, an overly general statement that does not exclude any strategy alternatives could be dysfunctional. Apple Computer's mission statement, for example, should not open the possibility for diversification into pesticides—or Ford Motor Company's into food processing.

Second, a mission statement needs to be broad to effectively reconcile differences among, and appeal to, an organization's diverse *stakeholders,* the individuals and groups of individuals who have a special stake or claim on the company. Stakeholders include employees, managers, stockholders, boards of directors, customers, suppliers, distributors, creditors, governments (local, state, federal, and foreign), unions, competitors, environmental groups, and the general public. Stakeholders affect and are affected by an organization's strategies, yet the claims and concerns of diverse constituencies vary and often conflict. For example, the general public is especially interested in social responsibility, whereas stockholders are more interested in profitability. Claims on any business literally may number in the thousands, and they often include clean air, jobs, taxes, investment opportunities, career opportunities, equal employment opportunities, employee benefits, salaries, wages, clean water, and community services. All stakeholders' claims on an organization cannot be pursued with equal emphasis. A good mission statement indicates the relative attention that an organization will devote to meeting the claims of various stakeholders. Many firms are environmentally proactive in response to the concerns of stakeholders, as indicated in the "Natural Environment Perspective" box.

The fine balance between specificity and generality is difficult to achieve, but it is well worth the effort. George Steiner offers the following insight on the need for a mission statement to be broad in scope:

> Most business statements of mission are expressed at high levels of abstraction. Vagueness nevertheless has its virtues. Mission statements are not designed to express concrete ends, but rather to provide motivation,

NATURAL ENVIRONMENT PERSPECTIVE

Is Your Firm Environmentally Proactive?

Conducting business in a way that preserves the natural environment is more than just good public relations; it is good business. Preserving the environment is a permanent part of doing business for the following reasons:

1. Consumer demand for environmentally safe products and packages is high.

2. Public opinion demanding that firms conduct business in ways that preserve the natural environment is strong.

3. Environmental advocacy groups now have over 20 million Americans as members.

4. Federal and state environmental regulations are changing rapidly and becoming more complex.

5. More lenders are examining the environmental liabilities of businesses seeking loans.

6. Many consumers, suppliers, distributors, and investors shun doing business with environmentally weak firms.

7. Liability suits and fines against firms having environmental problems are on the rise.

More firms are becoming environmentally proactive, which means they are taking the initiative to develop and implement strategies that preserve the environment while enhancing their efficiency and effectiveness. The old undesirable alternative is to be environmentally reactive—waiting until environmental pressures are thrust upon a firm by law or consumer pressure. A reactive environmental policy often leads to high cleanup costs, numerous liability suits, loss in market share, reduced customer loyalty, and higher medical costs. In contrast, a proactive policy views environmental pressures as opportunities and includes such actions as develop-

ing green products and packages, conserving energy, reducing waste, recycling, and creating a corporate culture that is environmentally sensitive.

A proactive policy forces a company to innovate and upgrade processes; this leads to reduced waste, improved efficiency, better quality, and greater profits. Successful firms today assess "the profit in preserving the environment" in decisions ranging from developing a mission statement to determining plant location, manufacturing technology, design, products, packaging, and consumer relations. A proactive environmental policy is simply good business.

Exemplary companies leading the way to reduce diesel fuel emissions on the highway are FedEx and UPS. Both companies are rapidly replacing their 100,000 old diesel trucks with new trucks that have cleaner technologies such as electric hybrids and hydrogen fuel cells, which these two firms are finding to be cheaper to maintain and operate. Trucks produce more than 30 percent of urban smog in the United States, so hopefully the other 5 million delivery truck fleets will follow the FedEx and UPS lead. FedEx just purchased 30,000 new hybrid electric vans and UPS is replacing its 142,300 trucks with low-emission vehicles. The scale of these two companies' commitment to air quality will likely transform the economies of hybrid commercial trucks to affordable and desirable rather than impractical. The era of smoke-belching delivery vans may end in the United States this decade.

Sources: Adapted from "The Profit in Preserving America," *Forbes* (November 11, 1991): 181–189; Forest Beinhardt, "Bringing the Environment Down to Earth," *Harvard Business Review* (July–August 1999): 149–158; Christine Rosen; "Environmental Strategy and Competitive Advantage," *California Management Review* 43, 3 (Spring 2001): 8–15; and Charles Haddad, "FedEx and Brown Are Going Green," *BusinessWeek* (August 11, 2003): 60–61.

general direction, an image, a tone, and a philosophy to guide the enterprise. An excess of detail could prove counterproductive since concrete specification could be the base for rallying opposition. Precision might stifle creativity in the formulation of an acceptable mission or purpose. Once an aim is cast in concrete, it creates a rigidity in an organization and resists change. Vagueness leaves room for other managers to fill in the details, perhaps even to modify general patterns. Vagueness permits more flexibility in adapting to changing environments and internal operations. It facilitates flexibility in implementation.[13]

An effective mission statement should not be too lengthy; recommended length is less than 200 words. An effective mission statement also arouses positive feelings and emotions about an organization; it is inspiring in the sense that it motivates readers to action. An effective mission statement generates the impression that a firm is successful, has direction, and is worthy of time, support, and investment—from all socioeconomic groups of people.

It reflects judgments about future growth directions and strategies that are based upon forward-looking external and internal analyses. A business mission should provide useful criteria for selecting among alternative strategies. A clear mission statement provides a basis for generating and screening strategic options. The statement of mission should be dynamic in orientation, allowing judgments about the most promising growth directions and those considered less promising.

A Customer Orientation

A good mission statement describes an organization's purpose, customers, products or services, markets, philosophy, and basic technology. According to Vern McGinnis, a mission statement should (1) define what the organization is and what the organization aspires to be, (2) be limited enough to exclude some ventures and broad enough to allow for creative growth, (3) distinguish a given organization from all others, (4) serve as a framework for evaluating both current and prospective activities, and (5) be stated in terms sufficiently clear to be widely understood throughout the organization.[14]

A good mission statement reflects the anticipations of customers. Rather than developing a product and then trying to find a market, the operating philosophy of organizations should be to identify customers' needs and then provide a product or service to fulfill those needs. Since more and more customers are using the Internet, all firms should post their vision and mission statements at the company's home page—as indicated in the "E-Commerce Perspective."

Good mission statements identify the utility of a firm's products to its customers. This is why AT&T's mission statement focuses on communication rather than on telephones; it is why ExxonMobil's mission statement focuses on energy rather than on oil and gas; it is why Union Pacific's mission statement focuses on transportation rather than on railroads; it is why Universal Studio's mission statement focuses on entertainment rather than on movies. The following utility statements are relevant in developing a mission statement:

> Do not offer me things.
> Do not offer me clothes. Offer me attractive looks.
> Do not offer me shoes. Offer me comfort for my feet and the pleasure of walking.
> Do not offer me a house. Offer me security, comfort, and a place that is clean and happy.
> Do not offer me books. Offer me hours of pleasure and the benefit of knowledge.
> Do not offer me records. Offer me leisure and the sound of music.
> Do not offer me tools. Offer me the benefits and the pleasure that come from making beautiful things.
> Do not offer me furniture. Offer me comfort and the quietness of a cozy place.
> Do not offer me things. Offer me ideas, emotions, ambience, feelings, and benefits.
> Please, do not offer me *things*.

E-COMMERCE PERSPECTIVE

Business Over the Internet Skyrocketing Globally

Business-to-business (B2B) e-commerce now exceeds $2.6 trillion annually and consumer ecommerce exceeds $130 billion. The Internet has truly connected people and businesses around the world, enabled companies to slash costs, and increased productivity. Businesses everywhere now communicate with their customers, suppliers, distributors, shareholders, and creditors instantaneously and inexpensively and are passing these cost savings on to consumers. Thousands of new consumers and businesses are coming online around the world every day.

Internet-based companies now dominate business in many industries. For example, eBay is the largest U.S. used car dealer and Expedia is the largest U.S. travel agency. Internet firms such as LendingTree, WebMD, Amazon, Phoenix University, and Dell Computer by some measures dominate their respective industries.

U.S. online retail sales are expected to increase 22 percent to $172 billion in 2005, spurred by growth in categories such as cosmetics and jewelry. The largest category of online sales in the United States is travel, exceeding $63 billion in 2005. Excluding travel, Internet sales reached $110 billion in 2005, or 5.5 percent of all retail sales, up from $89 billion, or 4.6 percent of retails sales in 2004.

Consumers globally are getting more comfortable with e-commerce, and this data represents key opportunities and threats in strategic planning for thousands of firms. For example, as indicated in the following table, online sales in Europe are expected to grow 33 percent annually between 2005 and 2009, compared to 14 percent in the United States. Forrester Research recently provided a forecast for Europe's online sales by country as given in the following table. This type of information impacts where firms choose to focus global efforts. Note, for example, that the annual growth rate of Internet sales in Greece is nearly three times the growth in the United States of America.

Country	Annual Growth Rate in Consumer Purchases Over the Internet (%)	# of Purchasers in 2005 (in millions)	# of Purchasers in 2009 (in millions)
Greece	61	174	1,118
Italy	53	3,073	16,188
Portugal	50	308	1,488
Spain	49	1,282	6,087
France	44	5,585	22,448
Finland	39	697	2,488
Ireland	39	441	1,520
Austria	38	1,089	3,658
Belgium	36	948	3,009
Luxembourg	36	82	252
Denmark	35	1,029	3,138
Sweden	35	1,856	5,764
Norway	35	1,034	3,206
Germany	32	15,237	42,765
Switzerland	32	2,498	6,794
Netherlands	24	3,295	7,316
United Kingdom	23	14,116	40,003
Total Europe	**33**	**57,498**	**167,241**
United States	**22**		

Source: Adapted from Beckey Bright, "How Do You Say "Web"? *Wall Street Journal* (May 23, 2005): R11. Also, Mylene Mangalindan, "Online Retail Sales Are Expected to Rise to $172 Billion This Year," *Wall Street Journal* (May 24, 2005): D5.

Mission statements attract customers that give mission~

A major reason for developing a business mission statement is to attract customers who give meaning to an organization. Hotel customers today want to use the Internet, so more and more hotels are providing Internet service. A classic description of the purpose of a business reveals the relative importance of customers in a statement of mission:

> It is the customer who determines what a business is. It is the customer alone whose willingness to pay for a good or service converts economic resources into wealth and things into goods. What a business thinks it produces is not of first importance, especially not to the future of the business and to its success. What the customer thinks he/she is buying, what he/she considers value, is decisive—it determines what a business is, what it produces, and whether it will prosper. And what the customer buys and considers value is never a product. It is always utility, meaning what a product or service does for him or her. The customer is the foundation of a business and keeps it in existence.[15]

A Declaration of Social Policy

The term *social policy* embraces managerial philosophy and thinking at the highest levels of an organization. For this reason, social policy affects the development of a business mission statement. Social issues mandate that strategists consider not only what the organization owes its various stakeholders but also what responsibilities the firm has to consumers, environmentalists, minorities, communities, and other groups. After decades of debate on the topic of social responsibility, many firms still struggle to determine appropriate social policies.

As indicated in the "Global Perspective", corporate policies related to mandatory retirement are a growing social concern in many countries.

The issue of social responsibility arises when a company establishes its business mission. The impact of society on business and vice versa is becoming more pronounced each year. Social policies directly affect a firm's customers, products and services, markets, technology, profitability, self-concept, and public image. An organization's social policy should be integrated into all strategic-management activities, including the development of a mission statement. Corporate social policy should be designed and articulated during strategy formulation, set and administered during strategy implementation, and reaffirmed or changed during strategy evaluation.[16] The emerging view of social responsibility holds that social issues should be attended to both directly and indirectly in determining strategies. In 2005, the top companies for social responsibility were as follows[17]:

1. Fannie Mae
2. Procter & Gamble
3. Intel Corporation
4. St. Paul Companies
5. Green Mountain Coffee Roasters
6. Deere & Company
7. Avon Products, Inc.
8. Hewlett-Packard Company
9. Agilent Technologies Inc.
10. Ecolab Inc.
11. Imation Corporation
12. IBM

GLOBAL PERSPECTIVE

Social Policies on Retirement: Japan Versus the World

Some countries around the world are facing severe workforce shortages associated with their aging populations. The percentage of persons aged 65 or older will reach 20 percent in 2006 in both Japan and Italy, but will reach 20 percent in 2036 in China and the United States. Persons aged 65 and older will reach 20 percent of the population in Germany and France in 2009 and 2018 respectively. Unlike the United States, Japan is reluctant to rely on large-scale immigration to bolster its workforce. Instead, Japan is providing incentives for its elderly to work until age 65 to 75. Western European countries are doing the opposite, providing incentives for its elderly to retire at age 55 to 60. The International Labor Organization says 71 percent of Japanese men ages 60 to 64 work, compared to 57 percent of American men and just 17 percent of Frenchmen in the same age group.

Mr. Sachiko Ichioka, a typical 67-year-old man in Japan, says, "I want to work as long as I'm healthy. The extra money means I can go on trips, and I'm not a burden on my children." Better diet and healthcare have raised Japan's life expectancy now to 82, the highest in the world. Japanese women are having on average only 1.28 children compared to 2.04 in the United States. Keeping the elderly at work, coupled with reversing the old fashion trend of keeping women at home, are Japan's two key remedies for sustaining its workforce in factories and businesses. This prescription for dealing with problems associated with an aging society should be considered by many countries around the world. The Japanese government is phasing in a shift from ages 60 to 65 as the date when a person may begin receiving a pension, and premiums paid by Japanese employees are rising while payouts are falling. Unlike the United States, Japan has no law against discrimination based on age.

Source: Adapted from Sebastian Moffett, "Fat-Aging Japan Keeps Its Elders on the Job Longer," *Wall Street Journal* (June 15, 2005): A1, A8.

Firms should strive to engage in social activities that have economic benefits. For example, Merck & Co. recently developed the drug ivermectin for treating river blindness, a disease caused by a fly-borne parasitic worm endemic in poor, tropical areas of Africa, the Middle East, and Latin America. In an unprecedented gesture that reflected its corporate commitment to social responsibility, Merck then made ivermectin available at no cost to medical personnel throughout the world. Merck's action highlights the dilemma of orphan drugs, which offer pharmaceutical companies no economic incentive for development and distribution.

Despite differences in approaches, most U. S. companies try to ensure outsiders that they conduct their businesses in socially responsible ways. The mission statement is an effective instrument for conveying this message.

Some strategists agree with Ralph Nader, who proclaims that organizations have tremendous social obligations. Others agree with Milton Friedman, the economist, who maintains that organizations have no obligation to do any more for society than is legally required. Most strategists agree that the first social responsibility of any business must be to make enough profit to cover the costs of the future, because if this is not achieved, no other social responsibility can be met. Strategists should examine social problems in terms of potential costs and benefits to the firm, and they should address social issues that could benefit the firm most.

VISIT THE NET

Provides example mission and vision statements that can be critiqued.
(www.csuchico.edu/mgmt/strategy/module1/sld015.htm; www.csuchico.edu/mgmt/strategy/module1/sld014.htm; www.csuchico.edu/mgmt/strategy/module1/sld017.htm)

Mission Statement Components

Mission statements can and do vary in length, content, format, and specificity. Most practitioners and academicians of strategic management feel that an effective statement exhibits nine characteristics or components. Because a mission statement is often the most visible and public part of the strategic-management process, it is important that it includes all of these essential components:

1. *Customers*—Who are the firm's customers?
2. *Products or services*—What are the firm's major products or services?
3. *Markets*—Geographically, where does the firm compete?
4. *Technology*—Is the firm technologically current?
5. *Concern for survival, growth, and profitability*—Is the firm committed to growth and financial soundness?
6. *Philosophy*—What are the basic beliefs, values, aspirations, and ethical priorities of the firm?
7. *Self-concept*—What is the firm's distinctive competence or major competitive advantage?
8. *Concern for public image*—Is the firm responsive to social, community, and environmental concerns?
9. *Concern for employees*—Are employees a valuable asset of the firm?

Excerpts from the mission statements of different organizations are provided in Table 2-2 to examplify the nine essential mission statement components.

Writing and Evaluating Mission Statements

VISIT THE NET

Provides mission statement information on nonprofit firms.
(http://www.nonprofits.org/ npofaq/03/21.html)

Perhaps the best way to develop a skill for writing and evaluating mission statements is to study actual company missions. Therefore, six mission statements are presented in Table 2-3. These statements are then evaluated in Table 2-4 based on the nine criteria presented.

There is no one best mission statement for a particular organization, so good judgment is required in evaluating mission statements. In Table 2-4, a *Yes* indicates that the given mission statement answers satisfactorily the questions posed above for the respective evaluative criteria. Some individuals are more demanding than others in rating mission statements in this manner. For example, if a statement includes the word *employees or customer,* is that alone sufficient for the respective component? Some companies answer this question in the affirmative and some in the negative. You may ask yourself this question: "If I worked for this company, would I have done better with regard to including a particular component in its mission statement?" Perhaps the important issue here is that mission statements include each of the nine components in some manner.

As indicated in Table 2-4, the Dell Computer mission statement was rated to be the best among the six statements evaluated. Note, however, that the Dell Computer statement lacks inclusion of the "Philosophy" and the "Concern for Employees" components. The PepsiCo mission statement was evaluated as the worst because it included only three of the nine components. Note that only one of these six statements included the "Technology" component in its document.

TABLE 2-2 Examples of the Nine Essential Components of a Mission Statement

1. CUSTOMERS

We believe our first responsibility is to the doctors, nurses, patients, mothers, and all others who use our products and services. (Johnson & Johnson)

To earn our customers' loyalty, we listen to them, anticipate their needs, and act to create value in their eyes. (Lexmark International)

2. PRODUCTS OR SERVICES

AMAX's principal products are molybdenum, coal, iron ore, copper, lead, zinc, petroleum and natural gas, potash, phosphates, nickel, tungsten, silver, gold, and magnesium. (AMAX Engineering Company)

Standard Oil Company (Indiana) is in business to find and produce crude oil, natural gas, and natural gas liquids; to manufacture high-quality products useful to society from these raw materials; and to distribute and market those products and to provide dependable related services to the consuming public at reasonable prices. (Standard Oil Company)

3. MARKETS

We are dedicated to the total success of Corning Glass Works as a worldwide competitor. (Corning Glass Works)

Our emphasis is on North American markets, although global opportunities will be explored. (Blockway)

4. TECHNOLOGY

Control Data is in the business of applying micro-electronics and computer technology in two general areas: computer-related hardware; and computing-enhancing services, which include computation, information, education, and finance. (Control Data)

We will continually strive to meet the preferences of adult smokers by developing technologies that have the potential to reduce the health risks associated with smoking. (RJ Reynolds)

5. CONCERN FOR SURVIVAL, GROWTH, AND PROFITABILITY

In this respect, the company will conduct its operations prudently and will provide the profits and growth which will assure Hoover's ultimate success. (Hoover Universal)

To serve the worldwide need for knowledge at a fair profit by adhering, evaluating, producing, and distributing valuable information in a way that benefits our customers, employees, other investors, and our society. (McGraw-Hill)

6. PHILOSOPHY

Our world-class leadership is dedicated to a management philosophy that holds people above profits. (Kellogg)

It's all part of the Mary Kay philosophy—a philosophy based on the golden rule. A spirit of sharing and caring where people give cheerfully of their time, knowledge, and experience. (Mary Kay Cosmetics)

7. SELF-CONCEPT

Crown Zellerbach is committed to leapfrogging ongoing competition within 1,000 days by unleashing the constructive and creative abilities and energies of each of its employees. (Crown Zellerbach)

8. CONCERN FOR PUBLIC IMAGE

To share the world's obligation for the protection of the environment. (Dow Chemical)

To contribute to the economic strength of society and function as a good corporate citizen on a local, state, and national basis in all countries in which we do business. (Pfizer)

9. CONCERN FOR EMPLOYEES

To recruit, develop, motivate, reward, and retain personnel of exceptional ability, character, and dedication by providing good working conditions, superior leadership, compensation on the basis of performance, an attractive benefit program, opportunity for growth, and a high degree of employment security. (The Wachovia Corporation)

To compensate its employees with remuneration and fringe benefits competitive with other employment opportunities in its geographical area and commensurate with their contributions toward efficient corporate operations. (Public Service Electric & Gas Company)

TABLE 2-3   Mission Statements of Six Organizations

PepsiCo's mission is to increase the value of our shareholders' investment. We do this through sales growth, cost controls, and wise investment resources. We believe our commercial success depends upon offering quality and value to our consumers and customers; providing products that are safe, wholesome, economically efficient, and environmentally sound; and providing a fair return to our investors while adhering to the highest standards of integrity.

Ben & Jerry's mission is to make, distribute, and sell the finest quality all-natural ice cream and related products in a wide variety of innovative flavors made from Vermont dairy products. To operate the Company on a sound financial basis of profitable growth, increasing value for our shareholders, and creating career opportunities and financial rewards for our employees. To operate the Company in a way that actively recognizes the central role that business plays in the structure of society by initiating innovative ways to improve the quality of life of a broad community—local, national, and international.

The Mission of the Institute of Management Accountants (IMA) is to provide to members personal and professional development opportunities through education, association with business professionals, and certification in management accounting and financial management skills. The IMA is globally recognized by the financial community as a respected institution influencing the concepts and ethical practices of management accounting and financial management.

The Mission of Genentech, Inc., is to be the leading biotechnology company, using human genetic information to develop, manufacture, and market pharmaceuticals that address significant unmet medical needs. We commit ourselves to high standards of integrity in contributing to the best interests of patients, the medical profession, and our employees, and to seek significant returns to our stockholders based on the continued pursuit of excellent science.

The Mission of Barrett Memorial Hospital is to operate a high-quality health care facility, providing an appropriate mix of services to the residents of Beaverhead County and surrounding areas. Service is given with ultimate concern for patients, medical staff, hospital staff, and the community. Barrett Memorial Hospital assumes a strong leadership role in the coordination and development of health-related resources within the community.

Dell Computer's mission is to be the most successful computer company in the world at delivering the best customer experience in markets we serve. In doing so, Dell will meet customer expectations of highest quality; leading technology; competitive pricing; individual and company accountability; best-in-class service and support; flexible customization capability; superior corporate citizenship; financial stability.

TABLE 2-4   An Evaluation Matrix of Mission Statements

	COMPONENTS				
Organization	Customers	Products/ Services	Markets	Technology	Concern for Survival, Growth, Profitability
PepsiCo	Yes	No	No	No	Yes
Ben & Jerry's	No	Yes	Yes	No	Yes
Institute of Management Accountants	Yes	Yes	Yes	No	No
Genentech, Inc.	Yes	Yes	No	No	Yes

(Continued)

TABLE 2-4 Continued

Organization	Customers	Products/ Services	Markets	Technology	Concern for Survival, Growth, Profitability
Barrett Memorial Hospital	Yes	Yes	Yes	No	No
Dell Computer	Yes	Yes	Yes	Yes	Yes

	Philosophy	Self-Concept	Concern for Public Image	Concern for Employees
PepsiCo	Yes	No	No	No
Ben & Jerry's	No	Yes	Yes	Yes
Institute of Management Accountants	Yes	Yes	Yes	No
Genentech, Inc.	Yes	Yes	Yes	Yes
Barrett Memorial Hospital	No	Yes	Yes	Yes
Dell Computer	No	Yes	Yes	No

CONCLUSION

Every organization has a unique purpose and reason for being. This uniqueness should be reflected in vision and mission statements. The nature of a business vision and mission can represent either a competitive advantage or disadvantage for the firm. An organization achieves a heightened sense of purpose when strategists, managers, and employees develop and communicate a clear business vision and mission. Drucker says that developing a clear business vision and mission is the "first responsibility of strategists."

A good mission statement reveals an organization's customers; products or services; markets; technology; concern for survival, growth, and profitability; philosophy; self-concept; concern for public image; and concern for employees. These nine basic components serve as a practical framework for evaluating and writing mission statements. As the first step in strategic management, the vision and mission statements provide direction for all planning activities.

Well-designed vision and mission statements are essential for formulating, implementing, and evaluating strategy. Developing and communicating a clear business vision and mission are the most commonly overlooked tasks in strategic management. Without clear statements of vision and mission, a firm's short-term actions can be counterproductive to long-term interests. Vision and mission statements always should be subject to revision, but, if carefully prepared, they will require infrequent major changes. Organizations usually reexamine their vision and mission statements annually. Effective mission statements stand the test of time.

Vision and mission statements are essential tools for strategists, a fact illustrated in a short story told by Porsche former CEO Peter Schultz:

> Three people were at work on a construction site. All were doing the same job, but when each was asked what his job was, the answers varied: "Breaking rocks," the first replied; "Earning a living," responded the second; "Helping to build a cathedral," said the third. Few of us can build cathedrals. But to the extent we can see the cathedral in whatever cause we

are following, the job seems more worthwhile. Good strategists and a clear mission help us find those cathedrals in what otherwise could be dismal issues and empty causes.[18]

We invite you to visit the David page on the Prentice Hall Companion Web site at www.prenhall.com/david for this chapter's review quiz.

KEY TERMS AND CONCEPTS

Concern for Employees (p. 70)
Concern for Public Image (p. 70)
Concern for Survival, Growth, and Profitability (p. 70)
Creed Statement (p. 59)
Customers (p. 70)

Markets (p. 70)
Mission Statement (p. 59)
Mission Statement Components (p. 70)
Philosophy (p. 70)
Products or Services (p. 70)

Self-Concept (p. 70)
Social Policy (p. 68)
Stakeholders (p. 64)
Technology (p. 70)
Vision Statement (p. 60)

ISSUES FOR REVIEW AND DISCUSSION

1. Compare and contrast vision statements with mission statements in terms of composition and importance.
2. Do local service stations need to have written vision and mission statements? Why or why not?
3. Why do you think organizations that have a comprehensive mission tend to be high performers? Does having a comprehensive mission cause high performance?
4. Explain why a mission statement should not include strategies and objectives.
5. What is your college or university's self-concept? How would you state that in a mission statement?
6. Explain the principal value of a vision and a mission statement.
7. Why is it important for a mission statement to be reconciliatory?
8. In your opinion, what are the three most important components that should be included when writing a mission statement? Why?

9. How would the mission statements of a for-profit and a nonprofit organization differ?
10. Write a vision and mission statement for an organization of your choice.
11. Go to www.altavista.com and conduct a search with the key words *vision statement and mission statement.* Find various company vision and mission statements, and evaluate the documents.
12. Who are the major stakeholders of the bank that you locally do business with? What are the major claims of those stakeholders?
13. How could a strategist's attitude toward social responsibility affect a firm's strategy? What is your attitude toward social responsibility?
14. List the characteristics of a mission statement.
15. List the benefits of a having a clear mission statement.
16. How often do you think a firm's vision and mission statements should be changed?

NOTES

1. Barbara Bartkus, Myron Glassman, and Bruce McAfee, "Mission Statements: Are They Smoke and Mirrors?" *Business Horizons* (November–December 2000): 23.

2. Peter Drucker, *Management: Tasks, Responsibilities, and Practices* (New York: Harper & Row, 1974): 61.

3. Fred David, "How Companies Define Their Mission," *Long Range Planning* 22, no. 1 (February 1989): 90–92; John Pearce II and Fred David, "Corporate Mission Statements: The Bottom Line," *Academy of Management Executive* 1, no. 2 (May 1987): 110.

4. Joseph Quigley, "Vision: How Leaders Develop It, Share It and Sustain It," *Business Horizons* (September–October 1994): 39.

5. Andrew Campbell and Sally Yeung, "Creating a Sense of Mission," *Long Range Planning* 24, no. 4 (August 1991): 17.

6. Charles Rarick and John Vitton, "Mission Statements Make Cents," *Journal of Business Strategy* 16 (1995): 11. Also, Christopher Bart and Mark Baetz, "The Relationship Between Mission Statements and Firm Performance: An Exploratory Study," *Journal of Management Studies* 35 (1998): 823; "Mission Possible," *Business Week* (August 1999): F12.

7. W. R. King and D. I. Cleland, *Strategic Planning and Policy* (New York: Van Nostrand Reinhold, 1979): 124.

8. Brian Dumaine, "What the Leaders of Tomorrow See," *Fortune* (July 3, 1989): 50.

9. Drucker, 78, 79.

10. "How W. T. Grant Lost $175 Million Last Year," *BusinessWeek* (February 25, 1975): 75.

11. Drucker, 88.

12. John Pearce II, "The Company Mission as a Strategic Tool," *Sloan Management Review* 23, no. 3 (Spring 1982): 74.

13. George Steiner, *Strategic Planning: What Every Manager Must Know* (New York: The Free Press, 1979): 160.

14. Vern McGinnis, "The Mission Statement: A Key Step in Strategic Planning," *Business* 31, no. 6 (November–December 1981): 41.

15. Drucker, 61.

16. Archie Carroll and Frank Hoy, "Integrating Corporate Social Policy into Strategic Management," *Journal of Business Strategy* 4, no. 3 (Winter 1984): 57.

17. www.businessethics.com/chart_100_best_corporate_citizens_for_2004.htm

18. Robert Waterman, Jr., *The Renewal Factor: How the Best Get and Keep the Competitive Edge* (New York: Bantam, 1987); *BusinessWeek* (September 14, 1987): 120.

CURRENT READINGS

Baetz, Mark C., and Christopher K. Bart, "Developing Mission Statements Which Work." *Long Range Planning* 29, no. 4 (August 1996): 526–533.

Bartkus, Barbara, Myron Glassman, and R. Bruce McAfee. "Mission Statements: Are They Smoke and Mirrors?" *Business Horizons* 43, no. 6 (November–December 2000): 23.

Brabet, Julienne, and Mary Klemm. "Sharing the Vision: Company Mission Statements in Britain and France." *Long Range Planning* (February 1994): 84–94.

Collins, James C., and Jerry I. Porras. "Building a Visionary Company." *California Management Review* 37, no. 2 (Winter 1995): 80–100.

Collins, James C., and Jerry I. Porras. "Building Your Company's Vision." *Harvard Business Review* (September–October 1996): 65–78.

Cummings, Stephen, and John Davies. "Brief Case—Mission, Vision, Fusion." *Long Range Planning* 27, no. 6 (December 1994): 147–150.

Davies, Stuart W., and Keith W. Glaister. "Business School Mission Statements—The Bland Leading the Bland?" *Long Range Planning* 30, no. 4 (August 1997): 594–604.

Day, George S., and Paul Schoemaker, "Peripheral Vision: Sensing and Acting on Weak Signals." *Long Range Planning* 37, no. 2 (April 2004): 117.

Dowling, Grahame R. "Corporate Reputations: Should You Compete on Yours?" *California Management Review* 46, no. 3 (Spring 2004): 19.

Gratton, Lynda. "Implementing a Strategic Vision— Key Factors for Success." *Long Range Planning* 29, no. 3 (June 1996): 290–303.

Greenfield, W. M. "In the Name of Corporate Social Responsibility." *Business Horizons* 47, no. 1 (January–February 2004): 19.

Hollender, Jeffery. "What Matters Most: Corporate Values and Social Responsibility." *California Management Review* 46, no. 4 (Summer 2004): 111.

Larwood, Laurie, Cecilia M. Falbe, Mark P. Kriger, and Paul Miesing. "Structure and Meaning of Organizational Vision." *Academy of Management Journal* 38, no. 3 (June 1995): 740–769.

Lissak, Michael, and Johan Roos. "Be Coherent, Not Visionary." *Long Range Planning* 34, no. 1 (February 2001): 53.

McTavish, Ron. "One More Time: What Business Are You In?" *Long Range Planning* 28, no. 2 (April 1995): 49–60.

Oswald, S. L., K. W. Mossholder, and S. G. Harris. "Vision Salience and Strategic Involvement: Implications for Psychological Attachment to Organization and Job." *Strategic Management Journal* 15, no. 6 (July 1994): 477–490.

Pearce II, J. A., J. P. Doh. "The High Impact of Collaborative Social Initiatives." *MIT Sloan Management Review* 46, no. 3 (Spring 2005): 30.

experiential exercises

**Experiential
Exercise 2A**

*Evaluating Mission
Statements*

PURPOSE

A business mission statement is an integral part of strategic management. It provides direction for formulating, implementing, and evaluating strategic activities. This exercise will give you practice evaluating mission statements, a skill that is a prerequisite to writing a good mission statement.

INSTRUCTIONS

Step 1   Your instructor will select some or all of the following mission statements to evaluate. On a separate sheet of paper, construct an evaluation matrix like the one presented in Table 2-4. Evaluate the mission statements based on the nine criteria presented in this chapter.

Step 2   Record a *yes* in appropriate cells of the evaluation matrix when the respective mission statement satisfactorily meets the desired criteria. Record a *no* in appropriate cells when the respective mission statement does not meet the stated criteria.

MISSION STATEMENTS

Criterion Productions, Inc.

The mission statement of Criterion Productions, Inc., is to increase the success of all who avail themselves of our products and services by providing image enhancement and a medium that communicates our customer's corporate identity and unique message to a targeted audience. In this, our tenth year of business, Criterion Productions, Inc., pledges to offer a distinct advantage and a superior value in all of your video production needs. We will assist our customers in their endeavors to grow and prosper through celebrity associations that are "effectively appropriate" to their industry, and/or who possess the qualities and characteristics most respected by our customers.

Mid-America Plastics, Inc.

"Continuous Improvement Every Day, In Everything We Do."

In order for us to accomplish our mission, every employee must be "Committed to Excellence" in everything he or she does by performing his or her job right the first time.

Hatboro Area YMCA

To translate the principles of the YMCA's Christian heritage into programs that nurture children, strengthen families, build strong communities, and develop healthy minds, bodies, and spirits for all.

Integrated Communications, Inc.

Our mission is to be perceived by our customers as providing the highest quality of customer service and salesmanship, delivered with a sense of ownership, friendliness, individual pride, and team spirit. We will accomplish this with the quality of our Wireless Products that supply complete solutions to our customers' needs. And, through unyielding loyalty to our customers and suppliers, ICI will provide opportunities and security to our employees as well as [maximize] our long-term financial growth.

American Counseling Association (ACA)
The Mission of ACA is to promote public confidence and trust in the counseling profession.

Idaho Hospital Association
The mission of the Idaho Hospital Association is to provide representation, advocacy and assistance for member hospitals, healthcare systems and the healthcare services they provide. The Association, through leadership and collaboration among health-care providers and others, promotes quality healthcare that is adequately financed and accessible to all Idahoans.

Experiential Exercise 2B

Writing a Vision and Mission Statement for Google (GOOG)

PURPOSE

There is no one best vision or mission statement for a given organization. Analysts feel that Google needs a clear vision and mission statement to prosper. Writing a mission statement that includes desired components—and at the same time is inspiring and reconciliatory—requires careful thought. Mission statements should not be too lengthy; statements under 200 words are desirable.

INSTRUCTIONS

Step 1 Take 15 minutes to write vision and mission statements for Google. Scan the case for needed details as you prepare your statements.

Step 2 Join with three other classmates to form a group of four people. Silently read each others' statements. As a group, select the best vision statement and best mission statement from your group.

Step 3 Read those "best" statements to the class.

Experiential Exercise 2C

Writing a Vision and Mission Statement for My University

PURPOSE

Most universities have a vision and mission statement. The purpose of this exercise is to give you practice writing a vision and mission statement for a nonprofit organization such as your own university.

INSTRUCTIONS

Step 1 Take 15 minutes to write a vision statement and a mission statement for your university. Your mission statement should not exceed 200 words.

Step 2 Read your vision and mission statements to the class.

Step 3 Determine whether your institution has a vision and/or mission statement. Look in the front of the college handbook. If your institution has a written statement, contact an appropriate administrator of the institution to inquire as to how and when the statement was prepared. Share this information with the class. Analyze your college's mission statement in light of concepts presented in this chapter.

Experiential Exercise 2D

Conducting Mission Statement Research

PURPOSE

This exercise gives you the opportunity to study the nature and role of vision and mission statements in strategic management.

INSTRUCTIONS

Step 1 Call various organizations in your city or county to identify firms that have developed a formal vision and/or mission statement. Contact nonprofit organizations and government agencies in addition to small and large businesses. Ask to speak with the director, owner, or chief executive officer of each organization. Explain that you are studying vision and mission statements in class and are conducting research as part of a class activity.

Step 2 Ask several executives the following four questions, and record their answers.
1. When did your organization first develop its vision and/or mission statement? Who was primarily responsible for its development?
2. How long have your current statements existed? When were they last modified? Why were they modified at that point in time?
3. By what process are your firm's vision and mission statements altered?
4. How are your vision and mission statements used in the firm?

Step 3 Provide an overview of your findings to the class.

The External Assessment

chapter objectives

After studying this chapter, you should be able to do the following:

1. Describe how to conduct an external strategic-management audit.

2. Discuss 10 major external forces that affect organizations: economic, social, cultural, demographic, environmental, political, governmental, legal, technological, and competitive.

3. Identify key sources of external information, including the Internet.

4. Discuss important forecasting tools used in strategic management.

5. Discuss the importance of monitoring external trends and events.

6. Explain how to develop an EFE Matrix.

7. Explain how to develop a Competitive Profile Matrix.

8. Discuss the importance of gathering competitive intelligence.

9. Describe the trend toward cooperation among competitors.

10. Discuss the economic environment in Russia.

11. Discuss the global challenge facing American firms.

12. Discuss market commonality and resource similarity in relation to competitive analysis.

experiential exercises

"notable quotes"

If you're not faster than your competitor, you're in a tenuous position, and if you're only half as fast, you're terminal.
George Salk

The opportunities and threats existing in any situation always exceed the resources needed to exploit the opportunities or avoid the threats. Thus, strategy is essentially a problem of allocating resources. If strategy is to be successful, it must allocate superior resources against a decisive opportunity.
William Cohen

Organizations pursue strategies that will disrupt the normal course of industry events and forge new industry conditions to the disadvantage of competitors.
Ian C. Macmillan

The idea is to concentrate our strength against our competitor's relative weakness.
Bruce Henderson

If everyone is thinking alike, then somebody isn't thinking.
George Patton

It is not the strongest of the species that survive, nor the most intelligent, but the one most responsive to change.
Charles Darwin

Nothing focuses the mind better than the constant sight of a competitor who wants to wipe you off the map.
Wayne Calloway

This chapter examines the tools and concepts needed to conduct an external strategic management audit (sometimes called *environmental scanning or industry analysis*). An *external audit* focuses on identifying and evaluating trends and events beyond the control of a single firm, such as increased foreign competition, population shifts to the Sunbelt, an aging society, consumer fear of traveling, and stock market volatility. An external audit reveals key opportunities and threats confronting an organization so that managers can formulate strategies to take advantage of the opportunities and avoid or reduce the impact of threats. This chapter presents a practical framework for gathering, assimilating, and analyzing external information. The Industrial Organization (I/O) view of strategic management is introduced.

The Nature of an External Audit

VISIT THE NET

Reveals how strategic planning evolved from long-range planning and environmental scanning (external audit or assessment).
(horizon.unc.edu/projects/ seminars/futuresresearch/ strategic.asp#planning)

The purpose of an *external audit* is to develop a finite list of opportunities that could benefit a firm and threats that should be avoided. As the term *finite* suggests, the external audit is not aimed at developing an exhaustive list of every possible factor that could influence the business; rather, it is aimed at identifying key variables that offer actionable responses. Firms should be able to respond either offensively or defensively to the factors by formulating strategies that take advantage of external opportunities or that minimize the impact of potential threats. Figure 3-1 illustrates how the external audit fits into the strategic-management process.

FIGURE 3-1

A Comprehensive Strategic-Management Model

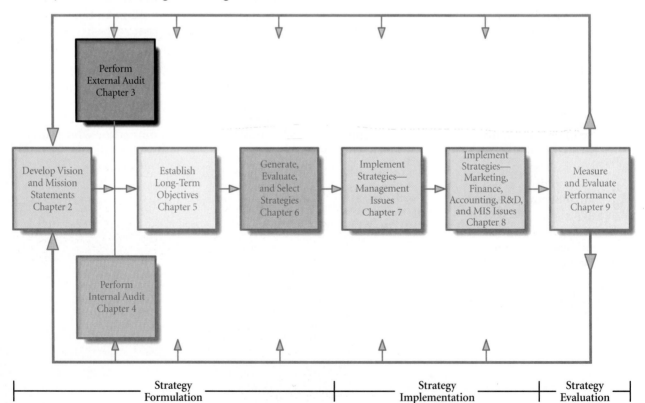

Key External Forces

External forces can be divided into five broad categories: (1) economic forces; (2) social, cultural, demographic, and environmental forces; (3) political, governmental, and legal forces; (4) technological forces; and (5) competitive forces. Relationships among these forces and an organization are depicted in Figure 3-2. External trends and events significantly affect all products, services, markets, and organizations in the world.

Changes in external forces translate into changes in consumer demand for both industrial and consumer products and services. External forces affect the types of products developed, the nature of positioning and market segmentation strategies, the type of services offered, and the choice of businesses to acquire or sell. External forces directly affect both suppliers and distributors. Identifying and evaluating external opportunities and threats enables organizations to develop a clear mission, to design strategies to achieve long-term objectives, and to develop policies to achieve annual objectives.

The increasing complexity of business today is evidenced by more countries developing the capacity and will to compete aggressively in world markets. Foreign businesses and countries are willing to learn, adapt, innovate, and invent to compete successfully in the marketplace. There are more competitive new technologies in Europe and the Far East today than ever before. U.S. businesses can no longer beat foreign competitors with ease.

The Process of Performing an External Audit

The process of performing an external audit must involve as many managers and employees as possible. As emphasized in earlier chapters, involvement in the strategic-management process can lead to understanding and commitment from organizational members. Individuals appreciate having the opportunity to contribute ideas and to gain a better understanding of their firms' industry, competitors, and markets.

FIGURE 3-2
Relationships Between Key External Forces and an Organization

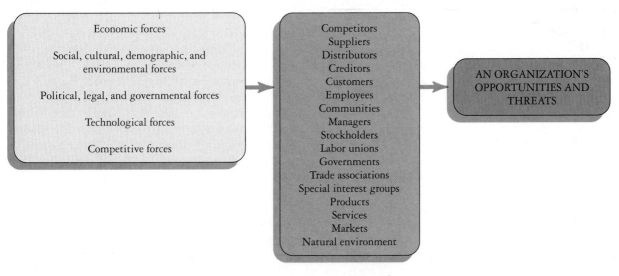

What to look [handwritten annotation in left margin]

To perform an external audit, a company first must gather competitive intelligence and information about economic, social, cultural, demographic, environmental, political, governmental, legal, and technological trends. Individuals can be asked to monitor various sources of information, such as key magazines, trade journals, and newspapers. These persons can submit periodic scanning reports to a committee of managers charged with performing the external audit. This approach provides a continuous stream of timely strategic information and involves many individuals in the external-audit process. The Internet provides another source for gathering strategic information, as do corporate, university, and public libraries. Suppliers, distributors, salespersons, customers, and competitors represent other sources of vital information.

Once information is gathered, it should be assimilated and evaluated. A meeting or series of meetings of managers is needed to collectively identify the most important opportunities and threats facing the firm. These key external factors should be listed on flip charts or a blackboard. A prioritized list of these factors could be obtained by requesting that all managers rank the factors identified, from 1 for the most important opportunity/threat to 20 for the least important opportunity/threat. These key external factors can vary over time and by industry. Relationships with suppliers or distributors are often a critical success factor. Other variables commonly used include market share, breadth of competing products, world economies, foreign affiliates, proprietary and key account advantages, price competitiveness, technological advancements, population shifts, interest rates, and pollution abatement.

Freund emphasized that these key external factors should be (1) important to achieving long-term and annual objectives, (2) measurable, (3) applicable to all competing firms, and (4) hierarchical in the sense that some will pertain to the overall company and others will be more narrowly focused on functional or divisional areas.[1] A final list of the most important key external factors should be communicated and distributed widely in the organization. Both opportunities and threats can be key external factors.

VISIT THE NET

Describes the external audit process in a university setting.
(horizon.unc.edu/projects/ seminars/futuresresearch/ stages.asp)

The Industrial Organization (I/O) View

external more important than internal factors to achieve CA [handwritten annotation in left margin]

The *Industrial Organization (I/O)* approach to competitive advantage advocates that external (industry) factors are more important than internal factors in a firm achieving competitive advantage. Proponents of the I/O view, such as Michael Porter, contend that organizational performance will be primarily determined by industry forces. Porter's Five-Forces Model, presented later in this chapter, is an example of the I/O perspective, which focuses upon analyzing external forces and industry variables as a basis for getting and keeping competitive advantage. Competitive advantage is determined largely by competitive positioning within an industry, according to I/O advocates. Managing strategically from the I/O perspective entails firms striving to compete in attractive industries, avoiding weak or faltering industries, and gaining a full understanding of key external factor relationships within that attractive industry. I/O research was mainly conducted from the 1960s to the 1980s and provided important contributions to our understanding of how to gain competitive advantage.

I/O theorists contend that the industry in which a firm chooses to compete has a stronger influence on the firm's performance than do the internal functional decisions managers make in marketing, finance, and the like. Firm performance, they contend, is primarily based more on industry properties, such as economies of scale, barriers to market entry, product differentiation, and level of competitiveness than on internal resources, capabilities, structure, and operations. Research findings suggest that approximately 20 percent of a firm's profitability can be explained by the industry, whereas 36 percent of the variance in profitability is attributed to the firm's internal factors (see the RBV discussion in the next chapter).[2]

The I/O view has enhanced our understanding of strategic management. However, it is not a question of whether external or internal factors are more important in gaining and maintaining competitive advantage. Effective integration and understanding of *both* external and internal factors is the key to securing and keeping a competitive advantage. In fact, as will be discussed in Chapter 6, matching key external opportunities/threats with key internal strengths/weaknesses provides the basis for successful strategy formulation.

Economic Forces

Increasing numbers of two-income households is an economic trend in the United States. Individuals place a premium on time. Improved customer service, immediate availability, trouble-free operation of products, and dependable maintenance and repair services are becoming more important. Americans today are more willing than ever to pay for good service if it limits inconvenience.

Economic factors have a direct impact on the potential attractiveness of various strategies. For example, when interest rates rise, funds needed for capital expansion become more costly or unavailable. Also, when interest rates rise, discretionary income declines, and the demand for discretionary goods falls. When stock prices increase, the desirability of equity as a source of capital for market development increases. Also, when the market rises, consumer and business wealth expands. A summary of economic variables that often represent opportunities and threats for organizations is provided in Table 3-1.

VISIT THE NET

Provides excellent narrative on NASA's strategic-management process, especially its external assessment activities. Provides NASA's entire strategic plan with outstanding narrative and illustrations about how to do strategic planning. (www.hq.nasa.gov/office/nsptoc.htm)

TABLE 3-1 Key Economic Variables to Be Monitored

Shift to a service economy in the United States	Import/export factors
Availability of credit	Demand shifts for different categories of goods and services
Level of disposable income	Income differences by region and consumer groups
Propensity of people to spend	
Interest rates	Price fluctuations
Inflation rates	Export of labor and capital from the United States
Money market rates	
Federal government budget deficits	Monetary policies
Gross domestic product trend	Fiscal policies
Consumption patterns	Tax rates
Unemployment trends	European Economic Community (EEC) policies
Worker productivity levels	
Value of the dollar in world markets	Organization of Petroleum Exporting Countries (OPEC) policies
Stock market trends	Coalitions of Lesser Developed Countries (LDC) policies
Foreign countries' economic conditions	

Trends in the dollar's value have significant and unequal effects on companies in different industries and in different locations. For example, the pharmaceutical, tourism, entertainment, motor vehicle, aerospace, and forest products industries benefit greatly when the dollar falls against the yen and euro. Agricultural and petroleum industries are hurt by the dollar's rise against the currencies of Mexico, Brazil, Venezuela, and Australia. Generally, a strong or high dollar makes U.S. goods more expensive in overseas markets. This worsens the U.S. trade deficit. When the value of the dollar falls, tourism-oriented firms benefit because Americans do not travel abroad as much when the value of the dollar is low; rather, foreigners visit and vacation more in the United States.

A low value of the dollar means lower imports and higher exports; it helps U.S. companies' competitiveness in world markets. In 2005, the dollar fell to five-year lows against the euro and yen, which makes U.S. goods cheaper to foreign consumers and combats deflation by pushing up prices of imports. However, European firms such as Volkswagen AG, Nokia Corp., and Michelin complain that the strong euro hurts their financial performance. The low value of the dollar benefits the U.S. economy in many ways. First, it helps to stave off the risks of deflation in the United States and also reduces the U.S. trade deficit. In addition, the low value of the dollar raises the foreign sales and profits of domestic firms, thanks to dollar-induced gains, and encourages foreign countries to lower interest rates and loosen fiscal policy, which stimulates worldwide economic expansion. Some sectors, such as consumer staples, energy, materials, technology, and health care, especially benefit from a low value of the dollar. Manufacturers in many domestic industries in fact benefit because of a weak dollar, which forces foreign rivals to raise prices and extinguish discounts. Domestic firms with big overseas sales, such as McDonald's, greatly benefit from a weak dollar.

In Europe, 10 countries from Eastern Europe, the Baltics, and the Mediterranean joined the 12-country European Union (EU) in 2004. These countries adopted the euro as their currency. However, Sweden, has rejected the euro as its currency although it has been an EU member since 1994. Denmark and Britain have delayed a vote until 2006 on whether to adopt the euro. Some European countries are having trouble meeting the euro requirement that a member country keep its federal budget deficits below 3 percent of gross domestic product (GDP). Germany and France have conspicuously and brazenly violated this rule since 2001, although they strongly demanded budget discipline as a condition for EU membership in 1997. Both countries' deficit is about 4 percent of GDP.

Every business day, thousands of U.S. workers learn that they will lose their jobs. More than 500,000 annual employee layoffs by U.S. firms in the 1990s led to terms such as *downsizing, rightsizing,* and *decruiting* becoming common. European firms, too, are downsizing. The United States and world economies face a sustained period of slow, low-inflationary expansion, global overcapacity, high unemployment, price wars, and increased competitiveness. Thousands of laid-off workers are being forced to become entrepreneurs to make a living. The United States is becoming more entrepreneurial every day.

The economic standard of living varies considerably across cities and countries, and this fact represents an opportunity or threat to firms and individuals relocating or building new facilities in new areas. Note in Table 3-2, that the cost of living in Rio de Janeiro is less than one-half the cost of living in Tokyo. Toronto has about the same cost of living as Atlanta. The cost of living in London is about 19 percent higher than in New York City, while the cost of living in Boston is about 25 percent less than in New York City.

TABLE 3-2 The Cost of Living in Various Cities Worldwide

CITY	OVERALL COST INDEX	MONTHLY RENT FOR A TWO-BEDROOM APARTMENT IN A GOOD AREA	CUP OF COFFEE WITH SERVICE
Tokyo	130.7	$4,536	$4.76
London	119.0	3,019	3.11
New York City	100.0	3,500	3.30
Sydney	91.8	1,381	2.42
Chicago	84.5	2,300	2.10
San Francisco	84.3	2,100	3.52
Boston	76.4	1,750	2.90
Atlanta	72.9	1,250	1.71
Toronto	71.8	1,383	2.11
Rio de Janeiro	59.3	1,366	0.94

Source: Adapted from Kelly Spors, "Keeping Up with Yourself," *Wall Street Journal* (April 11, 2005): R4.

Russia's Economy

According to the *Wall Street Journal,* political bureaucracy in Russia strangles economic progress, free enterprise, and entrepreneurship.[3] Russian businesspersons who do not show favor to local governments are today targeted with tax audits, punitive fines, and intrusive inspections and oftentimes are forced to close shop. Since coming to power in 2000, President Vladmir Putin has gradually weakened Russia's fledgling democratic institutions by restraining the media, stacking parliament with pro-Kremlin parties, and abolishing gubernatorial elections.[4] Russian businesses today are more likely to fall victim to illegal actions by officials and policemen than by criminals. Local governors across Russia are still largely former Communist leaders who give sweeping perks and preferences to businesses in which they have a vested interest, while most independent private businesses struggle to survive.

Russia's state-run gas monopoly, Gazprom, in 2005 purchased the country's leading newspaper, *Izvestia,* further strengthening the Kremlin's dominance of the media. This acquisition coupled with the breakup and partial nationalization of OAO Yukos, once Russia's largest oil producer, has shaken business confidence and slowed economic growth in Russia.[5] "Russia receives only about $65 per capita in annual foreign direct investment, compared to $220 in Hungary; potential investors say they are deterred by Russia's corrupt bureaucracy, weak rule of law, and the nebulousness of property rights."[6] Nations with the most 2004 foreign direct investment in Russia, in billions, were Cyprus ($10.1), the Netherlands ($8.8), the United States ($4.3), Germany ($2.6), and the United Kingdom ($1.6).

Social, Cultural, Demographic, and Environmental Forces

Social, cultural, demographic, and environmental changes have a major impact upon virtually all products, services, markets, and customers. Small, large, for-profit and nonprofit organizations in all industries are being staggered and challenged by the opportunities and threats arising from changes in social, cultural, demographic, and environmental variables. In every way, the United States is much different today than it was yesterday, and tomorrow promises even greater changes.

The United States is getting older and less Caucasian. The oldest members of America's 76 million baby boomers plan to retire in 2011, and this has lawmakers and younger taxpayers deeply concerned about who will pay their Social Security, Medicare, and Medicaid. Individuals age 65 and older in the United States as a percent of the population will rise to 18.5 percent by 2025.

By the year 2075, the United States will have no racial or ethnic majority. This forecast is aggravating tensions over issues such as immigration and affirmative action. Hawaii, California, and New Mexico already have no majority race or ethnic group.

Population of the world is approaching 7 billion; the United States has less than 300 million people. That leaves billions of people outside the United States who may be interested in the products and services produced through domestic firms. Remaining solely domestic is an increasingly risky strategy, especially as the world population continues to grow to an estimated 8 billion in 2028 and 9 billion in 2054.

Social, cultural, demographic, and environmental trends are shaping the way Americans live, work, produce, and consume. New trends are creating a different type of consumer and, consequently, a need for different products, different services, and different strategies. There are now more American households with people living alone or with unrelated people than there are households consisting of married couples with children. American households are making more and more purchases online. Beer consumption in the United States is growing at only 0.5 percent per year, whereas wine consumption is growing 3.5 percent and distilled spirits consumption is growing at 2.0 percent.[7] Beer is still the most popular alcoholic beverage in the United States, but its market share has dropped from 59.5 percent in its peak year of 1995 to 56.7 percent today. For a wine company such as Gallo, this trend is an opportunity whereas for a firm such as Adolph Coors Brewing, this trend is an external threat.

The U.S. Census Bureau projects that the number of Hispanics will increase to 15 percent of the population by 2021, when they will become a larger minority group than African Americans in America. The trend toward an older America is good news for restaurants, hotels, airlines, cruise lines, tours, resorts, theme parks, luxury products and services, recreational vehicles, home builders, furniture producers, computer manufacturers, travel services, pharmaceutical firms, automakers, and funeral homes. Older Americans are especially interested in healthcare, financial services, travel, crime prevention, and leisure. The world's longest-living people are the Japanese, with Japanese women living to 86.3 years and men living to 80.1 years on average. By 2050, the Census Bureau projects that the number of Americans age 100 and older will increase to over 834,000 from just under 100,000 centenarians in the United States in 2000. Senior citizens are also senior executives at hundreds of American companies. Examples include 89-year-old William Dillard at Dillard's Department Stores; 81-year-old Sumner Redstone, CEO of Viacom; 73-year-old Ellen Gordon, president of Tootsie Roll Industries; 79-year-old Richard Jacobs, CEO of the Cleveland Indians; 78-year-old Leslie Quick, CEO of Quick & Reilly; 85-year-old Ralph Roberts, chairman of Comcast; and 78-year-old Alan Greenspan, chairman of the Federal Reserve. Americans age 65 and over will increase from 12.6 percent of the U.S. population in 2000 to 20.0 percent by the year 2050.

The aging American population affects the strategic orientation of nearly all organizations. Apartment complexes for the elderly, with one meal a day, transportation, and utilities included in the rent, have increased nationwide. Called *lifecare facilities*, these complexes now exceed 2 million. Some well-known companies building these facilities include Avon, Marriott, and Hyatt. Individuals age 65 and older in the United States comprise 13 percent of the total population; Japan's elderly population ratio is 17 percent, and Germany's is 19 percent.

Americans are on the move in a population shift to the South and West (Sunbelt) and away from the Northeast and Midwest (Frostbelt). The Internal Revenue Service provides the Census Bureau with massive computer files of demographic data. By comparing individual address changes from year to year, the Census Bureau publishes extensive information about population shifts across the country. All of these facts represent major opportunities and threats for some companies. For example, Nevada is the fastest-growing state. Arizona, Colorado, and Florida are close behind. States incurring the greatest loss of people are North Dakota, West Virginia, Iowa, Louisiana, and Pennsylvania. This type of information can be essential for successful strategy formulation, including where to locate new plants and distribution centers and where to focus marketing efforts.

Americans are becoming less interested in fitness and exercise. Fitness participants declined annually in the United States by 3.5 percent in the 1990s. Makers of fitness products, such as Nike, Reebok International, and CML Group—which makes NordicTrack—are experiencing declines in sales growth. *American Sports Data* in Hartsdale, New York, reports that "the one American in five who exercises regularly is now outnumbered by three couch potatoes."

Except for terrorism, no greater threat to business and society exists than the voracious, continuous decimation and degradation of our natural environment. The U.S. Clean Air Act went into effect in 1994. The U.S. Clean Water Act went into effect in 1984. A summary of important social, cultural, demographic, and environmental variables that represent opportunities or threats for virtually all organizations is given in Table 3-3.

The U.S.–Mexico Border

Stretching 2,100 miles from the Pacific Ocean to the Gulf of Mexico, this 180-mile-wide strip of land is North America's fastest-growing region. The two nations meet along this border, where there are shantytowns just down the street from luxury residential neighborhoods.

There are now over 1,500 *maquiladoras* (assembly plants) on the Mexican side of the border. However, the *maquiladoras* have been under slow, steady assault from China despite the SARS epidemic there. China replaced Mexico in 2003 as the largest exporter to the United States. China has replaced the United States as the world's hottest destination for foreign direct investment. Because of China, Asia overtook Europe for the first time in 2003 as the continent receiving the most *foreign direct investment (FDI)*. China has cheaper labor than Mexico, and China gives companies more site location incentives than Mexico. An assembly-line worker in Guadalajara, Mexico, earns $2.50 to $3.50 an hour, whereas his counterpart in Guangdong, China, makes 50 cents to 80 cents. China joined the World Trade Organization (WTO) in 2001 and now has thousands of seasoned supplier companies available to firms locating there. China is a ferocious technological competitor, whereas Mexico recently ranked number 47 by the World Economic Forum behind Botswana in technological development. Mexico's corporate income tax rate is 34 percent, double China's rate. Mexico's electricity rates are 40 percent higher than China's. Not all companies are relocating from Mexico to China, but hundreds are, and thousands more are choosing China over Mexico for new operations. The impact of this trend on the economic well-being of both Mexico and the United States is profound.

TABLE 3-3 Key Social, Cultural, Demographic, and Environmental Variables

Childbearing rates	Attitudes toward retirement
Number of special-interest groups	Attitudes toward leisure time
Number of marriages	Attitudes toward product quality
Number of divorces	Attitudes toward customer service
Number of births	Pollution control
Number of deaths	Attitudes toward foreign peoples
Immigration and emigration rates	Energy conservation
Social Security programs	Social programs
Life expectancy rates	Number of churches
Per capita income	Number of church members
Location of retailing, manufacturing, and service businesses	Social responsibility
	Attitudes toward careers
Attitudes toward business	Population changes by race, age, sex, and level of affluence
Lifestyles	
Traffic congestion	Attitudes toward authority
Inner-city environments	Population changes by city, county, state, region, and country
Average disposable income	
Trust in government	Value placed on leisure time
Attitudes toward government	Regional changes in tastes and preferences
Attitudes toward work	
Buying habits	Number of women and minority workers
Ethical concerns	Number of high school and college graduates by geographic area
Attitudes toward saving	
Sex roles	Recycling
Attitudes toward investing	Waste management
Racial equality	Air pollution
Use of birth control	Water pollution
Average level of education	Ozone depletion
Government regulation	Endangered species.

Political, Governmental, and Legal Forces

Federal, state, local, and foreign governments are major regulators, deregulators, subsidizers, employers, and customers of organizations. Political, governmental, and legal factors, therefore, can represent key opportunities or threats for both small and large organizations.

For industries and firms that depend heavily on government contracts or subsidies, political forecasts can be the most important part of an external audit. Changes in patent laws, antitrust legislation, tax rates, and lobbying activities can affect firms significantly. The U.S. Justice Department offers excellent information at its Web site (www.usdoj.gov) on such topics.

In the world of biopolitics, Americans are still deeply divided over issues such as assisted suicide, genetic testing, genetic engineering, cloning, stem-cell research,

NATURAL ENVIRONMENT PERSPECTIVE

Environmentalists Are Concerned About Bush Administration Policies

Politicians and government policies can and do have tremendous impact on business, society, and—yes—the natural environment. The George Bush administration has come under increasing criticism from environmentalists who contend that U.S. government policies are too severely easing environmental standards regarding clean air, water, and land. For example, in 2003, the Environmental Protection Agency (EPA) created loopholes in the Clean Air Act that allow factories to upgrade facilities without installing improved pollution control devices. New rules also restrict jurisdiction of the Clean Water Act. Similarly, the U.S. Interior Department is pushing proposed lease sales that would allow offshore oil and gas development in the Beaufort Sea off Alaska's northern coast and the Arctic National Wildlife Refuge. Also, the Forest Service has refused to grant wilderness protection to 3 million acres of Alaska's Tongass National Forest, which is the largest roadless area in the United States. Logging and clear-cutting can now begin there. The Bush administration also has ended the 25-year-old ban on the sale of land polluted with polychlorinated biphenyls (PCBs). This ban was preventing hundreds of polluted sites from being redeveloped in ways that could spread the toxins and raise public health risks. More than 1,000 pieces of land nationwide are contaminated. The Department of Interior differs sharply with the Yellowstone National Park staff in its assessments of the threats facing that natural treasure. President Bush was the only major head of state who refused to attend 2003's most important environmental meeting—the World Summit on Sustainable Development held in South Africa. The list of such environmentalists' concerns is very extensive and should be a concern to all of us.

Increasingly in our world, what is good for the environment is good for business because a healthy environment is good for business and society. We should strive to protect rather than further harm our air, water, land, and oceans. Our belief that no one owns the ocean, for example, has allowed us seemingly to tolerate no one caring about the ocean's health. Scientists have documented that soot, which is too small to see in the air and arises from factories, power plants, cars, buses, and trucks, causes heart, lung, and other diseases. Cities in the United States with the most soot include Atlanta, Birmingham, Chicago, Cincinnati, Cleveland, Detroit, Indianapolis, Knoxville, Los Angeles, Louisville, Pittsburgh, and St. Louis. Soot levels exceed EPA limits in all these cities.

Facts such as those that follow exemplify our need to do as much as we can to preserve rather than harm the environment, and more than the Bush administration mandates.

1. Oil running off U.S. streets and driveways and ultimately flowing into the oceans is equal to an Exxon *Valdez* oil spill (10.9 million gallons) every eight months.

2. More than 13,000 U.S. beaches are closed or under pollution advisory this year, and this number increased 20 percent from last year.

3. U.S. coastal marshes, which filter pollutants and serve as nurseries for wildlife, are disappearing at a rate of 20,000 acres per year.

4. Global air temperature is expected to warm by 2.5 degrees to 10.4 degrees in the twenty-first century, raising the global sea level by 4 to 35 inches.

Sources: Adapted from Christopher Tulou (Executive Director), *Pew Oceans Commission Summary Report* (May 2003): 1–37. Peter Eisler, "EPA Lifts Ban on Selling PCB Sites," *USA Today* (September 2, 2003): 1A. Also, Traci Watson, "EPA Urges Look at Lower Soot Limits," *USA Today* (September 3, 2002): 3A; John Carey, "How Green Is the White House?" *BusinessWeek* (November 3, 2003): 96–98.

and abortion. Americans are also divided regarding feelings toward the natural environment policies and practices of the Bush administration—as indicated in the "Natural Environment Perspective." Political issues have great ramifications for companies in many industries, ranging from pharmaceuticals to computers.

The increasing global interdependence among economies, markets, governments, and organizations makes it imperative that firms consider the possible impact of political variables on the formulation and implementation of competitive strategies.

For example, the United States, Japan, and Europe are critical of the Chinese government for its fixed exchange rate, which analysts contend takes jobs from other countries and artificially cuts the cost of China's exports by significantly undervaluing its currency. A rise in the value of China's currency would make Chinese-made goods more expensive abroad. China's currency is called the yuan, which is fixed at 8.30 yuan to $1.00.

[handwritten margin note: China's exchange rate]

In Europe, many large multinational firms such as John Deere, Polo Ralph Lauren, Gillette, Cargill, and General Mills are moving their headquarters from France, Netherlands, and Germany to Switzerland and Ireland to avoid costs associated with *tax harmonization*—a term that refers to the EU's effort to end competitive tax breaks among member countries. Although the EU strives to standardize tax breaks, member countries vigorously defend their right to politically and legally set their own tax rates. Behind Switzerland as the most attractive European location for corporations, Ireland keeps its corporate tax rates low, which is why Ingersoll-Rand recently moved much of its operations there. About 650 U.S. companies already have operations in Switzerland.

Both France and Belgium voted "no" to the European Union's proposed constitution in mid 2005, raising concerns about the union itself. The two founding members of the EU heightened concern over the deep political conflicts within the 25-nation union. The euro currency fell further against the dollar. Nine countries, including Germany, have approved the charter, but it requires unanimous agreement among all member countries to go into effect. Votes in 14 more countries are planned for late 2005 and 2006. Political and strategic ramifications for companies doing business in Europe are substantial.

A world market has emerged from what previously was a multitude of distinct national markets, and the climate for international business today is much more favorable than yesterday. Mass communication and high technology are creating similar patterns of consumption in diverse cultures worldwide. This means that many companies may find it difficult to survive by relying solely on domestic markets.

> It is no exaggeration that in an industry that is, or is rapidly becoming, global, the riskiest possible posture is to remain a domestic competitor. The domestic competitor will watch as more aggressive companies use this growth to capture economies of scale and learning. The domestic competitor will then be faced with an attack on domestic markets using different (and possibly superior) technology, product design, manufacturing, marketing approaches, and economies of scale. A few examples suggest how extensive the phenomenon of world markets has already become. Hewlett-Packard's manufacturing chain reaches halfway around the globe, from well-paid, skilled engineers in California to low-wage assembly workers in Malaysia. General Electric has survived as a manufacturer of inexpensive audio products by centralizing its world production in Singapore.[8]

Local, state, and federal laws; regulatory agencies; and special-interest groups can have a major impact on the strategies of small, large, for-profit, and nonprofit organizations. Many companies have altered or abandoned strategies in the past because of political or governmental actions. A summary of political, governmental, and legal variables that can represent key opportunities or threats to organizations is provided in Table 3-4.

TABLE 3-4 Some Political, Governmental, and Legal Variables

Government regulations or deregulations	Sino-American relationships
Changes in tax laws	Russian-American relationships
Special tariffs	European-American relationships
Political action committees	African-American relationships
Voter participation rates	Import–export regulations
Number, severity, and location of government protests	Government fiscal and monetary policy changes
Number of patents	Political conditions in foreign countries
Changes in patent laws	Special local, state, and federal laws
Environmental protection laws	Lobbying activities
Level of defense expenditures	Size of government budgets
Legislation on equal employment	World oil, currency, and labor markets
Level of government subsidies	Location and severity of terrorist activities
Antitrust legislation	Local, state, and national elections

Technological Forces

Revolutionary technological changes and discoveries are having a dramatic impact on organizations. Superconductivity advancements alone, which increase the power of electrical products by lowering resistance to current, are revolutionizing business operations, especially in the transportation, utility, healthcare, electrical, and computer industries.

The *Internet* is acting as a national and global economic engine that is spurring productivity, a critical factor in a country's ability to improve living standards; and it is saving companies billions of dollars in distribution and transaction costs from direct sales to self-service systems.

The Internet is changing the very nature of opportunities and threats by altering the life cycles of products, increasing the speed of distribution, creating new products and services, erasing limitations of traditional geographic markets, and changing the historical trade-off between production standardization and flexibility. The Internet is altering economies of scale, changing entry barriers, and redefining the relationship between industries and various suppliers, creditors, customers, and competitors.

To effectively capitalize on e-commerce, a number of organizations are establishing two new positions in their firms: *chief information officer (CIO)* and *chief technology officer (CTO)*. This trend reflects the growing importance of *information technology (IT)* in strategic management. A CIO and CTO work together to ensure that information needed to formulate, implement, and evaluate strategies is available where and when it is needed. These individuals are responsible for developing, maintaining, and updating a company's information database. The CIO is more a manager, managing the overall external-audit process; the CTO is more a technician, focusing on technical issues such as data acquisition, data processing, decision-support systems, and software and hardware acquisition.

Technological forces represent major opportunities and threats that must be considered in formulating strategies. Technological advancements can dramatically affect organizations' products, services, markets, suppliers, distributors, competitors, customers, manufacturing processes, marketing practices, and competitive position.

STU
Threat

Technological advancements can create new markets, result in a proliferation of new and improved products, change the relative competitive cost positions in an industry, and render existing products and services obsolete. Technological changes can reduce or eliminate cost barriers between businesses, create shorter production runs, create shortages in technical skills, and result in changing values and expectations of employees, managers, and customers. Technological advancements can create new competitive advantages that are more powerful than existing advantages. No company or industry today is insulated against emerging technological developments. In high-tech industries, identification and evaluation of key technological opportunities and threats can be the most important part of the external strategic-management audit.

Organizations that traditionally have limited technology expenditures to what they can fund after meeting marketing and financial requirements urgently need a reversal in thinking. The pace of technological change is increasing and literally wiping out businesses every day. An emerging consensus holds that technology management is one of the key responsibilities of strategists. Firms should pursue strategies that take advantage of technological opportunities to achieve sustainable, competitive advantages in the marketplace.

> Technology-based issues will underlie nearly every important decision that strategists make. Crucial to those decisions will be the ability to approach technology planning analytically and strategically. . . . technology can be planned and managed using formal techniques similar to those used in business and capital investment planning. An effective technology strategy is built on a penetrating analysis of technology opportunities and threats, and an assessment of the relative importance of these factors to overall corporate strategy.[9]

In practice, critical decisions about technology too often are delegated to lower organizational levels or are made without an understanding of their strategic implications. Many strategists spend countless hours determining market share, positioning products in terms of features and price, forecasting sales and market size, and monitoring distributors; yet too often, technology does not receive the same respect.

Varying levels of threats

Not all sectors of the economy are affected equally by technological developments. The communications, electronics, aeronautics, and pharmaceutical industries are much more volatile than the textile, forestry, and metals industries. For strategists in industries affected by rapid technological change, identifying and evaluating technological opportunities and threats can represent the most important part of an external audit.

For example, in the office supply industry, business customers find that purchasing supplies over the Internet is more convenient than shopping in a store. Office Depot was the first office supply company to establish a Web site for this purpose and remains the largest Internet office supply retailer, with close to $1 billion in sales. Staples, Inc., has recently also entered the Internet office supply business with its staples.com Web site, but it has yet to make a profit on these operations, although revenue from the site is growing dramatically.

VISIT THE NET

Provides information regarding the importance of gathering information about competitors. This Web site offers audio answers to key questions about intelligence systems. (www.fuld.com)

Competitive Forces

The top five U.S. competitors in four different industries are identified in Table 3-5. An important part of an external audit is identifying rival firms and determining their strengths, weaknesses, capabilities, opportunities, threats, objectives, and strategies.

TABLE 3-5   The Top Five U.S. Competitors in Four Different Industries in 2004

	2004 SALES (IN MILLIONS)	% CHANGE FROM 2003	2004 PROFITS (IN MILLIONS)	% CHANGE FROM 2003
Beverages				
PepsiCo	29,261	+8	4,174	+17
Coca-Cola Enterprises	21,962	+4	4,847	+12
Anheuser-Busch	14,934	+6	2,240	+8
Pepsi Bottling Group	10,906	+6	457	+8
Molson Brewing	4,305	+8	196	+13
Pharmaceuticals				
Pfizer	52,516	+17	11,332	+596
Johnson & Johnson	47,348	+13	8,509	+18
Merck	22,938	+2	5,813	−12
Abbott Laboratories	19,680	+14	3,175	+27
Bristol-Myers Squibb	19,380	+ 4	2,378	−23
Machinery				
Caterpillar	30,251	+33	2,035	+85
Deere	20,629	+27	1,458	+95
Illinois Tool Works	11,731	+17	1,339	+29
Paccar	11,396	+39	906	+72
Ingersoll-Rand	9,393	+14	829	+56
Computers				
IBM	96,293	+8	8,448	+11
Hewlett-Packard	81,845	+10	3,504	+27
Dell	49,205	+19	3,043	+15
Sun Microsystems	11,230	0	−106	0
Apple Computer	9,763	+45	508	+271

Source: Adapted from *BusinessWeek,* April 4, 2005, pp. 113–148.

Collecting and evaluating information on competitors is essential for successful strategy formulation. Identifying major competitors is not always easy because many firms have divisions that compete in different industries. Most multidivisional firms generally do not provide sales and profit information on a divisional basis for competitive reasons. Also, privately held firms do not publish any financial or marketing information.

However, many businesses use the Internet to obtain most of their information on competitors. The Internet is fast, thorough, accurate, and increasingly indispensable in this regard. Addressing questions about competitors such as those presented in Table 3-6 is important in performing an external audit.

Competition in virtually all industries can be described as intense—and sometimes as cutthroat. For example, when Italian car maker Fiat Auto recently had financial troubles Ford Motor boosted advertising and marketing spending 10 to 20 percent in Italy, even though Ford was slashing expenses elsewhere. Renault SA and Peugeot SA, other rivals to Fiat, also boosted consumer incentives in the Italian market. Fiat's market share in Italy has recently dropped from 40 percent to 27 percent. If a firm detects weakness in a competitor, no mercy at all is shown in capitalizing on its problems.

TABLE 3-6   Key Questions About Competitors

1. What are the major competitors' strengths?
2. What are the major competitors' weaknesses?
3. What are the major competitors' objectives and strategies?
4. How will the major competitors most likely respond to current economic, social, cultural, demographic, environmental, political, governmental, legal, technological, and competitive trends affecting our industry?
5. How vulnerable are the major competitors to our alternative company strategies?
6. How vulnerable are our alternative strategies to successful counterattack by our major competitors?
7. How are our products or services positioned relative to major competitors?
8. To what extent are new firms entering and old firms leaving this industry?
9. What key factors have resulted in our present competitive position in this industry?
10. How have the sales and profit rankings of major competitors in the industry changed over recent years? Why have these rankings changed that way?
11. What is the nature of supplier and distributor relationships in this industry?
12. To what extent could substitute products or services be a threat to competitors in this industry?

Seven characteristics describe the most competitive companies:

1. Market share matters; the 90th share point isn't as important as the 91st, and nothing is more dangerous than falling to 89.
2. Understand and remember precisely what business you are in.
3. Whether it's broke or not, fix it—make it better; not just products, but the whole company, if necessary.
4. Innovate or evaporate; particularly in technology-driven businesses, nothing quite recedes like success.
5. Acquisition is essential to growth; the most successful purchases are in niches that add a technology or a related market.
6. People make a difference; tired of hearing it? Too bad.
7. There is no substitute for quality and no greater threat than failing to be cost-competitive on a global basis.

These are complementary concepts, not mutually exclusive ones.[10]

Competitive Intelligence Programs

What is competitive intelligence? *Competitive intelligence (CI)*, as formally defined by the Society of Competitive Intelligence Professionals (SCIP), is a systematic and ethical process for gathering and analyzing information about the competition's activities and general business trends to further a business's own goals (SCIP Web site).

Good competitive intelligence in business, as in the military, is one of the keys to success. The more information and knowledge a firm can obtain about its competitors, the more likely it is that it can formulate and implement effective strategies. Major competitors' weaknesses can represent external opportunities; major competitors' strengths may represent key threats.

According to *BusinessWeek,* there are more than 5,000 corporate spies now actively engaged in intelligence activities, and 9 out of 10 large companies have employees dedicated solely to gathering competitive intelligence.[11] The article contends that many large U.S. companies spend more than $1 million annually tracking their competitors. Evidence suggests that the benefits of corporate spying include increased revenues, lower costs, and better decision making.

Unfortunately, the majority of U.S. executives grew up in times when U.S. firms dominated foreign competitors so much that gathering competitive intelligence did not seem worth the effort. Too many of these executives still cling to these attitudes—to the detriment of their organizations today. Even most MBA programs do not offer a course in competitive and business intelligence, thus reinforcing this attitude. As a consequence, three strong misperceptions about business intelligence prevail among U.S. executives today:

1. Running an intelligence program requires lots of people, computers, and other resources.
2. Collecting intelligence about competitors violates antitrust laws; business intelligence equals espionage.
3. Intelligence gathering is an unethical business practice.[12]

All three of these perceptions are totally misguided. Any discussions with a competitor about price, market, or geography intentions could violate antitrust statutes, but this fact must not lure a firm into underestimating the need for and benefits of systematically collecting information about competitors for the purpose of enhancing a firm's effectiveness. The Internet has become an excellent medium for gathering competitive intelligence. Information gathering from employees, managers, suppliers, distributors, customers, creditors, and consultants also can make the difference between having superior or just average intelligence and overall competitiveness.

Firms need an effective competitive intelligence (CI) program. The three basic missions of a CI program are (1) to provide a general understanding of an industry and its competitors, (2) to identify areas in which competitors are vulnerable and to assess the impact strategic actions would have on competitors, and (3) to identify potential moves that a competitor might make that would endanger a firm's position in the market.[13] Competitive information is equally applicable for strategy formulation, implementation, and evaluation decisions. An effective CI program allows all areas of a firm to access consistent and verifiable information in making decisions. All members of an organization—from the chief executive officer to custodians—are valuable intelligence agents and should feel themselves to be a part of the CI process. Special characteristics of a successful CI program include flexibility, usefulness, timeliness, and cross-functional cooperation.

The increasing emphasis on *competitive analysis* in the United States is evidenced by corporations putting this function on their organizational charts under job titles such as Director of Competitive Analysis, Competitive Strategy Manager, Director of Information Services, or Associate Director of Competitive Assessment. The responsibilities of a *director of competitive analysis* include planning, collecting data, analyzing data, facilitating the process of gathering and analyzing data, disseminating intelligence on a timely basis, researching special issues, and recognizing what information is important and who needs to know. Competitive intelligence is not corporate espionage because 95 percent of the information a company needs to make strategic decisions is available and accessible to the public. Sources of competitive information include trade journals, want ads, newspaper articles, and government filings, as well as customers, suppliers, distributors, competitors themselves, and the Internet.

VISIT THE NET

Describes the nature and role of strategic planning in a firm.
(www.nonprofits.org/ npofaq/03/22.html)

Unethical tactics such as bribery, wiretapping, and computer break-ins should never be used to obtain information. Marriott and Motorola—two U.S. companies that do a particularly good job of gathering competitive intelligence—agree that all the information you could wish for can be collected without resorting to unethical tactics. They keep their intelligence staffs small, usually under five people, and spend less than $200,000 per year on gathering competitive intelligence.

Unilever recently sued Procter & Gamble (P&G) over that company's corporate-espionage activities to obtain the secrets of its Unilever hair-care business. After spending $3 million to establish a team to find out about competitors in the domestic hair-care industry, P&G allegedly took roughly 80 documents from garbage bins outside Unilever's Chicago offices. P&G produces Pantene and Head & Shoulders shampoos, while Unilver has hair-care brands such as ThermaSilk, Suave, Salon Selectives, and Finesse. Similarly, Oracle Corp. recently admitted that detectives it hired paid janitors to go through Microsoft Corp.'s garbage, looking for evidence to use in court.

An interesting aspect of any competitive analysis discussion is whether strategies themselves should be secret or open within firms. The Chinese warrior Sun Tzu and military leaders today strive to keep strategies secret, as war is based on deception. However, for a business organization, secrecy may not be best. Keeping strategies secret from employees and stakeholders at large could severely inhibit employee and stakeholder communication, understanding, and commitment and also forgo valuable input that these persons could have regarding formulation and/or implementation of that strategy. Thus strategists in a particular firm must decide for themselves whether the risk of rival firms easily knowing and exploiting a firm's strategies is worth the benefit of improved employee and stakeholder motivation and input. Most executives agree that some strategic information should remain confidential to top managers, and that steps should be taken to ensure that such information is not disseminated beyond the inner circle. For a firm that you may own or manage, would you advocate openness or secrecy in regard to strategies being formulated and implemented?

VISIT THE NET

Gives 30+ pages of excellent detail on "Developing a Business Strategy."
(www.planware.org/strategy.htm)

Cooperation Among Competitors

Strategies that stress cooperation among competitors are being used more. For example, Lockheed teamed up with British Aerospace PLC to compete against Boeing Company to develop the next-generation U.S. fighter jet. Lockheed's cooperative strategy with a profitable partner in the Airbus Industrie consortium encourages broader Lockheed–European collaboration as Europe's defense industry consolidates. The British firm offers Lockheed special expertise in the areas of short takeoff and vertical landing technologies, systems integration, and low-cost design and manufacturing.

Cooperative agreements between competitors are even becoming popular. For example, Boeing and Lockheed Martin formed a joint venture in 2005 to provide the U.S. government with lower-cost rockets to carry military, spy and civilian research satellites into space. This joint venture ended years of bitter rivalry and litigation between the two firms' money-losing government-rocket businesses. Recall that Boeing acknowledged in 2003 that it had stole and improperly used boxes of Lockheed proprietary documents to win a rocket competition five years earlier. Now the two rival firms cooperate more than compete in the rocket business—Boeing with Delta IV and Lockheed with Atlas V model rockets. The U.S. military had long desired a merger of these operations so it could save money by removing duplicate functions and operations. For collaboration between competitors to succeed, both firms must contribute something distinctive, such as technology, distribution, basic research, or manufacturing capacity. But a major risk is that unintended transfers of important skills or technology may occur at organizational levels below where the deal was signed.[14] Information not covered in the formal agreement often gets traded in the day-to-day interactions and dealings of engineers, marketers, and product developers. Firms often give away too much information to rival firms when operating under cooperative agreements! Tighter formal agreements are needed.

Fierce competitors America Online, Microsoft, and Yahoo! have joined forces to form a united front against spam. Spam costs U.S. companies nearly $10 billion annually and now accounts for one-half of all e-mail sent. "The Internet quality of life has deteriorated due to out-of-control spammers," says Nicholas Graham at AOL. Spammers, like hackers, change tactics frequently and are growing in numbers because it is a cheap way to reach millions of consumers. Worldwide spam messages sent daily grew from 4.0 to 8.8 billion from 2001 to 2004.[15] The three large competing ISP firms are jointly developing software and guidelines to combat spam, which bogs down Internet traffic worldwide and steals time from almost all Internet users.

Perhaps the best example of rival firms in an industry forming alliances to compete against each other is the airline industry. Today there are three major alliances. The Star Alliance has 16 airlines such as Air Canada, Mexicana, Spanair, United, and Varig, while the OneWorld Alliance has 8 airlines such as American, British Air, and LanChile, and finally, SkyTeam Alliance has 6 airlines such as Air France, Delta, and Korean Air. KLM is set to join SkyTeam soon, Swiss International is scheduled to join OneWorld, and USAirways is scheduled to join Star Alliance. Firms are moving to compete as groups within alliances more and more as it becomes increasingly difficult to survive alone in some industries.

alliances necessary for survival of firms

The idea of joining forces with a competitor is not easily accepted by Americans, who often view cooperation and partnerships with skepticism and suspicion. Indeed, joint ventures and cooperative arrangements among competitors demand a certain amount of trust if companies are to combat paranoia about whether one firm will injure the other. However, multinational firms are becoming more globally cooperative, and increasing numbers of domestic firms are joining forces with competitive foreign firms to reap mutual benefits. Kathryn Harrigan at Columbia University says, "Within a decade, most companies will be members of teams that compete against each other." Northrop Grumman is planning to partner with Airbus parent EADS in Europe to battle Boeing for a Pentagon contract for aerial-refueling planes. These talks are ongoing at this point in time. EADS is a French/German company but is perceived widely as French because Airbus planes are assembled in France. Northrop is based in Los Angeles.

U.S. companies often enter alliances primarily to avoid investments, being more interested in reducing the costs and risks of entering new businesses or markets than in acquiring new skills. In contrast, *learning from the partner* is a major reason why Asian and European firms enter into cooperative agreements. U.S. firms, too, should place learning high on the list of reasons to be cooperative with competitors. U.S. companies often form alliances with Asian firms to gain an understanding of their manufacturing excellence, but Asian competence in this area is not easily transferable. Manufacturing excellence is a complex system that includes employee training and involvement, integration with suppliers, statistical process controls, value engineering, and design. In contrast, U.S. know-how in technology and related areas more easily can be imitated. U.S. firms thus need to be careful not to give away more intelligence than they receive in cooperative agreements with rival Asian firms.

benefits of alliances

U.S. knowledge easier to mimic than Asian

Market Commonality and Resource Similarity

By definition, competitors are firms that offer similar products and services in the same market. Markets can be geographic or product areas or segments. For example, in the insurance industry the markets are broken down into commercial/consumer, health/life, and Europe/Asia. Researchers use the terms *market commonality* and *resource similarity* to study rivalry among competitors. *Market commonality* can be defined as the number and significance of markets that a firm competes in with rivals.[16] *Resource similarity* is the extent to which the type and amount of a firm's internal resources are comparable to a rival.[17] One way to analyze competitiveness between two or among several firms is to investigate market commonality and resource similarity issues while looking for areas of potential competitive advantage along each firm's value chain.

Competitive Analysis: Porter's Five-Forces Model

As illustrated in Figure 3-3, *Porter's Five-Forces Model* of competitive analysis is a widely used approach for developing strategies in many industries. The intensity of competition among firms varies widely across industries. Table 3-7 reveals the average return on equity for firms in 24 different industries in 2003 and 2004. Note the substantial change from year to year in these returns. Intensity of competition is highest in lower-return industries. The collective impact of competitive forces is so brutal in some industries that the market is clearly "unattractive" from a profit-making standpoint. Rivalry among existing firms is severe, new rivals can enter the industry with relative ease, and both suppliers and customers can exercise considerable bargaining leverage. Note in Table 3-7 that the average 2004 return on equity among firms in the hotel industry was 14.7 percent. According to Porter, the nature of competitiveness in a given industry can be viewed as a composite of five forces:

1. Rivalry among competing firms
2. Potential entry of new competitors
3. Potential development of substitute products
4. Bargaining power of suppliers
5. Bargaining power of consumers

FIGURE 3-3

The Five-Forces Model of Competition

TABLE 3-7 Intensity of Competition Among Firms in Different Industries—2003 and 2004 Results Provided

RANK	INDUSTRY	AVERAGE RETURN ON EQUITY	
		2003	2004
1	Materials	5.1	14.1
2	Semiconductors and Equipment	5.3	14.6
3	Real Estate	6.8	3.6
4	Technology Hardware	7.6	14.3
5	Transportation	8.8	4.1
6	Automobiles and Components	9.0	12.5
7	Media	9.0	−1.6
8	Utilities	9.1	11.6
9	Telecommunication Services	10.0	8.1
10	Hotels/Restaurants/Leisure	10.5	14.7
11	Insurance	11.5	12.5
12	Software and Services	12.6	16.6
13	Capital Goods	14.5	15.2
14	Retailing	14.6	15.9
15	Pharmaceuticals and Biotechnology	15.4	17.4
16	Diversified Financials	16.6	13.4
17	Commercial Services and Supplies	16.7	15.7
18	Food and Staples Retailing	17.9	17.5
19	Energy	18.3	20.8
20	Banks	18.3	13.6
21	Consumer Durables and Apparel	18.3	18.0
22	Health Care Equipment/Services	19.0	13.3
23	Food/Beverage/Tobacco	20.3	27.9
24	Household and Personal Products	36.6	40.5

Source: Adapted from *BusinessWeek,* February 23, 2004, pp. 60–84. Also, *Business Week,* April 4, 2005, pp. 113–139.

The following three steps for using Porter's Five-Forces Model can reveal whether competition in a given industry is such that the firm can make an acceptable profit:

1. Identify key aspects or elements of each competitive force that impact the firm.
2. Evaluate how strong and important each element is for the firm.
3. Decide whether the collective strength of the elements is worth the firm entering or staying in the industry.

Rivalry Among Competing Firms

Rivalry among competing firms is usually the most powerful of the five competitive forces. The strategies pursued by one firm can be successful only to the extent that they provide competitive advantage over the strategies pursued by rival firms. Changes in strategy by one firm may be met with retaliatory countermoves, such as lowering prices, enhancing quality, adding features, providing services, extending warranties, and increasing advertising.

VISIT THE NET

Gives good information about why employees may resist change.
(http://www.mindtools.com/)

In the Internet world, competitiveness is fierce. Amazon.com watches in dismay as customers use its site's easy-to-use format, in-depth reviews, expert recommendations—and then bypass the cash register as they click their way over to deep-discounted sites such as Buy.com to make their purchases. Buy.com's CEO says, "The Internet is going to shrink retailers' margins to the point where they will not survive." Price-comparison Web sites allow consumers to efficiently find the lowest-priced seller on the Internet. Kate Delhagen of Forrester Research says, "If you're a consumer and you're thinking about any kind of researched purchase, you're leaving thousands of dollars on the table if you don't at least look online."[18] The costs of setting up a great e-commerce site are nothing compared to the cost of acquiring real estate for building retail stores—or even printing and mailing catalogs.

Free-flowing information on the Internet is driving down prices and inflation worldwide. The Internet, coupled with the common currency in Europe, enables consumers to easily make price comparisons across countries. Just for a moment, consider the implications for car dealers who used to know everything about a new car's pricing, while you, the consumer, knew very little. You could bargain, but being in the dark, you rarely could win. Now you can go to Web sites such as CarPoint.com or Edmunds.com and know more about new car prices than the car salesperson, and you can even shop online in a few hours at every dealership within 500 miles to find the best price and terms. So you, the consumer, can win. This is true in many, if not most, business-to-consumer and business-to-business sales transactions today.

The intensity of rivalry among competing firms tends to increase as the number of competitors increases, as competitors become more equal in size and capability, as demand for the industry's products declines, and as price cutting becomes common. Rivalry also increases when consumers can switch brands easily; when barriers to leaving the market are high; when fixed costs are high; when the product is perishable; when consumer demand is growing slowly or declines such that rivals have excess capacity and/or inventory; when the products being sold are commodities (not easily differentiated such as gasoline); when rival firms are diverse in strategies, origins, and culture; and when mergers and acquisitions are common in the industry. As rivalry among competing firms intensifies, industry profits decline, in some cases to the point where an industry becomes inherently unattractive.

Potential Entry of New Competitors

Whenever new firms can easily enter a particular industry, the intensity of competitiveness among firms increases. Barriers to entry, however, can include the need to gain economies of scale quickly, the need to gain technology and specialized know-how, the lack of experience, strong customer loyalty, strong brand preferences, large capital requirements, lack of adequate distribution channels, government regulatory policies, tariffs, lack of access to raw materials, possession of patents, undesirable locations, counterattack by entrenched firms, and potential saturation of the market.

Despite numerous barriers to entry, new firms sometimes enter industries with higher-quality products, lower prices, and substantial marketing resources. The strategist's job, therefore, is to identify potential new firms entering the market, to monitor the new rival firms' strategies, to counterattack as needed, and to capitalize on existing strengths and opportunities. When the threat of new firms entering the market is strong, incumbent firms generally fortify their positions and take actions to deter new entrants, such as lowering prices, extending warranties, adding features, or offering financing specials. Recall in 2005 that General Motors was successful offering its "employee discounts" to all customers purchasing new vehicles.

Potential Development of Substitute Products

In many industries, firms are in close competition with producers of substitute products in other industries. Examples are plastic container producers competing with glass, paperboard, and aluminum can producers, and acetaminophen manufacturers competing with other manufacturers of pain and headache remedies. The presence of substitute products puts a ceiling on the price that can be charged before consumers will switch to the substitute product. Price ceilings equate to profit ceilings and more *effects* intense competition among rivals. Producers of eyeglasses and contact lenses, for example, face increasing competitive pressures from laser eye surgery. Producers of sugar face similar pressures from artificial sweetners. Newspapers and magazines face substitute-product competitive pressures from the Internet and 24-hour cable television. The magnitude of competitive pressure derived from development of substitute products is generally evidenced by rivals' plans for expanding production capacity, as well as by their sales and profit growth numbers.

Competitive pressures arising from substitute products increase as the relative price of substitute products declines and as consumers' switching costs decrease. The competitive strength of substitute products is best measured by the inroads into the market share those products obtain, as well as those firms' plans for increased capacity and market penetration.

Bargaining Power of Suppliers

The bargaining power of suppliers affects the intensity of competition in an industry, especially when there is a large number of suppliers, when there are only a few good substitute raw materials, or when the cost of switching raw materials is especially costly. It is often in the best interest of both suppliers and producers to assist each other with reasonable prices, improved quality, development of new services, just-in-time deliveries, and reduced inventory costs, thus enhancing long-term profitability for all concerned.

Firms may pursue a backward integration strategy to gain control or ownership of suppliers. This strategy is especially effective when suppliers are unreliable, too costly, or not capable of meeting a firm's needs on a consistent basis. Firms generally can negotiate more favorable terms with suppliers when backward integration is a commonly used strategy among rival firms in an industry.

However, in many industries it is more economical to use outside suppliers of component parts than to self-manufacture the items. This is true, for example, in the outdoor power equipment industry where producers of lawn mowers, rotary tillers, leaf blowers, and edgers such as Murray generally obtain their small engines from outside manufacturers such as Briggs & Stratton who specialize in such engines and have huge economies of scale.

In more and more industries, sellers are forging strategic partnerships with select suppliers in efforts to (1) reduce inventory and logistics costs (e.g., through just-in-time deliveries); (2) speed the availability of next-generation components; (3) enhance the quality of the parts and components being supplied and reduce defect rates; and (4) squeeze out important cost savings for both themselves and their suppliers.[19]

Bargaining Power of Consumers

When customers are concentrated or large or buy in volume, their bargaining power represents a major force affecting the intensity of competition in an industry. Rival firms may offer extended warranties or special services to gain customer loyalty whenever the bargaining power of consumers is substantial. Bargaining power of consumers also is higher when the products being purchased are standard or undifferentiated. When this is the case, consumers often can negotiate selling price, warranty coverage, and accessory packages to a greater extent.

The bargaining power of consumers can be the most important force impacting competitive advantage. Consumers gain increasing bargaining power under the following circumstances:

1. If they can inexpensively switch to competing brands or substitutes.
2. If they are particularly important to the seller.
3. If sellers are struggling in the face of falling consumer demand.
4. If they are informed about sellers' products, prices, and costs.
5. If they have discretion in whether and when they purchase the product.[20]

Sources of External Information

A wealth of strategic information is available to organizations from both published and unpublished sources. Unpublished sources include customer surveys, market research, speeches at professional and shareholders' meetings, television programs, interviews, and conversations with stakeholders. Published sources of strategic information include periodicals, journals, reports, government documents, abstracts, books, directories, newspapers, and manuals. The Internet has made it easier for firms to gather, assimilate, and evaluate information.

The Internet offers consumers and businesses a widening range of services and information resources from all over the world. Interactive services offer users not only access to information worldwide but also the ability to communicate with the person or company that created the information. Historical barriers to personal and business success—time zones and diverse cultures—are being eliminated. The Internet has become as important to our society as television and newspapers.

VISIT THE NET

Gives an extensive slide show presentation about strategic management, from beginning to the end of the process.
(www.csuchico.edu/mgmt/strategy/)

Forecasting Tools and Techniques

Forecasts are educated assumptions about future trends and events. Forecasting is a complex activity because of factors such as technological innovation, cultural changes, new products, improved services, stronger competitors, shifts in government priorities, changing social values, unstable economic conditions, and unforeseen events. Managers often must rely upon published forecasts to effectively identify key external opportunities and threats.

A sense of the future permeates all action and underlies every decision a person makes. People eat expecting to be satisfied and nourished—in the future. People sleep assuming that in the future they will feel rested. They invest energy, money, and time because they believe their efforts will be rewarded in the future. They build highways assuming that automobiles and trucks will need them in the future. Parents educate children on the basis of forecasts that they will need certain skills, attitudes, and knowledge when they grow up. The truth is we all make implicit forecasts throughout our daily lives. The question, therefore, is not whether we should forecast but rather how we can best forecast to enable us to move beyond our ordinarily unarticulated assumptions about the future. Can we obtain information and then make educated assumptions (forecasts) to better guide our current decisions to achieve a more desirable future state of affairs? We should go into the future with our eyes and our minds open, rather than stumble into the future with our eyes closed.[21]

Many publications and sources on the Internet forecast external variables. Several published examples include *Industry Week's* "Trends and Forecasts," *BusinessWeek's* "Investment Outlook," and Standard & Poor's *Industry Survey*. The reputation and continued success of these publications depend partly on accurate forecasts, so published sources of information can offer excellent projections. An especially good Web site for industry forecasts is finance.yahoo.com. Just insert a firm's stock symbol and go from there.

Sometimes organizations must develop their own projections. Most organizations forecast (project) their own revenues and profits annually. Organizations sometimes forecast market share or customer loyalty in local areas. Because forecasting is so important in strategic management and because the ability to forecast (in contrast to the ability to use a forecast) is essential, selected forecasting tools are examined further here.

Forecasting tools can be broadly categorized into two groups: quantitative techniques and qualitative techniques. Quantitative forecasts are most appropriate when historical data are available and when the relationships among key variables are expected to remain the same in the future. *Linear regression,* for example, is based on the assumption that the future will be just like the past—which, of course, it never is. As historical relationships become less stable, quantitative forecasts become less accurate.

No forecast is perfect, and some forecasts are even wildly inaccurate. This fact accents the need for strategists to devote sufficient time and effort to study the underlying bases for published forecasts and to develop internal forecasts of their own. Key external opportunities and threats can be effectively identified only through good forecasts. Accurate forecasts can provide major competitive advantages for organizations. Forecasts are vital to the strategic-management process and to the success of organizations.

Making Assumptions

Planning would be impossible without assumptions. McConkey defines assumptions as the "best present estimates of the impact of major external factors, over which the manager has little if any control, but which may exert a significant impact on performance or the ability to achieve desired results."[22] Strategists are faced with countless variables and imponderables that can be neither controlled nor predicted with 100 percent accuracy.

By identifying future occurrences that could have a major effect on the firm and by making reasonable assumptions about those factors, strategists can carry the strategic-management process forward. Assumptions are needed only for future trends and events that are most likely to have a significant effect on the company's business. Based on the best information at the time, assumptions serve as checkpoints on the validity of strategies. If future occurrences deviate significantly from assumptions, strategists know that corrective actions may be needed. Without reasonable assumptions, the strategy-formulation process could not proceed effectively. Firms that have the best information generally make the most accurate assumptions, which can lead to major competitive advantages.

The Global Challenge

Foreign competitors are battering U.S. firms in many industries. In its simplest sense, the international challenge faced by U.S. business is twofold: (1) how to gain and maintain exports to other nations and (2) how to defend domestic markets against imported goods. Few companies can afford to ignore the presence of international competition. Firms that seem insulated and comfortable today may be vulnerable tomorrow; for example, foreign banks do not yet compete or operate in most of the United States but this too is changing.

General Motors announced in mid-2005 that it will eliminate 25,000 manufacturing jobs in the United States by 2008 and close plants as part of a strategy to revive its North American business. With this retrenchment strategy, GM plans to save $2.5 billion. In just the last 12 months, GM's U.S. market share fell from 27 percent to 25.4 percent, much of that loss going to Toyota and Nissan. GM closed plants in Linden, New Jersey, in Baltimore, Maryland, and in Lansing, Michigan, just prior to the announcement of many more plants to come.

America's economy is becoming much less American. A world economy and monetary system are emerging. Corporations in every corner of the globe are taking advantage of the opportunity to share in the benefits of worldwide economic development. Markets are shifting rapidly and in many cases converging in tastes, trends, and prices. Innovative transport systems are accelerating the transfer of technology. Shifts in the nature and location of production systems, especially to China and India, are reducing the response time to changing market conditions.

More and more countries around the world are welcoming foreign investment and capital. As a result, labor markets have steadily become more international. East Asian countries have become market leaders in labor-intensive industries, Brazil offers abundant natural resources and rapidly developing markets, and Germany offers skilled labor and technology. The drive to improve the efficiency of global business operations is leading to greater functional specialization. This is not limited to a search for the familiar low-cost labor in Latin America or Asia. Other considerations include the cost of energy, availability of resources, inflation rates, existing tax rates, and the nature of trade regulations.

Multinational Corporations

Multinational corporations (MNCs) face unique and diverse risks, such as expropriation of assets, currency losses through exchange rate fluctuations, unfavorable foreign court interpretations of contracts and agreements, social/political disturbances, import/export restrictions, tariffs, and trade barriers. Strategists in MNCs are often confronted with the need to be globally competitive and nationally responsive at the same time. With the rise in world commerce, government and regulatory bodies are more closely monitoring foreign business practices. The United States Foreign Corrupt Practices Act, for example, defines corrupt practices in many areas of business. A sensitive issue is that some MNCs sometimes violate legal and ethical standards of the home country, but not of the host country.

Before entering international markets, firms should scan relevant journals and patent reports, seek the advice of academic and research organizations, participate in international trade fairs, form partnerships, and conduct extensive research to broaden their contacts and diminish the risk of doing business in new markets. Firms can also reduce the risks of doing business internationally by obtaining insurance from the U.S. government's Overseas Private Investment

GLOBAL PERSPECTIVE

The Old Way Versus the New Way to Take a Company Global

The old way to take a company global was to get in fast, do minimal research, strike deals with top officials, make quick acquisitions, focus on upscale consumers, and watch local customers begin buying up the company's products. That approach, however, failed more often than it succeeded.

The new, more effective approach to taking a company global is to do extensive homework regarding culture, distributors, suppliers, and customers before placing operations in a foreign land. Successful globalization today requires investing time and energy to understand the nature of business in those countries and to methodically build a presence from the ground up. Companies successfully going global today work closely with bureaucrats, entrepreneurs, social groups, and other potential customers at the grassroots level. These companies are also targeting individuals in countries where the average income is low yet whose numbers far exceed those of the richest 10 percent of countries and customers. These companies have come to realize that developing nations are growing much faster than the industrial nations. Fully 4 billion people who annually earn the equivalent of $1,500 or less live in developing nations, and this group is growing more rapidly than well-to-do citizens and countries.

A number of companies are using this new approach to be successful globally. Hewlett-Packard is presently marketing its products heavily in Central America and Africa. Citibank also is following this new approach by persuading its corporate customers in developing countries to set up retail bank accounts for their entire staffs—from janitors to top managers. General Electric announced in early 2005 that it is pursuing a new strategy focusing on developing countries rather than making acquisitions in the United States and Europe. Deane Dray, an analyst with Goldman Sachs, says, "GE's strategy is not by choice but by necessity. Developing countries are where the fastest growth is occurring and more sustainable growth." By 2007, GE expects its revenue from outside the United States to hit $82 billion, up 17 percent from its estimated $70 billion in 2005.

Source: Adapted from "Smart Globalization," *BusinessWeek* (August 27, 2001): 132–137. Also Kathryn Kranhold, "GE Pins Hopes on Emerging Markets," *Wall Street Journal* (March 2, 2005): A3.

Corporation (OPIC). Note in the "Global Perspective" section that U.S. firms are doing more extensive research today than ever before entering particular global markets.

Globalization

Globalization is a process of worldwide integration of strategy formulation, implementation, and evaluation activities. Strategic decisions are made based on their impact upon global profitability of the firm, rather than on just domestic or other individual country considerations. A global strategy seeks to meet the needs of customers worldwide, with the highest value at the lowest cost. This may mean locating production in countries with the lowest labor costs or abundant natural resources, locating research and complex engineering centers where skilled scientists and engineers can be found, and locating marketing activities close to the markets to be served. A global strategy includes designing, producing, and marketing products with global needs in mind, instead of considering individual countries alone. A global strategy integrates actions against competitors into a worldwide plan.

Globalization of industries is occurring for many reasons, including a worldwide trend toward similar consumption patterns, the emergence of global buyers and sellers, and e-commerce and the instant transmission of money and information across continents. The European Economic Community (EEC), religions, the Olympics, the World Bank, world trade centers, the Red Cross, the Internet, environmental conferences, telecommunications, and economic summits all contribute to global interdependencies and the emerging global marketplace.

It is clear that different industries become global for different reasons. The need to amortize massive R&D investments over many markets is a major reason why the aircraft manufacturing industry became global. Monitoring globalization in one's industry is an important strategic-management activity. Knowing how to use that information for one's competitive advantage is even more important. For example, firms may look around the world for the best technology and select one that has the most promise for the largest number of markets. When firms design a product, they design it to be marketable in as many countries as possible. When firms manufacture a product, they select the lowest-cost source, which may be Japan for semiconductors, Sri Lanka for textiles, Malaysia for simple electronics, and Europe for precision machinery. MNCs design manufacturing systems to accommodate world markets. One of the riskiest strategies for a domestic firm is to remain solely a domestic firm in an industry that is rapidly becoming global.

China: Opportunities and Threats

U.S. firms increasingly are doing business in China as market reforms daily create a more businesslike arena. Foreign direct investment in China is annually about $50 billion. As China prepares to join the World Trade Organization in 2007, its government is racing to modernize computer systems and telecom networks and revamping its legal system to meet international standards. Privacy and disregard for intellectual property rights is still a major problem in China, but the government is hurrying to institute new laws to protect and encourage foreign technological investment.

China continues to be the world's fastest-growing economy as its gross domestic product rose more than 9 percent in 2004. However, neighboring India's gross domestic product is growing annually, about 7 percent and many analysts think India's democratic government and huge English-speaking population will give it an edge over China in doing business with Western companies.

Risks that still deter firms from initiating business with China, however, include the following:

- Poor infrastructure
- Disregard for the natural environment
- Absence of a legal system
- Rampant corruption
- Lack of freedom of press, speech, and religion
- Severe human rights violations
- Little respect for patents, copyrights, brands, and logos
- Counterfeiting, fraud, and pirating of products
- Little respect for legal contracts
- No generally accepted accounting principles

The minimum wage in China is 12 cents per hour, but many firms pay even less. Chinese workers usually have no healthcare and no compensation for injury. Few factories have fire extinguishers. Bribes are often paid to officials to avoid fines and shutdowns. Labor unions are illegal and nonexistent in China. Child labor is commonplace. Political and religious oppression and imprisonment occur. Levi Strauss has pulled all its business operations out of China to protest human rights violations.

China's leaders are determined these days to minimize foreign policy problems so they can focus on domestic economic development. China's President Hu Jintao, has put China's economic goals at the forefront of policy and practice. China is expected to surpass India by 2006 as the country of choice for information technology (IT) outsourcing. China's economy is booming, and thousands of foreign companies have set up manufacturing bases on the Chinese mainland. In Shanghai, an engineer is paid on average $500 a month compared to $700 in India and $4,000 in the United States. As margins shrink in many industries due to increased competitiveness, more and more firms see China as more attractive even than Mexico or India for conducting business, especially IT operations.

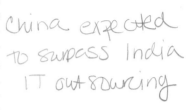

Hong Kong is the centerpiece of China's efforts to reform, privatize, and expand imports and exports worldwide. The map in Figure 3-4 illustrates Hong Kong's strategic location for China. With its 6.3 million people, magnificent harbor, financial wealth, 500 banks from 43 countries, the world's eighth-largest stock market, and minimum taxation, Hong Kong serves as the gateway to a fast-growing China. U.S. companies alone have 178 regional headquarters in Hong Kong and $10.5 billion in direct investment.

Hong Kong Chief Executive Tung Chee Hwa resigned in 2005, two years before his term expired, amid street protests demanding a more democratic state. Donald Ysang replaced Tung Hwa, but elections are being held soon for the next Hong Kong leader. Hong Kong's economy grew a rapid 7.8 percent in 2004.

Dell Inc. in 2006 completed construction of a second manufacturing plant in Xiamen, China, doubling its production capacity to make personal computers for China, Hong Kong, and Japan. Dell, the leading seller of PCs worldwide, opened the first Xiamen factory in 1998 and is now the fourth-largest seller of PC s in China with about 7 percent market share.

The number of Chinese traveling abroad hit 29 million in 2004, up 70 percent from 2002.[23] The World Tourism Organization estimates that the number of Chinese traveling abroad will reach 100 million by 2020. By comparison, slightly less than

FIGURE 3-4

Hong Kong's Strategic Location

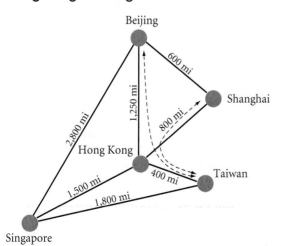

17 million Japanese traveled abroad in 2004. In response, many retailers worldwide are offering Chinese language publications and Web sites to lure the growing Chinese tourist business.

Industry Analysis: The External Factor Evaluation (EFE) Matrix

An *External Factor Evaluation (EFE) Matrix* allows strategists to summarize and evaluate economic, social, cultural, demographic, environmental, political, governmental, legal, technological, and competitive information. Illustrated in Table 3-8, the EFE Matrix can be developed in five steps:

1. List key external factors as identified in the external-audit process. Include a total of from 10 to 20 factors, including both opportunities and threats, that affect the firm and its industry. List the opportunities first and then the threats. Be as specific as possible, using percentages, ratios, and comparative numbers whenever possible.

2. Assign to each factor a weight that ranges from 0.0 (not important) to 1.0 (very important). The weight indicates the relative importance of that factor to being successful in the firm's industry. Opportunities often receive higher weights than threats, but threats too can receive high weights if they are especially severe or threatening. Appropriate weights can be determined by comparing successful with unsuccessful competitors or by discussing the factor and reaching a group consensus. The sum of all weights assigned to the factors must equal 1.0.

3. Assign a rating between 1 and 4 to each key external factor to indicate how effectively the firm's current strategies respond to the factor, where 4 = *the response is superior,* 3 = *the response is above average,* 2 = *the response is average,* and 1 = *the response is poor.* Ratings are based on effectiveness of the firm's strategies. Ratings are thus company-based, whereas the weights in step 2 are industry-based. It is important to note that both threats and opportunities can receive a 1, 2, 3, or 4.

4. Multiply each factor's weight by its rating to determine a weighted score.

5. Sum the weighted scores for each variable to determine the total weighted score for the organization.

Regardless of the number of key opportunities and threats included in an EFE Matrix, the highest possible total weighted score for an organization is 4.0 and the lowest possible total weighted score is 1.0. The average total weighted score is 2.5. A total weighted score of 4.0 indicates that an organization is responding in an outstanding way to existing opportunities and threats in its industry. In other words, the firm's strategies effectively take advantage of existing opportunities and minimize the potential adverse effects of external threats. A total score of 1.0 indicates that the firm's strategies are not capitalizing on opportunities or avoiding external threats.

An example of an EFE Matrix is provided in Table 3-8 for the large poultry producer Pilgrim's Pride based in Pittsburg, Texas. Note that Pilgrims Pride is capitalizing well on the "rising demand for both chicken and packaged foods" as indicated by the ratings of 4. However, the firm is doing poorly on handling the "leading competitor being for sale" opportunity and the "leading competitor increasing its ad expenses" threat as indicated by ratings of 1. The most important factor in the analysis is the "illegal immigrant problem" as indicated by a weight of 0.09. Note also that there are many percentage-based factors among the group. Be quantitative to the extent possible! Note also that the ratings range from 1 to 4 on both the opportunities and threats.

TABLE 3-8 EFE Matrix for the Poultry Firm: Pilgrim's Pride

KEY EXTERNAL FACTORS	WEIGHT	RATING	WEIGHTED SCORE
Opportunities			
1. Demand for chicken increasing 8 percent annually.	0.07	4	0.28
2. Demand for prepared food increasing 10 percent annually.	0.08	4	0.32
3. Exporting of chicken growing 12 percent annually.	0.05	3	0.15
4. Packaging technology offers 15 percent annual cost savings.	0.03	2	0.06
5. Genetic research offers 20 percent faster-growing of chicks.	0.03	2	0.06
6. Leading competitor could be acquired for $1 billion.	0.02	1	0.02
7. Chicken costs 40 percent less than other meats.	0.05	3	0.15
8. New treatment to reduce salmonella in chicks.	0.04	2	0.08
9. New laws governing migrant workers aid industry.	0.03	4	0.12
Threats			
10. Chicken industry reputation not good due to conditions.	0.05	3	0.15
11. Leading competitor increased its ad expenses 30 percent.	0.06	1	0.06
12. Increasing governmental regulation in the industry.	0.04	2	0.08
13. Salmonella scares crop up frequently.	0.06	2	0.12
14. Industry is highly labor intensive and subject to unions.	0.06	4	0.24
15. Interest rates are rising 1 percent annually.	0.04	2	0.08
16. Drought conditions raise grain prices.	0.05	2	0.10
17. Leading rival firms are more fully integrated.	0.07	2	0.14
18. Illegal immigrant problem plagues the firm.	0.09	3	0.27
19. Industry has profit margins less than 3 percent.	0.08	1	0.08
Total	**1.00**		**2.56**

The Competitive Profile Matrix (CPM)

The *Competitive Profile Matrix (CPM)* identifies a firm's major competitors and its particular strengths and weaknesses in relation to a sample firm's strategic position. The weights and total weighted scores in both a CPM and EFE have the same meaning. However, *critical success* factors in a CPM include both internal and external issues; therefore, the ratings refer to strengths and weaknesses, where 4 = major strength, 3 = minor strength, 2 = minor weakness, and 1 = major weakness. There are some important differences between the EFE and CPM. First of all, the critical success factors in a CPM are broader, they do not include specific or factual data and even may focus on internal issues. The critical success factors in a CPM also are not grouped into opportunities and threats as they are in an EFE. In a CPM, the ratings and total weighted scores for rival firms can be compared to the sample firm. This comparative analysis provides important internal strategic information.

A sample Competitive Profile Matrix is provided in Table 3-9. In this example, advertising and global expansion are the most important critical success factors, as indicated by a weight of 0.20. Avon's and L'Oreal's product quality is superior, as evidenced by a rating of 4; L'Oreal's "financial position" is good, as indicated by a rating of 3; Procter & Gamble is the weakest firm overall, as indicated by a total weighted score of 2.80.

Other than the critical success factors listed in the example CPM, factors often included in this analysis include breadth of product line, effectiveness of sales distribution,

TABLE 3-9   An Example Competitive Profile Matrix

Critical Success Factors	Weight	AVON Rating	AVON Score	L'OREAL Rating	L'OREAL Score	PROCTER & GAMBLE Rating	PROCTER & GAMBLE Score
Advertising	0.20	1	0.20	4	0.80	3	0.60
Product Quality	0.10	4	0.40	4	0.40	3	0.30
Price Competitiveness	0.10	3	0.30	3	0.30	4	0.40
Management	0.10	4	0.40	3	0.30	3	0.30
Financial Position	0.15	4	0.60	3	0.45	3	0.45
Customer Loyalty	0.10	4	0.40	4	0.40	2	0.20
Global Expansion	0.20	4	0.80	2	0.40	2	0.40
Market Share	0.05	1	0.05	4	0.20	3	0.15
Total	**1.00**		**3.15**		**3.25**		**2.80**

Note: (1) The ratings values are as follows: 1 = major weakness, 2 = minor weakness, 3 = minor strength, 4 = major strength. (2) As indicated by the total weighted score of 2.80, Competitor 3 is weakest. (3) Only eight critical success factors are included for simplicity; this is too few in actuality.

proprietary or patent advantages, location of facilities, production capacity and efficiency, experience, union relations, technological advantages, and e-commerce expertise.

A word on interpretation: Just because one firm receives a 3.2 rating and another receives a 2.80 rating in a Competitive Profile Matrix, it does not follow that the first firm is 20 percent better than the second. Numbers reveal the relative strengths of firms, but their implied precision is an illusion. Numbers are not magic. The aim is not to arrive at a single number, but rather to assimilate and evaluate information in a meaningful way that aids in decision making.

Another Competitive Profile Matrix is provided in Table 3-10 for Gateway Computer Company. Note that Apple has the best product quality and management experience; Dell has the best market share and inventory system; and Gateway has the best price as indicated by the ratings.

TABLE 3-10   Competitive Profile Matrix for Gateway Computer (2003)

Critical Success Factors	Weight	GATEWAY Rating	GATEWAY Weighted Score	APPLE Rating	APPLE Weighted Score	DELL Rating	DELL Weighted Score
Market share	0.15	3	0.45	2	0.30	4	0.60
Inventory system	0.08	2	0.16	2	0.16	4	0.32
Financial position	0.10	2	0.20	3	0.30	3	0.30
Product quality	0.08	3	0.24	4	0.32	3	0.24
Consumer loyalty	0.02	3	0.06	3	0.06	4	0.08
Sales distribution	0.10	3	0.30	2	0.20	3	0.30
Global expansion	0.15	3	0.45	2	0.30	4	0.60
Organization structure	0.05	3	0.15	3	0.15	3	0.15
Production capacity	0.04	3	0.12	3	0.12	3	0.12
E-commerce	0.10	3	0.30	3	0.30	3	0.30
Customer service	0.10	3	0.30	2	0.20	4	0.40
Price competitive	0.02	4	0.08	1	0.02	3	0.06
Management experience	0.01	2	0.02	4	0.04	2	0.02
Total	**1.00**		**2.83**		**2.47**		**3.49**

CONCLUSION

Increasing turbulence in markets and industries around the world means the external audit has become an explicit and vital part of the strategic-management process. This chapter provides a framework for collecting and evaluating economic, social, cultural, demographic, environmental, political, governmental, legal, technological, and competitive information. Firms that do not mobilize and empower their managers and employees to identify, monitor, forecast, and evaluate key external forces may fail to anticipate emerging opportunities and threats and, consequently, may pursue ineffective strategies, miss opportunities, and invite organizational demise. Firms not taking advantage of the Internet are technologically falling behind.

A major responsibility of strategists is to ensure development of an effective external-audit system. This includes using information technology to devise a competitive intelligence system that works. The external-audit approach described in this chapter can be used effectively by any size or type of organization. Typically, the external-audit process is more informal in small firms, but the need to understand key trends and events is no less important for these firms. The EFE Matrix and Porter's Five-Forces Model can help strategists evaluate the market and industry, but these tools must be accompanied by good intuitive judgment. Multinational firms especially need a systematic and effective external-audit system because external forces among foreign countries vary so greatly.

We invite you to visit the David page on the Prentice Hall Companion Web site at www.prenhall.com/david for this chapter's review quiz.

KEY TERMS AND CONCEPTS

Chief Information Officer (CIO) (p. 93)

Chief Technology Officer (CTO) (p. 93)

Competitive Analysis (p. 97)

Competitive Intelligence (CI) (p. 96)

Competitive Profile Matrix (CPM) (p. 111)

Decruiting (p. 86)

Director of Competitive Analysis (p. 97)

Downsizing (p. 86)

Environmental Scanning (p. 82)

External Audit (p. 82)

External Factor Evaluation (EFE) Matrix (p. 110)

External Forces (p. 83)

Foreign Direct Investment (FDI) (p. 89)

Industrial/Organization (I/O) (p. 84)

Industry Analysis (p. 82)

Information Technology (IT) (p. 93)

Internet (p. 93)

Learning from the Partner (p. 99)

Linear Regression (p. 105)

Lifecare Facilities (p. 88)

Market Commonality (p. 100)

Porter's Five-Forces Model (p. 100)

Resource Similarity (p. 100)

Rightsizing (p. 86)

Tax Harmonization (p. 92)

ISSUES FOR REVIEW AND DISCUSSION

1. Explain how to conduct an external strategic-management audit.
2. Identify a recent economic, social, political, or technological trend that significantly affects financial institutions.
3. Discuss the following statement: Major opportunities and threats usually result from an interaction among key environmental trends rather than from a single external event or factor.
4. Identify two industries experiencing rapid technological changes and three industries that are experiencing little technological change. How does the need for technological forecasting differ in these industries? Why?
5. Use Porter's Five-Forces Model to evaluate competitiveness within the U.S. banking industry.
6. What major forecasting techniques would you use to identify (1) economic opportunities and threats and (2) demographic opportunities and threats? Why are these techniques most appropriate?
7. How does the external audit affect other components of the strategic-management process?
8. As the owner of a small business, explain how you would organize a strategic-information scanning system. How would you organize such a system in a large organization?
9. Construct an EFE Matrix for an organization of your choice.
10. Make an appointment with a librarian at your university to learn how to use online databases. Report your findings in class.
11. Give some advantages and disadvantages of cooperative versus competitive strategies.
12. As strategist for a local bank, explain when you would use qualitative versus quantitative forecasts.
13. What is your forecast for interest rates and the stock market in the next several months? As the stock market moves up, do interest rates always move down? Why? What are the strategic implications of these trends?
14. Explain how information technology affects strategies of the organization where you worked most recently.
15. Let's say your boss develops an EFE Matrix that includes 62 factors. How would you suggest reducing the number of factors to 20?
16. Discuss the ethics of gathering competitive intelligence.
17. Discuss the ethics of cooperating with rival firms.
18. Visit the SEC Web site at www.sec.gov, and discuss the benefits of using information provided there.
19. What are the major differences between U.S. and multinational operations that affect strategic management?
20. Why is globalization of industries a common factor today?
21. Discuss the opportunities and threats a firm faces in doing business in China.
22. Do you agree with I/O theorists that external factors are more important than internal factors to a firm's achieving competitive advantage? Explain both your and their position.
23. Define, compare, and contrast the weights versus ratings in an EFEm versus IFEm Matrix.
24. Develop a Competitive Profile Matrix for your university. Include six factors.
25. List the 10 external areas that give rise to opportunities and threats.
26. Discuss recent trends in Russia's economic condition.
27. True or False: China replaced Mexico in 2003 as the largest exporter to the United States. Discuss this statement.
28. Define and discuss implications of "tax harmonization" in Europe.
29. Do you believe strategies themselves should be secret or open within firms? Explain.
30. True or False: For the first time in 100 years, China attracted more foreign direct investment (FDI) than the United States in the year 2002.

NOTES

1. York Freund, "Critical Success Factors," *Planning Review* 16, no. 4 (July–August 1988): 20.
2. A. M. McGahan, "Competition, Strategy and Business Performance," *California Management Review* 41, no. 3 (1999): 74–101; A. McGahan and M. Porter, "How Much Does Industry Matter Really?," *Strategic Management Journal* 18, no. 8 (1997): 15–30.
3. Guy Chazan, "In Putin's Russia, Business Struggles for a Foothold," *Wall Street Journal* (April 27, 2005): A1.
4. Ibid.
5. Guy Chazan and Gregory White, "Gazprom to Buy Control of Izvestia, Tightening Kremlin's Media Grip," *Wall Street Journal* (June 3, 2005): A3.
6. Ibid.
7. S&P Industry Surveys, Beverage Industry, 2005.
8. Frederick Gluck, "Global Competition in the 1990s," *Journal of Business Strategy* (Spring 1983): 22–24.
9. John Harris, Robert Shaw, Jr., and William Sommers, "The Strategic Management of Technology," *Planning Review* 11, no. 11 (January–February 1983): 28, 35.
10. Bill Saporito, "Companies that Compete Best," *Fortune* (May 22, 1989): 36.
11. Louis Lavelle, "The Case of the Corporate Spy," *BusinessWeek* (November 26, 2001): 56–57.
12. Kenneth Sawka, "Demystifying Business Intelligence," *Management Review* (October 1996): 49.
13. John Prescott and Daniel Smith, "The Largest Survey of 'Leading-Edge' Competitor Intelligence Managers," *Planning Review* 17, no. 3 (May–June 1989): 6–13.
14. Gary Hamel, Yves Doz, and C. K. Prahalad, "Collaborate with Your Competitors—and Win," *Harvard Business Review* 67, no. 1 (January–February 1989): 133.
15. Jon Swartz, "Rivals Form United Front Against Spam," *USA Today* (April 29, 2003): 2B.
16. M.J. Chen. "Competitor Analysis and Interfirm Rivalry: Toward a Theoretical Integration," *Academy of Management Review* 21 (1996): 106.
17. S. Jayachandran, J. Gimeno, and P. R. Varadarajan, "Theory of Multimarket Competition: A Synthesis and Implications for Marketing Strategy, *Journal of Marketing* 63, 3 (1999): 59. Also, M. J. Chen. "Competitor Analysis and Interfirm Rivalry: Toward a Theoretical Integration," *Academy of Management Review* 21 (1996): 107–108.
18. David Bank, "A Site-Eat-Site World," Wall Street *Journal* (July 12, 1999): R8.
19. Arthur Thompson, Jr., A. J. Strickland III, and John Gamble. *Crafting and Executing Strategy: Text and Readings.* New York: McGraw-Hill/Irwin (2005): 63.
20. Michael E. Porter, *Competitive Strategy: Techniques for Analyzing Industries and Competitors.* New York: Free Press (1980): 24–27.
21. horizon.unc.edu/projects/seminars/futuresresearch/rationale.asp
22. Dale McConkey, "Planning in a Changing Environment," *Business Horizons* 31, no. 5 (September–October 1988): 67.
23. Kristine Crane and Alex Ortolani, "Travel Industry Targets China," *Wall Street Journal* (June 15, 2005): A12.

CURRENT READINGS

Barr, P. S., and M. A. Glynn. "Cultural Variations in Strategic Issue Interpretation: Relating Cultural Uncertainty Avoidance to Controllability in Discriminating Threat and Opportunity." *Strategic Management Journal* 25, no. 1 (January 2004): 59.

Bendoly, E., A. Soni, and M. A. Venkataramanan. "Value Chain Resource Planning: Adding Value with Systems Beyond the Enterprise." *Business Horizons* 47, no. 2 (March–April 2004): 79.

Carter, J., and N. Sheehan. "From Competition to Cooperation: E-Tailing's Integration with

Retailing." *Business Horizons* 47, no. 2 (March–April 2004): 71.

Choi, Young Rok, and Dean A. Shepherd. "Entrepreneurs' Decisions to Exploit Opportunities." *Journal of Management* 30, no. 3 (2004): 377.

Chussil, Mark. "With All This Intelligence, Why Don't We Have Better Strategies?" *Journal of Business Strategy* 26, no. 1 (2005): 26.

Crane, A. "In the Company of Spies: When Competitive Intelligence Gathering Becomes Industrial Espionage." *Business Horizons* 48, no. 3 (May–June 2005): 233.

Ernst, D., and J. Bamford. "Best Practice: Your Alliances Are Too Stable." *Harvard Business Review* (June 2005): 133.

Hansen, M. T., and N. Nohria. "How to Build Collaborative Advantage." *MIT Sloan Management Review* 46, no. 1 (Fall 2004): 22.

Huffman, B. J. "Why Environmental Scanning Works Except When You Need It." *Business Horizons* 47, no. 3 (May–June 2004): 39.

———. "Intelligence." *MIT Sloan Management Review* 46, no. 3 (Spring 2005): 5.

Javidan, M., G. K. Stahl, F. Brodbeck, and C. P. M. Wilderom. "Cross-Border Transfer of Knowledge: Cultural Lessons from Project GLOBE." *The Academy of Management Executive* 19, no. 2 (May 2005): 59.

Ketchen, Jr., D. J., C. C. Snow, and V. L. Hoover. "Improving Firm Performance by Matching Strategic Decision-Making Processes to Competitive Dynamics." *The Academy of Management Executive* 18, no. 4 (November 2004): 29.

Kim, Eonsoo, Dae-il Nam, and J. L. Stimpert. "The Applicability of Porter's Generic Strategies in the Digital Age: Assumptions, Conjectures, and Suggestions." *Journal of Management* 30, no. 5 (2004): 569.

———. "The Many Dimensions of Culture." *The Academy of Management Executive* 18, no. 1 (February 2004): 88.

Robertson, C. J., and A. Watson. "Corruption and Change: The Impact of Foreign Direct Investment." *Strategic Management Journal* 25, no. 4 (April 2004): 385.

Spanos, Y. E., G. Zaralis, and S. Lioukas. "Strategy and Industry Effects on Profitability: Evidence from Greece." *Strategic Management Journal* 25, no. 2 (February 2004): 139.

Tan, J., and D. Tan. "Environment-Strategy Co-evolution and Co-alignment: A Staged Model of Chinese SOEs Under Transition." *Strategic Management Journal* 26, no. 2 (February 2005): 141.

Toh, Soo Min, and Angelo S. DeNisi. "A Local Perspective to Expatriate Success." *The Academy of Management Executive* 19, no. 1 (February 2005): 132.

experiential exercises

Experiential Exercise 3A

Developing an EFE Matrix for Google (GOOG)

PURPOSE

This exercise will give you practice developing an EFE Matrix. An EFE Matrix summarizes the results of an external audit. This is an important tool widely used by strategists.

INSTRUCTIONS

Step 1   Join with two other students in class, and jointly prepare an EFE Matrix for Google. Refer back to the Cohesion Case and to Experiential Exercise 1A, if necessary, to identify external opportunities and threats.

Step 2   All three-person teams participating in this exercise should record their EFE total weighted scores on the board. Put your initials after your score to identify it as your team's.

Step 3   Compare the total weighted scores. Which team's score came closest to the instructor's answer? Discuss reasons for variation in the scores reported on the board.

Experiential Exercise 3B

The External Assessment

PURPOSE

This exercise will help you become familiar with important sources of external information available in your college library. A key part of preparing an external audit is searching the Internet and examining published sources of information for relevant economic, social, cultural, demographic, environmental, political, governmental, legal, technological, and competitive trends and events. External opportunities and threats must be identified and evaluated before strategies can be formulated effectively.

INSTRUCTIONS

Step 1   Select a company or business where you currently or previously have worked. Conduct an external audit for this company. Find opportunities and threats in recent issues of newspapers and magazines. Search for information using the Internet.

Step 2   On a separate sheet of paper, list 10 opportunities and 10 threats that face this company. Be specific in stating each factor.

Step 3   Include a bibliography to reveal where you found the information.

Step 4   Write a three-page summary of your findings, and submit it to your instructor.

Experiential Exercise 3C

Developing an EFE Matrix for My University

PURPOSE

More colleges and universities are embarking upon the strategic-management process. Institutions are consciously and systematically identifying and evaluating external opportunities and threats facing higher education in your state, the nation, and the world.

INSTRUCTIONS

Step 1 Join with two other individuals in class, and jointly prepare an EFE Matrix for your institution.

Step 2 Go to the board and record your total weighted score in a column that includes the scores of all three-person teams participating. Put your initials after your score to identify it as your team's.

Step 3 Which team viewed your college's strategies most positively? Which team viewed your college's strategies most negatively? Discuss the nature of the differences.

**Experiential
Exercise 3D**

*Developing a Competitive
Profile Matrix for Google
(GOOG)*

PURPOSE

Monitoring competitors' performance and strategies is a key aspect of an external audit. This exercise is designed to give you practice evaluating the competitive position of organizations in a given industry and assimilating that information in the form of a Competitive Profile Matrix.

INSTRUCTIONS

Step 1 Turn back to the Cohesion Case and review the section on competitors.

Step 2 On a separate sheet of paper, prepare a Competitive Profile Matrix that includes Google and Yahoo!.

Step 3 Turn in your Competitive Profile Matrix for a classwork grade.

**Experiential
Exercise 3E**

*Developing a Competitive
Profile Matrix for My
University*

PURPOSE

Your college or university competes with all other educational institutions in the world, especially those in your own state. State funds, students, faculty, staff, endowments, gifts, and federal funds are areas of competitiveness. The purpose of this exercise is to give you practice thinking competitively about the business of education in your state.

INSTRUCTIONS

Step 1 Identify two colleges or universities in your state that compete directly with your institution for students. Interview several persons who are aware of particular strengths and weaknesses of those universities. Record information about the two competing universities.

Step 2 Prepare a Competitive Profile Matrix that includes your institution and the two competing institutions. Include the following factors in your analysis:
   1. Tuition costs
   2. Quality of faculty
   3. Academic reputation
   4. Average class size

5. Campus landscaping
6. Athletic programs
7. Quality of students
8. Graduate programs
9. Location of campus
10. Campus culture

Step 3   Submit your Competitive Profile Matrix to your instructor for evaluation.

The Internal Assessment

4

chapter objectives

After studying this chapter, you should be able to do the following:

1. Describe how to perform an internal strategic-management audit.

2. Discuss the Resource-Based View (RBV) in strategic management.

3. Discuss key interrelationships among the functional areas of business.

4. Compare and contrast culture in the United States with other countries.

5. Identify the basic functions or activities that make up management, marketing, finance/accounting, production/operations, research and development, and management information systems.

6. Explain how to determine and prioritize a firm's internal strengths and weaknesses.

7. Explain the importance of financial ratio analysis.

8. Discuss the nature and role of management information systems in strategic management.

9. Develop an Internal Factor Evaluation (IFE) Matrix.

10. Explain benchmarking as a strategic management tool.

experiential exercises

Experiential Exercise 4A
Performing a Financial Ratio Analysis for Google (GOOG)

Experiential Exercise 4B
Constructing an IFE Matrix for Google (GOOG)

Experiential Exercise 4C
Constructing an IFE Matrix for My University

"notable quotes"

Like a product or service, the planning process itself must be managed and shaped, if it is to serve executives as a vehicle for strategic decision-making.
Robert Lenz

The difference between now and five years ago is that information systems had limited function. You weren't betting your company on it. Now you are.
William Gruber

Weak leadership can wreck the soundest strategy.
Sun Zi

A firm that continues to employ a previously successful strategy eventually and inevitably falls victim to a competitor.
William Cohen

Sad but true, U.S. businesspeople have the lowest foreign language proficiency of any major trading nation. U.S. business schools do not emphasize foreign languages, and students traditionally avoid them.
Ronald Dulek

Great spirits have always encountered violent opposition from mediocre minds.
Albert Einstein

This chapter focuses on identifying and evaluating a firm's strengths and weaknesses in the functional areas of business, including management, marketing, finance/accounting, production/operations, research and development, and management information systems. Relationships among these areas of business are examined. Strategic implications of important functional area concepts are examined. The process of performing an internal audit is described. The Resource-Based View (RBV) of strategic management is introduced as is the Value Chain Analysis (VCA) concept.

The Nature of an Internal Audit

VISIT THE NET

Excellent strategic planning quotes.
(www.planware.org/quotes. htm#3)

All organizations have strengths and weaknesses in the functional areas of business. No enterprise is equally strong or weak in all areas. Maytag, for example, is known for excellent production and product design, whereas Procter & Gamble is known for superb marketing. Internal strengths/weaknesses, coupled with external opportunities/threats and a clear statement of mission, provide the basis for establishing objectives and strategies. Objectives and strategies are established with the intention of capitalizing upon internal strengths and overcoming weaknesses. The internal-audit part of the strategic-management process is illustrated in Figure 4-1.

FIGURE 4-1

A Comprehensive Strategic-Management Model

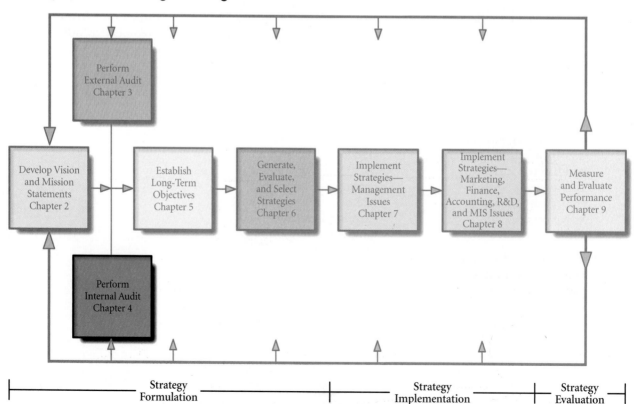

Key Internal Forces

It is not possible in a business policy text to review in depth all the material presented in courses such as marketing, finance, accounting, management, management information systems, and production/operations; there are many subareas within these functions, such as customer service, warranties, advertising, packaging, and pricing under marketing.

For different types of organizations, such as hospitals, universities, and government agencies, the functional business areas, of course, differ. In a hospital, for example, functional areas may include cardiology, hematology, nursing, maintenance, physician support, and receivables. Functional areas of a university can include athletic programs, placement services, housing, fund-raising, academic research, counseling, and intramural programs. Within large organizations, each division has certain strengths and weaknesses.

A firm's strengths that cannot be easily matched or imitated by competitors are called *distinctive competencies.* Building competitive advantages involves taking advantage of distinctive competencies. For example, 3M exploits its distinctive competence in research and development by producing a wide range of innovative products. Strategies are designed in part to improve on a firm's weaknesses, turning them into strengths—and maybe even into distinctive competencies.

Some researchers emphasize the importance of the internal audit part of the strategic-management process by comparing it to the external audit. Robert Grant concluded that the internal audit is more important, saying:

> In a world where customer preferences are volatile, the identity of customers is changing, and the technologies for serving customer requirements are continually evolving; an externally focused orientation does not provide a secure foundation for formulating long-term strategy. When the external environment is in a state of flux, the firm's own resources and capabilities may be a much more stable basis on which to define its identity. Hence, a definition of a business in terms of what it is capable of doing may offer a more durable basis for strategy than a definition based upon the needs which the business seeks to satisfy.[1]

The Process of Performing an Internal Audit

The process of performing an *internal audit* closely parallels the process of performing an external audit. Representative managers and employees from throughout the firm need to be involved in determining a firm's strengths and weaknesses. The internal audit requires gathering and assimilating information about the firm's management, marketing, finance/accounting, production/operations, research and development (R&D), and management information systems operations. Key factors should be prioritized as described in Chapter 3 so that the firm's most important strengths and weaknesses can be determined collectively.

Compared to the external audit, the process of performing an internal audit provides more opportunity for participants to understand how their jobs, departments, and divisions fit into the whole organization. This is a great benefit because managers and employees perform better when they understand how their work affects other areas and activities of the firm. For example, when marketing and manufacturing managers jointly discuss issues related to internal strengths and weaknesses, they gain a better appreciation of the issues, problems, concerns, and needs of all the functional areas. In organizations that do not use strategic management,

[handwritten: internal audit + improves departmental communication]

marketing, finance, and manufacturing managers often do not interact with each other in significant ways. Performing an internal audit thus is an excellent vehicle or forum for improving the process of communication in the organization. *Communication* may be the most important word in management.

Performing an internal audit requires gathering, assimilating, and evaluating information about the firm's operations. Critical success factors, consisting of both strengths and weaknesses, can be identified and prioritized in the manner discussed in Chapter 3. According to William King, a task force of managers from different units of the organization, supported by staff, should be charged with determining the 10 to 20 most important strengths and weaknesses that should influence the future of the organization. He says:

> The development of conclusions on the 10 to 20 most important organizational strengths and weaknesses can be, as any experienced manager knows, a difficult task, when it involves managers representing various organizational interests and points of view. Developing a 20-page list of strengths and weaknesses could be accomplished relatively easily, but a list of the 10 to 15 most important ones involves significant analysis and negotiation. This is true because of the judgments that are required and the impact which such a list will inevitably have as it is used in the formulation, implementation, and evaluation of strategies.[2]

VISIT THE NET

Provides the complete strategic plan for the Wyoming Insurance Department Agency, including its list of strengths and weaknesses.
(www.state.wy.us/state/ strategy/insurance.html)

[handwritten: SM is interactive ~ requires the coordination of many people]

Strategic management is a highly interactive process that requires effective coordination among management, marketing, finance/accounting, production/ operations, R&D, and management information systems managers. Although the strategic-management process is overseen by strategists, success requires that managers and employees from all functional areas work together to provide ideas and information. Financial managers, for example, may need to restrict the number of feasible options available to operations managers, or R&D managers may develop products for which marketing managers need to set higher objectives. A key to organizational success is effective coordination and understanding among managers from all functional business areas. Through involvement in performing an internal strategic-management audit, managers from different departments and divisions of the firm come to understand the nature and effect of decisions in other functional business areas in their firm. Knowledge of these relationships is critical for effectively establishing objectives and strategies.

A failure to recognize and understand relationships among the functional areas of business can be detrimental to strategic management, and the number of those relationships that must be managed increases dramatically with a firm's size, diversity, geographic dispersion, and the number of products or services offered. Governmental and nonprofit enterprises traditionally have not placed sufficient emphasis on relationships among the business functions. Some firms place too great an emphasis on one function at the expense of others. Ansoff explained:

[handwritten: Multi-function focus is key]

> During the first fifty years, successful firms focused their energies on optimizing the performance of one of the principal functions: production/operations, R&D, or marketing. Today, due to the growing complexity and dynamism of the environment, success increasingly depends on a judicious combination of several functional influences. This transition from a single function focus to a multifunction focus is essential for successful strategic management.[3]

Financial ratio analysis exemplifies the complexity of relationships among the functional areas of business. A declining return on investment or profit margin ratio could be the result of ineffective marketing, poor management policies, research and development errors, or a weak management information system. The effectiveness of strategy formulation, implementation, and evaluation activities hinges upon a clear understanding of how major business functions affect one another. For strategies to succeed, a coordinated effort among all the functional areas of business is needed. In the case of planning, George wrote:

> We may conceptually separate planning for the purpose of theoretical discussion and analysis, but in practice, neither is it a distinct entity nor is it capable of being separated. The planning function is mixed with all other business functions and, like ink once mixed with water, it cannot be set apart. It is spread throughout and is a part of the whole of managing an organization.[4]

The Resource-Based View (RBV)

Gaining in popularity in the 1990s and continuing today, the *Resource-Based View (RBV)* approach to competitive advantage contends that internal resources are more important for a firm than external factors in achieving and sustaining competitive advantage. In contrast to the I/O theory presented in the previous chapter, proponents of the RBV view contend that organizational performance will primarily be determined by internal resources that can be grouped into three all-encompassing categories: physical resources, human resources, and organizational resources.[5] Physical resources include all plant and equipment, location, technology, raw materials, machines; human resources include all employees, training, experience, intelligence, knowledge, skills, abilities; and organizational resources include firm structure, planning processes, information systems, patents, trademarks, copyrights, databases, and so on. RBV theory asserts that resources are actually what helps a firm exploit opportunities and neutralize threats.

The basic premise of the RBV is that the mix, type, amount, and nature of a firm's internal resources should be considered first and foremost in devising strategies that can lead to sustainable competitive advantage. Managing strategically according to the RBV involves developing and exploiting a firm's unique resources and capabilities, and continually maintaining and strengthening those resources. The theory asserts that it is advantageous for a firm to pursue a strategy that is not currently being implemented by any competing firm. When other firms are unable to duplicate a particular strategy, then the focal firm has a sustainable competitive advantage, according to RBV theorists. For a resource to be valuable, however, it must be either (1) rare, (2) hard to imitate, or (3) not easily substitutable. Often called *empirical indicators*, these three characteristics of resources enable a firm to implement strategies that improve its efficiency and effectiveness and lead to a sustainable competitive advantage. The more a resource(s) is rare, nonimitable, and nonsubstitutable, the stronger a firm's competitive advantage will be and the longer it will last.

Rare resources are resources that other competing firms do not possess. If many firms have the same resource, then those firms will likely implement similar strategies, thus giving no one firm a sustainable competitive advantage. This is not to say that resources that are common are not valuable; they do indeed aid the firm in its chance for economic prosperity. However, to sustain a competitive advantage, it is more advantageous if the resource(s) is also rare.

It is also important that these same resources be difficult to imitate. If firms cannot easily gain the resources, say RBV theorists, then those resources will lead to a competitive advantage more so than resources easily imitable. Even if a firm employs resources that are rare, a sustainable competitive advantage may be achieved only if other firms cannot easily obtain these resources.

The third empirical indicator that can make resources a source of competitive advantage is substitutability. Borrowing from Porter's Five-Forces Model, to the degree that there are no viable substitutes, a firm will be able to sustain its competitive advantage. However, even if a competing firm cannot perfectly imitate a firm's resource, it can still obtain a sustainable competitive advantage of its own by obtaining resource substitutes.

The RBV has continued to grow in popularity and continues to seek a better understanding of the relationship between resources and sustained competitive advantage in strategic management. However, as eluded to in Chapter 3, one cannot say with any degree of certainty that either external or internal factors will always or even consistently be more important in seeking competitive advantage. Understanding both external and internal factors, and more importantly, understanding the relationships among them, will be the key to effective strategy formulation (discussed in Chapter 6). Since both external and internal factors continually change, strategists seek to identify and take advantage of positive changes and buffer against negative changes in a continuing effort to gain and sustain a firm's competitive advantage. This is the essence and challenge of strategic management, and oftentimes survival of the firm hinges on this work.

Integrating Strategy and Culture

Relationships among a firm's functional business activities perhaps can be exemplified best by focusing on organizational culture, an internal phenomenon that permeates all departments and divisions of an organization. *Organizational culture* can be defined as "a pattern of behavior [that has been] developed by an organization as it learns to cope with its problem of external adaptation and internal integration, and that has worked well enough to be considered valid and to be taught to new members as the correct way to perceive, think, and feel."[6] This definition emphasizes the importance of matching external with internal factors in making strategic decisions.

Organizational culture captures the subtle, elusive, and largely unconscious forces that shape a workplace. Remarkably resistant to change, culture can represent a major strength or weakness for the firm. It can be an underlying reason for strengths or weaknesses in any of the major business functions.

Defined in Table 4-1, *cultural products* include values, beliefs, rites, rituals, ceremonies, myths, stories, legends, sagas, language, metaphors, symbols, heroes, and heroines. These products or dimensions are levers that strategists can use to influence and direct strategy formulation, implementation, and evaluation activities. An organization's culture compares to an individual's personality in the sense that no two organizations have the same culture and no two individuals have the same personality. Both culture and personality are fairly enduring and can be warm, aggressive, friendly, open, innovative, conservative, liberal, harsh, or likable.

VISIT THE NET

Provides an excellent "Business and Strategic Planning Bibliography." (home.att.net/~nichols/ strategy.htm)

TABLE 4-1   Cultural Products and Associated Definitions

Rites	Relatively elaborate, dramatic, planned sets of activities that consolidate various forms of cultural expressions into one event, carried out through social interactions, usually for the benefit of an audience
Ceremonial	A system of several rites connected with a single occasion or event
Ritual	A standardized, detailed set of techniques and behaviors that manage anxieties but seldom produce intended, technical consequences of practical importance
Myth	A dramatic narrative of imagined events, usually used to explain origins or transformations of something; also, an unquestioned belief about the practical benefits of certain techniques and behaviors that is not supported by facts
Saga	A historical narrative describing the unique accomplishments of a group and its leaders, usually in heroic terms
Legend	A handed-down narrative of some wonderful event that is based on history but has been embellished with fictional details
Story	A narrative based on true events, sometimes a combination of truth and fiction
Folktale	A completely fictional narrative
Symbol	Any object, act, event, quality, or relation that serves as a vehicle for conveying meaning, usually by representing another thing
Language	A particular form or manner in which members of a group use sounds and written signs to convey meanings to each other
Metaphors	Shorthand of words used to capture a vision or to reinforce old or new values
Values	Life-directing attitudes that serve as behavioral guidelines
Belief	An understanding of a particular phenomenon
Heroes/Heroines	Individuals whom the organization has legitimized to model behavior for others

Source: Adapted from H. M. Trice and J. M. Beyer, "Studying Organizational Cultures through Rites and Ceremonials," *Academy of Management Review* 9, no. 4 (October 1984): 655.

Dimensions of organizational culture permeate all the functional areas of business. It is something of an art to uncover the basic values and beliefs that are deeply buried in an organization's rich collection of stories, language, heroes, and rituals, but cultural products can represent both important strengths and weaknesses. Culture is an aspect of an organization that can no longer be taken for granted in performing an internal strategic-management audit because culture and strategy must work together.

The strategic-management process takes place largely within a particular organization's culture. Lorsch found that executives in successful companies are emotionally committed to the firm's culture, but he concluded that culture can inhibit strategic management in two basic ways. First, managers frequently miss the significance of changing external conditions because they are blinded by strongly held beliefs. Second, when a particular culture has been effective in the past, the natural response is to stick with it in the future, even during times of major strategic change.[7] An organization's culture must support the collective commitment of its people to a common purpose. It must foster competence and enthusiasm among managers and employees.

Organizational culture significantly affects business decisions and thus must be evaluated during an internal strategic-management audit. If strategies can capitalize on cultural strengths, such as a strong work ethic or highly ethical beliefs, then management often can swiftly and easily implement changes. However, if the firm's culture is not supportive, strategic changes may be ineffective or even counterproductive. A firm's culture can become antagonistic to new strategies, with the result being confusion and disorientation. An organization's culture should infuse individuals with enthusiasm for implementing strategies. Allarie and Firsirotu emphasized the need to understand culture:

> Culture provides an explanation for the insuperable difficulties a firm encounters when it attempts to shift its strategic direction. Not only has the "right" culture become the essence and foundation of corporate excellence, it is also claimed that success or failure of reforms hinges on management's sagacity and ability to change the firm's driving culture in time and in time with required changes in strategies.[8]

The potential value of organizational culture has not been realized fully in the study of strategic management. Ignoring the effect that culture can have on relationships among the functional areas of business can result in barriers to communication, lack of coordination, and an inability to adapt to changing conditions. Some tension between culture and a firm's strategy is inevitable, but the tension should be monitored so that it does not reach a point at which relationships are severed and the culture becomes antagonistic. The resulting disarray among members of the organization would disrupt strategy formulation, implementation, and evaluation. On the other hand, a supportive organizational culture can make managing much easier.

Internal strengths and weaknesses associated with a firm's culture sometimes are overlooked because of the interfunctional nature of this phenomenon. It is important, therefore, for strategists to understand their firm as a sociocultural system. Success is often determined by linkages between a firm's culture and strategies. The challenge of strategic management today is to bring about the changes in organizational culture and individual mind-sets that are needed to support the formulation, implementation, and evaluation of strategies.

U.S. Versus Foreign Cultures

To successfully compete in world markets, U.S. managers must obtain a better knowledge of historical, cultural, and religious forces that motivate and drive people in other countries. In Japan, for example, business relations operate within the context of *Wa*, which stresses group harmony and social cohesion. In China, business behavior revolves around *guanxi*, or personal relations. In Korea, activities involve concern for *inhwa*, or harmony based on respect of hierarchical relationships, including obedience to authority.[9]

In Europe, it is generally true that the farther north on the continent, the more participatory the management style. Most European workers are unionized and enjoy more frequent vacations and holidays than U.S. workers. A 90-minute lunch break plus 20-minute morning and afternoon breaks are common in European firms. Guaranteed permanent employment is commonly a part of employment contracts in Europe. In socialist countries such as France, Belgium, and the United Kingdom, the only ground for immediate dismissal from work is a criminal offense. A six-month trial period at the beginning of employment is usually part of the contract with a European firm. Many Europeans resent pay-for-performance, commission salaries, and objective measurement and reward systems. This is true especially of workers in southern Europe. Many

Europeans also find the notion of team spirit difficult to grasp because the unionized environment has dichotomized worker–management relations throughout Europe.

A weakness that U.S. firms have in competing with Pacific Rim firms is a lack of understanding of Far Eastern cultures, including how Asians think and behave. Spoken Chinese, for example, has more in common with spoken English than with spoken Japanese or Korean. Managers around the world face the responsibility of having to exert authority while at the same time trying to be liked by subordinates. U.S. managers consistently put more weight on being friendly and liked, whereas Asian and European managers exercise authority often without this concern. Americans tend to use first names instantly in business dealings with foreigners, but foreigners find this presumptuous. In Japan, for example, first names are used only among family members and intimate friends; even longtime business associates and coworkers shy away from the use of first names. Other cultural differences or pitfalls that U.S. managers need to know about are given in Table 4-2.

differences among cultures

U.S. managers have a low tolerance for silence, whereas Asian managers view extended periods of silence as important for organizing and evaluating one's thoughts. U.S. managers are much more action-oriented than their counterparts around the world; they rush to appointments, conferences, and meetings—and then feel the day has been productive. But for foreign managers, resting, listening, meditating, and thinking is considered productive. Sitting through a conference without talking is unproductive in the United States, but it is viewed as positive in Japan if one's silence helps preserve unity.

U.S. managers also put greater emphasis on short-term results than foreign managers do. In marketing, for example, Japanese managers strive to achieve "ever-lasting customers," whereas many Americans strive to make a one-time sale. Marketing managers in Japan see making a sale as the beginning, not the end, of the selling process. This is an important distinction. Japanese managers often criticize U.S. managers for worrying more about shareholders, whom they do not know, than

TABLE 4-2   Cultural Pitfalls That You Need to Know

- Waving is a serious insult in Greece and Nigeria, particularly if the hand is near someone's face.
- Making a "good-bye" wave in Europe can mean "No," but it means "Come here" in Peru.
- In China, last names are written first.
- A man named Carlos Lopez-Garcia should be addressed as Mr. Lopez in Latin America, but as Mr. Garcia in Brazil.
- Breakfast meetings are considered uncivilized in most foreign countries.
- Latin Americans are on average 20 minutes late to business appointments.
- Direct eye contact is impolite in Japan.
- Don't cross your legs in any Arab or many Asian countries—it's rude to show the sole of your shoe.
- In Brazil, touching your thumb and first finger—an American "Okay" sign—is the equivalent of raising your middle finger.
- Nodding or tossing your head back in southern Italy, Malta, Greece, and Tunisia means "No." In India, this body motion means "Yes."
- Snapping your fingers is vulgar in France and Belgium.
- Folding your arms across your chest is a sign of annoyance in Finland.
- In China, leave some food on your plate to show that your host was so generous that you couldn't finish.
- Do not eat with your left hand when dining with clients from Malaysia or India.
- One form of communication works the same worldwide. It's the smile—so take that along wherever you go.

employees, whom they do know. Americans refer to "hourly employees," whereas many Japanese companies still refer to "lifetime employees."

Rose Knotts recently summarized some important cultural differences between U.S. and foreign managers:[10]

1. Americans place an exceptionally high priority on time, viewing time as an asset. Many foreigners place more worth on relationships. This difference results in foreign managers often viewing U.S. managers as "more interested in business than people."

2. Personal touching and distance norms differ around the world. Americans generally stand about three feet from each other when carrying on business conversations, but Arabs and Africans stand about one foot apart. Touching another person with the left hand in business dealings is taboo in some countries. American managers need to learn the personal-space rules of foreign managers with whom they interact in business.

3. People in some cultures do not place the same significance on material wealth as American managers often do. Lists of the "largest corporations" and "highest-paid" executives abound in the United States. "More is better" and "bigger is better" in the United States, but not everywhere. This can be a consideration in trying to motivate individuals in other countries.

4. Family roles and relationships vary in different countries. For example, males are valued more than females in some cultures, and peer pressure, work situations, and business interactions reinforce this phenomenon.

5. Language differs dramatically across countries, even in countries where people speak the same language. Words and expressions commonly used in one country may be disrespectful in another.

6. Business and daily life in some societies are governed by religious factors. Prayer times, holidays, daily events, and dietary restrictions, for example, need to be respected by American managers not familiar with these practices in some countries.

7. Time spent with the family and the quality of relationships are more important in some cultures than the personal achievement and accomplishments espoused by the traditional U.S. manager. For example, where a person stands in the hierarchy of a firm's organizational structure, how large the firm is, and where the firm is located are much more important factors to U.S. managers than to many foreign managers.

8. Many cultures around the world value modesty, team spirit, collectivity, and patience much more than the competitiveness and individualism that are so important in the United States.

9. Punctuality is a valued personal trait when conducting business in the United States, but it is not revered in many of the world's societies. Eating habits also differ dramatically across cultures. For example, belching is acceptable in many countries as evidence of satisfaction with the food that has been prepared. Chinese culture considers it good manners to sample a portion of each food served.

10. To prevent social blunders when meeting with managers from other lands, one must learn and respect the rules of etiquette of others. Sitting on a toilet seat is viewed as unsanitary in most countries, but not in the United States. Leaving food or drink after dining is considered impolite in some countries, but not in China. Bowing instead of shaking hands is customary in many countries. Many cultures view Americans as unsanitary for locating toi-

let and bathing facilities in the same area, whereas Americans view people of some cultures as unsanitary for not taking a bath or shower every day.

11. Americans often do business with individuals they do not know, but this practice is not accepted in many other cultures. In Mexico and Japan, for example, an amicable relationship is often mandatory before conducting business.

In many countries, effective managers are those who are best at negotiating with government bureaucrats rather than those who inspire workers. Many U.S. managers are uncomfortable with nepotism and bribery, which are common in many countries. In almost every country except the United States, bribery is tax deductible.

The United States has gained a reputation for defending women from sexual harassment and minorities from discrimination, but not all countries embrace the same values. For example, in the Czech Republic, it is considered a compliment when the boss openly flirts with his female secretary and invites her to dinner. U.S. managers in the Czech Republic who do not flirt seem cold and uncaring to some employees.

American managers in China have to be careful about how they arrange office furniture because Chinese workers believe in *feng shui,* the practice of harnessing natural forces. U.S. managers in Japan have to be careful about *nemaswashio,* whereby Japanese workers expect supervisors to alert them privately of changes rather than informing them in a meeting. Japanese managers have little appreciation for versatility, expecting all managers to be the same. In Japan, "If a nail sticks out, you hit it into the wall," says Brad Lashbrook, an international consultant for Wilson Learning.

Probably the biggest obstacle to the effectiveness of U.S. managers—or managers from any country working in another—is the fact that it is almost impossible to change the attitude of a foreign workforce. "The system drives you; you cannot fight the system or culture," says Bill Parker, president of Phillips Petroleum in Norway.

Management

The *functions of management* consist of five basic activities: planning, organizing, motivating, staffing, and controlling. An overview of these activities is provided in Table 4-3.

Planning
The only thing certain about the future of any organization is change, and *planning* is the essential bridge between the present and the future that increases the likelihood of achieving desired results. Planning is the process by which one determines whether to attempt a task, works out the most effective way of reaching desired objectives, and prepares to overcome unexpected difficulties with adequate resources. Planning is the start of the process by which an individual or business may turn empty dreams into achievements. Planning enables one to avoid the trap of working extremely hard but achieving little.

Planning is an up-front investment in success. Planning helps a firm achieve maximum effect from a given effort. Planning enables a firm to take into account relevant factors and focus on the critical ones. Planning helps ensure that the firm can be prepared for all reasonable eventualities and for all changes that will be needed. Planning enables a firm to gather the resources needed and carry out tasks in the most efficient way possible. Planning enables a firm to conserve its own resources, avoid wasting ecological resources, make a fair profit, and be seen as an effective, useful firm. Planning enables a firm to identify precisely what is to be achieved and to detail precisely the who,

TABLE 4-3   The Basic Functions of Management

FUNCTION	DESCRIPTION	STAGE OF STRATEGIC-MANAGEMENT PROCESS WHEN MOST IMPORTANT
Planning	Planning consists of all those managerial activities related to preparing for the future. Specific tasks include forecasting, establishing objectives, devising strategies, developing policies, and setting goals.	Strategy Formulation
Organizing	Organizing includes all those managerial activities that result in a structure of task and authority relationships. Specific areas include organizational design, job specialization, job descriptions, job specifications, span of control, unity of command, coordination, job design, and job analysis.	Strategy Implementation
Motivating	Motivating involves efforts directed toward shaping human behavior. Specific topics include leadership, communication, work groups, behavior modification, delegation of authority, job enrichment, job satisfaction, needs fulfillment, organizational change, employee morale, and managerial morale.	Strategy Implementation
Staffing	Staffing activities are centered on personnel or human resource management. Included are wage and salary administration, employee benefits, interviewing, hiring, firing, training, management development, employee safety, affirmative action, equal employment opportunity, union relations, career development, personnel research, discipline policies, grievance procedures, and public relations.	Strategy Implementation
Controlling	Controlling refers to all those managerial activities directed toward ensuring that actual results are consistent with planned results. Key areas of concern include quality control, financial control, sales control, inventory control, expense control, analysis of variances, rewards, and sanctions.	Strategy Evaluation

what, when, where, why, and how needed to achieve desired objectives. Planning enables a firm to assess whether the effort, costs, and implications associated with achieving desired objectives are warranted.[11] Planning is the cornerstone of effective strategy formulation. But even though it is considered the foundation of management, it is commonly the task that managers neglect most. Planning is essential for successful strategy implementation and strategy evaluation, largely because organizing, motivating, staffing, and controlling activities depend upon good planning.

The process of planning must involve managers and employees throughout an organization. The time horizon for planning decreases from two to five years for top-level to less than six months for lower-level managers. The important point is that all managers do planning and should involve subordinates in the process to facilitate employee understanding and commitment.

Planning can have a positive impact on organizational and individual performance. Planning allows an organization to identify and take advantage of external opportunities as well as minimize the impact of external threats. Planning is more than extrapolating from the past and present into the future. It also includes developing a mission, forecasting future events and trends, establishing objectives, and choosing strategies to pursue.

An organization can develop synergy through planning. *Synergy* exists when everyone pulls together as a team that knows what it wants to achieve; synergy is the $2 + 2 = 5$ effect. By establishing and communicating clear objectives, employees and managers can work together toward desired results. Synergy can result in powerful competitive advantages. The strategic-management process itself is aimed at creating synergy in an organization.

Planning allows a firm to adapt to changing markets and thus to shape its own destiny. Strategic management can be viewed as a formal planning process that allows an organization to pursue proactive rather than reactive strategies. Successful organizations strive to control their own futures rather than merely react to external forces and events as they occur. Historically, organisms and organizations that have not adapted to changing conditions have become extinct. Swift adaptation is needed today more than ever because changes in markets, economies, and competitors worldwide are accelerating.

Organizing

The purpose of *organizing* is to achieve coordinated effort by defining task and authority relationships. Organizing means determining who does what and who reports to whom. There are countless examples in history of well-organized enterprises successfully competing against—and in some cases defeating—much stronger but less-organized firms. A well-organized firm generally has motivated managers and employees who are committed to seeing the organization succeed. Resources are allocated more effectively and used more efficiently in a well-organized firm than in a disorganized firm.

The organizing function of management can be viewed as consisting of three sequential activities: breaking down tasks into jobs (work specialization), combining jobs to form departments (departmentalization), and delegating authority. Breaking down tasks into jobs requires the development of job descriptions and job specifications. These tools clarify for both managers and employees what particular jobs entail. In *The Wealth of Nations,* published in 1776, Adam Smith cited the advantages of work specialization in the manufacture of pins:

> One man draws the wire, another straightens it, a third cuts it, a fourth points it, a fifth grinds it at the top for receiving the head. Ten men working in this manner can produce 48,000 pins in a single day, but if they had all wrought separately and independently, each might at best produce twenty pins in a day.[12]

Combining jobs to form departments results in an organizational structure, span of control, and a chain of command. Changes in strategy often require changes in structure because positions may be created, deleted, or merged. Organizational structure dictates how resources are allocated and how objectives are established in a firm. Allocating resources and establishing objectives geographically, for example, is much different from doing so by product or customer.

The most common forms of departmentalization are functional, divisional, strategic business unit, and matrix. These types of structure are discussed further in Chapter 7.

Delegating authority is an important organizing activity, as evidenced in the old saying "You can tell how good a manager is by observing how his or her department functions when he or she isn't there." Employees today are more educated and more capable of participating in organizational decision making than ever before. In most cases, they expect to be delegated authority and responsibility and to be held accountable for results. Delegation of authority is embedded in the strategic-management process.

Motivating

Motivating can be defined as the process of influencing people to accomplish specific objectives.[13] Motivation explains why some people work hard and others do not. Objectives, strategies, and policies have little chance of succeeding if employees and managers are not motivated to implement strategies once they are formulated. The motivating function of management includes at least four major components: leadership, group dynamics, communication, and organizational change.

When managers and employees of a firm strive to achieve high levels of productivity, this indicates that the firm's strategists are good leaders. Good leaders establish rapport with subordinates, empathize with their needs and concerns, set a good example, and are trustworthy and fair. Leadership includes developing a vision of the firm's future and inspiring people to work hard to achieve that vision. Kirkpatrick and Locke reported that certain traits also characterize effective leaders: knowledge of the business, cognitive ability, self-confidence, honesty, integrity, and drive.[14]

Research suggests that democratic behavior on the part of leaders results in more positive attitudes toward change and higher productivity than does autocratic behavior. Drucker said:

> Leadership is not a magnetic personality. That can just as well be demagoguery. It is not "making friends and influencing people." That is flattery. Leadership is the lifting of a person's vision to higher sights, the raising of a person's performance to a higher standard, the building of a person's personality beyond its normal limitations.[15]

Group dynamics play a major role in employee morale and satisfaction. Informal groups or coalitions form in every organization. The norms of coalitions can range from being very positive to very negative toward management. It is important, therefore, that strategists identify the composition and nature of informal groups in an organization to facilitate strategy formulation, implementation, and evaluation. Leaders of informal groups are especially important in formulating and implementing strategy changes.

Communication, perhaps the most important word in management, is a major component in motivation. An organization's system of communication determines whether strategies can be implemented successfully. Good two-way communication is vital for gaining support for departmental and divisional objectives and policies. Top-down communication can encourage bottom-up communication. The strategic-management process becomes a lot easier when subordinates are encouraged to discuss their concerns, reveal their problems, provide recommendations, and give suggestions. A primary reason for instituting strategic management is to build and support effective communication networks throughout the firm.

> The manager of tomorrow must be able to get his people to commit themselves to the business, whether they are machine operators or junior vice-presidents. Ah, you say, participative management. Have a cigar. But just because most managers tug a forelock at the P word doesn't mean they know how to make it work. Today, throwing together a few quality circles won't suffice. The key issue will be empowerment, a term whose strength suggests the need to get beyond merely sharing a little information and a bit of decision making.[16]

Staffing

The management function of *staffing,* also called *personnel management* or *human resource management,* includes activities such as recruiting, interviewing, testing, selecting, orienting, training, developing, caring for, evaluating, rewarding, disciplining, promoting, transferring, demoting, and dismissing employees, as well as managing union relations.

Staffing activities play a major role in strategy-implementation efforts, and for this reason, human resource managers are becoming more actively involved in the strategic-management process. It is important to identify strengths and weaknesses in the staffing area.

The complexity and importance of human resource activities have increased to such a degree that all but the smallest organizations now need a full-time human resource manager. Numerous court cases that directly affect staffing activities are decided each day. Organizations and individuals can be penalized severely for not following federal, state, and local laws and guidelines related to staffing. Line managers simply cannot stay abreast of all the legal developments and requirements regarding staffing. The human resources department coordinates staffing decisions in the firm so that an organization as a whole meets legal requirements. This department also provides needed consistency in administering company rules, wages, and policies.

Human resource management is particularly challenging for international companies. For example, the inability of spouses and children to adapt to new surroundings has become a major staffing problem in overseas transfers. The problems include premature returns, job performance slumps, resignations, discharges, low morale, marital discord, and general discontent. Firms such as Ford Motor and ExxonMobil have begun screening and interviewing spouses and children before assigning persons to overseas positions. The 3M Corporation introduces children to peers in the target country and offers spouses educational benefits.

Strategists are becoming increasingly aware of how important human resources are to effective strategic management. Human resource managers are becoming more involved and more proactive in formulating and implementing strategies. They provide leadership for organizations that are restructuring, or they allow employees to work at home.

Controlling

The *controlling* function of management includes all of those activities undertaken to ensure that actual operations conform to planned operations. All managers in an organization have controlling responsibilities, such as conducting performance evaluations and taking necessary action to minimize inefficiencies. The controlling function of management is particularly important for effective strategy evaluation. Controlling consists of four basic steps:

1. Establishing performance standards
2. Measuring individual and organizational performance
3. Comparing actual performance to planned performance standards
4. Taking corrective actions

Measuring individual performance is often conducted ineffectively or not at all in organizations. Some reasons for this shortcoming are that evaluations can create confrontations that most managers prefer to avoid, can take more time than most managers are willing to give, and can require skills that many managers lack.

No single approach to measuring individual performance is without limitations. For this reason, an organization should examine various methods, such as the graphic rating scale, the behaviorally anchored rating scale, and the critical incident method, and then develop or select a performance-appraisal approach that best suits the firm's needs. Increasingly, firms are striving to link organizational performance with managers' and employees' pay. This topic is discussed further in Chapter 7.

Management Audit Checklist of Questions

The following checklist of questions can help determine specific strengths and weaknesses in the functional area of business. An answer of *no* to any question could indicate a potential weakness, although the strategic significance and implications of negative answers, of course, will vary by organization, industry, and severity of the weakness. Positive or yes answers to the checklist questions suggest potential areas of strength.

1. Does the firm use strategic-management concepts?
2. Are company objectives and goals measurable and well communicated?
3. Do managers at all hierarchical levels plan effectively?
4. Do managers delegate authority well?
5. Is the organization's structure appropriate?
6. Are job descriptions and job specifications clear?
7. Is employee morale high?
8. Are employee turnover and absenteeism low?
9. Are organizational reward and control mechanisms effective?

Marketing

Marketing can be described as the process of defining, anticipating, creating, and fulfilling customers' needs and wants for products and services. There are seven basic *functions of marketing:* (1) customer analysis, (2) selling products/services, (3) product and service planning, (4) pricing, (5) distribution, (6) marketing research, and (7) opportunity analysis.[17] Understanding these functions helps strategists identify and evaluate marketing strengths and weaknesses.

Customer Analysis

Customer analysis—the examination and evaluation of consumer needs, desires, and wants—involves administering customer surveys, analyzing consumer information, evaluating market positioning strategies, developing customer profiles, and determining optimal market segmentation strategies. The information generated by customer analysis can be essential in developing an effective mission statement. Customer profiles can reveal the demographic characteristics of an organization's customers. Buyers, sellers, distributors, salespeople, managers, wholesalers, retailers, suppliers, and creditors can all participate in gathering information to successfully identify customers' needs and wants. Successful organizations continually monitor present and potential customers' buying patterns.

Selling Products/Services

Successful strategy implementation generally rests upon the ability of an organization to sell some product or service. *Selling* includes many marketing activities, such as advertising, sales promotion, publicity, personal selling, sales force management, customer relations, and dealer relations. These activities are especially critical when a firm pursues a market penetration strategy. The effectiveness of various selling tools for consumer and industrial products varies. Personal selling is most important for industrial goods companies, and advertising is most important for consumer goods companies. During the CBS telecast of Super Bowl XXXVIII on February 1, 2004, a 30-second advertisement cost $2.3 million, up 9 percent from 2003. There were 62 ad slots sold by CBS for this Super Bowl. Determining organizational strengths and weaknesses in the selling function of marketing is an important part of performing an internal strategic-management audit.

With regard to advertising products and services on the Internet, a new trend is to exclusively base advertising rates on sales rates. This new accountability contrasts sharply with traditional broadcast and print advertising, which bases rates on the number of persons expected to see a given advertisement. The new cost-per-sale online advertising rates are possible because any Web site can monitor which user clicks on which advertisement and then can record whether that consumer actually buys the product. If there are no sales, then the advertisement is free.

The fastest-growing segments of U.S. advertising spending in 2004 compared to 2003 were as follows: Internet (up 27.9 percent), outdoor advertising (up 20.1 percent), cable TV (up 13.8 percent), spot TV (up 11.7 percent), consumer magazines (up 11.2 percent), and network TV (up 10.7 percent).[18] The U.S. firm advertising more than any other is Procter & Gamble, which spent $3 billion on ads in 2004, roughly $2.5 billion of that on television. But P&G plans to significantly scale back its ad spending on television in 2005–2006.[19]

In a major strategic shift, pharmaceutical companies are significantly reducing the number of their salespersons who call on primary-care doctors such as internists and general practitioners. For example, drug maker Wyeth is reducing by 30 percent its sales force to less than 5,000 persons in 2005. The strategic shift among drug firms is to drastically reduce multiple salespeople calling on identical doctors. This common but costly strategy, called *mirroring,* has alienated physicians. Pfizer, which has the world's largest drug sales force, is cutting its sales force by 5 percent to less than 11,000 persons in 2005.

Product and Service Planning

Product and service planning includes activities such as test marketing; product and brand positioning; devising warranties; packaging; determining product options, product features, product style, and product quality; deleting old products; and providing for customer service. Product and service planning is particularly important when a company is pursuing product development or diversification.

One of the most effective product and service planning techniques is *test marketing.* Test markets allow an organization to test alternative marketing plans and to forecast future sales of new products. In conducting a test market project, an organization must decide how many cities to include, which cities to include, how long to run the test, what information to collect during the test, and what action to take after the test has been completed. Test marketing is used more frequently by consumer goods companies than by industrial goods companies. Test marketing can allow an organization to avoid substantial losses by revealing weak products and ineffective marketing approaches before large-scale production begins.

Pricing

Five major stakeholders affect *pricing* decisions: consumers, governments, suppliers, distributors, and competitors. Sometimes an organization will pursue a forward integration strategy primarily to gain better control over prices charged to consumers. Governments can impose constraints on price fixing, price discrimination, minimum prices, unit pricing, price advertising, and price controls. For example, the Robinson-Patman Act prohibits manufacturers and wholesalers from discriminating in price among channel member purchasers (suppliers and distributors) if competition is injured.

Competing organizations must be careful not to coordinate discounts, credit terms, or condition of sale; not to discuss prices, markups, and costs at trade association meetings; and not to arrange to issue new price lists on the same date, to rotate low bids on contracts, or to uniformly restrict production to maintain high prices. Strategists should view price from both a short-run and a long-run perspective, because competitors can copy price changes with relative ease. Often a dominant firm will aggressively match all price cuts by competitors.

With regard to pricing, as the value of the dollar increases, U.S. multinational companies have a choice. They can raise prices in the local currency of a foreign country or risk losing sales and market share. Alternatively, multinational firms can keep prices steady and face reduced profit when their export revenue is reported in the United States in dollars.

Wrigley's recently raised the price of its chewing gum by 5 cents, to 30 cents, the first such price hike in 16 years. The price of plasma televisions has dropped to below $2,000 from above $8,000 several years ago. Intense price competition coupled with Internet price-comparative shopping in most industries has reduced profit margins to bare minimum levels for most companies. For example, airline tickets, rental car prices, and even computer prices are lower today than they have been in many years.

Prices on handheld computers are falling dramatically because distributors have excess inventory due to slowing consumer demand. Analysts contend that handheld computers will soon become as inexpensive as cellphones—and eventually may be given away when a consumer purchases the company's wireless Internet service. Palm is the largest handheld-computer maker, but other competitors include Casio, Handspring, and Hewlett-Packard. While the current economic downturn has wreaked havoc for companies on Wall Street, it has benefited consumers on Main Street, who have seen lower prices almost everywhere they shop.

Distribution

Distribution includes warehousing, distribution channels, distribution coverage, retail site locations, sales territories, inventory levels and location, transportation carriers, wholesaling, and retailing. Most producers today do not sell their goods directly to consumers. Various marketing entities act as intermediaries; they bear a variety of names such as wholesalers, retailers, brokers, facilitators, agents, vendors—or simply distributors.

Distribution becomes especially important when a firm is striving to implement a market development or forward integration strategy. Some of the most complex and challenging decisions facing a firm concern product distribution. Intermediaries flourish in our economy because many producers lack the financial resources and expertise to carry out direct marketing. Manufacturers who could afford to sell directly to the public often can gain greater returns by expanding and improving their manufacturing operations. Even General Motors would find it very difficult to buy out its more than 18,000 independent dealers.

Successful organizations identify and evaluate alternative ways to reach their ultimate market. Possible approaches vary from direct selling to using just one or many wholesalers and retailers. Strengths and weaknesses of each channel alternative should be determined according to economic, control, and adaptive criteria. Organizations should consider the costs and benefits of various wholesaling and retailing options. They must consider the need to motivate and control channel members and the need to adapt to changes in the future. Once a marketing channel is chosen, an organization usually must adhere to it for an extended period of time.

Marketing Research

Marketing research is the systematic gathering, recording, and analyzing of data about problems relating to the marketing of goods and services. Marketing research can uncover critical strengths and weaknesses, and marketing researchers employ numerous scales, instruments, procedures, concepts, and techniques to gather information. Marketing research activities support all of the major business functions of an organization. Organizations that possess excellent marketing research skills have a definite strength in pursuing generic strategies.

> The President of PepsiCo said, "Looking at the competition is the company's best form of market research. The majority of our strategic successes are ideas that we borrow from the marketplace, usually from a small regional or local competitor. In each case, we spot a promising new idea, improve on it, and then out-execute our competitor."[20]

As indicated in the "E-Commerce Perspective," market researchers should be careful not to use spam as a marketing tool because consumers intensely reject this method of gathering information. Spam slows down business for millions of firms.

Opportunity Analysis

The seventh function of marketing is *opportunity analysis,* which involves assessing the costs, benefits, and risks associated with marketing decisions. Three steps are required to perform a *cost/benefit analysis:* (1) compute the total costs associated with a decision, (2) estimate the total benefits from the decision, and (3) compare the total costs with the total benefits. When expected benefits exceed total costs, an opportunity becomes more attractive. Sometimes the variables included in a cost/benefit analysis cannot be quantified or even measured, but usually reasonable estimates can be made to allow the analysis to be performed. One key factor to be considered is risk. Cost/benefit analysis should also be performed when a company is evaluating alternative ways to be socially responsible.

Marketing Audit Checklist of Questions

The following questions about marketing, much like the earlier questions for management, are pertinent:

1. Are markets segmented effectively?
2. Is the organization positioned well among competitors?
3. Has the firm's market share been increasing?
4. Are present channels of distribution reliable and cost-effective?
5. Does the firm have an effective sales organization?

E-COMMERCE PERSPECTIVE

Spam Is Choking E-Commerce

Spam, unwanted, unsolicited, undesirable e-mail messages, is globally choking e-commerce. Spam now accounts for over 50 percent of all Internet traffic and annually delivers more than 1,000 mailings to every person who uses the Internet. This traffic jams individual and business servers and computers around the globe and clogs and slows down transactions. Companies are being forced to buy more and more hardware and software to handle the avalanche of spam while their workers waste precious time every day combing through it. Current estimates are that spam is costing companies $874 a year per worker. Spammers are as bad for e-commerce as vandals who create worms and viruses or thieves who steal credit card numbers and extort. The FBI now lists cybercrime as its third-ranking priority, behind only the war against terror and counterespionage.

California has the nation's toughest anti-spam law because it requires e-mail marketers either to have an existing business relationship with each recipient or to receive permission from the recipient to send a commercial e-mail. Also, California law allows lawyers to sue the senders of unwanted e-mail; the law carries penalties of $1,000 for each unsolicited message sent and a $1 million fine for each "campaign." Since there is as yet no U.S. federal law against spamming, e-mail marketers still frequently change their e-mail address, route their e-mails through multiple computers to disguise their identity, and send e-mails from outside the United States. Thirty-five states have laws regulating spam in some form, but California's and Delaware's are more stringent.

In an attempt to halt the spread of disruptive computer viruses and spam, more and more companies are eliminating employee use of AOL, Yahoo!, and other outside e-mail services to protect their own networks. Companies are also eliminating Web surfing by employees. Phone4U, a mobile-phone retailer in England, for example, now prohibits its 2,500 employees from e-mailing one another, although customers can still e-mail the company. Analysts estimate that roughly half of all external corporate e-mail, or more than two trillion messages, was spam. Market researcher Cipher-Trust Research says that up to 80 percent of all U.S. businesses have policies in place to combat spam and viruses.

Sources: Adapted from Heather Green, Ira Sager, Steve Rosenbush, and Andrew Park, "Where Danger Lurks," *BusinessWeek* (August 25, 2003): 114-118; Mylene Mangalindan, "California Gets Serious About Spam," *Wall Street Journal* (September 24, 2003): A4; Jon Swartz, "More Workers Get Shut Out of E-mail," *USA Today* (September 29, 2003): B1.

6. Does the firm conduct market research?
7. Are product quality and customer service good?
8. Are the firm's products and services priced appropriately?
9. Does the firm have an effective promotion, advertising, and publicity strategy?
10. Are marketing, planning, and budgeting effective?
11. Do the firm's marketing managers have adequate experience and training?

Finance/Accounting

Financial condition is often considered the single best measure of a firm's competitive position and overall attractiveness to investors. Determining an organization's financial strengths and weaknesses is essential to effectively formulating strategies. A firm's liquidity, leverage, working capital, profitability, asset utilization, cash flow, and equity can eliminate some strategies as being feasible alternatives. Financial factors often alter existing strategies and change implementation plans.

An especially good Web site to obtain financial information about a company is https://us.etrade.com/e/t/invest/markets, which provides excellent financial ratio, stock, and valuation information on all publicly held companies. Simply insert the company's stock symbol when the screen first loads and a wealth of information follows. Another nice site for obtaining financial information is www.forbes.com. Be sure to access the Manufacturing and Service section of www.strategyclub.com for excellent financial-related Web sites.

Finance/Accounting Functions

According to James Van Horne, the *functions of finance/accounting* comprise three decisions: the investment decision, the financing decision, and the dividend decision.[21] Financial ratio analysis is the most widely used method for determining an organization's strengths and weaknesses in the investment, financing, and dividend areas. Because the functional areas of business are so closely related, financial ratios can signal strengths or weaknesses in management, marketing, production, research and development, and management information systems activities. It is important to note here that financial ratios are equally applicable in for-profit and nonprofit organizations. Even though nonprofit organizations obviously would not have return-on-investment or earnings-per-share ratios, they would routinely monitor many other special ratios. For example, a church would monitor the ratio of dollar contributions to number of members, while a zoo would monitor dollar food sales to number of visitors. A university would monitor number of students divided by number of professors. Therefore, be creative when performing ratio analysis for nonprofit organizations because they strive to be financially sound just as for-profit firms do.

The *investment decision,* also called *capital budgeting,* is the allocation and reallocation of capital and resources to projects, products, assets, and divisions of an organization. Once strategies are formulated, capital budgeting decisions are required to successfully implement strategies. The *financing decision* determines the best capital structure for the firm and includes examining various methods by which the firm can raise capital (for example, by issuing stock, increasing debt, selling assets, or using a combination of these approaches). The financing decision must consider both short-term and long-term needs for working capital. Two key financial ratios that indicate whether a firm's financing decisions have been effective are the debt-to-equity ratio and the debt-to-total-assets ratio.

Dividend decisions concern issues such as the percentage of earnings paid to stockholders, the stability of dividends paid over time, and the repurchase or issuance of stock. Dividend decisions determine the amount of funds that are retained in a firm compared to the amount paid out to stockholders. Three financial ratios that are helpful in evaluating a firm's dividend decisions are the earnings-per-share ratio, the dividends-per-share ratio, and the price-earnings ratio. The benefits of paying dividends to investors must be balanced against the benefits of internally retaining funds, and there is no set formula on how to balance this trade-off. For the reasons listed here, dividends are sometimes paid out even when funds could be better reinvested in the business or when the firm has to obtain outside sources of capital:

1. Paying cash dividends is customary. Failure to do so could be thought of as a stigma. A dividend change is considered a signal about the future.
2. Dividends represent a sales point for investment bankers. Some institutional investors can buy only dividend-paying stocks.
3. Shareholders often demand dividends, even in companies with great opportunities for reinvesting all available funds.
4. A myth exists that paying dividends will result in a higher stock price.

Maytag cut its dividend payout from 18 cents per share, which had been in place since 1998, to 9 cents per share following an 80 percent collapse in first-quarter 2005 company earnings. Maytag has been slow to move its manufacturing outside the United States to capitalize on lower labor costs. Only 12 percent of Maytag products are made outside the United States, although it just closed a refrigerator factory in Galesburg, Illinois, and reopened that factory in Reynosa, Mexico.

Basic Types of Financial Ratios

Financial ratios are computed from an organization's income statement and balance sheet. Computing financial ratios is like taking a picture because the results reflect a situation at just one point in time. Comparing ratios over time and to industry averages is more likely to result in meaningful statistics that can be used to identify and evaluate strengths and weaknesses. Trend analysis, illustrated in Figure 4-2, is a useful technique that incorporates both the time and industry average dimensions of financial ratios. Note that the dotted lines reveal projected ratios. Some Web sites, such as https://us.etrade.com/e/t/invest/markets, calculate financial ratios and provide data with charts. Four major sources of industry-average financial ratios follow:

VISIT THE NET

Enter your stock symbol and then access the up-to-date financial news about the company. (http://finance.yahoo.com)

1. Dun & Bradstreet's *Industry Norms and Key Business Ratios*—Fourteen different ratios are calculated in an industry-average format for 800 different types of businesses. The ratios are presented by Standard Industrial Classification (SIC) number and are grouped by annual sales into three size categories.

FIGURE 4-2

A Financial Ratio Trend Analysis

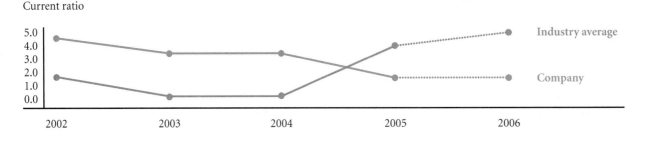

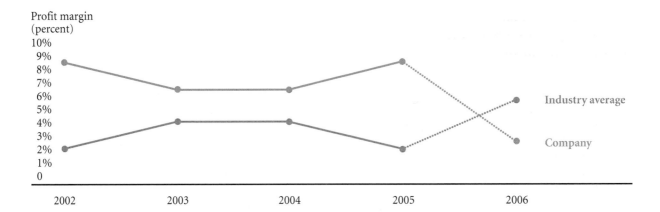

2. Robert Morris Associates' *Annual Statement Studies*—Sixteen different ratios are calculated in an industry-average format. Industries are referenced by SIC numbers published by the Bureau of the Census. The ratios are presented in four size categories by annual sales for all firms in the industry.

3. *Almanac of Business & Industrial Financial Ratios*—Twenty-two financial ratios and percentages are provided in an industry-average format for all major industries. The ratios and percentages are given for 12 different company-size categories for all firms in a given industry.

4. *Federal Trade Commission Reports*—The FTC publishes quarterly financial data, including ratios on manufacturing companies. FTC reports include analyses by industry group and asset size.

Table 4-4 provides a summary of key financial ratios showing how each ratio is calculated and what each ratio measures. However, all the ratios are not significant for all industries and companies. For example, accounts receivable turnover and average collection period are not very meaningful to a company that primarily does a cash receipts business. Key financial ratios can be classified into the following five types:

1. *Liquidity ratios* measure a firm's ability to meet maturing short-term obligations.
   Current ratio
   Quick (or acid-test) ratio

2. *Leverage ratios* measure the extent to which a firm has been financed by debt.
   Debt-to-total-assets ratio
   Debt-to-equity ratio
   Long-term debt-to-equity ratio
   Times-interest-earned (or coverage) ratio

3. *Activity ratios* measure how effectively a firm is using its resources.
   Inventory turnover
   Fixed assets turnover
   Total assets turnover
   Accounts receivable turnover
   Average collection period

4. *Profitability ratios* measure management's overall effectiveness as shown by the returns generated on sales and investment.
   Gross profit margin
   Operating profit margin
   Net profit margin
   Return on total assets (ROA)
   Return on stockholders' equity (ROE)
   Earnings per share (EPS)
   Price-earnings ratio

5. *Growth ratios* measure the firm's ability to maintain its economic position in the growth of the economy and industry.
   Sales
   Net income
   Earnings per share
   Dividends per share

TABLE 4-4 A Summary of Key Financial Ratios

RATIO	HOW CALCULATED	WHAT IT MEASURES
Liquidity Ratios		
Current Ratio	$\dfrac{\text{Current assets}}{\text{Current liabilities}}$	The extent to which a firm can meet its short-term obligations
Quick Ratio	$\dfrac{\text{Current assets minus inventory}}{\text{Current liabilities}}$	The extent to which a firm can meet its short-term obligations without relying upon the sale of its inventories
Leverage Ratios		
Debt-to-Total-Assets Ratio	$\dfrac{\text{Total debt}}{\text{Total assets}}$	The percentage of total funds that are provided by creditors
Debt-to-Equity Ratio	$\dfrac{\text{Total debt}}{\text{Total stockholders' equity}}$	The percentage of total funds provided by creditors versus by owners
Long-Term Debt-to-Equity Ratio	$\dfrac{\text{Long-term debt}}{\text{Total stockholders' equity}}$	The balance between debt and equity in a firm's long-term capital structure
Times-Interest-Earned Ratio	$\dfrac{\text{Profits before interest and taxes}}{\text{Total interest charges}}$	The extent to which earnings can decline without the firm becoming unable to meet its annual interest costs
Activity Ratios		
Inventory Turnover	$\dfrac{\text{Sales}}{\text{Inventory of finished goods}}$	Whether a firm holds excessive stocks of inventories and whether a firm is slowly selling its inventories compared to the industry average
Fixed Assets Turnover	$\dfrac{\text{Sales}}{\text{Fixed assets}}$	Sales productivity and plant and equipment utilization
Total Assets Turnover	$\dfrac{\text{Sales}}{\text{Total assets}}$	Whether a firm is generating a sufficient volume of business for the size of its asset investment
Accounts Receivable Turnover	$\dfrac{\text{Annual credit sales}}{\text{Accounts receivable}}$	The average length of time it takes a firm to collect credit sales (in percentage terms)
Average Collection Period	$\dfrac{\text{Accounts receivable}}{\text{Total credit sales/365 days}}$	The average length of time it takes a firm to collect on credit sales (in days)
Profitability Ratios		
Gross Profit Margin	$\dfrac{\text{Sales minus cost of goods sold}}{\text{Sales}}$	The total margin available to cover operating expenses and yield a profit
Operating Profit Margin	$\dfrac{\text{Earnings before interest and taxes (EBIT)}}{\text{Sales}}$	Profitability without concern for taxes and interest
Net Profit Margin	$\dfrac{\text{Net income}}{\text{Sales}}$	After-tax profits per dollar of sales

(Continued)

TABLE 4-4 Continued

RATIO	HOW CALCULATED	WHAT IT MEASURES
Profitability Ratios		
Return on Total Assets (ROA)	$\dfrac{\text{Net income}}{\text{Total assets}}$	After-tax profits per dollar of assets; this ratio is also called return on investment (ROI)
Return on Stockholders' Equity (ROE)	$\dfrac{\text{Net income}}{\text{Total stockholders' equity}}$	After-tax profits per dollar of stockholders' investment in the firm
Earnings Per Share (EPS)	$\dfrac{\text{Net income}}{\text{Number of shares of common stock outstanding}}$	Earnings available to the owners of common stock
Price-Earnings Ratio	$\dfrac{\text{Market price per share}}{\text{Earnings per share}}$	Attractiveness of firm on equity markets
Growth Ratios		
Sales	Annual percentage growth in total sales	Firm's growth rate in sales
Net Income	Annual percentage growth in profits	Firm's growth rate in profits
Earnings Per Share	Annual percentage growth in EPS	Firm's growth rate in EPS
Dividends Per Share	Annual percentage growth in dividends per share	Firm's growth rate in dividends per share

Financial ratio analysis must go beyond the actual calculation and interpretation of ratios. The analysis should be conducted on three separate fronts:

1. *How has each ratio changed over time?* This information provides a means of evaluating historical trends. It is important to note whether each ratio has been historically increasing, decreasing, or nearly constant. For example, a 10 percent profit margin could be bad if the trend has been down 20 percent each of the last three years. But a 10 percent profit margin could be excellent if the trend has been up, up, up. Therefore, calculate the percentage change in each ratio from one year to the next to assess historical financial performance on that dimension. Identify and examine large percent changes in a financial ratio from one year to the next.

2. *How does each ratio compare to industry norms?* A firm's inventory turnover ratio may appear impressive at first glance but may pale when compared to industry standards or norms. Industries can differ dramatically on certain ratios. For example grocery companies, such as Kroger, have a high inventory turnover whereas automobile dealerships have a lower turnover. Therefore, comparison of a firm's ratios within its particular industry can be essential in determining strength/weakness.

3. *How does each ratio compare with key competitors?* Oftentimes competition is more intense between several competitors in a given industry or location than across all rival firms in the industry. When this is true, financial ratio analysis should include comparison to those key competitors. For example, if a firm's profitability ratio is trending up over time and compares favorably to the industry average, but it is trending down relative to its leading competitor, there may be reason for concern.

Financial ratio analysis is not without some limitations. First of all, financial ratios are based on accounting data, and firms differ in their treatment of such items as depreciation, inventory valuation, research and development expenditures, pension plan costs, mergers, and taxes. Also, seasonal factors can influence comparative ratios.

Therefore, conformity to industry composite ratios does not establish with certainty that a firm is performing normally or that it is well managed. Likewise, departures from industry averages do not always indicate that a firm is doing especially well or badly. For example, a high inventory turnover ratio could indicate efficient inventory management and a strong working capital position, but it also could indicate a serious inventory shortage and a weak working capital position.

It is important to recognize that a firm's financial condition depends not only on the functions of finance, but also on many other factors that include (1) management, marketing, management production/operations, research and development, and management information systems decisions; (2) actions by competitors, suppliers, distributors, creditors, customers, and shareholders; and (3) economic, social, cultural, demographic, environmental, political, governmental, legal, and technological trends. Even natural environment liabilities can affect financial ratios, as indicated in the "Natural Environment Perspective. " So financial ratio analysis, like all other analytical tools, should be used wisely.

NATURAL ENVIRONMENT PERSPECTIVE

Is Your Business Polluting the Air or Water?

Air

More than 1.5 billion people around the world live in urban areas with dangerous levels of air pollution. Alarmingly, cities are growing too rapidly to reverse this trend. Seven of the 10 worst cities for sulfur dioxide and carbon monoxide are in developing countries. These and other pollutants cause acute and chronic lung disease, heart disease, lung cancer, and lead-induced neurological damage in children. Lung cancer alone kills over one million people annually, and more than a million new cases of lung cancer are diagnosed annually. There is no effective treatment for lung cancer—only 10 percent of patients are alive five years after diagnosis. Polluted air knows no city, state, country, or continent boundaries.

Water

Is your business polluting the water? Contaminated water is blamed for as much as 80 percent of all disease in developing countries. Well over one billion people in the world still are without safe water to drink, bathe, cook, and clean. Less than 2 percent of the domestic and industrial wastewater generated in developing countries receives any kind of treatment; it just runs into rivers and groundwater resources, thus poisoning populations, the environment, and the planet. Unsafe drinking water is a prime cause of diarrhea, malaria, cancer, infant deformities, and

infant mortality. A few statistics reveal the severity, harshness, and effect of water pollution.

- More than five million babies born in developing countries die annually in the first month of life, mainly because of polluted water.
- About four million babies are born with deformities annually.
- Diarrhea and dysentery kill 2.5 million people annually.
- Malaria kills 2.1 million people annually.

Industrial discharge, a major water problem even in the United States, contributes significantly to the dramatic rise in cancer both here and abroad. More than 10 million new cases of cancer are diagnosed annually, and about 6.5 million people die of cancer annually. More than 1.2 billion of these deaths are caused by stomach and colon cancer, two types often associated with poor water and eating habits. Besides deaths, the anguish, sickness, suffering, and expense inflicted upon people directly or indirectly because of contaminated water is immeasurably high even in the United States. Dangerous industrial chemicals are used here as fertilizers, pesticides, solvents, food additives, fuels, medicines, cosmetics, and in a wide range of manufacturing processes.

Source: Adapted from William Miller, "Clean-Air Contention," *Industry Week* (May 5, 1997): 14. Also, *World Health Organization Report* (1997).

Finance/Accounting Audit Checklist

The following finance/accounting questions, like the similar questions about marketing and management earlier, should be examined:

1. Where is the firm financially strong and weak as indicated by financial ratio analyses?
2. Can the firm raise needed short-term capital?
3. Can the firm raise needed long-term capital through debt and/or equity?
4. Does the firm have sufficient working capital?
5. Are capital budgeting procedures effective?
6. Are dividend payout policies reasonable?
7. Does the firm have good relations with its investors and stockholders?
8. Are the firm's financial managers experienced and well trained?

Production/Operations

The *production/operations function* of a business consists of all those activities that transform inputs into goods and services. Production/operations management deals with inputs, transformations, and outputs that vary across industries and markets. A manufacturing operation transforms or converts inputs such as raw materials, labor, capital, machines, and facilities into finished goods and services. As indicated in Table 4-5, Roger Schroeder suggested that production/operations management comprises five functions or decision areas: process, capacity, inventory, workforce, and quality.

transform inputs into goods and services

Most automakers require a 30-day notice to build vehicles, but Toyota Motor fills a buyer's new car order in just 5 days. Honda Motor was considered the industry's fastest producer, filling orders in 15 days. Automakers have for years operated under

TABLE 4-5 The Basic Functions of Production Management

FUNCTION	DESCRIPTION
1. Process	Process decisions concern the design of the physical production system. Specific decisions include choice of technology, facility layout, process flow analysis, facility location, line balancing, process control, and transportation analysis.
2. Capacity	Capacity decisions concern determination of optimal output levels for the organization—not too much and not too little. Specific decisions include forecasting, facilities planning, aggregate planning, scheduling, capacity planning, and queuing analysis.
3. Inventory	Inventory decisions involve managing the level of raw materials, work-in-process, and finished goods. Specific decisions include what to order, when to order, how much to order, and materials handling.
4. Workforce	Workforce decisions are concerned with managing the skilled, unskilled, clerical, and managerial employees. Specific decisions include job design, work measurement, job enrichment, work standards, and motivation techniques.
5. Quality	Quality decisions are aimed at ensuring that high-quality goods and services are produced. Specific decisions include quality control, sampling, testing, quality assurance, and cost control.

Source: Adapted from R. Schroeder, *Operations Management* (New York: McGraw-Hill Book Co., 1981): 12.

just-in-time inventory systems, but Toyota's 360 suppliers are linked to the company via computers on a virtual assembly line. The new Toyota production system was developed in the company's Cambridge, Ontario, plant and now applies to its Solara, Camry, Corolla, and Tacoma vehicles.

Capacity utilization for light trucks in the automobile industry has dropped from 107 percent in 2000 to 75 percent in 2005, due to oversupply and falling demand. Light trucks, which include SUVs, minivans, and pickups, account for much of the profits for Ford, DaimlerChrysler, and General Motors. U.S. automobile producers have been slow to upgrade their car models, and consequently, foreign makes of cars now comprise more than half of the market share for all cars sold in the United States.

Production/operation

Production/operations activities often represent the largest part of an organization's human and capital assets. In most industries, the major costs of producing a product or service are incurred within operations, so production/operations can have great value as a competitive weapon in a company's overall strategy. Strengths and weaknesses in the five functions of production can mean the success or failure of an enterprise. For example, a major production strength for the JCPenney company is its inventory control system, as explained in the "Global Perspective."

GLOBAL PERSPECTIVE

JCPenney's Global Inventory Control System Best in the Industry

JCPenney is widely considered to have the best inventory control system in the mass merchandising industry, and its system is global in all respects. When a Penney's store in Atlanta sells a dress shirt, a record of that sale goes to a Hong Kong computer company, TAL Apparel Ltd., which instructs a factory worker in Taiwan that same day to ship another identical shirt to that Atlanta store. Penney stores today keep almost no extra inventory of dress shirts, whereas a decade ago, Penney would have had warehouses across the United States keeping thousands of dress shirts in inventory, tying up capital as the shirts slowly went out of style. Formerly, Penney stores would each keep three months of inventory on hand and the warehouses would keep six months of inventory on hand. This was very expensive. Now, the Taiwanese manufacturer ships shirts directly to Penney's stores, bypassing warehouses and corporate decision makers.

As mass retailers today cut costs to bare minimum and respond swiftly to changing consumer needs, they are relying on suppliers more and more to manage their own inventory. And these suppliers are increasingly located in the Far East, rather than in Mexico or South America. TAL in Hong Kong supplies apparel name brands J. Crew, Calvin Klein, Banana Republic, Tommy Hilfiger, Liz Claiborne, Ralph Lauren, and Brooks Brothers to U.S. retailers and does so on a minute's notice. TAL is also actively involved in sales forecasting and inventory management as suppliers today become active production/operations consultants. TAL has manufacturing operations for apparel in Guangdong, Thailand, Malaysia, Taiwan, and Hong Kong.

For other companies such as Lands' End, TAL stitches made-to-measure pants in Malaysia and flies them straight to U.S. consumers with a Lands' End invoice included. Wal-Mart Stores actually pioneered this type of inventory control system years ago when it opened its computer systems to suppliers worldwide, who track sales and replenish inventory on a just-in-time basis. Penney has turned over immense power to TAL. Wai Chan Chan, a principal at McKinsey & Co. in Hong Kong says, "You are giving away a pretty important function when you outsource your inventory management. That's something most retailers do not want to part with." JCPenney is considering allowing TAL to do for its underwear what it does for its shirts. In fact, TAL and Penney are discussing a joint venture to allow TAL to control all of Penney's inventory.

Source: Adapted from Gabriel Kahn, "Invisible Supplier Has Penney's Shirts All Buttoned Up," *Wall Street Journal* (September 11, 2003): A1.

Many production/operations managers are finding that cross-training of employees can help their firms respond faster to changing markets. Cross-training of workers can increase efficiency, quality, productivity, and job satisfaction. For example, at General Motors' Detroit gear and axle plant, costs related to product defects were reduced 400 percent in two years as a result of cross-training workers. A shortage of qualified labor in the United States is another reason cross-training is becoming a common management practice.

Singapore rivals Hong Kong as an attractive site for locating production facilities in Southeast Asia. Singapore is a city-state near Malaysia. An island nation of about 4 million, Singapore is changing from an economy built on trade and services to one built on information technology. A large-scale program in computer education for older (over age 26) residents is very popular. Singapore children receive outstanding computer training in schools. All government services are computerized nicely. Singapore lures multinational businesses with great tax breaks, world-class infrastructure, excellent courts that efficiently handle business disputes, exceptionally low tariffs, large land giveaways, impressive industrial parks, excellent port facilities, and a government very receptive to and cooperative with foreign businesses. Foreign firms now account for 70 percent of manufacturing output in Singapore.

There is much reason for concern that many organizations have not taken sufficient account of the capabilities and limitations of the production/operations function in formulating strategies. Scholars contend that this neglect has had unfavorable consequences on corporate performance in America. As shown in Table 4-6, James Dilworth outlined several types of strategic decisions that a company might make with the production/operations implications of those decisions. Production capabilities and policies can also greatly affect strategies.

Production/Operations Audit Checklist

Questions such as the following should be examined:

1. Are supplies of raw materials, parts, and subassemblies reliable and reasonable?
2. Are facilities, equipment, machinery, and offices in good condition?
3. Are inventory-control policies and procedures effective?
4. Are quality-control policies and procedures effective?
5. Are facilities, resources, and markets strategically located?
6. Does the firm have technological competencies?

Research and Development

The fifth major area of internal operations that should be examined for specific strengths and weaknesses is *research and development (R&D)*. Many firms today conduct no R&D, and yet many other companies depend on successful R&D activities for survival. Firms pursuing a product development strategy especially need to have a strong R&D orientation.

Organizations invest in R&D because they believe that such an investment will lead to a superior product or service and will give them competitive advantages. Research and development expenditures are directed at developing new products before competitors do at improving product quality or at improving manufacturing processes to reduce costs.

TABLE 4-6 Implications of Various Strategies on the Production/Operations Function

VARIOUS STRATEGIES	IMPLICATIONS
1. Compete as low-cost provider of goods or services	Creates high barriers to entry Creates larger market Requires longer production runs and fewer product changes Requires special-purpose equipment and facilities
2. Compete as high-quality provider	Offers more total profit from a smaller volume of sales Requires more quality-assurance effort and higher operating cost Requires more precise equipment, which is more expensive Requires highly skilled workers, necessitating higher wages and greater training efforts
3. Stress customer service	Requires more service people, service parts, and equipment Requires rapid response to customer needs or changes in customer tastes Requires a higher inventory investment
4. Provide rapid and frequent introduction of new products	Requires versatile equipment and people Has higher research and development costs Has high retraining and tooling costs Provides lower volumes for each product and fewer opportunities for improvements due to the learning curve
5. Vertical integration	Enables company to control more of the process May require entry into unfamilar business areas May require high capital investment as well as technology and skills beyond those currently available
6. Consolidate processing (Centralize)	Can result in economies of scale Can locate near one major customer or supplier Vulnerability: one strike, fire, or flood can halt the entire operation
7. Disperse processing of service (Decentralize)	Can be near more customers and resources Requires more complex coordination and duplication of some personnel and equipment at each location If each location produces one product in the line, then other products still must be transported to be available at all locations If each location specializes in a type of component for all products, the company is vulnerable to strike, fire, flood, and so on If each location provides total product line, then economies of scale may not be realized
8. Stress the use of mechanization, automation, robots	Requires high capital investment Reduces flexibility May affect labor relations Makes maintenance more crucial
9. Stress stability of employment	Serves the security needs of employees and may develop employee loyalty Helps to attract and retain highly skilled employees May require revisions of make-or-buy decisions, use of idle time, inventory, and subcontractors as demand fluctuates

Source: Adapted from: J. Dilworth, *Production and Operations Management: Manufacturing and Nonmanufacturing,* 2nd ed. Copyright © 1983 by Random House, Inc. Reprinted by permission of Random House, Inc.

Effective management of the R&D function requires a strategic and operational partnership between R&D and the other vital business functions. A spirit of partnership and mutual trust between general and R&D managers is evident in the best-managed firms today. Managers in these firms jointly explore; assess; and decide the what, when, where, why, and how much of R&D. Priorities, costs, benefits, risks, and rewards associated with R&D activities are discussed openly and shared. The overall mission of R&D thus has become broad-based, including supporting existing businesses, helping launch new businesses, developing new products, improving product quality, improving manufacturing efficiency, and deepening or broadening the company's technological capabilities.[22]

The best-managed firms today seek to organize R&D activities in a way that breaks the isolation of R&D from the rest of the company and promotes a spirit of partnership between R&D managers and other managers in the firm. R&D decisions and plans must be integrated and coordinated across departments and divisions by having the departments share experiences and information. The strategic-management process facilitates this cross-functional approach to managing the R&D function.

Internal and External R&D

Cost distributions among R&D activities vary by company and industry, but total R&D costs generally do not exceed manufacturing and marketing start-up costs. Four approaches to determining R&D budget allocations commonly are used: (1) financing as many project proposals as possible, (2) using a percentage-of-sales method, (3) budgeting about the same amount that competitors spend for R&D, or (4) deciding how many successful new products are needed and working backward to estimate the required R&D investment.

R&D in organizations can take two basic forms: (1) internal R&D, in which an organization operates its own R&D department, and/or (2) contract R&D, in which a firm hires independent researchers or independent agencies to develop specific products. Many companies use both approaches to develop new products. A widely used approach for obtaining outside R&D assistance is to pursue a joint venture with another firm. R&D strengths (capabilities) and weaknesses (limitations) play a major role in strategy formulation and strategy implementation.

Most firms have no choice but to continually develop new and improved products because of changing consumer needs and tastes, new technologies, shortened product life cycles, and increased domestic and foreign competition. A shortage of ideas for new products, increased global competition, increased market segmentation, strong special-interest groups, and increased government regulations are several factors making the successful development of new products more and more difficult, costly, and risky. In the pharmaceutical industry, for example, only one out of every few thousand drugs created in the laboratory ends up on pharmacists' shelves. Scarpello, Boulton, and Hofer emphasized that different strategies require different R&D capabilities:

> The focus of R&D efforts can vary greatly depending on a firm's competitive strategy. Some corporations attempt to be market leaders and innovators of new products, while others are satisfied to be market followers and developers of currently available products. The basic skills required to support these strategies will vary, depending on whether R&D becomes the driving force behind competitive strategy. In cases where new product introduction is the driving force for strategy, R&D activities

must be extensive. The R&D unit must then be able to advance scientific and technological knowledge, exploit that knowledge, and manage the risks associated with ideas, products, services, and production requirements.[23]

U.S. companies have been lowering their R&D expenditures as a percentage of sales. For example, Hewlett-Packard's R&D spending historically has been about 6 percent of sales, but it has dropped to 4.4 percent. Cisco Systems' R&D budget has declined from its historical 17 percent to 14.5 percent. The R&D percentage of sales figures are falling also for Motorola, Lucent Technologies, Ericsson, Dell, Nortel, and Nokia Corp.

Research and Development Audit

Questions such as the following should be asked in performing an R&D audit:

1. Does the firm have R&D facilities? Are they adequate?
2. If outside R&D firms are used, are they cost-effective?
3. Are the organization's R&D personnel well qualified?
4. Are R&D resources allocated effectively?
5. Are management information and computer systems adequate?
6. Is communication between R&D and other organizational units effective?
7. Are present products technologically competitive?

Management Information Systems

Information ties all business functions together and provides the basis for all managerial decisions. It is the cornerstone of all organizations. Information represents a major source of competitive management advantage or disadvantage. Assessing a firm's internal strengths and weaknesses in information systems is a critical dimension of performing an internal audit. The company motto of Mitsui, a large Japanese trading company, is "Information is the lifeblood of the company." A satellite network connects Mitsui's 200 worldwide offices.

A management information system's purpose is to improve the performance of an enterprise by improving the quality of managerial decisions. An effective information system thus collects, codes, stores, synthesizes, and presents information in such a manner that it answers important operating and strategic questions. The heart of an information system is a database containing the kinds of records and data important to managers.

A *management information system* receives raw material from both the external and internal evaluation of an organization. It gathers data about marketing, finance, production, and personnel matters internally, and social, cultural, demographic, environmental, economic, political, governmental, legal, technological, and competitive factors externally. Data are integrated in ways needed to support managerial decision making.

There is a logical flow of material in a computer information system, whereby data are input to the system and transformed into output. Outputs include computer printouts, written reports, tables, charts, graphs, checks, purchase orders, invoices, inventory records, payroll accounts, and a variety of other documents. Payoffs from alternative strategies can be calculated and estimated. *Data* become *information* only when they are evaluated, filtered, condensed, analyzed, and organized for a specific purpose, problem, individual, or time.

An effective management information system utilizes computer hardware, software, models for analysis, and a database. Some people equate information systems with the advent of the computer, but historians have traced recordkeeping and non-computer data processing to Babylonian merchants living in 3500 B.C. Benefits of an effective information system include an improved understanding of business functions, improved communications, more informed decision making, a better analysis of problems, and improved control.

Because organizations are becoming more complex, decentralized, and globally dispersed, the function of information systems is growing in importance. Spurring this advance is the falling cost and increasing power of computers. There are costs and benefits associated with obtaining and evaluating information, just as with equipment and land. Like equipment, information can become obsolete and may need to be purged from the system. An effective information system is like a library, collecting, categorizing, and filing data for use by managers throughout the organization. Information systems are a major strategic resource, monitoring internal and external issues and trends, identifying competitive threats, and assisting in the implementation, evaluation, and control of strategy.

We are truly in an information age. Firms whose information-system skills are weak are at a competitive disadvantage. On the other hand, strengths in information systems allow firms to establish distinctive competencies in other areas. Low-cost manufacturing and good customer service, for example, can depend on a good information system.

Strategic-Planning Software

Some strategic decision support systems, however, are too sophisticated, expensive, or restrictive to be used easily by managers in a firm. This is unfortunate because the strategic-management process must be a people process to be successful. People make the difference! Strategic-planning software should thus be simple and unsophisticated. Simplicity allows wide participation among managers in a firm and participation is essential for effective strategy implementation.

One strategic-planning software product that parallels this text and offers managers and executives a simple yet effective approach for developing organizational strategies is CheckMATE. This personal computer software performs planning analyses and generates strategies a firm could pursue. CheckMATE incorporates the most modern strategic-planning techniques. No previous experience with computers or knowledge of strategic planning is required of the user. CheckMATE thus promotes communication, understanding, creativity, and forward thinking among users.

CheckMATE is not a spreadsheet program or database; it is an expert system that carries a firm through strategy formulation and implementation. A major strength of CheckMATE strategic-planning software is its simplicity and participative approach. The user is asked appropriate questions, responses are recorded, information is assimilated, and results are printed. Individuals can independently work through the software, and then the program will develop joint recommendations for the firm.

Specific analytical procedures included in the CheckMATE program are Strategic Position and Action Evaluation (SPACE) analysis, Strengths-Weaknesses-Opportunities-Threats (SWOT) analysis, Internal-External (IE) analysis, and Grand Strategy Matrix analysis. These widely used strategic-planning analyses are described in Chapter 6.

An individual license for CheckMATE costs $295. More information about CheckMATE can be obtained at www.checkmateplan.com or 910–579–5744 (phone).

Management Information Systems Audit

Questions such as the following should be asked when conducting this audit:

1. Do all managers in the firm use the information system to make decisions?
2. Is there a chief information officer or director of information systems position in the firm?
3. Are data in the information system updated regularly?
4. Do managers from all functional areas of the firm contribute input to the information system?
5. Are there effective passwords for entry into the firm's information system?
6. Are strategists of the firm familiar with the information systems of rival firms?
7. Is the information system user-friendly?
8. Do all users of the information system understand the competitive advantages that information can provide firms?
9. Are computer training workshops provided for users of the information system?
10. Is the firm's information system continually being improved in content and user-friendliness?

Value Chain Analysis (VCA)

According to Porter, the business of a firm can best be described as a *value chain,* in which total revenues minus total costs of all activities undertaken to develop and market a product or service yields value. All firms in a given industry have a similar value chain, which includes activities such as obtaining raw materials, designing products, building manufacturing facilities, developing cooperative agreements, and providing customer service. A firm will be profitable as long as total revenues exceed the total costs incurred in creating and delivering the product or service. Firms should strive to understand not only their own value chain operations but also their competitors', suppliers', and distributors' value chains.

Value chain analysis (VCA) refers to the process whereby a firm determines the costs associated with organizational activities from purchasing raw materials to manufacturing product(s) to marketing those products. VCA aims to identify where low-cost advantages or disadvantages exist anywhere along the value chain from raw material to customer service activities. VCA can enable a firm to better identify its own strengths and weaknesses, especially as compared to competitors' value chain analyses and their own data examined over time.

Substantial judgment may be required in performing a VCA because different items along the value chain may impact other items positively or negatively, so there exist complex interrelationships. For example, exceptional customer service may be especially expensive yet may reduce the costs of returns and increase revenues. Cost and price differences among rival firms can have their origins in activities performed by suppliers, distributors, creditors, or even shareholders. Despite the complexity of VCA, the initial step in implementing this procedure is to divide a firm's operations into specific activities or business processes. Then the analyst attempts to attach a cost to each discrete activity and the costs could be in terms of both time and money. Finally, the analyst converts the cost data into information by looking for competitive cost strengths and weaknesses that may yield competitive advantage or disadvantage. Conducting a VCA is supportive of the RBV's examination of a firm's assets and capabilities as sources of distinctive competence.

When a major competitor or new market entrant offers products or services at very low prices, this may be because that firm has substantially lower value chain costs or perhaps the rival firm is just waging a desperate attempt to gain sales or market share. Thus value chain analysis can be critically important for a firm in monitoring whether its prices and costs are competitive. An example value chain is illustrated in Figure 4-3. There can be more than a hundred particular value-creating activities associated with the business of producing and marketing

FIGURE 4-3
An Example of a Value Chain for a Typical Manufacturing Firm

Supplier Costs
- Raw materials
- Fuel
- Energy
- Transportation
- Truck drivers
- Truck maintenance
- Component parts
- Inspection
- Storing
- Warehouse

Production Costs
- Inventory system
- Receiving
- Plant layout
- Maintenance
- Plant location
- Computer
- R&D
- Cost accounting

Distribution Costs
- Loading
- Shipping
- Budgeting
- Personnel
- Internet
- Trucking
- Railroads
- Fuel
- Maintenance

(*Continued*)

FIGURE 4-3   Continued

Sales and Marketing Costs	____
Salespersons	____
Web site	____
Internet	____
Publicity	____
Promotion	____
Advertising	____
Transportation	____
Food and Lodging	____
Customer Service Costs	____
Postage	____
Phone	____
Internet	____
Warranty	____
Management Costs	____
Human resources	____
Administration	____
Employee benefits	____
Labor relations	____
Managers	____
Employees	____
Finance and Legal	____

a product or service, and each one of the activities can represent a competitive advantage or disadvantage for the firm. The combined costs of all the various activities in a company's value chain define the firm's cost of doing business. Firms should determine where cost advantages and disadvantages in their value chain occur relative to the value chain of rival firms.

Value chains differ immensely across industries and firms. Whereas a paper products company, such as Stone Container, would include on its value chain timber farming, logging, pulp mills, and papermaking, a computer company such as Hewlett-Packard would include programming, peripherals, software, hardware, and laptops. A motel would include food, housekeeping, check-in and check-out operations, Web site, reservations system, and so on. However all firms should use value-chain analysis to develop and nurture a core competence and convert this competence into a distinctive competence. A *core competence* is a value-chain activity that a firm performs especially well. When a core competence evolves into a major competitive advantage, then it is called a distinctive competence. Figure 4-4 illustrates this process.

More and more companies are using VCA to gain and sustain competitive advantage by being especially efficient and effective along various parts of the value chain. For example, Wal-Mart has built powerful value advantages by focusing on exceptionally tight inventory control, volume purchasing of products,

FIGURE 4-4

Translating Company Performance of Value Chain Activities into Competitive Advantage

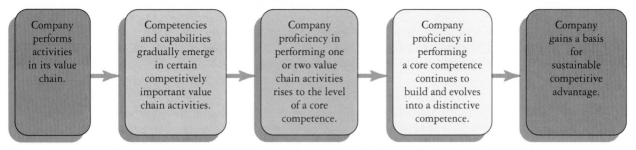

Source: Arthur Thompson, Jr., A. J. Strickland III, and John Gamble. Crafting and Executing Strategy: Text and Readings. (New York: McGraw-Hill/Irwin, 2005): 108. Used by permission of McGraw-Hill.

and offering exemplary customer service. Computer companies in contrast compete aggressively along the distribution end of the value chain. Of course, price competitiveness is a key component of effectiveness among both mass retailers and computer firms.

Benchmarking

Benchmarking is an analytical tool used to determine whether a firm's value chain activities are competitive compared to rivals and thus conducive to winning in the marketplace. Benchmarking entails measuring costs of value chain activities across an industry to determine "best practices" among competing firms for the purpose of duplicating or improving upon those best practices. Benchmarking enables a firm to take action to improve its competitiveness by identifying (and improving upon) value chain activities where rival firms have comparative advantages in cost, service, reputation, or operation.

determine best practices of competition + imitate

The hardest part of benchmarking can be gaining access to other firms' value chain activities with associated costs. Typical sources of benchmarking information, however, include published reports, trade publications, suppliers, distributors, customers, partners, creditors, shareholders, lobbyists, and willing rival firms. Some rival firms share benchmarking data. However, the International Benchmarking Clearinghouse provides guidelines to help ensure that restraint of trade, price fixing, bid rigging, bribery, and other improper business conduct do not arise between participating firms.

Due to the popularity of benchmarking today, numerous consulting firms such as Accenture, AT Kearney, Best Practices Benchmarking & Consulting, as well as the Strategic Planning Institute's Council on Benchmarking, gather benchmarking data, conduct benchmarking studies, and distribute benchmark information without identifying the sources.

The Internal Factor Evaluation (IFE) Matrix

A summary step in conducting an internal strategic-management audit is to construct an *Internal Factor Evaluation (IFE) Matrix*. This strategy-formulation tool summarizes and evaluates the major strengths and weaknesses in the functional

IFE

areas of a business, and it also provides a basis for identifying and evaluating relationships among those areas. Intuitive judgments are required in developing an IFE Matrix, so the appearance of a scientific approach should not be interpreted to mean this is an all-powerful technique. A thorough understanding of the factors included is more important than the actual numbers. Similar to the EFE Matrix and Competitive Profile Matrix described in Chapter 3, an IFE Matrix can be developed in five steps:

1. List key internal factors as identified in the internal-audit process. Use a total of from 10 to 20 internal factors, including both strengths and weaknesses. List strengths first and then weaknesses. Be as specific as possible, using percentages, ratios, and comparative numbers.

2. Assign a weight that ranges from 0.0 (not important) to 1.0 (all-important) to each factor. The weight assigned to a given factor indicates the relative importance of the factor to being successful in the firm's industry. Regardless of whether a key factor is an internal strength or weakness, factors considered to have the greatest effect on organizational performance should be assigned the highest weights. The sum of all weights must equal 1.0.

3. Assign a 1-to-4 rating to each factor to indicate whether that factor represents a major weakness (rating = 1), a minor weakness (rating = 2), a minor strength (rating = 3), or a major strength (rating = 4). Note that strengths must receive a 3 or 4 rating and weaknesses must receive a 1 or 2 rating. Ratings are thus company-based, whereas the weights in step 2 are industry-based.

4. Multiply each factor's weight by its rating to determine a weighted score for each variable.

5. Sum the weighted scores for each variable to determine the total weighted score for the organization.

Regardless of how many factors are included in an IFE Matrix, the total weighted score can range from a low of 1.0 to a high of 4.0, with the average score being 2.5. Total weighted scores well below 2.5 characterize organizations that are weak internally, whereas scores significantly above 2.5 indicate a strong internal position. Like the EFE Matrix, an IFE Matrix should include from 10 to 20 key factors. The number of factors has no effect upon the range of total weighted scores because the weights always sum to 1.0.

When a key internal factor is both a strength and a weakness, the factor should be included twice in the IFE Matrix, and a weight and rating should be assigned to each statement. For example, the Playboy logo both helps and hurts Playboy Enterprises; the logo attracts customers to *Playboy* magazine, but it keeps the Playboy cable channel out of many markets. Be as quantitative as possible when stating factors. Use $'s, %'s, #'s, and ratios to the extent possible.

An example of an IFE Matrix for E*Trade is provided in Table 4-7. Note that the firm's major strengths are its flat commission, banking accounts, and services to investors, as indicated by the rating of 4. The major weaknesses are declining broherage accounts and limited number of branches. The total weighted score of 2.67 indicates that this large brokerage firm is above average in its overall internal strength.

In multidivisional firms, each autonomous division or strategic business unit should construct an IFE Matrix. Divisional matrices then can be integrated to develop an overall corporate IFE Matrix.

TABLE 4-7 A Sample Internal Factor Evaluation Matrix for E*Trade Financial Corp.

KEY INTERNAL FACTORS	WEIGHT	RATING	WEIGHTED SCORE
Strengths			
1. E*Trade provides 24-hour, 7-day services.	0.08	3	0.24
2. E*Trade has a customer base in 119 countries.	0.06	3	0.18
3. E*Trade has more than 20,000 ATMs, making it the second largest ATM network in the United States.	0.03	3	0.09
4. E*Trade's "Power E" offers a flat commission of $9.99 per trade for investors who trade 27 or more times per quarter.	0.1	4	0.40
5. E*Trade's recent earnings were $0.59 per share from ongoing operations compared to $0.45 per share a year ago.	0.08	4	0.32
6. E*Trade Bank is an excellent online banking platform.	0.05	3	0.15
7. E*Trade's new banking accounts increased from 127,047 in 2003 to over 140,000 in 2005.	0.09	4	0.36
8. E*Trade provides research database and personal assistance services to investors.	0.05	4	0.20
9. E*Trade's "Total Protection Guarantee" provides customers 100 percent fraud coverage and privacy protection.	0.05	3	0.15
10. No E*Trade Board of Director member is an E*Trade executive.	0.03	3	0.09
Weaknesses			
11. E*Trade's total debt-to-equity ratio is 0.36 compared to the industry average of 0.9.	0.03	2	0.06
12. Active retail brokerage accounts decreased from 3,690,917 in 2002 to 2,848,625 in 2003.	0.1	1	0.10
13. E*Trade currently has a limited number of branches for customers to go to for assistance.	0.07	1	0.07
14. E*Trade has experienced computer system failures.	0.03	2	0.06
15. E*Trade's revenues (97 percent) come from the United States, Europe, or Southeast Asia.	0.1	1	0.10
16. E*Trade's return on assets (ROA) is considerably lower than the industry average.	0.03	2	0.06
17. CEO Kris Kasotkos's $80 million severance payoff was hidden in the financial statements	0.02	2	0.04
Total	**1.00**		**2.67**

CONCLUSION

Management, marketing, finance/accounting, production/operations, research and development, and management information systems represent the core operations of most businesses. A strategic-management audit of a firm's internal operations is vital to organizational health. Many companies still prefer to be judged solely on their bottom-line performance. However, an increasing number of successful organizations are using the internal audit to gain competitive advantages over rival firms.

Systematic methodologies for performing strength-weakness assessments are not well developed in the strategic-management literature, but it is clear that strategists must identify and evaluate internal strengths and weaknesses in order to effectively formulate and choose among alternative strategies. The EFE Matrix, Competitive Profile Matrix, IFE Matrix, and clear statements of vision and mission provide the basic information needed to successfully formulate competitive strategies. The process of performing an internal audit represents an opportunity for managers and employees throughout the organization to participate in determining the future of the firm. Involvement in the process can energize and mobilize managers and employees.

We invite you to visit the David page on the Prentice Hall Companion Web site at www.prenhall.com/david for this chapter's review quiz.

KEY TERMS AND CONCEPTS

Activity Ratios (p. 143)

Benchmarking (p. 157)

Capital Budgeting (p. 141)

Communication (p. 124)

Controlling (p. 135)

Core Competence (p. 156)

Cost/Benefit Analysis (p. 139)

Cultural Products (p. 126)

Customer Analysis (p. 136)

Distinctive Competencies (p. 123)

Distribution (p. 138)

Dividend Decisions (p. 141)

Empirical Indicators (p. 125)

Financial Ratio Analysis (p. 125)

Financing Decision (p. 141)

Functions of Finance/
  Accounting (p. 141)

Functions of Management (p. 131)

Functions of Marketing (p. 136)

Functions of Production/
  Operations (p. 147)

Growth Ratios (p. 143)

Human Resource Management
  (p. 135)

Internal Audit (p. 123)

Internal Factor Evaluation (IFE)
  Matrix (p. 157)

Investment Decision (p. 141)

Leverage Ratios (p. 143)

Liquidity Ratios (p. 143)

Management Information System
  (p. 152)

Marketing Research (p. 139)

Mirroring (p. 137)

Motivating (p. 134)

Opportunity Analysis (p. 139)

Organizational Culture (p. 126)

Organizing (p. 133)

Personnel Management (p. 135)

Planning (p. 131)

Pricing (p. 138)

Product and Service Planning
  (p. 137)

Production/Operations Function
  (p. 147)

Profitability Ratios (p. 143)

Research and Development (R&D)
  (p. 149)

Resource-Based View (RBV)
  (p. 125)

Selling (p. 137)

Staffing (p. 135)

Synergy (p. 133)

Test Marketing (p. 137)

Value Chain Analysis (VCA)
  (p. 154)

ISSUES FOR REVIEW AND DISCUSSION

1. Explain why prioritizing the relative importance of strengths and weaknesses in an IFE Matrix is an important strategic-management activity.

2. How can delegation of authority contribute to effective strategic management?

3. Diagram a formal organizational chart that reflects the following positions: a president, 2 executive officers, 4 middle managers, and 18 lower-level managers. Now, diagram three overlapping and hypothetical informal group structures. How

can this information be helpful to a strategist in formulating and implementing strategy?

4. Which of the three basic functions of finance/accounting do you feel is most important in a small electronics manufacturing concern? Justify your position.

5. Do you think aggregate R&D expenditures for U.S. firms will increase or decrease next year? Why?

6. Explain how you would motivate managers and employees to implement a major new strategy.

7. Why do you think production/operations managers often are not directly involved in strategy-formulation activities? Why can this be a major organizational weakness?

8. Give two examples of staffing strengths and two examples of staffing weaknesses of an organization with which you are familiar.

9. Would you ever pay out dividends when your firm's annual net profit is negative? Why? What effect could this have on a firm's strategies?

10. If a firm has zero debt in its capital structure, is that always an organizational strength? Why or why not?

11. Describe the production/operations system in a police department.

12. After conducting an internal audit, a firm discovers a total of 100 strengths and 100 weaknesses. What procedures then could be used to determine the most important of these? Why is it important to reduce the total number of key factors?

13. Why do you believe cultural products affect all the functions of business?

14. Do you think cultural products affect strategy formulation, implementation, or evaluation the most? Why?

15. Identify cultural products at your college or university. Do these products, viewed collectively or separately, represent a strength or weakness for the organization?

16. Describe the management information system at your college or university.

17. Explain the difference between data and information in terms of each being useful to strategists.

18. What are the most important characteristics of an effective management information system?

19. Compare and contrast U.S. versus foreign cultures in terms of doing business.

20. Do you agree or disagree with the RBV theorists that internal resources are more important for a firm than external factors in achieving and sustaining competitive advantage? Explain your and their position.

21. Define and discuss "empirical indicators."

22. Define and discuss the "spam" problem in the United States.

23. Discuss JCPenney's inventory control system. Why is that a competitive advantage for the firm?

24. Define and explain value chain analysis (VCA).

25. List five financial ratios that may be used by your university to monitor operations.

26. Explain benchmarking.

NOTES

1. Robert Grant, "The Resource-Based Theory of Competitive Advantage: Implications for Strategy Formulation," *California Management Review* (Spring 1991): 116.

2. Reprinted by permission of the publisher from "Integrating Strength–Weakness Analysis into Strategic Planning," by William King, *Journal of Business Research* 2, no. 4: p. 481. Copyright 1983 by Elsevier Science Publishing Co., Inc.

3. Igor Ansoff, "Strategic Management of Technology" *Journal of Business Strategy* 7, no. 3 (Winter 1987): 38.

4. Claude George, Jr., *The History of Management Thought*, 2nd ed. (Upper Saddle River, N.J.: Prentice-Hall, 1972): 174.

5. J. B. Barney, "Firm Resources and Sustained Competitive Advantage," *Journal of Management* 17 (1991): 99–120; J.B. Barney, "The Resource-Based Theory of the Firm," *Organizational Science* 7 (1996): 469; J.B. Barney, "Is the Resource-Based 'View' a Useful Perspective for Strategic Management Research? Yes." *Academy of Management Review* 26, no. 1 (2001): 41–56.

6. Edgar Schein, *Organizational Culture and Leadership* (San Francisco: Jossey-Bass, 1985): 9.

7. John Lorsch, "Managing Culture: The Invisible Barrier to Strategic Change," *California Management Review* 28, no. 2 (1986): 95–109.

8. Y. Allarie and M. Firsirotu, "How to Implement Radical Strategies in Large Organizations," *Sloan Management Review* (Spring 1985): 19.

9. Jon Alston, "Wa, Guanxi, and Inhwa: Managerial Principles in Japan, China and Korea," *Business Horizons* 32, no. 2 (March–April 1989): 26.

10. Rose Knotts, "Cross-Cultural Management: Transformations and Adaptations," *Business Horizons* (January–February 1989): 29–33.

11. www.mindtools.com/plfailpl.html

12. Adam Smith, *The Wealth of Nations* (New York: Modern Library, 1937): 3–4.

13. Richard Daft, *Management*, 3rd ed. (Orlando, FL: Dryden Press, 1993): 512.

14. Shelley Kirkpatrick and Edwin Locke, "Leadership: Do Traits Matter?" *Academy of Management Executive* 5, no. 2 (May 1991): 48.

15. Peter Drucker, *Management Tasks, Responsibilities, and Practice* (New York: Harper & Row, 1973): 463.

16. Brian Dumaine, "What the Leaders of Tomorrow See," *Fortune* (July 3, 1989): 51.

17. J. Evans and B. Bergman, *Marketing* (New York: Macmillan, 1982): 17.

18. Adapted from Kevin Delaney, "Google to Target Brands in Revenue Push," *Wall Street Journal* (April 25, 2005): B1.

19. Joe Flint and Brian Steinberg, "Ad Icon P&G Cuts Commitment to TV Commercials," *Wall Street Journal,* (June 13, 2005): A1.

20. Quoted in Robert Waterman, Jr., "The Renewal Factor," *BusinessWeek* (September 14, 1987): 108.

21. J. Van Horne, *Financial Management and Policy* (Upper Saddle River, N.J.: Prentice-Hall, 1974): 10.

22. Philip Rousebl, Kamal Saad, and Tamara Erickson, "The Evolution of Third Generation R&D," *Planning Review* 19, no. 2 (March–April 1991): 18–26.

23. Vida Scarpello, William Boulton, and Charles Hofer, "Reintegrating R&D into Business Strategy," *Journal of Business Strategy* 6, no. 4 (Spring 1986): 50–51.

CURRENT READINGS

Ahuja, G., and R. Katila. "Where Do Resources Come From? The Role of Idiosyncratic Situations." *Strategic Management Journal* 25, no. 8–9 (August–September 2004): 887.

Barron, Jennifer, and Jim Hollingshead. "Brand Globally, Market Locally." *Journal of Business Strategy* 25, no. 1 (2004): 9.

Bhattacharya, C. B., N. Craig Smith, and David Vogel. "Integrating Social Responsibility and Marketing Strategy: An Introduction." *California Management Review* 47, no. 1 (Fall 2004): 6.

Colbert, Barry A. "The Complex Resource-Based View: Implications for Theory and Practice in Strategic Human Resource Management." *The Academy of Management Review* 29, No. 3 (July 2004): 341.

Dalton, Catherine M. "Values, Relationships, and Organizational Culture: Principled Leadership at Brightpoint, Inc." *Business Horizons* 48, no. 1 (January–February 2005): 5.

Ehrenfeld, J. R. "Contraria: The Roots of Sustainability." *MIT Sloan Management Review* 46, no. 2 (Winter 2005): 23.

Hansen, M. H., L. T. Perry, and C. S. Reese. "A Bayesian Operationalization of the Resource-Based View." *Strategic Management Journal* 25, no. 13 (December 2004): 1279.

Tomas, G., M. Hult, David J. Ketchen, Jr., and Stanley F. Slater. "Information Processing, Knowledge Development, and Strategic Supply Chain Performance." *The Academy of Management Journal* 47, no. 2 (April 2004): 241.

Lei, David, and John W. Slocum. "Strategic and Organizational Requirements for Competitive Advantage." *The Academy of Management Executive* 19, no. 1 (February 2005): 31.

Luthans, F., K. W. Luthans, B. C. Luthans. "Positive Psychological Capital: Beyond Human and Social Capital." *Business Horizons* 47, no. 1 (January–February 2004): 45.

Mishina, Y., T. G. Pollock, and J. F. Porac. "Are More Resources Always Better for Growth? Resource Stickiness in Market and Product Expansion." *Strategic Management Journal* 25, no. 12 (December 2004): 1179.

Park, Namgyoo K., John M. Mezias, and Jaeyong Song. "A Resource-Based View of Strategic Alliances and Firm Value in the Electronic Marketplace." *Journal of Management* 30, no. 1 (2004): 7.

Ray, G., J. B. Barney, and W. A. Muhanna. "Capabilities, Business Processes, and Competitive Advantage: Choosing the Dependent Variable in Empirical Tests of the Resource-Based View." *Strategic Management Journal* 25, no. 1 (January 2004): 23.

Robichaud, Daniel, Hélène Giroux, and James R. Taylor. "The Metaconversation: The Recursive

Property of Language as a Key to Organizing." *The Academy of Management Review* 29, no. 4 (October 2004): 617.

Rosen, C., J. Case, M. Staubus. "Every Employee an Owner. Really." *Harvard Business Review* (June 2005): 122.

Song, M., C. Droge, S. Hanvanich, and R. Calantone. "Marketing and Technology Resource Complementarity: An Analysis of Their Interaction Effect in Two Environmental Contexts." *Strategic Management Journal* 26, no. 3 (March 2005): 259.

Swann, Jr., William B., Jeffrey T. Polzer, Daniel Conor Seyle, and Sei Jin Ko. "Finding Value in Diversity: Verification of Personal and Social Self-Views in Diverse Groups." *The Academy of Management Review* 29, no. 1 (January 2004): 9.

experiential exercises

Experiential Exercise 4A

Performing a Financial Ratio Analysis for Google (GOOG)

PURPOSE

Financial ratio analysis is one of the best techniques for identifying and evaluating internal strengths and weaknesses. Potential investors and current shareholders look closely at firms' financial ratios, making detailed comparisons to industry averages and to previous periods of time. Financial ratio analyses provide vital input information for developing an IFE Matrix.

INSTRUCTIONS

Step 1   On a separate sheet of paper, number from 1 to 20. Referring to Google's income statement and balance sheet (pp. 144–145), calculate 20 financial ratios for 2004 for the company. Use Table 4-4 as a reference.

Step 2   Go to https://us.etrade.com/e/t/invest/markets and find financial ratio information for Microsoft (stock symbol = MSFT). Microsoft is a GOOG competitor. Record the MSFT values in the second column on your paper. Calculate by hand any MSFT ratios that you cannot find on the Internet.

Step 3   In a third column, indicate whether you consider each ratio to be a strength, a weakness, or a neutral factor for Google.

Experiential Exercise 4B

Constructing an IFE Matrix for Google (GOOG)

PURPOSE

This exercise will give you experience in developing an IFE Matrix. Identifying and prioritizing factors to include in an IFE Matrix fosters communication among functional and divisional managers. Preparing an IFE Matrix allows human resource, marketing, production/operations, finance/accounting, R&D, and management information systems managers to articulate their concerns and thoughts regarding the business condition of the firm. This results in an improved collective understanding of the business.

INSTRUCTIONS

Step 1   Join with two other individuals to form a three-person team. Develop a team IFE Matrix for Google.

Step 2   Compare your team's IFE Matrix to other teams' IFE Matrices. Discuss any major differences.

Step 3   What strategies do you think would allow Google to capitalize on its major strengths? What strategies would allow Google to improve upon its major weaknesses?

Experiential Exercise 4C

Constructing an IFE Matrix for My University

PURPOSE

This exercise gives you the opportunity to evaluate your university's major strengths and weaknesses. As will become clearer in the next chapter, an organization's strategies are largely based upon striving to take advantage of strengths and improving upon weaknesses.

INSTRUCTIONS

Step 1   Join with two other individuals to form a three-person team. Develop a team IFE Matrix for your university. You may use the strengths/weaknesses determined in Experimental Exercise 1D.

Step 2   Go to the board and diagram your team's IFE Matrix.

Step 3   Compare your team's IFE Matrix to other teams' IFE Matrices. Discuss any major differences.

Step 4   What strategies do you think would allow your university to capitalize on its major strengths? What strategies would allow your university to improve upon its major weaknesses?

Strategies in Action

chapter objectives

After studying this chapter, you should be able to do the following:

1. Discuss the value of establishing long-term objectives.

2. Identify 16 types of business strategies.

3. Identify numerous examples of organizations pursuing different types of strategies.

4. Discuss guidelines when particular strategies are most appropriate to pursue.

5. Discuss Porter's five generic strategies.

6. Describe strategic management in nonprofit, governmental, and small organizations.

7. Discuss joint ventures as a way to enter the Russian market.

8. Discuss the Balanced Scorecard.

9. Compare and contrast financial with strategic objectives.

10. Discuss the levels of strategies in large versus small firms.

11. Explain the First Mover Advantages concept.

12. Discuss recent trends in outsourcing.

13. Discuss strategies for competing in turbulent, high-velocity markets.

"notable quotes"

Alice said, "Would you please tell me which way to go from here?" The cat said, "That depends on where you want to get to."
Lewis Carroll

Tomorrow always arrives. It is always different. And even the mightiest company is in trouble if it has not worked on the future. Being surprised by what happens is a risk that even the largest and richest company cannot afford, and even the smallest business need not run.
Peter Drucker

Planning. Doing things today to make us better tomorrow. Because the future belongs to those who make the hard decisions today.
Eaton Corporation

One big problem with American business is that when it gets into trouble, it redoubles its effort. It's like digging for gold. If you dig down twenty feet and haven't found it, one of the strategies you could use is to dig twice as deep. But if the gold is twenty feet to the side, you could dig a long time and not find it.
Edward De Bono

Even if you're on the right track, you'll get run over if you just sit there.
Will Rogers

Strategies for taking the hill won't necessarily hold it.
Amar Bhide

The early bird may get the worm, but the second mouse gets the cheese.
Unknown

Hundreds of companies today, including Sears, IBM, Searle, and Hewlett-Packard, have embraced strategic planning fully in their quest for higher revenues and profits. Kent Nelson, former chair of UPS, explains why his company has created a new strategic-planning department: "Because we're making bigger bets on investments in technology, we can't afford to spend a whole lot of money in one direction and then find out five years later it was the wrong direction."[1]

This chapter brings strategic management to life with many contemporary examples. Sixteen types of strategies are defined and exemplified, including Michael Porter's generic strategies: cost leadership, differentiation, and focus. Guidelines are presented for determining when it is most appropriate to pursue different types of strategies. An overview of strategic management in nonprofit organizations, governmental agencies, and small firms is provided.

Long-Term Objectives

Long-term objectives represent the results expected from pursuing certain strategies. Strategies represent the actions to be taken to accomplish long-term objectives. The time frame for objectives and strategies should be consistent, usually from two to five years.

The Nature of Long-Term Objectives

VISIT THE NET

Gives the basic principles of strategic planning.
(www.eaglepoint consulting.com/ sp_principles.html)

Objectives should be quantitative, measurable, realistic, understandable, challenging, hierarchical, obtainable, and congruent among organizational units. Each objective should also be associated with a timeline. Objectives are commonly stated in terms such as growth in assets, growth in sales, profitability, market share, degree and nature of diversification, degree and nature of vertical integration, earnings per share, and social responsibility. Clearly established objectives offer many benefits. They provide direction, allow synergy, aid in evaluation, establish priorities, reduce uncertainty, minimize conflicts, stimulate exertion, and aid in both the allocation of resources and the design of jobs.

Long-term objectives are needed at the corporate, divisional, and functional levels of an organization. They are an important measure of managerial performance. Many practitioners and academicians attribute a significant part of U.S. industry's competitive decline to the short-term, rather than long-term, strategy orientation of managers in the United States. Arthur D. Little argues that bonuses or merit pay for managers today must be based to a greater extent on long-term objectives and strategies. A general framework for relating objectives to performance evaluation is provided in Table 5-1. A particular organization could tailor these guidelines to meet its own needs, but incentives should be attached to both long-term and annual objectives.

Clearly stated and communicated objectives are vital to success for many reasons. First, objectives help stakeholders understand their role in an organization's future. They also provide a basis for consistent decision making by managers whose values and attitudes differ. By reaching a consensus on objectives during strategy-formulation activities, an organization can minimize potential conflicts later during implementation. Objectives set forth organizational priorities and stimulate exertion and accomplishment. They serve as standards by which individuals, groups, departments, divisions, and entire organizations can be evaluated. Objectives provide the basis for designing jobs and organizing activities to be performed in an organization. They also provide direction and allow for organizational synergy.

TABLE 5-1 Varying Performance Measures by Organizational Level

ORGANIZATIONAL LEVEL	BASIS FOR ANNUAL BONUS OR MERIT PAY
Corporate	75% based on long-term objectives 25% based on annual objectives
Division	50% based on long-term objectives 50% based on annual objectives
Function	25% based on long-term objectives 75% based on annual objectives

Without long-term objectives, an organization would drift aimlessly toward some unknown end. It is hard to imagine an organization or individual being successful without clear objectives. Success only rarely occurs by accident; rather, it is the result of hard work directed toward achieving certain objectives.

Financial Versus Strategic Objectives

Two types of objectives are especially common in organizations: financial and strategic objectives. Financial objectives include those associated with growth in revenues, growth in earnings, higher dividends, larger profit margins, greater return on investment, higher earnings per share, a rising stock price, improved cash flow, and so on; while strategic objectives include things such as a larger market share, quicker on-time delivery than rivals, shorter design-to-market times than rivals, lower costs than rivals, higher product quality than rivals, wider geographic coverage than rivals, achieving ISO 14001 certification, achieving technological leadership, consistently getting new or improved products to market ahead of rivals, and so on.

Although financial objectives are especially important in firms, oftentimes there is a trade-off between financial and strategic objectives such that crucial decisions have to be made. For example, a firm can do certain things to maximize short-term financial objectives that would harm long-term strategic objectives. To improve financial position in the short run through higher prices may, for example, jeopardize long-term market share. The dangers associated with trading off long-term strategic objectives with near-term bottom-line performance are especially severe if competitors relentlessly pursue increased market share at the expense of short-term profitability. And there are other trade-offs between financial and strategic objectives, related to riskiness of actions, concern for business ethics, need to preserve the natural environment, and social responsibility issues. Both financial and strategic objectives should include both annual and long-term performance targets. Ultimately, the best way to sustain competitive advantage over the long run is to relentlessly pursue strategic objectives that strengthen a firm's business position over rivals. Financial objectives can best be met by focusing first and foremost on achievement of strategic objectives that improve a firm's competitiveness and market strength.

Dell Computer has a corporate objective to grow revenues by 15 percent annually through 2006 and to reach $60 billion in total revenues by that year. To achieve this goal, Dell established specific annual objectives on a per-segment basis. These are shown in Table 5-2.

TABLE 5-2   Dell Computer's Revenue Objectives
Through 2006 (in $ Billions)

DIVISION	2004	2005	2006
PC's	$27	$29	$30
Servers/Storage	8	9	10
Services	5	7	9
Software/Peripherals	7	10	13
Total	**$47**	**$54**	**$62**

Source: Adapted from Andrew Park and Peter Burrows, "What You Don't Know About Dell," *BusinessWeek* (November 3, 2003): 81.

VISIT THE NET

Provides a short essay about the resurgence of strategic planning in companies.
(www.businessweek.com/1996/35/b34901.htm)

Not Managing by Objectives

An unknown educator once said, "If you think education is expensive, try ignorance." The idea behind this saying also applies to establishing objectives. Strategists should avoid the following alternative ways to "not managing by objectives."

- *Managing by Extrapolation*—adheres to the principle "If it ain't broke, don't fix it." The idea is to keep on doing about the same things in the same ways because things are going well.

- *Managing by Crisis*—based on the belief that the true measure of a really good strategist is the ability to solve problems. Because there are plenty of crises and problems to go around for every person and every organization, strategists ought to bring their time and creative energy to bear on solving the most pressing problems of the day. Managing by crisis is actually a form of reacting rather than acting and of letting events dictate the what and when of management decisions.

- *Managing by Subjectives*—built on the idea that there is no general plan for which way to go and what to do; just do the best you can to accomplish what you think should be done. In short, "Do your own thing, the best way you know how" (sometimes referred to as *the mystery approach to decision making* because subordinates are left to figure out what is happening and why).

- *Managing by Hope*—based on the fact that the future is laden with great uncertainty and that if we try and do not succeed, then we hope our second (or third) attempt will succeed. Decisions are predicted on the hope that they will work and the good times are just around the corner, especially if luck and good fortune are on our side![2]

The Balanced Scorecard

Developed in 1993 by Harvard Business School professors Robert Kaplan and David Norton, and refined continually through today, the Balanced Scorecard is a strategy evaluation and control technique.[3] Balanced Scorecard derives its name from the perceived need of firms to "balance" financial measures that are oftentimes used exclusively in strategy evaluation and control with nonfinancial measures such as product quality and customer service. An effective Balanced Scorecard contains a carefully chosen combination of strategic and financial objectives tailored to the company's business. As a tool to manage and evaluate strategy, the Balanced Scorecard is currently in use at Sears, United Parcel Service, 3M Corporation, Heinz, and hundreds of other firms. For example, 3M Corporation has a financial objective to achieve annual growth in earnings per share of 10 percent or better, as well as a strategic objective to have at least 30 percent of sales come from products introduced in the past four years. The overall aim of the Balanced Scorecard is to "balance" shareholder objectives with customer and operational objectives. Obviously, these sets of objectives interrelate and many even conflict. For example, customers want low price and high service, which may conflict with shareholders' desire for a high return on their investment. The Balanced Scorecard concept is consistent with the notions of continuous improvement in management (CIM) and total quality management (TQM).

Although the Balanced Scorecard concept will be covered in more detail in Chapter 9 as it relates to evaluating strategies, it should be noted here that clearly firms should establish objectives and evaluate strategies on items other than financial measures. This is the basic tenet of the Balanced Scorecard. Financial measures and ratios are vitally important. However, of equal importance are factors such as customer service, employee morale, product quality, pollution abatement, business ethics, social responsibility, community involvement, and other such items. In conjunction with financial measures, these "softer" factors comprise an integral part of both the objective-setting process and the strategy-evaluation process. These factors can vary by organization, but such items, along with financial measures, comprise the essence of a Balanced Scorecard. A Balanced Scorecard for a firm is simply a listing of all key objectives to work toward, along with an associated time dimension of when each objective is to be accomplished, as well as a primary responsibility or contact person, department, or division for each objective.

Types of Strategies

The model illustrated in Figure 5-1 provides a conceptual basis for applying strategic management. Defined and exemplified in Table 5-3 alternative strategies that an enterprise could pursue can be categorized into 11 actions—forward integration, backward integration, horizontal integration, market penetration, market development, product development, related diversification, unrelated diversification, retrenchment, divestiture, and liquidation. Each alternative strategy has countless variations. For example, market penetration can include adding salespersons, increasing advertising expenditures, couponing, and using similar actions to increase market share in a given geographic area.

Many, if not most, organizations simultaneously pursue a combination of two or more strategies, but a *combination strategy* can be exceptionally risky if carried too far. No organization can afford to pursue all the strategies that might benefit the firm. Difficult decisions must be made. Priority must be established. Organizations, like individuals, have limited resources. Both organizations and individuals must choose among alternative strategies and avoid excessive indebtedness.

Hansen and Smith recently explained that strategic planning involves "choices that risk resources" and "trade-offs that sacrifice opportunity." In other words, if you have a strategy to go north, then you must buy snowshoes and warm jackets (spend resources) and forgo the opportunity of population increases you would have by going south. You cannot have a strategy to go north and then take a step east, south, or west "just to be on the safe side." Firms spend resources and focus on a finite number of opportunities in pursuing strategies to achieve an uncertain outcome in the future. Strategic planning is much more than a roll of the dice; it is a wager based on predictions and hypotheses that are continually tested and refined by knowledge, research, experience, and learning. Survival of the firm itself may hinge on your strategic plan.[4]

FIGURE 5-1

A Comprehensive Strategic-Management Model

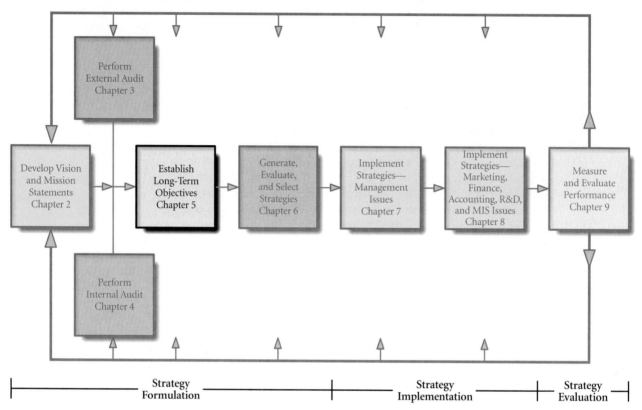

Organizations cannot do too many things well because resources and talents get spread thin and competitors gain advantage. In large diversified companies, a combination strategy is commonly employed when different divisions pursue different strategies. Also, organizations struggling to survive may simultaneously employ a combination of several defensive strategies, such as divestiture, liquidation, and retrenchment.

Levels of Strategies

Strategy making is not just a task for top executives. As discussed in Chapter 1, middle- and lower-level managers too must be involved in the strategic-planning process to the extent possible. In large firms, there are actually four levels of strategies: corporate, divisional, functional, and operational—as illustrated in Figure 5-2. However, in small firms, there are actually three levels of strategies: company, functional, and operational.

In large firms, the persons primarily responsible for having effective strategies at the various levels include the CEO at the corporate level; the president or executive vice president at the divisional level; the respective chief finance officer (CFO), chief information officer (CIO), human resource manager (HRM), chief marketing officer (CMO), and so on, at the functional level; and the plant manager, regional sales manager, and so on, at the operational level. In small firms, the persons primarily responsible for having effective strategies at the various levels include the

TABLE 5-3   Alternative Strategies Defined and Exemplified

STRATEGY	DEFINITION	2005 EXAMPLES
Forward Integration	Gaining ownership or increased control over distributors or retailers	Budget Rent-a-Car is opening car rental shops in Wal-Mart stores.
Backward Integration	Seeking ownership or increased control of a firm's suppliers	Hotels, Inc. purchased a furniture producer.
Horizontal Integration	Seeking ownership or increased control over competitors	Federated Department Stores, the parent of Macy's and Bloomingdale's, acquired May Department Stores.
Market Penetration	Seeking increased market share for present products or services in present markets through greater marketing efforts	Coca-Cola Co. is spending millions to advertise its new zero calorie drink called Coca-Cola Zero.
Market Development	Introducing present products or services into new geographic area	Bank of America recently purchased a 9 percent stake in China Construction Bank, China's fourth largest lender. This is Bank of America's first big move into China.
Product Development	Seeking increased sales by improving present products or services or developing new ones	Advanced Medical Optics is using acquisition to obtain all medical aspects of eye care, from laser surgery to contacts to implants for all ages.
Related Diversification	Adding new but related products or services	UPS acquired Overnite to diversify its packaging business into the trucking business. Now UPS carries packages over 150 lbs. which for 98 years it has not done.
Unrelated Diversification	Adding new, unrelated products or services	Tupperware Corp., the direct seller of kitchenware, has entered and is growing its skin and beauty business through BeautiControl.
Retrenchment	Regrouping through cost and asset reduction to reverse declining sales and profit	Viacom is selling noncore assets including its theme parks, publishing business, radio stations, and movie theaters.
Divestiture	Selling a division or part of an organization	Goodyear Tire & Rubber Co. sold its North American farm-tire business to Titan International.
Liquidation	Selling all of a company's assets, in parts, for their tangible worth	Britain's last major car manufacturer, MG Rover Group Ltd., liquidated in 2005 and laid off its 5,000 employees. The firm had major manufacturing facilities at Longbridge in central England.

business owner or president at the company level and then the same range of persons at the lower two levels, as with a large firm.

It is important to note that all persons responsible for strategic planning at the various levels ideally participate and understand the strategies at the other organizational levels to help ensure coordination, facilitation, and commitment while avoiding inconsistency, inefficiency, and miscommunication. Plant managers, for

FIGURE 5-2

Levels of Strategies with Persons Most Responsible

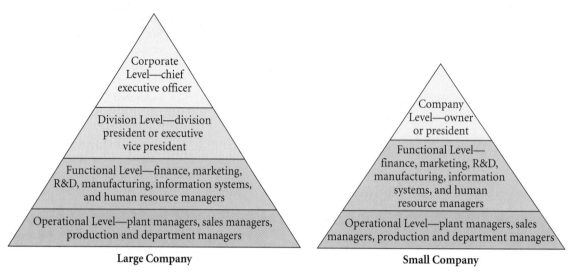

example, need to understand and be supportive of the overall corporate strategic plan (game plan) while the president and the CEO need to be knowledgeable of strategies being employed in various sales territories and manufacturing plants.

Integration Strategies

Forward integration, backward integration, and horizontal integration are sometimes collectively referred to as *vertical integration* strategies. Vertical integration strategies allow a firm to gain control over distributors, suppliers, and/or competitors.

Forward Integration

Forward integration involves gaining ownership or increased control over distributors or retailers. Increasing numbers of manufacturers (suppliers) today are pursuing a forward integration strategy by establishing Web sites to directly sell products to consumers. This strategy is causing turmoil in some industries. For example, Dell Computer recently began pursuing forward integration by establishing its own stores-within-a-store in Sears, Roebuck. This strategy supplements Dell's mall-based kiosks, which enable customers to see and try Dell computers before they purchase one. Neither the Dell kiosks nor the Dell stores-within-a-store will stock computers. Customers still will order Dells exclusively by phone or over the Internet, which historically differentiated Dell from other computer firms.

Another company betting heavily on forward integration today is Staples, which is adding "delivery of office products to businesses" as a service at more and more of its 1,400 stores nationwide and in Europe. Staples, however, is playing catch-up to Office Depot, which recently acquired a French delivery business that doubled its European sales.

An effective means of implementing forward integration is *franchising*. Approximately 2,000 companies in about 50 different industries in the United States use franchising to distribute their products or services. Businesses can expand rapidly by franchising because costs and opportunities are spread among many individuals. Total sales by franchises in the United States are annually about $1 trillion.

However, a growing trend is for franchisees, who for example may operate 10 franchised restaurants, stores, or whatever, to buy out their part of the business from their franchiser (corporate owner). There is a growing rift between franchisees and franchisers as the segment often outperforms the parent. For example, often to increase growth, a franchiser will allow new owners to locate near existing franchisee operations, or will cut back on services and training to reduce costs.[5]

The huge forest products firm Boise Cascade, which owns 2.3 million acres of timberlands and more than two dozen paper and building-products mills, continues to pursue forward integration, as evidenced by its recent acquisition of OfficeMax, the third-largest retail-office-products company after Staples and Office Depot. OfficeMax has more than 1,000 superstores and has lately focused on boosting domestic sales and on remodeling stores, rather than expanding internationally. A risk to Boise Cascade in making this acquisition is that Staples and Office Depot could drop the Boise Cascade line of products, viewing the company now to be more a competitor than a supplier.

Six guidelines for when forward integration may be an especially effective strategy are:[6]

- When an organization's present distributors are especially expensive, or unreliable, or incapable of meeting the firm's distribution needs.
- When the availability of quality distributors is so limited as to offer a competitive advantage to those firms that integrate forward.
- When an organization competes in an industry that is growing and is expected to continue to grow markedly; this is a factor because forward integration reduces an organization's ability to diversify if its basic industry falters.
- When an organization has both the capital and human resources needed to manage the new business of distributing its own products.
- When the advantages of stable production are particularly high; this is a consideration because an organization can increase the predictability of the demand for its output through forward integration.
- When present distributors or retailers have high profit margins; this situation suggests that a company profitably could distribute its own products and price them more competitively by integrating forward.

Backward Integration

Both manufacturers and retailers purchase needed materials from suppliers. *Backward integration* is a strategy of seeking ownership or increased control of a firm's suppliers. This strategy can be especially appropriate when a firm's current suppliers are unreliable, too costly, or cannot meet the firm's needs.

When you buy a box of Pampers diapers at Wal-Mart, a scanner at the store's checkout counter instantly zaps an order to Procter & Gamble Company. In contrast, in most hospitals, reordering supplies is a logistical nightmare. Inefficiency caused by lack of control of suppliers in the healthcare industry is, however, rapidly changing as many giant healthcare purchasers, such as the U.S. Defense Department and Columbia/HCA Healthcare Corporation, move to require electronic bar codes on every supply item purchased. This allows instant tracking and recording without invoices and paperwork. Of the estimated $83 billion spent annually on hospital supplies, industry reports indicate that $11 billion can be eliminated through more effective backward integration.

Some industries in the United States, such as the automotive and aluminum industries, are reducing their historical pursuit of backward integration. Instead of owning their suppliers, companies negotiate with several outside suppliers. Ford and DaimlerChrysler buy over half of their component parts from outside suppliers such as TRW, Eaton, General Electric, and Johnson Controls. *De-integration* makes sense in industries that have global sources of supply. Companies today shop around, play one seller against another, and go with the best deal. Global competition is also spurring firms to reduce their number of suppliers and to demand higher levels of service and quality from those they keep. Although traditionally relying on many suppliers to ensure uninterrupted supplies and low prices, American firms now are following the lead of Japanese firms, which have far fewer suppliers and closer, long-term relationships with those few. "Keeping track of so many suppliers is onerous," says Mark Shimelonis, formerly of Xerox.

Small steel manufacturers such as Arrowhead Steel Company and Worthington Steel Company are pursuing backward integration today through the use of the Internet. Owners of most small steel firms now click on Web sites, such as MetalSite LP, based in Pittsburgh, or e-Steel Corporation, based in New York, to find the lowest-priced supplier of scrap steel that they need. These two sites give buyers and sellers of steel the opportunity to trade, buy, and sell metal from a variety of companies. Many steel companies now have Web sites to capitalize on backward integration opportunities in the industry.

Seven guidelines for when backward integration may be an especially effective strategy are:[7]

- When an organization's present suppliers are especially expensive, or unreliable, or incapable of meeting the firm's needs for parts, components, assemblies, or raw materials.
- When the number of suppliers is small and the number of competitors is large.
- When an organization competes in an industry that is growing rapidly; this is a factor because integrative-type strategies (forward, backward, and horizontal) reduce an organization's ability to diversify in a declining industry.
- When an organization has both capital and human resources to manage the new business of supplying its own raw materials.
- When the advantages of stable prices are particularly important; this is a factor because an organization can stabilize the cost of its raw materials and the associated price of its product(s) through backward integration.
- When present supplies have high profit margins, which suggests that the business of supplying products or services in the given industry is a worthwhile venture.
- When an organization needs to quickly acquire a needed resource.

Horizontal Integration

Horizontal integration refers to a strategy of seeking ownership of or increased control over a firm's competitors. One of the most significant trends in strategic management today is the increased use of horizontal integration as a growth strategy. Mergers, acquisitions, and takeovers among competitors allow for increased economies of scale and enhanced transfer of resources and competencies. Kenneth Davidson makes the following observation about horizontal integration:

> The trend towards horizontal integration seems to reflect strategists' misgivings about their ability to operate many unrelated businesses. Mergers between direct competitors are more likely to create efficiencies

than mergers between unrelated businesses, both because there is a greater potential for eliminating duplicate facilities and because the management of the acquiring firm is more likely to understand the business of the target.[8]

Pernod Ricard SA of France and U.S.-based Fortune Brands recently acquired Allied Domecq PLC of the United Kingdom for $14 billion. This was the largest merger in Europe to date in 2005 and represented further consolidation of liquor companies seeking to gain economics of scale by merging. Pernod and Fortune purchased the Bristol, England-based company for 670 pence ($12.85) per share. A major competitor of the merged firms is Constellation Brands based in Fairport, New York. Other recent horizontal integration mergers in the spirits and distillery market include the Bacardi purchase of Sidney Frank Importing, Scottish & Newcastle's purchase of Hartwall Oyj Abp, and the Diageo purchase of Seagram (61 percent; Pernod Ricard purchased the other 39 percent of Seagram).

Adidas, in late 2005, acquired Reebok for $3.8 billion, or $59 a share, which was a 34 percent premium over Reebok's $44 stock price the day of purchase. Based in Germany, Adidas now can negotiate better shelf-space contracts with retailers, such as Foot Locker, as it strives to compete with industry-leader Nike.

Five guidelines for when horizontal integration may be an especially effective strategy are:[9]

- When an organization can gain monopolistic characteristics in a particular area or region without being challenged by the federal government for "tending substantially" to reduce competition.
- When an organization competes in a growing industry.
- When increased economies of scale provide major competitive advantages.
- When an organization has both the capital and human talent needed to successfully manage an expanded organization.
- When competitors are faltering due to a lack of managerial expertise or a need for particular resources that an organization possesses; note that horizontal integration would not be appropriate if competitors are doing poorly, because in that case overall industry sales are declining.

Intensive Strategies

Market penetration, market development, and product development are sometimes referred to as *intensive strategies* because they require intensive efforts if a firm's competitive position with existing products is to improve.

Market Penetration

A *market penetration* strategy seeks to increase market share for present products or services in present markets through greater marketing efforts. This strategy is widely used alone and in combination with other strategies. Market penetration includes increasing the number of salespersons, increasing advertising expenditures, offering extensive sales promotion items, or increasing publicity efforts. Japanese electronics giant Sony Corporation is spending over $140 million in a new advertising and promotion drive to market its high-definition television sets in the United States. The new sets are being sold under the name Bravia. Sony is also setting up special tents to promote

Bravia at 1,000 stores in the United States. Advertising expenditures at Avon Products Inc. jumped 50 percent in the second half of 2005 from the first half for a yearly total exceeding $150 million. Avon is introducing a premium line of anti-aging skin cremes.

Five guidelines for when market penetration may be an especially effective strategy are:[10]

- When current markets are not saturated with a particular product or service.
- When the usage rate of present customers could be increased significantly.
- When the market shares of major competitors have been declining while total industry sales have been increasing.
- When the correlation between dollar sales and dollar marketing expenditures historically has been high.
- When increased economies of scale provide major competitive advantages.

Market Development

Market development involves introducing present products or services into new geographic areas. For example, Adidas, in May 2005, had 1,500 stores in China and stated that it would open another 40 stores every month in China for the next 40 months. Already the number-two sportwear company in the world behind Nike, Adidas has been nominated as the official outfitter of the National Olympic Committee in China in 2008.

Lowe's, the huge home-improvement retailer based in Mooresville, North Carolina, plans to open 6 to 10 stores in Toronto, Canada, in 2007. This expansion is Lowe's first entry into Canada. Currently operating more than 1,100 stores, Lowe's plans at least 100 new stores in Canada this decade.

United Parcel Service (UPS) is building a new cargo hub in Shanghai, its first in mainland China. Based in Atlanta, UPS is launching a domestic Chinese express-delivery service. With this new facility, UPS plans to compete in China with FedEx and DHL, a unit of Deutsche Post AG of Germany. International express deliveries in China have ballooned along with the country's export-led economic growth.[11] During the first five months of 2005, the value of China's exports reached $276.4 billion, up 33.2 percent from a year earlier. DHL's business in China grew about 60 percent in 2005. UPS has only about 15 percent market share in China at present, whereas FedEx has about 20 percent and DHL about 33 percent.

Discount airlines such as AirTran, JetBlue, and Southwest are pursuing market development by expanding routes nationwide, just as the large airlines are cutting back on routes and employees. Both JetBlue and AirTran recently purchased 100 new planes to fly to new cities in the Americas. However, JetBlue recently stopped flying into Atlanta due to heavy competition in that market.

Six guidelines for when market development may be an especially effective strategy are:[12]

- When new channels of distribution are available that are reliable, inexpensive, and of good quality.
- When an organization is very successful at what it does.
- When new untapped or unsaturated markets exist.
- When an organization has the needed capital and human resources to manage expanded operations.
- When an organization has excess production capacity.
- When an organization's basic industry is becoming rapidly global in scope.

Product Development

Product development is a strategy that seeks increased sales by improving or modifying present products or services. Product development usually entails large research and development expenditures.

Fast-food chains from Arby's to McDonald's are pursuing product development, testing gourmet-like sandwiches, because customers increasingly are willing to pay more for fast food crafted with quality ingredients. People more and more want food that not only tastes good but that they can feel good about eating. McDonald's now has design-your-own deli sandwiches and Arby's sells chi-chi sandwiches, which is a chicken salad blended with pecans, apples, and grapes. Subway is testing a healthy Kids Pak, and Wendy's is testing fruit cups and milk as options in its Kids Meals.

Verizon Communications, the largest local phone company in the United States, recently began installing wireless Internet service at its pay phones, including 1,000 pay phones in New York City alone. A similar product-development strategy is being pursued by rival SBC Communications, another large phone company, and by rival Comcast, a large cable company. Phone companies currently have 35 percent of the high-speed Internet market in the United States compared to 62 percent for cable. Phone and cable companies aggressively compete against each other in the Internet service business.

In 2005, the Dutch brewer Heineken developed and introduced its first brand-name, low-calorie, low-carbohydrate beer into the United States. Called "Heineken Light," the company recently hired actors Brad Pitt and John Travolta to promote its new product. Light beers have grown to account for more than half of the 200-million-barrel U.S. beer market. Domestic light beers grew 3.9 percent in 2004 compared to 0.7 percent for the overall beer industry. Heineken Light will compete with Anheuser's Michelob Ultra, which increased 45 percent in sales in 2004 alone.

Coca-Cola Company, based in Atlanta, and PepsiCo, based in Purchase, New York, are introducing Coca-Cola Zero and Pepsi One, respectively, which underscore the growing popularity of diet soft drinks at the expense of sugary drinks. Sales of sugary drinks, such as Coca-Cola Classic and Pepsi, fell 3 percent and 2.5 percent, respectively, last year. Diet drinks now have 29.1 percent market share and that is growing. Many teenagers and young adults have ditched regular colas in favor of bottled water and diet drinks.

Nucor is developing steel-framed housing material to replace wood-framed houses. Nucor is pushing steel's ability to withstand hurricanes, termites, and earthquakes and to keep a house cool. Steel framing makes up less than 2 percent of new, single-family home construction in the United States. Steel framing accounts for 72 percent of new house construction in Hawaii, where insects wreak havoc on wood. Nucor's product development strategy is working well because wood prices have been annually climbing more than 10 percent of late.

Five guidelines for when product development may be an especially effective strategy to pursue are:[13]

- When an organization has successful products that are in the maturity stage of the product life cycle; the idea here is to attract satisfied customers to try new (improved) products as a result of their positive experience with the organization's present products or services.
- When an organization competes in an industry that is characterized by rapid technological developments.
- When major competitors offer better-quality products at comparable prices.
- When an organization competes in a high-growth industry.
- When an organization has especially strong research and development capabilities.

Diversification Strategies

There are two general types of *diversification strategies*: related and unrelated. Businesses are said to be *related* when their value chains posses competitively valuable cross-business strategic fits; businesses are said to be *unrelated* when their value chains are so dissimilar that no competitively valuable cross-business relationships exist.[14] Most companies favor related diversification strategies in order to capitalize on synergies as follows:

- Transferring competitively valuable expertise, technological know-how, or other capabilities from one business to another.
- Combining the related activities of separate businesses into a single operation to achieve lower costs.
- Exploiting common use of a well-known brand name.
- Cross-business collaboration to create competitively valuable resource strengths and capabilities.[15]

Diversification strategies are becoming less popular as organizations are finding it more difficult to manage diverse business activities. In the 1960s and 1970s, the trend was to diversify so as not to be dependent on any single industry, but the 1980s saw a general reversal of that thinking. Diversification is now on the retreat. Michael Porter, of the Harvard Business School, says, "Management found it couldn't manage the beast." Hence, businesses are selling, or closing, less profitable divisions in order to focus on core businesses.

The greatest risk of being in a single industry is having all of the firm's eggs in one basket. Although many firms are successful operating in a single industry, new technologies, new products, or fast-shifting buyer preferences can decimate a particular business. For example, digital cameras are decimating the film and film processing industry, and cell phones have permanently altered the long-distance telephone calling industry.

Diversification must do more than simply spread business risk across different industries, however, because shareholders could accomplish this by simply purchasing equity in different firms across different industries or by investing in mutual funds. Diversification makes sense only to the extent the strategy adds more to shareholder value than what shareholders could accomplish acting individually. Thus, the chosen industry for diversification must be attractive enough to yield consistently high returns on investment and offer potential across the operating divisions for synergies greater than those entities could achieve alone.

A few companies today, however, pride themselves on being conglomerates, from small firms such as Pentair Inc., and Blount International to huge companies such as Textron, Allied Signal, Emerson Electric, General Electric, Viacom, and Samsung. Samsung, for example, now has global market share leadership in many diverse areas, including cell phones (10 percent), big-screen televisions (32 percent), MP3 players (13 percent), DVD players (11 percent), and microwave ovens (25 percent).[16] Similarly, Textron, through numerous diverse acquisitions, now produces and sells Cessna airplanes, Bell helicopters, Jacobsen lawn mowers, golf products, transmissions, consumer loans, and telescopic machinery. Conglomerates prove that focus and diversity are not always mutually exclusive.

Many strategists contend that firms should "stick to the knitting" and not to stray too far from the firm's basic areas of competence. However, diversification is still sometimes an appropriate strategy, especially when the company is competing in an unattractive industry. For example, United Technologies is diversifying away from its core aviation business due to the slumping airline industry. Most recently, United Technologies acquired British electronic-security company Chubb PLC, which follows up its acquisition of Otis Elevator Company and Carrier air conditioning to reduce its dependence on the volatile airline industry. Hamish Maxwell, Philip Morris's former CEO, says, "We want to become a consumer-products company." Diversification makes sense for Philip Morris because cigarette consumption is declining, product liability suits are a risk, and some investors reject tobacco stocks on principle.

Related Diversification

An example of related diversification is Amazon.com Inc.'s recent move to sell personal computers through its online store. Rather than keeping the computers in its warehouses, however, Amazon will simply transmit orders for computers to wholesaler Ingram Micro, based in Santa Ana, California. Ingram will package and send the computers to customers, so Amazon is minimizing its own risk in this diversification initiative. If Amazon were to begin to sell songbirds, this would be related diversification. (See the Natural Environment insert on the next page).

Dell Computer is pursuing related diversification by manufacturing and marketing consumer electronics products such as flat-panel televisions and MP3 players. Also, Dell has recently opened an online music-downloading store. Dell sees the personal computer business becoming more aligned with the entertainment business because both are becoming more and more digital. Simply put, computing and consumer electronics are converging into one industry. Dell, as well as Hewlett-Packard and Gateway, are among the computer firms that now compete with Sony, Matsushita, and Samsung in consumer electronics.

Motorola exited the television-producing business in 1974 in order to focus on semiconductors and wireless products. However, Motorola recently reentered the television-making business by hiring a Chinese company, Proview International Holdings of Hong Kong, to produce flat-panel screens, televisions, and other products under the Motorola name. Motorola's related diversification strategy also involves the firm trying to divest its semiconductor division so it can focus more on wireless and electronic household products.

Rite Aid Corp., one of the largest drugstore chains in the United States, is pursuing related diversification by entering the mail-order pharmacy benefit-management (PBM) business to combat mail-order pharmacies managed by stand-alone companies. Rite Aid now provides PBM services to employers, health plans, and insurance companies. Two other big drugstore chains, Walgreens and CVS, both refuse to participate in new prescription-drug programs using mail-order operations.

Six guidelines for when related diversification may be an effective strategy are provided as follows.[17]

- When an organization competes in a no-growth or a slow-growth industry.
- When adding new, but related, products would significantly enhance the sales of current products.
- When new, but related, products could be offered at highly competitive prices.
- When new, but related, products have seasonal sales levels that counterbalance an organization's existing peaks and valleys.
- When an organization's products are currently in the declining stage of the product's life cycle.
- When an organization has a strong management team.

NATURAL ENVIRONMENT PERSPECTIVE

Songbirds and Coral Reefs in Trouble

Songbirds

Bluebirds are one of 76 songbird species in the United States that have dramatically declined in numbers in the last two decades. Not all birds are considered songbirds, and why birds sing is not clear. Some scientists say they sing when calling for mates or warning of danger, but many scientists now contend that birds sing for sheer pleasure. Songbirds include chickadees, orioles, swallows, mockingbirds, warblers, sparrows, vireos, and the wood thrush. "These birds are telling us there's problem, something's out of balance in our environment," says Jeff Wells, bird conservation director for the National Audubon Society. Songbirds may be telling us that their air or water is too dirty or that we are destroying too much of their habitat. People collect Picasso paintings and save historic buildings. "Songbirds are part of our natural heritage. Why should we be willing to watch songbirds destroyed anymore than allowing a great work of art be destroyed?" asks Wells. Whatever message songbirds are singing to us today about their natural environment, the message is becoming less and less heard nationwide. Listen when you go outside today. Each of us as individuals, companies, states, and countries should do what we reasonably can to help improve the natural environment for songbirds.

Coral Reefs

The ocean covers more than 71 percent of the Earth. The destructive effect of commercial fishing on ocean habitats coupled with increasing pollution runoff into the ocean and global warming of the ocean have decimated fisheries, marine life, and coral reefs around the world. The unfortunate consequence of fishing over the last century has been *overfishing*—with the principal reasons being politics and greed. Trawl fishing with nets destroys coral reefs and has been compared to catching squirrels by cutting down forests, since bottom nets scour and destroy vast areas of the ocean. The great proportion of marine life caught in a trawl is "by-catch" juvenile fish and other life that are killed and discarded. Warming of the ocean due to CO_2 emissions also kills thousands of acres of coral reefs annually. The total area of fully protected marine habitats in the United States is only about 50 square miles, compared to some 93 million acres of national wildlife refuges and national parks on the nation's land. A healthy ocean is vital to the economic and social future of the nation—and, indeed, all countries of the world. Everything we do on land ends up in the ocean, so we all must become better stewards of this last frontier on Earth in order to sustain human survival and the quality of life.

Sources: Adapted from Tom Brook, "Declining Numbers Mute Many Birds' Songs," *USA Today* (September 11, 2001): 4A. Also adapted from John Ogden, "Maintaining Diversity in the Oceans," *Environment* (April 2001): 29–36.

Unrelated Diversification

An unrelated diversification strategy favors capitalizing upon a portfolio of businesses that are capable of delivering excellent financial performance in their respective industries, rather than striving to capitalize on value chain strategic fits among the businesses. Firms that employ unrelated diversification continually search across different industries for companies that can be acquired for a deal and yet have potential to provide a high return on investment. Pursuing unrelated diversification entails being on the hunt to acquire companies whose assets are undervalued, or companies that are financially distressed, or companies that have high growth prospects but are short on investment capital. An obvious drawback of unrelated diversification is that the parent firm must have an excellent top management team that plans, organizes, motivates, delegates, and controls effectively. It is much more difficult to manage businesses in many industries than in a single industry. However some firms are successful pursuing unrelated diversification, such as Walt Disney that owns ABC, Viacom that owns CBS, and General Electric that owns NBC. Thus the three major television networks are all owned by diversified firms.

Many more firms have failed at unrelated diversification than have succeeded due to immense management challenges. However, unrelated diversification can be good, as it is for Cendant Corp., which owns the real-estate firm Century 21, the car-rental agency Avis, the travel-booking sites Orbitz and Flairview Travel, and the hotel brands Days Inn and Howard Johnson. For the first quarter of 2005, Century 21 revenues jumped 16 percent, Avis revenues jumped 9 percent, Orbitz and Flairview revenues jumped 22 percent, and hotel revenues jumped 19 percent. Cendant operates from a strategic business unit organizational structure (to be discussed in Chapter 7).

Real-estate magnate Donald Trump, CEO of Trump Entertainment Resorts, began diversifying his empire in 2005 by starting Trump University, an online business university. Trump's for-profit university consists of online courses, CD-ROMs, consulting services, and Learning Annex-type seminars. Courses at the new Trump University cost $300. The President of Trump University is Michael Sexton. This is another example of unrelated diversification.

E. W. Scripps, which owns television stations and newspapers, recently purchased Shopzilla, thus entering the popular field of online shopping services. Based in Cincinnati, Scripps plans to retain the Shopzilla founders and most managers and operate the business as a separate division. Most Shopzilla revenues are derived from referral fees paid by participating online retailers.

Even the huge toy company, Mattel, Inc., is pursuing unrelated diversification by moving into entertainment. Mattel will soon provide musical tours nationwide to promote its toys and characters. Mattel's "Barbie Live in Fairytopia!" tour will run in 2006 and 2007 and feature real, live Barbies and fairies, such as Elina. This 80-city tour is a partnership between Mattel and Clear Channel Entertainment.

An increasing number of hospitals are creating miniature malls by offering banks, bookstores, coffee shops, restaurants, drugstores, and other retail stores within their buildings. Many hospitals previously had only cafeterias, gift shops, and maybe a pharmacy, but the movement into malls and retail stores is aimed at improving the ambiance for patients and their visitors. The new University Pointe Hospital in West Chester, Ohio, has 75,000 square feet of retail space. The CEO says, "Unless we diversify our revenue, we won't be able to fulfill our mission of providing healthcare. We want our hospital to be a place that people want to go to."[18]

Another example of unrelated diversification strategy would be the recent General Electric (GE) acquisition of Vivendi Universal Entertainment (VUE). VUE is a television and theme park empire, while GE is a highly diversified conglomerate. VUE owns and operates Universal Studios theme parks. GE owns the National Broadcasting Corporation (NBC) and also produces home appliances and scores of other products. General Electric is a classic firm that is highly diversified. GE makes locomotives, lightbulbs, power plants, and refrigerators; GE manages more credit cards than American Express; GE owns more commercial aircraft than American Airlines.

Ten guidelines for when unrelated diversification may be an especially effective strategy are:[19]

- When revenues derived from an organization's current products or services would increase significantly by adding the new, unrelated products.
- When an organization competes in a highly competitive and/or a no-growth industry, as indicated by low industry profit margins and returns.
- When an organization's present channels of distribution can be used to market the new products to current customers.
- When the new products have countercyclical sales patterns compared to an organization's present products.
- When an organization's basic industry is experiencing declining annual sales and profits.
- When an organization has the capital and managerial talent needed to compete successfully in a new industry.
- When an organization has the opportunity to purchase an unrelated business that is an attractive investment opportunity.
- When there exists financial synergy between the acquired and acquiring firm. (Note that a key difference between related and unrelated diversification is that the former should be based on some commonality in markets, products, or technology, whereas the latter should be based more on profit considerations.)
- When existing markets for an organization's present products are saturated.
- When antitrust action could be charged against an organization that historically has concentrated on a single industry.

Defensive Strategies

In addition to integrative, intensive, and diversification strategies, organizations also could pursue retrenchment, divestiture, or liquidation.

Retrenchment

Retrenchment occurs when an organization regroups through cost and asset reduction to reverse declining sales and profits. Sometimes called a *turnaround* or *reorganizational strategy,* retrenchment is designed to fortify an organization's basic distinctive competence. During retrenchment, strategists work with limited resources and face pressure from shareholders, employees, and the media. Retrenchment can entail selling off land and buildings to raise needed cash, pruning product lines, closing marginal businesses, closing obsolete factories, automating processes, reducing the number of employees, and instituting expense control systems.

Winn-Dixie is pursuing a retrenchment strategy in 2005 to 2006 by closing one-third of its stores and eliminating 22,000 jobs, representing 28 percent of its workforce. The struggling supermarket chain is trying to emerge from Chapter 11 bankruptcy protection. The retrenchment involves closing 326 stores and pulling out completely from 14 markets across the Southeast, including Atlanta, Charlotte, and Jackson, Mississippi. Based in Jacksonville, Florida, this is the second round of retrenchment for Winn-Dixie, which in 2004 eliminated 156 stores and cut about 10,000 jobs.

In an unusual strategic move by a Japanese firm, Sanyo Electric is cutting its global workforce by 15 percent in 2006. The firm is closing factories and reducing its debt. Based in Osaka, Sanyo says 8,000 of the 14,000 job cuts will be in Japan, which is accustomed to lifetime employment, low rates of joblessness, and unobtrusive (rather than highly visible) job cuts. Sanyo has been especially hurt by falling prices of cell phones and cameras, and it plans to shift emphasis to batteries and compressors.

In some cases, *bankruptcy* can be an effective type of retrenchment strategy. Bankruptcy can allow a firm to avoid major debt obligations and to void union contracts. There are five major types of bankruptcy: Chapter 7, Chapter 9, Chapter 11, Chapter 12, and Chapter 13.

Chapter 7 bankruptcy is a liquidation procedure used only when a corporation sees no hope of being able to operate successfully or to obtain the necessary creditor agreement. All the organization's assets are sold in parts for their tangible worth.

Chapter 9 bankruptcy applies to municipalities. A municipality that successfully declared bankruptcy is Camden, New Jersey, the state's poorest city and the fifth-poorest city in the United States. A crime-ridden city of 87,000, Camden received $62.5 million in state aid and has withdrawn its bankruptcy petition. Between 1980 and 2000, only 18 U.S. cities declared bankruptcy. Some states do not allow municipalities to declare bankruptcy.

Chapter 11 bankruptcy allows organizations to reorganize and come back after filing a petition for protection. Pharmaceutical firm AaiPharma, based in Wilmington, North Carolina, declared Chapter 11 bankruptcy in 2005 and liquidated (sold) the assets of its pharmaceuticals divisions for $170 million. Collins & Aikman, a large auto parts supplier based in Troy, Michigan, also filed for Chapter 11 bankruptcy. Two rival auto suppliers, Meridian Automotive Systems and Tower Automotive, also recently declared bankruptcy. Based in San Jose, California, Proxim Corporation, a maker of wireless Internet hardware, filed for Chapter 11 bankruptcy-court protection in mid-2005 and agreed to sell itself to Moseley Associates Inc. for $21 million. At the time, Proxim had assets of $55.4 million and debts of $101.8 million. Also during 2005, Brazil's flagship airline, Viacao Aerea Riograndense SA, or Varig, declared bankruptcy. Varig has over $3.75 billion in debt, which equates to about 9 billion reals (Brazil's currency).

Chapter 12 bankruptcy was created by the Family Farmer Bankruptcy Act of 1986. This law became effective in 1987 and provides special relief to family farmers with debt equal to or less than $1.5 million.

Chapter 13 bankruptcy is a reorganization plan similar to Chapter 11, but it is available only to small businesses owned by individuals with unsecured debts of less than $100,000 and secured debts of less than $350,000. The Chapter 13 debtor is allowed to operate the business while a plan is being developed to provide for the successful operation of the business in the future.

Five guidelines for when retrenchment may be an especially effective strategy to pursue are as follows:[20]

- When an organization has a clearly distinctive competence but has failed consistently to meet its objectives and goals over time.
- When an organization is one of the weaker competitors in a given industry.
- When an organization is plagued by inefficiency, low profitability, poor employee morale, and pressure from stockholders to improve performance.
- When an organization has failed to capitalize on external opportunities, minimize external threats, take advantage of internal strengths, and overcome internal weaknesses over time; that is, when the organization's

strategic managers have failed (and possibly will be replaced by more competent individuals).

- When an organization has grown so large so quickly that major internal reorganization is needed.

Divestiture

Selling a division or part of an organization is called *divestiture*. Divestiture often is used to raise capital for further strategic acquisitions or investments. Divestiture can be part of an overall retrenchment strategy to rid an organization of businesses that are unprofitable, that require too much capital, or that do not fit well with the firm's other activities. For example, Morgan Stanley plans to divest its Discover credit card division, to be purchased by a group of shareholders and former executives who have convinced CEO Phillip Purcell and Morgan Stanley's board that the division should be divested. Unilever recently sold its perfume business, including brands Calvin Klein and Vera Wang, to Coty Inc. for $800 million. Unilever also owns Ben & Jerry's ice cream, Dove soap, and Lipton tea, among other products. Jacuzzi Brands, Inc., based in West Palm Beach, Florida, recently divested its Eljer Plumbingware and Rhone Capital LLC divisions to Sun Capital Partners and Rhone Capital LLC respectively. Adidas recently divested its ski-equipment maker Salomon, which was its least profitable division. Danish toy maker Lego recently divested its Legoland theme-park business to Blackstone Group for about $470 million. More examples of divestitures in 2005 are listed in Table 5-4.

Six guidelines for when divestiture may be an especially effective strategy to pursue follows:[21]

- When an organization has pursued a retrenchment strategy and failed to accomplish needed improvements.
- When a division needs more resources to be competitive than the company can provide.
- When a division is responsible for an organization's overall poor performance.
- When a division is a misfit with the rest of an organization; this can result from radically different markets, customers, managers, employees, values, or needs.
- When a large amount of cash is needed quickly and cannot be obtained reasonably from other sources.
- When government antitrust action threatens an organization.

Liquidation

Selling all of a company's assets, in parts, for their tangible worth is called *liquidation*. Liquidation is a recognition of defeat and consequently can be an emotionally difficult strategy. However, it may be better to cease operating than to continue losing large sums of money. For example, Canadian discount airline, Jetsgo, in 2005, halted operations, filed for bankruptcy, and then liquidated. Canada's third-largest airline, Jetsgo was launched three years earlier from Montreal. Jetsgo competed against WestJet, based in Calgary, Alberta, and Air Canada, based in Montreal. Analysts had long predicted that Jetsgo would fail, given the company's rock-bottom ticket prices and aggressive expansion.

America Online Latin America Inc. filed for bankruptcy protection in mid-2005 and announced plans to liquidate its business. Since its founding in 1999, AOL Latin America had never been cash-flow positive.

TABLE 5-4 Recent Divestitures

PARENT COMPANY	PART BEING DIVESTED	ACQUIRING COMPANY
Computer Sciences	Health Plans Solutions	DST Systems
General Electric	Self Storage Business	Prudential Financial
Instinet Group	Computerized Trading	Nasdaq Stock Market
Clear Channel	Entertainment Unit	Pending
Duke Energy	Natural-gas transmission	Pending
Duke Energy	Real estate	Pending
Leonard Green & Partners	Liberty Group Publishing	Fortress Capital Group
General Electric	Medical Protective Corp.	National Indemnity
DaimlerChrysler AG	Motor manufacturing	Pending
Veronis Suhler Stevenson	European telephone directory	Macquarie Capital Alliance
E.On AG	Real-estate division	Terra Firma Capital Ltd.
Tiscali SpA	Excite Italia BV	Ask Jeeves Inc.
Bertelsmann	U.S. magazine unit	Pending
Bertelsmann	YM Magazine	Condé Nast
Pfizer	Surgical ophthalmology	Advanced Medical Optics
Enel SpA	Wind SpA	Naguib Sawiris
Morgan Stanley	Discover Financial Services	Pending
Calpine Corp.	Saltend power plant	Mitsui & Co
Abbott Laboratories	Determine/DainaScreen	Inverness Medical
El Paso Corp.	Lakeside Technology	Digital Realty
Federated Dept. Stores	Credit-card business	Citigroup
May Dept. Stores	Credit-card business	Citigroup
Precision Drilling	Energy services	Weatherford
Precision Drilling	Contract drilling	Weatherford
Pernod	Bushmills	Diageo
Allied Domecq	Montana	Diageo
Wyeth Pharmaceuticals	Solgar Vitamin & Herb	NBTY Inc.
American Express	Financial advisory	Pending
Agilent	Semiconductor division	Pending
Viacom	Famous Players	Cineplex Galaxy
Cargill Investor Services	Brokerage operations	Refco Group Ltd.
E.On AG	Ruhrgas Industries GmbH	CVC Capital Partners Ltd.
Danone	HP Foods	Heinz Foods
Clayton Homes	Manufactured housing	Fleetwood Enterprises
Colgate-Palmolive	Laundry detergent brands	Phoenix Brands LLC

Thousands of small businesses in the United States liquidate annually without ever making the news. It is tough to start and successfully operate a small business. In China and Russia, thousands of government-owned businesses liquidate annually as those countries try to privatize and consolidate industries.

Three guidelines for when liquidation may be an especially effective strategy to pursue are:[22]

- When an organization has pursued both a retrenchment strategy and a divestiture strategy, and neither has been successful.
- When an organization's only alternative is bankruptcy. Liquidation represents an orderly and planned means of obtaining the greatest possible cash for an organization's assets. A company can legally declare bankruptcy first and then liquidate various divisions to raise needed capital.
- When the stockholders of a firm can minimize their losses by selling the organization's assets.

Michael Porter's Five Generic Strategies

Probably the three most widely read books on competitive analysis in the 1980s were Michael Porter's *Competitive Strategy* (Free Press, 1980), *Competitive Advantage* (Free Press, 1985), and *Competitive Advantage* of Nations (Free Press, 1989). According to Porter, strategies allow organizations to gain competitive advantage from three different bases: cost leadership, differentiation, and focus. Porter calls these bases *generic strategies. Cost leadership* emphasizes producing standardized products at a very low per-unit cost for consumers who are price-sensitive. Two alternative types of cost leadership strategies can be defined. Type 1 is a *low-cost* strategy that offers products or services to a wide range of customers at the lowest price available on the market. Type 2 is *best-value* strategy that offers products or services to a wide range of customers at the best price-value available on the market; the best-value strategy aims to offer customers a range of products or services at the lowest price available compared to a rival's products with similar attributes. Both Type 1 and Type 2 strategies target a large market.

Porter's Type 3 generic strategy is *differentiation. Differentiation* is a strategy aimed at producing products and services considered unique industrywide and directed at consumers who are relatively price-insensitive.

Focus means producing products and services that fulfill the needs of small groups of consumers. Two alternative types of focus strategies are Type 4 and Type 5. Type 4 is a *low-cost focus* strategy that offers products or services to a small range (niche group) of customers at the lowest price available on the market. Examples of firms that use the Type 4 strategy include Jiffy Lube International and Pizza Hut, as well as local used car dealers and hot dog restaurants. Type 5 is a *best-value focus* strategy that offers products or services to a small range of customers at the best price-value available on the market. Sometimes called "focused differentiation," the best-value focus strategy aims to offer a niche group of customers products or services that meet their tastes and requirements better than rivals' products do. Both Type 4 and Type 5 focus strategies target a small market. However, the difference is that Type 4 strategies offer products services to a niche group at the lowest price, whereas Type 5 offers products/services to a niche group at higher prices but loaded with features so the offerings are perceived as the best value. Examples of firms that use the Type 5 strategy include Cannondale (top-of-the-line mountain bikes), Maytag (washing machines), and Lone Star Restaurants (steak house), as well as bed-and-breakfast inns and local retail boutiques.

Porter's five strategies imply different organizational arrangements, control procedures, and incentive systems. Larger firms with greater access to resources

FIGURE 5-3

Porter's Five Generic Strategies

Type 1: Cost Leadership—Low Cost

Type 2: Cost Leadership—Best Value

Type 3: Differentiation

Type 4: Focus—Low Cost

Type 5: Focus—Best Value

GENERIC STRATEGIES

	Cost Leadership	Differentiation	Focus
Large	Type 1 Type 2	Type 3	—
Small	—	Type 3	Type 4 Type 5

SIZE OF MARKET

Source: Adapted from Michael E. Porter, *Competitive Strategy: Techniques for Analyzing Industries and Competitors* (New York: Free Press, 1980): 35–40.

typically compete on a cost leadership and/or differentiation basis, whereas smaller firms often compete on a focus basis. Porter's five generic strategies are illustrated in Figure 5-3. Note that a differentiation strategy (Type 3) can be pursued with either a small target market or a large target market. However, it is not effective to pursue a cost leadership strategy in a small market because profits margins are generally too small. Likewise, it is not effective to pursue a focus strategy in a large market because economies of scale would generally favor a low-cost or best-value cost leaderships strategy to gain and/or sustain competitive advantage.

Porter stresses the need for strategists to perform cost-benefit analyses to evaluate "sharing opportunities" among a firm's existing and potential business units. Sharing activities and resources enhances competitive advantage by lowering costs or increasing differentiation. In addition to prompting sharing, Porter stresses the need for firms to effectively "transfer" skills and expertise among autonomous business units in order to gain competitive advantage. Depending upon factors such as type of industry, size of firm, and nature of competition, various strategies could yield advantages in cost leadership, differentiation, and focus.

Cost Leadership Strategies (Type 1 and Type 2)

A primary reason for pursuing forward, backward, and horizontal integration strategies is to gain low-cost or best-value cost leadership benefits. But cost leadership generally must be pursued in conjunction with differentiation. A number of cost elements affect the relative attractiveness of generic strategies, including economies or diseconomies of scale achieved, learning and experience curve effects, the percentage of capacity utilization achieved, and linkages with suppliers and distributors. Other cost elements to consider in choosing among alternative strategies include the potential for sharing costs and knowledge within the organization, R&D costs associated with new product development or modification of existing products, labor costs, tax rates, energy costs, and shipping costs.

Striving to be the low-cost producer in an industry can be especially effective when the market is composed of many price-sensitive buyers, when there are few ways to achieve product differentiation, when buyers do not care much about differences from brand to brand, or when there are a large number of buyers with significant bargaining power. The basic idea is to underprice competitors and thereby gain market share and sales, entirely driving some competitors out of the market. Companies employing a low-cost (Type 1) or best-value (Type 2) cost leadership strategy must achieve their competitive advantage in ways that are difficult for competitors to copy or match. If rivals find it relatively easy or inexpensive to imitate the leader's cost leadership methods, the leaders' advantage will be not last long enough to yield a valuable edge in the marketplace. Recall that for a resource to be valuable, it must be either rare, hard to imitate, or not easily substitutable. To successfully employ a cost leadership strategy, a firm must ensure that its total costs across its overall value chain are lower than competitors' total costs. There are two ways to accomplish this:[23]

1. Perform value chain activities more efficiently than rivals and control the factors that drive the costs of value chain activities. Such activities could include altering the plant layout, mastering newly introduced technologies, using common parts or components in different products, simplifying product design, finding ways to operate close to full capacity year-round, and so on.

2. Revamp the firm's overall value chain to eliminate or bypass some cost-producing activities. Such activities could include securing new suppliers or distributors, selling products online, relocating manufacturing facilities, avoiding the use of union labor, and so on.

When employing a cost leadership strategy, a firm must be careful not to use such aggressive price cuts that their own profits are low or nonexistent. Constantly be mindful of cost-saving technological breakthroughs or any other value chain advancements that could erode or destroy the firm's competitive advantage. A Type 1 or Type 2 cost leadership strategy can be especially effective under the following conditions:[24]

1. When price competition among rival sellers is especially vigorous.

2. When the products of rival sellers are essentially identical and supplies are readily available from any of several eager sellers.

3. When there are few ways to achieve product differentiation that have value to buyers.

4. When most buyers use the product in the same ways.

5. When buyers incur low costs in switching their purchases from one seller to another.

6. When buyers are large and have significant power to bargain down prices.

7. When industry newcomers use introductory low prices to attract buyers and build a customer base.

A successful cost leadership strategy usually permeates the entire firm, as evidenced by high efficiency, low overhead, limited perks, intolerance of waste, intensive screening of budget requests, wide spans of control, rewards linked to cost containment, and broad employee participation in cost control efforts. Some risks of pursuing cost leadership are that competitors may imitate the strategy, thus driving overall industry profits down; that technological breakthroughs in the industry may make the strategy ineffective; or that buyer interest may swing to other differentiating features besides price. Several example firms that are well-known for their low-cost leadership strategies are Wal-Mart, BIC, McDonald's, Black and Decker, Lincoln Electric, and Briggs and Stratton.

Differentiation Strategies (Type 3)

Different strategies offer different degrees of differentiation. Differentiation does not guarantee competitive advantage, especially if standard products sufficiently meet customer needs or if rapid imitation by competitors is possible. Durable products protected by barriers to quick copying by competitors are best. Successful differentiation can mean greater product flexibility, greater compatibility, lower costs, improved service, less maintenance, greater convenience, or more features. Product development is an example of a strategy that offers the advantages of differentiation.

A differentiation strategy should be pursued only after a careful study of buyers' needs and preferences to determine the feasibility of incorporating one or more differentiating features into a unique product that features the desired attributes. A successful differentiation strategy allows a firm to charge a higher price for its product and to gain customer loyalty because consumers may become strongly attached to the differentiation features. Special features that differentiate one's product can include superior service, spare parts availability, engineering design, product performance, useful life, gas mileage, or ease of use.

A risk of pursuing a differentiation strategy is that the unique product may not be valued highly enough by customers to justify the higher price. When this happens, a cost leadership strategy easily will defeat a differentiation strategy. Another risk of pursuing a differentiation strategy is that competitors may quickly develop ways to copy the differentiating features. Firms thus must find durable sources of uniqueness that cannot be imitated quickly or cheaply by rival firms.

Common organizational requirements for a successful differentiation strategy include strong coordination among the R&D and marketing functions and substantial amenities to attract scientists and creative people. Firms can pursue a differentiation (Type 3) strategy based on many different competitive aspects. For example, Mountain Dew and root beer have a unique taste; Lowe's, Home Depot, and Wal-Mart offer wide selection and one-stop shopping; Dell Computer and FedEx offer superior service; BMW and Porsche offer engineering design and performance; IBM and Hewlett-Packard offer a wide range of products; and E*Trade and Ameritrade offer Internet convenience. Differentiation opportunities exist or can potentially be developed anywhere along the firm's value chain, including supply chain activities, product R&D activities, production and technological activities, manufacturing activities, human resource management activities, distribution activities, or marketing activities.

The most effective differentiation bases are those that are hard or expensive for rivals to duplicate. Competitors are continually trying to imitate, duplicate, and outperform rivals along any differentiation variable that has yielded competitive advantage. For example, when U.S. Airways cut its prices, Delta quickly followed suit. When Caterpillar instituted its quick-delivery-of-spare-parts policy,

John Deere soon followed suit. To the extent that differentiating attributes are tough for rivals to copy, a differentiation strategy will be especially effective, but the sources of uniqueness must be time-consuming, cost prohibitive, and simply too burdensome for rivals to match. A firm, therefore, must be careful when employing a differentiation (Type 3) strategy. Buyers will not pay the higher differentiation price unless their perceived value exceeds the price they are paying.[25] Based upon such matters as attractive packaging, extensive advertising, quality of sales presentations, quality of Web site, list of customers, professionalism, size of the firm, and/or profitability of the company, perceived value may be more important to customers than actual value.

A Type 3 differentiation strategy can be especially effective under the following conditions:[26]

1. When there are many ways to differentiate the product or service and many buyers perceive these differences as having value.
2. When buyer needs and uses are diverse.
3. When few rival firms are following a similar differentiation approach.
4. When technological change is fast paced and competition revolves around rapidly evolving product features.

Focus Strategies (Type 4 and Type 5)

A successful focus strategy depends on an industry segment that is of sufficient size, has good growth potential, and is not crucial to the success of other major competitors. Strategies such as market penetration and market development offer substantial focusing advantages. Midsize and large firms can effectively pursue focus-based strategies only in conjunction with differentiation or cost leadership-based strategies. All firms in essence follow a differentiated strategy. Because only one firm can differentiate itself with the lowest cost, the remaining firms in the industry must find other ways to differentiate their products.

Focus strategies are most effective when consumers have distinctive preferences or requirements and when rival firms are not attempting to specialize in the same target segment. Starbucks, the largest U.S. coffeehouse chain, is pursuing a focus strategy as it recently acquired Seattle Coffee's U.S. and Canadian operations for $72 million. Based in Seattle, Starbucks now owns Seattle's 150 coffee shops and its wholesale contracts with about 12,000 grocery stores and food service stores that distribute Seattle coffee beans.

In the insurance industry, Safeco recently divested its life insurance and investment management divisions to focus exclusively on property casualty insurance operations. The Seattle-based company's strategy is just one of many examples of consolidation in the insurance industry where firms strive to focus on one type of insurance rather than many types.

Risks of pursuing a focus strategy include the possibility that numerous competitors will recognize the successful focus strategy and copy it or that consumer preferences will drift toward the product attributes desired by the market as a whole. An organization using a focus strategy may concentrate on a particular group of customers, geographic markets, or on particular product-line segments to serve a well-defined but narrow market better than competitors who serve a broader market.

A low-cost (Type 4) or best-value (Type 5) focus strategy can be especially attractive under the following conditions:[27]

1. When the target market niche is large, profitable, and growing.
2. When industry leaders do not consider the niche to be crucial to their own success.

3. When industry leaders consider it too costly or difficult to meet the specialized needs of the target market niche while taking care of their mainstream customers.

4. When the industry has many different niches and segments, thereby allowing a focuser to pick a competitively attractive niche suited to its own resources.

5. When few, if any, other rivals are attempting to specialize in the same target segment.

Strategies for Competing in Turbulent, High-Velocity Markets

The world is changing more and more rapidly, and consequently industries and firms themselves are changing faster than ever. Some industries are changing so fast that researchers call them *turbulent, high-velocity markets,* such as telecommunications, medical, biotechnology, pharmaceuticals, computer hardware, software, and virtually all Internet-based industries. High-velocity change is clearly becoming more and more the rule rather than the exception, even in such industries as toys, phones, banking, defense, publishing, and communication.

As illustrated in Figure 5-4, meeting the challenge of high-velocity change presents the firm with a choice of whether to react, anticipate, or lead the market in terms of its own strategies. To primarily react to changes in the industry would be a defensive strategy used to counter, for example, unexpected shifts in buyer tastes and technological breakthroughs. The react-to-change strategy would not be as effective as the anticipate-change strategy, which would entail devising and following through with plans for dealing with the expected changes. However, firms ideally strive to be in a position to lead the changes in high-velocity markets, whereby they pioneer new and better technologies and products and set industry standards. As illustrated, being the leader or pioneer of change in a high-velocity market is an aggressive, offensive strategy that includes rushing next-generation products to market ahead of rivals and being continually proactive in shaping the market to one's own benefit. Although a lead-change strategy is best whenever the firm has the resources to pursue this approach, on occasion even the strongest firms in turbulent industries have to employ the react-to-the-market strategy and the anticipate-the-market strategy.

Means for Achieving Strategies

Joint Venture/Partnering

Joint venture is a popular strategy that occurs when two or more companies form a temporary partnership or consortium for the purpose of capitalizing on some opportunity. Often, the two or more sponsoring firms form a separate organization and have shared equity ownership in the new entity. Other types of *cooperative arrangements* include research and development partnerships, cross-distribution agreements, cross-licensing agreements, cross-manufacturing agreements, and joint-bidding consortia. Burger King recently formed a "conceptual agreement" with its fierce rival, Hungry Jacks, in Australia, whereby the two firms will join forces against market leader McDonald's. All Burger Kings in Australia are being renamed Hungry Jacks, but Burger King retains ownership under the unusual agreement. With this agreement, Australia becomes Burger King's fourth-largest country market, tied with Spain.

Nestlé SA and Colgate-Palmolive recently formed a joint venture to develop and sell candy and chewing gum that can reduce plaque and clean teeth. This

FIGURE 5-4

Meeting the Challenge of High-Velocity Change

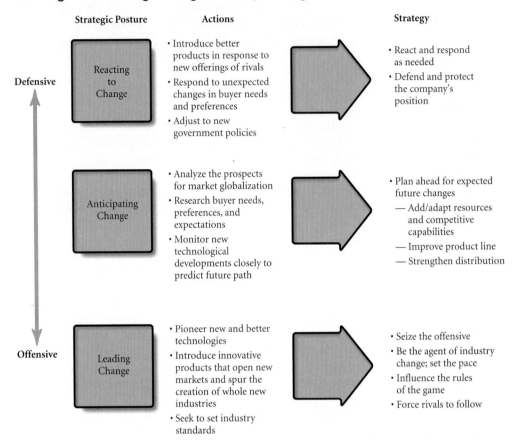

Source: Reprinted by permission of Harvard Business School Press. From *Competing on the Edge: Strategy as Structured Chaos* by Shona L. Brown and Kathleen M. Eisenhardt, Boston, MA, 1998, p. 5. Copyright © 1998 by the Harvard Business School Publishing Corporation; all rights reserved.

intensely competitive industry is dominated by Cadbury Schweppes PLC's Adams and Chicago-based Wm. Wrigley Jr. Co. Called the "functional confectionary segment," gum and candy sales that have health or aesthetic benefits are annually growing almost 6 percent, twice the growth rate of standard gum and candy. Nestlé had no functional confectionary products prior to the joint venture. Adams is the world leader in functional confectionery, with a 26 percent share and products such as tooth-whitening Trident White and Recaldent. Wrigley has 21 percent of the market with products such as Orbit White and Airwaves.

Joint ventures and cooperative arrangements are being used increasingly because they allow companies to improve communications and networking, to globalize operations, and to minimize risk. Joint ventures and partnerships are often used to pursue an opportunity that is too complex, uneconomical, or risky for a single firm to pursue alone. Such business creations also are used when achieving and sustaining competitive advantage when an industry requires a broader range of competencies and know-how than any one firm can marshal. Three non real estate companies better known for tractors, fish, and fashion are entered into joint ventures with luxury-property developers to attach their brands to high-end homes and lodging. John Deere, of Moline, Illinois, has joined with St. Lawrence Homes of Raleigh, North Carolina, to create a "John Deere Signature Community" in Durham, North Carolina. The $500,000 homes in the development come with a garage full of John Deere lawn equipment and two years of free maintenance. Orvis, the Manchester, Vermont, outdoors retailer has formed a joint venture with commercial real estate services firm Cushman & Wakefield to sell luxury ranch and recreational properties. Armani's joint venture is with Emaar Hotels & Resorts LLC to create, among others, the tallest building in the world in 2008: a 2,000-foot-tall hotel in Dubai's Burj Dubai. Kathryn Rudie Harrigan, professor of strategic management at Columbia University, summarizes the trend toward increased joint venturing:

> In today's global business environment of scarce resources, rapid rates of technological change, and rising capital requirements, the important question is no longer "Shall we form a joint venture?" Now the question is "Which joint ventures and cooperative arrangements are most appropriate for our needs and expectations?" followed by "How do we manage these ventures most effectively?"[28]

In a global market tied together by the Internet, joint ventures, and partnerships, alliances are proving to be a more effective way to enhance corporate growth than mergers and acquisitions.[29] Strategic partnering takes many forms, including outsourcing, information sharing, joint marketing, and joint research and development. Many companies, such as Eli Lilly, even now host partnership training classes for their managers and partners. There are today more than 10,000 joint ventures formed annually, more than all mergers and acquisitions. There are countless examples of successful strategic alliances, such as Starbucks' recent joint venture with China's President Coffee to open hundreds of new Starbuck coffee shops in China. For 4,500 years, China has been a country of tea drinkers, but Seattle-based Starbucks is having success building Chinese taste for coffee. Microsoft's online-services division in 2005 formed a joint venture with Shanghai Alliance Investment to launch MSN China throughout China. The new company, Shanghai MSN Network Communications Technology, serves China's online consumers: 100 million (and growing) at that time. As evidence of Microsoft's determination to enter the telecom market, the firm has formed a partnership with France Telecom SA, one of the world's largest telecommunications operators. Since people increasingly interact with the Internet using either a cell phone or television, Microsoft is using the alliance to push its voice-over-Internet protocol (VOIP), which is a handheld device that combines cell phone usage with Internet coverage.

A major reason why firms are using partnering as a means to achieve strategies is globalization. Wal-Mart's successful joint venture with Mexico's Cifra is indicative of how a domestic firm can benefit immensely by partnering with a foreign company to gain substantial presence in that new country. Technology also is a major reason behind the need to form strategic alliances, with the Internet linking widely dispersed partners. The Internet paved the way and legitimized the need for alliances to serve as the primary means for corporate growth.

Evidence is mounting that firms should use partnering as a means for achieving strategies. However, the sad fact is that most U.S. firms in many industries—such as financial services, forest products, metals, and retailing—still operate in a merger or acquire mode to obtain growth. Partnering is not yet taught at most business schools and is often viewed within companies as a financial issue rather than a strategic issue. However, partnering has become a core competency, a strategic issue of such importance that top management involvement initially and throughout the life of an alliance is vital.[30] European Aeronautic Defence & Space (EADS) recently formed a partnership with Raytheon to bid on a large Pentagon contract for Army transport aircraft. Based in Europe, EADS is the majority (80 percent) owner of aircraft maker Airbus. EADS is also negotiating a joint venture with Northrop Grumman for the Pentagon's Air Force tanker-plane contract.

Joint ventures among once rival firms are commonly being used to pursue strategies ranging from retrenchment to market development.

Although ventures and partnerships are preferred over mergers as a means for achieving strategies, certainly they are not all successful. The good news is that joint ventures and partnerships are less risky for companies than mergers, but the bad news is that many alliances fail. *Forbes* has reported that about 30 percent of all joint ventures and partnership alliances are outright failures, while another 17 percent have limited success and then dissipate due to problems.[31] There are countless examples of failed joint ventures. A few common problems that cause joint ventures to fail are as follows:

1. Managers who must collaborate daily in operating the venture are not involved in forming or shaping the venture.
2. The venture may benefit the partnering companies but may not benefit customers who then complain about poorer service or criticize the companies in other ways.
3. The venture may not be supported equally by both partners. If supported unequally, problems arise.
4. The venture may begin to compete more with one of the partners than the other.[32]

Six guidelines for when a joint venture may be an especially effective strategy to pursue are:[33]

- When a privately owned organization is forming a joint venture with a publicly owned organization; there are some advantages to being privately held, such as closed ownership; there are some advantages of being publicly held, such as access to stock issuances as a source of capital. Sometimes, the unique advantages of being privately and publicly held can be synergistically combined in a joint venture.
- When a domestic organization is forming a joint venture with a foreign company; a joint venture can provide a domestic company with the opportunity for obtaining local management in a foreign country, thereby reducing risks such as expropriation and harassment by host country officials.
- When the distinct competencies of two or more firms complement each other especially well.
- When some project is potentially very profitable but requires overwhelming resources and risks; the Alaskan pipeline is an example.
- When two or more smaller firms have trouble competing with a large firm.
- When there exists a need to quickly introduce a new technology.

Joint Ventures in Russia

A joint venture strategy offers a possible way to enter the Russian market. Joint ventures create a mechanism to generate hard currency, which is important because of problems valuing the ruble. Russia's joint venture law has been revised to allow foreigners to own up to 99 percent of the venture and to allow a foreigner to serve as chief executive officer.

The following guidelines are appropriate when considering a joint venture in Russia. First, avoid regions with ethnic conflicts and violence. Also, make sure the potential partner has a proper charter that has been amended to permit joint venture participation. Be aware that businesspeople in these lands have little knowledge of marketing, contract law, corporate law, fax machines, voice mail, and other business practices that Westerners take for granted.

Business contracts with Russian firms should address natural-environment issues because Westerners often get the blame for air and water pollution problems and habitat destruction. Work out a clear means of converting rubles to dollars before entering a proposed joint venture, because neither Russian banks nor authorities can be counted on to facilitate foreign firms' getting dollar profits out of a business. Recognize that chronic shortages of raw materials hamper business in Russia, so make sure an adequate supply of competitively priced, good-quality raw materials is reliably available. Finally, make sure the business contract limits the circumstances in which expropriation would be legal. Specify a lump sum in dollars if expropriation should occur unexpectedly, and obtain expropriation insurance before signing the agreement.

Merger/Acquisition

Merger and acquisition are two commonly used ways to pursue strategies. A *merger* occurs when two organizations of about equal size unite to form one enterprise. An *acquisition* occurs when a large organization purchases (acquires) a smaller firm, or vice versa. When a merger or acquisition is not desired by both parties, it can be called a *takeover* or *hostile takeover*. For example, Omnicare, Inc., recently raised its hostile bid for drug and medical-supply distributor NeighborCare to $1.45 billion. Based in Covington, Kentucky, Omnicare is a provider of long-term care and pharmacy services. NeighborCare has refused Omnicare's bid.

In contrast, if the acquisition is desired by both firms, it is termed a *friendly merger*. Most mergers are friendly. There are numerous and powerful forces driving once-fierce rivals to merge around the world. Some of these forces are deregulation, technological change, excess capacity, inability to boost profits through price increases, a depressed stock market, and the need to gain economies of scale. Other forces spurring acquisitions include increased market power, reduced entry barriers, reduced cost of new product development, increased speed of products to market, lowered risk compared to developing new products, increased diversification, avoidance of excessive competition, and opportunity to learn and develop new capabilities.

Bargains are available as companies struggle and while stock prices are low. Among domestic media companies, for example, numerous mergers are expected since the Federal Communications Commission recently lifted the decades-old restrictions on the size of media firms. That ruling allows newspapers to now own television and radio stations in the markets where they publish. Also, network television companies can now own stations reaching up to 45 percent of the nation's viewers, up from 35 percent. Companies such as Tribune, Media General, Sinclair Broadcast Group, LIN TV, NewsCorp, Fox, NBC, ABC, CBS, and others are expected to be merging in the 2006 to 2008 time period.

Not all mergers are effective and successful. Pricewaterhouse Coopers LLP recently researched mergers and found that the average acquirer's stock was 3.7 percent lower than its industry peer group a year later. *BusinessWeek* and the *Wall Street Journal* studied mergers and concluded that about half produced negative returns to shareholders. Warren Buffett once said in a speech that "too-high purchase price for the stock of an excellent company can undo the effects of a subsequent decade of favorable business developments." Research suggests that perhaps 20 percent of all mergers and acquisitions are successful, approximately 60 percent produce disappointing results, and the last 20 percent are clear failures.[34] So a merger between two firms can yield great benefits, but the price and reasoning must be right.

Some key reasons why many mergers and acquisitions fail are:

- Integration difficulties
- Inadequate evaluation of target
- Large or extraordinary debt
- Inability to achieve synergy
- Too much diversification
- Managers overly focused on acquisitions
- Too large an acquisition
- Difficult to integrate different organizational cultures
- Reduced employee morale due to layoffs and relocations

Among mergers, acquisitions, and takeovers in recent years, same-industry combinations have predominated. A general market consolidation is occurring in many industries, especially banking, insurance, defense, and healthcare, but also in pharmaceuticals, food, airlines, accounting, publishing, computers, retailing, financial services, and biotechnology.

Domestic movie attendance was down 8 percent in 2005 as fancy home-theater systems and DVDs increasingly encouraged people to stay home. To combat this trend, two of the nation's leading theater chains, AMC Entertainment and Loews Cineplex Entertainment, merged in mid-2005 into a 5,900-screen entity with operations throughout the United States and in multiple overseas markets. The new company, AMC Entertainment, is now second only to Regal Entertainment Group, which has 558 theaters with 6,273 screens.

UnitedHealth Group recently acquired (merged with) PacifiCare Health Systems for $8.11 billion, soon after purchasing Oxford Health Plans and Mid Atlantic Medical Services. Less than 50 percent of full-time U.S. workers are now covered by company-paid health insurance, down from 80 percent in 1989. Due to skyrocketing costs, employers are today dropping or trimming healthcare benefits to employees. The recent merger narrows the gap between UnitedHealth Group and the industry leader, WellPoint Health Networks, which recently merged with Anthem.

Table 5-5 shows some mergers and acquisitions completed in 2005. There are many reasons for mergers and acquisitions, including the following:

- To provide improved capacity utilization
- To make better use of the existing sales force
- To reduce managerial staff
- To gain economies of scale
- To smooth out seasonal trends in sales
- To gain access to new suppliers, distributors, customers, products, and creditors
- To gain new technology
- To reduce tax obligations

The volume of mergers completed annually worldwide is growing dramatically and exceeds $1 trillion. There are annually more than 10,000 mergers in the

TABLE 5-5 Some Mergers in 2005

ACQUIRING FIRM	ACQUIRED FIRM	PRICE	TYPE OF BUSINESS
Crompton Corp.	Great Lakes Chemical	$1.75 Bil	Specialty chemical
Gardner Denver	Thomas Industries	740 Mil	Compressors
Noranda	Falconbridge	2.47 Bil	Mining
Yellow Pages Group	Advertising Directory Sol	2.07 Bil	Yellow pages
IBM	Ascential Software	1.10 Bil	Software
Philip Morris	PT Hanjaya Mandala Samp	5.00 Bil	Cigarettes
Siemens	CTI Molecular	1.00 Bil	Medical equipment
Solvay SA	Fournier Pharma	1.03 Bil	Pharmaceutical
Medicis	Inamed	2.80 Bil	Skin-care products
Quiksilver	Groupe Rossignol SA	320 Mil	Ski equipment
Entegris	Mykrolis Crop	578 Mil	Semiconductors
Avid Technology	Pinnacle Systems	422 Mil	Video equipment
Juniper Networks	Kagoor Networks	67.5 Mil	Telecom networks
Thomson SA	Inventel	128 Mil	Electronics
Acxiom Corp	Digital Impact	140 Mil	Consumer data
FPL Group Inc.	Gexa Corp.	81 Mil	Utilities
Oracle	Oblix	n/a	Software
Oracle	Retek	670 Mil	Software
Oracle	PeopleSoft	10.6 Bil	Software
Silver Lake Partners	SunGard Data Systems	10.8 Bil	Financial services
Computer Associates	Concord Communications	330 Mil	Software
ChevronTexaco	Unocal	16.8 Bil	Oil and gas
OSIM International Ltd	Brookstone	450 Mil	Specialty retailing
Adobe Systems	Macromedia	3.4 Bil	Software
General Electric	Bombardier	1.4 Bil	Finance
GameStop	Electronics Boutique	1.44 Bil	Videogame retailing
Valero Energy	Premcor	6.9 Bil	Crude Oil Refining
Hellman & Friedman	DoubleClick	1.1 Bil	Internet advertising
Bandai	Namco	1.7 Bil	Toys and games
WellPoint	Lumenos	185 Mil	Healthcare programs
Fresenius	Renal Care	3.5 Bil	Kidney dialysis
American Tower	SpectraSite	3.0 Bil	Communication towers
Genzyme Corp.	Bone Care	719 Mil	Kidney treatment
Archipelago Holdings	New York Stock Exchange	20 Mil	Stock market
Archipelago Holdings	PCS Holdings	51 Mil	Stock options
Duke Energy	Cinergy	9.1 Bil	Utility
Maersk	P&O Nedlloyd	2.95 Bil	Container shipping
3M	Cuno Inc.	1.3 Bil	Water-purification
Sabre Holdings	lastminute.com PLC	1.08 Bil	Online travels
Aetna	ActiveHealth Management	400 Mil	Medical management
United Parcel Service	Overnite Corp.	1.25 Bil	Trucking
Viasys Healthcare	Pulmonetic Systems	98 Mil	Home ventilators

(Continued)

TABLE 5-5 Continued

ACQUIRING FIRM	ACQUIRED FIRM	PRICE	TYPE OF BUSINESS
US Airways	America West	—	Airlines
Ripplewood Holdings	Maytag	1.13 Bil	Appliances
L'Oreal SA	Skin-Ceuticals	—	Skin-care products
Sysco Corp.	Royalty Foods Inc	—	Beef distribution
Actavis Group	Amide Pharmaceutical	600 Mil	Generic drugs
JDS Uniphase	Acterna	760 Mil	Telecom equipment
Advanced Medical Optics	Visx	1.3 Bil	Eye care
Advanced Medical Optics	Quest Vision Tech	—	Eye care
eBay	Shopping.com	620 Mil	Shopping comparison
Johnson & Johnson	Guidant	25.4 Bil	Medical devices
Stride Rite	Saucony	170 Mil	Children's shoes
Sun Microsystems	Storage Tek	4.1 Bil	Data storage
Washington Mutual	Providian	6.45 Bil	Insurance
Scripps	Shopzilla	525 Mil	Online shopping
Unicredito Italiano SpA	HVB Group AG	18.81 Bil	Banking
L-3	Titan	2.08 Bil	Defense contractor
BNP Paribas SA	Commercial Federal Corp.	1.36 Bil	Banking
AMC Entertainment	Loews Cineplex Entertainment	4.0 Bil	Theater chains
Ameritrade	TD Waterhouse	2.9 Bil	Brokerage firms
Omnicare	NeighborCare	1.55 Bil	Drug distribution
Mohawk	Unilin	2.65 Bil	Flooring/carpet
Procter & Gamble	Gillete	53 Bil	Consumer products

United States that total more than $700 billion. The proliferation of mergers is fueled by companies' drive for market share, efficiency, and pricing power, as well as by globalization, the need for greater economies of scale, reduced regulation and antitrust concerns, the Internet, and e-commerce.

A *leveraged buyout* (LBO) occurs when a corporation's shareholders are bought (hence *buyout*) by the company's management and other private investors using borrowed funds (hence *leverage*).[35] Besides trying to avoid a hostile takeover, other reasons for initiating an LBO are senior management decisions that particular divisions do not fit into an overall corporate strategy or must be sold to raise cash, or receipt of an attractive offering price. An LBO takes a corporation private.

First Mover Advantages

First mover advantages refer to the benefits a firm may achieve by entering a new market or developing a new product or service prior to rival firms.[36] Some advantages of being a first mover include securing access to rare resources, gaining new knowledge of key factors and issues, and carving out market share and a position that is easy to defend and costly for rival firms to overtake. First mover advantages are analogous to taking the high ground first, which puts one in an excellent strategic position to launch aggressive campaigns and to defend territory. Being the first mover can be especially wise when such actions (1) build a firm's image and reputation with buyers, (2) produce cost advantages over rivals in terms of new technologies, new components, new distribution channels, and so on, (3) create strongly loyal customers,

(4) make imitation or duplication by a rival hard or unlikely.[37] To sustain the competitive advantage gained by being the first mover, such a firm also needs to be a fast learner. There would, however, be risks associated with being the first mover, such as unexpected and unanticipated problems and costs that occur from being the first firm doing business in the new market. Therefore, being a slow mover (also called fast follower or late mover) can be effective when a firm can easily copy or imitate the lead firm's products or services. If technology is advancing rapidly, slow movers can often leapfrog a first mover's products with improved second-generation products. However, slow movers often are relegated to relying on the first mover being a slow mover and making strategic and tactical mistakes. This situation does not occur often, so first mover advantages clearly offset the first mover disadvantages most of the time.

Strategic-management research indicates that first mover advantages tend to be greatest when competitors are roughly the same size and possess similar resources. If competitors are not similar in size, then larger competitors can wait while others make initial investments and mistakes, and then respond with greater effectiveness and resources.

Outsourcing

Business-process outsourcing (BPO) is a rapidly growing new business that involves companies taking over the functional operations, such as human resources, information systems, payroll, accounting, customer service, and even marketing of other firms. Companies are choosing to outsource their functional operations more and more for several reasons: (1) it is less expensive, (2) it allows the firm to focus on its core businesses, and (3) it enables the firm to provide better services. Other advantages of outsourcing are that the strategy (1) allows the firm to align itself with "best-in-world" suppliers who focus on performing the special task, (2) provides the firm flexibility should customer needs shift unexpectedly, and (3) allows the firm to concentrate on other internal value chain activities critical to sustaining competitive advantage. BPO is a means for achieving strategies that are similar to partnering and joint venturing. According to the *Wall Street Journal,* the worldwide BPO market rose 10.5 percent in 2003 to $122 billion and is expected to exceed $173 billion by 2007.[38]

Two of many firms selling BPO services today are IBM and Affiliated Computer Services (ACS). IBM has a $400 million, 10-year contract to handle Procter & Gamble's human resources tasks. ACS generated nearly 70 percent of its $3.8 billion in 2003 revenues from BPO services, up 63 percent from 2002. ACS handles all of Motorola's human resources but also does extensive BPO work for government agencies and even academic institutions.

Many firms, such as Dearborn, Michigan-based Visteon Corp. and J. P. Morgan Chase & Co., outsource their computer operations to IBM, which competes with firms such as Electronic Data Systems and Computer Sciences Corp., in the computer outsourcing business. 3M Corp., in 2004, is outsourcing all of its manufacturing operations to Flextronics International Ltd. of Singapore or Jabil Circuit in Florida. 3M is also outsourcing all design and manufacturing of low-end standardized volume products by building a new design center in Taiwan.

U. S. and European companies for more than a decade have been outsourcing their manufacturing, tech support, and back-office work, but most insisted on keeping research and development activities in-house. However, an ever-growing number of firms today are outsourcing their product design to Asian developers. China and India are becoming increasingly important suppliers of intellectual property. For companies that include Hewlett-Packard, PalmOne, Dell, Sony, Apple, Kodak, Motorola, Nokia, Ericsson, Lucent, Cisco, and Nortel, the design of PDA's today are 70 percent outsourced, notebook

PC designs are 65 percent outsourced, digital camera designs are 30 percent outsourced, and mobile phones 20 percent.[39] Leading Asian design companies include HTC, Compal, Inventec, Quanta, Wistron, Asustek, Sanyo, Premier, Altek, Primax, Cellon, BenQ, Gemtek, Delta, CyerTAN, and Huawei. Asian firms have become major forces in nearly every tech device, from laptops and high-definition TVs to MP3 music players and digital cameras. Procter & Gamble has an objective for 50 percent of its new product ideas to be generated from outside by firm by 2010, compared with 20 percent in 2005. As indicated in the Global Perspective, India has become a booming place for outsourcing.

In the airline industry, outsourcing of maintenance and repair work nearly doubled from 2002 to 2004 for many carriers, including Jet Blue (39 percent to 63 percent, United 33 percent to 54 percent, ATA 22 percent to 43 percent, Air Tran 31 percent to 46 percent, and Frontier 20 percent to 33 percent.[40] Southwest outsources 64 percent of its maintenance and repair work, compared to 80 percent for Alaska Airlines, 72 percent for American West, and 60 percent for US Airways.

GLOBAL PERSPECTIVE

India's Lure Growing Dramatically

Ten years ago, India was so uncompetitive that the conveyor belts in the port of Mumbai (formerly called Bombay) went one way: to unload goods from ships. Today, those belts go both ways, with more goods leaving Mumbai than arriving. Those belts used to symbolize India's lack of roads, congested railways, bad runways at major airports, and high wage rates. Today, India is a booming place to do business. Indian companies are very efficient and shareholder return–focused as compared to Chinese firms that are very driven by market share. Intel plans to build a huge chip-making plant in New Delhi rather than in China or Vietnam. Currently most Intel employees in India work in Bangalore, Mumbai, and New Delhi.

Reliance Energy Ltd. has begun building an $11 billion power plant in India's eastern state of Orissa in a move to help meet the country's surging demand for power. Power is a problem in India with almost half of the Indian population having no access to electricity. Also in Orissa, Posco is building a $12 billion steel plant that is the largest foreign investment in India ever. In India's state of Maharashtra, power is rationed to just nine hours per day in some areas. Although India has the world's fourth-largest coal reserves, mining of that resource is the exclusive domain of the inefficient, fiercely protected, state monopoly: Coal India Ltd. India's coal unions, concerned about job losses, threaten nationwide strikes if coal production is boosted.

In the spirits business, Indians drink a lot of whiskey but not beer. India is one of the last major markets where consumption of whiskey far outweighs that of beer. Even Russians have started drinking more beer than vodka in recent years. The beer-market size in 2004 in billion of gallons was 6.3 in the United States, 7.3 in China, and only 0.2 in India, although the populations of those three countries in 2005 in billions was 0.3, 1.3, and 1.1 respectively. In India, only 50,000 bars and liquor stores can be found in the whole country. A government-imposed ban applies to all liquor advertising. Taxes on beer in India are exceptionally high compared to taxes on whiskey, and this also encourages consumption of the latter. However, beer breweries, such as SAB Miller India and Scottish & Newcastle PLC, are eyeing the huge untapped market in India and are expanding aggressively there.

India is a democratic, young, educated country with a booming economy. More than half of India's population is under the age of 25, and analysts expect demand for goods and services, such as banking, telecommunications, and cars, will grow dramatically in the next 10 years.

Source: Adapted from Henny Sender, "India Comes of Age, as Stronger Returns Lure Foreign Capital," *Wall Street Journal* (June 6, 2005): A2. Also, John Larkin and Eric Bellman, "Reliance Project Could Help Fill India Energy Void," *Wall Street Journal* (June 9, 2005): A12; Cris Prystay, "India's Brewers Cleverly Dodge Alcohol-Ad Ban," *Wall Street Journal* (June 16, 2005): B1; and John Larkin, "India's Energy Woes Go Deep," *Wall Street Journal* (July 11, 2005): A11.

Strategic Management in Nonprofit and Governmental Organizations

The strategic-management process is being used effectively by countless nonprofit and governmental organizations, such as the Girl Scouts, Boy Scouts, the Red Cross, chambers of commerce, educational institutions, medical institutions, public utilities, libraries, government agencies, and churches. The nonprofit sector, surprisingly, is by far America's largest employer. Many nonprofit and governmental organizations outperform private firms and corporations on innovativeness, motivation, productivity, and strategic management. For many nonprofit examples of strategic planning in practice, click on Strategic Planning Links found at the www.strategyclub.com Web site.

Compared to for-profit firms, nonprofit and governmental organizations may be totally dependent on outside financing. Especially for these organizations, strategic management provides an excellent vehicle for developing and justifying requests for needed financial support.

Educational Institutions

Educational institutions are more frequently using strategic-management techniques and concepts. Richard Cyert, president of Carnegie Mellon University, says, "I believe we do a far better job of strategic management than any company I know." Population shifts nationally from the Northeast and Midwest to the Southeast and West are but one factor causing trauma for educational institutions that have not planned for changing enrollments. Ivy League schools in the Northeast are recruiting more heavily in the Southeast and West. This trend represents a significant change in the competitive climate for attracting the best high school graduates each year.

The first all-Internet law school, Concord University School of Law, boasts nearly 200 students who can access lectures anytime and chat at fixed times with professors. Online college degrees are becoming common and represent a threat to traditional colleges and universities. "You can put the kids to bed and go to law school," says Andrew Rosen, chief operating officer of Kaplan Education Centers, a subsidiary of the Washington Post Company, which owns Concord. Concord is not accredited by the American Bar Association, which prohibits study by correspondence and requires more than a thousand hours of classroom time.

For a list of college strategic plans, click on Strategic Planning Links found at the www.strategyclub.com Web site, and scroll down through the academic sites.

Medical Organizations

The $200 billion U.S. hospital industry is experiencing declining margins, excess capacity, bureaucratic overburdening, poorly planned and executed diversification strategies, soaring healthcare costs, reduced federal support, and high administrator turnover. The seriousness of this problem is accented by a 20 percent annual decline in use by inpatients nationwide. Declining occupancy rates, deregulation, and accelerating growth of health maintenance organizations, preferred provider organizations, urgent care centers, outpatient surgery centers, diagnostic centers, specialized clinics, and group practices are other major threats facing hospitals today. Many private and state-supported medical institutions are in financial trouble as a result of traditionally taking a reactive rather than a proactive approach in dealing with their industry.

Hospitals—originally intended to be warehouses for people dying of tuberculosis, smallpox, cancer, pneumonia, and infectious diseases—are creating new strategies today as advances in the diagnosis and treatment of chronic diseases are undercutting that earlier mission. Hospitals are beginning to bring services to the patient as much as bringing the patient to the hospital; healthcare is more and more being concentrated in the home and in the residential community, not on the hospital campus. Chronic care will require day-treatment facilities, electronic monitoring at home, user-friendly ambulatory services, decentralized service networks, and laboratory testing. A successful hospital strategy for the future will require renewed and deepened collaboration with physicians, who are central to hospitals' well-being, and a reallocation of resources from acute to chronic care in home and community settings.

Current strategies being pursued by many hospitals include creating home health services, establishing nursing homes, and forming rehabilitation centers. Backward integration strategies that some hospitals are pursuing include acquiring ambulance services, waste disposal services, and diagnostic services. Millions of persons annually research medical ailments online, which is causing a dramatic shift in the balance of power between doctor, patient, and hospitals.[41] The number of persons using the Internet to obtain medical information is skyrocketing. A motivated patient using the Internet can gain knowledge on a particular subject far beyond his or her doctor's knowledge, because no person can keep up with the results and implications of billions of dollars' worth of medical research reported weekly. Patients today often walk into the doctor's office with a file folder of the latest articles detailing research and treatment options for their ailments. On Web sites such as America's Doctor (www.americasdoctor.com), consumers can consult with a physician in an online chat room 24 hours a day. Excellent consumer health Web sites are proliferating, boosted by investments from such firms as Microsoft, AOL, Reader's Digest, and CBS. Drug companies, such as Glaxo Wellcome, are getting involved, as are hospitals. The whole strategic landscape of healthcare is changing because of the Internet. Intel recently began offering a new secure medical service whereby doctors and patients can conduct sensitive business on the Internet, such as sharing results of medical tests and prescribing medicine. The 10 most successful hospital strategies today are providing free-standing outpatient surgery centers, outpatient surgery and diagnostic centers, physical rehabilitation centers, home health services, cardiac rehabilitation centers, preferred provider services, industrial medicine services, women's medicine services, skilled nursing units, and psychiatric services.[42]

Governmental Agencies and Departments

Federal, state, county, and municipal agencies and departments, such as police departments, chambers of commerce, forestry associations, and health departments, are responsible for formulating, implementing, and evaluating strategies that use taxpayers' dollars in the most cost-effective way to provide services and programs. Strategic-management concepts are generally required and thus widely used to enable governmental organizations to be more effective and efficient. For a list of government agency strategic plans, click on Strategic Planning Links found at the www.strategyclub.com Web site, and scroll down through the government sites.

Strategists in governmental organizations operate with less strategic autonomy than their counterparts in private firms. Public enterprises generally cannot diversify into unrelated businesses or merge with other firms. Governmental strategists usually enjoy little freedom in altering the organizations' missions or redirecting objectives. Legislators and politicians often have direct or indirect control over major decisions and resources. Strategic issues get discussed and debated in the media and legislatures. Issues become politicized, resulting in fewer strategic choice alternatives. There is now more predictability in the management of public sector enterprises.

Government agencies and departments are finding that their employees get excited about the opportunity to participate in the strategic-management process and thereby have an effect on the organization's mission, objectives, strategies, and policies. In addition, government agencies are using a strategic-management approach to develop and substantiate formal requests for additional funding.

Strategic Management in Small Firms

Strategic management is vital for large firms' success, but what about small firms? The strategic-management process is just as vital for small companies. From their inception, all organizations have a strategy, even if the strategy just evolves from day-to-day operations. Even if conducted informally or by a single owner/entrepreneur, the strategic-management process can significantly enhance small firms' growth and prosperity. Recent data clearly show that an ever-increasing number of men and women in the United States are starting their own businesses. This means that more individuals are becoming strategists. Widespread corporate layoffs have contributed to an explosion in small businesses and new ideas.

Numerous magazine and journal articles have focused on applying strategic-management concepts to small businesses.[43] A major conclusion of these articles is that a lack of strategic-management knowledge is a serious obstacle for many small business owners. Other problems often encountered in applying strategic-management concepts to small businesses are a lack of both sufficient capital to exploit external opportunities and a day-to-day cognitive frame of reference. Research also indicates that strategic management in small firms is more informal than in large firms, but small firms that engage in strategic management outperform those that do not.[44]

VISIT THE NET

Site provides 60 sample business plans for small businesses.
(www.bplans.com/sp/index.cfm?a=bc)

CONCLUSION

The main appeal of any managerial approach is the expectation that it will enhance organizational performance. This is especially true of strategic management. Through involvement in strategic-management activities, managers and employees achieve a better understanding of an organization's priorities and operations. Strategic management allows organizations to be efficient, but more important, it allows them to be effective. Although strategic management does not guarantee organizational success, the process allows proactive rather than reactive decision making. Strategic management may represent a radical change in philosophy for some organizations, so strategists must be trained to anticipate and constructively respond to questions and issues as they arise. The 16 strategies discussed in this chapter can represent a new beginning for many firms, especially if managers and employees in the organization understand and support the plan for action.

We invite you to visit the David page on the Prentice Hall Companion Web site at www.prenhall.com/david for this chapter's review quiz.

KEY TERMS AND CONCEPTS

Acquisition (p. 197)

Backward Integration (p. 175)

Bankruptcy (p. 185)

Business-Processing Outsourcing (BPO) (p. 201)

Combination Strategy (p. 171)

Cooperative Arrangements (p. 193)

Cost Leadership (p. 188)

De-integration (p. 176)

Differentiation (p. 188)

Diversification Strategies (p. 180)

Divestiture (p. 186)

First Mover Advantages (p. 200)

Focus (p. 188)

Forward Integration (p. 174)

Franchising (p. 174)

Friendly Merger (p. 197)

Generic Strategies (p. 188)

Horizontal Integration (p. 176)

Hostile Takeover (p. 197)

Integration Strategies (p. 174)

Intensive Strategies (p. 177)

Joint Venture (p. 193)

Leveraged Buyout (p. 200)

Liquidation (p. 186)

Long-Term Objectives (p. 168)

Market Development (p. 178)

Market Penetration (p. 177)

Merger (p. 197)

Product Development (p. 179)

Related Diversification (p. 180)

Retrenchment (p. 184)

Takeover (p. 197)

Turbulent, High-Velocity Markets (p. 193)

Unrelated Diversification (p. 180)

Vertical Integration (p. 174)

ISSUES FOR REVIEW AND DISCUSSION

1. How does strategy formulation differ for a small versus a large organization? How does it differ for a for-profit versus a nonprofit organization?
2. Give recent examples of market penetration, market development, and product development.
3. Give recent examples of forward integration, backward integration, and horizontal integration.
4. Give recent examples of concentric diversification, horizontal diversification, and conglomerate diversification.
5. Give recent examples of joint venture, retrenchment, divestiture, and liquidation.
6. Do you think hostile takeovers are unethical? Why or why not?
7. What are the major advantages and disadvantages of diversification?
8. What are the major advantages and disadvantages of an integrative strategy?
9. How does strategic management differ in for-profit and nonprofit organizations?
10. Why is it not advisable to pursue too many strategies at once?
11. Consumers can purchase tennis shoes, food, cars, boats, and insurance on the Internet. Are there any products today than cannot be purchased online? What is the implication for traditional retailers?

12. What are the pros and cons of a firm merging with a rival firm?
13. Does the United States globally lead in small business start-ups?
14. Visit the CheckMATE strategic-planning software Web site at www.checkmateplan.com, and discuss the benefits offered.
15. Compare and contrast financial objectives with strategic objectives. Which type is more important in your opinion? Why?
16. Diagram a two-division organizational chart that includes a CEO, COO, CIO, CSO, CFO, CMO, HRM, R&D, and two division presidents. *Hint:* Division presidents report to the COO.
17. How do the levels of strategy differ in a large firm versus a small firm?
18. List 10 types of strategies. Give a hypothetical example of each strategy listed.
19. Discuss the nature of as well as the pros and cons of a "friendly merger" versus "hostile takeover" in acquiring another firm. Give an example of each.
20. Define and explain "first mover advantages."
21. Define and explain "outsourcing."
22. Discuss the business of offering a BBA or MBA degree online.
23. What strategies are best for turbulent, high-velocity markets?

NOTES

1. John Byrne, "Strategic Planning—It's Back," *BusinessWeek* (August 26, 1996): 46.
2. Steven C. Brandt, *Strategic Planning in Emerging Companies* (Reading, MA: Addison-Wesley, 1981). Reprinted with permission of the publisher.
3. R. Kaplan and D. Norton, "Putting the Balanced Scorecard to Work," *Harvard Business Review* (September–October, 1993): 147.
4. F. Hansen and M. Smith, "Crisis in Corporate America: The Role of Strategy," *Business Horizons* (January–February 2003): 9.
5. Jeff Bailey, "Franchisees Group to Take Control," *Wall Street Journal* (December 24, 2002): B2.
6. Adapted from F. R. David, "How Do We Choose Among Alternative Growth Strategies?" *Managerial Planning* 33, no. 4 (January–February 1985): 14–17, 22.
7. Ibid.
8. Kenneth Davidson, "Do Megamergers Make Sense?" *Journal of Business Strategy* 7, no. 3 (Winter 1987): 45.
9. Op. cit., David.
10. Ibid.
11. Bruce Stanley, "United Parcel Service to Open a Hub in Shanghai," *Wall Street Journal* (July 8, 2005): B2.
12. Op. cit., David.
13. Ibid.
14. Arthur Thompson, Jr., A. J. Strickland III, and John Gamble. *Crafting and Executing Strategy: Text and Readings* (New York: McGraw-Hill/Irwin, 2005): 241.
15. Michael E. Porter, *Competitive Strategy: Techniques for Analyzing Industries and Competitors* (New York: Free Press, 1980): 53–57, 318–319.
16. "The Samsung Way," *BusinessWeek* (June 16, 2003): 56–60.
17. Sheila Muto, "Seeing a Boost, Hospitals Turn to Retail Stores," *Wall Street Journal* (November 7, 2001): B1, B8.
18. Op. cit., David.
19. Op. cit., David.
20. Op. cit., David.
21. Ibid.
22. Ibid.

23. Michael Porter, *Competitive Advantage* (New York: Free Press, 1985): 97. Also, Arthur Thompson, Jr., A. J. Strickland III, and John Gamble. *Crafting and Executing Strategy: Text and Readings* (New York: McGraw-Hill/Irwin, 2005): 117.
24. Arthur Thompson, Jr., A. J. Strickland III, and John Gamble. *Crafting and Executing Strategy: Text and Readings* (New York: McGraw-Hill/Irwin, 2005): 125–126.
25. Porter, *Competitive Advantage,* pp. 160–162.
26. Thompson, Strickland, and Gamble: 129–130.
27. Ibid: 134.
28. Kathryn Rudie Harrigan, "Joint Ventures: Linking for a Leap Forward," *Planning Review* 14, no. 4 (July–August 1986): 10.
29. Matthew Schifrin, "Partner or Perish," *Forbes* (May 21, 2001): 26.
30. Ibid., p. 28.
31. Nikhil Hutheesing, "Marital Blisters," *Forbes* (May 21, 2001): 32.
32. Ibid., p. 32.
33. Steven Rattner, "Mergers: Windfalls or Pitfalls?" *Wall Street Journal* (October 11, 1999): A22; Nikhil Deogun, "Merger Wave Spurs More Stock Wipeouts," *Wall Street Journal* (November 29, 1999): C1.
34. J. A. Schmidt, "Business Perspective on Mergers and Acquisitions," in J. A. Schmidt, ed., *Making Mergers Work,* Alexandria, VA: Society for Human Resource Management, (2002): 23–46.
35. Joel Millman, "Mexican Mergers/Acquisitions Triple from 2001," *Wall Street Journal* (December 27, 2002): A2.
36. Robert Davis, "Net Empowering Patients," *USA Today* (July 14, 1999): 1A.
37. M. J. Gannon, K. G. Smith, and C. Grimm, "An Organizational Information-Processing Profile of First Movers," *Journal of Business Research* 25 (1992): 231–241; M. B. Lieberman and D. B. Montgomery, "First Mover Advantages," *Strategic Management Journal* 9 (Summer 1988): 41–58.
38. Jeffrey Covin, Dennis Slevin, and Michael Heeley, "Pioneers and Followers: Competitive Tactics, Environment, and Growth," *Journal of Business Venturing* 15, no. 2 (March 1999): 175–210.

39. Peter Loftus, "Outsourcing Gets Expanded Uses by Businesses," *Wall Street Journal* (September 24, 2003): B13B.

40. Pete Engardio and Bruce Hinhorn, "Outsourcing," *BusinessWeek* (March 21, 2005): 88.

41. Andy Pasztor, "Airline Turmoil Raises Safety Issues," *Wall Street Journal* (June 9, 2005): D5.

42. *Hospital* (May 5, 1991): 16.

43. Some articles are Keith D. Brouthers, Floris Andriessen, and Igor Nicolaes, "Driving Blind: Strategic Decision-Making in Small Companies," *Long Range Planning* 31 (1998): 130–138; Javad Kargar, "Strategic Planning System Characteristics and Planning Effectiveness in Small Mature Firms," *Mid-Atlantic Journal of*

Business 32, no. 1 (1996): 19–35; Michael J. Peel and John Bridge, "How Planning and Capital Budgeting Improve SME Performance," *Long Range Planning* 31, no. 6 (1998): 848–856; Larry R. Smeltzer, Gail L. Fann, and V. Neal Nikolaisen, "Environmental Scanning Practices in Small Business," *Journal of Small Business Management* 26, no. 3 (1988): 55–63; and Michael P. Steiner and Olaf Solem, "Factors for Success in Small Manufacturing Firms," *Journal of Small Business Management* 26, no. 1 (1988): 51–57.

44. Anne Carey and Grant Jerding, "Internet's Reach on Campus," *USA Today* (August 26, 1999): A1; Bill Meyers, "It's a Small-Business World," *USA Today* (July 30, 1999): B1–2.

CURRENT READINGS

Akgün, Ali E., Gary S. Lynn, and John C. Byrne. "Taking the Guesswork Out of New Product Development: How Successful High-Tech Companies Get That Way." *Journal of Business Strategy* 25, no. 4 (2004): 41.

Anslinger, Patricia, and Justin Jenk. "Creating Successful Alliances." *Journal of Business Strategy* 25, no. 2 (2004): 18.

Arino, A., and J. J. Reuer. "Designing and Renegotiating Strategic Alliance Contracts." *The Academy of Management Executive* 18, no. 3 (August 2004): 37.

Baxendale, S. J. "Outsourcing Opportunities for Small Business: A Quantiative Analysis." *Business Horizons* 47, no. 1 (January–February 2004): 51.

Carow, K., R. Heron, and T. Saxton. "Do Early Birds Get the Returns? An Empirical Investigation of Early-Mover Advantages in Acquisitions." *Strategic Management Journal* 25, no. 6 (June 2004): 563.

Chatterjee, Sayan. "Core Objectives: Clarity in Designing Strategy." *California Management Review* 47, no. 2 (Winter 2005): 33.

de Camara, Don, and Punit Renjen. "The Secrets of Successful Mergers: Dispatches from the Front Lines." *Journal of Business Strategy* 25, no. 3 (2004): 10.

Epstein, Marc J. "The Determinants and Evaluation of Merger Success." *Business Horizons* 48, no. 1 (January–February 2005): 37.

Franko, L. G. "The Death of Diversification? The Focusing of the World's Industrial Firms, 1980–2000." *Business Horizons* 47, no. 4 (July–August 2004): 41.

Gerwin, Donald. "Coordinating New Product Development in Strategic Alliances." *The Academy of Management Review* 29, no. 2 (April 2004): 241.

Goerzen, A., and P. W. Beamish. "The Effect of Alliance Network Diversity on Multinational Enterprise Performance." *Strategic Management Journal* 26, no. 4 (April 2005): 333.

Hoang, H., and F. T. Rothaermel, "The Effect of General and Partner-Specific Alliance Experience on Joint R&D Project Performance." *The Academy of Management Journal* 48, no. 2 (April 2005): 332.

Jagersma, Pieter Klaas. "Cross-Border Alliances: Advice from the Executive Suite." *Journal of Business Strategy* 26, no. 1 (2005): 41.

Karim, Samina, and Will Mitchell. "Innovating Through Acquisition and Internal Development: A Quarter-Century of Boundary Evolution at Johnson & Johnson." *Long Range Planning* 37, no. 6 (December 2004): 525.

Khanna, T., K. G. Palepu, and J. Sinha. "Strategies That Fit Emerging Markets." *Harvard Business Review* (June 2005): 63.

Kim, H., R. E. Hoskisson, and W. P. Wan. "Power Dependence, Diversification Strategy, and Performance in Keiretsu Member Firms." *Strategic Management Journal* 25, no. 7 (July 2004): 613.

Krishnan, R. A., S. Joshi, and H. Krishnan. "The Influence of Mergers on Firms' Product-Mix Strategies." *Strategic Management Journal* 25, no. 6 (June 2004): 587.

Kumar, M. V. S. "The Value from Acquiring and Divesting a Joint Venture: A Real Options Approach." *Strategic Management Journal* 26, no. 4 (April 2005): 321.

Lu, J. W., and P. W. Beamish. "International Diversification and Firm Performance: The SCurve Hypothesis." *The Academy of Management Journal* 47, no. 4 (August 2004): 598.

Makino, S., T. Isobe, and C. M. Chan. "Does Country Matter?" *Strategic Management Journal* 25, no. 10 (October 2004): 1027.

Miller, D. J. "Firms' Technological Resources and the Performance Effects of Diversification: A Longitudinal Study." *Strategic Management Journal* 25, no. 11 (November 2004): 1097.

Morrow Jr., J. L., Richard A. Johnson, and Lowell W. Busenitz. "The Effects of Cost and Asset Retrenchment on Firm Performance: The Overlooked Role of a Firm's Competitive Environment." *Journal of Management* 30, no. 2 (2004): 189.

Pearce II, J. A., and R. B. Robinson, Jr. "Hostile Takeover Defenses That Maximize Shareholder Wealth." *Business Horizons* 47, no. 5 (September–October 2004): 15.

Power, Mark, Carlo Bonifazi, and Kevin Desouza. "The Ten Outsourcing Traps to Avoid." *Journal of Business Strategy* 25, no. 2 (2004): 37.

Reuer, J. J., and T. W. Tong. "Real Options in International Joint Ventures." *Journal of Management* 31, no. 3 (June 2005): 403.

Sampson, R. C. "The Scope and Governance of International R&D Alliances." *Strategic Management Journal* 25, no. 8–9 (August–September 2004): 723.

Sheremata, Willow A. "Competing Through Innovation in Network Markets: Strategies for Challengers." *The Academy of Management Review* 29, no. 3 (July 2004): 359.

Shimizu, Katsuhiko, and Michael A. Hitt. "What Constrains or Facilitates Divestitures of Formerly Acquired Firms? The Effects of Organizational Inertia." *Journal of Management* 31, no. 1 (February 2005): 50.

Suarez, F., and G. Lanzolla. "Best Practice: The Half-Truth of First-Mover Advantage." *Harvard Business Review* (April 2005): 121.

Vestring, T., T. Rouse, and S. Rovit. "In Practice: Integrate Where It Matters." *MIT Sloan Management Review* 46, no. 1 (Fall 2004): 15.

Williamson, P. J. "Strategies for Asia's New Competitive Game." *Journal of Business Strategy* 26, no. 2 (2005): 37.

experiential exercises

Experiential Exercise 5A

What Strategies Should Google Pursue in 2006–2007?

PURPOSE

In performing business policy case analysis, you can find information about the respective company's actual and planned strategies. Comparing what is planned versus *what you recommend* is an important part of case analysis. Do not recommend what the firm actually plans, unless in-depth analysis of the situation reveals those strategies to be best among all feasible alternatives. This exercise gives you experience conducting library and Internet research to determine what Google should do in 2006.

INSTRUCTIONS

Step 1 Look up Google and Yahoo! on the Internet. Find some recent articles about firms in this industry. Scan Moody's, Dun & Bradstreet, and Standard & Poor's publications for information. Check the finance.yahoo.com Web site and the www.strategyclub.com Web site.

Step 2 Summarize your findings in a three-page report entitled "Strategies for Google in 2006."

Experiential Exercise 5B

Examining Strategy Articles

PURPOSE

Strategy articles can be found weekly in journals, magazines, and newspapers. By reading and studying strategy articles, you can gain a better understanding of the strategic-management process. Several of the best journals in which to find corporate strategy articles are *Advanced Management Journal, Business Horizons, Long Range Planning, Journal of Business Strategy,* and *Strategic Management Journal.* These journals are devoted to reporting the results of empirical research in management. They apply strategic-management concepts to specific organizations and industries. They introduce new strategic-management techniques and provide short case studies on selected firms.

Other good journals in which to find strategic-management articles are *Harvard Business Review, Sloan Management Review, California Management Review, Academy of Management Review, Academy of Management Journal, Academy of Management Executive, Journal of Management,* and *Journal of Small Business Management.*

In addition to journals, many magazines regularly publish articles that focus on business strategies. Several of the best magazines in which to find applied strategy articles are *Dun's Business Month, Fortune, Forbes, BusinessWeek, Inc.,* and *Industry Week.* Newspapers such as *USA Today, Wall Street Journal, New York Times,* and *Barrons* cover strategy events when they occur—for example, a joint venture announcement, a bankruptcy declaration, a new advertising campaign start, acquisition of a company, divestiture of a division, a chief executive officer's hiring or firing, or a hostile takeover attempt.

In combination, journal, magazine, and newspaper articles can make the strategic-management course more exciting. They allow current strategies of for-profit and non-profit organizations to be identified and studied.

INSTRUCTIONS

Step 1 Go to your college library and find a recent journal article that focuses on a strategic-management topic. Select your article from one of the journals listed previously, not from a magazine. Copy the article and bring it to class.

Step 2   Give a 3-minute oral report summarizing the most important information in your article. Include comments giving your personal reaction to the article. Pass your article around in class.

Experiential Exercise 5C

Classifying Some Year 2005 Strategies

PURPOSE

This exercise can improve your understanding of various strategies by giving you experience classifying strategies. This skill will help you use the strategy-formulation tools presented later. Consider the following 12 (actual or possible) year-2005 strategies by various firms:

1. The wholesale retailer, Big Lots, expands into Mexico.
2. The food manufacturer, Campbell Soup, begins massive tomato farming operations.
3. Delta Air Lines acquires an ocean cruise lines company.
4. The specialty retailer, Gap, enters the radio broadcasting business.
5. The online auction company, eBay, acquires an online auction firm in Russia.
6. The food giant, McDonald's, closes 100 restaurants and lays off 2,000 employees.
7. General Electric sells its NBC Broadcasting division.
8. Hilton Hotels acquires a large furniture manufacturer.
9. Ford Motor Company acquires its automobile dealers.
10. The appliance maker, Maytag, introduces a wireless refrigerator.
11. The drug firm, Eli Lilly, doubles its number of salespersons.
12. The sports firm, Nike, enters the boat manufacturing business.

INSTRUCTIONS

Step 1   On a separate sheet of paper, number from 1 to 12. These numbers correspond to the strategies described.

Step 2   What type of strategy best describes the 12 actions cited? Indicate your answers.

Step 3   Exchange papers with a classmate, and grade each other's paper as your instructor gives the right answers.

Experiential Exercise 5D

How Risky Are Various Alternative Strategies?

PURPOSE

This exercise focuses on how risky various alternative strategies are for organizations to pursue. Different degrees of risk are based largely on varying degrees of *externality*, defined as movement away from present business into new markets and products. In general, the greater the degree of externality, the greater the probability of loss resulting from unexpected events. High-risk strategies generally are less attractive than low-risk strategies.

INSTRUCTIONS

Step 1   On a separate sheet of paper, number vertically from 1 to 10. Think of 1 as "most risky," 2 as "next most risky," and so forth to 10, "least risky."

Step 2 Write the following strategies beside the appropriate number to indicate how risky you believe the strategy is to pursue: horizontal integration, related diversification, liquidation, forward integration, backward integration, product development, market development, market penetration, retrenchment, and unrelated diversification.

Step 3 Grade your paper as your teacher gives you the right answers and supporting rationale. Each correct answer is worth 10 points.

Experiential Exercise 5E

Developing Alternative Strategies for My University

PURPOSE

It is important for representatives from all areas of a college or university to identify and discuss alternative strategies that could benefit faculty, students, alumni, staff, and other constituencies. As you complete this exercise, notice the learning and understanding that occurs as people express differences of opinion. Recall that *the process of planning is more important than the document.*

INSTRUCTIONS

Step 1 Recall or locate the external opportunity/threat and internal strength/weakness factors that you identified as part of Experiential Exercise 1D. If you did not do that exercise, discuss now as a class important external and internal factors facing your college or university.

Step 2 Identify and put on the chalkboard alternative strategies that you feel could benefit your college or university. Your proposed actions should allow the institution to capitalize on particular strengths, improve upon certain weaknesses, avoid external threats, and/or take advantage of particular external opportunities. List 12 possible strategies on the board. Number the strategies as they are written on the board.

Step 3 On a separate sheet of paper, number from 1 to 12. Everyone in class individually should rate the strategies identified, using a 1 to 3 scale, where 1 = *I do not support implementation*, 2 = *I am neutral about implementation*, and 3 = *I strongly support implementation*. In rating the strategies, recognize that your institution cannot do everything desired or potentially beneficial.

Step 4 Go to the board and record your ratings in a row beside the respective strategies. Everyone in class should do this, going to the board perhaps by rows in the class.

Step 5 Sum the ratings for each strategy so that a prioritized list of recommended strategies is obtained. This prioritized list reflects the collective wisdom of your class. Strategies with the highest score are deemed best.

Step 6 Discuss how this process could enable organizations to achieve understanding and commitment from individuals.

Step 7 Share your class results with a university administrator, and ask for comments regarding the process and top strategies recommended.

Experiential Exercise 5F

Lessons in Globally Doing Business

PURPOSE

The purpose of this exercise is to discover some important lessons learned by local businesses that internationally do businesses .

INSTRUCTIONS

Contact several local business leaders by phone. Find at least three firms that engage in international or export operations. Visit the owner or manager of each business in person. Ask the businessperson to give you several important lessons that his or her firm has learned in globally doing business. Record the lessons on paper, and report your findings to the class.

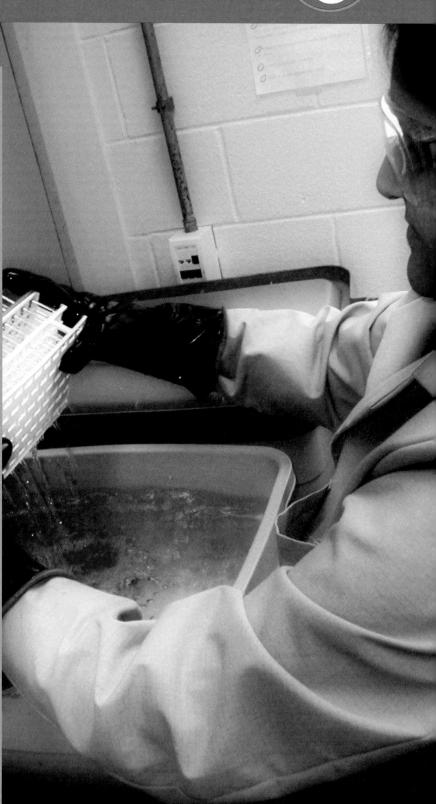

chapter objectives

After studying this chapter, you should be able to do the following:

1. Describe a three-stage framework for choosing among alternative strategies.

2. Explain how to develop a SWOT Matrix, SPACE Matrix, BCG Matrix, IE Matrix, and QSPM.

3. Identify important behavioral, political, ethical, and social responsibility considerations in strategy analysis and choice.

4. Discuss the role of intuition in strategic analysis and choice.

5. Discuss the role of organizational culture in strategic analysis and choice.

6. Discuss the role of a board of directors in choosing among alternative strategies.

"notable quotes"

Strategic management is not a box of tricks or a bundle of techniques. It is analytical thinking and commitment of resources to action. But quantification alone is not planning. Some of the most important issues in strategic management cannot be quantified at all.
Peter Drucker

Objectives are not commands; they are commitments. They do not determine the future; they are the means to mobilize resources and energies of an organization for the making of the future.
Peter Drucker

Life is full of lousy options.
General P. X. Kelley

When a crisis forces choosing among alternatives, most people will choose the worst possible one.
Rudin's Law

Strategy isn't something you can nail together in slapdash fashion by sitting around a conference table.
Terry Haller

Planning is often doomed before it ever starts, either because too much is expected of it or because not enough is put into it.
T. J. Cartwright

Whether it's broke or not, fix it—make it better. Not just products, but the whole company if necessary.
Bill Saporito

basis for decisions

Strategy analysis and choice largely involve making subjective decisions based on objective information. This chapter introduces important concepts that can help strategists generate feasible alternatives, evaluate those alternatives, and choose a specific course of action. Behavioral aspects of strategy formulation are described, including politics, culture, ethics, and social responsibility considerations. Modern tools for formulating strategies are described, and the appropriate role of a board of directors is discussed.

The Nature of Strategy Analysis and Choice

As indicated by Figure 6-1, this chapter focuses on generating and evaluating alternative strategies, as well as selecting strategies to pursue. Strategy analysis and choice seek to determine alternative courses of action that could best enable the firm to achieve its mission and objectives. The firm's present strategies, objectives, and mission, coupled with the external and internal audit information, provide a basis for generating and evaluating feasible alternative strategies.

Unless a desperate situation confronts the firm, alternative strategies will likely represent incremental steps that move the firm from its present position to a desired future position. Alternative strategies do not come out of the wild blue yonder; they are derived from the firm's vision, mission, objectives, external audit, and internal

alternative courses of action that could best enable the firm to achieve its obj. + mission

FIGURE 6-1

A Comprehensive Strategic-Management Model

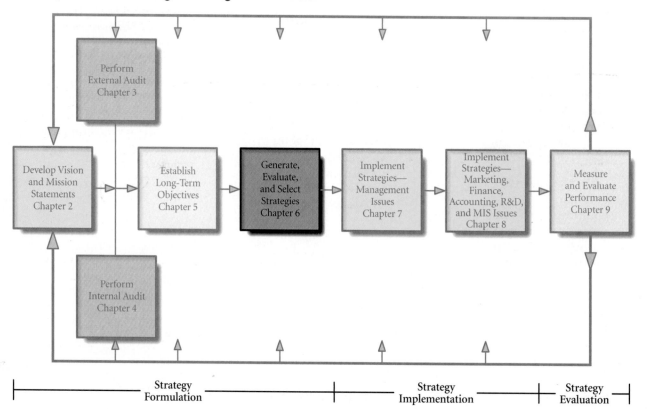

What Is a Pollution Register?

No business wants a reputation as being a big polluter; that could hurt it in the marketplace, jeopardize its standing in the community, and invite scrutiny by regulators, investors, and environmentalists. Accordingly, governments increasingly encourage businesses to behave responsibly. Various governments mandate that businesses publicly report the pollutants and wastes their facilities produce.

Perhaps the best-known pollution register is the Toxics Release Inventory (TRI) administered by the EPA in the United States. The TRI is a plant-by-plant accounting of industrial pollution that the government makes publicly accessible via the Internet and published reports. The TRI has been instrumental in cutting industrial pollutant releases of tracked chemicals by 48 percent from 1988 to 2000, pressuring some firms not only to comply with government regulations but also to reduce pollution beyond their legal obligation.

The United States, Canada, the Netherlands, Norway, and the United Kingdom all have at least a decade of experience operating comprehensive pollution registers like the TRI. In response to the success of these registers, other countries have instituted or are in the process of creating their own national pollution registers, which are generically termed "Pollutant Release and Transfer Registers" or "PRTRs." Today, about 60 countries have developed or are in the process of developing such registers. The attractiveness of a country to foreign direct investment, to some extent, hinges on that country's environmental policies and practices.

Pollution registers clearly provide information that interests and empowers citizens, investors, and reporters. Since the first release of TRI data in 1989, these pollution listings have become the subject of media reports. Journalists were particularly likely to report on a company with pollution concentrated at a few facilities or on chemical releases from companies that were not traditionally considered big polluters. The TRI data have affected the decisions of stock market investors as well. On the day in 1989 that TRI data first became available, the companies included in the inventory suffered statistically significant declines in the market value of their stock. For companies whose emissions were the subject of a media story, the loss in stock value

was greater—an average of $6.2 million, according to one analysis. In other words, investors were surprised by the quantity of pollution their companies produced, and they were worried about negative publicity and potential cleanup costs.

The TRI can provide useful data for communities to pressure companies to reduce emissions from local factories. Citizens in any community in the United States can use the Internet to print a tailored emission report from the TRI database for their county and can even send a message or question about their findings to the government. Similarly, in Canada, the Canadian National Pollutant Release Inventory (NPRI) provides communities and consumers with information that they have used to pressure Canadian companies to reduce their emissions. Within two days of its rollout, some 3 million Internet users visited the Pollution Watch Web site created by Canadian NGOs to give easy access to NPRI data and sent roughly 1,200 faxes to polluting companies listed there.

Countries operating a pollution register in 2004 were Australia, Ireland, Korea, Norway, United Kingdom, Canada, Japan, Netherlands, the Slovak Republic, the United States, and Mexico. Countries that did not have a pollution register in 2004, but as members of the EU are required to participate in the European Polluting Emissions Register, are Austria, Estonia, Hungary, Luxembourg, Slovenia, Belgium, Finland, Italy, Malta, Spain, Cyprus, France, Latvia, Poland, Sweden, the Czech Republic, Germany, Lithuania, Portugal, Switzerland, Denmark, and Greece. Countries without a pollution register that have indicated some interest in designing one or that participate in the Aarhus Protocol on Pollutant Release and Transfer Registers are Albania, Brazil, Ecuador, Kazakhstan, South Africa, Argentina, Bulgaria, Egypt, Romania, Ukraine, Armenia, Chile, Georgia, Russia, Uzbekistan, Azerbaijan, Costa Rica, Macedonia, Serbia, Montenegro, Taiwan, Belarus, Croatia, Moldova, Tajikistan, Turkey, Bosnia, Herzegovina, Cuba, and Monaco. All other countries, including **China**, indicate no interest in pollution registers.

Sources: Adapted from World Resources Institute 2002–2004, *Decisions for the Earth: Balance, Voice, and Power;* United Nations Development Programme, United Nations Environment Programme, World Bank; USEPA 2002:12.

[handwritten margin notes: Alt. strategies build on past successful strategies. / environmental mngmt or sustainibility]

audit; they are consistent with, or build on, past strategies that have worked well. Note from the "Natural Environment Perspective" box that the strategies of both companies and countries are increasingly scrutinized and evaluated from a natural environment perspective, as indicated by the presence of pollution registers. Even the *Wall Street Journal* is advocating and reporting that a growing number of business schools offer separate courses and even a concentration in environmental management or *sustainability*, the idea that a business can meet its financial goals without hurting the environment.[1] Note that China is among the countries that shun the idea of companies having to publicly report the pollutants and wastes their facilities produce.

The Process of Generating and Selecting Strategies

VISIT THE NET

Cautions that planners must not usurp the responsibility of line managers in strategic planning.

(www.csuchico.edu/mgmt /strategy/module1/ sld050.htm)

Strategists never consider all feasible alternatives that could benefit the firm because there are an infinite number of possible actions and an infinite number of ways to implement those actions. Therefore, a manageable set of the most attractive alternative strategies must be developed. The advantages, disadvantages, trade-offs, costs, and benefits of these strategies should be determined. This section discusses the process that many firms use to determine an appropriate set of alternative strategies.

Identifying and evaluating alternative strategies should involve many of the managers and employees who earlier assembled the organizational vision and mission statements, performed the external audit, and conducted the internal audit. Representatives from each department and division of the firm should be included in this process, as was the case in previous strategy-formulation activities. Recall that involvement provides the best opportunity for managers and employees to gain an understanding of what the firm is doing and why and to become committed to helping the firm accomplish its objectives.

All participants in the strategy analysis and choice activity should have the firm's external and internal audit information by their sides. This information, coupled with the firm's mission statement, will help participants crystallize in their own minds particular strategies that they believe could benefit the firm most. Creativity should be encouraged in this thought process.

*[handwritten margin note: Process *]*

Alternative strategies proposed by participants should be considered and discussed in a meeting or series of meetings. Proposed strategies should be listed in writing. When all feasible strategies identified by participants are given and understood, the strategies should be ranked in order of attractiveness by all participants, with 1 = should not be implemented, 2 = possibly should be implemented, 3 = probably should be implemented, and 4 = definitely should be implemented. This process will result in a prioritized list of best strategies that reflects the collective wisdom of the group.

A Comprehensive Strategy-Formulation Framework

Important strategy-formulation techniques can be integrated into a three-stage decision-making framework, as shown in Figure 6-2. The tools presented in this framework are applicable to all sizes and types of organizations and can help strategists identify, evaluate, and select strategies.

FIGURE 6-2

The Strategy-Formulation Analytical Framework

STAGE 1: THE INPUT STAGE

External Factor Evaluation (EFE) Matrix	Competitive Profile Matrix (CPM)	Internal Factor Evaluation (IFE) Matrix

STAGE 2: THE MATCHING STAGE

Strengths-Weaknesses-Opportunities-Threats (SWOT) Matrix	Strategic Position and Action Evaluation (SPACE) Matrix	Boston Consulting Group (BCG) Matrix	Internal-External (IE) Matrix	Grand Strategy Matrix

STAGE 3: THE DECISION STAGE

Quantitative Strategic Planning Matrix (QSPM)

Stage 1 of the formulation framework consists of the EFE Matrix, the IFE Matrix, and the Competitive Profile Matrix (CPM). Called the *Input Stage*, Stage 1 summarizes the basic input information needed to formulate strategies. Stage 2, called the *Matching Stage*, focuses upon generating feasible alternative strategies by aligning key external and internal factors. Stage 2 techniques include the Strengths-Weaknesses-Opportunities-Threats (SWOT) Matrix, the Strategic Position and Action Evaluation (SPACE) Matrix, the Boston Consulting Group (BCG) Matrix, the Internal-External (IE) Matrix, and the Grand Strategy Matrix. Stage 3, called the *Decision Stage*, involves a single technique, the Quantitative Strategic Planning Matrix (QSPM). A QSPM uses input information from Stage 1 to objectively evaluate feasible alternative strategies identified in Stage 2. A QSPM reveals the relative attractiveness of alternative strategies and thus provides objective basis for selecting specific strategies.

All nine techniques included in the *strategy-formulation framework* require the integration of intuition and analysis. Autonomous divisions in an organization commonly use strategy-formulation techniques to develop strategies and objectives. Divisional analyses provide a basis for identifying, evaluating, and selecting among alternative corporate-level strategies.

Strategists themselves, not analytic tools, are always responsible and accountable for strategic decisions. Lenz emphasized that the shift from a words-oriented to a numbers-oriented planning process can give rise to a false sense of certainty; it can reduce dialogue, discussion, and argument as a means for exploring understandings, testing assumptions, and fostering organizational learning.[2] Strategists, therefore, must be wary of this possibility and use analytical tools to facilitate, rather than to diminish, communication. Without objective information and analysis, personal biases, politics, emotions, personalities, and *halo error* (the tendency to put too much weight on a single factor) unfortunately may play a dominant role in the strategy-formulation process.

The Input Stage

Procedures for developing an EFE Matrix, an IFE Matrix, and a CPM were presented in Chapters 3 and 4. The information derived from these three matrices provides basic input information for the matching and decision stage matrices described later in this chapter.

VISIT THE NET

Gives purpose and characteristics of objectives.
(www.csuchico.edu/ mgmt/strategy/ module1/sld022.htm)

The input tools require strategists to quantify subjectivity during early stages of the strategy-formulation process. Making small decisions in the input matrices regarding the relative importance of external and internal factors allows strategists to more effectively generate and evaluate alternative strategies. Good intuitive judgment is always needed in determining appropriate weights and ratings.

The Matching Stage

VISIT THE NET

Gives example objectives.
(www.csuchico.edu/mgmt/
strategy/module1/
sld024.htm)

Strategy is sometimes defined as the match an organization makes between its internal resources and skills and the opportunities and risks created by its external factors.[3] The matching stage of the strategy-formulation framework consists of five techniques that can be used in any sequence: the SWOT Matrix, the SPACE Matrix, the BCG Matrix, the IE Matrix, and the Grand Strategy Matrix. These tools rely upon information derived from the input stage to match external opportunities and threats with internal strengths and weaknesses. *Matching* external and internal critical success factors is the key to effectively generating feasible alternative strategies. For example, a firm with excess working capital (an internal strength) could take advantage of the cell phone industry's 20 percent annual growth rate (an external opportunity) by acquiring Cellfone, Inc., a firm in the cell phone industry. This example portrays simple one-to-one matching. In most situations, external and internal relationships are more complex, and the matching requires multiple alignments for each strategy generated. The basic concept of matching is illustrated in Table 6-1.

Any organization, whether military, product-oriented, service-oriented, governmental, or even athletic, must develop and execute good strategies to win. A good offense without a good defense, or vice versa, usually leads to defeat. Developing strategies that use strengths to capitalize on opportunities could be considered an offense, whereas strategies designed to improve upon weaknesses while avoiding threats could be termed defensive. Every organization has some external opportunities and threats and internal strengths and weaknesses that can be aligned to formulate feasible alternative strategies.

TABLE 6-1 Matching Key External and Internal Factors to Formulate Alternative Strategies

KEY INTERNAL FACTOR		KEY EXTERNAL FACTOR		RESULTANT STRATEGY
Excess working capacity (an internal strength)	+	20 percent annual growth in the cell phone industry (an external opportunity)	=	Acquire Cellfone, Inc.
Insufficient capacity (an internal weakness)	+	Exit of two major foreign competitors from the industry (an external opportunity)	=	Pursue horizontal integration by buying competitors' facilities
Strong R&D expertise (an internal strength)	+	Decreasing numbers of younger adults (an external threat)	=	Develop new products for older adults
Poor employee morale (an internal weakness)	+	Strong union activity (an external threat)	=	Develop a new employee benefits package

The Strengths-Weaknesses-Opportunities-Threats (SWOT) Matrix

The *Strengths-Weaknesses-Opportunities-Threats (SWOT) Matrix* is an important matching tool that helps managers develop four types of strategies: SO (strengths-opportunities) Strategies, WO (weaknesses-opportunities) Strategies, ST (strengths-threats) Strategies, and WT (weaknesses-threats) Strategies.[4] Matching key external and internal factors is the most difficult part of developing a SWOT Matrix and requires good judgment—and there is no one best set of matches. Note in Table 6-1 that the first, second, third, and fourth strategies are SO, WO, ST, and WT strategies, respectively.

SO Strategies use a firm's internal strengths to take advantage of external opportunities. All managers would like their organizations to be in a position in which internal strengths can be used to take advantage of external trends and events. Organizations generally will pursue WO, ST, or WT strategies to get into a situation in which they can apply SO Strategies. When a firm has major weaknesses, it will strive to overcome them and make them strengths. When an organization faces major threats, it will seek to avoid them to concentrate on opportunities.

WO Strategies aim at improving internal weaknesses by taking advantage of external opportunities. Sometimes key external opportunities exist, but a firm has internal weaknesses that prevent it from exploiting those opportunities. For example, there may be a high demand for electronic devices to control the amount and timing of fuel injection in automobile engines (opportunity), but a certain auto parts manufacturer may lack the technology required for producing these devices (weakness). One possible WO Strategy would be to acquire this technology by forming a joint venture with a firm having competency in this area. An alternative WO Strategy would be to hire and train people with the required technical capabilities.

ST Strategies use a firm's strengths to avoid or reduce the impact of external threats. This does not mean that a strong organization should always meet threats in the external environment head-on. An example of ST Strategy occurred when Texas Instruments used an excellent legal department (a strength) to collect nearly $700 million in damages and royalties from nine Japanese and Korean firms that infringed on patents for semiconductor memory chips (threat). Rival firms that copy ideas, innovations, and patented products are a major threat in many industries. This is still a major problem for U.S. firms selling products in China.

WT Strategies are defensive tactics directed at reducing internal weakness and avoiding external threats. An organization faced with numerous external threats and internal weaknesses may indeed be in a precarious position. In fact, such a firm may have to fight for its survival, merge, retrench, declare bankruptcy, or choose liquidation.

A schematic representation of the SWOT Matrix is provided in Figure 6-3. Note that a SWOT Matrix is composed of nine cells. As shown, there are four key factor cells, four strategy cells, and one cell that is always left blank (the upper-left cell). The four strategy cells, labeled *SO, WO, ST,* and *WT,* are developed after completing four key factor cells, labeled *S, W, O,* and *T.* There are eight steps involved in constructing a SWOT Matrix:

1. List the firm's key external opportunities.
2. List the firm's key external threats.
3. List the firm's key internal strengths.
4. List the firm's key internal weaknesses.
5. Match internal strengths with external opportunities, and record the resultant SO Strategies in the appropriate cell.

FIGURE 6-3

The SWOT Matrix For A Cruise Line Company

	STRENGTHS—S	WEAKNESSES—W
	1. Holds 34% market share 2. Largest fleet of ships 3. Six different cruise lines 4. Innovator in cruise travel industry 5. Largest variety of ships 6. Building largest cruise ship 7. High brand recognition 8. Headquartered in Tampa 9. Internet friendly with online booking = 30% of total	1. Major loss in affiliated operations 2. Increased debt from building new ships 3. Not serving Asian market 4. ROI ratio is 4%
OPPORTUNITIES—O	SO STRATEGIES	WO STRATEGIES
1. Air travel has decreased (9/11) 2. Asian market not being served 3. Possible acquisition of Princess Cruise Lines 4. New weather forecasting systems available 5. Rising demand for all-inclusive vacation packages 6. Families have increased disposable incomes 7. Marriage rates are up—more honeymoons	1. Increase capacity of ships to obtain travelers from air industry (S6, O1, O3) 2. Display the weather of vacation locations on Web site (S9, O4) 3. Offer Trans-Atlantic cruises (S6, O4) 4. Acquire P & O Princess (S1, O3)	1. Begin serving Japan and Pacific Islands (W3, O2, O3, O4) 2. Use weather forecasting to alert customers of potential storm during their vacation (W1, O4)
THREATS—T	ST STRATEGIES	WT STRATEGIES
1. Decrease in travel since 9/11 2. Terrorism 3. Competition within industry 4. Competition among other types of vacations 5. Economic recession 6. Chance of natural disasters 7. Increasing fuel prices 8. Changing government regulations	1. Advertise ship variety, brand recognition, and safety policies (S3, S7, T1, T2, T5) 2. Advertise alternate vacations that are not affected by hurricane season (S3, T5, T7) 3. Offer discounts on Web site (S9, T6)	1. Lower prices of cruises during hurricane season (W1, T6) 2. Research viability of entering other foreign markets (W2, W3, T8, S9)

6. Match internal weaknesses with external opportunities, and record the resultant WO Strategies.

7. Match internal strengths with external threats, and record the resultant ST Strategies.

8. Match internal weaknesses with external threats, and record the resultant WT Strategies.

FIGURE 6-4
SWOT Matrix for the Riverbanks Zoo (2005)

	STRENGTHS—S	WEAKNESSES—W
	1. The Riverbanks Zoo and Garden are ranked among the top zoos in North America.	1. Weak advertising effort.
	2. Winner of the 2002 Governor's cup for most outstanding tourist attraction in South Carolina.	2. Few foul-weather retreats at the zoo.
	3. Riverbank Zoo and Garden is the premium choice for education and recreation, including school programs, educational classes, and overnight and day camps.	3. Not actively soliciting businesses.
	4. Riverbanks Zoo is home to some of the Earth's most popular and spectacular creatures, like African lions and tigers.	
	5. Education and conservation efforts increase the number of visitors.	
	6. The zoo has been treating endangered species for over 25 years.	
	7. Riverbanks Zoo is home to more than 2,000 magnificent, fascinating, and exotic animals.	
	8. Guests are able to feed lots of the animals, including the giraffes.	
	9. Riverbanks Zoo and Garden supports conservation and science by being an active member of American Zoo and Aquarium (AZA).	
	10. Excellent financial condition.	
OPPORTUNITIES—O	**SO STRATEGIES**	**WO STRATEGIES**
1. Increase in revenue annually.	1. A program that offers credit to high school seniors by helping care for and feed the animals. (S3, S5, S7, S8, S9, O2, O4, O5)	1. Interactive Web site that allows customers to vote on a feature animal or plant of the month. (W1, O3, O6)
2. Governmental support increased to 26.8% for the year 2001.	2. A program that offers credit to college students who help care for and feed the animals. (S3, S5, S7, O3)	2. Seek more business/corporate sponsorships of animals. (W1, W3, O3, O4)
3. Columbia, S.C., is a growing area.		
4. Active memberships increased from 27,000 in 2001 to about 32,000 in 2002.		
5. Attendance increased from around 800,000 in 2001 to over 1,000,000 visitors in 2002, including 25% who came from outside the state.		
6. The Internet enables visitors to access information about the zoo and garden before attending.		
7. Families spending more time on entertainment.		

FIGURE 6-4
Continued

THREATS—T	ST STRATEGIES	WT STRATEGIES
1. Weak economy.	1. Conduct a monthly scavenger hunt for youth and adults with prizes given. (S3, S5, S10, T2)	1. Add a prehistoric/extinct animal museum in the zoo area. (W1, T3)
2. Local attractions remain a big part of the zoo's competition.	2. Develop partnerships with local Columbia events such as USC ballgames and coliseum concerts. (S1, T2)	2. Add a covered walkway trail in and about the zoo. (W2, T5)
3. Animal extinctions; less than 1.5 million elephants survive in all of Africa. There are only about 400 African elephants in zoos in North America.		
4. The black rhino is highly endangered. There are only about 2,500 rhinos left in the wild.		
5. Admission revenues are affected by weather conditions because most of the attractions are outdoors.		
6. Animal movement can be costly and risky (from overseas to the zoos). It cost $49,000 to import, e.g., Warthogs from Africa or Asia to United States for each pair.		
7. Animal diet can be costly. For example, elephants alone feed up to 16 hours per day (10 pounds of mixed vegetables and fruits, one to two bales of coastal grass hay per day, and 60 gallons of water per day).		

The purpose of each Stage 2 matching tool is to generate feasible alternative strategies, not to select or determine which strategies are best. Not all of the strategies developed in the SWOT Matrix, therefore, will be selected for implementation. A sample SWOT Matrix for the Riverbanks Zoo located in Columbia, South Carolina is provided in Figure 6-4.

The strategy-formulation guidelines provided in Chapter 5 can enhance the process of matching key external and internal factors. For example, when an organization has both the capital and human resources needed to distribute its own products (internal strength) and distributors are unreliable, costly, or incapable of meeting the firm's needs (external threat), forward integration can be an attractive ST Strategy. When a firm has excess production capacity (internal weakness) and its basic industry is experiencing declining annual sales and profits (external threat), related diversification can be an effective WT Strategy. It is important to use specific, rather than general, strategy terms when developing a SWOT Matrix. In addition, it is important to include the "S1, O2"-type notation after each strategy in the SWOT Matrix. This notation reveals the rationale for each alternative strategy.

Although the SWOT matrix is widely used in strategic planning, the analysis does have some limitations.[5] First, SWOT does not show how to achieve a competitive advantage, so it must not be an end in itself. The matrix should be the starting point for discussion on how proposed strategies could be implemented as well as cost-benefit considerations that ultimately could lead to competitive advantage. Secondly, SWOT is a static assessment (or snapshot) in time. A SWOT matrix can be like studying a single frame of a motion picture where you see the lead characters and the setting but have no clue as to the plot. As circumstances, capabilities, threats, and strategies change, the dynamics of a competitive environment may not be revealed in a single matrix. Thirdly, SWOT analysis may lead the firm to overemphasize a single internal or external factor in formulating strategies. There are interrelationships among the key internal and external factors that SWOT does not reveal that may be important in devising strategies.

snapshot

VISIT THE NET

Gives excellent information about the need for planning.
(http://www.mindtools.com/)

may lead to over emphasizing one factor

The Strategic Position and Action Evaluation (SPACE) Matrix

The *Strategic Position and Action Evaluation* (SPACE) Matrix, another important Stage 2 matching tool, is illustrated in Figure 6-5. Its four-quadrant framework indicates whether aggressive, conservative, defensive, or competitive strategies are most appropriate for a given organization. The axes of the SPACE Matrix represent two internal dimensions (*financial strength [FS]* and *competitive advantage [CA]*) and two external dimensions (*environmental stability [ES]* and *industry strength [IS]*). These four factors are perhaps the most important determinants of an organization's overall strategic position.[6]

FIGURE 6-5

The SPACE Matrix

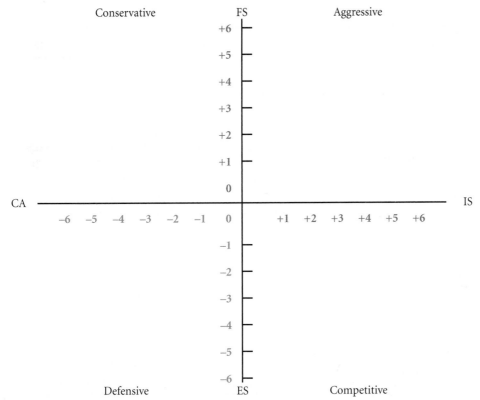

Source: H. Rowe, R. Mason, and K. Dickel, *Strategic Management and Business Policy: A Methodological Approach* (Reading, MA: Addison-Wesley Publishing Co. Inc., © 1982): 155. Reprinted with permission of the publisher.

Depending upon the type of organization, numerous variables could make up each of the dimensions represented on the axes of the SPACE Matrix. Factors that were included earlier in the firm's EFE and IFE Matrices should be considered in developing a SPACE Matrix. Other variables commonly included are given in Table 6-2. For example, return on investment, leverage, liquidity, working capital, and cash flow are commonly considered to be determining factors of an organization's financial strength. Like the SWOT Matrix, the SPACE Matrix should be both tailored to the particular organization being studied and based on factual information as much as possible.

The steps required to develop a SPACE Matrix are as follows:

1. Select a set of variables to define financial strength (FS), competitive advantage (CA), environmental stability (ES), and industry strength (IS).

2. Assign a numerical value ranging from +1 (worst) to +6 (best) to each of the variables that make up the FS and IS dimensions. Assign a numerical value ranging from −1 (best) to −6 (worst) to each of the variables that make up the ES and CA dimensions. On the FS and CA axes, make comparison to competitors. On the IS and ES axes, make comparison to other industries.

3. Compute an average score for FS, CA, IS, and ES by summing the values given to the variables of each dimension and then by dividing by the number of variables included in the respective dimension.

TABLE 6-2   Example Factors That Make Up the SPACE Matrix Axes

INTERNAL STRATEGIC POSITION	EXTERNAL STRATEGIC POSITION
Financial Strength (FS)	*Environmental Stability (ES)*
Return on investment	Technological changes
Leverage	Rate of inflation
Liquidity	Demand variability
Working capital	Price range of competing products
Cash flow	Barriers to entry into market
	Competitive pressure
	Ease of exit from market
	Price elasticity of demand
	Risk involved in business
Competitive Advantage (CA)	*Industry Strength (IS)*
Market share	Growth potential
Product quality	Profit potential
Product life cycle	Financial stability
Customer loyalty	Technological know-how
Competition's capacity utilization	Resource utilization
Technological know-how	Ease of entry into market
Control over suppliers and distributors	Productivity, capacity utilization

Source: H. Rowe, R. Mason, and K. Dickel, *Strategic Management and Business Policy: A Methodological Approach* (Reading, MA: Addison-Wesley Publishing Co. Inc., © 1982): 155–156. Reprinted with permission of the publisher.

4. Plot the average scores for FS, IS, ES, and CA on the appropriate axis in the SPACE Matrix.

5. Add the two scores on the *x*-axis and plot the resultant point on X. Add the two scores on the *y*-axis and plot the resultant point on Y. Plot the intersection of the new *xy* point.

6. Draw a *directional vector* from the origin of the SPACE Matrix through the new intersection point. This vector reveals the type of strategies recommended for the organization: aggressive, competitive, defensive, or conservative.

Some examples of strategy profiles that can emerge from a SPACE analysis are shown in Figure 6-6. The directional vector associated with each profile suggests the type of strategies to pursue: aggressive, conservative, defensive, or competitive. When a firm's directional vector is located in the *aggressive quadrant* (upper-right quadrant) of the SPACE Matrix, an organization is in an excellent position to use its internal strengths to (1) take advantage of external opportunities, (2) overcome internal weaknesses, and (3) avoid external threats. Therefore, market penetration, market development, product development, backward integration, forward integration, horizontal integration, conglomerate diversification, concentric diversification, horizontal diversification, or a combination strategy all can be feasible, depending on the specific circumstances that face the firm.

The directional vector may appear in the *conservative quadrant* (upper-left quadrant) of the SPACE Matrix, which implies staying close to the firm's basic competencies and not taking excessive risks. Conservative strategies most often include market penetration, market development, product development, and concentric diversification. The directional vector may be located in the lower-left or *defensive quadrant* of the SPACE Matrix, which suggests that the firm should focus on rectifying internal weaknesses and avoiding external threats. Defensive strategies include retrenchment, divestiture, liquidation, and concentric diversification. Finally, the directional vector may be located in the lower-right or *competitive quadrant* of the SPACE Matrix, indicating competitive strategies. Competitive strategies include backward, forward, and horizontal integration; market penetration; market development; product development; and joint ventures.

A SPACE Matrix analysis for a bank is provided in Table 6-3. Note that competitive type strategies are recommended.

The Boston Consulting Group (BCG) Matrix

Autonomous divisions (or profit centers) of an organization make up what is called a *business portfolio*. When a firm's divisions compete in different industries, a separate strategy often must be developed for each business. The *Boston Consulting Group (BCG) Matrix* and the *Internal-External (IE) Matrix* are designed specifically to enhance a multidivisional firm's efforts to formulate strategies. (BCG is a private management consulting firm based in Boston. BCG employs about 1,400 consultants worldwide.

The BCG Matrix graphically portrays differences among divisions in terms of relative market share position and industry growth rate. The BCG Matrix allows a multidivisional organization to manage its portfolio of businesses by examining the relative market share position and the industry growth rate of each division relative to all other divisions in the organization. *Relative market share position* is defined as the ratio of a division's own market share in a particular industry to the market share

FIGURE 6-6

Example Strategy Profiles

Aggressive Profiles

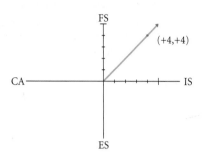

A financially strong firm that has achieved major competitive advantages in a growing and stable industry

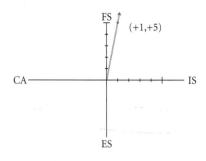

A firm whose financial strength is a dominating factor in the industry

Conservative Profiles

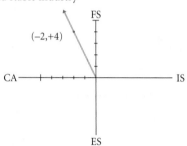

A firm that has achieved financial strength in a stable industry that is not growing; the firm has no major competitive advantages

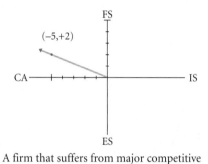

A firm that suffers from major competitive disadvantages in an industry that is technologically stable but declining in sales

Competitive Profiles

A firm with major competitive advantages in a high-growth industry

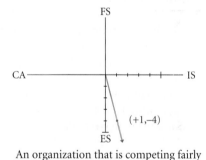

An organization that is competing fairly well in an unstable industry

Defensive Profiles

A firm that has a very weak competitive position in a negative growth, stable industry

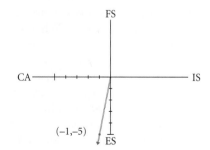

A financially troubled firm in a very unstable industry

Source: H. Rowe, R. Mason, and K. Dickel, *Strategic Management and Business Policy: A Methodological Approach* (Reading, MA: Addison-Wesley Publishing Co. Inc., © 1982): 155. Reprinted with permission of the publisher.

TABLE 6-3   A SPACE Matrix for a Bank

FINANCIAL STRENGTH	RATINGS
The bank's primary capital ratio is 7.23 percent, which is 1.23 percentage points over the generally required ratio of 6 percent.	1.0
The bank's return on assets is negative 0.77, compared to a bank industry average ratio of positive 0.70.	1.0
The bank's net income was $183 million, down 9 percent from a year earlier.	3.0
The bank's revenues increased 7 percent to $3.46 billion.	4.0
	9.0

INDUSTRY STRENGTH	
Deregulation provides geographic and product freedom.	4.0
Deregulation increases competition in the banking industry.	2.0
Pennsylvania's interstate banking law allows the bank to acquire other banks in New Jersey, Ohio, Kentucky, the District of Columbia, and West Virginia.	4.0
	10.0

ENVIRONMENTAL STABILITY	
Less-developed countries are experiencing high inflation and political instability.	-4.0
Headquartered in Pittsburgh, the bank historically has been heavily dependent on the steel, oil, and gas industries. These industries are depressed.	-5.0
Banking deregulation has created instability throughout the industry.	-4.0
	-13.0

COMPETITIVE ADVANTAGE	
The bank provides data processing services for more than 450 institutions in 38 states.	-2.0
Superregional banks, international banks, and nonbanks are becoming increasingly competitive.	-5.0
The bank has a large customer base.	-2.0
	-9.0

CONCLUSION

ES Average is $-13.0 \div 3 = -4.33$ IS Average is $+ 10.0 \div 3 = 3.33$
CA Average is $-9.0 \div 3 = -3.00$ FS Average is $+ 9.0 \div 4 = 2.25$
Directional Vector Coordinates: x-axis: $-3.00 + (+3.33) = +0.33$
y-axis: $-4.33 + (+2.25) = -2.08$
The bank should pursue Competitive Strategies.

held by the largest rival firm in that industry. Note in Table 6-4 that Miller Lite's relative market share position in 2004 is $238.7/532.0 = 0.45$.

Relative market share position is given on the x-axis of the BCG Matrix. The midpoint on the x-axis usually is set at .50, corresponding to a division that has half the market share of the leading firm in the industry. The y-axis represents the industry growth rate in sales, measured in percentage terms. The growth rate percentages on the y-axis could range from -20 to $+20$ percent, with 0.0 being the midpoint. These numerical ranges on the x- and y-axes are often used, but other numerical values could be established as deemed appropriate for particular organizations.

TABLE 6-4   Market Share Data for Selected Industries in 2005

U.S. LIGHT-BEER CONSUMPTION

Domestic Beers	*Cases Consumed*
Bud Lite	532.0
Coors Light	224.4
Miller Lite	238.7
Sam Adams Light	1.7
Total Domestic Lights	**1,395.1**

Imported Light Beers	*Cases Consumed*
Amstel Light	10.4
Corona Light	8.7
Labatt Blue Light	5.7
Molson Canadian Light	0.7
Beck's Light	0.4
Total Imported Lights	**26.4**
Grand Total	**1,421.5**

BEER CONSUMPTION IN RUSSIA

Heineken	8.3% (up from 7.5% with recent purchase of Patra)
Baltic Beverages	34.2%
Sun Interbrew	14.2%
Other brewers	43.3%

Source: Adapted from Christopher Lawton, "Heineken to Enter Light-Beer Fray," *Wall Street Journal* (March 11, 2005): B3. Also see (May 9, 2005): 19.

An example of a BCG Matrix appears in Figure 6-7. Each circle represents a separate division. The size of the circle corresponds to the proportion of corporate **revenue** generated by that business unit, and the pie slice indicates the proportion of corporate **profits** generated by that division. Divisions located in Quadrant I of the BCG Matrix are called "Question Marks," those located in Quadrant II are called "Stars," those located in Quadrant III are called "Cash Cows," and those divisions located in Quadrant IV are called "Dogs."

- *Question Marks*—Divisions in Quadrant I have a low relative market share position, yet they compete in a high-growth industry. Generally these firms' cash needs are high and their cash generation is low. These businesses are called *Question Marks* because the organization must decide whether to strengthen them by pursuing an intensive strategy (market penetration, market development, or product development) or to sell them.

- *Stars*—Quadrant II businesses (*Stars*) represent the organization's best long-run opportunities for growth and profitability. Divisions with a high relative market share and a high industry growth rate should receive substantial investment to maintain or strengthen their dominant positions. Forward, backward, and horizontal integration; market penetration; market development; and product development are appropriate strategies for these divisions to consider.

FIGURE 6-7

The BCG Matrix

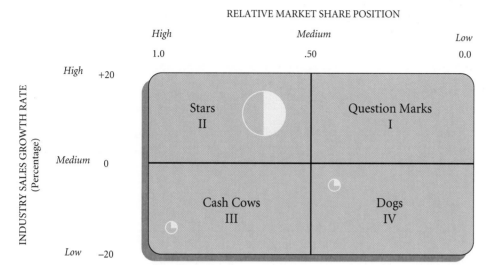

Source: Adapted from Boston Consulting Group, *Perspectives on Experience* (Boston: The Boston Consulting Group, 1974).

- *Cash Cows*—Divisions positioned in Quadrant III have a high relative market share position but compete in a low-growth industry. Called *Cash Cows* because they generate cash in excess of their needs, they are often milked. Many of today's Cash Cows were yesterday's Stars. Cash Cow divisions should be managed to maintain their strong position for as long as possible. Product development or concentric diversification may be attractive strategies for strong Cash Cows. However, as a Cash Cow division becomes weak, retrenchment or divestiture can become more appropriate.

- *Dogs*—Quadrant IV divisions of the organization have a low relative market share position and compete in a slow- or no-market-growth industry; they are *Dogs* in the firm's portfolio. Because of their weak internal and external position, these businesses are often liquidated, divested, or trimmed down through retrenchment. When a division first becomes a Dog, retrenchment can be the best strategy to pursue because many Dogs have bounced back, after strenuous asset and cost reduction, to become viable, profitable divisions.

The major benefit of the BCG Matrix is that it draws attention to the cash flow, investment characteristics, and needs of an organization's various divisions. The divisions of many firms evolve over time: Dogs become Question Marks, Question Marks become Stars, Stars become Cash Cows, and Cash Cows become Dogs in an ongoing counterclockwise motion. Less frequently, Stars become Question Marks, Question Marks become Dogs, Dogs become Cash Cows, and Cash Cows become Stars (in a clockwise motion). In some organizations, no cyclical motion is apparent. Over time, organizations should strive to achieve a portfolio of divisions that are Stars.

One example of a BCG Matrix is provided in Figure 6-8, which illustrates an organization composed of five divisions with annual sales ranging from $5,000 to

FIGURE 6-8

An Example BCG Matrix

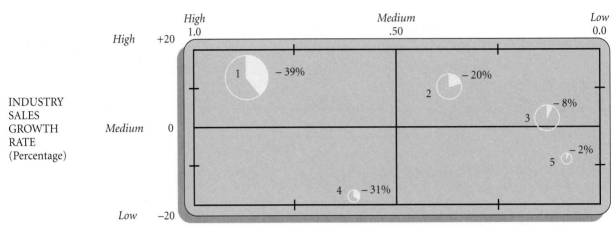

Division	Revenues	Percent Revenues	Profits	Percent Profits	Percent Market Share	Percent Growth Rate
1	$60,000	37	$10,000	39	80	+15
2	40,000	24	5,000	20	40	+10
3	40,000	24	2,000	8	10	+1
4	20,000	12	8,000	31	60	−20
5	5,000	3	500	2	5	−10
Total	**$165,000**	**100**	**$25,500**	**100**	—	—

$60,000. Division 1 has the greatest sales volume, so the circle representing that division is the largest one in the matrix. The circle corresponding to Division 5 is the smallest because its sales volume ($5,000) is least among all the divisions. The pie slices within the circles reveal the percent of corporate profits contributed by each division. As shown, Division 1 contributes the highest profit percentage, 39 percent. Notice in the diagram that Division 1 is considered a Star, Division 2 is a Question Mark, Division 3 is also a Question Mark, Division 4 is a Cash Cow, and Division 5 is a Dog.

The BCG Matrix, like all analytical techniques, has some limitations. For example, viewing every business as either a Star, Cash Cow, Dog, or Question Mark is an oversimplification; many businesses fall right in the middle of the BCG Matrix and thus are not easily classified. Furthermore, the BCG Matrix does not reflect whether or not various divisions or their industries are growing over time; that is, the matrix has no temporal qualities, but rather it is a snapshot of an organization at a given point in time. Finally, other variables besides relative market share position and industry growth rate in sales, such as size of the market and competitive advantages, are important in making strategic decisions about various divisions.

An example BCG Matrix for Limited Brands, Inc., is provided in Figure 6-9. Headquartered in Columbus, Ohio, Limited Brands has six divisions, led by Victoria's Secret Stores, which generate nearly one-half of company profits. Also note in Figure 6-9 that the Henri Bendel/Mast Industries division had an operating loss of $188 million. Take note how the % profit column is calculated because oftentimes a firm will have a division that incurs a loss for a year. In terms of the pie slice in circle 6 of the

FIGURE 6-9

An Example BCG Matrix for The Limited (2004 year-end)

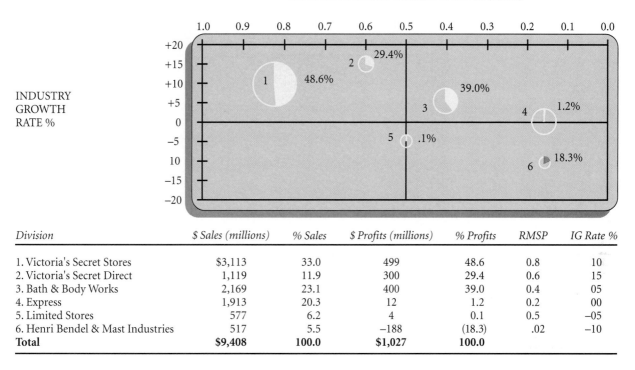

Division	$ Sales (millions)	% Sales	$ Profits (millions)	% Profits	RMSP	IG Rate %
1. Victoria's Secret Stores	$3,113	33.0	499	48.6	0.8	10
2. Victoria's Secret Direct	1,119	11.9	300	29.4	0.6	15
3. Bath & Body Works	2,169	23.1	400	39.0	0.4	05
4. Express	1,913	20.3	12	1.2	0.2	00
5. Limited Stores	577	6.2	4	0.1	0.5	−05
6. Henri Bendel & Mast Industries	517	5.5	−188	(18.3)	.02	−10
Total	**$9,408**	**100.0**	**$1,027**	**100.0**		

diagram, note that it is a different color from the positive profit segments in the other circles.

Another example BCG Matrix is given in Figure 6-10 for General Electric. Although GE is structured based on product divisions (as we will see), the company also keeps an up-to-date portfolio matrix based on continents. As shown in Figure 6-10, GE has greater greater revenues and profits in Europe than in the Americas.

The Internal-External (IE) Matrix

The *Internal-External (IE) Matrix* positions an organization's various divisions in a nine-cell display, illustrated in Figure 6-11. The IE Matrix is similar to the BCG Matrix in that both tools involve plotting organization divisions in a schematic diagram; this is why they are both called "portfolio matrices." Also, the size of each circle represents the percentage sales contribution of each division, and pie slices reveal the percentage profit contribution of each division in both the BCG and IE Matrix.

But there are some important differences between the BCG Matrix and the IE Matrix. First, the axes are different. Also, the IE Matrix requires more information about the divisions than the BCG Matrix. Furthermore, the strategic implications of each matrix are different. For these reasons, strategists in multidivisional firms often develop both the BCG Matrix and the IE Matrix in formulating alternative strategies. A common practice is to develop a BCG Matrix and an IE Matrix for the present and then develop projected matrices to reflect expectations of the future. This before-and-after analysis forecasts the expected effect of strategic decisions on an organization's portfolio of divisions.

FIGURE 6-10

An Example BCG Matrix for General Electric (2004 year-end; in millions)

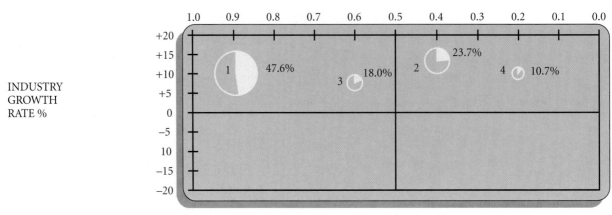

Division	$ Sales (millions)	% Sales	$ Profits (millions)	% Profits	RMSP	IG Rate %
1. Europe	$37,000	59.0	5,800	47.6	0.9	10
2. Pacific Basin	13,100	20.9	2,900	23.7	0.4	15
3. Americas	7,200	11.5	2,200	18.0	0.6	08
4. Other Global	5,400	8.6	1,300	10.7	0.2	12
Total	**$62,700**	**100.0**	**$12,200**	**100.0**		

GLOBAL PERSPECTIVE

Japanese Woman Is a Role Model for Her Peers

Ms. Fumiko Hayashi, CEO of Daiei Inc. in Tokyo, Japan, is a rarity in the male-dominated world of corporate Japan. Ms. Hayashi heads a short list of Japanese female top managers that include Tomomi Ishigara, president of skin-care cosmetics maker, Dr. Ci Labo; and Shoko Ikeda, president of Bull-Dog Sauce. Ms. Tomoyo Nonaka was recently named the chairwoman and CEO of Sanyo Electric Company.

Japan is far behind other major industrialized countries when it comes to women in top corporate posts. Women hold about 40 percent of the jobs in Japan but only about 8.9 percent of administrative and managerial positions, which is among the world's lowest for all countries. By contrast in the United States, women make up about 50 percent of the workforce and hold 45.9 percent of all administrative and managerial jobs.

Research shows that about 5.64 percent of the 1.23 million companies in Japan have a female president. Japan's government is considering ways to increase the number of female managers and has instituted a goal for at least 30 percent of all managers to be women by 2020. Ms. Hayashi plans to turn around Daiei by making the grocery stores more comfortable places for women to shop. Daiei is Japan's third-largest supermarket by sales, but the company reported a loss of $4.8 billion in 2004. Ms. Hayashi is working hard to be a great role model for other women in Japan to become managers and top executives. As has been proven in many parts of the world, women can be just as effective—or even more effective—than men as top managers in both public and private organizations.

Source: Adapted from Miyako Takebe, "Japanese CEO Is Model for Her Peers," *Wall Street Journal* (June 9, 2005): A15.

FIGURE 6-11

The Internal–External (IE) Matrix

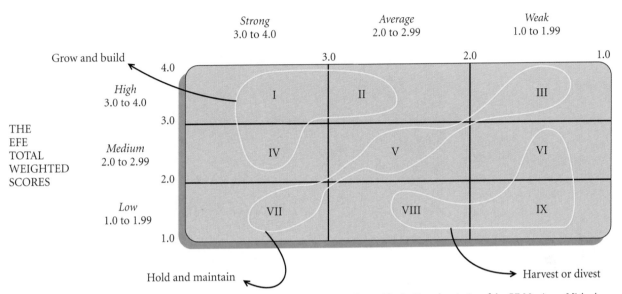

Source: Adapted. The IE Matrix was developed from the General Electric (GE) Business Screen Matrix. For a description of the GE Matrix see Michael Allen, "Diagramming GE's Planning for What's WATT," in R. Allio and M. Pennington, eds., *Corporate Planning: Techniques and Applications* (New York: AMACOM, 1979).

The IE Matrix is based on two key dimensions: the IFE total weighted scores on the *x*-axis and the EFE total weighted scores on the *y*-axis. Recall that each division of an organization should construct an IFE Matrix and an EFE Matrix for its part of the organization. The total weighted scores derived from the divisions allow construction of the corporate-level IE Matrix. On the *x*-axis of the IE Matrix, an IFE total weighted score of 1.0 to 1.99 represents a weak internal position; a score of 2.0 to 2.99 is considered average; and a score of 3.0 to 4.0 is strong. Similarly, on the *y*-axis, an EFE total weighted score of 1.0 to 1.99 is considered low; a score of 2.0 to 2.99 is medium; and a score of 3.0 to 4.0 is high.

The IE Matrix can be divided into three major regions that have different strategy implications. First, the prescription for divisions that fall into cells I, II, or IV can be described as *grow and build*. Intensive (market penetration, market development, and product development) or integrative (backward integration, forward integration, and horizontal integration) strategies can be most appropriate for these divisions. Second, divisions that fall into cells III, V, or VII can be managed best with *hold and maintain* strategies; market penetration and product development are two commonly employed strategies for these types of divisions. Third, a common prescription for divisions that fall into cells VI, VIII, or IX is *harvest or divest*. Successful organizations are able to achieve a portfolio of businesses positioned in or around cell I in the IE Matrix.

An example of a completed IE Matrix is given in Figure 6-12, which depicts an organization composed of four divisions. As indicated by the positioning of the circles, *grow and build* strategies are appropriate for Division 1, Division 2, and

FIGURE 6-12

An Example IE Matrix

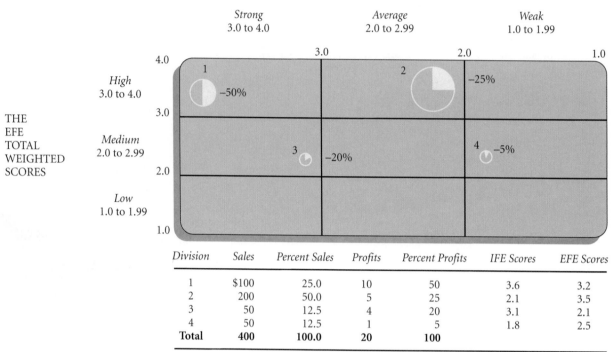

THE IFE TOTAL WEIGHTED SCORES

Division	Sales	Percent Sales	Profits	Percent Profits	IFE Scores	EFE Scores
1	$100	25.0	10	50	3.6	3.2
2	200	50.0	5	25	2.1	3.5
3	50	12.5	4	20	3.1	2.1
4	50	12.5	1	5	1.8	2.5
Total	**400**	**100.0**	**20**	**100**		

Division 3. Division 4 is a candidate for *harvest or divest*. Division 2 contributes the greatest percentage of company sales and thus is represented by the largest circle. Division 1 contributes the greatest proportion of total profits; it has the largest-percentage pie slice.

As indicated in Figure 6-13 and Figure 6-14, Harrah's recently constructed two IE Matrices, one for its four geographic segments and one for its five product segments. Note that its Central Region and its Casino Division have the largest revenues (as indicated by the largest circles) and the largest profits (as indicated by the largest pie slices) in the matrices, respectively. Harrah's could also develop a Land-Based versus Riverboat versus Indian Gaming IE Matrix with three circles. It is common for organizations to develop both geographic and product-based IE Matrices to more effectively formulate strategies and allocate resources among divisions. In addition, firms often prepare an IE (or BCG) Matrix for competitors. Furthermore, firms will often prepare "before and after" IE (or BCG) Matrices to reveal the situation at present versus the expected situation after one year. This latter idea minimizes the limitation of these matrices being a "snapshot in time." In performing case analysis, feel free to estimate the IFE and EFE scores for the various divisions based upon your research into the company and industry—rather than preparing a separate IE Matrix for each division.

Note in Figure 6-15 that General Electric (GE) has 11 divisions. The firm's top 2 revenue-generating divisions are 1) Commercial Finance and 2) Insurance. GE is one of the premier diversified firms in the United States.

FIGURE 6-13
The Internal-External (IE) Matrix for Harrah's (2004) (Based on Region)

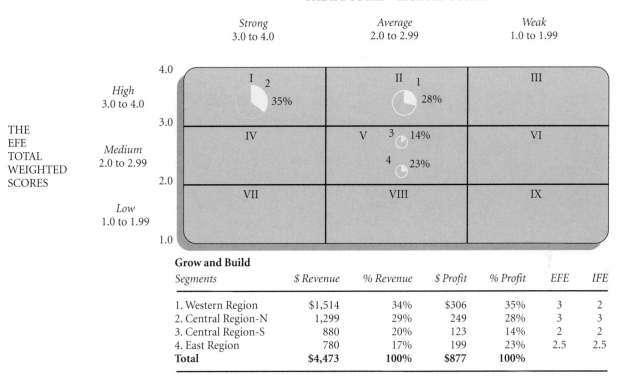

THE IFE TOTAL WEIGHTED SCORES

	Strong 3.0 to 4.0	Average 2.0 to 2.99	Weak 1.0 to 1.99

THE EFE TOTAL WEIGHTED SCORES

Grow and Build

Segments	$ Revenue	% Revenue	$ Profit	% Profit	EFE	IFE
1. Western Region	$1,514	34%	$306	35%	3	2
2. Central Region-N	1,299	29%	249	28%	3	3
3. Central Region-S	880	20%	123	14%	2	2
4. East Region	780	17%	199	23%	2.5	2.5
Total	**$4,473**	**100%**	**$877**	**100%**		

The Grand Strategy Matrix

In addition to the SWOT Matrix, SPACE Matrix, BCG Matrix, and IE Matrix, the *Grand Strategy Matrix* has become a popular tool for formulating alternative strategies. All organizations can be positioned in one of the Grand Strategy Matrix's four strategy quadrants. A firm's divisions likewise could be positioned. As illustrated in Figure 6-16, the Grand Strategy Matrix is based on two evaluative dimensions: competitive position and market growth. Appropriate strategies for an organization to consider are listed in sequential order of attractiveness in each quadrant of the matrix.

Firms located in Quadrant I of the Grand Strategy Matrix are in an excellent strategic position. For these firms, continued concentration on current markets (market penetration and market development) and products (product development) is an appropriate strategy. It is unwise for a Quadrant I firm to shift notably from its established competitive advantages. When a Quadrant I organization has excessive resources, then backward, forward, or horizontal integration may be effective strategies. When a Quadrant I firm is too heavily committed to a single product, then related diversification may reduce the risks associated with a narrow product line. Quadrant I firms can afford to take advantage of external opportunities in several areas. They can take risks aggressively when necessary.

Firms positioned in Quadrant II need to evaluate their present approach to the marketplace seriously. Although their industry is growing, they are unable to

FIGURE 6-14

The Internal-External (IE) for Harrah's (2004) (Based on Product)

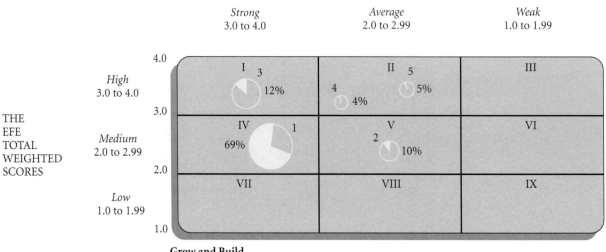

Grow and Build						
Segments	$ Revenue	% Revenue	$ Profit	% Profit	EFE Scores	IFE Scores
1. Casinos	$4,077	76%	$2,016	71%	2.5	3
2. Rooms	390	7%	323	11%	2	2
3. Food and Beverages	665	12%	387	14%	3	3
4. Managed Properties	60	1%	20	1%	2.5	2.5
5. Other	217	4%	77	3%	3	2
Total	**$5,409**	**100%**	**$2,823**	**100%**	—	—

compete effectively, and they need to determine why the firm's current approach is ineffective and how the company can best change to improve its competitiveness. Because Quadrant II firms are in a rapid-market-growth industry, an intensive strategy (as opposed to integrative or diversification) is usually the first option that should be considered. However, if the firm is lacking a distinctive competence or competitive advantage, then horizontal integration is often a desirable alternative. As a last resort, divestiture or liquidation should be considered. Divestiture can provide funds needed to acquire other businesses or buy back shares of stock.

Quadrant III organizations compete in slow-growth industries and have weak competitive positions. These firms must make some drastic changes quickly to avoid further decline and possible liquidation. Extensive cost and asset reduction (retrenchment) should be pursued first. An alternative strategy is to shift resources away from the current business into different areas (diversify). If all else fails, the final options for Quadrant III businesses are divestiture or liquidation.

Finally, Quadrant IV businesses have a strong competitive position but are in a slow-growth industry. These firms have the strength to launch diversified programs into more promising growth areas: Quadrant IV firms have characteristically high cash-flow levels and limited internal growth needs and often can pursue related or unrelated diversification successfully. Quadrant IV firms also may pursue joint ventures.

FIGURE 6-15

An Example IE Matrix for General Electric (2004 year-end; in millions)

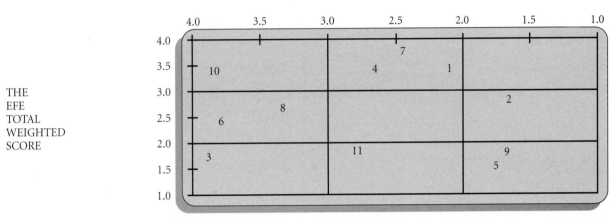

Division	$ Sales (millions)	% Sales	$ Profits (millions)	% Profits	IFE Scores	EFE Scores
1. Advanced Materials	$8,290	5.4	$710	3.33	2.13	3.45
2. Commercial Finance	23,489	15.4	4,465	20.98	1.68	2.59
3. Consumer Finance	15,734	10.3	2,520	11.84	3.88	1.77
4. Consumer/Industrial	13,767	9.3	716	3.34	2.65	3.44
5. Energy	17,348	11.3	2,845	13.37	1.77	1.88
6. Equipment/Services	8,986	5.8	833	3.91	3.66	2.44
7. Healthcare	13,456	8.8	2,286	10.74	2.44	3.78
8. Infrastructure	3,447	2.2	563	2.64	3.22	2.66
9. Insurance	23,070	15.0	569	2.65	1.55	1.88
10. NBC Universal	12,886	8.4	2,558	12.10	3.88	3.41
11. Transportation	15,562	10.1	3,213	15.10	2.67	1.99
Corporate Items	(3,169)	(2.0)	—	—		
Total	**$152,866**	**100.0**	**$21,278**	**100.00**		

The Decision Stage

Analysis and intuition provide a basis for making strategy-formulation decisions. The matching techniques just discussed reveal feasible alternative strategies. Many of these strategies will likely have been proposed by managers and employees participating in the strategy analysis and choice activity. Any additional strategies resulting from the matching analyses could be discussed and added to the list of feasible alternative options. As indicated earlier in this chapter, participants could rate these strategies on a 1 to 4 scale so that a prioritized list of the best strategies could be achieved.

The Quantitative Strategic Planning Matrix (QSPM)

Other than ranking strategies to achieve the prioritized list, there is only one analytical technique in the literature designed to determine the relative attractiveness of feasible alternative actions. This technique is the *Quantitative Strategic Planning Matrix (QSPM)*, which comprises Stage 3 of the strategy-formulation analytical framework.[7] This technique objectively indicates which alternative strategies are best.

FIGURE 6-16

The Grand Strategy Matrix

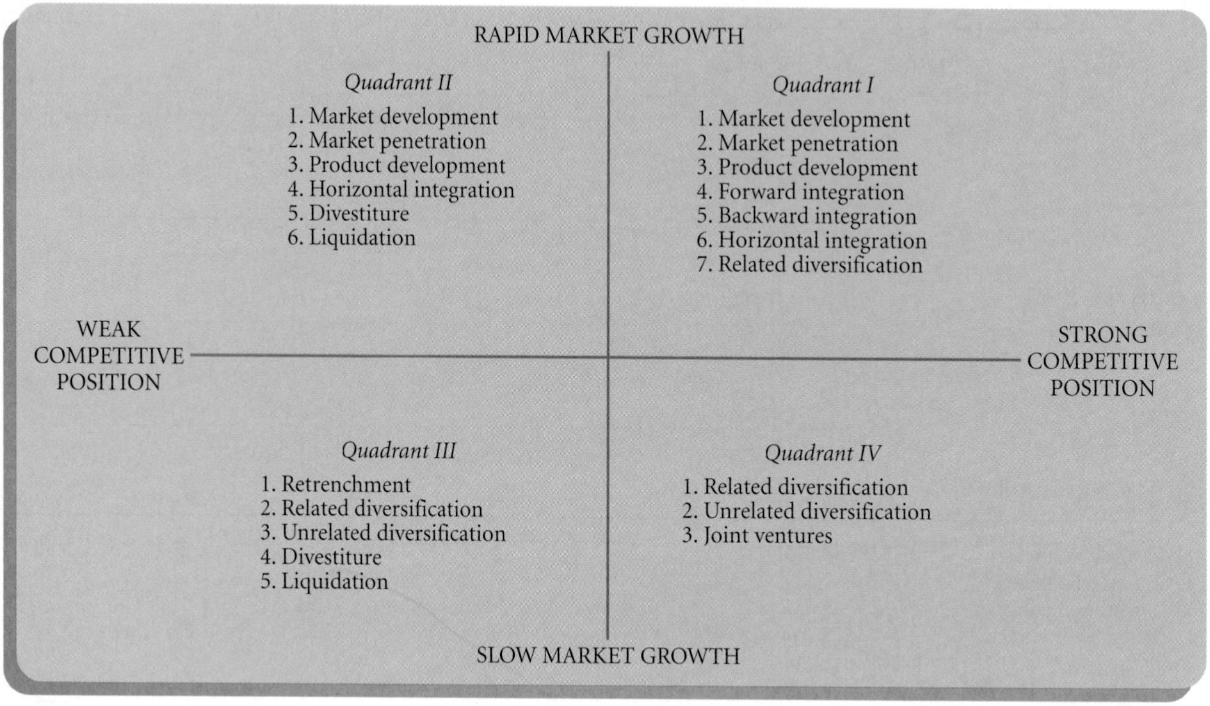

RAPID MARKET GROWTH

Quadrant II
1. Market development
2. Market penetration
3. Product development
4. Horizontal integration
5. Divestiture
6. Liquidation

Quadrant I
1. Market development
2. Market penetration
3. Product development
4. Forward integration
5. Backward integration
6. Horizontal integration
7. Related diversification

WEAK COMPETITIVE POSITION — — — — — — STRONG COMPETITIVE POSITION

Quadrant III
1. Retrenchment
2. Related diversification
3. Unrelated diversification
4. Divestiture
5. Liquidation

Quadrant IV
1. Related diversification
2. Unrelated diversification
3. Joint ventures

SLOW MARKET GROWTH

Source: Adapted from Roland Christensen, Norman Berg, and Malcolm Salter, *Policy Formulation and Administration* (Homewood, IL: Richard D. Irwin, 1976): 16–18.

The QSPM uses input from Stage 1 analyses and matching results from Stage 2 analyses to decide objectively among alternative strategies. That is, the EFE Matrix, IFE Matrix, and Competitive Profile Matrix that make up Stage 1, coupled with the SWOT Matrix, SPACE Matrix, BCG Matrix, IE Matrix, and Grand Strategy Matrix that make up Stage 2, provide the needed information for setting up the QSPM (Stage 3). The QSPM is a tool that allows strategists to evaluate alternative strategies objectively, based on previously identified external and internal critical success factors. Like other strategy-formulation analytical tools, the QSPM requires good intuitive judgment.

The basic format of the QSPM is illustrated in Table 6-5. Note that the left column of a QSPM consists of key external and internal factors (from Stage 1), and the top row consists of feasible alternative strategies (from Stage 2). Specifically, the left column of a QSPM consists of information obtained directly from the EFE Matrix and IFE Matrix. In a column adjacent to the critical success factors, the respective weights received by each factor in the EFE Matrix and the IFE Matrix are recorded.

The top row of a QSPM consists of alternative strategies derived from the SWOT Matrix, SPACE Matrix, BCG Matrix, IE Matrix, and Grand Strategy Matrix. These matching tools usually generate similar feasible alternatives. However, not every strategy suggested by the matching techniques has to be evaluated in a QSPM. Strategists should use good intuitive judgment in selecting strategies to include in a QSPM.

TABLE 6-5 The Quantitative Strategic Planning Matrix—QSPM

		STRATEGIC ALTERNATIVES		
Key Factors	*Weight*	*Strategy 1*	*Strategy 2*	*Strategy 3*
Key External Factors				
Economy				
Political/Legal/Governmental				
Social/Cultural/Demographic/Environmental				
Technological				
Competitive				
Key Internal Factors				
Management				
Marketing				
Finance/Accounting				
Production/Operations				
Research and Development				
Management Information Systems				

Conceptually, the QSPM determines the relative attractiveness of various strategies based on the extent to which key external and internal critical success factors are capitalized upon or improved. The relative attractiveness of each strategy within a set of alternatives is computed by determining the cumulative impact of each external and internal critical success factor. Any number of sets of alternative strategies can be included in the QSPM, and any number of strategies can make up a given set, but only strategies within a given set are evaluated relative to each other. For example, one set of strategies may include diversification, whereas another set may include issuing stock and selling a division to raise needed capital. These two sets of strategies are totally different, and the QSPM evaluates strategies only within sets. Note in Table 6-5 that three strategies are included, and they make up just one set.

A QSPM for Campbell Soup Company is provided in Table 6-6. This example illustrates all the components of the QSPM: Strategic Alternatives, Key Factors, Weights, Attractiveness Scores (AS), Total Attractiveness Scores (TAS), and the Sum Total Attractiveness Score. The three new terms just introduced—(1) Attractiveness Scores, (2) Total Attractiveness Scores, and (3) the Sum Total Attractiveness Score—are defined and explained as the six steps required to develop a QSPM are discussed:

Step 1   *Make a list of the firm's key external opportunities/threats and internal strengths/weaknesses in the left column of the QSPM.*
This information should be taken directly from the EFE Matrix and IFE Matrix. A minimum of 10 external critical success factors and 10 internal critical success factors should be included in the QSPM.

TABLE 6-6   A QSPM for Campbell Soup Company

		STRATEGIC ALTERNATIVES			
		Joint Venture in Europe		Joint Venture in Asia	
Key Factors	Weight	AS	TAS	AS	TAS
Opportunities					
1. One European currency—euro	.10	4	.40	2	.20
2. Rising health consciousness in selecting foods	.15	4	.60	3	.45
3. Free market economies arising in Asia	.10	2	.20	4	.40
4. Demand for soups increasing 10% annually	.15	3	.45	4	.60
5. NAFTA	.05	—	—	—	—
Threats					
1. Food revenues increasing only 1% annually	.10	3	.30	4	.40
2. ConAgra's Banquet TV dinners lead market with 27.4 percent share	.05	—	—	—	—
3. Unstable economies in Asia	.10	4	.40	1	.10
4. Tin cans are not biodegradable	.05	—	—	—	—
5. Low value of the dollar	.15	4	.60	2	.30
	1.00				
Strengths					
1. Profits rose 30%	.10	4	.40	2	.20
2. New North American division	.10	—	—	—	—
3. New health-conscious soups are successful	.10	4	.40	2	.20
4. Swanson TV dinners' market share has increased to 25.1%	.05	4	.20	3	.15
5. One-fifth of all managers' bonuses is based on overall corporate performance	.05	—	—	—	—
6. Capacity utilization increased from 60% to 80%	.15	3	.45	4	.60
Weaknesses					
1. Pepperidge Farm sales have declined 7%	.05	—	—	—	—
2. Restructuring cost $302 million	.05	—	—	—	—
3. The company's European operation is losing money	.15	2	.30	4	.60
4. The company is slow in globalizing	.15	4	.60	3	.45
5. Pretax profit margin of 8.4% is only one-half industry average	.05	—	—	—	—
Sum Total Attractiveness Score	1.00		5.30		4.65

AS = Attractiveness Score; TAS = Total Attractiveness Score
Attractiveness Score: 1 = not attractive; 2 = somewhat attractive; 3 = reasonably attractive; 4 = highly attractive.

Step 2 *Assign weights to each key external and internal factor.* These weights are identical to those in the EFE Matrix and the IFE Matrix. The weights are presented in a straight column just to the right of the external and internal critical success factors.

Step 3 *Examine the Stage 2 (matching) matrices, and identify alternative strategies that the organization should consider implementing.*

Record these strategies in the top row of the QSPM. Group the strategies into mutually exclusive sets if possible.

Step 4   ***Determine the Attractiveness Scores (AS)*** defined as numerical values that indicate the relative attractiveness of each strategy in a given set of alternatives. *Attractiveness Scores (AS)* are determined by examining each key external or internal factor, one at a time, and asking the question "Does this factor affect the choice of strategies being made?" If the answer to this question is *yes*, then the strategies should be compared relative to that key factor. Specifically, Attractiveness Scores should be assigned to each strategy to indicate the relative attractiveness of one strategy over others, considering the particular factor. The range for Attractiveness Scores is 1 = not attractive, 2 = somewhat attractive, 3 = reasonably attractive, and 4 = highly attractive. Work row by row in developing a QSPM. If the answer to the previous question is *no,* indicating that the respective key factor has no effect upon the specific choice being made, then do not assign Attractiveness Scores to the strategies in that set. Use a dash to indicate that the key factor does not affect the choice being made. *Note:* If you assign an AS score to one strategy, then assign AS score(s) to the other. In other words, if one strategy receives a dash, then all others must receive a dash in a given row.

Step 5   ***Compute the Total Attractiveness Scores.*** *Total Attractiveness Scores (TAS)* are defined as the product of multiplying the weights (Step 2) by the Attractiveness Scores (Step 4) in each row. The Total Attractiveness Scores indicate the relative attractiveness of each alternative strategy, considering only the impact of the adjacent external or internal critical success factor. The higher the Total Attractiveness Score, the more attractive the strategic alternative (considering only the adjacent critical success factor).

Step 6   ***Compute the Sum Total Attractiveness Score.*** Add Total Attractiveness Scores in each strategy column of the QSPM. The *Sum Total Attractiveness Scores (STAS)* reveal which strategy is most attractive in each set of alternatives. Higher scores indicate more attractive strategies, considering all the relevant external and internal factors that could affect the strategic decisions. The magnitude of the difference between the Sum Total Attractiveness Scores in a given set of strategic alternatives indicates the relative desirability of one strategy over another.

In Table 6-6, two alternative strategies—establishing a joint venture in Europe and establishing a joint venture in Asia—are being considered by Campbell Soup.

Note that NAFTA has no impact on the choice being made between the two strategies, so a dash (–) appears several times across that row. Several other factors also have no effect on the choice being made, so dashes are recorded in those rows as well. If a particular factor affects one strategy but not the other, it affects the choice being made, so attractiveness scores should be recorded. The sum total attractiveness score of 5.30 in Table 6-6 indicates that the joint venture in Europe is a more attractive strategy when compared to the joint venture in Asia.

You should have a rationale for each AS score assigned. In Table 6-5, the rationale for the AS scores in the first row is that the unification of Western Europe creates more stable business conditions in Europe than in Asia. The AS score of 4 for the joint venture

AS should be - - - - -

in Europe and 2 for the joint venture in Asia indicate that the European venture is highly attractive and the Asian venture is somewhat attractive, considering only the first critical success factor. AS scores, therefore, are not mere guesses; they should be rational, defensible, and reasonable. Avoid giving each strategy the same AS score. Note in Table 6-6 that dashes are inserted all the way across the row when used. Also note that double 4s, or double 3s, or double 2s, or double 1s are never in a given row. Again work row by row, not column by column. These are important guidelines to follow in constructing a QSPM.

Positive Features and Limitations of the QSPM

A positive feature of the QSPM is that sets of strategies can be examined sequentially or simultaneously. For example, corporate-level strategies could be evaluated first, followed by division-level strategies, and then function-level strategies. There is no limit to the number of strategies that can be evaluated or the number of sets of strategies that can be examined at once using the QSPM.

Another positive feature of the QSPM is that it requires strategists to integrate pertinent external and internal factors into the decision process. Developing a QSPM makes it less likely that key factors will be overlooked or weighted inappropriately. A QSPM draws attention to important relationships that affect strategy decisions. Although developing a QSPM requires a number of subjective decisions, making small decisions along the way enhances the probability that the final strategic decisions will be best for the organization. A QSPM can be adapted for use by small and large for-profit and nonprofit organizations so can be applied to virtually any type of organization. A QSPM can especially enhance strategic choice in multinational firms because many key factors and strategies can be considered at once. It also has been applied successfully by a number of small businesses.[8]

The QSPM is not without some limitations. First, it always requires intuitive judgments and educated assumptions. The ratings and attractiveness scores require judgmental decisions, even though they should be based on objective information. Discussion among strategists, managers, and employees throughout the strategy-formulation process, including development of a QSPM, is constructive and improves strategic decisions. Constructive discussion during strategy analysis and choice may arise because of genuine differences of interpretation of information and varying opinions. Another limitation of the QSPM is that it can be only as good as the prerequisite information and matching analyses upon which it is based.

Cultural Aspects of Strategy Choice

Culture

All organizations have a culture. *Culture* includes the set of shared values, beliefs, attitudes, customs, norms, personalities, heroes, and heroines that describe a firm. Culture is the unique way an organization does business. It is the human dimension that creates solidarity and meaning, and it inspires commitment and productivity in an organization when strategy changes are made. All human beings have a basic need to make sense of the world, to feel in control, and to make meaning. When events threaten meaning, individuals react defensively. Managers and employees may even sabotage new strategies in an effort to recapture the status quo.

Success depends on firms culture

It is beneficial to view strategic management from a cultural perspective because success often rests upon the degree of support that strategies receive from a firm's culture. If a firm's strategies are supported by cultural products such as values, beliefs, rites, rituals, ceremonies, stories, symbols, language, heroes, and heroines, then managers often can implement changes swiftly and easily. However, if a supportive culture does not exist and is not cultivated, then strategy changes may be ineffective or even counterproductive. A firm's culture can become antagonistic to new strategies, and the result of that antagonism may be confusion and disarray.

Strategies that require fewer cultural changes may be more attractive because extensive changes can take considerable time and effort. Whenever two firms merge, it becomes especially important to evaluate and consider culture-strategy linkages. For example, Hewlett-Packard (HP) and Compaq merged, and their company cultures were quite different. Compaq's culture was top-down–oriented, whereas the HP culture, called the "HP Way," was based on "management by walking around." Compaq was a marketer that spent only 3.5 percent of revenues on R&D, whereas HP is an inventor that spends 6 percent of its revenues annually on R&D. Compaq focused on a few major products, whereas HP boasts a wide array of products in many categories. Compaq's management style was described as outgoing, whereas HP's is introspective and analytical.[9] Compaq's workforce was highly competitive, aggressive, and took risks, whereas the HP Way is to base decisions more on experience, professionalism, and careful analysis.

Culture provides an explanation for the difficulties a firm encounters when it attempts to shift its strategic direction, as the following statement explains:

> Not only has the "right" corporate culture become the essence and foundation of corporate excellence, but success or failure of needed corporate reforms hinges on management's sagacity and ability to change the firm's driving culture in time and in tune with required changes in strategies.[10]

The Politics of Strategy Choice

All organizations are political. Unless managed, political maneuvering consumes valuable time, subverts organizational objectives, diverts human energy, and results in the loss of some valuable employees. Sometimes political biases and personal preferences get unduly embedded in strategy choice decisions. Internal politics affect the choice of strategies in all organizations. The hierarchy of command in an organization, combined with the career aspirations of different people and the need to allocate scarce resources, guarantees the formation of coalitions of individuals who strive to take care of themselves first and the organization second, third, or fourth. Coalitions of individuals often form around key strategy issues that face an enterprise. A major responsibility of strategists is to guide the development of coalitions, to nurture an overall team concept, and to gain the support of key individuals and groups of individuals.

In the absence of objective analyses, strategy decisions too often are based on the politics of the moment. With development of improved strategy-formation tools, political factors become less important in making strategic decisions. In the absence of objectivity, political factors sometimes dictate strategies, and this is unfortunate. Managing political relationships is an integral part of building enthusiasm and esprit de corps in an organization.

A classic study of strategic management in nine large corporations examined the political tactics of successful and unsuccessful strategists.[11] Successful strategists were found to let weakly supported ideas and proposals die through inaction and to establish additional hurdles or tests for strongly supported ideas considered unacceptable but not openly opposed. Successful strategists kept a low political profile on unacceptable proposals and strived to let most negative decisions come from subordinates or a group consensus, thereby reserving their personal vetoes for big issues and crucial moments. Successful strategists did a lot of chatting and informal questioning to stay abreast of how things were progressing and to know when to intervene. They led strategy but did not dictate it. They gave few orders, announced few decisions, depended heavily on informal questioning, and sought to probe and clarify until a consensus emerged.

Successful strategists generously and visibly rewarded key thrusts that succeeded. They assigned responsibility for major new thrusts to *champions*, the individuals most strongly identified with the idea or product and whose futures were linked to its success. They stayed alert to the symbolic impact of their own actions and statements so as not to send false signals that could stimulate movements in unwanted directions.

Successful strategists ensured that all major power bases within an organization were represented in, or had access to, top management. They interjected new faces and new views into considerations of major changes. This is important because new employees and managers generally have more enthusiasm and drive than employees who have been with the firm a long time. New employees do not see the world the same old way; nor do they act as screens against changes. Successful strategists minimized their own political exposure on highly controversial issues and in circumstances in which major opposition from key power centers was likely. In combination, these findings provide a basis for managing political relationships in an organization.

Because strategies must be effective in the marketplace and capable of gaining internal commitment, the following tactics used by politicians for centuries can aid strategists:

- *Equifinality*—It is often possible to achieve similar results using different means or paths. Strategists should recognize that achieving a successful outcome is more important than imposing the method of achieving it. It may be possible to generate new alternatives that give equal results but with far greater potential for gaining commitment.
- *Satisfying*—Achieving satisfactory results with an acceptable strategy is far better than failing to achieve optimal results with an unpopular strategy.
- *Generalization*—Shifting focus from specific issues to more general ones may increase strategists' options for gaining organizational commitment.
- *Focus on Higher-Order Issues*—By raising an issue to a higher level, many short-term interests can be postponed in favor of long-term interests. For instance, by focusing on issues of survival, the airline and automotive industries were able to persuade unions to make concessions on wage increases.
- *Provide Political Access on Important Issues*—Strategy and policy decisions with significant negative consequences for middle managers will motivate intervention behavior from them. If middle managers do not have an opportunity to take a position on such decisions in appropriate political forums, they are capable of successfully resisting the decisions after they are made. Providing such political access provides strategists with information that otherwise might not be available and that could be useful in managing intervention behavior.[12]

Governance Issues

A "director," according to Webster's Dictionary, is "one of a group of persons entrusted with the overall direction of a corporate enterprise." A *board of directors* is a group of individuals who are elected by the ownership of a corporation to have oversight and guidance over management and who look out for shareholders' interests. The act of oversight and direction is referred to as *governance.* The National Association of Corporate Directors defines governance as "the characteristic of ensuring that long-term strategic objectives and plans are established and that the proper management structure is in place to achieve those objectives, while at the same time making sure that the structure functions to maintain the corporation's integrity, reputation, and responsibility to its various constituencies." This broad scope of responsibility for the board shows how boards are being held accountable for the entire performance of the firm. In the Worldcom, Tyco, and Enron bankruptcies and scandals, the firms' boards of directors were sued by shareholders for mismanaging their interests. New accounting rules in the United States and Europe are being passed to enhance corporate-governance codes and to require much more extensive financial disclosure among publicly-held firms. The roles and duties of a board of directors can be divided into four broad categories, as indicated in Table 6-7.

Until recently, boards of directors did most of their work sitting around polished wooden tables. However, Hewlett-Packard's directors, among many others, now log onto their own special board Web site twice a week and conduct business based on extensive confidential briefing information posted there by the firm's top management team. Then the board members meet face to face and fully informed every two months to discuss the biggest issues facing the firm. The "E-Commerce Perspective" focuses on "doing governance online."

Today, boards of directors are composed mostly of outsiders who are becoming more involved in organizations' strategic management. The trend in the United States is toward much greater board member accountability with smaller boards, now averaging 12 members rather than 18 as they did a few years ago. *BusinessWeek* recently evaluated the boards of most large U.S. companies and provided the following "principles of good governance":

1. No more than two directors are current or former company executives.
2. No directors do business with the company or accept consulting or legal fees from the firm.
3. The audit, compensation, and nominating committees are made up solely of outside directors.
4. Each director owns a large equity stake in the company, excluding stock options.
5. At least one outside director has extensive experience in the company's core business and at least one has been CEO of an equivalent-size company.
6. Fully employed directors sit on no more than four boards and retirees sit on no more than seven.
7. Each director attends at least 75 percent of all meetings.
8. The board meets regularly without management present and evaluates its own performance annually.
9. The audit committee meets at least four times a year.
10. The board is frugal on executive pay, diligent in CEO succession oversight responsibilities, and prompt to act when trouble arises.
11. The CEO is not also the Chairperson of the Board.
12. Shareholders have considerable power and information to choose and replace directors.
13. Stock options are considered a corporate expense.
14. There are no interlocking directorships (where a director or CEO sits on another director's board).[13]

TABLE 6-7 Board of Director Duties and Responsibilities

1. CONTROL AND OVERSIGHT OVER MANAGEMENT
   a. Select the Chief Executive Officer (CEO).
   b. Sanction the CEO's team.
   c. Provide the CEO with a forum.
   d. Ensure managerial competency.
   e. Evaluate management's performance.
   f. Set management's salary levels, including fringe benefits.
   g. Guarantee managerial integrity through continuous auditing.
   h. Chart the corporate course.
   i. Devise and revise policies to be implemented by management.

2. ADHERENCE TO LEGAL PRESCRIPTIONS
   a. Keep abreast of new laws.
   b. Ensure the entire organization fulfills legal prescriptions.
   c. Pass bylaws and related resolutions.
   d. Select new directors.
   e. Approve capital budgets.
   f. Authorize borrowing, new stock issues, bonds, and so on.

3. CONSIDERATION OF STAKEHOLDERS' INTERESTS
   a. Monitor product quality.
   b. Facilitate upward progression in employee quality of work life.
   c. Review labor policies and practices.
   d. Improve the customer climate.
   e. Keep community relations at the highest level.
   f. Use influence to better governmental, professional association, and educational contacts.
   g. Maintain good public image.

4. ADVANCEMENT OF STOCKHOLDERS' RIGHTS
   a. Preserve stockholders' equity.
   b. Stimulate corporate growth so that the firm will survive and flourish.
   c. Guard against equity dilution.
   d. Ensure equitable stockholder representation.
   e. Inform stockholders through letters, reports, and meetings.
   f. Declare proper dividends.
   g. Guarantee corporate survival.

BusinessWeek identified some of the "worst" boards as those at Apple, Conseco, Gap, Kmart, Qwest, Tyson Foods, and Xerox the "best" boards were those at 3M, Apria Healthcare, Colgate-Palmolive, General Electric, Home Depot, Intel, Johnson & Johnson, Medtronic, Pfizer, and Texas Instruments. Being a member of a board of directors today requires much more time, is much more difficult, and requires much more technical knowledge and financial commitment than in the past. Jeff Sonnerfeld, associate dean of the Yale School of Management, says, "Boards of directors are now rolling up their sleeves and becoming much more closely involved with management decision-making." Since

E-COMMERCE PERSPECTIVE

Board of Directors Doing Their Work Online

Directors today must have a better understanding of their firms' operations and doing business online on their own private, secure sites is now the practice of 23 percent of corporations in the United States. In addition to HP, other firms that have boards doing most of their business online include Cinergy, Albertson's, Intel, Motorola, and Tyco International. Some of these firms say they feel safer sending out confidential information electronically than relying on couriers to hand-deliver briefing packets.

The Sarbanes-Oxley Act of 2002 includes governance reforms that require audit committees of boards to meet far more frequently than in the past, so online meetings are especially well received by these members of boards. This act establishes "best practices" of boards of directors of public firms; even private firms are rapidly moving to adopt these new standards and procedures.

Several lessons that pioneering firms offer to others in bringing boards of directors online are these:

1. Establish strong security, password protected log-in, and firewalls on the special board of directors Web site.

2. Keep bulky graphics to a minimum since many directors at home or in hotels do not have fast Internet access.

3. Establish a telephone hotline to provide directors with technical support as needed.

4. Design the site in an easy manner where directors can easily access historical speeches and so on.

5. Establish instant messaging, e-mail, and Web conferencing so directors can interact vigorously even though they may be thousands of miles apart.

An advantage of online board meetings is that the most talkative, strong-willed directors are less able to dominate discussions. E-mail allows more private contact between directors, and this is an advantage. However, some CEOs feel threatened by directors who can scheme and plan together on their own through the special board Web site.

Source: Adapted from George Anders, "Run a Board Meeting," *Wall Street Journal* (September 15, 2003): R6.

---

the Enron and Worldcom scandals, company CEOs and boards are required to personally certify financial statements; company loans to company executives and directors are illegal, and there is faster reporting of insider stock transactions.

Just as directors are beginning to place more emphasis on staying informed about an organization's health and operations, they are also taking a more active role in ensuring that publicly-issued documents are accurate representations of a firm's status. It is becoming widely recognized that a board of directors has legal responsibilities to stockholders and society for all company activities, for corporate performance, and for ensuring that a firm has an effective strategy. Failure to accept responsibility for auditing or evaluating a firm's strategy is considered a serious breach of a director's duties. Stockholders, government agencies, and customers are filing legal suits against directors for fraud, omissions, inaccurate disclosures, lack of due diligence, and culpable ignorance about a firm's operations with increasing frequency. Liability insurance for directors has become exceptionally expensive and has caused numerous directors to resign.

More than 50 percent of outside directors at Fortune 500 firms have quit in recent years.[14] The 12 former Worldcom directors paid $25 million out of pocket to settle shareholder claims, and this has set a precedent for director liability. Among the

Fortune 1,000 firms, board member average pay increased 32 percent since Sarbanes-Oxley was enacted in 2002 to $57,000 annually. This is commensurate with members' increased responsibility and liability. In the last 10 years, the percentage of those boards that include at least one woman rose from 63 to 82 percent; the percentage of those boards that have a least one member of an ethnic minority rose from 44 to 76 percent.

The Sarbanes-Oxley Act resulted in scores of boardroom overhauls among publicly-traded companies. The jobs of chief executive and chairman are now held by separate persons, and board audit committees must now have at least one financial expert as a member. Board audit committees now meet 10 or more times per year, rather than 3 or 4 times as they did prior to the Act. The Act put an end to the "country club" atmosphere of most boards and has shifted power from CEOs to directors. Although aimed at public companies, the Act has also had a similar impact on privately owned companies.[15]

In Sweden, a new law has recently been passed requiring 25 percent female representation in boardrooms. The Norwegian government has passed a similar law that requires 40 percent of corporate director seats to go to women. In the United States, women currently hold about 13 percent of board seats at S&P 500 firms and 10 percent at S&P 1,500 firms. The Investor Responsibility Research Center in Washington, D.C. reports that minorities hold just 8.8 percent of board seats of S&P 1,500 companies. Progressive firms realize that women and minorities ask different questions and make different suggestions in boardrooms than white men, which is helpful because women and minorities comprise much of the consumer base everywhere.

A direct response of increased pressure on directors to stay informed and execute their responsibilities is that audit committees are becoming commonplace. A board of directors should conduct an annual strategy audit in much the same fashion that it reviews the annual financial audit. In performing such an audit, a board could work jointly with operating management and/or seek outside counsel. Boards should play a role beyond that of performing a strategic audit. They should provide greater input and advice in the strategy-formulation process to ensure that strategists are providing for the long-term needs of the firm. This is being done through the formation of three particular board committees: nominating committees to propose candidates for the board and senior officers of the firm; compensation committees to evaluate the performance of top executives and determine the terms and conditions of their employment; and audit committees to give board-level attention to company accounting and financial policies and performance.

CONCLUSION

VISIT THE NET

Provides answers to "Frequently Asked Questions About Strategic Planning." (www.allianceonline.org/ faqs.html)

The essence of strategy formulation is an assessment of whether an organization is doing the right things and how it can be more effective in what it does. Every organization should be wary of becoming a prisoner of its own strategy, because even the best strategies become obsolete sooner or later. Regular reappraisal of strategy helps management avoid complacency. Objectives and strategies should be consciously developed and coordinated and should not merely evolve out of day-to-day operating decisions.

An organization with no sense of direction and no coherent strategy precipitates its own demise. When an organization does not know where it wants to go, it usually ends up some place it does not want to be. Every organization needs to consciously establish and communicate clear objectives and strategies.

Modern strategy-formulation tools and concepts are described in this chapter and integrated into a practical three-stage framework. Tools such as the SWOT Matrix, SPACE Matrix, BCG Matrix, IE Matrix, and QSPM can significantly enhance the quality of strategic decisions, but they should never be used to dictate the choice of strategies. Behavioral, cultural, and political aspects of strategy generation and selection are always important to consider and manage. Because of increased legal pressure from outside groups, boards of directors are assuming a more active role in strategy analysis and choice. This is a positive trend for organizations.

We invite you to visit the David page on the Prentice Hall Companion Web site at www.prenhall.com/david for this chapter's review quiz.

KEY TERMS AND CONCEPTS

Aggressive Quadrant (p. 227)

Attractiveness Scores (AS) (p. 243)

Board of Directors (p. 246)

Boston Consulting Group (BCG) Matrix (p. 227)

Business Portfolio (p. 227)

Cash Cows (p. 231)

Champions (p. 246)

Competitive Advantage (CA) (p. 225)

Competitive Quadrant (p. 227)

Conservative Quadrant (p. 227)

Culture (p. 244)

Decision Stage (p. 219)

Defensive Quadrant (p. 227)

Directional Vector (p. 227)

Dogs (p. 231)

Environmental Stability (ES) (p. 225)

Financial Strength (FS) (p. 225)

Governance (p. 247)

Grand Strategy Matrix (p. 237)

Halo Error (p. 219)

Industry Strength (IS) (p. 225)

Input Stage (p. 219)

Internal-External (IE) Matrix (p. 227)

Matching (p. 220)

Matching Stage (p. 219)

Quantitative Strategic Planning Matrix (QSPM) (p. 239)

Question Marks (p. 230)

Relative Market Share Position (p. 227)

SO Strategies (p. 221)

Stars (p. 230)

Strategic Position and Action Evaluation (SPACE) Matrix (p. 225)

Strategy-Formulation Framework (p. 219)

Strengths-Weaknesses-Opportunities-Threats (SWOT) Matrix (p. 221)

ST Strategies (p. 221)

Sum Total Attractiveness Scores (STAS) (p. 243)

Sustainability (p. 218)

Total Attractiveness Scores (TAS) (p. 243)

WO Strategies (p. 221)

WT Strategies (p. 221)

ISSUES FOR REVIEW AND DISCUSSION

1. How would application of the strategy-formulation framework differ from a small to a large organization?
2. What types of strategies would you recommend for an organization that achieves total weighted scores of 3.6 on the IFE and 1.2 on the EFE Matrix?
3. Given the following information, develop a SPACE Matrix for the XYZ Corporation: FS = +2; ES = −6; CA = −2; IS = +4.
4. Given the information in the following table, develop a BCG Matrix and an IE Matrix:

Divisions	1	2	3
Profits	$10	$15	$25
Sales	$100	$50	$100
Relative Market Share	0.2	0.5	0.8
Industry Growth Rate	+.20	+.10	−.10
IFE Total Weighted Scores	1.6	3.1	2.2
EFE Total Weighted Scores	2.5	1.8	3.3

5. Explain the steps involved in developing a QSPM.
6. How would you develop a set of objectives for your school or business?
7. What do you think is the appropriate role of a board of directors in strategic management? Why?
8. Discuss the limitations of various strategy-formulation analytical techniques.
9. Explain why cultural factors should be an important consideration in analyzing and choosing among alternative strategies.
10. How are the SWOT Matrix, SPACE Matrix, BCG Matrix, IE Matrix, and Grand Strategy Matrix similar? How are they different?
11. How would for-profit and nonprofit organizations differ in their applications of the strategy-formulation framework?
12. Develop a SPACE Matrix for a company that is weak financially and is a weak competitor. The industry for this company is pretty stable, but the industry's projected growth in revenues and profits is not good. Label all axes and quadrants.
13. List four limitations of a BCG Matrix.
14. Make up an example to show clearly and completely that you can develop an IE Matrix for a three-division company, where each division has $10, $20, and $40 in revenues and $2, $4, and $1 in profits. State other assumptions needed. Label axes and quadrants.
15. What procedures could be necessary if the SPACE vector falls right on the axis between the Competitive and Defensive quadrants?
16. In a BCG Matrix or the Grand Strategy Matrix, what would you consider to be a rapid market (or industry) growth rate?
17. What are the pros and cons of a company (and country) participating in a Pollution Register?
18. How does the Sarbanes-Oxley Act of 2002 impact boards of directors?
19. Rank *BusinessWeek's* "principles of good governance" from 1 to 14 (1 being most important and 14 least important) to reveal your assessment of these new rules.
20. Why is it important to work row by row instead of column by column in preparing a QSPM?
21. Why should one avoid putting double 4's in a row in preparing a QSPM?
22. Envision a QSPM with no weight column. Would that still be a useful analysis? Why or why not? What do you lose by deleting the weight column?
23. Prepare a BCG Matrix for a two-division firm with sales of $5 and $8 versus profits of $3 and $1, respectively? State assumptions for the RMSP and IGR axes to enable you to construct the diagram.
24. Consider developing a before-and-after BCG or IE Matrix to reveal the expected results of your proposed strategies. What limitation of the analysis would this procedure overcome somewhat?
25. If a firm has the leading market share in its industry, where on the BCG Matrix would the circle lie?
26. If a firm competes in a very unstable industry, such as telecommunications, where on the ES axis of the SPACE Matrix would you plot the appropriate point?
27. Why do you think the SWOT Matrix is the most widely used of all strategy matrices?
28. The strategy templates described at the www.strategyclub.com Web site have templates for all of the Chapter 6 matrices. How could those templates be useful in preparing an example BCG or IE Matrix?

NOTES

1. Jane Kim, "Business Schools Take a Page from Kinder, Gentler Textbook," *Wall Street Journal* (October 22, 2003): B2C.
2. R. T. Lenz, "Managing the Evolution of the Strategic Planning Process," *Business Horizons* 30, no. 1 (January–February 1987): 37.
3. Robert Grant, "The Resource-Based Theory of Competitive Advantage: Implications for Strategy Formulation," *California Management Review* (Spring 1991): 114.
4. Heinz Weihrich, "The TOWS Matrix: A Tool for Situational Analysis," *Long Range Planning* 15,

no. 2 (April 1982): 61. Note: Although Dr. Weihrich first modified SWOT analysis to form the TOWS matrix, the acronym SWOT is much more widely used than TOWS in practice, so this eleventh edition reflects a change to SWOT from the use of TOWS in previous editions.

5. Greg, Dess, G. T. Lumpkin and Alan, Eisner, *Strategic Management: Text and Cases*, (New York: McGraw-Hill/Irwin, 2006): 72.

6. H. Rowe, R. Mason, and K. Dickel, *Strategic Management and Business Policy: A Methodological Approach* (Reading, MA: Addison-Wesley Publishing Co. Inc., 1982): 155–156. Reprinted with permission of the publisher.

7. Fred David, "The Strategic Planning Matrix— A Quantitative Approach," *Long Range Planning* 19, no. 5 (October 1986): 102; Andre Gib and Robert Margulies, "Making Competitive Intelligence Relevant to the User," *Planning Review* 19, no. 3 (May–June 1991): 21.

8. Fred David, "Computer-Assisted Strategic Planning in Small Businesses," *Journal of Systems Management* 36, no. 7 (July 1985): 24–34.

9. Jon Swartz, "How Will Compaq, H-P Fit Together?" *USA Today* (September 6, 2001): 3B.

10. Y. Allarie and M. Firsirotu, "How to Implement Radical Strategies in Large Organizations," *Sloan Management Review* 26, no. 3 (Spring 1985): 19. Another excellent article is P. Shrivastava, "Integrating Strategy Formulation with Organizational Culture," *Journal of Business Strategy* 5, no. 3 (Winter 1985): 103–111.

11. James Brian Quinn, *Strategies for Changes: Logical Incrementalism* (Homewood, IL: Richard D. Irwin, 1980): 128–145. These political tactics are listed in A. Thompson and A. Strickland, *Strategic Management: Concepts and Cases* (Plano, TX: Business Publications, 1984): 261.

12. William Guth and Ian MacMillan, "Strategy Implementation Versus Middle Management Self-Interest," *Strategic Management Journal* 7, no. 4 (July–August 1986): 321.

13. Louis Lavelle, "The Best and Worst Boards," *BusinessWeek* (October 7, 2002): 104–110.

14. Anne Fisher, "Board Seats Are Going Begging," *Fortune* (May 16, 2005): 204.

15. Matt Murray, "Private Companies Also Feel Pressure to Clean Up Acts," *Wall Street Journal* (July 22, 2003): B1.

CURRENT READINGS

Buswick, Ted, Clare Morgan, and Kirsten Lange. "Poetry in the Boardroom: Thinking Beyond the Facts." *Journal of Business Strategy* 26, no. 1 (2005): 34.

Dalton, D. R., and C. M. Dalton. "Executive Digest: Spotlight on Corporate Governance." *Business Horizons* 48, no. 2 (March–April 2005): 95.

Delmas, M., Y. Tokat. "Deregulation, Goverance Structures, and Efficiency: The U.S. Electric Utility." *Strategic Management Journal* 26, no. 5 (May 2005): 441.

Deutsch, Y. "The Impact of Board Composition on Firms' Critical Decisions: A Meta-Analytic Review." *Journal of Management* 31, no. 3 (June 2005): 424.

Fram, E. H. "Governance Reform—It's Only Just Begun." *Business Horizons* 47, no. 6 (November–December 2004): 10.

Hillman, A. J. "Politicians on the Board of Directors: Do Connections Affect the Bottom Line?" *Journal of Management* 31, no. 3 (June 2005): 464.

Morris, D. "A New Tool for Strategy Analysis: The Opportunity Model." *Journal Business Strategy* 26, no. 3 (2005): 50.

Peng, M. W. "Outside Directors and Firm Performance During Institutional Transitions." *Strategic Management Journal* 25, no. 5 (May 2004): 453.

Roos, J. "Opinion: Sparking Strategic Imagination." *MIT Sloan Management Review* 46, no. 1 (Fall 2004): 96.

Shafer, S. M., H. J. Smith, and J. C. Linder. "The Power of Business Models." *Business Horizons* 48, no. 3 (May–June 2005): 199.

Sussland, Willy A. "Business Value and Corporate Governance: A New Approach." *Journal of Business Strategy* 25, no. 1 (2004): 49.

Yin, X., and E. J. Zajac. "The Strategy/Governance Structure Fit Relationship: Theory and Evidence in Franchising Arrangements." *Strategic Management Journal* 25, no. 4 (April 2004): 365.

experiential exercises

Experiential Exercise 6A

Developing a SWOT Matrix for Google

PURPOSE

The most widely used strategy-formulation technique among U.S. firms is the SWOT Matrix. This exercise requires the development of a SWOT Matrix for Google. Matching key external and internal factors in a SWOT Matrix requires good intuitive and conceptual skills. You will improve with practice in developing a SWOT Matrix.

INSTRUCTIONS

Recall from Experiential Exercise 1A that you already may have determined Google's external opportunites/threats and internal strengths/weaknesses. This information could be used to complete this exercise. Follow the steps outlined as follows:

Step 1   On a separate sheet of paper, construct a large nine-cell diagram that will represent your SWOT Matrix. Appropriately label the cells.

Step 2   Appropriately record Google's opportunities/threats and strengths/weaknesses in your diagram.

Step 3   Match external and internal factors to generate feasible alternative strategies for Google. Record SO, WO, ST, and WT strategies in the appropriate cells of the SWOT Matrix. Use the proper notation to indicate the rationale for the strategies. You do not necessarily have to have strategies in all four strategy cells.

Step 4   Compare your SWOT Matrix to another student's SWOT Matrix. Discuss any major differences.

Experiential Exercise 6B

Developing a SPACE Matrix for Google

PURPOSE

Should Google pursue aggressive, conservative, competitive, or defensive strategies? Develop a SPACE Matrix for Google to answer this question. Elaborate on the strategic implications of your directional vector. Be specific in terms of strategies that could benefit Google.

INSTRUCTIONS

Step 1   Join with two other people in class and develop a joint SPACE Matrix for Google.

Step 2   Diagram your SPACE Matrix on the board. Compare your matrix with other team's matrices.

Step 3   Discuss the implications of your SPACE Matrix.

Experiential Exercise 6C

Developing a BCG Matrix for Google

PURPOSE

Portfolio matrices are widely used by multidivisional organizations to help identify and select strategies to pursue. A BCG analysis identifies particular divisions that should receive fewer resources than others. It may identify some divisions that need to be divested. This exercise can give you practice developing a BCG Matrix.

INSTRUCTIONS

Step 1   Place the following five column headings at the top of a separate sheet of paper: Divisions, Revenues, Profits, Relative Market Share Position, Industry Growth Rate.

Step 2   Complete a BCG Matrix for Google.

Step 3   Compare your BCG Matrix to other students' matrices. Discuss any major differences.

**Experiential
Exercise 6D**

*Developing a QSPM
for Google*

PURPOSE

This exercise can give you practice developing a Quantitative Strategic Planning Matrix to determine the relative attractiveness of various strategic alternatives.

INSTRUCTIONS

Step 1   Join with two other students in class to develop a joint QSPM for Google.

Step 2   Go to the blackboard and record your strategies and their Sum Total Attractiveness Score. Compare your team's strategies and Sum Total Attractiveness Score to those of other teams. Be sure not to assign the same AS score in a given row. Recall that dashes should be inserted all the way across a given row when used.

Step 3   Discuss any major differences.

**Experiential
Exercise 6E**

*Formulating Individual
Strategies*

PURPOSE

Individuals and organizations are alike in many ways. Each has competitors, and each should plan for the future. Every individual and organization faces some external opportunities and threats and has some internal strengths and weaknesses. Both individuals and organizations establish objectives and allocate resources. These and other similarities make it possible for individuals to use many strategic-management concepts and tools. This exercise is designed to demonstrate how the SWOT Matrix can be used by individuals to plan their futures. As one nears completion of a college degree and begins interviewing for jobs, planning can be particularly important.

INSTRUCTIONS

On a separate sheet of paper, construct a SWOT Matrix. Include what you consider to be your major external opportunities, your major external threats, your major strengths, and your major weaknesses. An internal weakness may be a low grade point average. An external opportunity may be that your university offers a graduate program that interests you. Match key external and internal factors by recording in the appropriate cell of the matrix alternative strategies or actions that would allow you to capitalize upon your strengths, overcome your weaknesses, take advantage of your external opportunities, and minimize the impact of external threats. Be sure to use the appropriate matching notation in the strategy cells of the matrix. Because every individual (and organization) is unique, there is no one right answer to this exercise.

Experiential Exercise 6F

The Mach Test

PURPOSE

The purpose of this exercise is to enhance your understanding and awareness of the impact that behavioral and political factors can have on strategy analysis and choice.

INSTRUCTIONS

Step 1 On a separate sheet of paper, number from 1 to 10. For each of the 10 statements given as follows, record a *1, 2, 3, 4,* or *5* to indicate your attitude, where

1 = I disagree a lot.
2 = I disagree a little.
3 = My attitude is neutral.
4 = I agree a little.
5 = I agree a lot.

1. The best way to handle people is to tell them what they want to hear.
2. When you ask someone to do something for you, it is best to give the real reason for wanting it, rather than a reason that might carry more weight.
3. Anyone who completely trusts anyone else is asking for trouble.
4. It is hard to get ahead without cutting corners here and there.
5. It is safest to assume that all people have a vicious streak, and it will come out when they are given a chance.
6. One should take action only when it is morally right.
7. Most people are basically good and kind.
8. There is no excuse for lying to someone else.
9. Most people forget more easily the death of their father than the loss of their property.
10. Generally speaking, people won't work hard unless they're forced to do so.

Step 2 Add up the numbers you recorded beside statements 1, 3, 4, 5, 9, and 10. This sum is Subtotal One. For the other four statements, reverse the numbers you recorded, so a 5 becomes a *1*, 4 becomes *2*, 2 becomes *4*, 1 becomes *5*, and 3 remains *3*. Then add those four numbers to get Subtotal Two. Finally, add Subtotal One and Subtotal Two to get your Final Score.

YOUR FINAL SCORE

Your Final Score is your Machiavellian Score. Machiavellian principles are defined in a dictionary as "manipulative, dishonest, deceiving, and favoring political expediency over morality." These tactics are not desirable, are not ethical, and are not recommended in the strategic-management process! You may, however, encounter some highly Machiavellian individuals in your career, so beware. It is important for strategists not to manipulate others in the pursuit of organizational objectives. Individuals today recognize and resent manipulative tactics more than ever before. J. R. Ewing (on a television show in the 1980s, *Dallas*) was a good example of someone who was a high Mach (score over 30). The National Opinion Research Center used this short quiz in a random sample of U.S. adults and found the national average Final Score to be 25.[1] The higher your score, the more Machiavellian (manipulative) you tend to be. The following scale is descriptive of individual scores on this test:

- Below 16: Never uses manipulation as a tool.
- 16 to 20: Rarely uses manipulation as a tool.
- 21 to 25: Sometimes uses manipulation as a tool.
- 26 to 30: Often uses manipulation as a tool.
- Over 30: Always uses manipulation as a tool.

TEST DEVELOPMENT

The Mach (Machiavellian) test was developed by Dr. Richard Christie, whose research suggests the following tendencies:

1. Men generally are more Machiavellian than women.
2. There is no significant difference between high Machs and low Machs on measures of intelligence or ability.
3. Although high Machs are detached from others, they are detached in a pathological sense.
4. Machiavellian scores are not statistically related to authoritarian values.
5. High Machs tend to be in professions that emphasize the control and manipulation of individuals—for example, law, psychiatry, and behavioral science.
6. Machiavellianism is not significantly related to major demographic characteristics such as educational level or marital status.
7. High Machs tend to come from a city or have urban backgrounds.
8. Older adults tend to have lower Mach scores than younger adults.[2]

A classic book on power relationships, *The Prince*, was written by Niccolo Machiavelli. Several excerpts from *The Prince* follow:

> Men must either be cajoled or crushed, for they will revenge themselves for slight wrongs, while for grave ones they cannot. The injury therefore that you do to a man should be such that you need not fear his revenge.
>
> We must bear in mind . . . that there is nothing more difficult and dangerous, or more doubtful of success, than an attempt to introduce a new order of things in any state. The innovator has for enemies all those who derived advantages from the old order of things, while those who expect to be benefitted by the new institution will be but lukewarm defenders.
>
> A wise prince, therefore, will steadily pursue such a course that the citizens of his state will always and under all circumstances feel the need for his authority, and will therefore always prove faithful to him.
>
> A prince should seem to be merciful, faithful, humane, religious, and upright, and should even be so in reality, but he should have his mind so trained that, when occasion requires it, he may know how to change to the opposite.[3]

Notes

1. Richard Christie and Florence Geis, *Studies in Machiavellianism* (Orlando, FL: Academic Press, 1970). Material in this exercise adapted with permission of the authors and the Academic Press.
2. Ibid., 82–83.
3. Niccolo Machiavelli, *The Prince* (New York: The Washington Press, 1963).

Experiential Exercise 6G

Developing a BCG Matrix for My University

PURPOSE

Developing a BCG Matrix for many nonprofit organizations, including colleges and universities, is a useful exercise. Of course, there are no profits for each division or department—and in some cases no revenues. However, you can be creative in performing a BCG Matrix. For example, the pie slice in the circles can represent the number of majors receiving jobs upon graduation, the number of faculty teaching in that area, or some other variable that you believe is important to consider. The size of the circles can represent the number of students majoring in particular departments or areas.

INSTRUCTIONS

Step 1 On a separate sheet of paper, develop a BCG Matrix for your university. Include all academic schools, departments, or colleges.

Step 2 Diagram your BCG Matrix on the blackboard.

Step 3 Discuss differences among the BCG Matrices on the board.

Experiential Exercise 6H

The Role of Boards of Directors

PURPOSE

This exercise will give you a better understanding of the role of boards of directors in formulating, implementing, and evaluating strategies.

INSTRUCTIONS

Identify a person in your community who serves on a board of directors. Make an appointment to interview that person, and seek answers to the following questions. Summarize your findings in a five-minute oral report to the class.

- On what board are you a member?
- How often does the board meet?
- How long have you served on the board?
- What role does the board play in this company?
- How has the role of the board changed in recent years?
- What changes would you like to see in the role of the board?
- To what extent do you prepare for the board meeting?
- To what extent are you involved in strategic management of the firm?

Experiential Exercise 6I

Locating Companies in a Grand Strategy Matrix

PURPOSE

The Grand Strategy Matrix is a popular tool for formulating alternative strategies. All organizations can be positioned in one of the Grand Strategy Matrix's four strategy quadrants. The divisions of a firm likewise could be positioned. The Grand Strategy Matrix is based on two evaluative dimensions: competitive position and market growth. Appropriate strategies for an organization to consider are listed in sequential order of attractiveness in each quadrant of the matrix. This exercise gives you experience using a Grand Strategy Matrix.

INSTRUCTIONS

Using the year-end 2004 financial information provided, prepare a Grand Strategy Matrix on a separate sheet of paper. Write the respective company names in the appropriate quadrant of the matrix. Based on this analysis, what strategies are recommended for each company?

COMPANY	COMPANY SALES/PROFIT GROWTH (%)	INDUSTRY	INDUSTRY SALES/PROFIT GROWTH (%)
McDonald's	+11/+51	Restaurant	+16/+38
New York Times	+2/−3	Newspapers	+8/0
JCPenney	+4/+83	Retailers	+9/+1
Sears, Roebuck	−12/−90	Retailers	+9/+1
Anheuser-Busch	+6/+8	Beverages	+7/+29
Washington Mutual	−11/−35	Insurance	−15/−3
Merck	+2/−12	Pharmaceuticals	+12/+33
Southwest Airlines	+10/−29	Airlines	+11/−53
AT&T	−12/0	Telecommunications	+1/−29

Source: Adapted from *BusinessWeek* (April 4, 2005): 114–122.

Implementing Strategies: Management and Operations Issues

chapter objectives

After studying this chapter, you should be able to do the following:

1. Explain why strategy implementation is more difficult than strategy formulation.

2. Discuss the importance of annual objectives and policies in achieving organizational commitment for strategies to be implemented.

3. Explain why organizational structure is so important in strategy implementation.

4. Compare and contrast restructuring and reengineering.

5. Describe the relationships between production/operations and strategy implementation.

6. Explain how a firm can effectively link performance and pay to strategies.

7. Discuss employee stock ownership plans (ESOPs) as a strategic-management concept.

8. Describe how to modify an organizational culture to support new strategies.

9. Discuss the culture in Mexico, Russia, and Japan.

10. Describe the glass ceiling in the United States.

experiential exercises

"notable quotes"

You want your people to run the business as if it were their own.
William Fulmer

Poor Ike; when he was a general, he gave an order and it was carried out. Now, he's going to sit in that office and give an order and not a damn thing is going to happen.
Harry Truman

Changing your pay plan is a big risk, but not changing it could be a bigger one.
Nancy Perry

Objectives can be compared to a compass bearing by which a ship navigates. A compass bearing is firm, but in actual navigation, a ship may veer off its course for many miles. Without a compass bearing, a ship would neither find its port nor be able to estimate the time required to get there.
Peter Drucker

The best game plan in the world never blocked or tackled anybody.
Vince Lombardi

Pretend that every single person you meet has a sign around his or her neck that says, "Make me feel important."
Mary Kay Ash

The strategic-management process does not end when the firm decides what strategy or strategies to pursue. There must be a translation of strategic thought into strategic action. This translation is much easier if managers and employees of the firm understand the business, feel a part of the company, and through involvement in strategy-formulation activities have become committed to helping the organization succeed. Without understanding and commitment, strategy-implementation efforts face major problems.

Implementing strategy affects an organization from top to bottom; it affects all the functional and divisional areas of a business. It is beyond the purpose and scope of this text to examine all of the business administration concepts and tools important in strategy implementation. This chapter focuses on management issues most central to implementing strategies in the year 2005, and Chapter 8 focuses on marketing, finance/accounting, R&D, and management information systems issues.

VISIT THE NET

Gives a good definition of strategy implementation.
(www.csuchico.edu/mgmt/ strategy/module/ sld044.htm)

> Even the most technically perfect strategic plan will serve little purpose if it is not implemented. Many organizations tend to spend an inordinate amount of time, money, and effort on developing the strategic plan, treating the means and circumstances under which it will be implemented as afterthoughts! Change comes through implementation and evaluation, not through the plan. A technically imperfect plan that is implemented well will achieve more than the perfect plan that never gets off the paper on which it is typed.[1]

The Nature of Strategy Implementation

The strategy-implementation stage of strategic management is revealed in Figure 7-1. Successful strategy formulation does not guarantee successful strategy implementation. It is always more difficult to do something (strategy implementation) than to say you are going to do it (strategy formulation)! Although inextricably linked, strategy implementation is fundamentally different from strategy formulation. Strategy formulation and implementation can be contrasted in the following ways:

- Strategy formulation is positioning forces before the action.
- Strategy implementation is managing forces during the action.
- Strategy formulation focuses on effectiveness.
- Strategy implementation focuses on efficiency.
- Strategy formulation is primarily an intellectual process.
- Strategy implementation is primarily an operational process.
- Strategy formulation requires good intuitive and analytical skills.
- Strategy implementation requires special motivation and leadership skills.
- Strategy formulation requires coordination among a few individuals.
- Strategy implementation requires coordination among many individuals.

Strategy-formulation concepts and tools do not differ greatly for small, large, for-profit, or nonprofit organizations. However, strategy implementation varies substantially among different types and sizes of organizations. Implementing strategies requires such actions as altering sales territories, adding new departments, closing facilities, hiring new employees, changing an organization's pricing strategy,

FIGURE 7-1

Comprehensive Strategic-Management Model

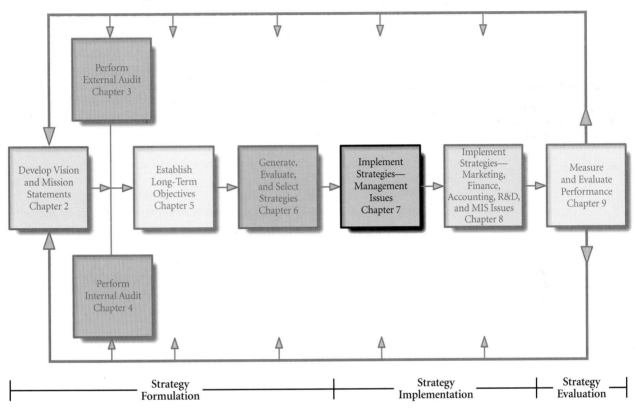

developing financial budgets, developing new employee benefits, establishing cost-control procedures, changing advertising strategies, building new facilities, training new employees, transferring managers among divisions, and building a better management information system. These types of activities obviously differ greatly between manufacturing, service, and governmental organizations.

required for implementing strategies

Management Perspectives

In all but the smallest organizations, the transition from strategy formulation to strategy implementation requires a shift in responsibility from strategists to divisional and functional managers. Implementation problems can arise because of this shift in responsibility, especially if strategy-formulation decisions come as a surprise to middle- and lower-level managers. Managers and employees are motivated more by perceived self-interests than by organizational interests, unless the two coincide. Therefore, it is essential that divisional and functional managers be involved as much as possible in strategy-formulation activities. Of equal importance, strategists should be involved as much as possible in strategy-implementation activities.

a shift in responsibility

mngrs + employees are motivated by self-interest

Management issues central to strategy implementation include establishing annual objectives, devising policies, allocating resources, altering an existing organizational structure, restructuring and reengineering, revising reward and incentive plans, minimizing resistance to change, matching managers with strategy, developing a strategy-supportive culture, adapting production/operations processes, developing an effective human resources function, and, if necessary, downsizing. Management changes are necessarily more extensive when strategies to be implemented move a firm in a major new direction.

Managers and employees throughout an organization should participate early and directly in strategy-implementation decisions. Their role in strategy implementation should build upon prior involvement in strategy-formulation activities. Strategists' genuine personal commitment to implementation is a necessary and powerful motivational force for managers and employees. Too often, strategists are too busy to actively support strategy-implementation efforts, and their lack of interest can be detrimental to organizational success. The rationale for objectives and strategies should be understood and clearly communicated throughout an organization. Major competitors' accomplishments, products, plans, actions, and performance should be apparent to all organizational members. Major external opportunities and threats should be clear, and managers' and employees' questions should be answered. Top-down flow of communication is essential for developing bottom-up support.

Firms need to develop a competitor focus at all hierarchical levels by gathering and widely distributing competitive intelligence; every employee should be able to benchmark her or his efforts against best-in-class competitors so that the challenge becomes personal. This is a challenge for strategists of the firm. Firms should provide training for both managers and employees to ensure that they have and maintain the skills necessary to be world-class performers.

Annual Objectives

Establishing annual objectives is a decentralized activity that directly involves all managers in an organization. Active participation in establishing annual objectives can lead to acceptance and commitment. *Annual objectives* are essential for strategy implementation because they (1) represent the basis for allocating resources; (2) are a primary mechanism for evaluating managers; (3) are the major instrument for monitoring progress toward achieving long-term objectives; and (4) establish organizational, divisional, and departmental priorities. Considerable time and effort should be devoted to ensuring that annual objectives are well conceived, consistent with long-term objectives, and supportive of strategies to be implemented. Approving, revising, or rejecting annual objectives is much more than a rubber-stamp activity. The purpose of annual objectives can be summarized as follows:

> Annual objectives serve as guidelines for action, directing and channeling efforts and activities of organization members. They provide a source of legitimacy in an enterprise by justifying activities to stakeholders. They serve as standards of performance. They serve as an important source of employee motivation and identification. They give incentives for managers and employees to perform. They provide a basis for organizational design.[2]

Clearly stated and communicated objectives are critical to success in all types and sizes of firms. Annual objectives, stated in terms of profitability, growth, and market share by business segment, geographic area, customer groups, and product, are common in organizations. Figure 7-2 illustrates how the Stamus Company could establish annual objectives based on long-term objectives. Table 7-1 reveals associated

FIGURE 7-2

The Stamus Company's Hierarchy of Aims

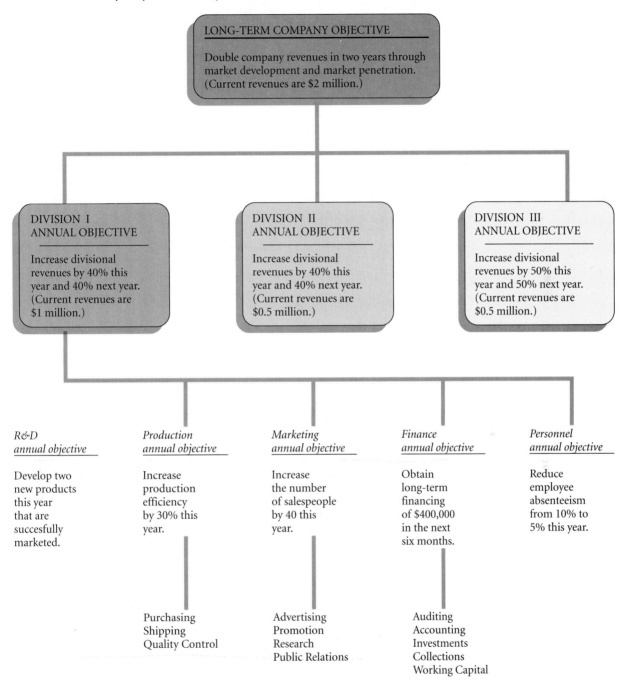

revenue figures that correspond to the objectives outlined in Figure 7-2. Note that, according to plan, the Stamus Company will slightly exceed its long-term objective of doubling company revenues between 2006 and 2008.

Figure 7-2 also reflects how a hierarchy of annual objectives can be established based on an organization's structure. Objectives should be consistent across

TABLE 7-1   The Stamus Company's Revenue
Expectations (in millions of dollars)

	2006	2007	2008
Division I Revenues	1.0	1.400	1.960
Division II Revenues	0.5	0.700	0.980
Division III Revenues	0.5	0.750	1.125
Total Company Revenues	**2.0**	**2.850**	**4.065**

hierarchical levels and form a network of supportive aims. *Horizontal consistency of objectives* is as important as *vertical consistency of objectives.* For instance, it would not be effective for manufacturing to achieve more than its annual objective of units produced if marketing could not sell the additional units.

Annual objectives should be measurable, consistent, reasonable, challenging, clear, communicated throughout the organization, characterized by an appropriate time dimension, and accompanied by commensurate rewards and sanctions. Too often, objectives are stated in generalities, with little operational usefulness. Annual objectives, such as "to improve communication" or "to improve performance," are not clear, specific, or measurable. Objectives should state quantity, quality, cost, and time—and also be verifiable. Terms and phrases such as *maximize, minimize, as soon as possible,* and *adequate* should be avoided.

Annual objectives should be compatible with employees' and managers' values and should be supported by clearly stated policies. More of something is not always better. Improved quality or reduced cost may, for example, be more important than quantity. It is important to tie rewards and sanctions to annual objectives so that employees and managers understand that achieving objectives is critical to successful strategy implementation. Clear annual objectives do not guarantee successful strategy implementation, but they do increase the likelihood that personal and organizational aims can be accomplished. Overemphasis on achieving objectives can result in undesirable conduct, such as faking the numbers, distorting the records, and letting objectives become ends in themselves. Managers must be alert to these potential problems.

Policies

Changes in a firm's strategic direction do not occur automatically. On a day-to-day basis, policies are needed to make a strategy work. Policies facilitate solving recurring problems and guide the implementation of strategy. Broadly defined, *policy* refers to specific guidelines, methods, procedures, rules, forms, and administrative practices established to support and encourage work toward stated goals. Policies are instruments for strategy implementation. Policies set boundaries, constraints, and limits on the kinds of administrative actions that can be taken to reward and sanction behavior; they clarify what can and cannot be done in pursuit of an organization's objectives. For example, Carnival's *Paradise* ship has a no-smoking policy anywhere, anytime aboard ship. It is the first cruise ship to comprehensively ban smoking. Another example of corporate policy relates to surfing the Web while at work. About 40 percent of companies today do not have a formal policy preventing employees from surfing the Internet, but software is being marketed now that allows firms to monitor how, when, where, and how long various employees use the Internet at work.

Policies let both employees and managers know what is expected of them, thereby increasing the likelihood that strategies will be implemented successfully. They provide a basis for management control, allow coordination across organizational units, and reduce the amount of time managers spend making decisions. Policies also clarify what work is to be done and by whom. They promote delegation of decision making to appropriate managerial levels where various problems usually arise. Many organizations have a policy manual that serves to guide and direct behavior. Wal-Mart has a policy that it calls the "10 Foot" Rule, whereby customers can find assistance within 10 feet of anywhere in the store. This is a welcomed policy in Japan where Wal-Mart is trying to gain a foothold; 58 percent of all retailers in Japan are mom-and-pop stores and consumers historically have had to pay "top yen" rather than "discounted prices" for merchandise.

Policies can apply to all divisions and departments (for example, "We are an equal opportunity employer"). Some policies apply to a single department ("Employees in this department must take at least one training and development course each year"). Whatever their scope and form, policies serve as a mechanism for implementing strategies and obtaining objectives. Policies should be stated in writing whenever possible. They represent the means for carrying out strategic decisions. Examples of policies that support a company strategy, a divisional objective, and a departmental objective are given in Table 7-2.

Some example issues that may require a management policy are as follows:

- To offer extensive or limited management development workshops and seminars
- To centralize or decentralize employee-training activities
- To recruit through employment agencies, college campuses, and/or newspapers
- To promote from within or to hire from the outside
- To promote on the basis of merit or on the basis of seniority
- To tie executive compensation to long-term and/or annual objectives
- To offer numerous or few employee benefits
- To negotiate directly or indirectly with labor unions
- To delegate authority for large expenditures or to centrally retain this authority
- To allow much, some, or no overtime work
- To establish a high- or low-safety stock of inventory
- To use one or more suppliers
- To buy, lease, or rent new production equipment
- To greatly or somewhat stress quality control
- To establish many or only a few production standards
- To operate one, two, or three shifts
- To discourage using insider information for personal gain
- To discourage sexual harassment
- To discourage smoking at work
- To discourage insider trading
- To discourage moonlighting

TABLE 7-2   A Hierarchy of Policies

Company Strategy

Acquire a chain of retail stores to meet our sales growth and profitability objectives.

Supporting Policies

1. "All stores will be open from 8 A.M. to 8 P.M. Monday through Saturday." (This policy could increase retail sales if stores currently are open only 40 hours a week.)
2. "All stores must submit a Monthly Control Data Report." (This policy could reduce expense-to-sales ratios.)
3. "All stores must support company advertising by contributing 5 percent of their total monthly revenues for this purpose." (This policy could allow the company to establish a national reputation.)
4. "All stores must adhere to the uniform pricing guidelines set forth in the Company Handbook." (This policy could help assure customers that the company offers a consistent product in terms of price and quality in all its stores.)

Divisional Objective

Increase the division's revenues from $10 million in 2005 to $15 million in 2006.

Supporting Policies

1. "Beginning in January 2005, each one of this division's salespersons must file a weekly activity report that includes the number of calls made, the number of miles traveled, the number of units sold, the dollar volume sold, and the number of new accounts opened." (This policy could ensure that salespersons do not place too great an emphasis in certain areas.)
2. "Beginning in January 2005, this division will return to its employees 5 percent of its gross revenues in the form of a Christmas bonus." (This policy could increase employee productivity.)
3. "Beginning in January 2005, inventory levels carried in warehouses will be decreased by 30 percent in accordance with a Just-in-Time (JIT) manufacturing approach." (This policy could reduce production expenses and thus free funds for increased marketing efforts.)

Production Department Objective

Increase production from 20,000 units in 2005 to 30,000 units in 2006.

Supporting Policies

1. "Beginning in January 2005, employees will have the option of working up to 20 hours of overtime per week." (This policy could minimize the need to hire additional employees.)
2. "Beginning in January 2005, perfect attendance awards in the amount of $100 will be given to all employees who do not miss a workday in a given year." (This policy could decrease absenteeism and increase productivity.)
3. "Beginning in January 2005, new equipment must be leased rather than purchased." (This policy could reduce tax liabilities and thus allow more funds to be invested in modernizing production processes.)

Resource Allocation

Resource allocation is a central management activity that allows for strategy execution. In organizations that do not use a strategic-management approach to decision making, resource allocation is often based on political or personal factors. Strategic management enables resources to be allocated according to priorities established by annual objectives.

Nothing could be more detrimental to strategic management and to organizational success than for resources to be allocated in ways not consistent with priorities indicated by approved annual objectives.

All organizations have at least four types of resources that can be used to achieve desired objectives: financial resources, physical resources, human resources, and technological resources. Allocating resources to particular divisions and departments does not mean that strategies will be successfully implemented. A number of factors commonly prohibit effective resource allocation, including an overprotection of resources, too great an emphasis on short-run financial criteria, organizational politics, vague strategy targets, a reluctance to take risks, and a lack of sufficient knowledge.

Below the corporate level, there often exists an absence of systematic thinking about resources allocated and strategies of the firm. Yavitz and Newman explain why:

> Managers normally have many more tasks than they can do. Managers must allocate time and resources among these tasks. Pressure builds up. Expenses are too high. The CEO wants a good financial report for the third quarter. Strategy formulation and implementation activities often get deferred. Today's problems soak up available energies and resources. Scrambled accounts and budgets fail to reveal the shift in allocation away from strategic needs to currently squeaking wheels.[3]

The real value of any resource allocation program lies in the resulting accomplishment of an organization's objectives. Effective resource allocation does not guarantee successful strategy implementation because programs, personnel, controls, and commitment must breathe life into the resources provided. Strategic management itself is sometimes referred to as a "resource allocation process."

Managing Conflict

Interdependency of objectives and competition for limited resources often leads to conflict. *Conflict* can be defined as a disagreement between two or more parties on one or more issues. Establishing annual objectives can lead to conflict because individuals have different expectations and perceptions, schedules create pressure, personalities are incompatible, and misunderstandings between line managers (such as production supervisors) and staff managers (such as human resource specialists) occur. For example, a collection manager's objective of reducing bad debts by 50 percent in a given year may conflict with a divisional objective to increase sales by 20 percent.

Establishing objectives can lead to conflict because managers and strategists must make trade-offs, such as whether to emphasize short-term profits or long-term growth, profit margin or market share, market penetration or market development, growth or stability, high risk or low risk, and social responsiveness or profit maximization. Conflict is unavoidable in organizations, so it is important that conflict be managed and resolved before dysfunctional consequences affect organizational performance. Conflict is not always bad. An absence of conflict can signal indifference and apathy. Conflict can serve to energize opposing groups into action and may help managers identify problems.

Various approaches for managing and resolving conflict can be classified into three categories: avoidance, defusion, and confrontation. *Avoidance* includes such actions as ignoring the problem in hopes that the conflict will resolve itself or physically separating the conflicting individuals (or groups). *Defusion* can include playing down differences between conflicting parties while accentuating similarities and common interests, compromising so that there is neither a clear winner nor loser, resorting to majority rule, appealing to a higher authority, or redesigning present positions. *Confrontation* is exemplified by exchanging members of conflicting parties so that each can gain an appreciation of the other's point of view or holding a meeting at which conflicting parties present their views and work through their differences.

Matching Structure with Strategy

VISIT THE NET

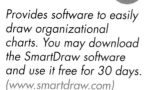

Provides software to easily draw organizational charts. You may download the SmartDraw software and use it free for 30 days. (www.smartdraw.com)

Changes in strategy often require changes in the way an organization is structured for two major reasons. First, structure largely dictates how objectives and policies will be established. For example, objectives and policies established under a geographic organizational structure are couched in geographic terms. Objectives and policies are stated largely in terms of products in an organization whose structure is based on product groups. The structural format for developing objectives and policies can significantly impact all other strategy-implementation activities.

The second major reason why changes in strategy often require changes in structure is that structure dictates how resources will be allocated. If an organization's structure is based on customer groups, then resources will be allocated in that manner. Similarly, if an organization's structure is set up along functional business lines, then resources are allocated by functional areas. Unless new or revised strategies place emphasis in the same areas as old strategies, structural reorientation commonly becomes a part of strategy implementation.

Changes in strategy lead to changes in organizational structure. Structure should be designed to facilitate the strategic pursuit of a firm and, therefore, follow strategy. Without a strategy or reasons for being (mission), companies find it difficult to design an effective structure. Chandler found a particular structure sequence to be often repeated as organizations grow and change strategy over time; this sequence is depicted in Figure 7-3.

There is no one optimal organizational design or structure for a given strategy or type of organization. What is appropriate for one organization may not be appropriate for a similar firm, although successful firms in a given industry do tend to organize

FIGURE 7-3
Chandler's Strategy-Structure Relationship

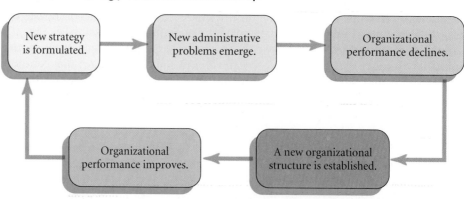

Source: Adapted from Alfred Chandler, *Strategy and Structure* (Cambridge, MA: MIT Press, 1962).

themselves in a similar way. For example, consumer goods companies tend to emulate the divisional structure-by-product form of organization. Small firms tend to be functionally structured (centralized). Medium-sized firms tend to be divisionally structured (decentralized). Large firms tend to use a strategic business unit (SBU) or matrix structure. As organizations grow, their structures generally change from simple to complex as a result of concatenation, or the linking together of several basic strategies.

Numerous external and internal forces affect an organization; no firm could change its structure in response to every one of these forces, because to do so would lead to chaos. However, when a firm changes its strategy, the existing organizational structure may become ineffective. Symptoms of an ineffective organizational structure include too many levels of management, too many meetings attended by too many people, too much attention being directed toward solving interdepartmental conflicts, too large a span of control, and too many unachieved objectives. Changes in structure can facilitate strategy-implementation efforts, but changes in structure should not be expected to make a bad strategy good, to make bad managers good, or to make bad products sell.

Structure undeniably can and does influence strategy. Strategies formulated must be workable, so if a certain new strategy required massive structural changes it would not be an attractive choice. In this way, structure can shape the choice of strategies. But a more important concern is determining what types of structural changes are needed to implement new strategies and how these changes can best be accomplished. We examine this issue by focusing on seven basic types of organizational structure: functional, divisional by geographic area, divisional by product, divisional by customer, divisional process, strategic business unit (SBU), and matrix.

The Functional Structure

The most widely used structure is the functional or centralized type because this structure is the simplest and least expensive of the seven alternatives. A *functional structure* groups tasks and activities by business function, such as production/operations, marketing, finance/accounting, research and development, and management information systems. A university may structure its activities by major functions that include academic affairs, student services, alumni relations, athletics, maintenance, and accounting. Besides being simple and inexpensive, a functional structure also promotes specialization of labor, encourages efficient use of managerial and technical talent, minimizes the need for an elaborate control system, and allows rapid decision making.

Some disadvantages of a functional structure are that it forces accountability to the top, minimizes career development opportunities, and is sometimes characterized by low employee morale, line/staff conflicts, poor delegation of authority, and inadequate planning for products and markets.

A functional structure often leads to short-term and narrow thinking that may undermine what is best for the firm as a whole. For example, the research and development department may strive to overdesign products and components to achieve technical elegance, while manufacturing may argue for low-frills products that can be mass produced more easily. Thus, communication is often not as good in a functional structure. Schein gives an example of a communication problem in a functional structure:

> The word "marketing" will mean product development to the engineer, studying customers through market research to the product manager, merchandising to the salesperson, and constant change in design to the manufacturing manager. Then when these managers try to work together, they often attribute disagreements to personalities and fail to notice the deeper, shared assumptions that vary and dictate how each function thinks.[4]

VISIT THE NET

Lists some items that strategy implementation must include.
(www.csuchico.edu/mgmt/ strategy/module1/ sld045.htm)

Most large companies have abandoned the functional structure in favor of decentralization and improved accountability. However, two large firms that still successfully use a functional firm are Nucor Steel based in Charlotte, North Carolina, and Sharp, the $17 billion consumer electronics firm.

The Divisional Structure

The *divisional* or *decentralized structure* is the second-most common type used by U.S. businesses. As a small organization grows, it has more difficulty managing different products and services in different markets. Some form of divisional structure generally becomes necessary to motivate employees, control operations, and compete successfully in diverse locations. The divisional structure can be organized in one of four ways: *by geographic area*, *by product* or *service*, *by customer*, or *by process*. With a divisional structure, functional activities are performed both centrally and in each separate division.

Cisco Systems recently discarded its divisional structure by customer and reorganized into a functional structure. CEO John Chambers replaced the three-customer structure based on big businesses, small businesses, and telecoms, and now the company has centralized its engineering and marketing units so that they focus on technologies such as wireless networks. Chambers says the goal was to eliminate duplication, but the change should not be viewed as a shift in strategy. Chambers's span of control in the new structure is reduced from 15 to 12 managers reporting directly to him. He continues to operate Cisco without a chief operating officer or a number-two executive.

Kodak recently reduced its number of business units from seven by-customer divisions to five by-product divisions. As consumption patterns become increasingly similar worldwide, a by-product structure is becoming more effective than a by-customer or a by-geographic type divisional structure. In the restructuring, Kodak eliminated its global operations division and distributed those responsibilities across the new by-product divisions.

A divisional structure has some clear advantages. First and perhaps foremost, accountability is clear. That is, divisional managers can be held responsible for sales and profit levels. Because a divisional structure is based on extensive delegation of authority, managers and employees can easily see the results of their good or bad performances. As a result, employee morale is generally higher in a divisional structure than it is in a centralized structure. Other advantages of the divisional design are that it creates career development opportunities for managers, allows local control of situations, leads to a competitive climate within an organization, and allows new businesses and products to be added easily.

The divisional design is not without some limitations, however. Perhaps the most important limitation is that a divisional structure is costly, for a number of reasons. First, each division requires functional specialists who must be paid. Second, there exists some duplication of staff services, facilities, and personnel; for instance, functional specialists are also needed centrally (at headquarters) to coordinate divisional activities. Third, managers must be well qualified because the divisional design forces delegation of authority; better-qualified individuals require higher salaries. A divisional structure can also be costly because it requires an elaborate, headquarters-driven control system. Fourth, competition between divisions may become so intense that it is dysfunctional and leads to limited sharing of ideas and resources for the common good of the firm. Ghoshal and Bartlett, two leading scholars in strategic management, note the following:

> As their label clearly warns, divisions divide. The divisional model fragments companies' resources; it creates vertical communication channels that insulate business units and prevents them from sharing their strengths with one

another. Consequently, the whole of the corporation is often less than the sum of its parts. A final limitation of the divisional design is that certain regions, products, or customers may sometimes receive special treatment, and it may be difficult to maintain consistent, companywide practices. Nonetheless, for most large organizations and many small firms, the advantages of a divisional structure more than offset the potential limitations.[5]

[handwritten: difficult to maintain system-wide practices]

A *divisional structure by geographic area* is appropriate for organizations whose strategies need to be tailored to fit the particular needs and characteristics of customers in different geographic areas. This type of structure can be most appropriate for organizations that have similar branch facilities located in widely dispersed areas. A divisional structure by geographic area allows local participation in decision making and improved coordination within a region. Hershey Foods is an example of a company organized using the divisional by geographic region type of structure. Hershey's divisions are United States, Canada, Mexico, Brazil, and Other. Analysts contend that this type of structure may not be best for Hershey since consumption patterns for candy are quite similar worldwide. An alternative—and perhaps better—type of structure for Hershey would be divisional by product since the company produces and sells three types of products worldwide: (1) chocolate, (2) nonchocolate, and (3) grocery.

[handwritten: geographic is good if needs must be tailored]

The *divisional structure by product (or services)* is most effective for implementing strategies when specific products or services need special emphasis. Also, this type of structure is widely used when an organization offers only a few products or services or when an organization's products or services differ substantially. The divisional structure allows strict control over and attention to product lines, but it may also require a more skilled management force and reduced top management control. General Motors, DuPont, and Procter & Gamble use a divisional structure by product to implement strategies. Huffy, the largest bicycle company in the world, is another firm that is highly decentralized based on a divisional-by-product structure. Based in Ohio, Huffy's divisions are the Bicycle division, the Gerry Baby Products division, the Huffy Sports division, YLC Enterprises, and Washington Inventory Service. Harry Shaw, Huffy's chairman, believes decentralization is one of the keys to Huffy's success.

[handwritten: most effective for strategies when products need emphasis]

Eastman Chemical established a new by-product divisional organizational structure. The company's two new divisions, Eastman Company and Voridian Company, focus on chemicals and polymers, respectively. The Eastman division focuses on coatings, adhesives, inks, and plastics, whereas the Voridian division focuses on fibers, polyethylene, and other polymers. In late 2005, Microsoft reorganized the whole corporation into three large divisions-by-product. Headed by a President, the new divisions are (1) Platform Products and Services, (2) Business, and (3) Entertainment and Devices. Also in 2005, the swiss electrical-engineering company ABB Ltd. scrapped its two core divisions, (1) power technologies and (2) automation technologies, and replaced them with five new divisions: (1) power products, (2) power systems, (3) automation products, (4) process automation, and (5) robotics.

When a few major customers are of paramount importance and many different services are provided to these customers, then a *divisional structure by customer* can be the most effective way to implement strategies. This structure allows an organization to cater effectively to the requirements of clearly defined customer groups. For example, book publishing companies often organize their activities around customer groups, such as colleges, secondary schools, and private commercial schools. Some airline companies have two major customer divisions: passengers and freight or cargo services. Merrill Lynch is organized into separate divisions that cater to different groups of customers, including wealthy individuals, institutional investors, and small corporations. Motorola's semiconductor chip division is also organized divisionally by customer, having three separate segments that sell to (1) the automotive and industrial market, (2) the mobile phone market, and (3) the data-networking market. The automotive and industrial segment is doing well, but the other two segments are faltering, which is a reason why Motorola is trying to divest its semiconductor operations.

A *divisional structure by process* is similar to a functional structure, because activities are organized according to the way work is actually performed. However, a key difference between these two designs is that functional departments are not accountable for profits or revenues, whereas divisional process departments are evaluated on these criteria. An example of a divisional structure by process is a manufacturing business organized into six divisions: electrical work, glass cutting, welding, grinding, painting, and foundry work. In this case, all operations related to these specific processes would be grouped under the separate divisions. Each process (division) would be responsible for generating revenues and profits. The divisional structure by process can be particularly effective in achieving objectives when distinct production processes represent the thrust of competitiveness in an industry.

The Strategic Business Unit (SBU) Structure

As the number, size, and diversity of divisions in an organization increase, controlling and evaluating divisional operations become increasingly difficult for strategists. Increases in sales often are not accompanied by similar increases in profitability. The span of control becomes too large at top levels of the firm. For example, in a large conglomerate organization composed of 90 divisions, such as ConAgra, the chief executive officer could have difficulty even remembering the first names of divisional presidents. In multidivisional organizations, an SBU structure can greatly facilitate strategy-implementation efforts. ConAgra has put its many divisions into three primary SBUs: (1) food service (restaurants), (2) retail (grocery stores), and (3) agricultural products.

The SBU structure groups similar divisions into strategic business units and delegates authority and responsibility for each unit to a senior executive who reports directly to the chief executive officer. This change in structure can facilitate strategy implementation by improving coordination between similar divisions and channeling accountability to distinct business units. In a 100-division conglomerate, the divisions could perhaps be regrouped into 10 SBUs according to certain common characteristics, such as competing in the same industry, being located in the same area, or having the same customers.

Two disadvantages of an SBU structure are that it requires an additional layer of management, which increases salary expenses. Also, the role of the group vice president is often ambiguous. However, these limitations often do not outweigh the advantages of improved coordination and accountability. Another advantage of the SBU structure is that it makes the tasks of planning and control by the corporate office more manageable.

Honeywell International reorganized its aerospace division in 2005 from a products-based structure based on engines, electronics, wheels, brakes, and so on to three strategic business units: (1) air transport and regional transport, (2) business and general aviation, and (3) defense and space. Honeywell is not shedding any businesses in this reorganization. The firm wants to simplify its interactions with customers by

FIGURE 7-4

Sonoco Product's SBU Organizational Chart

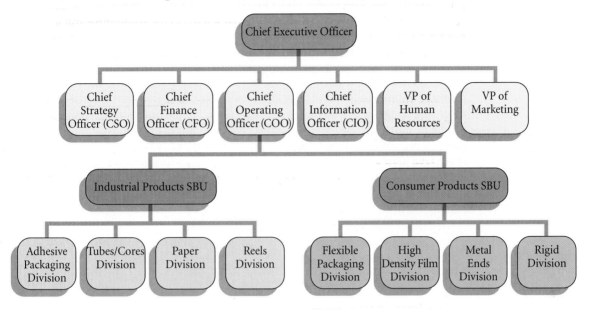

reducing the number of layers in its organization. Atlantic Richfield and Fairchild Industries are examples of firms that successfully use an SBU-type structure.

As illustrated in Figure 7-4, Sonoco Products Corporation, based in Hartsville, South Carolina, utilizes an SBU organizational structure. Note that Sonoco's SBUs—Industrial Products and Consumer Products—each have four autonomous divisions that have their own sales, manufacturing, R&D, finance, HRM, and MIS functions.

The Matrix Structure

A *matrix structure* is the most complex of all designs because it depends upon both vertical and horizontal flows of authority and communication (hence the term *matrix*). In contrast, functional and divisional structures depend primarily on vertical flows of authority and communication. A matrix structure can result in higher overhead because it creates more management positions. Other disadvantages of a matrix structure that contribute to overall complexity include dual lines of budget authority (a violation of the unity-of-command principle), dual sources of reward and punishment, shared authority, dual reporting channels, and a need for an extensive and effective communication system.

Despite its complexity, the matrix structure is widely used in many industries, including construction, healthcare, research, and defense. Some advantages of a matrix structure are that project objectives are clear, there are many channels of communication, workers can see the visible results of their work, and shutting down a project can be accomplished relatively easily. Another advantage of a matrix structure is that it facilitates the use of specialized personnel, equipment, and facilities. Functional resources are shared in a matrix structure, rather than duplicated as in a divisional structure. Individuals with a high degree of expertise can divide their time as needed among projects, and they in turn develop their own skills and

[handwritten margin note: matrix the most complex vertical + horizontal communication authority]

competencies more than in other structures. Walt Disney Corp. relies on a matrix structure.

A typical matrix structure is illustrated in Figure 7-5. Note that the letters (A thru Z^4) refer to managers. For example, if you were manager A, you would be responsible for financial aspects of Project 1, and you would have two bosses: the Project 1 Manager onsite and the CFO off site.

For a matrix structure to be effective, organizations need participative planning, training, clear mutual understanding of roles and responsibilities, excellent internal communication, and mutual trust and confidence. The matrix structure is being used more frequently by U.S. businesses because firms are pursuing strategies that add new products, customer groups, and technology to their range of activities. Out of these changes are coming product managers, functional managers, and geographic-area managers, all of whom have important strategic responsibilities. When several variables, such as product, customer, technology, geography, functional area, and line of business, have roughly equal strategic priorities, a matrix organization can be an effective structural form.

FIGURE 7-5
An Example Matrix Structure

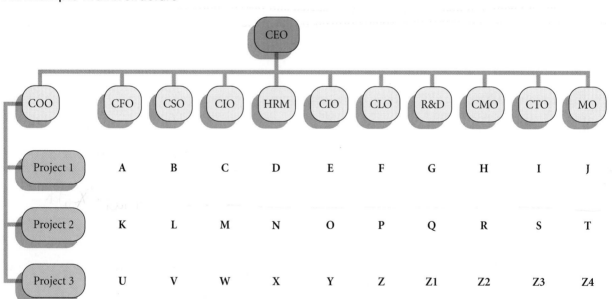

Notes: Titles spelled out as follows.

Chief Executive Officer (CEO)
Chief Finance Officer (CFO)
Chief Strategy Officer (CSO)
Chief Information Officer (CIO)
Human Resources Manager (HRM)
Chief Operating Officer (COO)
Chief Legal Officer (CLO)
Research & Development Officer (R&D)
Chief Marketing Officer (CMO)
Chief Technology Officer (CTO)
Competitive Intelligence Officer (CIO)
Maintenance Officer (MO)

Some Do's and Don'ts in Developing Organizational Charts

Students analyzing strategic management cases are often asked to revise and develop a firm's organizational structure. This section provides some basic guidelines for this endeavor. There are some basic do's and don'ts in regard to devising or constructing organizational charts, especially for midsize to large firms. First of all, reserve the title CEO for the top executive of the firm. Don't use the title "president" for the top person; use it for the division top managers if there are divisions within the firm. Also, do not use the title "president" for functional business executives. They should have the title "chief," or "vice president," or "manager," or "officer," such as "Chief Information Officer," or "VP of Human Resources." Further, do not recommend a dual title (such as "CEO and President") for just one executive. The Chairman of the Board and CEO of Bristol-Myers Squibb, Peter Dolan, gave up his title as chairman in 2005. Actually, "chairperson" is much better than "chairman" for this title.

Why?

   Directly below the CEO, it is best to have a COO (chief operating officer) with any division presidents reporting directly to the COO. On the same level as the COO and also reporting to the CEO, draw in your functional business executives, such as a CFO (chief financial officer), VP of Human Resources, a CSO (Chief Strategy Officer), a CIO (Chief Information Officer), a CMO (Chief Marketing Officer), a VP of R&D, a VP of Legal Affairs, a Investment Relations Officer, Maintenance Superintendent, and so on. Note in Figure 7-6 that these positions are labeled and placed appropriately. Note that a controller and/or treasurer would normally report to the CFO.

FIGURE 7-6

Typical Top Managers of a Large Firm

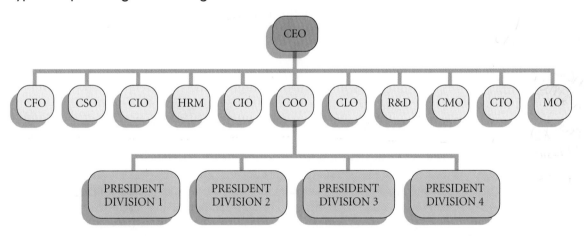

Notes: Titles spelled out as follows.

Chief Executive Officer (CEO)
Chief Finance Officer (CFO)
Chief Strategy Officer (CSO)
Chief Information Officer (CIO)
Human Resources Manager (HRM)
Chief Operating Officer (COO)
Chief Legal Officer (CLO)
Research & Development Officer (R&D)
Chief Marketing Officer (CMO)
Chief Technology Officer (CTO)
Competitive Intelligence Officer (CIO)
Maintenance Officer (MO)

In developing an organizational chart, avoid having a particular person reporting to more than one person above them in the chain of command. This would violate the unity-of-command principle of management that "every employee should have just one boss." Also, do not have the CFO, CIO, CSO, Human Resource Officer, or other functional positions report to the COO. All these positions report directly to the CEO.

A key consideration in devising an organizational structure concerns the divisions. Note whether the divisions (if any) of a firm presently are established based upon geography, customer, product, or process. If the firm's organizational chart is not available, you oftentimes can devise a chart based on the titles of executives. An important case analysis activity is for you to decide how the divisions of a firm should be organized for maximum effectiveness. Even if the firm presently has no divisions, determine whether the firm would operate better with divisions. In other words, which type of divisional breakdown do you (or your group or team) feel would be best for the firm in allocating resources, establishing objectives, and devising compensation incentives? This important strategic decision faces many midsize and large firms (and teams of students analyzing a strategic-management case). As consumption patterns become more and more similar worldwide, the divisional-by-product form of structure is increasingly the most effective. Be mindful that all firms have functional staff below their top executive and often readily provide this information, so be wary of concluding prematurely that a particular firm utilizes a functional structure. If you see the word "president" in the titles of executives, coupled with financial-reporting segments, such as by product or geographic region, then the firm is divisionally structured.

If the firm is large with numerous divisions, decide whether an SBU type of structure would be more appropriate to reduce the span of control reporting to the COO. Note in Figure 7-4 that the Sonoco Products' strategic business units (SBUs) are based on product groupings. An alternative SBU structure would have been to base the division groupings on location. One never knows for sure if a proposed or actual structure is indeed most effective for a particular firm. Note from Chandler's strategy-structure relationship illustrated previously in this chapter that declining financial performance signals a need for altering the structure.

Restructuring, Reengineering, and E-Engineering

Restructuring and reengineering are becoming commonplace on the corporate landscape across the United States and Europe. *Restructuring*—also called *downsizing*, rightsizing, or *delayering*—involves reducing the size of the firm in terms of number of employees, number of divisions or units, and number of hierarchical levels in the firm's organizational structure. This reduction in size is intended to improve both efficiency and effectiveness. Restructuring is concerned primarily with shareholder well-being rather than employee well-being.

Recessionary economic conditions have forced many European companies to downsize, laying off managers and employees. This was almost unheard of prior to the mid-1990s because European labor unions and laws required lengthy negotiations or huge severance checks before workers could be terminated. In contrast to the United States, labor union executives of large European firms sit on most boards of directors.

Job security in European companies is slowly moving toward a U.S. scenario, in which firms lay off almost at will. From banks in Milan to factories in Mannheim, European employers are starting to show people the door in an effort to streamline operations, increase efficiency, and compete against already slim and trim

U.S. firms. Massive U.S.-style layoffs are still rare in Europe, but unemployment rates throughout the continent are rising quite rapidly. European firms still prefer to downsize by attrition and retirement rather than by blanket layoffs because of culture, laws, and unions.

In contrast, *reengineering* is concerned more with employee and customer well-being than shareholder well-being. Reengineering—also called process management, process innovation, or process redesign—involves reconfiguring or redesigning work, jobs, and processes for the purpose of improving cost, quality, service, and speed. Reengineering does not usually affect the organizational structure or chart, nor does it imply job loss or employee layoffs. Whereas restructuring is concerned with eliminating or establishing, shrinking or enlarging, and moving organizational departments and divisions, the focus of reengineering is changing the way work is actually carried out.

Reengineering is characterized by many tactical (short-term, business-function-specific) decisions, whereas restructuring is characterized by strategic (long-term, affecting all business functions) decisions.

The Internet is ushering in a new wave of business transformation. No longer is it enough for companies to put up simple Web sites for customers and employees. To take full advantage of the Internet, companies must change the way they distribute goods, deal with suppliers, attract customers, and serve customers. The Internet eliminates the geographic protection/monopoly of local businesses. Basically, companies must reinvent the way they do business to take full advantage of the Internet. This whole process is being called e-engineering.[6] Dow Corning Corporation and many others have recently appointed an e-commerce top executive.

Restructuring

Firms often employ restructuring when various ratios appear out of line with competitors as determined through benchmarking exercises. Recall that *benchmarking* simply involves comparing a firm against the best firms in the industry on a wide variety of performance-related criteria. Some benchmarking ratios commonly used in rationalizing the need for restructuring are headcount-to-sales-volume, or corporate-staff-to-operating-employees, or span-of-control figures.

The primary benefit sought from restructuring is cost reduction. For some highly bureaucratic firms, restructuring can actually rescue the firm from global competition and demise. But the downside of restructuring can be reduced employee commitment, creativity, and innovation that accompanies the uncertainty and trauma associated with pending and actual employee layoffs. During 2005, IBM restructured by laying off 13,000 people, mostly from their European operations. IBM restructured those operations to report to either its Zurich or its Madrid base. The firm's restructuring came on the heels of disappointing financial figures for the first half of the year. IBM employs about 320,000 people worldwide and roughly 100,000 in Europe.

Another downside of restructuring is that many people today do not aspire to become managers, and many present-day managers are trying to get off the management track.[7] Sentiment against joining management ranks is higher today than ever. About 80 percent of employees say they want nothing to do with management, a major shift from just a decade ago when 60 to 70 percent hoped to become managers. Managing others historically led to enhanced career mobility, financial rewards, and executive perks; but in today's global, more competitive, restructured arena, managerial jobs demand more hours and headaches with fewer financial rewards. Managers today manage more people spread over different locations, travel

focuses on the employee and the way work is carried out.

companies must take adv of internet

head count-to-sales
corporate staff to operating employees
span of control figures

• seek cost reduction

managing more difficult now

more, manage diverse functions, and are change agents even when they have nothing to do with the creation of the plan or disagree with its approach. Employers today are looking for people who can do things, not for people who make other people do things. Restructuring in many firms has made a manager's job an invisible, thankless role. More workers today are self-managed, entrepreneurs, interpreneurs, or team-managed. Managers today need to be counselors, motivators, financial advisors, and psychologists. They also run the risk of becoming technologically behind in their areas of expertise. "Dilbert" cartoons commonly portray managers as enemies or as morons.

It is interesting to note that laying off employees in France is almost impossible due to labor laws that require lengthy negotiations and expensive severance packages for any individuals who are laid off. French CEOs feel that the strict layoff policies are crippling France's economy and companies. This is true because other European countries, such as Germany, have recently made it much easier for companies to lay off employees to stay competitive—and indeed to survive. Moulinex is an example of a French company that recently tried to lay off 670 employees but was denied this option, so the firm fell into bankruptcy and possible liquidation.

Reengineering

The argument for a firm engaging in reengineering usually goes as follows: Many companies historically have been organized vertically by business function. This arrangement has led over time to managers' and employees' mind-sets being defined by their particular functions rather than by overall customer service, product quality, or corporate performance. The logic is that all firms tend to bureaucratize over time. As routines become entrenched, turf becomes delineated and defended, and politics takes precedence over performance. Walls that exist in the physical workplace can be reflections of "mental" walls.

In reengineering, a firm uses information technology to break down functional barriers and create a work system based on business processes, products, or outputs rather than on functions or inputs. Cornerstones of reengineering are decentralization, reciprocal interdependence, and information sharing. A firm that exemplifies complete information sharing is Springfield Remanufacturing Corporation, which provides to all employees a weekly income statement of the firm, as well as extensive information on other companies' performances.

The *Wall Street Journal* noted that reengineering today must go beyond knocking down internal walls that keep parts of a company from cooperating effectively; it must also knock down the external walls that prohibit or discourage cooperation with other firms—even rival firms.[8] A maker of disposable diapers echoes this need differently when it says that to be successful "cooperation at the firm must stretch from stump to rump."

Hewlett-Packard is a good example of a company that has knocked down the external barriers to cooperation and practices modern reengineering. The HP of today shares its forecasts with all of its supply-chain partners and shares other critical information with its distributors and other stakeholders. HP does all the buying of resin for its many manufacturers, giving it a volume discount of up to 5 percent. HP has established many alliances and cooperative agreements of the kind discussed in Chapter 5.

A benefit of reengineering is that it offers employees the opportunity to see more clearly how their particular jobs affect the final product or service being marketed by the firm. However, reengineering can also raise manager and employee anxiety, which, unless calmed, can lead to corporate trauma.

Linking Performance and Pay to Strategies

Most companies today are practicing some form of pay-for-performance for employees and managers other than top executives. The average employee performance bonus is 6.8 percent of pay for individual performance, 5.5 percent of pay for group productivity, and 6.4 percent of pay for companywide profitability.

Staff control of pay systems often prevents line managers from using financial compensation as a strategic tool. Flexibility regarding managerial and employee compensation is needed to allow short-term shifts in compensation that can stimulate efforts to achieve long-term objectives.

How can an organization's reward system be more closely linked to strategic performance? How can decisions on salary increases, promotions, merit pay, and bonuses be more closely aligned to support the long-term strategic objectives of the organization? There are no widely accepted answers to these questions, but a dual bonus system based on both annual objectives and long-term objectives is becoming common. The percentage of a manager's annual bonus attributable to short-term versus long-term results should vary by hierarchical level in the organization. A chief executive officer's annual bonus could, for example, be determined on a 75 percent short-term and 25 percent long-term basis. It is important that bonuses not be based solely on short-term results because such a system ignores long-term company strategies and objectives.

DuPont Canada has a 16 percent return-on-equity objective. If this objective is met, the company's 4,000 employees receive a "performance sharing cash award" equal to 4 percent of pay. If return-on-equity falls below 11 percent, employees get nothing. If return-on-equity exceeds 28 percent, workers receive a 10 percent bonus.

In an effort to cut costs and increase productivity, more and more Japanese companies are switching from seniority-based pay to performance-based approaches. Toyota has switched to a full merit system for 20,000 of its 70,000 white-collar workers. Fujitsu, Sony, Matsushita Electric Industrial, and Kao also have switched to merit pay systems. Nearly 30 percent of all Japanese companies have switched to merit pay from seniority pay.[9] This switching is hurting morale at some Japanese companies, which have trained workers for decades to cooperate rather than to compete and to work in groups rather than individually.

Richard Brown, CEO of Electronic Data Systems (EDS), recently removed the bottom 20 percent of EDS's sales force and said,

> You have to start with an appraisal system that gives genuine feedback and differentiates performance. Some call it ranking people. That seems a little harsh. But you can't have a manager checking a box that says you're either stupendous, magnificent, very good, good, or average. Concise, constructive feedback is the fuel workers use to get better. A company that doesn't differentiate performance risks losing its best people.[10]

Profit sharing is another widely used form of incentive compensation. More than 30 percent of U.S. companies have profit sharing plans, but critics emphasize that too many factors affect profits for this to be a good criterion. Taxes, pricing, or an acquisition would wipe out profits, for example. Also, firms try to minimize profits in a sense to reduce taxes.

Still another criterion widely used to link performance and pay to strategies is gain sharing. *Gain sharing* requires employees or departments to establish performance

[handwritten margin notes:]
flexibility needed in compensation

dual systems link long-term + short-term performance goals.

profit sharing widely used, but is criticized

targets; if actual results exceed objectives, all members get bonuses. More than 26 percent of U.S. companies use some form of gain sharing; about 75 percent of gain sharing plans have been adopted since 1980. Carrier, a subsidiary of United Technologies, has had excellent success with gain sharing in its six plants in Syracuse, New York; Firestone's tire plant in Wilson, North Carolina, has experienced similar success with gain sharing.

Criteria such as sales, profit, production efficiency, quality, and safety could also serve as bases for an effective *bonus system.* If an organization meets certain understood, agreed-upon profit objectives, every member of the enterprise should share in the harvest. A bonus system can be an effective tool for motivating individuals to support strategy-implementation efforts. BankAmerica, for example, recently overhauled its incentive system to link pay to sales of the bank's most profitable products and services. Branch managers receive a base salary plus a bonus based both on the number of new customers and on sales of bank products. Every employee in each branch is also eligible for a bonus if the branch exceeds its goals. Thomas Peterson, a top BankAmerica executive, says, "We want to make people responsible for meeting their goals, so we pay incentives on sales, not on controlling costs or on being sure the parking lot is swept."

Five tests are often used to determine whether a performance-pay plan will benefit an organization:

1. ***Does the plan capture attention?*** Are people talking more about their activities and taking pride in early successes under the plan?
2. ***Do employees understand the plan?*** Can participants explain how it works and what they need to do to earn the incentive?
3. ***Is the plan improving communication?*** Do employees know more than they used to about the company's mission, plans, and objectives?
4. ***Does the plan pay out when it should?*** Are incentives being paid for desired results—and being withheld when objectives are not met?
5. ***Is the company or unit performing better?*** Are profits up? Has market share grown? Have gains resulted in part from the incentives?[11]

In addition to a dual bonus system, a combination of reward strategy incentives, such as salary raises, stock options, fringe benefits, promotions, praise, recognition, criticism, fear, increased job autonomy, and awards, can be used to encourage managers and employees to push hard for successful strategic implementation. The range of options for getting people, departments, and divisions to actively support strategy-implementation activities in a particular organization is almost limitless. Merck, for example, recently gave each of its 37,000 employees a 10-year option to buy 100 shares of Merck stock at a set price of $127. Steven Darien, Merck's vice president of human resources, says, "We needed to find ways to get everyone in the workforce on board in terms of our goals and objectives. Company executives will begin meeting with all Merck workers to explore ways in which employees can contribute more."

Increasing criticism aimed at chief executive officers for their high pay has resulted in executive compensation being linked more closely than ever before to performance of their firms. Although the linkage between CEO pay and corporate performance is getting closer, CEO pay in the United States still can be astronomical. The average CEO's pay increased 3.4 percent in 2004 to a median $7.4 million among the Fortune 500 firms.[12] The five best-paid and worst-paid Fortune 500 CEOs in 2004 are listed in Table 7-3. Note that CEO Steve Jobs at Apple Computer and Richard Kinder at Kinder Morgan Energy accepted only $1.00 in annual compensation.

TABLE 7-3   CEO Compensation Among Fortune 500 Firms in 2004

HIGHEST-PAID CEOs	COMPANY	AMOUNT
John Wilder	TXU	$55.2 million
Robert Toll	Toll Brothers	44.3 million
Ray Irani	Occidental Petroleum	41.7 million
Bob Nardelli	Home Depot	39.5 million
Edward Zander	Motorola	38.9 million

LOWEST-PAID CEOs	COMPANY	AMOUNT
Richard Kinder	Kinder Morgan Energy	$1.00
Steve Jobs	Apple Computer	1.00
Jeff Bezos	Amazon	81,840
Warren Buffett	Berkshire Hathaway	311,000
Paul Anderson	Duke Energy	365,296

Source: Adapted from Matthew Boyle, "KA-CHING! CEOs Grab Record Perks." *Fortune* (May 2, 2005): 22.

Managing Resistance to Change

No organization or individual can escape change. But the thought of change raises anxieties because people fear economic loss, inconvenience, uncertainty, and a break in normal social patterns. Almost any change in structure, technology, people, or strategies has the potential to disrupt comfortable interaction patterns. For this reason, people resist change. The strategic-management process itself can impose major changes on individuals and processes. Reorienting an organization to get people to think and act strategically is not an easy task.

Resistance to change can be considered the single greatest threat to successful strategy implementation. Resistance regularly occurs in organizations in the form of sabotaging production machines, absenteeism, filing unfounded grievances, and an unwillingness to cooperate. People often resist strategy implementation because they do not understand what is happening or why changes are taking place. In that case, employees may simply need accurate information. Successful strategy implementation hinges upon managers' ability to develop an organizational climate conducive to change. Change must be viewed as an opportunity rather than as a threat by managers and employees.

Resistance to change can emerge at any stage or level of the strategy-implementation process. Although there are various approaches for implementing changes, three commonly used strategies are a force change strategy, an educative change strategy, and a rational or self-interest change strategy. A *force change strategy* involves giving orders and enforcing those orders; this strategy has the advantage of being fast, but it is plagued by low commitment and high resistance. The *educative change strategy* is one that presents information to convince people of the need for change; the disadvantage of an educative change strategy is that implementation becomes slow and difficult. However, this type of strategy evokes greater commitment and less resistance than does the force change strategy. Finally, a *rational* or *self-interest change strategy* is one that attempts to convince individuals that the change is to their

VISIT THE NET

Provides a PowerPoint presentation on organizational change and managing resistance to change.
(www.cl.uh.edu/bpa/ hadm/HADM_5731/ ppt_presentations/ 5orgchg/index.htm)

personal advantage. When this appeal is successful, strategy implementation can be relatively easy. However, implementation changes are seldom to everyone's advantage.

The rational change strategy is the most desirable, so this approach is examined a bit further. Managers can improve the likelihood of successfully implementing change by carefully designing change efforts. Jack Duncan described a rational or self-interest change strategy as consisting of four steps. First, employees are invited to participate in the process of change and in the details of transition; participation allows everyone to give opinions, to feel a part of the change process, and to identify their own self-interests regarding the recommended change. Second, some motivation or incentive to change is required; self-interest can be the most important motivator. Third, communication is needed so that people can understand the purpose for the changes. Giving and receiving feedback is the fourth step: everyone enjoys knowing how things are going and how much progress is being made.[13]

Igor Ansoff summarized the need for strategists to manage resistance to change as follows:

> Observation of the historical transitions from one orientation to another shows that, if left unmanaged, the process becomes conflict-laden, prolonged, and costly in both human and financial terms. Management of resistance involves anticipating the focus of resistance and its intensity. Second, it involves eliminating unnecessary resistance caused by misperceptions and insecurities. Third, it involves mustering the power base necessary to assure support for the change. Fourth, it involves planning the process of change. Finally, it involves monitoring and controlling resistance during the process of change.[14]

Because of diverse external and internal forces, change is a fact of life in organizations. The rate, speed, magnitude, and direction of changes vary over time by industry and organization. Strategists should strive to create a work environment in which change is recognized as necessary and beneficial so that individuals can more easily adapt to change. Adopting a strategic-management approach to decision making can itself require major changes in the philosophy and operations of a firm.

Strategists can take a number of positive actions to minimize managers' and employees' resistance to change. For example, individuals who will be affected by a change should be involved in the decision to make the change and in decisions about how to implement the change. Strategists should anticipate changes and develop and offer training and development workshops so that managers and employees can adapt to those changes. They also need to effectively communicate the need for changes. The strategic-management process can be described as a process of managing change. Robert Waterman describes how successful organizations involve individuals to facilitate change:

> Implementation starts with, not after, the decision. When Ford Motor Company embarked on the program to build the highly successful Taurus, management gave up the usual, sequential design process. Instead it showed the tentative design to the workforce and asked its help in devising a car that would be easy to build. Team Taurus came up with no less than 1,401 items suggested by Ford employees. What a contrast from the secrecy that characterized the industry before. When people are treated as the main engine rather than interchangeable parts, motivation, creativity, quality, and commitment to implementation go up.[15]

Organizational change should be viewed today as a continuous process rather than as a project or event. The most successful organizations today continuously adapt to changes in the competitive environment, which themselves continue to change at an accelerating rate. It is not sufficient today to simply react to change. Managers need to anticipate change and ideally be the creator of change. Viewing change as a continuous process is in stark contrast to an old management doctrine regarding change, which was to unfreeze behavior, change the behavior, and then refreeze the new behavior. The new "continuous organizational change" philosophy should mirror the popular "continuous quality improvement philosophy."

Org change should be a continuos process

Managing the Natural Environment

All business functions are affected by natural environment considerations or by striving to make a profit. However, both employees and consumers are especially resentful of firms that take from more than give to the natural environment; likewise, people today are especially appreciative of firms that conduct operations in a way that mend rather than harm the environment. But a rapidly increasing number of companies are implementing tougher environmental regulation because it makes economic sense. General Electric, for example, plans to achieve $20 billion in sales by 2010 in eco-friendly technologies that include cleaner coal-fired power plants, a diesel-and-electric hybrid locomotive, and agricultural silicon that cuts the amount of water and pesticide used in spraying fields. This is double GE's sales today in "green" products.[16] GE has a goal to improve its energy efficiency by 30 percent between 2005 and 2012.

Earth itself has become a stakeholder for all business firms. Consumer interest in businesses preserving nature's ecological balance and fostering a clean, healthy environment is high. As indicated in the "Natural Environment Perspective," an increasing number of businesses today are considering the amount of formal training in environmental matters that prospective managers have received. The annual Business-Environment-Learning-Leadership (BELL) Conference focuses on which colleges and universities do an especially good or bad job in covering natural environment issues in business administration curricula.

The ecological challenge facing all organizations requires managers to formulate strategies that preserve and conserve natural resources and control pollution. Special natural environment issues include ozone depletion, global warming, depletion of rain forests, destruction of animal habitats, protecting endangered species, developing biodegradable products and packages, waste management, clean air, clean water, erosion, destruction of natural resources, and pollution control. Firms increasingly are developing green product lines that are biodegradable and/or are made from recycled products. Green products sell well.

The Environmental Protection Agency recently reported that U.S. citizens and organizations annually spend more than about $200 billion on pollution abatement. Environmental concerns touch all aspects of a business's operations, including workplace risk exposures, packaging, waste reduction, energy use, alternative fuels, environmental cost accounting, and recycling practices.

Managing as if Earth matters requires an understanding of how international trade, competitiveness, and global resources are connected. Managing environmental affairs can no longer be simply a technical function performed by specialists in a firm; more emphasis must be placed on developing an environmental

VISIT THE NET

Gives the strategic plan for a community police consortium, including a section on strategy implementation.
(www.communitypolicing.org/outline.html)

NATURAL ENVIRONMENT PERSPECTIVE

In Hiring, Do Companies Consider Environmental Training of Students?

The *Wall Street Journal* reports that companies actively consider environmental training in employees they hire. A recent study reported that 77 percent of corporate recruiters said "it is important to hire students with an awareness of social and environmental responsibility." According to Ford Motor Company's director of corporate governance, "We want students who will help us find solutions to societal challenges and we have trouble hiring students with such skills" (Alsop, 2001). The Aspen Institute contends that most business schools currently do not, but should, incorporate environmental training in all facets of their core curriculum, not just in special elective courses. The Institute reports that the University of Texas, the University of North Carolina, and the University of Michigan, among others, are at the cutting edge in providing environmental coverage at their respective MBA levels. Companies today do consider business schools with the best environmental programs to prepare students more effectively for the business world; companies favor hiring graduates from these universities.

Findings from research suggest that business schools at the undergraduate level are doing a poor job of educating students on environmental issues. Since business students with limited knowledge on environmental issues may make poor decisions, business schools should address environmental issues more in their curricula. Failure to do so could result in graduates making inappropriate business decisions in regard to the natural environment. Failing to provide adequate coverage of natural environment issues and decisions in their training could make those students less attractive to employers than graduates from other universities.

Bruce Nelson, chairman and CEO of Office Depot, addressed business leaders and professors from around the world as part of the World Resources Institute's (WRI) 2003 BELL Conference at Florida Atlantic University's Fort Lauderdale campus. More than 200 business educators and corporate professionals attended this annual Business-Environment-Learning-Leadership (BELL) Conference. "It's important to have today's business leaders support the concept of environmental education for the business leaders of tomorrow," said Jonathan Lash, president of the World Resources Institute (WRI). "Stated sustainability commitments by companies like Office Depot should encourage business educators to add environmental content to their core curriculum."

The annual BELL conference exposes business schools to new tools and ideas designed to integrate social and environmental curricula into traditional business tracks that will train thousands of future business leaders. WRI launched the BELL program in 1991 to fill a void in business education. In 1990, no business school in the United States offered an environment class. Today, the BELL network includes business professors and programs from most of the top business schools across North America and has spawned a series of environment programs within business schools throughout China and Latin America.

The 2003 BELL conference was co-hosted by the Council for Sustainable Florida (CSF), Florida Department of Environmental Protection, Educational Alliance for a Sustainable Florida (EASF), and Florida Atlantic University College of Business. The World Resources Institute (www.wri.org.wri) is an environmental research and policy organization that creates solutions to protect Earth and improve people's lives.

Sources: Adapted from R. Alsop, "Corporations Still Put Profits First, But Social Concerns Gain Ground," *Wall Street Journal* (2001): B14, Jane Kim, "Business Schools Take a Page from Kinder, Gentler Textbook," *Wall Street Journal* (October 22, 2003): B2C. Also, www.worldresourcesinstitute.com; www.wri.org.wri; www.beyondgreypinstripes.org; and bell.wri.org.

perspective among all employees and managers of the firm. Many companies are moving environmental affairs from the staff side of the organization to the line side, thus making the corporate environmental group report directly to the chief operating officer.

Societies have been plagued by environmental disasters to such an extent recently that firms failing to recognize the importance of environmental issues and challenges could suffer severe consequences. Managing environmental affairs can no longer be an incidental or secondary function of company operations. Product design, manufacturing, and ultimate disposal should not merely reflect environmental considerations, but also be driven by them. Firms that manage environmental affairs will enhance relations with consumers, regulators, vendors, and other industry players—substantially improving their prospects of success.

Firms should formulate and implement strategies from an environmental perspective. Environmental strategies could include developing or acquiring green businesses, divesting or altering environment-damaging businesses, striving to become a low-cost producer through waste minimization and energy conservation, and pursuing a differentiation strategy through green-product features. In addition to creating strategies, firms could include an environmental representative on the board of directors, conduct regular envrionmental audits, implement bonuses for favorable environmental results, become involved in environmental issues and programs, incorporate environmental values in mission statements, establish environmentally oriented objectives, acquire environmental skills, and provide environmental training programs for company employees and managers.

Creating a Strategy-Supportive Culture

Strategists should strive to preserve, emphasize, and build upon aspects of an existing *culture* that support proposed new strategies. Aspects of an existing culture that are antagonistic to a proposed strategy should be identified and changed. Substantial research indicates that new strategies are often market-driven and dictated by competitive forces. For this reason, changing a firm's culture to fit a new strategy is usually more effective than changing a strategy to fit an existing culture. Numerous techniques are available to alter an organization's culture, including recruitment, training, transfer, promotion, restructure of an organization's design, role modeling, and positive reinforcement.

Jack Duncan described *triangulation* as an effective, multi-method technique for studying and altering a firm's culture.[17] Triangulation includes the combined use of obtrusive observation, self-administered questionnaires, and personal interviews to determine the nature of a firm's culture. The process of triangulation reveals changes that need to be made to a firm's culture to benefit strategy.

Schein indicated that the following elements are most useful in linking culture to strategy:

1. Formal statements of organizational philosophy, charters, creeds, materials used for recruitment and selection, and socialization.
2. Designing of physical spaces, facades, buildings.
3. Deliberate role modeling, teaching, and coaching by leaders.
4. Explicit reward and status system, promotion criteria.
5. Stories, legends, myths, and parables about key people and events.

6. What leaders pay attention to, measure, and control.
7. Leader reactions to critical incidents and organizational crises.
8. How the organization is designed and structured.
9. Organizational systems and procedures.
10. Criteria used for recruitment, selection, promotion, leveling off, retirement, and "excommunication" of people.[18]

In the personal and religious side of life, the impact of loss and change is easy to see.[19] Memories of loss and change often haunt individuals and organizations for years. Ibsen wrote, "Rob the average man of his life illusion and you rob him of his happiness at the same stroke."[20] When attachments to a culture are severed in an organization's attempt to change direction, employees and managers often experience deep feelings of grief. This phenomenon commonly occurs when external conditions dictate the need for a new strategy. Managers and employees often struggle to find meaning in a situation that changed many years before. Some people find comfort in memories; others find solace in the present. Weak linkages between strategic management and organizational culture can jeopardize performance and success. Deal and Kennedy emphasized that making strategic changes in an organization always threatens a culture:

> People form strong attachments to heroes, legends, the rituals of daily life, the hoopla of extravaganza and ceremonies, and all the symbols of the workplace. Change strips relationships and leaves employees confused, insecure, and often angry. Unless something can be done to provide support for transitions from old to new, the force of a culture can neutralize and emasculate strategy changes.[21]

The Mexican Culture

VISIT THE NET

Provides nice information on "What Is Culture" and also provides additional excellent links to other culture sites.
(http://www. managementhelp.org/ org_thry/culture/ culture.htm)

Mexico always has been and still is an authoritarian society in terms of schools, churches, businesses, and families. Employers seek workers who are agreeable, respectful, and obedient, rather than innovative, creative, and independent. Mexican workers tend to be activity oriented rather than problem solvers. When visitors walk into a Mexican business, they are impressed by the cordial, friendly atmosphere. This is almost always true because Mexicans desire harmony rather than conflict; desire for harmony is part of the social fabric in worker–manager relations. There is a much lower tolerance for adversarial relations or friction at work in Mexico as compared to the United States.

Mexican employers are paternalistic, providing workers with more than a paycheck, but in return they expect allegiance. Weekly food baskets, free meals, free bus service, and free day care are often part of compensation. The ideal working condition for a Mexican worker is the family model, with people all working together, doing their share, according to their designated roles. Mexican workers do not expect or desire a work environment in which self-expression and initiative are encouraged. Whereas U.S. business embodies individualism, achievement, competition, curiosity, pragmatism, informality, spontaneity, and doing more than expected on the job, Mexican businesses stress collectivism, continuity, cooperation, belongingness, formality, and doing exactly what you're told.

In Mexico, business associates rarely entertain each other at their homes, which are places reserved exclusively for close friends and family. Business meetings and entertaining are nearly always done at a restaurant. Preserving one's honor, saving face, and looking important are also exceptionally important in Mexico. This is why

Mexicans do not accept criticism and change easily; many find it humiliating to acknowledge having made a mistake. A meeting among employees and managers in a business located in Mexico is a forum for giving orders and directions rather than for discussing problems or participating in decision making. Mexican workers want to be closely supervised, cared for, and corrected in a civil manner. Opinions expressed by employees are often regarded as back talk in Mexico. Mexican supervisors are viewed as weak if they explain the rationale for their orders to workers.

Mexicans do not feel compelled to follow rules that are not associated with a particular person in authority they work for or know well. Thus, signs to wear earplugs or safety glasses, or attendance or seniority policies, and even one-way street signs are often ignored. Whereas Americans follow the rules, Mexicans often do not.

Life is slower in Mexico than in the United States. People do not wear watches. The first priority is often assigned to the last request, rather than to the first. Telephone systems break down. Banks may suddenly not have pesos. Phone repair can take months. Electricity for an entire plant or town can be down for hours or even days. Business and government offices open and close at different hours. Buses and taxis may be hours off schedule. Meeting times for appointments are not rigid. Tardiness is common everywhere. Effectively doing business in Mexico requires knowledge of the Mexican way of life, culture, beliefs, and customs.

The Russian Culture

In the United States, unsuccessful business entrepreneurs are viewed negatively as failures, whereas successful small-business owners enjoy high esteem and respect. In Russia, however, there is substantial social pressure against becoming a successful entrepreneur. Being a winner in Russia makes you the object of envy and resentment, a member of the elite rather than of the masses. Although this is slowly changing, personal ambition and success in Russia are often met with vindictiveness and derision. Initiative is met with indifference at best and punishment at worst. In the face of public ridicule and organized crime, however, thousands of Russians, particularly young persons, are opening all kinds of businesses. Public scorn and their own guilt from violating the values they were raised with do not deter many. Because Russian society scorns success, publicizing achievements, material possessions, awards, or privileges earned by Russian workers is not an effective motivational tool for those workers.

The Russian people are best known for their drive, boundless energy, tenacity, hard work, and perseverance in spite of immense obstacles. This is as true today as ever. The notion that the average Russian is stupid or lazy is nonsense; Russians on average are more educated than their American counterparts and bounce up more readily from failure.

In the United States, business ethics and personal ethics are essentially the same. Deception is deception and a lie is a lie whether in business or personal affairs in the United States. However, in Russia, business and personal ethics are separate. To deceive someone, bribe someone, or lie to someone to promote a business transaction is ethical in Russia, but to deceive a friend or trusted colleague is unethical. There are countless examples of foreign firms being cheated by Russian business partners. The implication of this fact for U.S. businesses is to forge strong personal relationships with their Russian business partners whenever possible; spend time with the Russians, eating, relaxing, and exercising; and in the absence of a personal relationship, be exceptionally cautious with agreements, partnerships, payments, and when granting credit.

The Russian people have great faith and confidence in, as well as respect for, U.S. products and services. Russians generally have low self-confidence. U.S. ideas, technology, and production practices are viewed by Russians as a panacea that can save them from a gloomy existence. For example, their squeaky telephone system and lack of fax machines make them feel deprived. This mind-set presents great opportunity in Russia for U.S. products of all kinds.

Russia has historically been an autocratic state. This cultural factor is evident in business; Russian managers generally exercise power without ever being challenged by subordinates. Delegation of authority and responsibility is difficult and often nonexistent in Russian businesses. The U.S. participative management style is not well received in Russia.

The Russian republic of Ingushetia recently passed a decree legalizing the practice of polygamy that allows men to have multiple wives, even a harem. The new law is a direct challenge to the Russian government, which has jurisdiction over 89 republics. The Russian Constitution prohibits polygamy, but the criminal code does not provide for any penalty. Ingushetian men take more than one wife, especially when the first wife does not have a son, despite the scientific discovery in 1959 that the father's contribution alone in procreation determines a child's sex.

The Japanese Culture

The Japanese place great importance upon group loyalty and consensus, a concept called *Wa*. Nearly all corporate activities in Japan encourage *Wa* among managers and employees. *Wa* requires that all members of a group agree and cooperate; this results in constant discussion and compromise. Japanese managers evaluate the potential attractiveness of alternative business decisions in terms of the long-term effect on the group's *Wa*. This is why silence, used for pondering alternatives, can be a plus in a formal Japanese meeting. Discussions potentially disruptive to *Wa* are generally conducted in very informal settings, such as at a bar, so as to minimize harm to the group's *Wa*. Entertaining is an important business activity in Japan because it strengthens *Wa*. Formal meetings are often conducted in informal settings. When confronted with disturbing questions or opinions, Japanese managers tend to remain silent, whereas Americans tend to respond directly, defending themselves through explanation and argument.

Note in the "Global Perspective" that when negotiating orally with Japanese executives, one must periodically allow for a time of silence and must not ask, "How was your weekend?" which could be viewed as intrusive.

Most Japanese managers are reserved, quiet, distant, introspective, and other oriented, whereas most U.S. managers are talkative, insensitive, impulsive, direct, and individual oriented. Americans often perceive Japanese managers as wasting time and carrying on pointless conversations, whereas U.S. managers often use blunt criticism, ask prying questions, and make quick decisions. These kinds of cultural differences have disrupted many potentially productive Japanese–American business endeavors. Viewing the Japanese communication style as a prototype for all Asian cultures is a stereotype that must be avoided.

Americans have more freedom to control their own fates than do the Japanese. Life in the United States and life in Japan are very different; the United States offers more upward mobility to its people. This is a great strength of the United States. Sherman explained:

> America is not like Japan and can never be. America's strength is the opposite:
> It opens its doors and brings the world's disorder in. It tolerates social change
> that would tear most other societies apart. This openness encourages
> Americans to adapt as individuals rather than as a group. Americans go west
> to California to get a new start; they move east to Manhattan to try to make

GLOBAL PERSPECTIVE

American Versus Foreign Communication Differences

As Americans increasingly interact with managers in other countries, it is important to be sensitive to foreign business cultures. Americans too often come across as intrusive, manipulative, and garrulous, and this impression reduces their effectiveness in communication. *Forbes* recently provided the following cultural hints from Charis Intercultural Training:

1. Italians, Germans, and French generally do not soften up executives with praise before they criticize. Americans do soften up folks, and this practice seems manipulative to Europeans.

2. Israelis are accustomed to fast-paced meetings and have little patience for American informality and small talk.

3. British executives often complain that American executives chatter too much. Informality, egalitarianism, and spontaneity from Americans in business settings jolt many foreigners.

4. Europeans feel they are being treated like children when asked to wear name tags by Americans.

5. Executives in India are used to interrupting one another. Thus, when American executives listen without asking for clarification or posing questions, they are viewed by Indians as not paying attention.

6. When negotiating orally with Malaysian or Japanese executives, it is appropriate to periodically allow for a time of silence. However, no pause is needed when negotiating in Israel.

Refrain from asking foreign managers questions such as "How was your weekend?" That is intrusive to foreigners, who tend to regard their business and private lives as totally separate.

Source: Adapted from Lalita Khosla, "You Say Tomato," *Forbes* (May 21, 2001): 36.

---

the big time; they move to Vermont or to a farm to get close to the soil. They break away from their parents' religions or values or class; they rediscover their ethnicity. They go to night school; they change their names.[22]

Production/Operations Concerns When Implementing Strategies

Production/operations capabilities, limitations, and policies can significantly enhance or inhibit the attainment of objectives. Production processes typically constitute more than 70 percent of a firm's total assets. A major part of the strategy-implementation process takes place at the production site. Production-related decisions on plant size, plant location, product design, choice of equipment, kind of tooling, size of inventory, inventory control, quality control, cost control, use of standards, job specialization, employee training, equipment and resource utilization, shipping and packaging, and technological innovation can have a dramatic impact on the success or failure of strategy-implementation efforts.

Examples of adjustments in production systems that could be required to implement various strategies are provided in Table 7-4 for both for-profit and non-profit organizations. For instance, note that when a bank formulates and selects a strategy to add 10 new branches, a production-related implementation concern is site

TABLE 7-4   Production Management and Strategy Implementation

TYPE OF ORGANIZATION	STRATEGY BEING IMPLEMENTED	PRODUCTION SYSTEM ADJUSTMENTS
Hospital	Adding a cancer center (Product Development)	Purchase specialized equipment and add specialized people.
Bank	Adding 10 new branches (Market Development)	Perform site location analysis.
Beer brewery	Purchasing a barley farm operation (Backward Integration)	Revise the inventory control system.
Steel manufacturer	Acquiring a fast-food chain (Unrelated Diversification)	Improve the quality control system.
Computer company	Purchasing a retail distribution chain (Forward Integration)	Alter the shipping, packaging, and transportation systems.

location. The largest bicycle company in the United States, Huffy, recently ended its own production of bikes and now contracts out those services to Asian and Mexican manufacturers. Huffy focuses instead on the design, marketing, and distribution of bikes, but it no longer produces bikes itself. The Dayton, Ohio, company closed its plants in Ohio, Missouri, and Mississippi.

Just-in-Time (JIT) production approaches have withstood the test of time. JIT significantly reduces the costs of implementing strategies. With JIT, parts and materials are delivered to a production site just as they are needed, rather than being stockpiled as a hedge against later deliveries. Harley-Davidson reports that at one plant alone, JIT freed $22 million previously tied up in inventory and greatly reduced reorder lead time.

Factors that should be studied before locating production facilities include the availability of major resources, the prevailing wage rates in the area, transportation costs related to shipping and receiving, the location of major markets, political risks in the area or country, and the availability of trainable employees.

For high-technology companies, production costs may not be as important as production flexibility because major product changes can be needed often. Industries such as biogenetics and plastics rely on production systems that must be flexible enough to allow frequent changes and the rapid introduction of new products. An article in *Harvard Business Review* explained why some organizations get into trouble:

> They too slowly realize that a change in product strategy alters the tasks of a production system. These tasks, which can be stated in terms of requirements for cost, product flexibility, volume flexibility, product performance, and product consistency, determine which manufacturing policies are appropriate. As strategies shift over time, so must production policies covering the location and scale of manufacturing facilities, the choice of manufacturing process, the degree of vertical integration of each manufacturing facility, the use of R&D units, the control of the production system, and the licensing of technology.[23]

A common management practice, cross-training of employees, can facilitate strategy implementation and can yield many benefits. Employees gain a better understanding of the whole business and can contribute better ideas in planning sessions. Production/operations managers need to realize, however, that cross-training employees can create problems related to the following issues:

1. It can thrust managers into roles that emphasize counseling and coaching over directing and enforcing.
2. It can necessitate substantial investments in training and incentives.
3. It can be very time-consuming.
4. Skilled workers may resent unskilled workers who learn their jobs.
5. Older employees may not want to learn new skills.

Human Resource Concerns When Implementing Strategies

The job of human resource manager is changing rapidly as companies continue to downsize and reorganize. Strategic responsibilities of the human resource manager include assessing the staffing needs and costs for alternative strategies proposed during strategy formulation and developing a staffing plan for effectively implementing strategies. This plan must consider how best to manage spiraling healthcare insurance costs. Employers' health coverage expenses consume an average 26 percent of firms' net profits, even though most companies now require employees to pay part of their health insurance premiums. The plan must also include how to motivate employees and managers during a time when layoffs are common and workloads are high.

The human resource department must develop performance incentives that clearly link performance and pay to strategies. The process of empowering managers and employees through their involvement in strategic-management activities yields the greatest benefits when all organizational members understand clearly how they will benefit personally if the firm does well. Linking company and personal benefits is a major new strategic responsibility of human resource managers. Other new responsibilities for human resource managers may include establishing and administering an *employee stock ownership plan (ESOP)*, instituting an effective child-care policy, and providing leadership for managers and employees in a way that allows them to balance work and family.

A well-designed strategic-management system can fail if insufficient attention is given to the human resource dimension. Human resource problems that arise when businesses implement strategies can usually be traced to one of three causes: (1) disruption of social and political structures, (2) failure to match individuals' aptitudes with implementation tasks, and (3) inadequate top management support for implementation activities.[24]

Strategy implementation poses a threat to many managers and employees in an organization. New power and status relationships are anticipated and realized. New formal and informal groups' values, beliefs, and priorities may be largely unknown. Managers and employees may become engaged in resistance behavior as their roles, prerogatives, and power in the firm change. Disruption of social and political structures that accompany strategy execution must be anticipated and considered during strategy formulation and managed during strategy implementation.

A concern in matching managers with strategy is that jobs have specific and relatively static responsibilities, although people are dynamic in their personal development. Commonly used methods that match managers with strategies to be implemented include transferring managers, developing leadership workshops, offering career development activities, promotions, job enlargement, and job enrichment.

A number of other guidelines can help ensure that human relationships facilitate rather than disrupt strategy-implementation efforts. Specifically, managers should do a lot of chatting and informal questioning to stay abreast of how things are progressing and to know when to intervene. Managers can build support for strategy-implementation efforts by giving few orders, announcing few decisions, depending heavily on informal questioning, and seeking to probe and clarify until a consensus emerges. Key thrusts that succeed should be rewarded generously and visibly.

It is surprising that so often during strategy formulation, individual values, skills, and abilities needed for successful strategy implementation are not considered. It is rare that a firm selecting new strategies or significantly altering existing strategies possesses the right line and staff personnel in the right positions for successful strategy implementation. The need to match individual aptitudes with strategy-implementation tasks should be considered in strategy choice.

Inadequate support from strategists for implementation activities often undermines organizational success. Chief executive officers, small business owners, and government agency heads must be personally committed to strategy implementation and express this commitment in highly visible ways. Strategists' formal statements about the importance of strategic management must be consistent with actual support and rewards given for activities completed and objectives reached. Otherwise, stress created by inconsistency can cause uncertainty among managers and employees at all levels.

Perhaps the best method for preventing and overcoming human resource problems in strategic management is to actively involve as many managers and employees as possible in the process. Although time-consuming, this approach builds understanding, trust, commitment, and ownership and reduces resentment and hostility. The true potential of strategy formulation and implementation resides in people.

Employee Stock Ownership Plans (ESOPs)

An *ESOP* is a tax-qualified, defined-contribution, employee-benefit plan whereby employees purchase stock of the company through borrowed money or cash contributions. ESOPs empower employees to work as owners; this is a primary reason why the number of ESOPs grew dramatically throughout the 1980s and 1990s to more than 10,000 plans covering more than 15 million employees. ESOPs now control more than $80 billion in corporate stock in the United States.

Besides reducing worker alienation and stimulating productivity, ESOPs allow firms other benefits, such as substantial tax savings. Principal, interest, and dividend payments on ESOP-funded debt are tax deductible. Banks lend money to ESOPs at interest rates below prime. This money can be repaid in pretax dollars, lowering the debt service as much as 30 percent in some cases.

If an ESOP owns more than 50 percent of the firm, those who lend money to the ESOP are taxed on only 50 percent of the income received on the loans. ESOPs are not for every firm, however, because the initial legal, accounting, actuarial, and appraisal fees to set up an ESOP are about $50,000 for a small or midsized firm, with annual administration expenses of about $15,000. Analysts say ESOPs also do not work well in firms that have fluctuating payrolls and profits. Human resource managers in many firms conduct preliminary research to determine the desirability of an ESOP, and then they facilitate its establishment and administration if benefits outweigh the costs.

Many companies are following the lead of Polaroid, which established an ESOP as a tactic for preventing a hostile takeover. Polaroid's CEO MacAllister Booth says, "Twenty years from now we'll find that employees have a sizable stake in every major American corporation." (It is interesting to note here that Polaroid is chartered in the state of Delaware, which requires corporate suitors to acquire 85 percent of a target company's shares to complete a merger; over 50 percent of all U.S. corporations are incorporated in Delaware for this reason.) Wyatt Cafeterias, a southwestern United States operator of 120 cafeterias, also adopted the ESOP concept to prevent a hostile takeover. Employee productivity at Wyatt has greatly increased since the ESOP began, as illustrated in the following quote:

> The key employee in our entire organization is the person serving the customer on the cafeteria line. In the past, because of high employee turnover and entry-level wages for many line jobs, these employees received far less attention and recognition than managers. We now tell the tea cart server, "You own the place. Don't wait for the manager to tell you how to do your job better or how to provide better service. You take care of it." Sure, we're looking for productivity increases, but since we began pushing decisions down to the level of people who deal directly with customers, we've discovered an awesome side effect—suddenly the work crews have this "happy to be here" attitude that the customers really love.[25]

Balancing Work Life and Home Life

Work/family strategies have become so popular among companies today that the strategies now represent a competitive advantage for those firms that offer such benefits as elder care assistance, flexible scheduling, job sharing, adoption benefits, an on-site summer camp, employee help lines, pet care, and even lawn service referrals. New corporate titles such as Work/Life Coordinator and Director of Diversity are becoming common.

Working Mother magazine annually published its listing of "The 100 Best Companies for Working Mothers" (workingmother.com/bestlist.html). Three especially important variables used in the ranking were availability of flextime, advancement opportunities, and equitable distribution of benefits among companies. *Working Mother's* top 10 best companies for working women in 2005 are provided in Table 7-5.

Working Mother also conducts extensive research to determine the best U.S. firms for women of color. In 2005, the top six firms for women of color to work for were Allstate, American Express, Fannie Mae, General Mills, IBM, and JP Morgan Chase (www.workingmother/wocbest.html).

Human resource managers need to foster a more effective balancing of professional and private lives because nearly 60 million people in the United States are now part of two-career families. A corporate objective to become more lean and mean must today include consideration for the fact that a good home life contributes immensely to a good work life.

The work/family issue is no longer just a women's issue. Some specific measures that firms are taking to address this issue are providing spouse relocation assistance as an employee benefit; providing company resources for family recreational and educational use; establishing employee country clubs, such as those at IBM and Bethlehem Steel; and creating family/work interaction opportunities. A study by Joseph Pleck of Wheaton College found that in companies that do not offer paternity leave for fathers as a benefit, most men take short, informal paternity leaves anyway by combining vacation time and sick days.

Some organizations have developed family days, when family members are invited into the workplace, taken on plant or office tours, dined by management, and given a chance to see exactly what other family members do each day. Family days are inexpensive and increase the employee's pride in working for the organization. Flexible working hours during the week are another human resource response to the need for individuals to balance work life and home life. The work/family topic is being made part of the agenda at meetings and thus is being discussed in many organizations.

VISIT THE NET

Provides a great overview of the strategic planning process.
(www.mapnp.org/library/plan_dec/str_plan.html)

TABLE 7-5   The 10 Best Firms for Women to Work for in 2005 (listed alphabetically)

Bristol-Myers Squibb Company. Widely uses flex-scheduling options and on-site child-care facilities. High numbers of women on staff attend advancement and leadership training.

Discovery Communications Inc. This media and entertainment company has generous paid maternity leave, comprehensive lactation support services, and heavily utilized flexible work arrangements.

Eli Lilly and Company. This large pharmaceutical firm offers extensive paid parental leave, generous adoption aid, and a variety of well-attended advancement programs for women.

IBM. This hardware and software developer boasts high usage of flex-scheduling options, 156 weeks of job-protected parental leave, and a full menu of child-care services.

Johnson & Johnson. This pharmaceutical and medical products manufacturer offers great on-site child-care benefits, manager training and accountability on work/life issues, and family-friendly resources.

JPMorgan Chase. This financial services firm offers a stellar paid maternity benefit, manager work/life training, and formal compensation policies that reward managers who help women advance.

PricewaterhouseCoopers LLP. A full range of flexible scheduling options, a generous paid parental leave policy, and highly attended programs designed to train and advance women characterize this global accounting firm.

Prudential Financial Inc. This insurance and financial services provider offers a comprehensive lactation program, a range of flexible work arrangements, and a commitment to women's advancement programs.

S. C. Johnson & Son, Inc. This manufacturer of household products offers an extensive array of family-friendly concierge services, manager training on work/life issues, and ample paid leave for new parents.

Wachovia Corporation. This banking and financial services company offers extensive child-care benefits, a long menu of concierge services, and some widely utilized flexible-scheduling options.

Source: Adapted from www.workingmother.com/top10.html.

According to Catalyst, a New York–based women's advocacy group, women comprise about 16 percent of the top-ranking executives at America's largest companies. This is up from less than 9 percent in 1995. This is good news for women because more than 2,000 out of 14,000 corporate officers among the Fortune 500 companies now are women. However, only five of the Fortune 500 firms have a woman CEO and 70 of the Fortune 500 firms have no women corporate officers at all. Thus there is great room for improvement in removing the *glass ceiling* domestically, especially considering that women make up 47 percent of the U.S. labor force. Glass ceiling refers to the invisible barrier in many firms that bars women and minorities from top level management positions. As listed in Table 7-6 female CEOs (strategists) among large U.S. firms include Patricia Russo at Lucent, Anne Mulcahy at Xerox, Andrea Jung at Avon, and Besty Holden at Kraft Foods. The United States leads the world in promoting women and minorities into mid- and top-level managerial positions in business. Wal-Mart is an example of a company in some legal trouble, since about 15 percent of its managers are female, yet women make up about 70 percent of the Wal-Mart workforce.

Boeing's recent firing of CEO Harry Stonecipher for having an extramarital affair has raised public awareness of office romance. However, just 12 percent of 391 companies surveyed by the American Management Association have written guidelines on office dating.[26] The fact of the matter is that most employers in the United States turn a blind eye to martial cheating. Some employers, such as Southwest Airlines, which employs more than 1,000 married couples, explicitly allow consensual office relationships. Research suggests that more men than women engage in extramarital affairs at work, roughly 22 percent to 15 percent; however, the percentage of women having extramarital affairs is increasing steadily whereas the percentage of men having affairs with co-workers is holding steady.[27] If an affair is disrupting your work, then "the first

TABLE 7-6 Some Women CEOs in the United States in 2005

CEO	COMPANY	CEO'S AGE
1. Meg Whitman	eBay	49
2. Andrea Jung	Avon Products	47
3. Anne Mulcahy	Xerox	52
4. Majorie Magner	Citigroup	56
5. Betsy Holden	Kraft Foods	49
6. Ann Moore	AOL Time Warner	57
7. Sallie Krawcheck	Smith Barney	40
8. Shelly Lazarus	Ogilvy & Mather Worldwide	58
9. Pat Russo	Lucent Technologies	53
10. Mary Sammons	Rite Aid	55
11. Maria Lagomasino	J. P. Morgan Chase	47

step is to go to the offending person privately and try to resolve the matter. If that fails, then go to the human-resources manager seeking assistance."[28] Filing a discrimination lawsuit based on the affair is recommended only as a last resort because courts generally rule that co-workers' injuries are not pervasive enough to warrant any damages.

Benefits of a Diverse Workforce

Toyota has committed almost $8 billion over 10 years to diversify its workforce and to use more minority suppliers. Hundreds of other firms, such as Ford Motor Company and Coca-Cola, are also striving to become more diversified in their workforces. TJX Companies, the parent of 1,500 T. J. Maxx and Marshall's stores, has reaped great benefits and is an exemplary company in terms of diversity. A recent *Wall Street Journal* article listed, in order of importance, the following major benefits of having a diverse workforce:[29]

1. Improves corporate culture
2. Improves employee morale
3. Leads to a higher retention of employees
4. Leads to an easier recruitment of new employees
5. Decreases complaints and litigation
6. Increases creativity
7. Decreases interpersonal conflict between employees
8. Enables the organization to move into emerging markets
9. Improves client relations
10. Increases productivity
11. Improves the bottom line
12. Maximizes brand identity
13. Reduces training costs

An organization can perhaps be most effective when its workforce mirrors the diversity of its customers. For global companies, this goal can be optimistic, but it is a worthwhile goal. It is interesting that online shopping by Hispanics is growing at more than three times overall online shopping.[30] Consequently, many retailers are launching Spanish language Web sites. JetBlue Airways, Nissan North America, Office Depot, and Honda Motors are among dozens of companies that now offer Spanish-language Web sites. Hispanics today almost outnumber African Americans as the largest minority group in the United States. Although only 16 Hispanics serve as president or chief executive of Fortune 1,000 companies, many firms are committed to attracting, developing, and retaining Hispanic leaders. For example PepsiCo has increased its Latino executives by more than 75 percent in the first half of this decade. The CEO of Alcoa, the world's largest producer of aluminum, is Alain Belda, a Hispanic. Another is James Padilla, president and COO of Ford Motor Company. Nike president and CEO is William Perez. The COO of Eastman Kodak is Antonio Perez. Hector J. de Ruiz is CEO of Advanced Micro Devices (AMD). Linda Alvarado, Claudio Gonzales, and Enrique Hernandez, Jr., are on four or more boards of directors of Fortune 1,000 firms.

CONCLUSION

Successful strategy formulation does not at all guarantee successful strategy implementation. Although inextricably interdependent, strategy formulation and strategy implementation are characteristically different. In a single word, strategy implementation means *change*. It is widely agreed that "the real work begins after strategies are formulated." Successful strategy implementation requires the support of, as well as discipline and hard work from, motivated managers and employees. It is sometimes frightening to think that a single individual can irreparably sabotage strategy-implementation efforts.

Formulating the right strategies is not enough, because managers and employees must be motivated to implement those strategies. Management issues considered central to strategy implementation include matching organizational structure with strategy, linking performance and pay to strategies, creating an organizational climate conducive to change, managing political relationships, creating a strategy-supportive culture, adapting production/operations processes, and managing human resources. Establishing annual objectives, devising policies, and allocating resources are central strategy-implementation activities common to all organizations. Depending on the size and type of the organization, other management issues could be equally important to successful strategy implementation.

We invite you to visit the David page on the Prentice Hall Companion Web site at www.prenhall.com/david for this chapter's review quiz.

KEY TERMS AND CONCEPTS

Annual Objectives (p. 264)

Avoidance (p. 269)

Benchmarking (p. 279)

Bonus System (p. 282)

Conflict (p. 269)

Confrontation (p. 270)

Culture (p. 287)

Defusion (p. 269)

Delayering (p. 278)

Decentralized Structure (p. 272)

Divisional Structure by Geographic Area, Product, Customer, or Process (p. 272)

Downsizing (p. 278)

Educative Change Strategy (p. 283)

Employee Stock Ownership
Plans (ESOP) (p. 293)
Establishing Annual Objectives
(p. 264)
Force Change Strategy (p. 283)
Functional Structure (p. 271)
Gain Sharing (p. 281)
Glass Ceiling (p. 296)
Horizontal Consistency
of Objectives (p. 266)

Just-in-Time (JIT) (p. 292)
Matrix Structure (p. 275)
Policy (p. 266)
Profit Sharing (p. 281)
Rational Change Strategy (p. 283)
Reengineering (p. 279)
Resistance to Change (p. 283)
Resource Allocation (p. 268)
Restructuring (p. 278)

Rightsizing (p. 278)
Self-Interest Change
Strategy (p. 283)
Strategic Business Unit (SBU)
Structure (p. 274)
Triangulation (p. 287)
Vertical Consistency
of Objectives (p. 266)

ISSUES FOR REVIEW AND DISCUSSION

1. Allocating resources can be a political and an ad hoc activity in firms that do not use strategic management. Why is this true? Does adopting strategic management ensure easy resource allocation? Why?
2. Compare strategy formulation with strategy implementation in terms of each being an art or a science.
3. Describe the relationship between annual objectives and policies.
4. Identify a long-term objective and two supporting annual objectives for a familiar organization.
5. Identify and discuss three policies that apply to your present business policy class.
6. Explain the following statement: Horizontal consistency of goals is as important as vertical consistency.
7. Describe several reasons why conflict may occur during objective-setting activities.
8. In your opinion, what approaches to conflict resolution would be best for resolving a disagreement between a personnel manager and a sales manager over the firing of a particular salesperson? Why?
9. Describe the organizational culture of your college or university.
10. Explain why organizational structure is so important in strategy implementation.
11. In your opinion, how many separate divisions could an organization reasonably have without using an SBU-type organizational structure? Why?
12. Would you recommend a divisional structure by geographic area, product, customer, or process for a medium-sized bank in your local area? Why?
13. What are the advantages and disadvantages of decentralizing the wage and salary functions of an organization? How could this be accomplished?

14. Consider a college organization with which you are familiar. How did management issues affect strategy implementation in that organization?
15. As production manager of a local newspaper, what problems would you anticipate in implementing a strategy to increase the average number of pages in the paper by 40 percent?
16. Do you believe expenditures for child care or fitness facilities are warranted from a cost-benefit perspective? Why or why not?
17. Explain why successful strategy implementation often hinges on whether the strategy-formulation process empowers managers and employees.
18. Compare and contrast the cultures in Mexico, Russia, and Japan.
19. Discuss the glass ceiling in the United States, giving your ideas and suggestions.
20. Discuss three ways discussed in this book for linking performance and pay to strategies.
21. List the different types of organizational structure. Diagram what you think is the most complex of these structures and label your chart clearly.
22. List the advantages and disadvantages of a functional versus a divisional organizational structure.
23. Compare and contrast the U.S. business culture with the Mexican business culture.
24. Discuss recent trends in women and minorities becoming top executives in the United States.
25. Discuss recent trends in firms downsizing family-friendly programs.
26. Research the latest developments in the class-action lawsuit involving women managers versus Wal-Mart Stores and report your findings to the class.
27. List seven guidelines to follow in developing an organizational chart.

NOTES

1. Dale McConkey, "Planning in a Changing Environment," *Business Horizons* (September–October 1988): 66.

2. A. G. Bedeian and W. F. Glueck, *Management*, 3rd ed. (Chicago: The Dryden Press, 1983): 212.

3. Boris Yavitz and William Newman, *Strategy in Action: The Execution, Politics, and Payoff of Business Planning* (New York: The Free Press, 1982): 195.

4. Schein, E. H. "Three Cultures of Management: The Key to Organizational Learning," *Sloan Management Review* 38, 1 (1996): 9–20.

5. Ghoshal, S. and Bartlett, C. A., "Changing the Role of Management: Beyond Structure to Processes." *Harvard Business Review* 73, 1 (1995): 88.

6. Steve Hamm and Marcia Stepanek, "From Reengineering to E-engineering," *BusinessWeek* (March 22, 1999): EB15.

7. "Want to Be a Manager? Many People Say No, Calling Job Miserable," *Wall Street Journal* (April 4, 1997): 1; Also, Stephanie Armour, "Management Loses Its Allure," *USA Today* (October 10, 1997): 1B.

8. Paul Carroll, "No More Business as Usual, Please. Time to Try Something Different," *Wall Street Journal* (October 23, 2001): A24.

9. Julie Schmit, "Japan Shifts to Merit Pay," *USA Today* (July 23, 1999): 5B.

10. Richard Brown, "Outsider CEO: Inspiring Change with Force and Grace," *USA Today* (July 19, 1999): 3B.

11. Yavitz and Newman, 58.

12. Matthew Boyle, "KA-CHING! CEOs Grab Record Perks." *Fortune* (May 2, 2005): 22.

13. Jack Duncan, *Management* (New York: Random House, 1983): 381–390.

14. H. Igor Ansoff, "Strategic Management of Technology," *Journal of Business Strategy* 7, no. 3 (Winter 1987): 38.

15. Robert Waterman, Jr., "How the Best Get Better," *BusinessWeek* (September 14, 1987): 104.

16. Kathernie Kranhold and Jeffrey Ball, "GE to Spend More on Projects Tied to Climate Change," *Wall Street Journal* (May 9, 2005): A2.

17. Jack Duncan, "Organizational Culture: Getting a Fix on an Elusive Concept," *Academy of Management Executive* 3, no. 3 (August 1989): 229.

18. E. H. Schein, "The Role of the Founder in Creating Organizational Culture," *Organizational Dynamics* (Summer 1983): 13–28.

19. T. Deal and A. Kennedy, "Culture: A New Look Through Old Lenses," *Journal of Applied Behavioral Science* 19, no. 4 (1983): 498–504.

20. H. Ibsen, "The Wild Duck," in O. G. Brochett and L. Brochett (eds.), *Plays for the Theater* (New York: Holt, Rinehart & Winston, 1967); R. Pascale, "The Paradox of 'Corporate Culture': Reconciling Ourselves to Socialization," *California Management Review* 28, no. 2 (1985): 26, 37–40.

21. T. Deal and A. Kennedy, *Corporate Cultures: The Rites and Rituals of Corporate Life* (Reading, MA: Addison-Wesley, 1982): 256.

22. Stratford Sherman, "How to Beat the Japanese," *Fortune* (April 10, 1989): 145.

23. Robert Stobaugh and Piero Telesio, "Match Manufacturing Policies and Product Strategy," *Harvard Business Review* 61, no. 2 (March–April 1983): 113.

24. R. T. Lenz and Marjorie Lyles, "Managing Human Resource Problems in Strategy Planning Systems," *Journal of Business Strategy* 60, no. 4 (Spring 1986): 58.

25. J. Warren Henry, "ESOPs with Productivity Payoffs," *Journal of Business Strategy* (July–August 1989): 33.

26. Sue Shellenbarger, "Employers Often Ignore Office Affairs, Leaving Co-workers in Difficult Spot," *Wall Street Journal* (March 10, 2005): D1.

27. Ibid.

28. Ibid.

29. Julie Bennett, "Corporate Downsizing Doesn't Deter Search for Diversity," *Wall Street Journal* (October 23, 2001): B18.

30. Jon Swartz, "Retailers Offer Web Sites in Spanish," *USA Today* (May 29, 2003): B1.

CURRENT READINGS

Argyres, N. S., and B. S. Silverman. "R&D, Organization Structure, and the Development of Corporate Technological Knowledge." *Strategic Management Journal* 25, no. 8–9 (August–September 2004): 929.

Bowen, David E., and Cheri Ostroff. "Understanding HRM-Firm Performance Linkages: The Role of the 'Strength' of the HRM System." *The Academy of Management Review* 29, no. 2 (April 2004): 203.

Chadwick, C., L. W. Hunter, and S. L. Walston. "Effects of Downsizing Practices on the Performance of Hospitals." *Strategic Management Journal* 25, no. 5 (May 2004): 405.

Charan, R. "Ending the CEO Succession Crisis." *Harvard Business Review* (February 2005): 72.

Chong, John K. S. "Six Steps to Better Crisis Management." *Journal of Business Strategy* 25, no. 2 (2004): 43.

Datta, Deepak K., James P. Guthrie, and Patrick M. Wright. "Human Resource Management and Labor Productivity: Does Industry Matter?" *The Academy of Management Journal* 48, no. 1 (February 2005): 135.

Dedrick, J., and K. L. Kraemer. "The Impacts of IT on Firm and Industry Structure: The Personal Computer Industry." *California Management Review* 47, no. 3 (Spring 2005): 122.

De Miguel, A., J. Pindado, and C. de la Torre. "Ownership Structure and Firm Value: New Evidence from Spain." *Strategic Management Journal* 25, no. 12 (December 2004): 1199.

Ginsberg, J. M., and P. N. Bloom. "Choosing the Right Green Marketing Strategy." *MIT Sloan Management Review* 46, no. 1 (Fall 2004): 79.

Gratton, L., and S. Ghoshal. "Beyond Best Practice." *MIT Sloan Management Review* 46, no. 3 (Spring 2005): 49.

Hoppe, M. H. "Introduction: Geert Hofstede's Culture's Consequences: International Differences in Work-Related Values." *The Academy of Management Executive* 18, no. 1 (February 2004): 73.

Howell, Jane M., and Boas Shamir. "The Role of Followers in the Charismatic Leadership Process: Relationships and Their Consequences." *The Academy of Management Review* 30, no. 1 (January 2005): 96.

Jarzabkowski, Paula, and Rosalind H. Searle. "Harnessing Diversity and Collective Action in the Top Management Team." *Long Range Planning* 37, no. 5 (October 2004): 399.

Meer, David. "Enter the Chief Growth Officer: Searching for Organic Growth." *Journal of Business Strategy* 26, no. 1 (2005): 13.

Minnick, Donald J., and R. Duane Ireland. "Inside the New Organization: a Blueprint for Surviving Restructuring, Downsizing, Acquisitions and Outsourcing." *Journal of Business Strategy* 26, no. 1 (2005): 18.

Nixon, R. D., M. A. Hitt, H. U. Lee, and E. Jeong. "Market Reactions to Announcements of Corporate Downsizing Action and Implementation Strategies." *Strategic Management Journal* 25, no. 11 (November 2004): 1121.

Olson, Eric M., Stanley F. Slater, G. Tomas, and M. Hult. "The Importance of Structure and Process to Strategy Implementation." *Business Horizons* 48, no. 1 (January–February 2005): 47.

Ravasi, Davide, and Gabriella Lojacono. "Managing Design and Designers for Strategic Renewal." *Long Range Planning* 38, no. 1 (February 2005): 51.

Richard, Orlando C., Tim Barnett, Sean Dwyer, and Ken Chadwick. "Cultural Diversity in Management, Firm Performance, and the Moderating Role of Entrepreneurial Orientation Dimensions." *The Academy of Management Journal* 47, no. 2 (April 2004): 255.

Schaffer, R. H., and M. K. McCreight. "Build Your Own Change Model." *Business Horizons* 47, no. 3 (May–June 2004): 33.

Shaw, Jason D., Nina Gupta, Atul Mitra, and Gerald E. Ledford Jr. "Success and Survival of Skill-Based Pay Plans." *Journal of Management* 31, no. 1 (February 2005): 28.

Singh, Val, and Sébastien Point. "Strategic Responses by European Companies to the Diversity Challenge: An Online Comparison." *Long Range Planning* 37, no. 4 (August 2004): 295.

Vera, Dusya, and Mary Crossan. "Strategic Leadership and Organizational Learning." *The Academy of Management Review* 29, no. 2 (April 2004): 222.

Von Glinow, Mary Ann, Debra L. Shapiro, and Jeanne M. Brett. "Can We *Talk*, and Should We? Managing Emotional Conflict in Multicultural Teams." *The Academy of Management Review* 29, no. 4 (October 2004): 578.

Werner, S., H. L. Tosi, and L. Gomez-Mejia. "Organizational Governance and Employee Pay: How Ownership Structure Affects the Firm's Compensation Strategy." *Strategic Management Journal* 26, no. 4 (April 2005): 377.

Yoshikawa, T., P. H. Phan, and P. David. "The Impact of Ownership Structure on Wages Intensity in Japanese Corporations." *Journal of Management* 31, no. 2 (April 2005): 278.

experiential exercises

Experiential Exercise 7A

Revising Google's Organizational Chart

PURPOSE

Developing and altering organizational charts is an important skill for strategists to possess. This exercise can improve your skill in altering an organization's hierarchical structure in response to new strategies being formulated.

INSTRUCTIONS

Step 1 Turn to the Google Cohesion Case (p. 34). On a separate sheet of paper, diagram an organizational chart that you believe would best suit Google's needs if the company decided to form a divisional by-product structure.

Step 2 Provide as much detail in your chart as possible, including the names of individuals and the titles of positions.

Experiential Exercise 7B

Do Organizations Really Establish Objectives?

PURPOSE

Objectives provide direction, allow synergy, aid in evaluation, establish priorities, reduce uncertainty, minimize conflicts, stimulate exertion, and aid in both the allocation of resources and the design of jobs. This exercise will enhance your understanding of how organizations use or misuse objectives.

INSTRUCTIONS

Step 1 Join with one other person in class to form a two-person team.

Step 2 Contact by telephone the owner or manager of an organization in your city or town. Request a 30-minute personal interview or meeting with that person for the purpose of discussing "business objectives." During your meeting, seek answers to the following questions:

1. Do you believe it is important for a business to establish and clearly communicate long-term and annual objectives? Why or why not?
2. Does your organization establish objectives? If yes, what type and how many? How are the objectives communicated to individuals? Are your firm's objectives in written form or simply communicated orally?
3. To what extent are managers and employees involved in the process of establishing objectives?
4. How often are your business objectives revised and by what process?

Step 3 Take good notes during the interview. Let one person be the note taker and one person do most of the talking. Have your notes typed up and ready to turn in to your professor.

Step 4 Prepare a 5-minute oral presentation for the class, reporting the results of your interview. Turn in your typed report.

Experiential Exercise 7C

Understanding My University's Culture

PURPOSE

It is something of an art to uncover the basic values and beliefs that are buried deeply in an organization's rich collection of stories, language, heroes, heroines, and rituals, yet culture can be the most important factor in implementing strategies.

INSTRUCTIONS

Step 1 On a separate sheet of paper, list the following terms: hero/heroine, belief, metaphor, language, value, symbol, story, legend, saga, folktale, myth, ceremony, rite, and ritual.

Step 2 For your college or university, give examples of each term. If necessary, speak with faculty, staff, alumni, administration, or fellow students of the institution to identify examples of each term.

Step 3 Report your findings to the class. Tell the class how you feel regarding cultural products being consciously used to help implement strategies.

Implementing Strategies: Marketing, Finance/Accounting, R&D, and MIS Issues

"notable quotes"

The greatest strategy is doomed if it's implemented badly.
Bernard Reimann

There is no "perfect" strategic decision. One always has to pay a price. One always has to balance conflicting objectives, conflicting opinions, and conflicting priorities. The best strategic decision is only an approximation—and a risk.
Peter Drucker

The real question isn't how well you're doing today against your own history, but how you're doing against your competitors.
Donald Kress

As market windows open and close more quickly, it is important that R&D be tied more closely to corporate strategy.
William Spenser

Most of the time, strategists should not be formulating strategy at all; they should be getting on with implementing strategies they already have.
Henry Mintzberg

It is human nature to make decisions based on emotion, rather than on fact. But nothing could be more illogical.
Toshiba Corporation

No business can do everything. Even if it has the money, it will never have enough good people. It has to set priorities. The worst thing to do is a little bit of everything. This makes sure that nothing is being accomplished. It is better to pick the wrong priority than none at all.
Peter Drucker

Strategies have no chance of being implemented successfully in organizations that do not market goods and services well, in firms that cannot raise needed working capital, in firms that produce technologically inferior products, or in firms that have a weak information system. This chapter examines marketing, finance/accounting, R&D, and management information systems (MIS) issues that are central to effective strategy implementation. Special topics include market segmentation, market positioning, evaluating the worth of a business, determining to what extent debt and/or stock should be used as a source of capital, developing pro forma financial statements, contracting R&D outside the firm, and creating an information support system. Manager and employee involvement and participation are essential for success in marketing, finance/accounting, R&D, and MIS activities.

The Nature of Strategy Implementation

The quarterback can call the best play possible in the huddle, but that does not mean the play will go for a touchdown. The team may even lose yardage unless the play is executed (implemented) well. Less than 10 percent of strategies formulated are successfully implemented! There are many reasons for this low success rate, including failing to appropriately segment markets, paying too much for a new acquisition, and falling behind competitors in R&D.

Strategy implementation directly affects the lives of plant managers, division managers, department managers, sales managers, product managers, project managers, personnel managers, staff managers, supervisors, and all employees. In some situations, individuals may not have participated in the strategy-formulation process at all and may not appreciate, understand, or even accept the work and thought that went into strategy formulation. There may even be foot dragging or resistance on their part. Managers and employees who do not understand the business and are not committed to the business may attempt to sabotage strategy-implementation efforts in hopes that the organization will return to its old ways. The strategy-implementation stage of the strategic-management process is highlighted in Figure 8-1.

Marketing Issues

Countless marketing variables affect the success or failure of strategy implementation, and the scope of this text does not allow us to address all those issues. Some examples of marketing decisions that may require policies are as follows:

1. To use exclusive dealerships or multiple channels of distribution.
2. To use heavy, light, or no TV advertising.
3. To limit (or not) the share of business done with a single customer.
4. To be a price leader or a price follower.
5. To offer a complete or limited warranty.
6. To reward salespeople based on straight salary, straight commission, or a combination salary/commission.
7. To advertise online or not.

FIGURE 8-1

A Comprehensive Strategic-Management Model

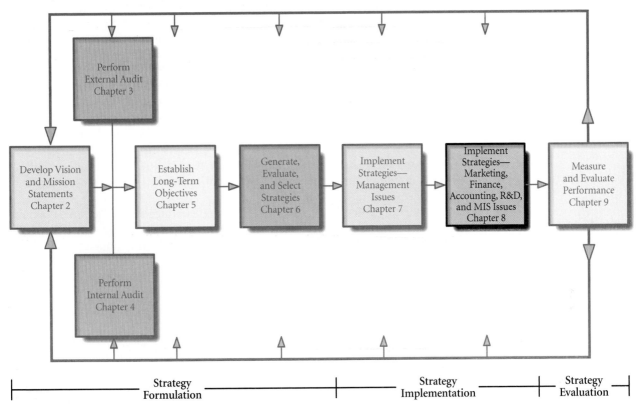

A marketing issue of increasing concern to consumers today is the extent to which companies can track individuals' movements on the Internet—and even be able to identify an individual by name and e-mail address. Individuals' wanderings on the Internet are no longer anonymous, as many persons still believe. Marketing companies such as Doubleclick, Flycast, AdKnowledge, AdForce, and Real Media have sophisticated methods to identify who you are and your particular interests.[1] If you are especially concerned about being tracked, visit the www.networkadvertising.org Web site that gives details about how marketers today are identifying you and your buying habits.

Two variables are of central importance to strategy implementation: *market segmentation* and *product positioning*. Market segmentation and product positioning rank as marketing's most important contributions to strategic management.

Market Segmentation

Market segmentation is widely used in implementing strategies, especially for small and specialized firms. Market segmentation can be defined as the subdividing of a market into distinct subsets of customers according to needs and buying habits.

Market segmentation is an important variable in strategy implementation for at least three major reasons. First, strategies such as market development, product development, market penetration, and diversification require increased sales through new markets and products. To successfully implement these strategies, new or improved market-segmentation approaches are required. Second, market segmentation allows a firm to operate with limited resources because mass production, mass distribution, and mass advertising are not required. Market segmentation enables a small firm to compete successfully with a large firm by maximizing per-unit profits and per-segment sales. Finally, market segmentation decisions directly affect *marketing mix variables:* product, place, promotion, and price, as indicated in Table 8-1. For example, SnackWells, a pioneer in reduced-fat snacks, has shifted its advertising emphasis from low-fat to great taste as part of its new market-segmentation strategy.

Perhaps the most dramatic new market-segmentation strategy is the targeting of regional tastes. Firms from McDonald's to General Motors are increasingly modifying their products to meet different regional preferences within the United States. Campbell's has a spicier version of its nacho cheese soup for the Southwest, and Burger King offers breakfast burritos in New Mexico but not in South Carolina. Geographic and demographic bases for segmenting markets are the most commonly employed, as illustrated in Table 8-2.

Evaluating potential market segments requires strategists to determine the characteristics and needs of consumers, to analyze consumer similarities and differences, and to develop consumer group profiles. Segmenting consumer markets is generally much simpler and easier than segmenting industrial markets, because industrial products, such as electronic circuits and forklifts, have multiple applications and appeal to diverse customer groups. Note in Figure 8-2 that customer age is used to segment automobile car purchases. Note that some older buyers especially like Cadillacs and Buicks.

Segmentation is a key to matching supply and demand, which is one of the thorniest problems in customer service. Segmentation often reveals that large, random fluctuations in demand actually consist of several small, predictable, and manageable patterns. Matching supply and demand allows factories to produce desirable levels without extra shifts, overtime, and subcontracting. Matching supply and demand also minimizes the number and severity of stock-outs. The demand for hotel rooms, for example, can be dependent on foreign tourists, businesspersons, and vacationers. Focusing separately on these three market segments, however, can allow hotel firms to more effectively predict overall supply and demand.

TABLE 8-1   The Marketing Mix Component Variables

PRODUCT	PLACE	PROMOTION	PRICE
Quality	Distribution channels	Advertising	Level
Features and options	Distribution coverage	Personal selling	Discounts and allowances
Style	Outlet location	Sales promotion	Payment terms
Brand name	Sales territories	Publicity	
Packaging	Inventory levels and locations		
Product line	Transportation carriers		
Warranty			
Service level			
Other services			

Source: E. Jerome McCarthy, *Basic Marketing: A Managerial Approach,* 9th ed. (Homewood, IL: Richard D. Irwin, Inc., 1987): 37–44.

TABLE 8-2 Alternative Bases for Market Segmentation

VARIABLE	TYPICAL BREAKDOWNS
GEOGRAPHIC	
Region	Pacific, Mountain, West North Central, West South Central, East North Central, East South Central, South Atlantic, Middle Atlantic, New England
County Size	A, B, C, D
City Size	Under 5,000; 5,000–20,000; 20,001–50,000; 50,001–100,000; 100,001–250,000; 250,001–500,000; 500,001–1,000,000; 1,000,001–4,000,000; 4,000,001 or over
Density	Urban, suburban, rural
Climate	Northern, southern
DEMOGRAPHIC	
Age	Under 6, 6–11, 12–19, 20–34, 35–49, 50–64, 65+
Gender	Male, female
Family Size	1–2, 3–4, 5+
Family Life Cycle	Young, single; young, married, no children; young, married, youngest child under 6; young, married, youngest child 6 or over; older, married, with children; older, married, no children under 18; older, single; other
Income	Under $10,000; $10,001–$15,000; $15,001–$20,000; $20,001–$30,000; $30,001–$50,000; $50,001–$70,000; $70,001–$100,000; over $100,000
Occupation	Professional and technical; managers, officials, and proprietors; clerical and sales; craftspeople; foremen; operatives; farmers; retirees; students; housewives; unemployed
Education	Grade school or less; some high school; high school graduate; some college; college graduate
Religion	Catholic, Protestant, Jewish, Islamic, other
Race	White, Asian, Hispanic, African American
Nationality	American, British, French, German, Scandinavian, Italian, Latin American, Middle Eastern, Japanese
PSYCHOGRAPHIC	
Social Class	Lower lowers, upper lowers, lower middles, upper middles, lower uppers, upper uppers
Personality	Compulsive, gregarious, authoritarian, ambitious
BEHAVIORAL	
Use Occasion	Regular occasion, special occasion
Benefits Sought	Quality, service, economy
User Status	Nonuser, ex-user, potential user, first-time user, regular user
Usage Rate	Light user, medium user, heavy user
Loyalty Status	None, medium, strong, absolute
Readiness Stage	Unaware, aware, informed, interested, desirous, intending to buy
Attitude Toward Product	Enthusiastic, positive, indifferent, negative, hostile

Source: Adapted from Philip Kotler, *Marketing Management: Analysis, Planning and Control,* © 1984: 256. Adapted by permission of Prentice-Hall, Inc., Upper Saddle River, New Jersey.

FIGURE 8-2

Average Age of Automobile Buyers, by Brand

Plymouth 38	Pontiac 42	Infiniti 45
Mitsubishi. 38	Acura 42	Subaru 45
Volkswagen. 38	Hyundai 42	Oldsmobile 46
Honda 41	Suzuki 42	Saturn 46
Isuzu 41	Audi 42	Chrysler 47
Kia 41	Daewoo 43	Lexus 47
Land Rover 41	Chevrolet 43	Jaguar 49
Mazda 41	Porsche 43	Mercury 50
Nissan 41	Saab 43	Lincoln 51
BMW. 42	GMC 44	Cadillac 53
Dodge 42	Toyota 44	Buick 57
Jeep 42	Volvo 44	
Ford. 42	Mercedes-Benz 45	

Source: Adapted from Norihiko Shirouzu, "This Is Not Your Father's Toyota," *Wall Street Journal* (March 26, 2002): B1.

Banks now are segmenting markets to increase effectiveness. "You're dead in the water if you aren't segmenting the market," says Anne Moore, president of a bank consulting firm in Atlanta. The Internet makes market segmentation easier today because consumers naturally form "communities" on the Web.

Does the Internet Make Market Segmentation Easier?

Yes. The segments of people who marketers want to reach online are much more precisely defined than the segments of people reached through traditional forms of media, such as television, radio, and magazines. For example, Quepasa.com is widely visited by Hispanics. Marketers aiming to reach college students, who are notoriously difficult to reach via traditional media, focus on sites such as collegeclub.com and studentadvantage.com. The gay and lesbian population, which is estimated to comprise about 5 percent of the U. S. population, has always been difficult to reach via traditional media but now can be focused on at sites such as gay.com. Marketers can reach persons interested in specific topics, such as travel or fishing, by placing banners on related Web sites.

People all over the world are congregating into virtual communities on the Web by becoming members/customers/visitors of Web sites that focus on an endless range of topics. People in essence segment themselves by nature of the Web sites that comprise their "favorite places," and many of these Web sites sell information regarding their "visitors." Businesses and groups of individuals all over the world pool their purchasing power in Web sites to get volume discounts.

Product Positioning

After markets have been segmented so that the firm can target particular customer groups, the next step is to find out what customers want and expect. This takes analysis and research. A severe mistake is to assume the firm knows what customers want and expect. Countless research studies reveal large differences between how customers define service and rank the importance of different service activities and how producers view services. Many firms have become successful by filling the gap between what customers and producers see as good service. What the customer believes is good service is paramount, not what the producer believes service should be.

Identifying target customers upon whom to focus marketing efforts sets the stage for deciding how to meet the needs and wants of particular consumer groups. Product positioning is widely used for this purpose. Positioning entails developing schematic representations that reflect how your products or services compare to competitors' on dimensions most important to success in the industry. The following steps are required in product positioning:

[handwritten: product positioning]

1. Select key criteria that effectively differentiate products or services in the industry.
2. Diagram a two-dimensional product-positioning map with specified criteria on each axis.
3. Plot major competitors' products or services in the resultant four-quadrant matrix.
4. Identify areas in the positioning map where the company's products or services could be most competitive in the given target market. Look for vacant areas (niches).
5. Develop a marketing plan to position the company's products or services appropriately.

[handwritten: Look for niches]

Because just two criteria can be examined on a single product-positioning map, multiple maps are often developed to assess various approaches to strategy implementation. Multidimensional scaling could be used to examine three or more criteria simultaneously, but this technique requires computer assistance and is beyond the scope of this text. Some examples of product-positioning maps are illustrated in Figure 8-3.

Some rules for using product positioning as a strategy-implementation tool are the following:

1. Look for the hole or *vacant niche*. The best strategic opportunity might be an unserved segment.
2. Don't squat between segments. Any advantage from squatting (such as a larger target market) is offset by a failure to satisfy one segment. In decision-theory terms, the intent here is to avoid suboptimization by trying to serve more than one objective function.
3. Don't serve two segments with the same strategy. Usually, a strategy successful with one segment cannot be directly transferred to another segment.
4. Don't position yourself in the middle of the map. The middle usually means a strategy that is not clearly perceived to have any distinguishing characteristics. This rule can vary with the number of competitors. For example, when there are only two competitors, as in U. S. presidential elections, the middle becomes the preferred strategic position.[2]

VISIT THE NET

Provides the 2007–2017 Strategic Plan of the National Archives and Records Administration, including Annual Performance Plans. (www.archives.gov/about_us /strategic_planning_and_ reporting/2003_ strategic_plan.html)

An effective product-positioning strategy meets two criteria: (1) it uniquely distinguishes a company from the competition, and (2) it leads customers to expect slightly less service than a company can deliver. Firms should not create expectations that exceed the service the firm can or will deliver. Network Equipment Technology is an example of

[handwritten: distinguished expectations < capabilities]

FIGURE 8-3

Examples of Product-Positioning Maps

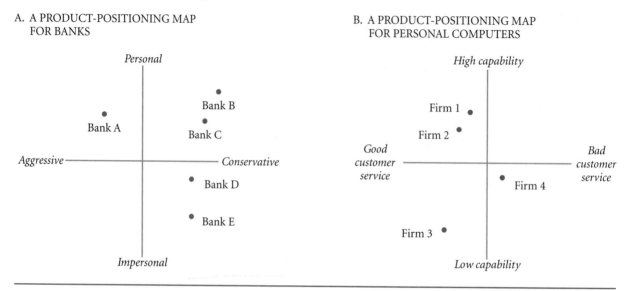

A. A PRODUCT-POSITIONING MAP
   FOR BANKS

B. A PRODUCT-POSITIONING MAP
   FOR PERSONAL COMPUTERS

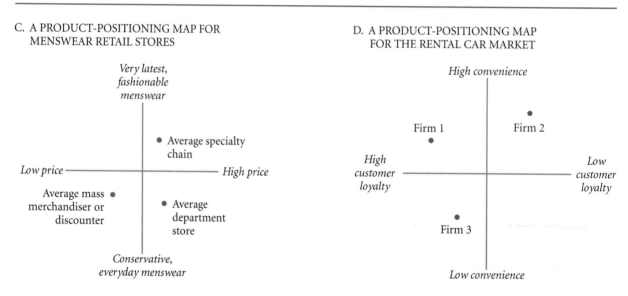

C. A PRODUCT-POSITIONING MAP FOR
   MENSWEAR RETAIL STORES

D. A PRODUCT-POSITIONING MAP
   FOR THE RENTAL CAR MARKET

a company that keeps customer expectations slightly below perceived performance. This is a constant challenge for marketers. Firms need to inform customers about what to expect and then exceed the promise. Underpromise and then overdeliver is the key!

Finance/Accounting Issues

In this section, we examine several finance/accounting concepts considered to be central to strategy implementation: acquiring needed capital, developing projected financial statements, preparing financial budgets, and evaluating the worth of a business. Some examples of decisions that may require finance/accounting policies are these:

1. To raise capital with short-term debt, long-term debt, preferred stock, or common stock.
2. To lease or buy fixed assets.
3. To determine an appropriate dividend payout ratio.
4. To use LIFO (Last-in, First-out), FIFO (First-in, First-out), or a market-value accounting approach.
5. To extend the time of accounts receivable.
6. To establish a certain percentage discount on accounts within a specified period of time.
7. To determine the amount of cash that should be kept on hand.

Acquiring Capital to Implement Strategies

Successful strategy implementation often requires additional capital. Besides net profit from operations and the sale of assets, two basic sources of capital for an organization are debt and equity. Determining an appropriate mix of debt and equity in a firm's capital structure can be vital to successful strategy implementation. An *Earnings Per Share/Earnings Before Interest and Taxes (EPS/EBIT) analysis* is the most widely used technique for determining whether debt, stock, or a combination of debt and stock is the best alternative for raising capital to implement strategies. This technique involves an examination of the impact that debt versus stock financing has on earnings per share under various assumptions as to EBIT.

[handwritten: common analysis]

Theoretically, an enterprise should have enough debt in its capital structure to boost its return on investment by applying debt to products and projects earning more than the cost of the debt. In low earning periods, too much debt in the capital structure of an organization can endanger stockholders' returns and jeopardize company survival. Fixed debt obligations generally must be met, regardless of circumstances. This does not mean that stock issuances are always better than debt for raising capital. Some special concerns with stock issuances are dilution of ownership, effect on stock price, and the need to share future earnings with all new shareholders.

Without going into detail on other institutional and legal issues related to the debt versus stock decision, EPS/EBIT may be best explained by working through an example. Let's say the Brown Company needs to raise $1 million to finance implementation of a market-development strategy. The company's common stock currently sells for $50 per share, and 100,000 shares are outstanding. The prime interest rate is 10 percent, and the company's tax rate is 50 percent. The company's earnings before interest and taxes next year are expected to be $2 million if a recession occurs, $4 million if the economy stays as is, and $8 million if the economy significantly improves. EPS/EBIT analysis can be used to determine if all stock, all debt, or some combination of stock and debt is the best capital financing alternative. The EPS/EBIT analysis for this example is provided in Table 8-3.

As indicated by the EPS values of 9.5, 19.50, and 39.50 in Table 8-3, debt is the best financing alternative for the Brown Company if a recession, boom, or normal year is expected. An EPS/EBIT chart can be constructed to determine the break-even point, where one financing alternative becomes more attractive than another. Figure 8-4 indicates that issuing common stock is the least attractive financing alternative for the Brown Company.

[handwritten: can determine the break-even point]

TABLE 8-3   EPS/EBIT Analysis for the Brown Company (in millions)

	COMMON STOCK FINANCING			DEBT FINANCING			COMBINATION FINANCING		
	Recession	*Normal*	*Boom*	*Recession*	*Normal*	*Boom*	*Recession*	*Normal*	*Boom*
EBIT	$2.0	$ 4.0	$ 8.0	$2.0	$ 4.0	$ 8.0	$2.0	$ 4.0	$ 8.0
Interest[a]	0	0	0	.10	.10	.10	.05	.05	.05
EBT	2.0	4.0	8.0	1.9	3.9	7.9	1.95	3.95	7.95
Taxes	1.0	2.0	4.0	.95	1.95	3.95	.975	1.975	3.975
EAT	1.0	2.0	4.0	.95	1.95	3.95	.975	1.975	3.975
#Shares[b]	.12	.12	.12	.10	.10	.10	.11	.11	.11
EPS[c]	8.33	16.66	33.33	9.5	19.50	39.50	8.86	17.95	36.14

[a]The annual interest charge on $1 million at 10% is $100,000 and on $0.5 million is $50,000. This row is in $, not %.
[b]To raise all of the needed $1 million with stock, 20,000 new shares must be issued, raising the total to 120,000 shares outstanding. To raise one-half of the needed $1 million with stock, 10,000 new shares must be issued, raising the total to 110,000 shares outstanding.
[c]EPS = Earnings After Taxes (EAT) divided by shares (number of shares outstanding).

EPS/EBIT analysis is a valuable tool for making the capital financing decisions needed to implement strategies, but several considerations should be made whenever using this technique. First, profit levels may be higher for stock or debt alternatives when EPS levels are lower. For example, looking only at the earnings after taxes (EAT) values in Table 8-3, you can see that the common stock option is the best alternative, regardless of economic conditions. If the Brown Company's mission includes strict profit maximization, as opposed to the maximization of stockholders' wealth or some other criterion, then stock rather than debt is the best choice of financing.

Another consideration when using EPS/EBIT analysis is flexibility. As an organization's capital structure changes, so does its flexibility for considering future capital needs. Using all debt or all stock to raise capital in the present may impose fixed obligations, restrictive covenants, or other constraints that could severely reduce a firm's ability to raise additional capital in the future. Control is also a concern. When additional stock is

FIGURE 8-4

An EPS/EBIT Chart for the Brown Company

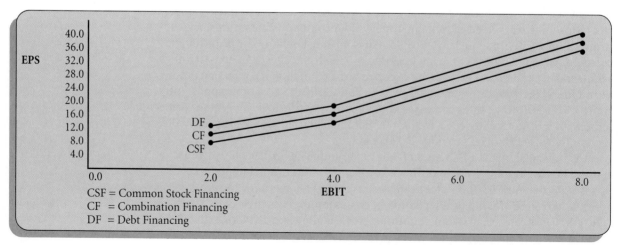

issued to finance strategy implementation, ownership and control of the enterprise are diluted. This can be a serious concern in today's business environment of hostile takeovers, mergers, and acquisitions.

Dilution of ownership can be an overriding concern in closely held corporations in which stock issuances affect the decision-making power of majority stockholders. For example, the Smucker family owns 30 percent of the stock in Smucker's, a well-known jam and jelly company. When Smucker's acquired Dickson Family, Inc., the company used mostly debt rather than stock in order not to dilute the family ownership.

When using EPS/EBIT analysis, timing in relation to movements of stock prices, interest rates, and bond prices becomes important. In times of depressed stock prices, debt may prove to be the most suitable alternative from both a cost and a demand standpoint. However, when cost of capital (interest rates) is high, stock issuances become more attractive.

Tables 8-4 and 8-5 provide EPS/EBIT analyses for two companies—Gateway and Boeing. Notice in those analyses that the combination stock/debt options vary from 30/70 to 70/30. Any number of combinations could be explored. However, sometimes in preparing the EPS/EBIT graphs, the lines will intersect, thus revealing break-even points at which one financing alternative becomes more or less attractive than another. The slope of these lines will be determined by a combination of factors including stock price, interest rate, number of shares, and amount of capital needed. Also, it should be noted here that the best financing alternatives are indicated by the highest EPS values. In Tables 8-4 and 8-5, note that the tax rates for the companies vary considerably and should be computed from the respective income statements by dividing taxes paid by income before taxes.

In Table 8-4, the higher EPS values indicate that Gateway should use stock to raise capital in recession or normal economic conditions but should use debt financing under boom conditions. Stock is the best alternative for Gateway under all three conditions if EAT (profit maximization) were the decision criteria, but EPS (maximize shareholders' wealth) is the better ratio to make this decision. Firms can do many things in the short run to maximize profits, so investors and creditors consider maximizing shareholders' wealth to be the better criteria for making financing decisions.

In Table 8-5, note that Boeing should use stock to raise capital in recession (see 0.92) or normal (see 2.29) economic conditions but should use debt financing under boom conditions (see 5.07). Let's calculate here the number of shares figure of 1014.68 given under Boeing's stock alternative. Divide $10,000 M funds needed by the stock price of $53 = 188.68 M new shares to be issued + the 826 M shares outstanding already = 1014.68 M shares under the stock scenario. Along the final row, EPS is the number of shares outstanding divided by EAT in all columns.

Note in Table 8-4 and Table 8-5 that a dividends row is absent from both the Gateway and Boeing analyses. The more shares outstanding, the more dividends to be paid (if the firm indeed pays dividends). Paying dividends lowers EAT, which lowers the stock EPS values whenever this aspect is included. To consider dividends in an EPS/EBIT analysis, simply insert another row for "Dividends" right below the "EAT" row and then insert an "Earnings After Taxes and Dividends" row. Considering dividends would make the analysis more robust.

Note in both the Gateway and Boeing graphs, there is a break-even point between the normal and boom range of EBIT where the debt option overtakes the 70% Debt/30% Stock option as the best financing alternative. A break-even point

TABLE 8-4   EPS/EBIT Analysis for Gateway (year-end 2004, M = in millions)

Amount Needed: $1,000 M
EBIT Range: − $500 M to + $100 M to + $500 M
Interest Rate: 5%
Tax Rate: 0% (because the firm has been incurring a loss annually)
Stock Price: $6.00
# of Shares Outstanding: 371 M

	COMMON STOCK FINANCING			DEBT FINANCING		
	Recession	*Normal*	*Boom*	*Recession*	*Normal*	*Boom*
EBIT	(500.00)	100.00	500.00	(500.00)	100.00	500.00
Interest	0.00	0.00	0.00	50.00	50.00	50.00
EBT	(500.00)	100.00	500.00	(550.00)	50.00	450.00
Taxes	0.00	0.00	0.00	0.00	0.00	0.00
EAT	(500.00)	100.00	500.00	(550.00)	50.00	450.00
#Shares	537.67	537.67	537.67	371.00	371.00	371.00
EPS	**(0.93)**	**0.19**	**0.93**	**(1.48)**	**0.13**	**1.21**

	70 PERCENT STOCK—30 PERCENT DEBT			70 PERCENT DEBT—30 PERCENT STOCK		
	Recession	*Normal*	*Boom*	*Recession*	*Normal*	*Boom*
EBIT	(500.00)	100.00	500.00	(500.00)	100.00	500.00
Interest	15.00	15.00	15.00	35.00	35.00	35.00
EBT	(515.00)	85.00	485.00	(535.00)	65.00	465.00
Taxes	0.00	0.00	0.00	0.00	0.00	0.00
EAT	(515.00)	85.00	485.00	(535.00)	65.00	465.00
#Shares	487.67	487.67	487.67	421.00	421.00	421.00
EPS	**(1.06)**	**0.17**	**0.99**	**(1.27)**	**0.15**	**1.10**

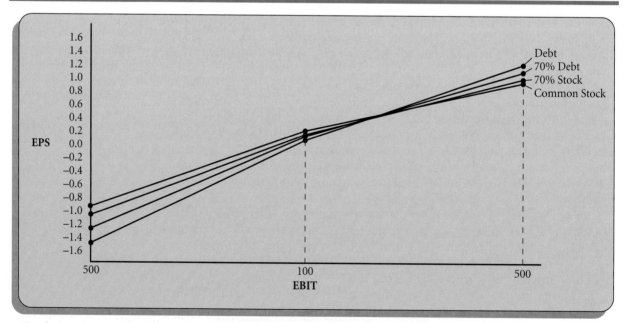

Conclusion: Gateway should use common stock to raise capital in recession or normal economic conditions but should use debt financing under boom conditions. Note that stock is the best alternative under all three conditions according to EAT (profit maximization), but EPS (maximize shareholders' wealth) is the better ratio to make this decision.

TABLE 8-5 EPS/EBIT Analysis for Boeing (year-end 2004, M = in millions)

Amount Needed: $10,000 M
Interest Rate: 5%
Tax Rate: 7%
Stock Price: $53.00
# of Shares Outstanding: 826 M

	COMMON STOCK FINANCING			DEBT FINANCING		
	Recession	*Normal*	*Boom*	*Recession*	*Normal*	*Boom*
EBIT	1,000.00	2,500.00	5,000.00	1,000.00	2,500.00	5,000.00
Interest	0.00	0.00	0.00	500.00	500.00	500.00
EBT	1,000.00	2,500.00	5,000.00	500.00	2,000.00	4,500.00
Taxes	70.00	175.00	350.00	35.00	140.00	315.00
EAT	930.00	2,325.00	4,650.00	465.00	1,860.00	4,185.00
# Shares	1,014.68	1,014.68	1,014.68	826.00	826.00	826.00
EPS	**0.92**	**2.29**	**4.58**	**0.56**	**2.25**	**5.07**

	70% STOCK—30% DEBT			70% DEBT—30% STOCK		
	Recession	*Normal*	*Boom*	*Recession*	*Normal*	*Boom*
EBIT	1,000.00	2,500.00	5,000.00	1,000.00	2,500.00	5,000.00
Interest	150.00	150.00	150.00	350.00	350.00	350.00
EBT	850.00	2,350.00	4,850.00	650.00	2,150.00	4,650.00
Taxes	59.50	164.50	339.50	45.50	150.50	325.50
EAT	790.50	2,185.50	4,510.50	604.50	1,999.50	4,324.50
# Shares	958.08	958.08	958.08	882.60	882.60	882.60
EPS	**0.83**	**2.28**	**4.71**	**0.68**	**2.27**	**4.90**

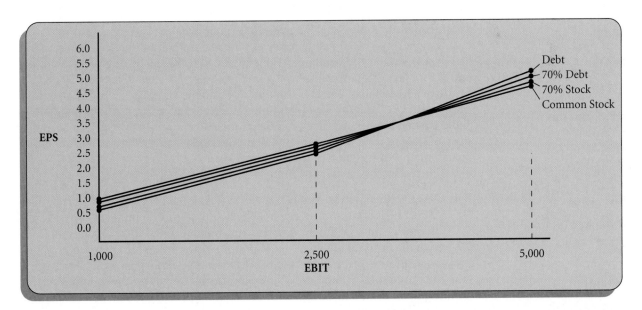

Conclusion: Boeing should use common stock to raise capital in recession (see 0.92) or normal (see 2.29) economic conditions but should use debt financing under boom conditions (see 5.07). Note that a dividends row is absent from this analysis. The more shares outstanding, the more dividends to be paid (if the firm pays dividends), which would lower the common stock EPS values.

is where two lines cross each other. A break-even point is the EBIT level where various financing alternative represented by lines crossing are equally attractive in terms of EPS. Both the Gateway and Boeing graphs indicate that EPS values are highest for the 100 percent Debt option at high EBIT levels. The two graphs also reveal that the EPS values for 100 percent debt increase faster than the other financing options as EBIT levels increase beyond the break-even point. At low levels of EBIT however, both the Gateway and Boeing graphs indicate that 100 percent stock is the best financing alternative because the EPS values are highest.

Projected Financial Statements

Projected financial statement analysis is a central strategy-implementation technique because it allows an organization to examine the expected results of various actions and approaches. This type of analysis can be used to forecast the impact of various implementation decisions (for example, to increase promotion expenditures by 50 percent to support a market-development strategy, to increase salaries by 25 percent to support a market-penetration strategy, to increase research and development expenditures by 70 percent to support product development, or to sell $1 million of common stock to raise capital for diversification). Nearly all financial institutions require at least three years of projected financial statements whenever a business seeks capital. A projected income statement and balance sheet allow an organization to compute projected financial ratios under various strategy-implementation scenarios. When compared to prior years and to industry averages, financial ratios provide valuable insights into the feasibility of various strategy-implementation approaches.

Primarily as a result of the Enron collapse and accounting scandal and the reassuring Sarbanes-Oxley Act, companies today are being much more diligent in preparing projected financial statements to "reasonably rather than too optimistically" project future expenses and earnings. There is much more care not to mislead shareholders and other constituencies.[3]

A 2006 projected income statement and a balance sheet for the Litten Company are provided in Table 8-6. The projected statements for Litten are based on five assumptions: (1) The company needs to raise $45 million to finance expansion into foreign markets; (2) $30 million of this total will be raised through increased debt and $15 million through common stock; (3) sales are expected to increase 50 percent; (4) three new facilities, costing a total of $30 million, will be constructed in foreign markets; and (5) land for the new facilities is already owned by the company. Note in Table 8-6 that Litten's strategies and their implementation are expected to result in a sales increase from $100 million to $150 million and in a net increase in income from $6 million to $9.75 million in the forecasted year.

There are six steps in performing projected financial analysis:

1. Prepare the projected income statement before the balance sheet. Start by forecasting sales as accurately as possible. Be careful not to blindly push historical percentages into the future with regard to revenue (sales) increases. Be mindful of what the firm did to achieve those past sales increases, which may not be appropriate for the future unless the firm takes similar or analogous actions (such as opening a similar number of stores, for example). If dealing with a manufacturing firm, also be mindful that if the firm is operating at 100 percent capacity running three eight-hour shifts per day, then probably new manufacturing facilities (land, plant, and equipment) will be needed to increase sales further.

2. Use the percentage-of-sales method to project cost of goods sold (CGS) and the expense items in the income statement. For example, if CGS is 70 percent of sales

TABLE 8-6   A Projected Income Statement and Balance Sheet for the Litten Company (in millions)

	PRIOR YEAR 2005	PROJECTED YEAR 2006	REMARKS
PROJECTED INCOME STATEMENT			
Sales	$100	$150.00	50% increase
Cost of Goods Sold	70	105.00	70% of sales
Gross Margin	30	45.00	
Selling Expense	10	15.00	10% of sales
Administrative Expense	5	7.50	5% of sales
Earnings Before Interest and Taxes	15	22.50	
Interest	3	3.00	
Earnings Before Taxes	12	19.50	
Taxes	6	9.75	50% rate
Net Income	**6**	**9.75**	
Dividends	2	5.00	
Retained Earnings	4	4.75	
PROJECTED BALANCE SHEET			
Assets			
Cash	5	7.75	Plug figure
Accounts Receivable	2	4.00	100% increase
Inventory	20	45.00	
Total Current Assets	27	56.75	
Land	15	15.00	
Plant and Equipment	50	80.00	Add three new plants at $10 million each
Less Depreciation	10	20.00	
Net Plant and Equipment	40	60.00	
Total Fixed Assets	55	75.00	
Total Assets	**82**	**131.75**	
Liabilities			
Accounts Payable	10	10.00	
Notes Payable	10	10.00	
Total Current Liabilities	20	20.00	
Long-term Debt	40	70.00	Borrowed $30 million
Additional Paid-in-Capital	20	35.00	Issued 100,000 shares at $150 each
Retained Earnings	2	6.75	$2 + $4.75
Total Liabilities and Net Worth	**82**	**131.75**	

in the prior year (as it is in Table 8-6), then use that same percentage to calculate CGS in the future year—unless there is a reason to use a different percentage. Items such as interest, dividends, and taxes must be treated independently and cannot be forecasted using the percentage-of-sales method.

3. Calculate the projected net income.

4. Subtract from the net income any dividends to be paid for that year. This remaining net income is retained earnings (RE). Bring this retained earnings amount for that year (NI − DIV = RE) over to the balance sheet by adding it to the prior year's RE shown on the balance sheet. In other words, every year

a firm adds its RE for that particular year (from the income statement) to its historical RE total on the balance sheet. Therefore, the RE amount on the balance sheet is a cumulative number rather than money available for strategy implementation! Note that RE is the **first** projected balance sheet item to be entered. Due to this accounting procedure in developing projected financial statements, the RE amount on the balance sheet is usually a large number. However, it also can be a low or even negative number if the firm has been incurring losses. The only way for RE to decrease from one year to the next on the balance sheet is (1) if the firm incurred an earnings loss that year or (2) the firm had positive net income for the year but paid out dividends more than the net income. Be mindful that RE is the key link between a projected income statement and balance sheet, so be careful to make this calculation correctly.

5. Project the balance sheet items, beginning with retained earnings and then forecasting stockholders' equity, long-term liabilities, current liabilities, total liabilities, total assets, fixed assets, and current assets (in that order). Use the cash account as the plug figure—that is, use the cash account to make the assets total the liabilities and net worth. Then make appropriate adjustments. For example, if the cash needed to balance the statements is too small (or too large), make appropriate changes to borrow more (or less) money than planned.

6. List comments (remarks) on the projected statements. Any time a significant change is made in an item from a prior year to the projected year, an explanation (remark) should be provided. Remarks are essential because otherwise pro formas are meaningless.

The U. S. Securities and Exchange Commission (SEC) conducts fraud investigations if projected numbers are misleading or if they omit information that's important to investors. Projected statements must conform with generally accepted accounting principles (GAAP) and must not be designed to hide poor expected results. The Sarbanes-Oxley Act requires CEOs and CFOs of corporations to personally sign their firms' financial statements attesting to their accuracy. These executives could thus be held personally liable for misleading or inaccurate statements. The collapse of the Arthur Andersen accounting firm, along with its client Enron, fostered a "zero tolerance" policy among auditors and shareholders with regard to a firm's financial statements. But, plenty of firms still "inflate" their financial projections and call them "pro formas," so investors, shareholders, and other stakeholders must still be wary of different companies' financial projections.[4]

Financial Budgets

A *financial budget* is a document that details how funds will be obtained and spent for a specified period of time. Annual budgets are most common, although the period of time for a budget can range from one day to more than 10 years. Fundamentally, financial budgeting is a method for specifying what must be done to complete strategy implementation successfully. Financial budgeting should not be thought of as a tool for limiting expenditures but rather as a method for obtaining the most productive and profitable use of an organization's resources. Financial budgets can be viewed as the planned allocation of a firm's resources based on forecasts of the future.

There are almost as many different types of financial budgets as there are types of organizations. Some common types of budgets include cash budgets, operating budgets, sales budgets, profit budgets, factory budgets, capital budgets, expense budgets, divisional budgets, variable budgets, flexible budgets, and fixed budgets. When an organization is experiencing financial difficulties, budgets are especially important in guiding strategy implementation.

Perhaps the most common type of financial budget is the *cash budget*. The Financial Accounting Standards Board (FASB) has mandated that every publicly held company in the United States must issue an annual cash-flow statement in addition to the usual financial reports. The statement includes all receipts and disbursements of cash in operations, investments, and financing. It supplements the Statement on Changes in Financial Position formerly included in the annual reports of all publicly held companies. A cash budget for the year 2007 for the Toddler Toy Company is provided in Table 8-7. Note that Toddler is not expecting to have surplus cash until November 2007.

Financial budgets have some limitations. First, budgetary programs can become so detailed that they are cumbersome and overly expensive. Overbudgeting or underbudgeting can cause problems. Second, financial budgets can become a substitute for objectives. A budget is a tool and not an end in itself. Third, budgets can hide inefficiencies if based solely on precedent rather than on periodic evaluation of circumstances and standards. Finally, budgets are sometimes used as instruments of tyranny that result in frustration, resentment, absenteeism, and high turnover. To minimize the effect of this last concern, managers should increase the participation of subordinates in preparing budgets.

TABLE 8-7 A Six-Month Cash Budget for the Toddler Toy Company in 2007

CASH BUDGET (IN THOUSANDS)	JULY	AUG.	SEPT.	OCT.	NOV.	DEC.	JAN.
Receipts							
Collections	$12,000	$21,000	$31,000	$35,000	$22,000	$18,000	$11,000
Payments							
Purchases	14,000	21,000	28,000	14,000	14,000	7,000	
Wages and Salaries	1,500	2,000	2,500	1,500	1,500	1,000	
Rent	500	500	500	500	500	500	
Other Expenses	200	300	400	200	—	100	
Taxes	—	8,000	—	—	—	—	
Payment on Machine	—	—	10,000	—	—	—	
Total Payments	$16,200	$31,800	$41,400	$16,200	$16,000	$8,600	
Net Cash Gain (Loss) During Month	−4,200	−10,800	−10,400	18,800	6,000	9,400	
Cash at Start of Month if No Borrowing Is Done	6,000	1,800	−9,000	−19,400	−600	5,400	
Cumulative Cash (Cash at start plus gains or minus losses)	1,800	−9,000	−19,400	−600	5,400	14,800	
Less Desired Level of Cash	−5,000	−5,000	−5,000	−5,000	−5,000	−5,000	
Total Loans Outstanding to Maintain $5,000 Cash Balance	$3,200	$14,000	$24,400	$5,600	—	—	
Surplus Cash	—	—	—	—	400	9,800	

Evaluating the Worth of a Business

Evaluating the worth of a business is central to strategy implementation because integrative, intensive, and diversification strategies are often implemented by acquiring other firms. Other strategies, such as retrenchment and divestiture, may result in the sale of a division of an organization or of the firm itself. Thousands of transactions occur each year in which businesses are bought or sold in the United States. In all these cases, it is necessary to establish the financial worth or cash value of a business to successfully implement strategies.

All the various methods for determining a business's worth can be grouped into three main approaches: what a firm owns, what a firm earns, or what a firm will bring in the market. But it is important to realize that valuation is not an exact science. The valuation of a firm's worth is based on financial facts, but common sense and intuitive judgment must enter into the process. It is difficult to assign a monetary value to some factors—such as a loyal customer base, a history of growth, legal suits pending, dedicated employees, a favorable lease, a bad credit rating, or good patents—that may not be reflected in a firm's financial statements. Also, different valuation methods will yield different totals for a firm's worth, and no prescribed approach is best for a certain situation. Evaluating the worth of a business truly requires both qualitative and quantitative skills.

The first approach in evaluating the worth of a business is determining its net worth or stockholders' equity. Net worth represents the sum of common stock, additional paid-in capital, and retained earnings. After calculating net worth, add or subtract an appropriate amount for goodwill and overvalued or undervalued assets. This total provides a reasonable estimate of a firm's monetary value. If a firm has goodwill, it will be listed on the balance sheet, perhaps as "intangibles." It should be noted that Financial Accounting Standard Board (FASB) Rule 142 requires companies to admit once a year if the premiums they paid for acquisitions, called goodwill, were a waste of money. Goodwill is not a good thing to have on a balance sheet. Companies with "too much" goodwill in 2003 include AOL Time Warner ($81.7 billion, 51 percent of total assets), Viacom ($57.5 billion, 64 percent of total assets), and Kraft Foods ($36.4 billion, 64 percent of total assets). AOL converted $54 billion of its goodwill into an earnings loss in 2002 and another $45.5 billion "write down" in 2003, as the firm struggled to avoid bankruptcy.[5] As noted in the "Global Perspective" box, accounting standards worldwide are converging which is good.

The second approach to measuring the value of a firm grows out of the belief that the worth of any business should be based largely on the future benefits its owners may derive through net profits. A conservative rule of thumb is to establish a business's worth as five times the firm's current annual profit. A five-year average profit level could also be used. When using the approach, remember that firms normally suppress earnings in their financial statements to minimize taxes.

The third approach, letting the market determine a business's worth, involves three methods. First, base the firm's worth on the selling price of a similar company. A potential problem, however, is that sometimes comparable figures are not easy to locate, even though substantial information on firms that buy or sell to other firms is available in major libraries. The second approach is called the *price-earnings ratio method.* To use this method, divide the market price of the firm's common stock by the annual earnings per share and multiply this number by the firm's average net income for the past five years. The third method can be called the *outstanding shares* method. To use this method, simply multiply the number of shares outstanding by the market price per share and add a premium. The premium is simply a per-share dollar amount that a person or firm is willing to pay to control (acquire) the other company.

GLOBAL PERSPECTIVE

Globally Standardizing Accounting Standards

The Financial Accounting Standards Board (FASB) in the U.S. and its counterpart, the International Accounting Standards Board (IASB), are each modifying its "rules" in an effort to globally converge accounting standards. It is unusual for the FASB to change simply to meet the IASB, but there is more and more movement from both sides towards convergence. And yes, the FASB is changing too. Standard setters in both the United States and other countries mutually desire the financial statements of a company—say in France—one day be comparable to those in the U. S. Accounting standards convergence would greatly simplify cross-border investment, interaction, and trade.

The FASB and the IASB began meeting twice yearly in 2002 which is good. The European Union of countries has agreed to adopt the IASB's standards by 2005. Actually about 91 countries worldwide will require their companies to comply with IASB standards by 2005. However, there still exist many differences though between FASB and IASB standards. For example, the FASB does not allow for upward re-evaluation of property, plant, and equipment, whereas the IASB permits periodic re-evaluation up or down of assets. Thus, property, plant, and equipment on the statements of U. S. firms is often worth a lot more than reflected on the books. For another example, the IASB wants to remove net income from the income statement, but the FASB has not reached a decision on this issue. There are also differences between FASB and IASB in accounting for acquisitions as well as differences between when revenue should be booked.

One day decades in the future, there may be one currency worldwide. Certainly, convergence between accounting systems among countries worldwide would be step in that direction. Establishment of the Euro was a big step, too, in that direction. Convergence of accounting systems simply makes doing business much easier among businesses worldwide.

Source: Adapted from Cassell Bryan-Low, "Accounting's Global Rule Book," *Wall Street Journal* (November 28, 2003): C1.

Business evaluations are becoming routine in many situations. Businesses have many strategy-implementation reasons for determining their worth in addition to preparing to be sold or to buy other companies. Employee plans, taxes, retirement packages, mergers, acquisitions, expansion plans, banking relationships, death of a principal, divorce, partnership agreements, and IRS audits are other reasons for a periodic valuation. It is just good business to have a reasonable understanding of what your firm is worth. This knowledge protects the interests of all parties involved.

Table 8-8 provides the cash value analyses for three companies—Southwest Airlines, Target, and Revlon—for year-end 2004. Notice that there is significant variation among the four methods used to determine cash value. For example, the worth of Southwest Airlines ranged for $1.56 billion to $12.3 billion and the worth of Target ranged from $13 billion of $75 billion. Obviously, if you were selling your company, you would seek the larger values, while if purchasing a company you would seek the lower values. In practice, substantial negotiation takes place in reaching a final compromise (or averaged) amount. Also recognize that if a firm's net income is negative, theoretically the approaches involving that figure would result in a negative number, implying that the firm would pay you to acquire them. Of course, you obtain all of the firm's debt and liabilities in an acquisition, so theoretically this would be possible.

At year-end 2004, Southwest Airlines, Target, and Revlon had $0 million, $60 - million, and $186 million in goodwill respectively on their balance sheets. However, note in Table 8-8 that goodwill is not added to the stockholders' equity calculations. Some

TABLE 8-8 Worth of a Business Analysis for Southwest Airlines, Target, and Revlon (year-end 2004, M = in millions except stock price and EPS)

A. Southwest Airlines
Stockholders' Equity: $5,524
Net Income: $313
Stock Price: $15.70
EPS: $0.45
# of Shares Outstanding: 784

Company Worth Analysis	
Stockholders' Equity	$5,524
Net Income × 5	$1,565
(Share Price/EPS) × Net Income	$10,920
Number of Shares Outstanding × Share Price	$12,309
Method Average	**$7,580**

B. Target
Stockholders' Equity: $13,029
Net Income: $3,198
Stock Price: $51.70
EPS: $2.19
# of Shares Outstanding: 885

Company Worth Analysis	
Stockholders' Equity	$13,029
Net Income × 5	$15,990
(Share Price/EPS) × Net Income	$75,496
Number of Shares Outstanding × Share Price	$45,755
Method Average	**$37,567**

C. Revlon
Stockholders' Equity: (−$1,019)
Net Income: (−$142)
Share Price: $2.25
EPS: (−$0.36)
# of Shares Outstanding: 370

Company Worth Analysis	
Stockholders' Equity	(1019.00)
Net Income × 5	(710.00)
(Share Price/EPS) × Net Income	(887.50)
Number of Shares Outstanding × Share Price	832.50
Method Average	**(446.00)**

creditors and investors feel that goodwill indeed should be added to the stockholders' equity in calculating worth of a business, but some feel it should be subtracted, and still others feel it should not be included at all. Perhaps whether you are buying or selling the business may determine whether you negotiate to add or subtract goodwill in the analysis. Goodwill is sometimes listed as intangibles on the balance sheet.

Deciding Whether to Go Public

Going public means selling off a percentage of your company to others in order to raise capital; consequently, it dilutes the owners' control of the firm. Going public is not recommended for companies with less than $10 million in sales because the initial costs can be too high for the firm to generate sufficient cash flow to make going public worthwhile. One dollar in four is the average total cost paid to lawyers, accountants, and underwriters when an initial stock issuance is under $1 million; 1 dollar in 20 will go to cover these costs for issuances over $20 million.

In addition to initial costs involved with a stock offering, there are costs and obligations associated with reporting and management in a publicly-held firm. For firms with more than $10 million in sales, going public can provide major advantages: It can allow the firm to raise capital to develop new products, build plants, expand, grow, and market products and services more effectively.

Research and Development (R&D) Issues

Research and development (R&D) personnel can play an integral part in strategy implementation. These individuals are generally charged with developing new products and improving old products in a way that will allow effective strategy implementation. R&D employees and managers perform tasks that include transferring complex technology, adjusting processes to local raw materials, adapting processes to local markets, and altering products to particular tastes and specifications. Strategies such as product development, market penetration, and related diversification require that new products be successfully developed and that old products be significantly improved. But the level of management support for R&D is often constrained by resource availability.

Technological improvements that affect consumer and industrial products and services shorten product life cycles. Companies in virtually every industry are relying on the development of new products and services to fuel profitability and growth.[6] Surveys suggest that the most successful organizations use an R&D strategy that ties external opportunities to internal strengths and is linked with objectives. Well-formulated R&D policies match market opportunities with internal capabilities. R&D policies can enhance strategy implementation efforts to:

1. Emphasize product or process improvements.
2. Stress basic or applied research.
3. Be leaders or followers in R&D.
4. Develop robotics or manual-type processes.
5. Spend a high, average, or low amount of money on R&D.
6. Perform R&D within the firm or to contract R&D to outside firms.
7. Use university researchers or private-sector researchers.

There must be effective interactions between R&D departments and other functional departments in implementing different types of generic business strategies. Conflicts between marketing, finance/accounting, R&D, and information systems departments can be minimized with clear policies and objectives. Table 8-9 gives some examples of R&D activities that could be required for successful implementation of various strategies. Many U.S. utility, energy, and automotive companies are employing their research and development departments to determine how the firm can effectively reduce its gas emissions.

TABLE 8-9   Research and Development Involvement in Selected
Strategy-Implementation Situations

TYPE OF ORGANIZATION	STRATEGY BEING IMPLEMENTED	R&D ACTIVITY
Pharmaceutical company	Product development	Test the effects of a new drug on different subgroups.
Boat manufacturer	Related diversification	Test the performance of various keel designs under various conditions.
Plastic container manufacturer	Market penetration	Develop a biodegradable container.
Electronics company	Market development	Develop a telecommunications system in a foreign country.

Many firms wrestle with the decision to acquire R&D expertise from external firms or to develop R&D expertise internally. The following guidelines can be used to help make this decision:

1. If the rate of technical progress is slow, the rate of market growth is moderate, and there are significant barriers to possible new entrants, then in-house R&D is the preferred solution. The reason is that R&D, if successful, will result in a temporary product or process monopoly that the company can exploit.

2. If technology is changing rapidly and the market is growing slowly, then a major effort in R&D may be very risky, because it may lead to the development of an ultimately obsolete technology or one for which there is no market.

3. If technology is changing slowly but the market is growing quickly, there generally is not enough time for in-house development. The prescribed approach is to obtain R&D expertise on an exclusive or nonexclusive basis from an outside firm.

4. If both technical progress and market growth are fast, R&D expertise should be obtained through acquisition of a well-established firm in the industry.[7]

There are at least three major R&D approaches for implementing strategies. The first strategy is to be the first firm to market new technological products. This is a glamorous and exciting strategy but also a dangerous one. Firms such as 3M and General Electric have been successful with this approach, but many other pioneering firms have fallen, with rival firms seizing the initiative.

A second R&D approach is to be an innovative imitator of successful products, thus minimizing the risks and costs of start-up. This approach entails allowing a pioneer firm to develop the first version of the new product and to demonstrate that a market exists. Then, laggard firms develop a similar product. This strategy requires excellent R&D personnel and an excellent marketing department.

A third R&D strategy is to be a low-cost producer by mass-producing products similar to but less expensive than products recently introduced. As a new product is accepted by customers, price becomes increasingly important in the buying decision. Also, mass marketing replaces personal selling as the dominant selling strategy. This R&D strategy, requires substantial investment in plant and equipment but fewer expenditures in R&D than the two approaches described previously.

R&D activities among U.S. firms need to be more closely aligned to business objectives. There needs to be expanded communication between R&D managers and strategists. Corporations are experimenting with various methods to achieve this improved communication climate, including different roles and reporting arrangements for managers and new methods to reduce the time it takes research ideas to become reality.

Perhaps the most current trend in R&D management has been lifting the veil of secrecy whereby firms, even major competitors, are joining forces to develop new products. Collaboration is on the rise due to new competitive pressures, rising research costs, increasing regulatory issues, and accelerated product development schedules. Companies not only are working more closely with each other on R&D, but they are also turning to consortia at universities for their R&D needs. More than 600 research consortia are now in operation in the United States. Lifting of R&D secrecy among many firms through collaboration has allowed the marketing of new technologies and products even before they are available for sale. As indicated in the Natural Environment Perspective, several firms are collaborating on the efficient design of solar panels to power homes and businesses.

[handwritten margin note: lifting of secrecy]

Management Information Systems (MIS) Issues

Firms that gather, assimilate, and evaluate external and internal information most effectively are gaining competitive advantages over other firms. Recognizing the importance of having an effective *management information system (MIS)* will not be an option in the future; it will be a requirement. Information is the basis for understanding in a firm. In many industries, information is becoming the most important factor in differentiating successful from unsuccessful firms. The process of strategic management is facilitated immensely in firms that have an effective information system. Many companies are establishing a new approach to information systems, one that blends the technical knowledge of the computer experts with the vision of senior management.

Information collection, retrieval, and storage can be used to create competitive advantages in ways such as cross-selling to customers, monitoring suppliers, keeping managers and employees informed, coordinating activities among divisions, and managing funds. Like inventory and human resources, information is now recognized as a valuable organizational asset that can be controlled and managed. Firms that implement strategies using the best information will reap competitive advantages in the twenty-first century.

[handwritten margin note: adv of MIS]

A good information system can allow a firm to reduce costs. For example, online orders from salespersons to production facilities can shorten materials ordering time and reduce inventory costs. Direct communications between suppliers, manufacturers, marketers, and customers can link together elements of the value chain as though they were one organization. Improved quality and service often result from an improved information system.

Firms must increasingly be concerned about computer hackers and take specific measures to secure and safeguard corporate communications, files, orders, and business conducted over the Internet. Gap, Playboy Enterprises, Hitachi America, PeopleSoft, and Twentieth Century Fox average over 30 computer intrusion attempts daily. Thousands of companies today are plagued by computer hackers who include disgruntled employees, competitors, bored teens, sociopaths, thieves, spies, and hired agents. Computer vulnerability is a giant, expensive headache.

NATURAL ENVIRONMENT PERSPECTIVE

Should You Put a Solar Panel on Top of Your Home and Business?

Solar electricity is becoming more and more commonly used in both homes and businesses as a way to cut electricity bills. Once mainly used by ecologically-minded consumers, now installation costs have fallen sharply, and states are giving excellent tax breaks and rebates as incentives to install solar panels on roofs of homes and businesses. About 300,000 homes in the United States are equipped with solar electricity. Sales of residential solar panels grew 28 percent to about $500 million in 2004 and should rise another 20 percent in 2005, according to the Solar Energy Industries Association trade group. Incentives to cover almost all installation costs are available in more than 30 states, up from 4 states in 1999. In California, more than 5,000 residences have solar electricity. New Jersey offers the most generous rebates for solar power. Connecticut and Ohio pay $5 a watt, Nevada pays $4, and Oregon pays up to $3.50 per watt. Idaho offers no rebate but allows homeowners a 100 percent tax deduction up to $20,000.

The following three Web sites offer excellent information on the use of solar electricity for homes and businesses in the United States:

- www.dsireusa.org
- www.ncsc.ncsu.edu
- www.sela.org

Some states allow home and business owners to sell their excess electricity to the local utility. Known as "net metering," this practice also allows the home or business owner to purchase power from a utility at times when the solar panels are not generating enough electricity. Thirty-nine states mandate net metering but some sunny states do not, including North Carolina, Missouri, and Nebraska.

Depending on a firm's use of electricity and where it is located; solar energy may be worth considering as an alternative fuel source. Solar energy obviously is "green" energy and now increasingly may also be the most cost-effective energy.

Source: Adapted from Joseph Pereira, "Solar Power Heats Up," *Wall Street Journal* (June 2, 2005): D1.

Dun & Bradstreet is an example of a company that has an excellent information system. Every D&B customer and client in the world has a separate nine-digit number. The database of information associated with each number has become so widely used that it is like a business Social Security number. D&B reaps great competitive advantages from its information system.

In many firms, information technology is doing away with the workplace and allowing employees to work at home or anywhere, anytime. The mobile concept of work allows employees to work the traditional 9-to-5 workday across any of the 24 time zones around the globe. Affordable desktop videoconferencing software developed by AT&T, Lotus, or Vivo Software allows employees to "beam in" whenever needed. Any manager or employee who travels a lot away from the office is a good candidate for working at home rather than in an office provided by the firm. Salespersons or consultants are good examples, but any person whose job largely involves talking to others or handling information could easily operate at home with the proper computer system and software. The accounting firm Ernst & Young has reduced its office space requirements by 2 million square feet over the past three years by allowing employees to work at home.

Many people see the officeless office trend as leading to a resurgence of family togetherness in U.S. society. Even the design of homes may change from having large open areas to having more private small areas conducive to getting work done.[8]

CONCLUSION

Successful strategy implementation depends on cooperation among all functional and divisional managers in an organization. Marketing departments are commonly charged with implementing strategies that require significant increases in sales revenues in new areas and with new or improved products. Finance and accounting managers must devise effective strategy-implementation approaches at low cost and minimum risk to that firm. R&D managers have to transfer complex technologies or develop new technologies to successfully implement strategies. Information systems managers are being called upon more and more to provide leadership and training for all individuals in the firm. The nature and role of marketing, finance/accounting, R&D, and management information systems activities, coupled with the management activities described in Chapter 7, largely determine organizational success.

We invite you to visit the David page on the Prentice Hall Companion Web site at www.prenhall.com/david for this chapter's review quiz.

KEY TERMS AND CONCEPTS

Cash Budget (p. 321)

EPS/EBIT Analysis (p. 313)

Financial Budget (p. 320)

Management Information System (MIS) (p. 327)

Market Segmentation (p. 307)

Marketing Mix Variables (p. 308)

Outstanding Shares Method (p. 322)

Price-Earnings Ratio Method (p. 322)

Product Positioning (p. 307)

Projected Financial Statement Analysis (p. 318)

Research and Development (R&D) (p. 325)

Vacant Niche (p. 311)

ISSUES FOR REVIEW AND DISCUSSION

1. Suppose your company has just acquired a firm that produces battery-operated lawn mowers, and strategists want to implement a market-penetration strategy. How would you segment the market for this product? Justify your answer.
2. Explain how you would estimate the total worth of a business.
3. Diagram and label clearly a product-positioning map that includes six fast-food restaurant chains.
4. Explain why EPS/EBIT analysis is a central strategy-implementation technique.
5. How would the R&D role in strategy implementation differ in small versus large organizations?
6. Discuss the limitations of EPS/EBIT analysis.
7. Explain how marketing, finance/accounting, R&D, and management information systems

managers' involvement in strategy formulation can enhance strategy implementation.
8. Consider the following statement: "Retained earnings on the balance sheet are not monies available to finance strategy implementation." Is it true or false? Explain.
9. Explain why projected financial statement analysis is considered both a strategy-formulation and a strategy-implementation tool.
10. Describe some marketing, finance/accounting, R&D, and management information systems activities that a small restaurant chain might undertake to expand into a neighboring state.
11. Discuss the management information system at your college or university.
12. What effect is e-commerce having on firms' efforts to segment markets?

13. How has the Sarbanes-Oxley Act of 2002 changed CEOs' and CFOs' handling of financial statements?

14. To what extent have you been exposed to natural environment issues in your business courses? Which course has provided the most coverage? What percentage of your business courses provided no coverage? Comment.

15. Complete the following EPS/EBIT analysis for a company whose stock price is $20, interest rate on funds is 5 percent, tax rate is 20 percent, number of shares outstanding is 500 million, and EBIT range is $100 million to $300 million. The firm needs to raise $200 million in capital. Use the table on the following page to complete the work

16. Under what conditions would retained earnings on the balance sheet decrease from one year to the next?

17. In your own words, list all the steps in developing projected financial statements.

18. Based on the financial statements provided for Google how much dividends in dollars did Google pay in 2004?

19. Based on the financial statements provided in this chapter for the Litten Company, calculate the value of this company if you know that its stock price

is $20 and it has 1 million shares outstanding. Calculate four different ways and average.

20. Why should you be careful not to use historical percentages blindly in developing projected financial statements?

21. In developing projected financial statements, what should you do if the $ amount you must put in the cash account (to make the statement balance) is far more (or less) than desired?

22. Why is it both important and necessary to segment markets and target groups of customers, rather than market to all possible consumers?

23. In full detail, explain the following EPS/EBIT chart.

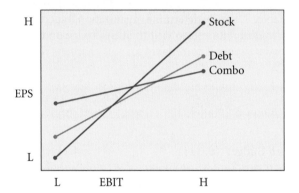

100% COMMON STOCK	100% DEBT FINANCING	20%DEBT–80%STOCK
EBIT		
Interest		
EBT		
Taxes		
EAT		
# Shares		
EPS		

NOTES

1. Leslie Miller and Elizabeth Weise, "E-Privacy—FTC Studies 'Profiling' by Web Sites," *USA Today* (November 8, 1999): 1A, 2A.

2. Ralph Biggadike, "The Contributions of Marketing to Strategic Management," *Academy of Management Review* 6, no. 4 (October 1981): 627.

3. Phyllis Plitch, "Companies in Many Sectors Give Earnings a Pro Forma Makeover, Survey Finds," *Wall Street Journal* (January 22, 2002): A4.

4. Michael Rapoport, "Pro Forma Is a Hard Habit to Break," *Wall Street Journal* (September 18, 2003): B3A.

5. Matt Krantz, "Accounting Rule Targets Goodwill," *USA Today* (February 6, 2003): 3B.

6. Amy Merrick, "U. S. Research Spending to Rise Only 3.2 Percent," *Wall Street Journal* (December 28, 2001): A2.

7. Pier Abetti, "Technology: A Key Strategic Resource," *Management Review* 78, no. 2 (February 1989): 38.

8. Adapted from Edward Baig, "Welcome to the Officeless Office," *BusinessWeek* (June 26, 1995).

CURRENT READINGS

Ballow, John J., Roland Burgman, and Micheal J. Molnar. "Managing for Shareholder Value: Intangibles, Future Value and Investment Decisions." *Journal of Business Strategy* 25, no. 3 (2004): 26.

Crittenden, V. L., and W. F. Crittenden. "Developing the Sales Force, Growing the Business: The Direct Selling Experience." *Business Horizons* 47, no. 5 (September–October 2004): 39.

Dhanaraj, C., and P. W. Beamish. "Effect of Equity Ownership on the Survival of International Joint Ventures." *Strategic Management Journal* 25, no. 3 (March 2004): 295.

Fodness, D. "Rethinking Strategic Marketing: Achieving Breakthrough Results." *Journal of Business Strategy* 26, no. 3 (2005): 20.

Grand, Simon, Georg von Krogh, Dorothy Leonard, and Walter Swap. "Resource Allocation Beyond Firm Boundaries: A Multi-Level Model for Open Source Innovation." *Long Range Planning* 37, no. 6 (December 2004): 591.

Hambrick, D. C., and A. A. Cannella, Jr. "CEOs Who Have COOs: Contingency Analysis of an Unexplored Structural Form." *Strategic Management Journal* 25, no. 10 (October 2004): 959.

Johnson, J. L., A. E. Ellstrand, D. R. Dalton, and C. M. Dalton. "The Influence of the Financial Press on Stockholder Wealth: The Case of Corporate Governance." *Strategic Management Journal* 26, no. 5 (May 2005): 461.

Longman, Andrew, and James Mullins. "Project Management: Key Tool for Implementing Strategy." *Journal of Business Strategy* 25, no. 5 (2004): 54.

Lorange, P. "Agenda: Memo to Marketing." *MIT Sloan Management Review* 46, no. 2 (Winter 2005): 16.

Miller, Susan, David Wilson, and David Hickson. "Beyond Planning: Strategies for Successfully Implementing Strategic Decisions." *Long Range Planning* 37, no. 3 (June 2004): 201.

Prince, E. T. "In Context: The Fiscal Behavior of CEOs." *MIT Sloan Management Review* 46, no. 3 (Spring 2005): 23.

Puffer, S. M. "Changing Organizational Structures: An Interview with Rosabeth Moss Kanter." *The Academy of Management Executive* 18, no. 2 (July 2004): 96.

Sanders, W. G., and S. Boivie. "Sorting Things Out: Valuation of New Firms in Uncertain Markets." *Strategic Management Journal* 25, no. 2 (February 2004): 167.

Toffel, Michael W. "Strategic Management of Product Recovery." *California Management Review* 46, no. 2 (Winter 2004): 120.

experiential exercises

Experiential Exercise 8A

Developing a Product-Positioning Map for Google

PURPOSE

Organizations continually monitor how their products and services are positioned relative to competitors. This information is especially useful for marketing managers but is also used by other managers and strategists.

INSTRUCTIONS

Step 1   On a separate sheet of paper, develop a product-positioning map for Google. Include Yahoo!, AOL, and Microsoft in your diagram.

Step 2   Go to the blackboard and diagram your product-positioning map.

Step 3   Compare your product-positioning map with those diagrammed by other students. Discuss any major differences.

Experiential Exercise 8B

Performing an EPS/EBIT Analysis for Google

PURPOSE

An EPS/EBIT analysis is one of the most widely used techniques for determining the extent that debt and/or stock should be used to finance strategies to be implemented. This exercise can give you practice performing EPS/EBIT analysis.

INSTRUCTIONS (1-1-06 DATA)

Let's say Google needs to raise $1 billion to expand around the world in 2006. Determine whether Google should have used all debt, all stock, or a 50-50 combination of debt and stock to finance this market-development strategy. Assume a 38 percent tax rate, 5 percent interest rate, Google stock price of $400 per share, and an annual dividend of $2.00 per share of common stock. The EBIT range for 2006 is between $1 billion and $500 million. A total of 300 million shares of common stock are outstanding. Develop an EPS/EBIT chart to reflect your analysis.

Experiential Exercise 8C

Preparing Projected Financial Statements for Google

PURPOSE

This exercise is designed to give you experience preparing projected financial statements. Pro forma analysis is a central strategy-implementation technique because it allows managers to anticipate and evaluate the expected results of various strategy-implementation approaches.

INSTRUCTIONS

Step 1   Work with a classmate. Develop a 2006 projected income statement and balance sheet for Google. Assume that Google plans to raise $900 million in 2006 to begin serving new countries and plans to obtain 50 percent financing from a bank and 50 percent financing from a stock issuance. Make other assumptions as needed, and state them clearly in written form.

Step 2   Compute Google's current ratio, debt-to-equity ratio, and return-on-investment ratio for 2004 and 2005. How do your 2006 projected ratios compare to the 2004 and 2005 ratios? Why is it important to make this comparison? Use http://finance.yahoo.com to obtain 2005 financial statements.

Step 3   Bring your projected statements to class, and discuss any problems or questions you encountered.

Step 4   Compare your projected statements to the statements of other students. What major differences exist between your analysis and the work of other students?

Experiential Exercise 8D

Determining the Cash Value of Google

PURPOSE

It is simply good business practice to periodically determine the financial worth or cash value of your company. This exercise gives you practice determining the total worth of a company using several methods. Use year-end 2004 data as given in the Cohesion Case on p. 46 & 47.

INSTRUCTIONS

Step 1   Calculate the financial worth of Google based on four methods: (1) the net worth or stockholders' equity, (2) the future value of Google earnings, (3) the price-earnings ratio, and (4) the outstanding shares method.

Step 2   In a dollar amount, how much is Google worth?

Step 3   Compare your analyses and conclusions with those of other students.

Experiential Exercise 8E

Developing a Product-Positioning Map for My University

PURPOSE

The purpose of this exercise is to give you practice developing product-positioning maps. Nonprofit organizations, such as universities, are increasingly using product-positioning maps to determine effective ways to implement strategies.

INSTRUCTIONS

Step 1   Join with two other people in class to form a group of three.

Step 2   Jointly prepare a product-positioning map that includes your institution and four other colleges or universities in your state.

Step 3   Go to the blackboard and diagram your product-positioning map.

Step 4   Discuss differences among the maps diagrammed on the board.

Experiential Exercise 8F

Do Banks Require Projected Financial Statements?

PURPOSE

The purpose of this exercise is to explore the practical importance and use of projected financial statements in the banking business.

INSTRUCTIONS

Contact two local bankers by phone and seek answers to the questions that follow. Record the answers you receive, and report your findings to the class.

1. Does your bank require projected financial statements as part of a business loan application?
2. How does your bank use projected financial statements when they are part of a business loan application?
3. What special advice do you give potential business borrowers in preparing projected financial statements?

chapter objectives

After studying this chapter, you should be able to do the following:

1. Describe a practical framework for evaluating strategies.

2. Explain why strategy evaluation is complex, sensitive, and yet essential for organizational success.

3. Discuss the importance of contingency planning in strategy evaluation.

4. Discuss the role of auditing in strategy evaluation.

5. Explain how computers can aid in evaluating strategies.

6. Discuss the Balanced Scorecard.

7. Discuss three twenty-first-century challenges in strategic management.

experiential exercises

Experiential Exercise 9A
Preparing a Strategy-Evaluation Report for Google

Experiential Exercise 9B
Evaluating My University's Strategies

Experiential Exercise 9C
Who Prepares an Environmental Audit?

"notable quotes"

Complicated controls do not work. They confuse. They misdirect attention from what is to be controlled to the mechanics and methodology of the control.
Seymour Tilles

Although Plan A may be selected as the most realistic . . . the other major alternatives should not be forgotten. They may well serve as contingency plans.
Dale McConkey

Organizations are most vulnerable when they are at the peak of their success.
R. T. Lenz

Strategy evaluation must make it as easy as possible for managers
to revise their plans and reach quick agreement on the changes.
Dale McConkey

While strategy is a word that is usually associated with the future, its link to the past is no less central. Life is lived forward but understood backward. Managers may live strategy in the future, but they understand it through the past.
Henry Mintzberg

Unless strategy evaluation is performed seriously and systematically, and unless strategists are willing to act on the results, energy will be used up defending yesterday. No one will have the time, resources, or will to work on
exploiting today, let alone to work on making tomorrow.
Peter Drucker

Executives, consultants, and B-school professors all agree that strategic planning is now the single most important management issue and will remain so for the next five years. Strategy has become a part of the main agenda at lots of organizations today. Strategic planning is back with a vengeance.
John Byrne

Planners should not plan, but serve as facilitators, catalysts, inquirers, educators, and synthesizers to guide the planning process effectively.
A. Hax and N. Majluf

The best-formulated and best-implemented strategies become obsolete as a firm's external and internal environments change. It is essential, therefore, that strategists systematically review, evaluate, and control the execution of strategies. This chapter presents a framework that can guide managers' efforts to evaluate strategic-management activities, to make sure they are working, and to make timely changes. Management information systems being used to evaluate strategies are discussed. Guidelines are presented for formulating, implementing, and evaluating strategies.

The Nature of Strategy Evaluation

VISIT THE NET

Gives excellent additional information about evaluating strategies, including some analytical tools.
(www.mindtools.com/ plevplan.html)

The strategic-management process results in decisions that can have significant, long-lasting consequences. Erroneous strategic decisions can inflict severe penalties and can be exceedingly difficult, if not impossible, to reverse. Most strategists agree, therefore, that strategy evaluation is vital to an organization's well-being; timely evaluations can alert management to problems or potential problems before a situation becomes critical. Strategy evaluation includes three basic activities: (1) examining the underlying bases of a firm's strategy, (2) comparing expected results with actual results, and (3) taking corrective actions to ensure that performance conforms to plans. The strategy-evaluation stage of the strategic-management process is illustrated in Figure 9-1.

FIGURE 9-1

A Comprehensive Strategic-Management Model

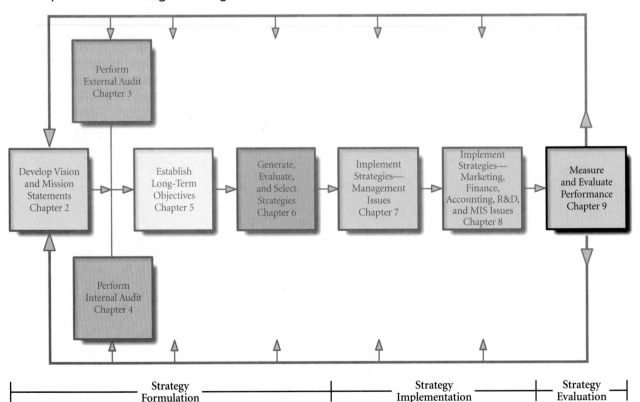

Adequate and timely feedback is the cornerstone of effective strategy evaluation. Strategy evaluation can be no better than the information on which it is based. Too much pressure from top managers may result in lower managers contriving numbers they think will be satisfactory.

Strategy evaluation can be a complex and sensitive undertaking. Too much emphasis on evaluating strategies may be expensive and counterproductive. No one likes to be evaluated too closely! The more managers attempt to evaluate the behavior of others, the less control they have. Yet too little or no evaluation can create even worse problems. Strategy evaluation is essential to ensure that stated objectives are being achieved.

In many organizations, strategy evaluation is simply an appraisal of how well an organization has performed. Have the firm's assets increased? Has there been an increase in profitability? Have sales increased? Have productivity levels increased? Have profit margin, return on investment, and earnings-per-share ratios increased? Some firms argue that their strategy must have been correct if the answers to these types of questions are affirmative. Well, the strategy or strategies may have been correct, but this type of reasoning can be misleading because strategy evaluation must have both a long-run and short-run focus. Strategies often do not affect short-term operating results until it is too late to make needed changes.

It is impossible to demonstrate conclusively that a particular strategy is optimal or even to guarantee that it will work. One can, however, evaluate it for critical flaws. Richard Rumelt offered four criteria that could be used to evaluate a strategy: consistency, consonance, feasibility, and advantage. Described in Table 9-1, *consonance* and *advantage* are mostly based on a firm's external assessment, whereas *consistency* and *feasibility* are largely based on an internal assessment.

Strategy evaluation is important because organizations face dynamic environments in which key external and internal factors often change quickly and dramatically. Success today is no guarantee of success tomorrow! An organization should never be lulled into complacency with success. Countless firms have thrived one year only to struggle for survival the following year. Organizational trouble can come swiftly, as further evidenced by the examples described in Table 9-2.

Strategy evaluation is becoming increasingly difficult with the passage of time, for many reasons. Domestic and world economies were more stable in years past, product life cycles were longer, product development cycles were longer, technological advancement was slower, change occurred less frequently, there were fewer competitors, foreign companies were weak, and there were more regulated industries. Other reasons why strategy evaluation is more difficult today include the following trends:

1. A dramatic increase in the environment's complexity
2. The increasing difficulty of predicting the future with accuracy
3. The increasing number of variables
4. The rapid rate of obsolescence of even the best plans
5. The increase in the number of both domestic and world events affecting organizations
6. The decreasing time span for which planning can be done with any degree of certainty[1]

A fundamental problem facing managers today is how to effectively control employees in light of modern organizational demands for greater flexibility, innovation, creativity, and initiative from employees.[2] How can managers today ensure that empowered employees acting in an entrepreneurial manner do not put the well-being of the business at risk? Recall that Kidder, Peabody & Company lost

VISIT THE NET

Describes the how and why of strategy evaluation. (www.csuchico.edu/mgmt/ strategy/module1/ sld046.htm)

TABLE 9-1   Rumelt's Criteria for Evaluating Strategies

CONSISTENCY

A strategy should not present inconsistent goals and policies. Organizational conflict and interdepartmental bickering are often symptoms of managerial disorder, but these problems may also be a sign of strategic inconsistency. Three guidelines help determine if organizational problems are due to inconsistencies in strategy:

- If managerial problems continue despite changes in personnel and if they tend to be issue-based rather than people-based, then strategies may be inconsistent.
- If success for one organizational department means, or is interpreted to mean, failure for another department, then strategies may be inconsistent.
- If policy problems and issues continue to be brought to the top for resolution, then strategies may be inconsistent.

CONSONANCE

Consonance refers to the need for strategists to examine *sets of trends*, as well as individual trends, in evaluating strategies. A strategy must represent an adaptive response to the external environment and to the critical changes occurring within it. One difficulty in matching a firm's key internal and external factors in the formulation of strategy is that most trends are the result of interactions among other trends. For example, the day-care explosion came about as a combined result of many trends that included a rise in the average level of education, increased inflation, and an increase in women in the workforce. Although single economic or demographic trends might appear steady for many years, there are waves of change going on at the interaction level.

FEASIBILITY

A strategy must neither overtax available resources nor create unsolvable subproblems. The final broad test of strategy is its feasibility; that is, can the strategy be attempted within the physical, human, and financial resources of the enterprise? The financial resources of a business are the easiest to quantify and are normally the first limitation against which strategy is evaluated. It is sometimes forgotten, however, that innovative approaches to financing are often possible. Devices, such as captive subsidiaries, sale-leaseback arrangements, and tying plant mortgages to long-term contracts, have all been used effectively to help win key positions in suddenly expanding industries. A less quantifiable, but actually more rigid, limitation on strategic choice is that imposed by individual and organizational capabilities. In evaluating a strategy, it is important to examine whether an organization has demonstrated in the past that it possesses the abilities, competencies, skills, and talents needed to carry out a given strategy.

ADVANTAGE

A strategy must provide for the creation and/or maintenance of a competitive advantage in a selected area of activity. Competitive advantages normally are the result of superiority in one of three areas: (1) resources, (2) skills, or (3) position. The idea that the positioning of one's resources can enhance their combined effectiveness is familiar to military theorists, chess players, and diplomats. Position can also play a crucial role in an organization's strategy. Once gained, a good position is defensible—meaning that it is so costly to capture that rivals are deterred from full-scale attacks. Positional advantage tends to be self-sustaining as long as the key internal and environmental factors that underlie it remain stable. This is why entrenched firms can be almost impossible to unseat, even if their raw skill levels are only average. Although not all positional advantages are associated with size, it is true that larger organizations tend to operate in markets and use procedures that turn their size into advantage, while smaller firms seek product/market positions that exploit other types of advantage. The principal characteristic of good position is that it permits the firm to obtain advantage from policies that would not similarly benefit rivals without the same position. Therefore, in evaluating strategy, organizations should examine the nature of positional advantages associated with a given strategy.

Source: Adapted from Richard Rumelt, "The Evaluation of Business Strategy," in W. F. Glueck (ed.), *Business Policy and Strategic Management* (New York: McGraw-Hill, 1980): 359–367.

TABLE 9-2 Examples of Organizational Demise

A. SOME LARGE COMPANIES THAT EXPERIENCED A LARGE DROP IN REVENUES IN 2004 VS. 2003		B. SOME LARGE COMPANIES THAT EXPERIENCED A LARGE DROP IN PROFITS IN 2004 VS. 2003	
Sears, Roebuck	−12%	Continental Airlines	−1055%
AT&T	−12%	Northwest Airlines	− 447%
JCPenney	−22%	Winn-Dixie Stores	− 142%
MCI	−17%	AT&T	− 446%
Washington Mutual	−11%	QWest Communications	− 218%
Citizens Communications	−14%	Kroger	− 140%
Janus Capital Group	−13%	Arvinmeritor	− 130%
Williams	−33%	CNF	− 225%
Newell Rubbermaid	−11%	Viacom	−1332%
CMS Energy	−10%	Sprint	− 178%
E1 Paso	−47%	Sears, Roebuck	− 114%

Source: Adapted from *BusinessWeek*, February 23, 2004, pp. 60–84.

$350 million when one of its traders allegedly booked fictitious profits; Sears, Roebuck and Company took a $60 million charge against earnings after admitting that its automobile service businesses were performing unnecessary repairs. The costs to companies such as these in terms of damaged reputations, fines, missed opportunities, and diversion of management's attention are enormous.

When empowered employees are held accountable for and pressured to achieve specific goals and are given wide latitude in their actions to achieve them, there can be dysfunctional behavior. For example, Nordstrom, the upscale fashion retailer known for outstanding customer service, was subjected to lawsuits and fines when employees underreported hours worked in order to increase their sales per hour—the company's primary performance criterion. Nordstrom's customer service and earnings were enhanced until the misconduct was reported, at which time severe penalties were levied against the firm.

The Process of Evaluating Strategies

Strategy evaluation is necessary for all sizes and kinds of organizations. Strategy evaluation should initiate managerial questioning of expectations and assumptions, should trigger a review of objectives and values, and should stimulate creativity in generating alternatives and formulating criteria of evaluation.[3] Regardless of the size of the organization, a certain amount of *management by wandering around* at all levels is essential to effective strategy evaluation. Strategy-evaluation activities should be performed on a continuing basis, rather than at the end of specified periods of time or just after problems occur. Waiting until the end of the year, for example, could result in a firm closing the barn door after the horses have already escaped.

Evaluating strategies on a continuous rather than on a periodic basis allows benchmarks of progress to be established and more effectively monitored. Some strategies take years to implement; consequently, associated results may not become apparent for years. Successful strategies combine patience with a willingness to promptly take corrective actions when necessary. There always comes a time when corrective actions

VISIT THE NET

Elaborates on the "taking corrective actions" phase of strategy evaluation.
(www.csuchico.edu/mgmt/ strategy/module1/ sld047.htm)

are needed in an organization! Centuries ago, a writer (perhaps Solomon) made the following observations about change:

> There is a time for everything,
> A time to be born and a time to die,
> A time to plant and a time to uproot,
> A time to kill and a time to heal,
> A time to tear down and a time to build,
> A time to weep and a time to laugh,
> A time to mourn and a time to dance,
> A time to scatter stones and a time to gather them,
> A time to embrace and a time to refrain,
> A time to search and a time to give up,
> A time to keep and a time to throw away,
> A time to tear and a time to mend,
> A time to be silent and a time to speak,
> A time to love and a time to hate,
> A time for war and a time for peace.[4]

Managers and employees of the firm should be continually aware of progress being made toward achieving the firm's objectives. As critical success factors change, organizational members should be involved in determining appropriate corrective actions. If assumptions and expectations deviate significantly from forecasts, then the firm should renew strategy-formulation activities, perhaps sooner than planned. In strategy evaluation, like strategy formulation and strategy implementation, people make the difference. Through involvement in the process of evaluating strategies, managers and employees become committed to keeping the firm moving steadily toward achieving objectives.

A Strategy-Evaluation Framework

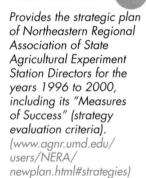

VISIT THE NET

Provides the strategic plan of Northeastern Regional Association of State Agricultural Experiment Station Directors for the years 1996 to 2000, including its "Measures of Success" (strategy evaluation criteria).
(www.agnr.umd.edu/ users/NERA/ newplan.html#strategies)

Table 9-3 summarizes strategy-evaluation activities in terms of key questions that should be addressed, alternative answers to those questions, and appropriate actions for an organization to take. Notice that corrective actions are almost always needed except when (1) external and internal factors have not significantly changed and (2) the firm is progressing satisfactorily toward achieving stated objectives. Relationships among strategy-evaluation activities are illustrated in Figure 9-2.

Reviewing Bases of Strategy

As shown in Figure 9-2, *reviewing the underlying bases of an organization's strategy* could be approached by developing a revised EFE Matrix and IFE Matrix. A *revised IFE Matrix* should focus on changes in the organization's management, marketing, finance/accounting, production/operations, R&D, and management information systems strengths and weaknesses. A *revised EFE Matrix* should indicate how effective a firm's strategies have been in response to key opportunities and threats. This analysis could also address such questions as the following:

1. How have competitors reacted to our strategies?
2. How have competitors' strategies changed?
3. Have major competitors' strengths and weaknesses changed?
4. Why are competitors making certain strategic changes?

TABLE 9-3 A Strategy-Evaluation Assessment Matrix

HAVE MAJOR CHANGES OCCURRED IN THE FIRM'S INTERNAL STRATEGIC POSITION?	HAVE MAJOR CHANGES OCCURRED IN THE FIRM'S EXTERNAL STRATEGIC POSITION?	HAS THE FIRM PROGRESSED SATISFACTORILY TOWARD ACHIEVING ITS STATED OBJECTIVES?	RESULT
No	No	No	Take corrective actions
Yes	Yes	Yes	Take corrective actions
Yes	Yes	No	Take corrective actions
Yes	No	Yes	Take corrective actions
Yes	No	No	Take corrective actions
No	Yes	Yes	Take corrective actions
No	Yes	No	Take corrective actions
No	No	Yes	Continue present strategic course

5. Why are some competitors' strategies more successful than others?
6. How satisfied are our competitors with their present market positions and profitability?
7. How far can our major competitors be pushed before retaliating?
8. How could we more effectively cooperate with our competitors?

Numerous external and internal factors can prohibit firms from achieving long-term and annual objectives. Externally, actions by competitors, changes in demand, changes in technology, economic changes, demographic shifts, and governmental actions may prohibit objectives from being accomplished. Internally, ineffective strategies may have been chosen or implementation activities may have been poor. Objectives may have been too optimistic. Thus, failure to achieve objectives may not be the result of unsatisfactory work by managers and employees. All organizational members need to know this to encourage their support for strategy-evaluation activities. Organizations desperately need to know as soon as possible when their strategies are not effective. Sometimes managers and employees on the front lines discover this well before strategists.

External opportunities and threats and internal strengths and weaknesses that represent the bases of current strategies should continually be monitored for change. It is not really a question of whether these factors will change but rather when they will change and in what ways. Some key questions to address in evaluating strategies follow:

1. Are our internal strengths still strengths?
2. Have we added other internal strengths? If so, what are they?
3. Are our internal weaknesses still weaknesses?
4. Do we now have other internal weaknesses? If so, what are they?
5. Are our external opportunities still opportunities?
6. Are there now other external opportunities? If so, what are they?
7. Are our external threats still threats?
8. Are there now other external threats? If so, what are they?
9. Are we vulnerable to a hostile takeover?

VISIT THE NET

The Small Business Administration Web site provides a 40-page Business Plan Outline. (www.sba.gov/starting_/business/planning/basic.html)

FIGURE 9-2

A Strategy-Evaluation Framework

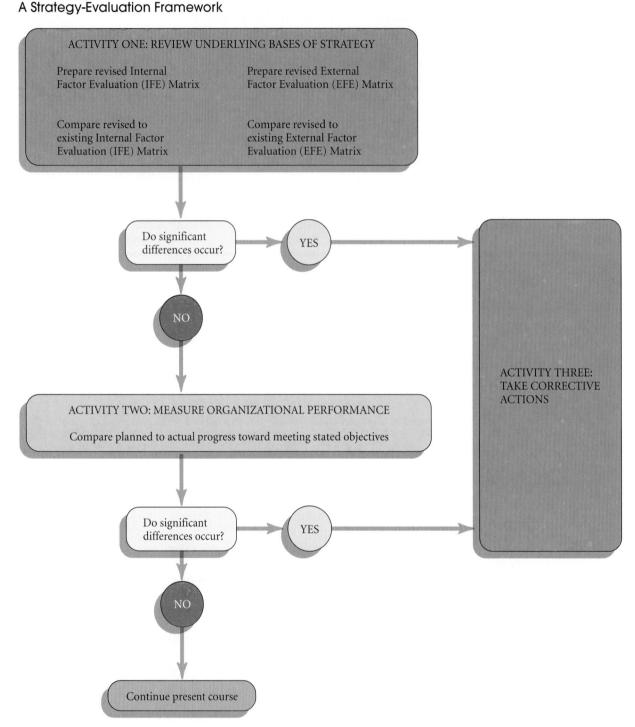

Measuring Organizational Performance

Another important strategy-evaluation activity is *measuring organizational performance*. This activity includes comparing expected results to actual results, investigating deviations from plans, evaluating individual performance, and examining progress being made toward meeting stated objectives. Both long-term and annual objectives are commonly used in this process. Criteria for evaluating strategies should be measurable and easily verifiable. Criteria that predict results may be more important than those that reveal what already has happened. For example, rather than simply being informed that sales in the last quarter were 20 percent under what was expected, strategists need to know that sales in the next quarter may be 20 percent below standard unless some action is taken to counter the trend. Really effective control requires accurate forecasting.

Failure to make satisfactory progress toward accomplishing long-term or annual objectives signals a need for corrective actions. Many factors, such as unreasonable policies, unexpected turns in the economy, unreliable suppliers or distributors, or ineffective strategies, can result in unsatisfactory progress toward meeting objectives. Problems can result from ineffectiveness (not doing the right things) or inefficiency (poorly doing the right things).

Determining which objectives are most important in the evaluation of strategies can be difficult. Strategy evaluation is based on both quantitative and qualitative criteria. Selecting the exact set of criteria for evaluating strategies depends on a particular organization's size, industry, strategies, and management philosophy. An organization pursuing a retrenchment strategy, for example, could have an entirely different set of evaluative criteria from an organization pursuing a market-development strategy. Quantitative criteria commonly used to evaluate strategies are financial ratios, which strategists use to make three critical comparisons: (1) comparing the firm's performance over different time periods, (2) comparing the firm's performance to competitors', and (3) comparing the firm's performance to industry averages. Some key financial ratios that are particularly useful as criteria for strategy evaluation are as follows:

1. Return on investment (ROI)
2. Return on equity (ROE)
3. Profit margin
4. Market share
5. Debt to equity
6. Earnings per share
7. Sales growth
8. Asset growth

But there are some potential problems associated with using quantitative criteria for evaluating strategies. First, most quantitative criteria are geared to annual objectives rather than long-term objectives. Also, different accounting methods can provide different results on many quantitative criteria. Third, intuitive judgments are almost always involved in deriving quantitative criteria. For these and other reasons, qualitative criteria are also important in evaluating strategies. Human factors such as high absenteeism and turnover rates, poor production quality and quantity rates, or low employee satisfaction can be underlying causes of declining performance. Marketing, finance/accounting, R&D, or management information systems factors can also cause financial problems. Seymour Tilles identified six qualitative questions that are useful in evaluating strategies:

1. Is the strategy internally consistent?
2. Is the strategy consistent with the environment?
3. Is the strategy appropriate in view of available resources?

4. Does the strategy involve an acceptable degree of risk?

5. Does the strategy have an appropriate time framework?

6. Is the strategy workable?[5]

Some additional key questions that reveal the need for qualitative or intuitive judgments in strategy evaluation are as follows:

1. How good is the firm's balance of investments between high-risk and low-risk projects?

2. How good is the firm's balance of investments between long-term and short-term projects?

3. How good is the firm's balance of investments between slow-growing markets and fast-growing markets?

4. How good is the firm's balance of investments among different divisions?

5. To what extent are the firm's alternative strategies socially responsible?

6. What are the relationships among the firm's key internal and external strategic factors?

7. How are major competitors likely to respond to particular strategies?

Taking Corrective Actions

The final strategy-evaluation activity, *taking corrective actions*, requires making changes to competitively reposition a firm for the future. Examples of changes that may be needed are altering an organization's structure, replacing one or more key individuals, selling a division, or revising a business mission. Other changes could include establishing or revising objectives, devising new policies, issuing stock to raise capital, adding additional salespersons, differently allocating resources, or developing new performance incentives. Taking corrective actions does not necessarily mean that existing strategies will be abandoned or even that new strategies must be formulated.

> The probabilities and possibilities for incorrect or inappropriate actions increase geometrically with an arithmetic increase in personnel. Any person directing an overall undertaking must check on the actions of the participants as well as the results that they have achieved. If either the actions or results do not comply with preconceived or planned achievements, then corrective actions are needed.[6]

No organization can survive as an island; no organization can escape change. Taking corrective actions is necessary to keep an organization on track toward achieving stated objectives. In his thought-provoking books *Future Shock* and *The Third Wave*, Alvin Toffler argued that business environments are becoming so dynamic and complex that they threaten people and organizations with *future shock*, which occurs when the nature, types, and speed of changes overpower an individual's or organization's ability and capacity to adapt. Strategy evaluation enhances an organization's ability to adapt successfully to changing circumstances. Brown and Agnew referred to this notion as *corporate agility*.[7]

Taking corrective actions raises employees' and managers' anxieties. Research suggests that participation in strategy-evaluation activities is one of the best ways to overcome individuals' resistance to change. According to Erez and Kanfer, individuals accept change best when they have a cognitive understanding of the changes, a sense of control over the situation, and an awareness that necessary actions are going to be taken to implement the changes.[8]

Strategy evaluation can lead to strategy-formulation changes, strategy-implementation changes, both formulation and implementation changes, or no changes at all. Strategists cannot escape having to revise strategies and implementation approaches sooner or later. Hussey and Langham offered the following insight on taking corrective actions:

> Resistance to change is often emotionally based and not easily overcome by rational argument. Resistance may be based on such feelings as loss of status, implied criticism of present competence, fear of failure in the new situation, annoyance at not being consulted, lack of understanding of the need for change, or insecurity in changing from well-known and fixed methods. It is necessary, therefore, to overcome such resistance by creating situations of participation and full explanation when changes are envisaged.[9]

Corrective actions should place an organization in a better position to capitalize upon internal strengths; to take advantage of key external opportunities; to avoid, reduce, or mitigate external threats; and to improve internal weaknesses. Corrective actions should have a proper time horizon and an appropriate amount of risk. They should be internally consistent and socially responsible. Perhaps most important, corrective actions strengthen an organization's competitive position in its basic industry. Continuous strategy evaluation keeps strategists close to the pulse of an organization and provides information needed for an effective strategic-management system. Carter Bayles described the benefits of strategy evaluation as follows:

> Evaluation activities may renew confidence in the current business strategy or point to the need for actions to correct some weaknesses, such as erosion of product superiority or technological edge. In many cases, the benefits of strategy evaluation are much more far-reaching, for the outcome of the process may be a fundamentally new strategy that will lead, even in a business that is already turning a respectable profit, to substantially increased earnings. It is this possibility that justifies strategy evaluation, for the payoff can be very large.[10]

An example company that today is taking major corrective actions is Sun Microsystems. For nearly two decades, Sun Microsystems dismissed the standard chips and software that ran most computers in favor of its own souped-up custom designs.[11] Although more powerful than Intel and Microsoft chips and servers, Sun products were also more expensive. However, today Intel and Microsoft and similar firms produce generic chips and software that are less expensive than Sun's and just as powerful, so Sun increasingly is unable to compete on price, quality, or power. Sun's revenues and profits are declining rapidly, and the firm is actively engaged in the strategy-evaluation process. This is an example of a company that basically began with step two in the process illustrated; today firms must begin with step one due to intense competition in virtually all industries.

The Balanced Scorecard

Introduced earlier in the Chapter 5 discussion of objectives, the Balanced Scorecard is an important strategy-evaluation tool. It is a process that allows firms to evaluate strategies from four perspectives: financial performance, customer knowledge, internal business processes, and learning and growth. The *Balanced Scorecard* analysis requires that firms seek answers to the following questions and utilize that information, in conjunction with financial measures, to adequately and more effectively evaluate strategies being implemented:

1. How well is the firm continually improving and creating value along measures, such as innovation, technological leadership, product quality, operational process efficiencies, and so on?
2. How well is the firm sustaining and even improving upon its core competencies and competitive advantages?
3. How satisfied are the firm's customers?

A sample Balanced Scorecard is provided in Table 9-4. Notice that the firm examines six key issues in evaluating its strategies: (1) Customers, (2) Managers/Employees, (3) Operations/Processes, (4) Community/Social Responsibility, (5) Business Ethics/Natural Environment, and (6) Financial. The basic form of a Balanced Scorecard may differ for different organizations. The Balanced Scorecard approach to strategy evaluation aims to balance long-term with short-term concerns, to balance financial with nonfinancial concerns, and to balance internal with external concerns. It can be an excellent management tool, and it is used successfully today by Chemical Bank, Exxon/Mobil Corporation, CIGNA Property and Casualty Insurance, and numerous other firms. For example, Unilever has a financial objective to grow revenues by 5 percent to 6 percent annually. The company also has a strategic objective to reduce its 1,200 food, household, and personal care products to 400 core brands within three years. The Balanced Scorecard would be constructed differently, that is, adapted, to particular firms in various industries with the underlying theme or thrust being the same, which is to evaluate the firm's strategies based upon both key quantitative and qualitative measures.

Published Sources of Strategy-Evaluation Information

A number of publications are helpful in evaluating a firm's strategies. For example, *Fortune* annually identifies and evaluates the Fortune 1,000 (the largest manufacturers) and the Fortune 50 (the largest retailers, transportation companies, utilities, banks, insurance companies, and diversified financial corporations in the United States). *Fortune* ranks the best and worst performers on various factors, such as return on investment, sales volume, and profitability. In its March issue each year, *Fortune* publishes its strategy-evaluation research in an article entitled "America's Most Admired Companies." Nine key attributes serve as evaluative criteria: quality of management; innovativeness; quality of products or services; long-term investment value; financial soundness; community and environmental responsibility; ability to attract, develop, and keep talented people; use of corporate assets; and international acumen. In October of each year, *Fortune* publishes additional strategy-evaluation research in an

TABLE 9-4   An Example Balanced Scorecard

AREA OF OBJECTIVES	MEASURE OR TARGET	TIME EXPECTATION	PRIMARY RESPONSIBILITY
Customers			
1.			
2.			
3.			
4.			
Managers/Employees			
1.			
2.			
3.			
4.			
Operations/Processes			
1.			
2.			
3.			
4.			
Community/Social Responsibility			
1.			
2.			
3.			
4.			
Business Ethics/Natural Environment			
1.			
2.			
3.			
4.			
Financial			
1.			
2.			
3.			
4.			

article entitled "The World's Most Admired Companies." *Fortune's* 2005 evaluation in Table 9-5 reveals the firms ranked as the top 10 most admired (best managed).

Another excellent evaluation of corporations in America, "The Annual Report on American Industry," is published annually in the January issue of *Forbes*. It provides a detailed and comprehensive evaluation of hundreds of U.S. companies in many different industries. *BusinessWeek*, *Industry Week*, and *Dun's Business Month* also periodically publish detailed evaluations of U.S. businesses and industries. Although published sources of strategy-evaluation information focus primarily on large, publicly held businesses, the comparative ratios and related information are widely used to evaluate small businesses and privately-owned firms as well.

TABLE 9-5 Most Admired Companies (2005)

RANK	COMPANY	TOTAL RETURN (2004)
1	Dell	24.0%
2	General Electric	20.7%
3	Starbucks	88.1%
4	Wal-Mart Stores	0.4%
5	Southwest Airlines	1.0%
6	FedEx	46.4%
7	Berkshire Hathaway	4.3%
8	Microsoft	9.1%
9	Johnson & Johnson	25.1%
10	Procter & Gamble	11.9%
Top 10 Average		23.1%
SIPSCO		10.88%

Source: Adapted from www.fortune.com/fortune/mostadmired/subs/2005/topten

Characteristics of an Effective Evaluation System

Strategy evaluation must meet several basic requirements to be effective. First, strategy-evaluation activities must be economical; too much information can be just as bad as too little information; and too many controls can do more harm than good. Strategy-evaluation activities also should be meaningful; they should specifically relate to a firm's objectives. They should provide managers with useful information about tasks over which they have control and influence. Strategy-evaluation activities should provide timely information; on occasion and in some areas, managers may daily need information. For example, when a firm has diversified by acquiring another firm, evaluative information may be needed frequently. However, in an R&D department, daily or even weekly evaluative information could be dysfunctional. Approximate information that is timely is generally more desirable as a basis for strategy evaluation than accurate information that does not depict the present. Frequent measurement and rapid reporting may frustrate control rather than give better control. The time dimension of control must coincide with the time span of the event being measured.

Strategy evaluation should be designed to provide a true picture of what is happening. For example, in a severe economic downturn, productivity and profitability ratios may drop alarmingly, although employees and managers are actually working harder. Strategy evaluations should fairly portray this type of situation. Information derived from the strategy-evaluation process should facilitate action and should be directed to those individuals in the organization who need to take action based on it. Managers commonly ignore evaluative reports that are provided only for informational purposes; not all managers need to receive all reports. Controls need to be action-oriented rather than information-oriented.

The strategy-evaluation process should not dominate decisions; it should foster mutual understanding, trust, and common sense. No department should fail to cooperate with another in evaluating strategies. Strategy evaluations should be simple, not too cumbersome, and not too restrictive. Complex strategy-evaluation systems often confuse people and accomplish little. The test of an effective evaluation system is its usefulness, not its complexity.

Large organizations require a more elaborate and detailed strategy-evaluation system because it is more difficult to coordinate efforts among different divisions and functional areas. Managers in small companies often communicate daily with each other and their employees and do not need extensive evaluative reporting systems. Familiarity with local environments usually makes gathering and evaluating information much easier for small organizations than for large businesses. But the key to an effective strategy-evaluation system may be the ability to convince participants that failure to accomplish certain objectives within a prescribed time is not necessarily a reflection of their performance.

There is no one ideal strategy-evaluation system. The unique characteristics of an organization, including its size, management style, purpose, problems, and strengths, can determine a strategy-evaluation and control system's final design. Robert Waterman offered the following observation about successful organizations' strategy-evaluation and control systems:

> Successful companies treat facts as friends and controls as liberating. Morgan Guaranty and Wells Fargo not only survive but thrive in the troubled waters of bank deregulation, because their strategy evaluation and control systems are sound, their risk is contained, and they know themselves and the competitive situation so well. Successful companies have a voracious hunger for facts. They see information where others see only data. They love comparisons, rankings, anything that removes decision making from the realm of mere opinion. Successful companies maintain tight, accurate financial controls. Their people don't regard controls as an imposition of autocracy but as the benign checks and balances that allow them to be creative and free.[12]

Contingency Planning

A basic premise of good strategic management is that firms plan ways to deal with unfavorable and favorable events before they occur. Too many organizations prepare contingency plans just for unfavorable events; this is a mistake, because both minimizing threats and capitalizing on opportunities can improve a firm's competitive position.

Regardless of how carefully strategies are formulated, implemented, and evaluated, unforeseen events, such as strikes, boycotts, natural disasters, arrival of foreign competitors, and government actions, can make a strategy obsolete. To minimize the impact of potential threats, organizations should develop contingency plans as part of their strategy-evaluation process. *Contingency plans* can be defined as alternative plans that can be put into effect if certain key events do not occur as expected. Only high-priority areas require the insurance of contingency plans. Strategists cannot and should not try to cover all bases by planning for all possible contingencies. But in any case, contingency plans should be as simple as possible.

Some contingency plans commonly established by firms include the following:

1. If a major competitor withdraws from particular markets as intelligence reports indicate, what actions should our firm take?
2. If our sales objectives are not reached, what actions should our firm take to avoid profit losses?
3. If demand for our new product exceeds plans, what actions should our firm take to meet the higher demand?

4. If certain disasters occur—such as loss of computer capabilities; a hostile takeover attempt; loss of patent protection; or destruction of manufacturing facilities because of earthquakes, tornados, or hurricanes—what actions should our firm take?

5. If a new technological advancement makes our new product obsolete sooner than expected, what actions should our firm take?

Too many organizations discard alternative strategies not selected for implementation although the work devoted to analyzing these options would render valuable information. Alternative strategies not selected for implementation can serve as contingency plans in case the strategy or strategies selected do not work. U.S. companies and governments are increasingly considering nuclear-generated electricity as the most efficient means of power generation. Many contingency plans certainly call for nuclear power rather than for coal- and gas-derived electricity. As indicated in the "Global Perspective", the United States is well below many countries in the world in the percentage of power derived from nuclear power plants.

When strategy-evaluation activities reveal the need for a major change quickly, an appropriate contingency plan can be executed in a timely way. Contingency plans

GLOBAL PERSPECTIVE

Eastern Europe, Western Europe, and the United States (In That Order) Embrace Atomic Energy

The United States and Western Europe continue to waver on the use of atomic energy, while Eastern European countries build new-generation nuclear power stations to meet rising demand. Note in the following list that the United States is well behind almost all European countries on the use of nuclear fuel for electricity generation.

Country	Percent of Electricity Derived from Nuclear Power in 2004
France	78.1%
Lithuania	72.1
Slovakia	55.2
Belgium	55.1
Sweden	51.8
Bulgaria	41.6
Switzerland	40.0
Slovenia	38.8
Hungary	33.8
Germany	32.1
Czech Republic	31.2
Finland	26.6
Spain	22.9
United States	19.9
United Kingdom	13.4

While coal and natural gas power plants may be safer (and that is debatable), the nuclear option surely is cleaner and more powerful. East European countries are thus building new nuclear plants to meet growing demand, while the United States and Western Europe have this option only in their contingency plans. New nuclear plants today are being built in France, the Czech Republic, Slovakia, Romania, Finland, and Bulgaria, while Germany, England, and the United States discuss closing some of their plants. Germany, in fact, is committed to being a nuclear-free state by 2021, which means closing 19 nuclear plants that today account for 30 percent of that country's power-generating capacity.

Source: Adapted from Nina Sovich, "Europe's New Nuclear Standoff: Eastern States Embrace Atomic Energy, as Western Neighbors Waver," *Wall Street Journal* (June 29, 2005): A13.

can promote a strategist's ability to respond quickly to key changes in the internal and external bases of an organization's current strategy. For example, if underlying assumptions about the economy turn out to be wrong and contingency plans are ready, then managers can make appropriate changes promptly.

In some cases, external or internal conditions present unexpected opportunities. When such opportunities occur, contingency plans could allow an organization to quickly capitalize on them. Linneman and Chandran reported that contingency planning gave users, such as DuPont, Dow Chemical, Consolidated Foods, and Emerson Electric, three major benefits: (1) It permitted quick response to change, (2) it prevented panic in crisis situations, and (3) it made managers more adaptable by encouraging them to appreciate just how variable the future can be. They suggested that effective contingency planning involves a seven-step process:

1. Identify both beneficial and unfavorable events that could possibly derail the strategy or strategies.
2. Specify trigger points. Calculate about when contingent events are likely to occur.
3. Assess the impact of each contingent event. Estimate the potential benefit or harm of each contingent event.
4. Develop contingency plans. Be sure that contingency plans are compatible with current strategy and are economically feasible.
5. Assess the counterimpact of each contingency plan. That is, estimate how much each contingency plan will capitalize on or cancel out its associated contingent event. Doing this will quantify the potential value of each contingency plan.
6. Determine early warning signals for key contingent events. Monitor the early warning signals.
7. For contingent events with reliable early warning signals, develop advance action plans to take advantage of the available lead time.[13]

Auditing

A frequently used tool in strategy evaluation is the audit. *Auditing* is defined by the American Accounting Association (AAA) as "a systematic process of objectively obtaining and evaluating evidence regarding assertions about economic actions and events to ascertain the degree of correspondence between these assertions and established criteria, and communicating the results to interested users."[14] Since the Enron, Worldcom, and Johnson & Johnson scandals, auditing has taken on greater emphasis and care in companies. Independent auditors basically are certified public accountants (CPAs) who provide their services to organizations for a fee; they examine the financial statements of an organization to determine whether they have been prepared according to generally accepted accounting principles (GAAP) and whether they fairly represent the activities of the firm. Independent auditors use a set of standards called *generally accepted auditing standards* (GAAS). Public accounting firms often have a consulting arm that provides strategy-evaluation services.

Two government agencies—the General Accounting Office (GAO) and the Internal Revenue Service (IRS)—employ government auditors responsible for making sure that organizations comply with federal laws, statutes, and policies. GAO and IRS auditors can audit any public or private organization. The third group of auditors consists of employees within an organization who are responsible for safeguarding company assets, for assessing the efficiency of company operations, and for ensuring that generally accepted business procedures are practiced.

The Environmental Audit

For an increasing number of firms, overseeing environmental affairs is no longer a technical function performed by specialists; rather, it has become an important strategic-management concern. Product design, manufacturing, transportation, customer use, packaging, product disposal, and corporate rewards and sanctions should reflect environmental considerations. Firms that effectively manage environmental affairs are benefiting from constructive relations with employees, consumers, suppliers, and distributors. As indicated in the Natural Environment Perspective, J.P. Morgan bank has made environmental policy an issue in its lending policy.

Shimell emphasized the need for organizations to conduct environmental audits of their operations and to develop a Corporate Environmental Policy (CEP).[15] Shimell contended that an environmental audit should be as rigorous as a financial audit and should include training workshops in which staff can help design and implement the policy. The CEP should be budgeted, and requisite funds should be allocated to ensure that it is not a public relations facade. A Statement of Environmental Policy should be published periodically to inform shareholders and the public of environmental actions taken by the firm.

NATURAL ENVIRONMENT PERSPECTIVE

J. P. Morgan Turning Green

J. P. Morgan, the third largest bank in the United States, in April 2005 issued a 10-page environmental policy that revealed sweeping new guidelines to restrict its lending and underwriting practices for industrial projects that are likely to have a negative environmental impact. The new policy takes an aggressive stance to curtail global warming by tying carbon-dioxide emissions to its loan-review process for power plants and other large polluters. The policy also instructs J. P. Morgan to lobby the U.S. government to adopt a national policy on greenhouse-gas emissions. This is the first large U.S. bank to pledge to put the natural environment above profitability if that is the cost.

Large banks have for several years been the target of environmentalists because of their potential role in financing activity such as energy development and logging. Rick Lazio, J. P. Morgan's director of global government affairs and policy and the Republican who lost to Hillary Rodham Clinton in the 2000 New York Senate race, says, "We are committed to establishing a significant leadership position on the environment, and we have achieved it."

The number of shareholder resolutions filed against companies on global warming issues is rising. These suits are largely aimed at auto, oil, utility, financial-services companies, and real-estate investment firms. J. P. Morgan's new policy sets up "No Go Zones," which are sensitive regions where the firm will not finance logging or any activity or project that poses an environmental threat.

Many companies are today being lobbied by Rainforest Action Network (RAN), based in San Francisco, and other activist groups, such as Greenpeace, to develop new environmental policies. Such groups have been largely unsuccessful lobbying the Bush administration on environmental issues, so they have taken their campaign directly to the shareholders of specific companies. RAN was primarily responsible for convincing J. P. Morgan to issue its new policy. Now RAN plans similar campaigns toward other banks and the large U.S. automobile manufacturers.

Source: Adapted from Jim Carlton, "J. P. Morgan Adopts 'Green' Lending Policies," *Wall Street Journal* (April 25, 2005): B1.

Instituting an environmental audit can include moving environmental affairs from the staff side of the organization to the line side. Some firms are also introducing environmental criteria and objectives in their performance appraisal instruments and systems. Conoco, for example, ties compensation of all its top managers to environmental action plans. Occidental Chemical includes environmental responsibilities in all its job descriptions for positions.

Twenty-First-Century Challenges in Strategic Management

Three particular challenges or decisions that face all strategists today are (1) deciding whether the process should be more an art or a science, (2) deciding whether strategies should be visible or hidden from stakeholders, and (3) deciding whether the process should be more top-down or bottom-up in their firm.[16]

The Art or Science Issue

This textbook is consistent with most of the strategy literature in advocating that strategic management be viewed more as a science than an art. This perspective contends that firms need to systematically assess their external and internal environments, conduct research, carefully evaluate the pros and cons of various alternatives, perform analyses, and then decide upon a particular course of action. In contrast, Mintzberg's notion of "crafting" strategies embodies the artistic model, which suggests that strategic decision making be based primarily on holistic thinking, intuition, creativity, and imagination.[17] Mintzberg and his followers reject strategies that result from objective analysis, preferring instead subjective imagination. "Strategy scientists" reject strategies that emerge from emotion, hunch, creativity, and politics. Proponents of the artistic view often consider strategic planning exercises to be time poorly spent. The Mintzberg philosophy insists on informality, whereas strategy scientists (and this text) insist on more formality. Mintzberg refers to strategic planning as an "emergent" process whereas strategy scientists use the term "deliberate" process.[18]

The answer to the art versus science question is one that strategists must decide for themselves, and certainly the two approaches are not mutually exclusive. In deciding which approach is more effective, however, consider that the business world today has become increasingly complex and more intensely competitive. There is less room for error in strategic planning. Recall that Chapter 1 discussed the importance of intuition and experience and subjectivity in strategic planning, and even the weights and ratings discussed in Chapters 3, 4, and 6 certainly require good judgment. But the idea of deciding upon strategies for any firm without thorough research and analysis, at least in the mind of this writer, is unwise. Certainly, in smaller firms there can be more informality in the process compared to larger firms, but even for smaller firms, a wealth of competitive information is available on the Internet and elsewhere and should be collected, assimilated, and evaluated before deciding on a course of action upon which survival of the firm may hinge. The livelihood of countless employees and shareholders may hinge on the effectiveness of strategies selected. Too much is at stake to be less than thorough in formulating strategies. It is not wise for a strategist to rely too heavily on gut feeling and opinion instead of research data, competitive intelligence, and analysis in formulating strategies.

The Visible or Hidden Issue

There are certainly good reasons to keep the strategy process and strategies themselves visible and open rather than hidden and secret. There are also good reasons to keep strategies hidden from all but top-level executives. Strategists must decide for themselves what is best for their firms. This text comes down largely on the side of being visible and open but certainly this may not be best for all strategists and all firms. As pointed out in Chapter 1, Sun Tzu argued that all war is based on deception and that the best maneuvers are those not easily predicted by rivals. Business is analogous to war.

Some reasons to be completely open with the strategy process and resultant decisions are these:

1. Managers, employees, and other stakeholders can readily contribute to the process. They often have excellent ideas. Secrecy would forgo many excellent ideas.
2. Investors, creditors, and other stakeholders have greater basis for supporting a firm when they know what the firm is doing and where the firm is going.
3. Visibility promotes democracy, whereas secrecy promotes autocracy. Domestic firms and most foreign firms prefer democracy over autocracy as a management style.
4. Participation and openness enhance understanding, commitment, and communication within the firm.

Reasons why some firms prefer to conduct strategic planning in secret and keep strategies hidden from all but the highest-level executives are as follows:

1. Free dissemination of a firm's strategies may easily translate into competitive intelligence for rival firms who could exploit the firm given that information.
2. Secrecy limits criticism, second guessing, and hindsight.
3. Participants in a visible strategy process become more attractive to rival firms who may lure them away.
4. Secrecy limits rival firms from imitating or duplicating the firm's strategies and undermining the firm.

The obvious benefits of the visible versus hidden extremes suggest that a working balance must be sought between the apparent contradictions. Parnell says that in a perfect world all key individuals both inside and outside the firm should be involved in strategic planning, but in practice particularly sensitive and confidential information should always remain strictly confidential to top managers.[19] This balancing act is difficult but essential for survival of the firm.

The Top-Down or Bottom-Up Approach

Proponents of the top-down approach contend that top executives are the only persons in the firm with the collective experience, acumen, and fiduciary responsibility to make key strategy decisions. In contrast, bottom-up advocates argue that lower- and middle-level managers and employees who will be implementing the strategies need to be actively involved in the process of formulating the strategies to ensure their support and commitment. Recent strategy research and this textbook emphasize the bottom-up approach, but earlier work by Schendel and Hofer stressed the need for firms to rely on perceptions of their top managers in strategic planning.[20] Strategists must reach a working balance of the two approaches in a manner deemed best for their firms at a particular time, while cognizant of the fact that current research supports the bottom-up approach, at least among U.S. firms. Increased education and diversity of the workforce at all levels are reasons why middle- and lower-level managers—and even nonmanagers—should be invited to participate in the firm's strategic planning process, at least to the extent that they are willing and able to contribute.

CONCLUSION

This chapter presents a strategy-evaluation framework that can facilitate accomplishment of annual and long-term objectives. Effective strategy evaluation allows an organization to capitalize on internal strengths as they develop, to exploit external opportunities as they emerge, to recognize and defend against threats, and to mitigate internal weaknesses before they become detrimental.

Strategists in successful organizations take the time to formulate, implement, and then evaluate strategies deliberately and systematically. Good strategists move their organization forward with purpose and direction, continually evaluating and improving the firm's external and internal strategic positions. Strategy evaluation allows an organization to shape its own future rather than allowing it to be constantly shaped by remote forces that have little or no vested interest in the well-being of the enterprise.

Although not a guarantee for success, strategic management allows organizations to make effective long-term decisions, to execute those decisions efficiently, and to take corrective actions as needed to ensure success. Computer networks and the Internet help to coordinate strategic-management activities and to ensure that decisions are based on good information. The Checkmate Strategic Planning Software is especially good in this regard (www.checkmateplan.com). A key to effective strategy evaluation and to successful strategic management is an integration of intuition and analysis:

> A potentially fatal problem is the tendency for analytical and intuitive issues to polarize. This polarization leads to strategy evaluation that is dominated by either analysis or intuition, or to strategy evaluation that is discontinuous, with a lack of coordination among analytical and intuitive issues.[21]

Strategists in successful organizations realize that strategic management is first and foremost a people process. It is an excellent vehicle for fostering organizational communication. People are what make the difference in organizations.

> The real key to effective strategic management is to accept the premise that the planning process is more important than the written plan, that the manager is continuously planning and does not stop planning when the written plan is finished. The written plan is only a snapshot as of the moment it is approved. If the manager is not planning on a continuous basis—planning, measuring, and revising—the written plan can become obsolete the day it is finished. This obsolescence becomes more of a certainty as the increasingly rapid rate of change makes the business environment more uncertain.[22]

We invite you to visit the David page on the Prentice Hall Companion Web site at www.prenhall.com/david for this chapter's review quiz.

KEY TERMS AND CONCEPTS

Advantage (p. 337)
Auditing (p. 351)
Balanced Scorecard (p. 346)
Consistency (p. 337)
Consonance (p. 337)
Contingency Plans (p. 349)
Corporate Agility (p. 344)

Feasibility (p. 337)
Future Shock (p. 344)
Management by Wandering
  Around (p. 339)
Measuring Organizational
  Performance (p. 342)

Reviewing the Underlying Bases
  of an Organization's Strategy
  (p. 340)
Revised EFE Matrix (p. 340)
Revised IFE Matrix (p. 340)
Taking Corrective Actions (p. 344)

ISSUES FOR REVIEW AND DISCUSSION

1. Why has strategy evaluation become so important in business today?
2. BellSouth Services is considering putting divisional EFE and IFE matrices online for continual updating. How would this affect strategy evaluation?
3. What types of quantitative and qualitative criteria do you think Meg Whitman, CEO of eBay, uses to evaluate the company's strategy?
4. As owner of a local, independent supermarket, explain how you would evaluate the firm's strategy.
5. Under what conditions are corrective actions not required in the strategy-evaluation process?
6. Identify types of organizations that may need to more frequently evaluate strategy than others. Justify your choices.
7. As executive director of the state forestry commission, in what way and how frequently would you evaluate the organization's strategies?
8. Identify some key financial ratios that would be important in evaluating a bank's strategy.
9. As owner of a chain of hardware stores, describe how you would approach contingency planning.
10. Strategy evaluation allows an organization to take a proactive stance toward shaping its own future. Discuss the meaning of this statement.
11. Explain and discuss the Balanced Scorecard.
12. Why is the Balanced Scorecard an important topic both in devising objectives and in evaluating strategies?
13. Develop a Balanced Scorecard for a local fast-food restaurant.
14. Do you believe strategic management should be more visible or hidden as a process in a firm? Explain.
15. Do you feel strategic management should be more a top-down or bottom-up process in a firm? Explain.
16. Do you believe strategic management is more an art or a science? Explain.

NOTES

1. Dale McConkey, "Planning in a Changing Environment," *Business Horizons* (September–October 1988): 64.
2. Robert Simons, "Control in an Age of Empowerment," *Harvard Business Review* (March–April 1995): 80.
3. Dale Zand, "Reviewing the Policy Process," *California Management Review* 21, no. 1 (Fall 1978): 37.
4. Eccles. 3: 1–8.
5. Seymour Tilles, "How to Evaluate Corporate Strategy," *Harvard Business Review* 41 (July–August 1963): 111–121.

6. Claude George, Jr., *The History of Management Thought* (Upper Saddle River, New Jersey: Prentice Hall, 1968): 165–166.

7. John Brown and Neil Agnew, "Corporate Agility," *Business Horizons* 25, no. 2 (March–April 1982): 29.

8. M. Erez and F. Kanfer, "The Role of Goal Acceptance in Goal Setting and Task Performance," *Academy of Management Review* 8, no. 3 (July 1983): 457.

9. D. Hussey and M. Langham, *Corporate Planning: The Human Factor* (Oxford, England: Pergamon Press, 1979): 138.

10. Carter Bayles, "Strategic Control: The President's Paradox," *Business Horizons* 20, no. 4 (August 1977): 18.

11. Pui-Wing Tam, "Cloud Over Sun Microsystems: Plummeting Computer Prices," *Wall Street Journal* (October 16, 2003): A1.

12. Robert Waterman, Jr., "How the Best Get Better," *BusinessWeek* (September 14, 1987): 105.

13. Robert Linneman and Rajan Chandran, "Contingency Planning: A Key to Swift Managerial Action in the Uncertain Tomorrow," *Managerial Planning* 29, no. 4 (January–February 1981): 23–27.

14. American Accounting Association, *Report of Committee on Basic Auditing Concepts* (1971): 15–74.

15. Pamela Shimell, "Corporate Environmental Policy in Practice," *Long Range Planning* 24, no. 3 (June 1991): 10.

16. John Parnell, "Five Critical Challenges in Strategy Making," *SAM Advanced Management Journal* 68, no. 2 (Spring 2003): 15–22.

17. Henry Mintzberg, "Crafting Strategy," *Harvard Business Review* (July–August, 1987): 66–75.

18. Henry Mintzberg and J. Waters, "Of Strategies, Deliberate and Emergent," *Strategic Management Journal* 6, no. 2: 257–272.

19. Parnell, 15–22.

20. D. E. Schendel and C. W. Hofer (Eds.), *Strategic Management* (Boston: Little, Brown, 1979).

21. Michael McGinnis, "The Key to Strategic Planning: Integrating Analysis and Intuition," *Sloan Management Review* 26, no. 1 (Fall 1984): 49.

22. McConkey, 72.

CURRENT READINGS

Barker III, V. L. "Traps in Diagnosing Organizational Failure." *Journal of Business Strategy* 26, no. 2 (2005): 44.

Braam, Geert J. M., and Edwin J. Nijssen. "Performance Effects of Using the Balanced Scorecard: A Note on the Dutch Experience." *Long Range Planning* 37, no. 4 (August 2004): 335.

Finkelstein, S. "When Bad Things Happen to Good Companies: Strategy Failure and Flawed Executives." *Journal of Business Strategy* 26, no. 2 (2005): 19.

Papalexandris, Alexandros, George Ioannou, and Gregory P. Prastacos. "Implementing the Balanced Scorecard in Greece: A Software Firm's Experience." *Long Range Planning* 37, no. 4 (August 2004): 351.

Probst, Gilbert, and Sebastian Raisch. "Organizational Crisis: The Logic of Failure." *The Academy of Management Executive* 19, no. 1 (February 2005): 90.

Roos, Johan, Bart Victor, and Matt Statler. "Playing Seriously with Strategy." *Long Range Planning* 37, no. 6 (December 2004): 549.

Scholey, C. "Strategy Maps: A Step-by-Step Guide to Measuring, Managing, and Communicating the Plan." *Journal of Business Strategy* 26, no. 3 (2005): 12.

Shimizu, K. and M. A. Hitt. "Strategic Flexibility: Organizational Preparedness to Reverse Ineffective Strategic Decisions." *The Academy of Management Executive* 18, no. 4 (November 2004): 44.

Tanriverdi, H., and N. Venkatraman. "Knowledge Relatedness and the Performance of Multibusiness Firms." *Strategic Management Journal* 26, no. 2 (February 2005): 97.

experiential exercises

**Experiential
Exercise 9A**

*Preparing a Strategy-
Evaluation Report for
Google*

PURPOSE

This exercise can give you experience locating strategy-evaluation information. Use of the Internet coupled with published sources of information can significantly enhance the strategy-evaluation process. Performance information on competitors, for example, can help put into perspective a firm's own performance.

INSTRUCTIONS

Step 1 Visit http://finance.yahoo.com to locate strategy-evaluation information on competitors. Read 5 to 10 articles written in the last six months that discuss the fast-food industry.

Step 2 Summarize your research findings by preparing a strategy-evaluation report for your instructor. Include in your report a summary of Google's strategies and performance in 2005 and a summary of your conclusions regarding the effectiveness of Google's strategies.

Step 3 Based on your analysis, do you feel that Google is pursuing effective strategies? What recommendations would you offer to Google's chief executive officer?

**Experiential
Exercise 9B**

*Evaluating My
University's Strategies*

PURPOSE

An important part of evaluating strategies is determining the nature and extent of changes in an organization's external opportunities/threats and internal strengths/weaknesses. Changes in these underlying critical success factors can indicate a need to change or modify the firm's strategies.

INSTRUCTIONS

As a class, discuss positive and negative changes in your university's external and internal factors during your college career. Begin by listing on the board new or emerging opportunities and threats. Then identify strengths and weaknesses that have changed significantly during your college career. In light of the external and internal changes that were identified, discuss whether your university's strategies need modifying. Are there any new strategies that you would recommend? Make a list to recommend to your department chair, dean, president, or chancellor.

**Experiential
Exercise 9C**

*Who Prepares an
Environmental Audit?*

PURPOSE

The purpose of this activity is to determine the nature and prevalence of environmental audits among companies in your state.

INSTRUCTIONS

Contact by phone at least five different plant managers or owners of large businesses in your area. Seek answers to the following questions. Present your findings in a written report to your instructor.

1. Does your company conduct an environmental audit? If yes, please describe the nature and scope of the audit.
2. Are environmental criteria included in the performance evaluation of managers? If yes, please specify the criteria.
3. Are environmental affairs more a technical function or a management function in your company?
4. Does your firm offer any environmental workshops for employees? If yes, please describe them.

How to Prepare and Present a Case Analysis

Objectives

After studying this chapter, you should be able to do the following:

1. Describe the case method for learning strategic-management concepts.

2. Identify the steps in preparing a comprehensive written case analysis.

3. Describe how to give an effective oral case analysis presentation.

4. Discuss special tips for doing case analysis.

steps in presenting an oral case analysis

Oral Presentation–Step 1
1. Introduction (2 minutes)

Oral Presentation–Step 2
2. Mission/Vision (4 minutes)

Oral Presentation–Step 3
3. Internal Assessment (8 minutes)

Oral Presentation–Step 4
4. External Assessment (8 minutes)

Oral Presentation–Step 5
5. Strategy Formulation (14 minutes)

Oral Presentation–Step 6
6. Strategy Implementation (8 minutes)

Oral Presentation–Step 7
7. Strategy Evaluation (2 minutes)

Oral Presentation–Step 8
8. Conclusion (4 minutes)

"notable quotes"

Two heads are better than one.
Unknown Author

One reaction frequently heard is "I don't have enough information." In reality strategists never have enough information because some information is not available and some is too costly.
William Glueck

I keep six honest serving men. They taught me all I know. Their names are What, Why, When, How, Where, and Who.
Rudyard Kipling

Don't recommend anything you would not be prepared to do yourself if you were in the decision maker's shoes.
A. J. Strickland III

A picture is worth a thousand words.
Unknown Author

The purpose of this section is to help you analyze strategic-management cases. Guidelines for preparing written and oral case analyses are given, and suggestions for preparing cases for class discussion are presented. Steps to follow in preparing case analyses are provided. Guidelines for making an oral presentation are described.

What Is a Strategic-Management Case?

A *strategic-management (or business policy) case* describes an organization's external and internal conditions and raises issues concerning the firm's mission, strategies, objectives, and policies. Most of the information in a business policy case is established fact, but some information may be opinions, judgments, and beliefs. Strategic-management cases are more comprehensive than those you may have studied in other courses. They generally include a description of related management, marketing, finance/accounting, production/operations, R&D, computer information systems, and natural environment issues. A strategic-management case puts the reader on the scene of the action by describing a firm's situation at some point in time. Strategic-management cases are written to give you practice applying strategic-management concepts. The case method for studying strategic management is often called *learning by doing*.

Guidelines for Preparing Case Analyses

The Need for Practicality
There is no such thing as a complete case, and no case ever gives you all the information you need to conduct analyses and make recommendations. Likewise, in the business world, strategists never have all the information they need to make decisions: information may be unavailable or too costly to obtain, or it may take too much time to obtain. So in preparing strategic-management cases, do what strategists do every day—make reasonable assumptions about unknowns, clearly state assumptions, perform appropriate analyses, and make decisions. *Be practical.* For example, in performing a projected financial analysis, make reasonable assumptions, appropriately state them, and proceed to show what impact your recommendations are expected to have on the organization's financial position. Avoid saying "I don't have enough information." You can always supplement the information provided in a case with Internet and library research.

The Need for Justification
The most important part of analyzing cases is not what strategies you recommend but rather how you support your decisions and how you propose that they be implemented. There is no single best solution or one right answer to a case, so give ample justification for your recommendations. This is important. In the business world, strategists usually do not know if their decisions are right until resources have been allocated and consumed. Then it is often too late to reverse a decision. This cold fact accents the need for careful integration of intuition and analysis in preparing business policy case analyses.

The Need for Realism
Avoid recommending a course of action beyond an organization's means. *Be realistic.* No organization can possibly pursue all the strategies that could potentially benefit the firm.

Estimate how much capital will be required to implement what you recommended. Determine whether debt, stock, or a combination of debt and stock could be used to obtain the capital. Make sure your recommendations are feasible. Do not prepare a case analysis that omits all arguments and information not supportive of your recommendations. Rather, present the major advantages and disadvantages of several feasible alternatives. Try not to exaggerate, stereotype, prejudge, or overdramatize. Strive to demonstrate that your interpretation of the evidence is reasonable and objective.

The Need for Specificity

Do not make broad generalizations such as "The company should pursue a market penetration strategy." Be specific by telling *what, why, when, how, where,* and *who*. Failure to use specifics is the single major shortcoming of most oral and written case analyses. For example, in an internal audit say, "The firm's current ratio fell from 2.2 in 2004 to 1.3 in 2005, and this is considered to be a major weakness," instead of "The firm's financial condition is bad." Rather than concluding from a Strategic Position and Action Evaluation (SPACE) Matrix that a firm should be defensive, be more specific, saying "The firm should consider closing three plants, laying off 280 employees, and divesting itself of its chemical division, for a net savings of $20.2 million in 2005." Use ratios, percentages, numbers, and dollar estimates. Businesspeople dislike generalities and vagueness.

The Need for Originality

Do not necessarily recommend the course of action that the firm plans to take or actually undertook, even if those actions resulted in improved revenues and earnings. The aim of case analysis is for you to consider all the facts and information relevant to the organization at the time, to generate feasible alternative strategies, to choose among those alternatives, and to defend your recommendations. Put yourself back in time to the point when strategic decisions were being made by the firm's strategists. Based on the information available then, what would you have done? Support your position with charts, graphs, ratios, analyses, and the like—not a revelation from the library. You can become a good strategist by thinking through situations, making management assessments, and proposing plans yourself. *Be original.* Compare and contrast what you recommend versus what the company plans to do or did.

The Need to Contribute

Strategy formulation, implementation, and evaluation decisions are commonly made by a group of individuals rather than by a single person. Therefore, your professor may divide the class into three- or four-person teams and ask you to prepare written or oral case analyses. Members of a strategic-management team, in class or in the business world, differ on their aversion to risk, their concern for short-run versus long-run benefits, their attitudes toward social responsibility, and their views concerning globalization. There are no perfect people, so there are no perfect strategies. Be open-minded to others' views. *Be a good listener and a good contributor.*

Preparing a Case for Class Discussion

Your professor may ask you to prepare a case for class discussion. Preparing a case for class discussion means that you need to read the case before class, make notes regarding the organization's external opportunities/threats and internal strengths/weaknesses, perform appropriate analyses, and come to class prepared to offer and defend some specific recommendations.

The Case Method Versus Lecture Approach

The case method of teaching is radically different from the traditional lecture approach, in which little or no preparation is needed by students before class. The *case method* involves a classroom situation in which students do most of the talking; your professor facilitates discussion by asking questions and encouraging student interaction regarding ideas, analyses, and recommendations. Be prepared for a discussion along the lines of "What would you do, why would you do it, when would you do it, and how would you do it?" Prepare answers to the following types of questions:

- What are the firm's most important external opportunities and threats?
- What are the organization's major strengths and weaknesses?
- How would you describe the organization's financial condition?
- What are the firm's existing strategies and objectives?
- Who are the firm's competitors, and what are their strategies?
- What objectives and strategies do you recommend for this organization? Explain your reasoning. How does what you recommend compare to what the company plans?
- How could the organization best implement what you recommend? What implementation problems do you envision? How could the firm avoid or solve those problems?

The Cross-Examination

Do not hesitate to take a stand on the issues and to support your position with objective analyses and outside research. Strive to apply strategic-management concepts and tools in preparing your case for class discussion. Seek defensible arguments and positions. Support opinions and judgments with facts, reasons, and evidence. Crunch the numbers before class! Be willing to describe your recommendations to the class without fear of disapproval. Respect the ideas of others, but be willing to go against the majority opinion when you can justify a better position.

Business policy case analysis gives you the opportunity to learn more about yourself, your colleagues, strategic management, and the decision-making process in organizations. The rewards of this experience will depend on the effort you put forth, so do a good job. Discussing business policy cases in class is exciting and challenging. Expect views counter to those you present. Different students will place emphasis on different aspects of an organization's situation and submit different recommendations for scrutiny and rebuttal. Cross-examination discussions commonly arise, just as they occur in a real business organization. Avoid being a silent observer.

Preparing a Written Case Analysis

In addition to asking you to prepare a case for class discussion, your professor may ask you to prepare a written case analysis. Preparing a written case analysis is similar to preparing a case for class discussion, except written reports are generally more structured and more detailed. There is no ironclad procedure for preparing a written case analysis because cases differ in focus; the type, size, and complexity of the organizations being analyzed also vary.

When writing a strategic-management report or case analysis, avoid using jargon, vague or redundant words, acronyms, abbreviations, sexist language, and ethnic or racial slurs. And watch your spelling! Use short sentences and paragraphs and simple words and phrases. Use quite a few subheadings. Arrange issues and ideas from the most important to the least important. Arrange recommendations from the least controversial to the most controversial. Use the active voice rather than the passive voice for all verbs; for example, say "Our team recommends that the company diversify" rather than "It is recommended by our team to diversify." Use many examples to add specificity and clarity. Tables, figures, pie charts, bar charts, timelines, and other kinds of exhibits help communicate important points and ideas. Sometimes a picture *is* worth a thousand words.

The Executive Summary

Your professor may ask you to focus the written case analysis on a particular aspect of the strategic-management process, such as (1) to identify and evaluate the organization's existing mission, objectives, and strategies; or (2) to propose and defend specific recommendations for the company; or (3) to develop an industry analysis by describing the competitors, products, selling techniques, and market conditions in a given industry. These types of written reports are sometimes called *executive summaries*. An executive summary usually ranges from three to five pages of text in length, plus exhibits.

The Comprehensive Written Analysis

Your professor may ask you to prepare a *comprehensive written analysis*. This assignment requires you to apply the entire strategic-management process to the particular organization. When preparing a comprehensive written analysis, picture yourself as a consultant who has been asked by a company to conduct a study of its external and internal environment and to make specific recommendations for its future. Prepare exhibits to support your recommendations. Highlight exhibits with some discussion in the paper. Comprehensive written analyses are usually about 10 pages in length, plus exhibits.

Steps in Preparing a Written Case Analysis

In preparing a **written** case analysis, you could follow the steps outlined here, which correlate to the stages in the strategic-management process and the chapters in this text. (Note - The steps in presenting an **oral** case analysis are given on p. 371, are more detailed, and could be used here).

Step 1   Identify the firm's existing vision, mission, objectives, and strategies.

Step 2   Develop vision and mission statements for the organization.

Step 3   Identify the organization's external opportunities and threats.

Step 4   Construct a Competitive Profile Matrix (CPM).

Step 5   Construct an External Factor Evaluation (EFE) Matrix.

Step 6   Identify the organization's internal strengths and weaknesses.

Step 7   Construct an Internal Factor Evaluation (IFE) Matrix.

Step 8   Prepare a Strengths-Weaknesses-Opportunities-Threats (SWOT) Matrix, Strategic Position and Action Evaluation (SPACE) Matrix, Boston

Consulting Group (BCG) Matrix, Internal-External (IE) Matrix, Grand Strategy Matrix, and Quantitative Strategic Planning Matrix (QSPM) as appropriate. Give advantages and disadvantages of alternative strategies.

Step 9 Recommend specific strategies and long-term objectives. Show how much your recommendations will cost. Clearly itemize these costs for each projected year. Compare your recommendations to actual strategies planned by the company.

Step 10 Specify how your recommendations can be implemented and what results you can expect. Prepare forecasted ratios and projected financial statements. Present a timetable or agenda for action.

Step 11 Recommend specific annual objectives and policies.

Step 12 Recommend procedures for strategy review and evaluation.

Making an Oral Presentation

Your professor may ask you to prepare a strategic-management case analysis, individually or as a group, and present your analysis to the class. Oral presentations are usually graded on two parts: content and delivery. *Content* refers to the quality, quantity, correctness, and appropriateness of analyses presented, including such dimensions as logical flow through the presentation, coverage of major issues, use of specifics, avoidance of generalities, absence of mistakes, and feasibility of recommendations. *Delivery* includes such dimensions as audience attentiveness, clarity of visual aids, appropriate dress, persuasiveness of arguments, tone of voice, eye contact, and posture. Great ideas are of no value unless others can be convinced of their merit through clear communication. The guidelines presented here can help you make an effective oral presentation.

Organizing the Presentation

Begin your presentation by introducing yourself and giving a clear outline of topics to be covered. If a team is presenting, specify the sequence of speakers and the areas each person will address. At the beginning of an oral presentation, try to capture your audience's interest and attention. You could do this by displaying some products made by the company, telling an interesting short story about the company, or sharing an experience you had that is related to the company, its products, or its services. You could develop or obtain a video to show at the beginning of class; you could visit a local distributor of the firm's products and tape a personal interview with the business owner or manager. A light or humorous introduction can be effective at the beginning of a presentation.

Be sure the setting of your presentation is well organized, with seats for attendees, flip charts, a transparency projector, and whatever else you plan to use. Arrive at the classroom at least 15 minutes early to organize the setting, and be sure your materials are ready to go. Make sure everyone can see your visual aids well.

Controlling Your Voice

An effective rate of speaking ranges from 100 to 125 words per minute. Practice your presentation aloud to determine if you are going too fast. Individuals commonly speak too fast when nervous. Breathe deeply before and during the presentation to help yourself slow down. Have a cup of water available; pausing to take a drink will wet your throat, give you time to collect your thoughts, control your nervousness, slow you down, and signal to the audience a change in topic.

Avoid a monotone by placing emphasis on different words or sentences. Speak loudly and clearly, but don't shout. Silence can be used effectively to break a monotone voice. Stop at the end of each sentence, rather than running sentences together with *and* or *uh*.

Managing Body Language

Be sure not to fold your arms, lean on the podium, put your hands in your pockets, or put your hands behind you. Keep a straight posture, with one foot slightly in front of the other. Do not turn your back to the audience; doing so is not only rude, but it also prevents your voice from projecting well. Avoid using too many hand gestures. On occasion, leave the podium or table and walk toward your audience, but do not walk around too much. Never block the audience's view of your visual aids.

Maintain good eye contact throughout the presentation. This is the best way to persuade your audience. There is nothing more reassuring to a speaker than to see members of the audience nod in agreement or smile. Try to look everyone in the eye at least once during your presentation, but focus more on individuals who look interested than on those who seem bored. To stay in touch with your audience, use humor and smiles as appropriate throughout your presentation. A presentation should never be dull!

Speaking from Notes

Be sure not to read to your audience because reading puts people to sleep. Perhaps worse than reading is merely reciting what you have memorized. Do not try to memorize anything. Rather, practice unobtrusively using notes. Make sure your notes are written clearly so you will not flounder when trying to read your own writing. Include only main ideas on your note cards. Keep note cards on a podium or table if possible so that you won't drop them or get them out of order; walking with note cards tends to be distracting.

Constructing Visual Aids

Make sure your visual aids are legible to individuals in the back of the room. Use color to highlight special items. Avoid putting complete sentences on visual aids; rather, use short phrases and then orally elaborate on issues as you make your presentation. Generally, there should be no more than four to six lines of text on each visual aid. Use clear headings and subheadings. Be careful about spelling and grammar; use a consistent style of lettering. Use masking tape or an easel for posters—do not hold posters in your hand. Transparencies and handouts are excellent aids; however, be careful not to use too many handouts or your audience may concentrate on them instead of you during the presentation.

Answering Questions

It is best to field questions at the end of your presentation, rather than during the presentation itself. Encourage questions, and take your time to respond to each one. Answering questions can be persuasive because it involves you with the audience. If a team is giving the presentation, the audience should direct questions to a specific person. During the question-and-answer period, be polite, confident, and courteous. Avoid verbose responses. Do not get defensive with your answers, even if a hostile or confrontational question is asked. Staying calm during potentially disruptive situations, such as a cross-examination, reflects self-confidence, maturity, poise, and command of the particular company and its industry. Stand up throughout the question-and-answer period.

Tips for Success in Case Analysis

Strategic-management students who have used this text over 10 editions offer you the following tips for success in doing case analysis. The tips are grouped into two basic sections: (1) Content Tips and (2) Process Tips. Content tips relate especially to the content of your case analysis, whereas the Process tips relate mostly to the process that you and your group mates undergo in preparing and delivering your case analysis/presentation.

Content Tips

1. Use the www.strategyclub.com Web site resources. The software described there is especially useful.
2. In preparing your external assessment, use the S&P Industry Survey material in your college library.
3. Go to the http://finance.yahoo.com or http://moneycentral.msn/investor/home.asp and enter your company's stock symbol.
4. View your case analysis and presentation as a product that must have some competitive factor to favorably differentiate it from the case analyses of other students.
5. Develop a mind-set of *why*, continually questioning your own and others' assumptions and assertions.
6. Since business policy is a capstone course, seek the help of professors in other specialty areas when necessary.
7. Read your case frequently as work progresses so you don't overlook details.
8. At the end of each group session, assign each member of the group a task to be completed for the next meeting.
9. Become friends with the library and the Internet.
10. Be creative and innovative throughout the case analysis process.
11. A goal of case analysis is to improve your ability to think clearly in ambiguous and confusing situations; do not get frustrated that there is no single best answer.
12. Do not confuse symptoms with causes; do not develop conclusions and solutions prematurely; recognize that information may be misleading, conflicting, or wrong.
13. Work hard to develop the ability to formulate reasonable, consistent, and creative plans; put yourself in the strategist's position.
14. Develop confidence in using quantitative tools for analysis. They are not inherently difficult, it is just practice and familiarity you need.
15. Strive for excellence in writing and in the technical preparation of your case. Prepare nice charts, tables, diagrams, and graphs. Use color and unique pictures. No messy exhibits! Use PowerPoint.
16. Do not forget that the objective is to learn; explore areas with which you are not familiar.
17. Pay attention to detail.
18. Think through alternative implications fully and realistically. The consequences of decisions are not always apparent. They often affect many different aspects of a firm's operations.

19. Provide answers to such fundamental questions as *what, when, where, why, who,* and *how.*
20. Do not merely recite ratios or present figures. Rather, develop ideas and conclusions concerning the possible trends. Show the importance of these figures to the corporation.
21. Support reasoning and judgment with factual data whenever possible.
22. Your analysis should be as detailed and specific as possible.
23. A picture speaks a thousand words, and a creative picture gets you an A in many classes.
24. Emphasize the Recommendations and Strategy Implementation sections. A common mistake is to spend too much time on the external or internal analysis parts of your paper. Always remember that the recommendations and implementation sections are the most important part of the paper or presentation.

Process Tips

1. When working as a team, encourage most of the work to be done individually. Use team meetings mostly to assimilate work. This approach is most efficient.
2. If allowed to do so, invite questions throughout your presentation.
3. During the presentation, keep good posture, eye contact, voice tone, and project confidence. Do not get defensive under any conditions or with any questions.
4. Prepare your case analysis in advance of the due date to allow time for reflection and practice. Do not procrastinate.
5. Maintain a positive attitude about the class, working *with* problems rather than against them.
6. Keep in tune with your professor, and understand his or her values and expectations.
7. Other students will have strengths in functional areas that will complement your weaknesses, so develop a cooperative spirit that moderates competitiveness in group work.
8. When preparing a case analysis as a group, divide into separate teams to work on the external analysis and internal analysis.
9. Have a good sense of humor.
10. Capitalize on the strengths of each member of the group; volunteer your services in your areas of strength.
11. Set goals for yourself and your team; budget your time to attain them.
12. Foster attitudes that encourage group participation and interaction. Do not be hasty to judge group members.
13. Be prepared to work. There will be times when you will have to do more than your share. Accept it, and do what you have to do to move the team forward.
14. Think of your case analysis as if it were really happening; do not reduce case analysis to a mechanical process.
15. To uncover flaws in your analysis and to prepare the group for questions during an oral presentation, assign one person in the group to actively play the devil's advocate.
16. Do not schedule excessively long group meetings; two-hour sessions are about right.

17. Push your ideas hard enough to get them listened to, but then let up; listen to others and try to follow their lines of thinking; follow the flow of group discussion, recognizing when you need to get back on track; do not repeat yourself or others unless clarity or progress demands repetition.

18. Develop a case-presentation style that is direct, assertive, and convincing; be concise, precise, fluent, and correct.

19. Have fun when at all possible. Preparing a case is frustrating at times, but enjoy it while you can; it may be several years before you are playing CEO again.

20. In group cases, do not allow personality differences to interfere. When they occur, they must be understood for what they are—and then put aside.

21. Get things written down (drafts) as soon as possible.

22. Read everything that other group members write, and comment on it in writing. This allows group input into all aspects of case preparation.

23. Adaptation and flexibility are keys to success; be creative and innovative.

24. Neatness is a real plus; your case analysis should look professional.

25. Let someone else read and critique your presentation several days before you present it.

26. Make special efforts to get to know your group members. This leads to more openness in the group and allows for more interchange of ideas. Put in the time and effort necessary to develop these relationships.

27. Be constructively critical of your group members' work. Do not dominate group discussions. Be a good listener and contributor.

28. Learn from past mistakes and deficiencies. Improve upon weak aspects of other case presentations.

29. Learn from the positive approaches and accomplishments of classmates.

Sample Case Analysis Outline

There are musicians who play wonderfully without notes and there are chefs who cook wonderfully without recipes, but most of us prefer a more orderly cookbook approach, at least in the first attempt at doing something new. Therefore the following eight steps may serve as a basic outline for you in presenting a strategic plan for your firm's future. This outline is not the only approach used in business and industry for communicating a strategic plan, but this approach is time-tested, it does work, and it does cover all of the basics. You may amend the content, tools, and concepts given to suit your own company, audience, assignment, and circumstances, but it helps to know and understand the rules before you start breaking them.

Depending upon whether your class is 50 minutes or 75 minutes and how much time your professor allows for your case presentation, the following outlines what generally needs to be covered. A recommended time (in minutes) as part of the presentation is given for an overall 50-minute event. Of course, all cases are different, some being about for-profit and some about not-for-profit organizations, for example, so the scope and content of your analysis may vary. Even if you do not have time to cover all areas in your oral presentation, you may be asked to prepare these areas and give them to your professor as a "written case analysis." Be sure in an oral presentation to manage time knowing that your recommendations and associated costs are the most important part. You should go to www.strategyclub.com and utilize that information and software in preparing your case analysis. Good luck.

steps in presenting an oral case analysis

Oral Presentation-Step 1

1. Introduction

(2 minutes)

a. Introduce yourselves by name and major. Establish the time setting of your case and analysis. Prepare your strategic plan for the three years 2005–2007 (or 2006–2008 if you have the 2005 year-end financials).

b. Introduce your company and its products/services; capture interest.

c. Show the outline of your presentation and tell who is doing what parts.

Oral Presentation-Step 2

2. Mission/Vision

(4 minutes)

a. Show existing mission and vision statements if available from the firm's Web site, or annual report, or elsewhere.

b. Show your "improved" mission and vision and tell why it is improved.

c. Compare your mission and vision to a leading competitor's statements.

d. Comment on your vision and mission in terms of how they support the strategies you envision for your firm.

Oral Presentation-Step 3

3. Internal Assessment

(8 minutes)

a. Give your financial ratio analysis. Highlight especially good and bad ratios. Do not give definitions of the ratios and do not highlight all the ratios.

b. Show the firm's organizational chart found or "created based on executive titles." Identify the type of chart as well as good and bad aspects. Unless all white males comprise the chart, peoples' names are generally not important because positions reveal structure as people come and go.

c. Present your improved/recommended organizational chart. Tell why you feel it is improved over the existing chart.

d. Show a market positioning map with firm and competitors. Discuss the map in light of strategies you envision for firm versus competitors' strategies.

e. Identify the marketing strategy of the firm in terms of good and bad points versus competitors and in light of strategies you envision for the firm.

f. Show a map locating the firm's operations. Discuss in light of strategies you envision. Also, perhaps show a Value Chain Analysis chart.

g. Discuss (and perhaps show) the firm's Web site and e-commerce efforts/abilities in terms of good and bad points.

h. Show your "value of the firm" analysis.

i. List up to 20 of the firm's strengths and weaknesses. Go over each one listed without "reading" them verbatim.

j. Show and explain your Internal Factor Evaluation (IFE) Matrix.

Oral Presentation-Step 4

4. External Assessment

(8 minutes)

a. Identify and discuss major competitors. Use pie charts, maps, tables, and/or figures to show the intensity of competition in the industry.

b. Show your Competitive Profile Matrix. Include at least 12 factors and two competitors.

c. Summarize key industry trends citing Standard & Poor's *Industry Survey* or Chamber of Commerce statistics, etc. Highlight key external trends as they impact the firm, in areas such as the economic, social, cultural, demographic, geographic, technological, political, legal, governmental, and natural environment.

d. List up to 20 of the firm's opportunities and threats. Make sure your opportunities are not stated as strategies. Go over each one listed without "reading" them verbatim.

e. Show and explain your External Factor Evaluation (EFE) Matrix.

Oral Presentation- Step 5

5. Strategy Formulation

(14 minutes)

a. Show and explain your SWOT Matrix, highlighting each of your strategies listed.

b. Show and explain your SPACE Matrix, using half of your "space time" on calculations and the other half on implications of those numbers. Strategy implications must be specific rather than generic. In other words, use of a term such as "market penetration" is not satisfactory alone as a strategy implication.

c. Show your Boston Consulting Group (BCG) Matrix. Again focus on both the numbers and the strategy implications. Do multiple BCG Matrices if possible, including domestic versus global, or another geographic breakdown. Develop a product BCG if at all possible. Comment on changes to this matrix as per strategies you envision. Develop this matrix even if you do not know the profits per division and even if you have to estimate the axes information. However, make no wild guesses on axes or revenue/profit information.

d. Show your Internal-External (IE) Matrix. Since this analysis is similar to the BCG, see the preceding comments.

e. Show your Grand Strategy Matrix. Again focus on implications after giving the quadrant selection. Reminder: Use of a term such as "market penetration" is not satisfactory alone as a strategy implication. Be more specific. Elaborate.

f. Show your Quantitative Strategic Planning Matrix (QSPM). Be sure to explain your strategies to start with here. Do not go back over the internal and external factors. Avoid having more than one 4, 3, 2, or 1 in a row. If you rate one strategy, you need to rate the other because, that particular factor is affecting the choice. Work row by row rather than column by column on preparing the QSPM.

g. Present your Recommendations Page. This is the most important page in your presentation. Be specific in terms of both strategies and estimated costs of those strategies. *Total up your estimated costs.* You should have six or more strategies. Divide your strategies into two groups: (1) Existing Strategies to Be Continued, and (2) New Strategies to Be Started.

Oral Presentation- Step 6

6. Strategy Implementation

(8 minutes)

a. Show and explain your EPS/EBIT analysis to reveal whether stock, debt, or a combination is best to finance your recommendations. Graph the analysis. Decide which approach to use if there are any given limitations of the analysis.

b. Show your projected income statement. Relate changes in the items to your recommendations rather than blindly going with historical percentage changes.

c. Show your projected balance sheet. Relate changes in your items to your recommendations. Be sure to show the retained earnings calculation and the results of your EPS/EBIT decision.

d. Show your projected financial ratios and highlight several key ratios to show the benefits of your strategic plan.

Oral Presentation–Step 7

7. Strategy Evaluation
(2 minutes)

a. Prepare a Balanced Scorecard to show your expected financial and non-financial objectives recommended for the firm.

Oral Presentation–Step 8

8. Conclusion (4 minutes)

a. Compare and contrast your strategic plan versus the company's own plans for the future.

b. Thank audience members for their attention. Seek and answer questions.

Index

Name

Subject